The Enjoyment of
MUSIC

SHORTER VERSION

Twelfth Edition

The Enjoyment of
MUSIC

SHORTER VERSION

Twelfth Edition

Kristine Forney
Professor of Music
California State University, Long Beach

Andrew Dell'Antonio
Distinguished Teaching Professor of Music
The University of Texas at Austin

Joseph Machlis
Late of Queens College of the City University of New York

W.W. NORTON & COMPANY
NEW YORK   LONDON

W. W. Norton & Company has been independent since its founding in 1923, when William Warder Norton and Mary D. Herter Norton first began publishing lectures delivered at the People's Institute, the adult education division of New York City's Cooper Union. The firm soon expanded its program beyond the Institute, publishing books by celebrated academics from America and abroad. By midcentury, the two major pillars of Norton's publishing program—trade books and college texts—were firmly established. In the 1950s, the Norton family transferred control of the company to its employees, and today—with a staff of four hundred and a comparable number of trade, college, and professional titles published each year—W. W. Norton & Company stands as the largest and oldest publishing house owned wholly by its employees.

Editors: Maribeth Payne and Chris Freitag
Developmental editor: Susan Gaustad
Media editor: Steve Hoge
Ancillaries editor: Michael Fauver
Managing editor, college: Marian Johnson
Managing editor, college digital media: Kim Yi
Production manager: Jane Searle
Editorial assistant, music media: Andrew Ralston
Media project editor: Jack Borrebach
Marketing manager, music: Mary Dudley
Design director: Jillian Burr
Designer: Lissi Sigillo
Photo editor: Nelson Colon
Permissions manager: Megan Jackson
Indexer: Marilyn Bliss
Page layout: Carole Desnoes
Composition: Jouve North America
Manufactured in the United States by RR Donnelley

The text of this book is composed in Dante with the display set in Neutraface Text.

Library of Congress Cataloging-in-Publication Data

Forney, Kristine, author.
The enjoyment of music / Kristine Forney, Professor of Music California State University, Long Beach ; Andrew Dell'Antonio, Distinguished Teaching Professor of Music, The University of Texas at Austin ; Joseph Machlis, Late of Queens College of the City University of New York.—Twelfth edition, shorter version.
    pages cm
Includes bibliographical references and index.
ISBN 978-0-393-93638-4 (pbk.)
1. Music appreciation. I. Dell'Antonio, Andrew, author. II. Machlis, Joseph, 1906-1998, author. III. Title.
MT90.F67 2015
780—dc23   2014022305

W. W. Norton & Company, Inc., 500 Fifth Avenue, New York, NY 10110-0017
wwnorton.com

W. W. Norton & Company Ltd., Castle House, 75/76 Wells Street, London W1T 3QT

2 3 4 5 6 7 8 9 0

CONTENTS

Materials of Music

PART 1

PART 2   The Middle Ages and Renaissance

The Baroque Era

PART 3

Eighteenth-Century Classicism   PART 4

PART 5 The Nineteenth Century

PART 6 Twentieth-Century Modernism

PART 7　Postmodernism: The Twentieth Century and Beyond

Online Video and Listening Examples

🎥 Video

Orchestra and Chamber Music

Bach: Contrapunctus I, from *The Art of Fugue* (string quartet)

Beethoven: Symphony No. 5 in C Minor, I

Britten: *The Young Person's Guide to the Orchestra*

Handel: "Rejoice greatly" and "Hallelujah Chorus," from *Messiah*

Mozart:
    Eine kleine Nachtmusik, I
    Piano Concerto in G Major, K. 453, I

Sousa: *Washington Post* March (wind band)

Tchaikovsky:
    Dance of the Sugar Plum Fairy and *Trepak*, from *The Nutcracker*
    Symphony No. 5 in E Minor, III

Telemann: *Tafelmusik*, selections (Baroque orchestra)

Metropolitan Opera

Adams: *Doctor Atomic*, excerpts

Berg: *Wozzeck*, Act III, excerpts

Bizet: *Habanera*, from *Carmen*

Mozart: *Don Giovanni*, Act I, excerpts

Puccini: "Un bel di," from *Madame Butterfly*

Verdi: *Rigoletto*, Act III, excerpts

Wagner: *Die Walküre*, Act III, excerpts

🎧 Listening Examples

Adams: "At the sight of this," from *Doctor Atomic*

Adhan: Call to Prayer and *Blessings on the Prophet* (Islamic chant)

Amazing Grace (traditional hymn, UK)

America (patriotic song)

Avaz of Bayate Esfahan (Iran)

Bach, J. S.:
    Contrapunctus I, from *The Art of Fugue*
    Contrapunctus I theme (original, inversion, retrograde, retrograde inversion, augmentation, diminution)
    Brandenburg Concerto No. 1, I
    Cantata No. 56, "Endlich, endlich wird mein Joch"
    Jesu, Joy of Man's Desiring
    Minuet in D Minor (from *Anna Magdalena Bach Notebook*)
    Sarabande, from Cello Suite No. 2
    Toccata in D Minor

Battle Cry of Freedom

Battle Hymn of the Republic (Civil War song)

Beethoven:
    Für Elise
    Moonlight Sonata, I
    Pathétique Sonata, II
    Symphony No. 5, I
    Symphony No. 9, IV ("Ode to Joy")

Berg: *Wozzeck*, Act I, scene 1

Berlioz: *Symphonie fantastique*, I (*idée fixe*)

Bernstein: *Tonight*, from *West Side Story*

Bhimpalasi (North India)

Bizet: *Toreador Song*, from *Carmen*

Brahms:
    Lullaby (*Wiegenlied*)
    Symphony No. 4, IV

Chopin:
    Prelude in A Minor, Op. 28, No. 2
    Prelude in E Minor, Op. 29, No. 4

El Cihualteco (Mexico, mariachi song)

Debussy: *Jeux de vagues*, from *La mer*

Dougla Dance (Trinidad)

Echigo Jishi (Japan)

Ensiriba ya munange Katego (East African drumming)

Er quan ying yue (*The Moon Reflected on the Second Springs*, China)

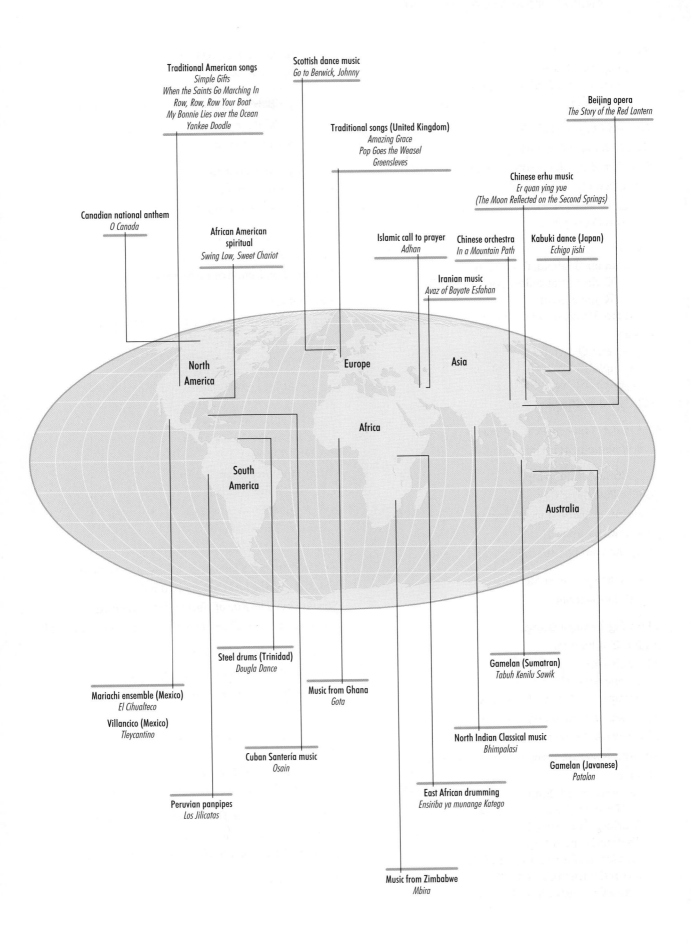

Traditional American songs
Simple Gifts
When the Saints Go Marching In
Row, Row, Row Your Boat
My Bonnie Lies over the Ocean
Yankee Doodle

Scottish dance music
Go to Berwick, Johnny

Beijing opera
The Story of the Red Lantern

Traditional songs (United Kingdom)
Amazing Grace
Pop Goes the Weasel
Greensleves

Chinese erhu music
Er quan ying yue
(The Moon Reflected on the Second Springs)

Canadian national anthem
O Canada

African American
spiritual
Swing Low, Sweet Chariot

Islamic call to prayer
Adhan

Chinese orchestra
In a Mountain Path

Kabuki dance (Japan)
Echigo jishi

Iranian music
Avaz of Bayate Esfahan

North
America

Europe

Asia

Africa

South
America

Australia

Steel drums (Trinidad)
Dougla Dance

Gamelan (Sumatran)
Tabuh Kenilu Sawik

Music from Ghana
Gota

Mariachi ensemble (Mexico)
El Cihualteco

Villancico (Mexico)
Tleycantino

Cuban Santería music
Osain

North Indian Classical music
Bhimpalasi

Gamelan (Javanese)
Patalon

Peruvian panpipes
Los Jilicatas

East African drumming
Ensiriba ya munange Katego

Music from Zimbabwe
Mbira

PREFACE

The Enjoyment of Music is a classic—it's been around for more than half a century. Its contents and pedagogical approach have been constantly updated to offer an exceptionally appealing listening repertory and the latest scholarship, integrated with unparalleled media resources every step of the way.

There is much that is new about this 12th edition. First, the book, while chronological by historical eras, is modular, with short chapters containing one or, at most, two works. These make for easier reading and will help you master the material more quickly. And the language aims to be direct and engaging, with comments focused toward you, the student.

Also new to this edition are **Your Turn to Explore** boxes at the end of each chapter, encouraging you to explore a work, genre, or style's relevance across historical, popular, and worldwide traditions; **Encounter** boxes that introduce a selection from non-Western, popular, or traditional music; and **Interface** boxes that make connections between music and other subjects you may be studying. You'll see these items described below, along with the other main features in the text and online. Understanding all these resources will greatly enhance your listening, help with study skills, and improve performance in class.

Using the Book

The Enjoyment of Music, 12th edition, is designed to help you discover for yourself the joy of studying music, with appealing musical selections and compelling and contemporary topics presented in clear prose.

- A **varied repertory** broadly represents classical masters, including women composers and living composers, as well as jazz, musical theater, film music, popular and traditional music, and non-Western styles.

- **Key Points**, at the beginning of each chapter, briefly summarize the terms and main ideas in that chapter.

- **Marginal sideheads** and **boldface type** identify key terms defined in the text and focus attention on important concepts.

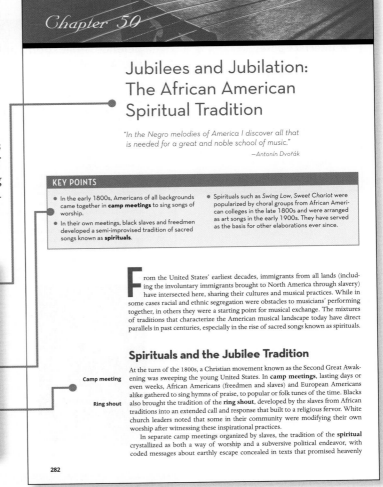

Chapter 50

Jubilees and Jubilation: The African American Spiritual Tradition

"In the Negro melodies of America I discover all that is needed for a great and noble school of music."
—Antonín Dvořák

KEY POINTS

- In the early 1800s, Americans of all backgrounds came together in **camp meetings** to sing songs of worship.
- In their own meetings, black slaves and freedmen developed a semi-improvised tradition of sacred songs known as **spirituals**.

- Spirituals such as *Swing Low, Sweet Chariot* were popularized by choral groups from African American colleges in the late 1800s and were arranged as art songs in the early 1900s. They have served as the basis for other elaborations ever since.

From the United States' earliest decades, immigrants from all lands (including the involuntary immigrants brought to North America through slavery) have intersected here, sharing their cultures and musical practices. While in some cases racial and ethnic segregation were obstacles to musicians' performing together, in others they were a starting point for musical exchange. The mixtures of traditions that characterize the American musical landscape today have direct parallels in past centuries, especially in the rise of sacred songs known as spirituals.

Spirituals and the Jubilee Tradition

At the turn of the 1800s, a Christian movement known as the Second Great Awakening was sweeping the young United States. In **camp meetings**, lasting days or even weeks, African Americans (freedmen and slaves) and European Americans alike gathered to sing hymns of praise, to popular or folk tunes of the time. Blacks also brought the tradition of the **ring shout**, developed by the slaves from African traditions into an extended call and response that built to a religious fervor. White church leaders noted that some in their community were modifying their own worship after witnessing these inspirational practices.

In separate camp meetings organized by slaves, the tradition of the **spiritual** crystallized as both a way of worship and a subversive political endeavor, with coded messages about earthly escape concealed in texts that promised heavenly

Camp meeting

Ring shout

282

Glo-ry,	glory!	Hallelu-jah!	Glo-ry,	glory!	Halle-lu-jah!
I			IV		I

Glo-ry,	glory!	Hallelu-jah! His	truth	is	marching	on.
I			IV	V		I

Battle Hymn of the Republic

- **Icons** direct you to the relevant online resources:
  Listening Examples (short clips from traditional, world, and classical selections) and recordings are represented by a headphone icon.
  Videos (operas and instrumental works streamed online) are represented by a video icon.

LISTENING GUIDE 46   4:44

Berg: *Wozzeck*, Act III, scene 4

DATE: 1922

GENRE: Opera, in three acts

BASIS: Expressionist play by Georg Büchner

CHARACTERS: Wozzeck, a soldier (baritone)   Captain (tenor)
Marie, his common-law wife (soprano)   Doctor (bass)
Marie and Wozzeck's son (treble)   Drum Major (tenor)

- **Interface** boxes help you make interdisciplinary connections, linking music to other studies you may undertake (including science, technology, philosophy, religion, politics, history, literature, and more).

Interface

Science, Philosophy, and Music in the Age of Enlightenment

In a major intellectual and cultural shift, the eighteenth century looked toward the advancement of knowledge through reason and science. Among those who spearheaded change were the philosopher Voltaire and the physicist who developed the laws of gravity, Isaac Newton. These thinkers embraced a new philosophy that sought to understand all things according to nature and mathematics rather than religion. Scholars arduously collected information to increase the overall body of knowledge, and society in general embraced a focus on learning. One result was the great French *Encyclopédie*, a thirty-five-volume reference source purporting to systematize all knowledge, written by the leading intellectuals of the day, including Voltaire and Jean-Jacques Rousseau. Musicians took

part in this effort to amass learning: Rousseau (also a composer) published a comprehensive dictionary of musical terms; Jean-Philippe Rameau wrote an important music theory treatise; and in 1776, the Englishman Charles Burney penned the first music history text (the ancestor of your textbook), which sought to record all knowledge about musicians and their works.

Some of the most celebrated technological achievements were connected to music: for example, "music boxes" with rotating cylinders and other mechanical means of plucking strings or striking metal plates when wound up. (Many of these musical machines were created by clock makers, who were making tremendous technological strides in miniaturizing time-keeping devices in the 1700s.) Some musical machines, known as automata, were made to resemble humans: a life-size human flute player played twelve separate melodies, and there's a famous automaton, now in the museum of Art and History in Neuchâtel, Switzerland, of a woman playing an organ, pressing the keys of the instrument with her fingers. While the "robotic" performer's bodily movements may seem less convincing to us in an age of sophisticated CGI animation, they were certainly among the most humanlike mechanical actions that had ever been seen at the time, and they demonstrated the power of human ingenuity.

Across the Atlantic, the statesman and scientist Benjamin Franklin was central to the American Enlightenment through his scientific experi-

A glass armonica from Boston, c. 1830.

ments with electricity and his diverse inventions, including the lightning rod, bifocal glasses, the Franklin stove, and the glass armonica—a musical instrument made of tuned water glasses, for which both Mozart and Beethoven composed works. Franklin was a musician himself (he played harp and guitar), and he wrote a treatise on musical aesthetics, in which he espoused a philosophy of simplicity in melody and harmony.

We can easily relate the Enlightenment's goals of reasoned thought and simplicity to the music we are studying from this period. Both the individual musical elements—melody, rhythm, and harmony—and the overall structures are designed to embody a clarity, balance, and logic new to composition. This was truly intended as a "universally understandable" language of sound, and it is partly because of this quasi-scientific clarity that many still point to the music of the Classical era as the most straightforward pathway into understanding the musical logic of the European tradition.

An automaton of a mandolin player, built by P. Gaultier (eighteenth century).

ENCOUNTER

North Indian Classical Music

We have seen how musical structures were expanded and developed in the Classical era, so that a single movement of a symphony or a concerto might take fifteen minutes or more to perform. Still, we can expect that its sections will be marked by predictable patterns of either repetition (or variation) or new material. Similar processes take place in the music of other cultures, although the end result is quite different. A case in point is North Indian classical music, a centuries-old performance tradition linked to Hinduism and its deities. This musical style is based not on entirely fixed musical works, but rather on long-standing traditional repertories of motives and themes elaborated by expert performers. Rather than featuring a key center, each semi-improvised elaboration introduces a **raga**, a series of pitches that also projects a particular mood and an association with a certain time of day.

We will consider *Raga Bhimpalasi*, performed by the venerable Indian musician Ravi Shankar (1920–2012), who plays a **sitar**, a long-necked plucked string instrument with metal strings and gourd resonators. He is

often accompanied by a performer who plays a complex rhythmic cycle (**tala**, meaning "clap") with a small set of hand drums called **tabla**. A typical Indian classical piece can take up to several hours to play; our selection, however, is a mere twelve minutes. Indian audiences understand that *Raga Bhimpalsi* is performed in the afternoon—at the height of the day's heat—and it projects a mood of tenderness and longing.

The raga provides the pitches for the highly ornamented melody, and its tala is an additive rhythmic cycle of fourteen; you can hear Shankar explain both the raga and tala in a brief demonstration at the beginning. Harmony is not really a part of this music, except for what's produced by the striking of strings that sound **drones** (sustained pitches). As in a sonata-allegro form, we can expect the work to play out in sections; but while there is a general outline to the overall structure, improvisation plays a key role throughout. As the performance progresses, the tempo gradually accelerates to an extended climax, with dazzling passagework on the sitar accompanied by animated rhythms on the tabla.

Indian musicians learn to play this

music by apprenticing to master players, who pass their performance techniques down to the next generation via an oral tradition. Ravi Shankar taught his daughter Anoushka this way, and she has herself become a great sitar artist. Shankar in fact introduced Indian classical music to the Western world, inspiring a genre of "raga-rock" in the 1960s and 70s. He gave a memorable performance at the original Woodstock Festival in August 1969, and the Beatles employed sitar on their recordings. Beatle George Harrison even studied sitar with Shankar and collaborated on projects with him, thus ensuring broad international visibility for the Indian master. A fortuitous example of the Eastern and Western worlds of music colliding.

Raga Bhimpalasi 🔊

What to listen for:

- Improvised melodic elaborations by the sitar on a series of pitches.
- Raga in its ascending and descending form.
- Complex rhythmic accompaniment on the tabla (2 + 4 + 4 + 4).

The introductory section (*alap*) is slow and unmetered, played by the sitar alone; the pitches of the raga are established in this improvisatory section. The second section (*gat*) begins with the entrance of the tabla, which sets up the rhythmic cycle (tala). With the third section (*jhala*), the tempo speeds up and the interplay between the instruments becomes more complex.

Composer and sitar player Ravi Shankar, performing here with his daughter Anoushka, was the most renowned and honored figure in Indian classical music of the twentieth century.

Igor Stravinsky (1882–1971)

Born in Russia, Stravinsky grew up in a musical environment and studied composition with Nikolai Rimsky-Korsakov. His music attracted the attention of impressario Serge Diaghilev, who commissioned him to write a series of ballets (*The Firebird, Petrushka, The Rite of Spring*) that launched the young composer to fame. The premiere of *The Rite of Spring* in 1913 was one of the most scandalous in music history. Just a year later, however, when presented at a symphony concert, it was received with enthusiasm and deemed a masterpiece. When war broke out in 1914, Stravinsky took refuge first in Switzerland and then in France. With the onset of the Second World War, he decided to settle his family in Los Angeles; he became an American citizen in 1945. His later concert tours around the world made him the most celebrated figure in twentieth-century music. He died in New York in 1971.

Stravinsky's musical style evolved throughout his career, from the post-Impressionism of *The Firebird* and the primitivism of *The Rite of Spring* to the controlled Classicism of his mature style (*Symphony of Psalms*), and finally to the twelve-tone method of his late works (*Agon*). In his ballets, which are strongly nationalistic, Stravinsky invigorated rhythm, creating a sense of furious and powerful movement. His lustrous orchestrations are so clear that, as Diaghilev remarked, "one can see through [them] with one's ears."

MAJOR WORKS: Orchestral music, including *Symphonies of Wind Instruments* (1920) and *Symphony in Three Movements* (1945) • Ballets, including *L'oiseau de feu* (*The Firebird*, 1910), *Petrushka* (1911), *Le sacre du printemps* (*The Rite of Spring*, 1913), *Agon* (1957) • Operas, including *Oedipus Rex* (1927) • Other theater works, including *L'histoire du soldat* (*The Soldier's Tale*, 1918) • Choral music, including *Symphony of Psalms* (1930) and *Threni: Lamentations of the Prophet Jeremiah* (1958) • Chamber music • Piano music • Songs.

 The Rite of Spring, Introduction

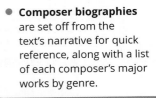

● **Encounter** boxes present extended discussion and listening guides for repertories outside the Euro-American "art" music tradition, including non-Western and popular styles that have relevance to the main repertory.

● **Composer biographies** are set off from the text's narrative for quick reference, along with a list of each composer's major works by genre.

In His Own Words

" Can you see the notes behave like waves? Up and down they go! Look, you can also see the mountains. You have to amuse yourself sometimes after being serious so long."

—Joseph Haydn

In His/Her Own Words offer relevant quotes throughout from composers and important historical figures.

At the end of each chapter:

- **Critical Thinking** questions raise issues for further study.
- **Your Turn to Explore** boxes offer suggestions for students' independent investigation of the issues raised in that chapter, whether within or beyond the confines of the course.

CRITICAL THINKING

1. What contributions did Haydn make to the genre of the symphony?
2. How is this second movement similar to the second movement of the Haydn quartet examined in Chapter 28? How is it different?

YOUR TURN TO EXPLORE

Look for (ideally video) recordings of large instrumental ensembles from several varied traditions—Western orchestras, but also (for example) gamelan ensembles from Indonesia, a Vietnamese Nha Nhac performance, a big-band jazz group. How does the range/variety of timbres differ from ensemble to ensemble? How is each similar to and different from a Western orchestra?

BAROQUE ERA

Events		Composers and Works
Death of Elizabeth I. **1603**	**1600**	**1567–1643** Claudio Monteverdi (operas and madrigals)
Gaspar Fernandes appointed choirmaster at Puebla Cathedral. **1606**		**1602–c. 1676** Chiara Margarita Cozzolani (*Magnificat*)
King James Version of the Bible printed. **1611**		
Dr. William Harvey explains the circulatory system. **1628**		
Bay Psalm Book printed in Massachusetts. **1628**		
Period of Commonwealth begins in England. **1649**		
John Milton's *Paradise Lost* published. **1667**	**1650**	**1659–1695** Henry Purcell (*Dido and Aeneas*)
French court of Louis XIV established at Versailles. **1682**		**1678–1741** Antonio Vivaldi (*The Four Seasons*)
Sir Isaac Newton's theory of gravitation published. **1687**		**1685–1750** Johann Sebastian Bach (Cantata *Wachet auf*; *The Art of Fugue*)
		1685–1759 George Frideric Handel (*Water Music*; *Messiah*)
	1700	**1746–1800** William Billings (*David's Lamentation*)
Reign of Louis XV begins. **1715**		
John Gay's *Beggar's Opera* performed. **1728**		
George Washington born. **1732**		
J. S. Bach's *Art of Fugue* published. **1751**	**1750**	

Timelines, placed at the beginning of each Part Opener, provide a chronological orientation for composers as well as world events and principal literary and historical figures.

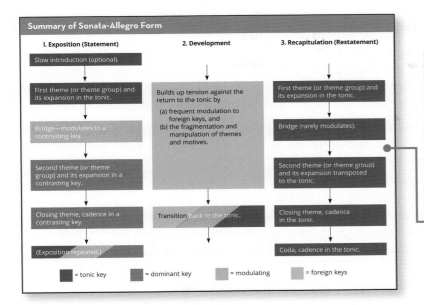

Summary of Sonata-Allegro Form

1. Exposition (Statement)	2. Development	3. Recapitulation (Restatement)
Slow introduction (optional).		
First theme (or theme group) and its expansion in the tonic.	Builds up tension against the return to the tonic by (a) frequent modulation to foreign keys, and (b) the fragmentation and manipulation of themes and motives.	First theme (or theme group) and its expansion in the tonic.
Bridge—modulates to a contrasting key.		Bridge (rarely modulates).
Second theme (or theme group) and its expansion in a contrasting key.		Second theme (or theme group) and its expansion transposed to the tonic.
Closing theme, cadence in a contrasting key.	Transition back to the tonic.	Closing theme, cadence in the tonic.
(Exposition repeated.)		Coda, cadence in the tonic.

■ = tonic key   ■ = dominant key   ■ = modulating   ■ = foreign keys

- **Maps** located throughout the book reinforce the location and names of composers associated with major musical centers. A **world map** is found at the back of the book, with detail on Europe, the United States, and Canada. **World music examples** from the online Listening Examples are indexed on a world map on p. xviii.
- Colorful **charts** visually reinforce concepts presented in the text.

- Color-coded **Materials of Music** chapters in Part 1 match the colors in the "What to Listen For" sections of each Listening Guide.
- Comprehensive **Preludes** in each part introduce historical eras in their cultural context—through political events as well as literary, artistic, and technological trends—and provide a window onto musicians' social and economic circumstances.

Appendixes:

- **Musical Notation** (Appendix I) gives explanations of musical symbols used for pitch and rhythm to assist in understanding musical examples.
- **Glossary** (Appendix II) offers concise definitions of all musical terms covered in the book.

Prelude 5

Music as Passion and Individualism

"Music, of all the liberal arts, has the greatest influence over the passions."
—Napoleon Bonaparte (1769–1821)

In His Own Words

❝ Our sweetest songs are those that tell of saddest thoughts.❞
— Percy Bysshe Shelley (1792–1822)

If the time frame of Classicism is hard to pin down, Romanticism is one of the artistic trends for which beginnings can be most readily identified, since it was a self-conscious break from the ideals of the Enlightenment. The artistic movement really comes into its own through music in the early decades of the 1800s. Indeed, it is a musician—Ludwig van Beethoven—who is often identified as the first great creative Romantic, and whose influence looms to the present day as an embodiment of passionate individual expression. Many of the common tenets of Romanticism are still very much with us: the artist struggling against rather than working within society and convention; the need for art to unsettle rather than soothe; the belief that works display their creator's distinctive originality and self-expression.

An Age of Revolutions

The Romantic era grew out of the social and political upheavals that followed the French Revolution in the last decade of the 1700s. The revolution signaled the transfer of power from a hereditary landholding aristocracy to the middle class. This change, firmly rooted in urban commerce and industry, emerged from the Industrial Revolution, which brought millions of people from the country into the cities. The new society, based on free enterprise, celebrated the individual as never before. The slogan of the French Revolution—"Liberty, Equality, Fraternity"—inspired hopes and visions to which artists responded with zeal. Sympathy for the oppressed, interest in peasants, workers, and children, faith in humankind and its destiny, all formed part of the increasingly democratic character of the Romantic period, and inspired a series of revolutions and rebellions that gradually led to the modern political landscape of Europe.

The spirit of the French Revolution is captured in *Liberty Leading the People*, by **Eugène Delacroix** (1798–1863).

Romantic Writers and Artists

Romantic poets and artists rebelled against the conventional concerns of their Classical predecessors and were

200

About the Listening Guides

The **Listening Guides** (LGs) are an essential feature of the book; follow along with them as you listen to the recordings. These guides will enhance your knowledge and appreciation of each piece. Interactive LGs (iLGs) and InQuizitive learning activities are available online and are compatible with tablets and mobiles.

1. The total duration of the piece is given in the bar at the top, at the right; some LGs will include the video icon (you can watch a performance online) as well as headphone icon.

2. The composer and title of each piece is followed by some basic information about the work, including its date and genre.

3. The "What to Listen For" box focuses your listening by drawing your attention to each musical element. These elements are color-coded to match chapter topics in Part 1 (for example, "Melody" is pink, as is Chapter 1, "Melody: Musical Line").

4. Cumulative timings are listed to the left throughout.

5. Text and translations (if necessary) are given for all vocal works.

6. A moment-by-moment description of events helps you follow the musical selection throughout.

7. Short examples of the main musical theme(s) are sometimes provided as a visual guide to what you hear.

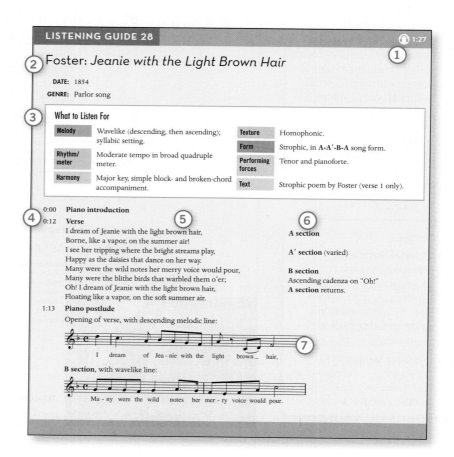

Media Resources: Total Access

With every new copy of *The Enjoyment of Music*, 12th Edition (Shorter Version), you have **total access** to all online media, whether from **StudySpace** or a Norton Coursepack installed within your campus learning-management system. Look for the unique registration code printed on a card at the front of your book, and register at http://www.wwnorton.com/college/music/enjoyment-of-music12/shorter to take advantage of a wealth of resources.

- **All 76 works** covered in the text (65 main repertory and 11 Encounter pieces) are **streamed from chapter playlists**.
- **Interactive Listening Guides (iLGs)** are now compatible with tablets and mobiles. Each iLG includes an overview of the work with a **"What to listen for" animated tutorial**. The iLG synchronizes music and description to convey the most important aspects of each work.
- **InQuizitive learning activities** for every chapter (designated with the icon at right) let you learn by doing, with varied types of questions supported by audio and video in a game-like environment. You receive feedback with each answer and links to the ebook and other resources, all to help you understand the music and the history that surrounds it.

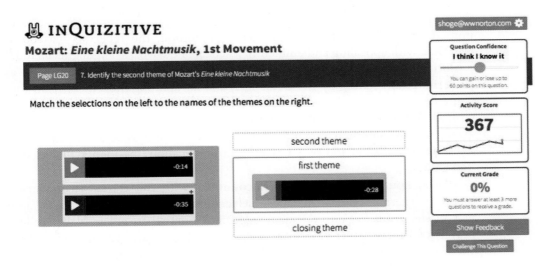

- For help in understanding musical concepts, styles, and genres, as well as musics from different cultures, additional **Listening Examples** are available for comparison; they are integrated into InQuizitive activities and chapter playlists.
- A **complete ebook**, compatible with tablets and mobiles, features links to all the iLGs, InQuizitive activities, Listening Examples, videos, and more.
- **Performance videos** showcase works by Britten, Bach, Telemann, Mozart, Beethoven, Sousa, Handel, and Tchaikovsky.
- **Instruments of the Orchestra videos**, recorded at the Eastman School of Music, allow you to see and hear how each instrument is played.
- **Metropolitan Opera video** features over two hours of stunning performances (of scenes from *Don Giovanni*, *Rigoletto*, *Die Walküre*, *Madame Butterfly*, and *Dr. Atomic*, among others).

- **Chapter Outlines** and **FlashCards** help you review important terms in each chapter.
- The **mp3 + iLG Recordings Disc** includes all 76 works of the repertory, plus the iLGs (with "What to listen for" animated tutorials). The disc can be packaged with the textbook at a discount for students.

For Instructors: What's New

This new edition encourages you to customize your teaching by providing a modular organization—short chapters featuring one or two works each. The overall plan is chronological by historical era and, within each era, genre by genre; however, the modular format enables you to personalize your choice of works to focus on and allows for greater flexibility. Indeed, a nonchronological approach is completely feasible. Less obvious but no less innovative are broad themes threaded throughout the discussion (e.g., music and technology, music and identity, music and hyper-reality, music and text, musical procedure and meaning, music and movement), which transcend chapters and eras, offering possible "teaching pathways" that you might explore in the classroom.

More than ever, the clear writing in this edition engages directly with today's undergraduates, and the chapter structure aims to provide arguments that are immediately compelling. As with each new edition, the repertory has been refreshed with appealing and eminently teachable new works. Highlights include a glorious *Magnificat* by the Benedictine nun Chiara Margarita Cozzolani, a powerful psalm setting by Lili Boulanger, and an uplifting movement from the Fauré *Requiem*; a hymn by William Billings, a jaunty piano work by Louis Moreau Gottschalk, and a familiar African American spiritual in two early twentieth-century arrangements; an ethereal hymn by John Tavener and a frenetic electric guitar work by Steve Reich; and two new film music selections, by John Williams and Tan Dun.

Throughout the book, boxed **Encounters** (with full tracks accompanied by short listening guides) juxtapose selections from popular, traditional, and non-Western music against the main repertory; among these are an Islamic call to prayer, a villancico from New Spain, a classical Indian raga, a Beijing opera, a Japanese kabuki dance, an American folk song, an Indonesian gamelan selection, an East African drumming song, a Chinese erhu work, a high-tech work for hyperinstruments, and an example of video game music. These serve to expand students' listening experiences and knowledge of other cultures, as well as noncanonic facets of the Western tradition.

Boxed **Interfaces,** another new feature, provide interdisciplinary discussions of music in connection with various fields that are frequently part of general studies or a liberal arts curriculum—among them science, philosophy, technology, history, religious studies, art, literature, gender studies, black studies, and pedagogy. The Interfaces are designed to help students integrate their studies while responding to a broad pedagogical push toward cultural diversity and creating world citizens.

New **Your Turn to Explore** boxes, concluding each chapter, invite students to investigate similar genres in other cultures, discover connections with music they listen to every day, observe performance behavior across all styles, and much more. Though the book's focus is on Western classical musical traditions, popular, traditional, and non-Western influences are integrated throughout, and coverage is given to jazz, musical theater, and film and video game music as well.

Of special note: Norton and the **Metropolitan Opera** have released a DVD of opera video correlated to the repertory in this edition (*Don Giovanni, Rigoletto, Die Walküre, Doctor Atomic,* among others). Over two hours of top-quality live performances are available to all *Enjoyment* users.

The **Instruments of the Orchestra DVD** combines all the instrument videos from Eastman School of Music performers into an easily navigable, high-quality, full-screen DVD. Videos can be accessed alphabetically or by instrument family, complete with basic descriptions of each one. They are also available online.

Coursepacks

Available at no cost to professors or students, Norton Coursepacks for online or hybrid courses are available in all versions of BlackBoard (WebCT), Angel, Moodle, Desire2Learn, and Canvas, and custom formats on request. With a simple download from our instructor website (wwnorton.com/instructors), you can bring high-quality Norton digital media into a new or existing online course. This customizable resource includes

- links to all online **Total Access** content—including chapter playlists, iLGs, InQuizitive learning activities, ebook, videos, and more;
- additional **Chapter** and **Listening Quizzes** that report directly to your learning-management system;
- links to **Assessment Activities**, which report to an individual course-management gradebook.

Instructor's Manual Cory Gavito, Oklahoma City University

Available online, this resource includes suggested syllabi and an overview for each chapter, learning objectives, lecture suggestions, writing assignments, advice for responding to the challenges of teaching music appreciation, and detailed annotated bibliographies of books and audiovisual resources. The manual also includes classroom-ready activities, many of which link to other components of the text's media package. Download free from wwnorton.com/instructors.

Instructor's Resource Disc (IRD)

This disc (order or download free from wwnorton.com/instructors) contains everything you need to start from scratch or to augment your music appreciation lectures:

- enhanced Lecture PowerPoint slides, with a suggested classroom-lecture script in the notes field;
- PowerPoint slides featuring all the photographs, art, and paintings from the text;
- PowerPoint-ready Instruments of the Orchestra videos;
- mp3 excerpts from the Listening Example bank;
- new orchestral performance videos.

Test Bank Roger Hickman, California State University, Long Beach

The Test Bank includes over 2,000 multiple-choice, true/false, and essay questions written in accordance with the Norton Assessment Guidelines. Each question is identified with a topic, question type, and difficulty level, enabling instructors to customize exams for their students. Download free or order the CD-ROM from wwnorton.com/instructors.

Acknowledgments

Any project of this size is dependent on the expertise and assistance of many individuals to make it a success. First, we wish to acknowledge the many loyal users of *The Enjoyment of Music* who have taken the time to comment on the text and media package. As always, their suggestions help us shape each new edition. We also wish to thank those instructors who reviewed the text or media for this 12th edition and provided invaluable feedback: Debra Brown (Johnson County Community College), Kevin R. Burke (Franklin College), Ellen J. Burns (University of Albany), Carey Campbell (Weber State University), Donald Foster (Moreno Valley College), Kurt Fowler (Indiana State University), Richard Freedman (Haverford College), Judith Hand (McNeese State University), Julie Hubbert (University of South Carolina), Miles M. Ishigaki (California State University, Fresno), Ellie Jenkins (Dalton State College), Heather Killmeyer (East Tennessee State University), Jonathan Kulp (University of Louisiana, Lafayette), Melissa Lesbines (Appalachian State University), Natalie Mann (Moreno Valley College), Nancy Newman (State University of New York, Albany), Carolyn L. Quin (Moreno Valley College), Donald C. Sanders (Samford University), Andrew Santander (University of North Georgia), Sarah Satterfield (College of Central Florida), Peter Schimpf (Metropolitan State University of Denver), Brian Short (Madison Area Technical College), Randall Sorensen (Louisiana Tech University), Nancy Stewart (Greenville Technical College), Michael Sundblad (Thomas Nelson Community College), Jonas Thoms (Wright State University), I-Ching Tsai (Riverside City College), Mary Wolinski (Western Kentucky University), and Inaki Zubizarreta (Norco College).

The team assembled to prepare the media and ancillary materials for this edition is unparalleled: it includes Jennifer L. Hund (Purdue University), author of the "What to listen for" tutorial storyboards, InQuizitive activities, and online Explorations; Alicia Doyle (California State University, Long Beach), who created InQuizitive assessments and iLG content for selections new to 12/e; Rebecca Marchand (Boston Conservatory), who provided additional InQuizitive assessments; Jessie Fillerup (University of Richmond), author of the iLGs; Melissa Lesbines (Appalachian State University), who wrote the chapter outlines; Carey Campbell (Weber State University), who prepared the PowerPoint presentations; and Erica Rothman and Jim Haverkamp of Nightlight Studio, responsible for producing the animations. Tom Laskey of the Sony BMG Custom Marketing Group assembled, licensed, and mastered the recording package; Roger Hickman (California State University, Long Beach) prepared the commentary for the Norton Scores, assisted with the recording selection and coordination with the scores, and updated and edited the Test Bank file; Cory Gavito (Oklahoma City University) prepared the Interactive Instructor's Guide; and our spouses, William Prizer (University of California, Santa Barbara) and Felicia Miyakawa, assisted in more ways than can possibly be named.

This 12th edition could not have been realized without the very capable assistance of the exceptional Norton team. We owe profound thanks to Maribeth Payne, music editor at Norton, for her heartfelt dedication and counsel to the whole project; to Chris Freitag, for his invaluable advice and guidance in the later stages of this edition; to Susan Gaustad, for her outstanding editing of the book and overseeing of all aspects of its production; to Steve Hoge, for creating and coordinating our stellar media package; to Lissi Sigillo, for her stunning design; to Jillian Burr, for overseeing the design process; to Carole Desnoes, for her artistic layout; to Michael Fauver, for his capable editing of the ancillaries; to Nelson Colon, for his invaluable assistance with selecting and licensing the illustrations; to Jane Searle, for handling the production of the *Enjoyment of Music* package; to Mary Dudley, for her insightful marketing strategies; to Andrew Ralston, for handling numerous details of the media package; to Marilyn Bliss, for her meticulous index; to Megan Jackson, for clearing permissions; and to David Botwinik, for his skilled music typesetting.

We wish finally to express our deep appreciation to three former music editors at Norton—Michael Ochs, Claire Brook, and David Hamilton—who over the years have guided and inspired *The Enjoyment of Music* to its continued success.

Kristine Forney
Andrew Dell'Antonio

The Enjoyment of
MUSIC

SHORTER VERSION

Twelfth Edition

OVERVIEW

Materials of Music

Melodies preserved through notation.	**800**	Middle Ages **400–1450**
Harmony developed.	**1000**	
Rhythmic concepts introduced.	**1200**	
Metric schemes developed.	**1400**	Renaissance **1450–1600**
Textures grow more complex, based on imitation.	**1500**	
First operas created. Modern string family developed.	**1600**	Baroque **1600–1750**
Western harmonic system of tonality established.	**1700**	Classical **1750–1825**
Symphony orchestra flourishes.	**1800**	Romantic **1820–1900**
Large-scale compositions written for orchestra and small ensemble.	**1850**	
		Post-Romantic and Impressionist **1890–1915**
Revolutionary concepts in harmony and rhythm introduced.	**1900**	Twentieth century and beyond
Electronic and computer music flourish. Global music concepts explored.	**2000**	

Part 1

Materials of Music

Listening to Music Today

"It's not that people don't like classical music. It's that they don't have the chance to understand and experience it."

—Gustavo Dudamel

As with any new endeavor, it takes practice to become an experienced listener. We often "listen" to music as a background to another activity—perhaps studying or just relaxing. In either case, we are probably not concentrating on the music. This type of "partial listening" is normal and appealing, but this book aims to develop listening skills that expand your musical memory.

You probably have favorite books, movies, or songs that you like to revisit again and again, and each time you may notice something new, or appreciate even more a moment you have grown to cherish. It's precisely through repeated encounters that we gain both familiarity with and understanding of the touchstones of our culture. And one of the wonders of the present-day world is that we have the opportunity to listen to recorded music almost any time we want. We encourage you to listen repeatedly to the examples this book provides: with this kind of repeated, attentive listening, you will gain skills you can then transfer to new repertories as well as to your favorite songs.

At the same time, while recordings facilitate repeated listening, it's important to hear music in performance, for nothing can equal the excitement of a live concert. The crowded hall, the visual and aural stimulation of a performance, and even the element of unpredictability—of what might happen on a particular night—all contribute to the unique communicative powers of people making music.

There are certain traditions surrounding concerts and concert-going: these include the way performers dress, the appropriate moments to applaud, and even the choice of seats. These aspects of performance differ between art-music and popular-music concerts. Understanding the differing traditions, and knowing what to expect, will contribute to your enjoyment of the event.

A Masai warrior in Kenya enjoys listening to music on his iPod.

Attending Concerts

Regardless of where you live, it's likely that you have a rich choice of musical events available. To explore concerts in your area, check with the Music Department for on-campus concerts, read local and college newspapers for a calendar of upcoming events, or consult websites for nearby concert venues and calendars.

Ticket prices vary, depending on the concert. For university events, tickets are usually reasonable (under $20). For a performance in a major

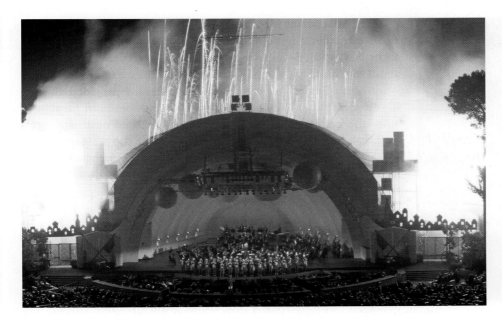

The audience delights in a fireworks display during a performance of Tchaikovsky's *1812 Overture* at the Hollywood Bowl, in Los Angeles.

concert hall, you will probably pay more, generally $35 to over $100, depending on the location of your seat. Today, most new concert halls are constructed so that virtually all the seats are satisfactory. For small chamber groups, try to get front orchestra seats, close to the performers. For large ensembles—orchestras and operas, or even popular concerts—the best places are probably near the middle of the hall or in the balcony, where you also have a good view. For some concerts, you may need to purchase tickets in advance, either by phone or online, paying with a credit card. Be sure to ask for student discounts when appropriate.

Before you attend a concert, you may want to prepare by doing some reading. First, find out what works will be performed. Then check your textbook and its online materials as well as the Internet for information about the composers and works. It's especially important to read about an opera before the performance because it may be sung in the original language (e.g., Italian), though many venues provide supertitle translations.

What you choose to wear should depend on the degree of formality and the location of the event. Whatever the occasion, you should be neatly attired out of respect for the performers.

In His Own Words

66 The life of the arts is close to the center of a nation's purpose, and is a test of the quality of a nation's civilization."

—John F. Kennedy

Summary: Attending Concerts

- Consult websites, your local and college newspapers, the Music Department, and bulletin boards on campus to learn about upcoming concerts in your area.
- Determine if you must purchase your tickets in advance or at the door.
- Read about the works in advance in your textbook or on the Internet.
- Consider what to wear; your attire should suit the occasion.
- Arrive early to purchase or pick up your ticket and to get a good seat.
- Review the program before the concert starts to learn about the music.
- Be respectful to the performers and those sitting near you by not making noise.
- Follow the program carefully to know when to applaud.
- Be aware of and respectful of concert hall traditions.
- Above all, enjoy the event!

Wynton Marsalis (b. 1961), one of the most successful jazz and classical trumpet players today.

Plan to arrive at least twenty minutes before a concert starts, and even earlier if it is open seating or you must pick up your ticket at the box office. Be sure to get a program from the usher and read about the music and the performers before the event begins. Translations into English of vocal texts are generally provided as well. If you arrive after the concert has begun, you will not be able to enter the hall until after the first piece is finished or an appropriate break in the music occurs. Be respectful of the performers and those around you by not talking and not leaving your seat except at intermission (the break that usually occurs about halfway through the performance).

The Concert Program

One key aspect of attending a concert is understanding the program. A sample program for a university orchestra concert appears below. The concert opens with an overture, with a familiar title based on Shakespeare's *A Midsummer Night's Dream*. We will see later that some works have a literary basis for the composer's ideas. Felix Mendelssohn's dates establish him as an early Romantic master.

The concert continues with a symphony by Wolfgang Amadeus Mozart, of whom you have undoubtedly heard. You can deduce by the title that Mozart wrote many symphonies; what you may not know is that this one (No. 41) is his last. The symphony is in four sections, or **movements**, with contrasting tempo indications for each movement, in Italian. (You can read more about the tempo terms in Chapter 7 and the forms of individual movements in Chapters 28–32.)

After the intermission, the second half is devoted to a single work: a piano concerto by the late nineteenth-century Russian composer Peter Ilyich Tchaikovsky. This concerto is in three movements, again a standard format (fast-slow-fast). The tempo markings are, however, much more descriptive than those for the Mozart

In Her Own Words

❝ Applause is the fulfillment. . . . Once you get on the stage, everything is right. I feel the most beautiful, complete, fulfilled."

—*Leontyne Price*

Program

Overture to *A Midsummer Night's Dream*	Felix Mendelssohn (1809–1847)
Symphony No. 41 in C Major, K. 551 (*Jupiter*) I. Allegro vivace II. Andante cantabile III. Menuetto (Allegretto) & Trio IV. Finale: Molto allegro	W. A. Mozart (1756–1791)

Intermission

Concerto No. 1 for Piano and Orchestra in B-flat Minor, Op. 23 I. Allegro non troppo e molto maestoso; Allegro con spirito II. Andantino semplice; Prestissimo; Tempo I III. Allegro con fuoco	P. I. Tchaikovsky (1840–1893)

Barbara Allen, piano

The University Symphony Orchestra
Eugene Castillo, conductor

symphony, using words like *maestoso* (majestic), *con spirito* (with spirit), and *con fuoco* (with fire). This is typical of the Romantic era, as is the work's expressive minor key. In the concerto, your interest will be drawn sometimes to the soloist, performing virtuoso passages, and at other times to the orchestra.

In addition to the works being performed, the program may include short notes about each composition and biographical sketches about the soloist and conductor.

During the Performance

At a typical concert, the house lights are usually dimmed just before it begins. Make sure your cell phone is turned off and that you do not make noise with candy wrappers or shuffling papers if you are taking notes. As you will see, it is customary to applaud at the entrance of performers, soloists, and conductors. In an orchestra concert, the **concertmaster** (the first-chair violinist) will make a separate entrance and then tune the orchestra by asking the oboe player to play a pitch, to which all the instruments tune in turn. When the orchestra falls silent, the conductor enters, and the performance begins.

Concert etiquette

Pianist Beatrice Rana performs with the Fort Worth Symphony, conducted by Leonard Slatkin, as part of the Van Cliburn Piano Competition.

Knowing when to applaud during a concert is part of the necessary etiquette. Generally, the audience claps after complete works such as a symphony, a concerto, a sonata, or a song cycle, rather than between movements or songs. Sometimes short works are grouped together on the program, suggesting that they are a set. In this case, applause is suitable at the close of the group. If you are unsure, follow the lead of others in the audience. At the opera, the conventions are a little different; the audience might interrupt with applause and "Bravo!" after a particularly fine delivery of an aria.

You might be surprised at the formality of the performers' dress. It is traditional for ensemble players to wear black—long dresses or black pants and tops for the women, tuxedos or tails for the men—to minimize visual distraction. Soloists, however, might dress more colorfully.

The entire orchestra usually stands at the entrance of the conductor, and a small group, such as a string quartet, will bow to the audience in unison. The performers often do not speak to the audience until the close of the program—although this tradition is changing—and then only if an additional piece is demanded by extended applause. In this case, the **encore** (French for "again") is generally announced. Some musicians, like pianists, perform long, complex works from memory. To do so requires intense concentration and many arduous hours of study and practice.

You will undoubtedly sense an aura of suspense surrounding concerts. Try to take full advantage of the opportunities available—try something completely unfamiliar, perhaps an opera or a symphony, as you continue to enjoy performances of whatever music you already like.

Chapter 1

Melody: Musical Line

"It is the melody which is the charm of music, and it is that which is most difficult to produce. The invention of a fine melody is a work of genius."

—Joseph Haydn

KEY POINTS

- A **melody** is a line, or the tune, in music.
- Each melody is unique in **contour** (how it moves up and down) and in **range**, or span of pitches.
- An **interval** is the distance between any two pitches. A melody that moves in small, connected intervals is **conjunct**, while one that moves by leaps is **disjunct**.
- The units that make up a melody are **phrases**; phrases end in resting places called **cadences**.
- A melody may be accompanied by a secondary melody, or a **countermelody**.

We tend to characterize any musical sound as one that has a perceivable and measurable **pitch**, determined by its **frequency** (number of vibrations per second). This pitch depends on the length or size of a vibrating object. For example, a short string vibrates faster (has a higher frequency) than a long string (which has a lower frequency). This is why a violin sounds higher than a cello: its strings are shorter overall. When a musician places a finger on the string of a violin or cello, the vibrating length of the string is shortened, and the pitch/frequency changes accordingly.

In the Western tradition, we represent each pitch with a symbol called a **note**, that's placed on a **staff** (five parallel lines; see Appendix I for more on notation). This symbol designates the frequency and the **duration**, or length of time, of the pitch. A pitch also has a certain **volume** (loudness or softness), and a distinct quality known as **tone color**, or **timbre**; this last quality distinguishes voices from instruments, a trumpet from a clarinet.

A **melody** is a succession of single pitches that we hear as a recognizable whole. We relate to the pitches of a melody in the same way we hear the words of a sentence—not singly but as an entire cohesive thought. We know a good melody when we hear one, and we recognize its power to move us, as do most musical cultures of the world.

Each melody goes up and down

This apartment building in Vejle, Denmark, called The Wave, was designed by architect **Henning Larsen** to blend in with the surrounding environment of hills and a fjord. Its wavelike shape resembles that heard in many melodies.

in its own distinct way, with one pitch being higher or lower than another; its **range** is the distance between the lowest and highest notes. This span can be very narrow, as in an easy children's song, or very wide, as in some melodies played on an instrument. Although this distance can be measured in the number of notes, we will describe range in approximate terms—narrow, medium, or wide. The **contour** of a melody is its overall shape as it turns upward or downward or remains static. You can visualize a melody in a line graph, resulting in an ascending or descending line, an arch, or a wave (see "Melodic Examples" below).

Range

Contour

The distance between any two pitches is called an **interval**. Melodies that move principally by small intervals in a joined, connected manner (like *Joy to the World*) are called **conjunct**, while those that move in larger, disconnected intervals (like *The Star-Spangled Banner*) are described as **disjunct**. A tune's movement need not necessarily remain the same throughout: it may, for example, begin with a small range and conjunct motion and, as it develops, expand its range and become more disjunct.

Interval

The Structure of Melody

The component units of a melody are like parts of a sentence. A **phrase** in music, as in language, is a unit of meaning within a larger structure. The phrase ends in a resting place, or **cadence**, which punctuates the music in the same way that a comma or period punctuates a sentence. The cadence may be inconclusive, leaving you with the impression that more is to come, or it may sound final, giving you the sense that the melody has reached the end. The cadence is where a singer or instrumentalist pauses to draw a breath.

Phrase

Cadence

If the melody has words, the text lines and the musical phrases will usually coincide. Consider the well-known hymn *Amazing Grace* (p. 10). Its four phrases, both the text and the music, are of equal length, and the **rhyme scheme** of the text (the way the last syllables in each line rhyme) is *a-b-a-b*. The first three cadences (at the end of each of the first three phrases) are inconclusive, or incomplete; notice the upward inflection like a question at the end of phrase 2. Phrase 4, with its final downward motion, provides the answer; it gives you a sense of closure.

Rhyme scheme

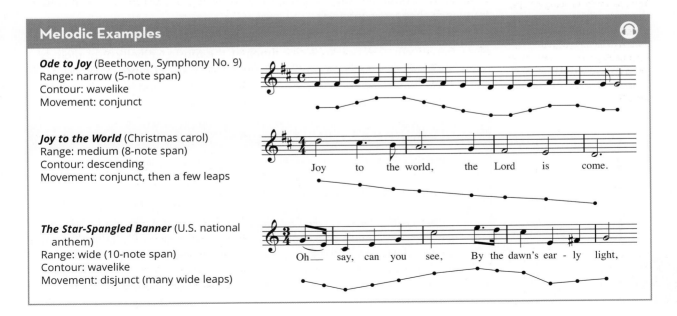

Melodic Examples

Ode to Joy (Beethoven, Symphony No. 9)
Range: narrow (5-note span)
Contour: wavelike
Movement: conjunct

Joy to the World (Christmas carol)
Range: medium (8-note span)
Contour: descending
Movement: conjunct, then a few leaps

Joy   to   the world,   the   Lord   is   come.

The Star-Spangled Banner (U.S. national
   anthem)
Range: wide (10-note span)
Contour: wavelike
Movement: disjunct (many wide leaps)

Oh—   say,   can   you   see,   By the dawn's ear - ly   light,

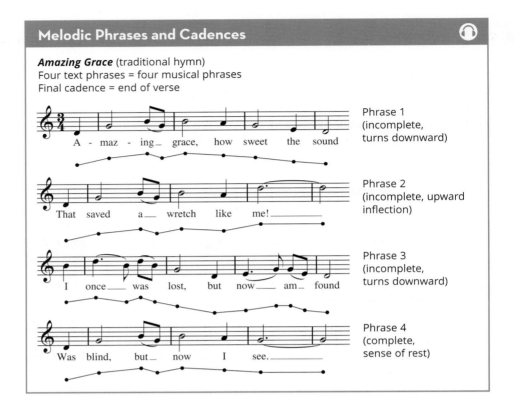

Melodic Phrases and Cadences

Amazing Grace (traditional hymn)
Four text phrases = four musical phrases
Final cadence = end of verse

A - maz - ing_ grace, how sweet the sound

Phrase 1
(incomplete,
turns downward)

That saved a_ wretch like me!_

Phrase 2
(incomplete, upward
inflection)

I once_ was lost, but now_ am_ found

Phrase 3
(incomplete,
turns downward)

Was blind, but_ now I see._

Phrase 4
(complete,
sense of rest)

In order to maintain the listener's interest, a melody must be shaped carefully, either by the composer or by the performer who invents it on the spot. What makes a striking effect is the **climax**, the high point in a melodic line, which usually represents a peak in intensity as well as in range. Sing through, or listen to, *The Star-Spangled Banner* and note its climax in the last stirring phrase, when the line rises to the words "O'er the land of the free."

The Star-Spangled Banner
The Stars and Stripes Forever

More complex music can feature several simultaneous melodies. Sometimes the relative importance of one over the other is clear, and the added tune is called a **countermelody** (literally, "against a melody"). You may have heard the high-range countermelody played by the piccolos in the famous *Stars and Stripes Forever* march by John Philip Sousa (Chapter 51). In other styles, each melodic line is of seemingly equal importance. For much of the music we will study, melody is the most basic element of communication between the composer or performer and the listener. It's what we remember, what we whistle and hum.

Melody

YOUR TURN TO EXPLORE

While melody is not the main element in some popular music (rap, for example), folk rock is all about the tune. Listen to Bob Dylan's *Mr. Tambourine Man* and consider the shape and structure of the opening chorus (after the short intro). There are four equal-length phrases: the first is a descending line, the second sounds incomplete ("there is no place I'm going to"), and with the end of the fourth phrase you know the chorus is done. Select another song with a prominent melody; think about the phrases, and where you feel a sense of incompleteness or rest. How does this end-of-phrase quality affect you?

Chapter 2

Rhythm and Meter: Musical Time

"I got rhythm, I got music . . ."
—Ira Gershwin (1896–1983)

KEY POINTS

- **Rhythm** is what moves music forward in time.
- **Meter,** marked off in **measures** (or **bars**), organizes the **beats** (the basic units) in music.
- Measures often begin with a strong **downbeat**.
- **Simple meters**—duple, triple, and quadruple—are the most common; each beat is divided into two.
- **Compound meters** divide each beat into three rather than two.
- Rhythmic complexities occur with **offbeats, syncopation,** and **polyrhythm**.
- Some music is **nonmetric**, with an obscured pulse.

Music is propelled forward by **rhythm**, the movement of music in time. Each individual note has a length, or duration—some long and some short. The **beat** is the basic unit of rhythm, a regular pulse that divides time into equal segments. Some beats are stronger than others; we perceive these as **accented** beats. In much of Western music, these strong beats occur at regular intervals—every other beat, every third beat, every fourth, and so on—and thus we hear groupings of two, three, or four. These organizing patterns are called **meters** and, in notation, are marked off in **measures** (or **bars**). Each measure contains a fixed number of beats, and the first beat in a measure usually receives the strongest accent. Measures are designated with **measure (bar) lines**, regular vertical lines through the staff (on which the music is notated; see Appendix I).

Beat

Meter and measure

Meter organizes the flow of rhythm in music. In Western music, its patterns are simple, paralleling the alternating accents heard in poetry. Consider, for example, this well-known stanza by the American poet Robert Frost. Its meter alternates a strong beat with a weak one (this is iambic meter, da DUM, da DUM, da DUM, da DUM). A metrical reading of the poem will bring out the regular pattern of accented (′) and unaccented (-) syllables:

In His Own Words

❝ Rhythm and motion, not the element of feeling, are the foundations of musical art."
—Igor Stravinsky

The woods are love-ly, dark and deep.

But I have prom-is-es to keep,

And miles to go be-fore I sleep,

And miles to go be-fore I sleep,

The Gothic arches of the Doge's Palace in Venice clearly show duple subdivisions, much like simple meters in music.

Metrical Patterns

You will hear the regularly recurring patterns of two, three, or four beats in much of the music we will study. As in poetry, these patterns, or meters, depend on regular accents. The first accented beat of each pattern is known as a **downbeat**, referring to the downward stroke of a conductor's hand (see conducting patterns, p. 51). The most basic pattern, known as **duple meter**, alternates a strong downbeat with a weak beat: ONE two, ONE two; or, if you marched it, LEFT right, LEFT right.

Triple meter, another basic pattern, has three beats to a measure—one strong beat and two weak ones (ONE two three). This meter is traditionally associated with dances such as the waltz and the minuet.

Quadruple meter contains four beats to the measure, with a primary accent on the first beat and a secondary accent on the third. Although it is sometimes difficult to distinguish duple and quadruple meter, quadruple meter usually has a broader feeling.

In **simple meters** (simple duple, simple triple, and simple quadruple), the beat is divided into two (ONE-and, two-and; or ONE-and, two-and, three-and). However, in some patterns, the beat is divided into three; these are known as **compound meters**. The most common compound meter is **sextuple meter** (compound duple), which has six beats to the measure, or two main beats that each divides into three (ONE-and-a, TWO-and-a). Marked by a gently flowing effect, this pattern is often found in lullabies and nursery rhymes:

> ′ ‾ ‾   ′ ‾ ‾   ′ ‾ ‾   ′ ‾ ‾
> Lit – tle Boy Blue, come blow your horn, the
>
> ′ ‾ ‾   ′   ‾ ‾ ′ ‾ ‾ ′   ‾ ‾
> sheep's in the meadow, the cow's in the corn.

The examples on page 13 illustrate the four basic patterns. Not all pieces begin on a downbeat (beat 1). For example, *Greensleeves,* in sextuple meter, begins with an **upbeat** (beat 6). (Notice that the Frost poem given earlier is in duple meter and begins with an upbeat on "the.")

Rhythmic Complexities

Composers have devised a number of ways to keep the recurrent accent from becoming monotonous. The most common technique is **syncopation**, a deliberate upsetting of the normal pattern of accents. Instead of falling on the strong beat of the measure, the accent is shifted to a weak beat, or **offbeat** (in between the stronger beats). Syncopation is heard in many kinds of music, and is particularly characteristic of the African American dance rhythms out of which jazz developed. The example opposite illustrates the technique.

Syncopation is only one technique that throws off the regular patterns. A composition may change meters during its course; certain twentieth-century pieces shift meters nearly every measure. Another technique is the simultaneous use of rhythmic patterns that conflict with the underlying beat, such as "two against three" or "three against four"—in a piano piece, for example, the left hand might play two notes to a beat, while the right hand plays three notes to the same beat. This is called **polyrhythm** ("many rhythms") and characterizes the music of several world cultures, including drum ensembles from Ghana and Uganda (p. 388) and gamelan music of Indonesia (p. 374). Some non-Western cultures create meter through **additive** rhythms, where larger patterns are built from combinations like

Like meter in music, basic repeated patterns can be found in nature, such as in this chambered nautilus shell.

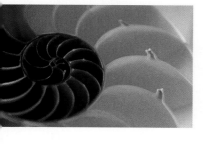

Examples of Meters

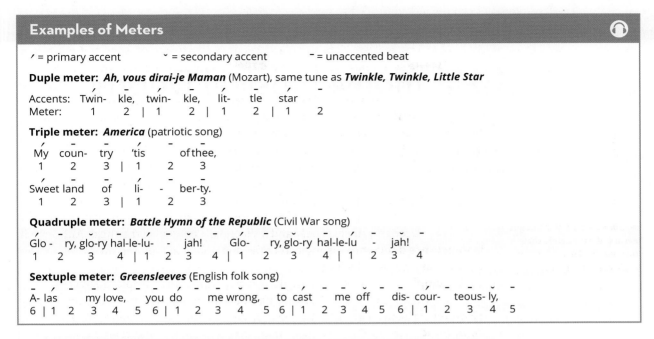

´ = primary accent   ˘ = secondary accent   ¯ = unaccented beat

Duple meter: *Ah, vous dirai-je Maman* (Mozart), same tune as ***Twinkle, Twinkle, Little Star***

Accents: Twin- kle, twin- kle, lit- tle star
Meter: 1   2 | 1   2 | 1   2

Triple meter: *America* (patriotic song)

My coun- try 'tis   of thee,
1   2   3 | 1   2   3

Sweet land of li- - ber-ty.
1   2   3 | 1   2   3

Quadruple meter: *Battle Hymn of the Republic* (Civil War song)

Glo - ry, glo-ry hal-le-lu- - jah!   Glo - ry, glo-ry hal-le-lu - jah!
1   2   3   4 | 1   2   3   4 | 1   2   3   4 | 1   2   3   4

Sextuple meter: *Greensleeves* (English folk song)

A- las   my love, you do   me wrong, to cast me off dis- cour- teous- ly,
6 | 1 2   3   4   5 6 | 1 2   3   4   5 6 | 1 2   3   4   5 6 | 1 2   3   4   5

Syncopation

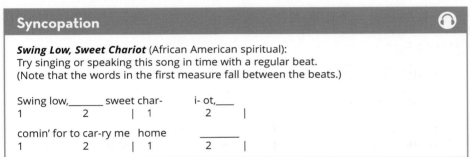

Swing Low, Sweet Chariot (African American spiritual):
Try singing or speaking this song in time with a regular beat.
(Note that the words in the first measure fall between the beats.)

Swing low,_____ sweet char-   i- ot,___
1   2 | 1   2 |

comin' for to car-ry me home   _____
1   2 | 1   2 |

$2 + 3 + 3 \ (= 8)$, rather than recurring patterns of two or three. This is typical of Indian classical music (p. 172).

Some music moves without any strong sense of beat or meter. We might say that such a work is **nonmetric** (this is the case in the chants of the early Christian church): the pulse is veiled or weak, with the music moving in a floating rhythm that typifies certain non-Western styles.

Nonmetric

Time is a crucial dimension in music. This is the element that binds together the parts within the whole: the notes within the measure and the measure within the phrase. It is therefore the most fundamental element of music.

Rhythm

YOUR TURN TO EXPLORE

The vast majority of popular songs are set in duple (usually 4/4) meter, and a strong beat usually makes the meter clear. Especially in styles influenced by African American or Latin American traditions, performers use various rhythmic devices to provide complexity and interest. Locate a recording of Public Enemy's *Don't Believe the Hype*, and listen for the strong offbeats in the drums and how the voices upset the beat, especially in the chorus ("Don't believe the hype"), with syncopation. Pick another song with a clear meter. What techniques are used to disguise the regularity of the beat? How do they affect your experience of the song?

Chapter 3

Harmony: Musical Depth

"We have learned to express the more delicate nuances of feeling by penetrating more deeply into the mysteries of harmony."

—Robert Schumann

KEY POINTS

- **Harmony** describes the vertical aspects of music: how notes (pitches) sound together.

- A **chord** is the simultaneous sounding of three or more pitches; chords are built from a particular **scale**, or sequence of pitches.

- The most common chord in Western music is a **triad**, three alternate pitches of a scale.

- Most Western music is based on **major** or **minor scales**, from which melody and harmony are derived.

- The **tonic** is the central pitch around which a melody and its harmonies are built; this principle of organization is called **tonality**.

- **Dissonance** is created by an unstable, or discordant, combination of pitches. **Consonance** occurs with a resolution of dissonance, producing a stable or restful sound.

To the linear movement of the melody, harmony adds another dimension: depth. **Harmony** is the simultaneous combination of sounds. It can be compared to the concept of perspective in artworks (see p. 15). Not all musics of the world rely on harmony, but it is central to most Western styles.

Harmony determines the relationships of intervals and chords. Intervals, the distance between any two notes, can occur successively or simultaneously. When three or more notes are sounded together, a **chord** is produced. Harmony describes a piece's chords and the progression from one chord to the next. It is the progression of harmony in a musical work that creates a feeling of order and unity.

The intervals from which chords and melodies are built are chosen from a particular collection of pitches arranged in ascending or descending order known as a **scale**. To the notes of the scale we assign syllables, *do–re–mi–fa–sol–la–ti–do,* or numbers, 1–2–3–4–5–6–7–8. An interval spanning eight notes is called an **octave**.

Chord

Scale

Octave

do	*re*	*mi*	*fa*	*sol*	*la*	*ti*	*do*
1	2	3	4	5	6	7	8

octave

The most common chord in Western music, a particular combination of three pitches, is known as a **triad**. Such a chord may be built on any note of the scale by combining every other note. For example, a triad built on the first pitch of a scale consists of the first, third, and fifth pitches of that scale *(do-mi-sol);* on the

Triad

second pitch, steps 2-4-6 *(re-fa-la)*; and so on. The triad is a basic formation in most music we know. In the example below, the melody of *Camptown Races* is harmonized with triads. You can see at a glance how melody is the horizontal aspect of music, while harmony, comprising blocks of notes (the chords), constitutes the vertical. Melody and harmony do not function independently of one another. On the contrary, the melody suggests the harmony that goes with it, and each constantly influences the other.

The Organization of Harmony

In all music, regardless of the style, certain notes assume greater importance than others. In most Western music, the first note of the scale, *do*, is considered the **tonic** and serves as a home base around which the others revolve and to which they ultimately gravitate. We observed this principle at work earlier with *Amazing Grace* (p. 10): the tune does not reach a final cadence, or stopping point, on the tonic note until its last phrase. It is this sense of a home base that helps us recognize when a piece of music ends.

The principle of organization around a central note, the tonic, is called **tonality**. The scale chosen as the basis of a piece determines the identity of the tonic and the key of the piece. Two different types of scales predominate in Western music written between about 1650 and 1900: major and minor. Each scale has a distinct sound because of its unique combination of intervals, as we will see in Chapter 4.

Harmony lends a sense of depth to music, as perspective does in this photograph, by **Fernand Ivaldi**, of a view down a tree-lined canal in France.

Tonality

Consonance and Dissonance

The movement of harmony toward resolution is the dynamic force in Western music. As music moves in time, we feel moments of tension and release. The tension results from **dissonance**, a combination of notes that sounds unstable, sometimes harsh, and in need of resolution. Dissonance introduces conflict into music in the same way that suspense creates tension in drama. Dissonance resolves in

Example of Harmony

Camptown Races (Stephen Foster)

Melody: The Camptown la-dies sing this song,

horizontal plane (melody)

vertical plane (harmony)

Harmony (chords)

Scale: *do re mi fa sol la ti do*
1 2 3 4 5 6 7 8

Just as dissonance provides tension in music, this image of global researchers sunbathing on the edge of a frozen fjord in the Arctic to emphasize the dramatic rate of global warming is discordant to the eye.

consonance, an agreeable-sounding combination of notes that provides a sense of relaxation and fulfillment. Each complements the other, and each is a necessary part of the artistic whole.

Drone   Harmony appeared much later historically (around 900) than melody, and its development took place largely in Western music. In many Asian cultures, harmony is relatively simple, consisting of a single sustained pitch, called a **drone**, against which melodic and rhythmic complexities unfold. This harmonic principle also occurs in some European folk music, where, for example, a bagpipe might play one or more accompanying drones to a lively dance tune.

Harmony   Our system of harmony has advanced steadily over the past millennium, continually responding to new needs. Composers have tested the rules, changing our notion of what sounds consonant, as they have experimented with innovative sounds and procedures. Yet their goal remains the same: to impose order on sound, organizing the pitches so that we perceive a unified idea.

YOUR TURN TO EXPLORE

Listen to Nirvana's *Smells Like Teen Spirit*. In addition to soft and loud sections, there are contrasting moments of consonance (in the solo verses) and dissonance (in the choruses and instrumental sections). How does consonance relieve the tension in this song? Choose another song you like, and listen for moments of tension or instability through dissonance, and release through consonance.

Chapter 4

The Organization of Musical Sounds

"If only the world could feel the power of harmony."

—W. A. Mozart

KEY POINTS

- An **octave** is the interval spanning eight notes of the scale. In Western music, the octave is divided into twelve **half steps**; two half steps make a **whole step**.

- The **chromatic scale** is made up of all twelve half steps, while a **diatonic scale** consists of seven whole and half steps whose patterns form **major** and **minor scales**.

- A **sharp** (♯) is a symbol that raises a pitch by a half step; a **flat** (♭) lowers a pitch by a half step.

- Other scale types are found around the world, sometimes using **microtones**, which are intervals smaller than half steps.

- The **tonic chord**, built on the first scale note, is the home base to which **active chords** (**dominant** and **subdominant**) need to resolve.

- Composers can shift the pitch level (**key**) of an entire work (**transposition**), or change the key during a work (**modulation**).

Here we consider how melody and harmony, two of the essential building blocks of musical compositions, function together to construct a musical system, both in the West and elsewhere.

Pitches are named using the first seven letters of the alphabet (A through G), which just start over again when you reach an octave. As noted earlier, an octave is an interval spanning eight notes of the scale. When we hear any two notes an octave apart, we recognize that they sound "the same." (These two notes take the same pitch name: for example, a C and the C an octave higher.)

One important variable in the different languages of music around the world is the way the octave is divided. In Western music, it is divided into twelve equal semitones, or **half steps**; from these are built different kinds of scales, which have constituted the basis of this musical language for nearly four hundred years. Some non-Western music features intervals even smaller than half steps, called **microtones**: for example, you can hear "bent," or inflected, pitches in Indian sitar music (p. 172) and microtonal sliding between pitches in Islamic chant (p. 68).

Octave

Half step

Microtones

The Chromatic Scale

The twelve half steps that make up the octave constitute what is known as the **chromatic scale**. You can see these twelve half steps on the keyboard (p. 18), counting all the white and black keys from C to the C above it. Virtually all

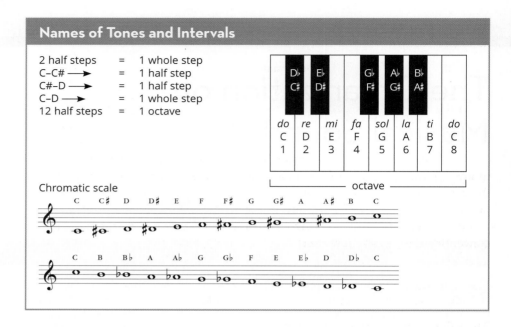

Names of Tones and Intervals

2 half steps   =   1 whole step
C–C# ⟶   =   1 half step
C#–D ⟶   =   1 half step
C–D ⟶   =   1 whole step
12 half steps   =   1 octave

Chromatic scale

Western music, no matter how intricate, is made up of the same twelve pitches and their duplications in higher and lower octaves.

You will notice that the black keys on the piano are named in relation to their white-key neighbors. The black key between C and D can be called C-sharp (♯) or D-flat (♭), depending on the context of the music. This plan applies to all the black keys. Thus, a **sharp** raises a note by a half step, and a **flat** lowers a note a half step. The distance between C and D is two half steps, or one **whole step**.

The Major Scale

Key

Chapter 3 introduced the notion that certain notes in music assume greater importance than others; in Western music, the first pitch of the scale, the tonic, is the home base to which the music gravitates. Two main scale types—major and minor—function within this organizational system known as tonality. When you listen to a composition in the **key** of C major, you hear a piece built around the central tone C, using the harmonies formed from the C major scale. Tonality is the basic harmonic principle at work in most Western music written from around 1600 to 1900 and in most popular music.

The **major scale** is the most familiar sequence of pitches. You can produce a C major scale (*do–re–mi–fa–sol–la–ti–do*) by playing only the white keys on the piano from one C to the next C. Looking at the keyboard above, you will see that there is no black key between E and F (*mi–fa*) or between B and C (*ti–do*). These notes are a half step apart, while the other white keys are a whole step apart. Consequently, a major scale is created by a specific pattern of whole (W) and half (H) steps— (W–W–H–W–W–W–H)—and can be built with this pattern starting on any pitch, even a black key.

Within each major scale are certain relationships based on tension and resolution. One of the most important is the thrust of the seventh pitch to the eighth (*ti* resolving to *do*). Similarly, we feel resolution when *re* moves to *do; fa* gravitates to *mi;* and *la* descends to *sol*. You can hear some of these relationships at work in the beginning of the well-known carol *Joy to the World*. It starts on the tonic note (*do*) ("Joy"), then descends and pauses on the **dominant** note (*sol*) ("world"), after

Dominant

which it continues downward, feeling a strong pull to the final *do* (on "come"; see melody on p. 9 and chart below).

Tonic			Dominant				Tonic
8	7	6	5	4	3	2	1
do →	*ti*	*la* →	*sol*	*fa* →	*mi*	*re* →	*do*
Joy	to	the	world,	the	Lord	is	come.

Joy to the World

Most important of all, the major scale defines two poles of traditional harmony: the tonic, the point of ultimate rest; and the dominant, which represents the active harmony. Tonic going to dominant and returning to tonic is a basic progression of harmony in Western music. Songs and pieces in a major key, like this carol, generally sound cheerful or triumphant to our ears (more a cultural convention than an absolute trait).

The Minor Scale

The **minor scale** sounds quite different from the major. One reason is that it has a lowered, or flatted, third note. Therefore, in the scale of C minor, there is an E-flat rather than the E-natural (white-key E) of the major scale; the interval C to E-flat is smaller than the interval C to E. Minor-key pieces sound sadder, darker than major-key. In the famous Bach theme to *The Art of Fugue,* you hear the smaller third interval right at the onset, as the melody outlines this interval (a minor third), then descends in a minor scale. The intervals of the minor scale (W–H–W–W–H–W–W) are shown in the table below.

The Art of Fugue

Diatonic vs. Chromatic

Music in a major or minor key focuses on the seven notes of the respective scale and is considered **diatonic**. In diatonic music, both the melody and the harmony are firmly rooted in the key. But some compositions introduce other notes that are foreign to the scale, drawing from the full gamut of the twelve half steps that span the octave. These works are considered **chromatic** (meaning "color").

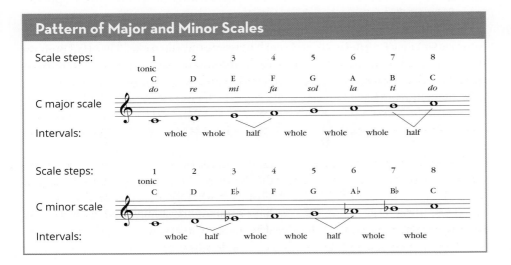

Sophie Taeuber-Arp (1889–1943), *Composition in Circles and Overlapping Angles* (1930). The overlapping and repeated shapes in this artwork can be compared, in music, to new pitch levels or to modulations to another key.

Romantic-era composers explored the possibilities of chromaticism to charge their music with emotion. In contrast, music of the Baroque and Classical eras is largely diatonic, centering on a tonic note and its related harmonies.

Other Scale Types

The Western musical system is only one way to structure music. The musical languages of other cultures often divide the octave differently, producing different scale patterns. Among the most common is the **pentatonic**, or five-note, scale, used in some African, Asian, and Native American musics. (*Amazing Grace*, on p. 9, is a pentatonic, folk-like melody.) Another non-Western scale type is **tritonic**, a three-note pattern also found in the music of some African cultures.

Some scales are not easily playable on Western instruments because they employ intervals smaller than the half step. Such intervals, known as **microtones**, may sound "off-key" to Western ears. One way of producing microtonal music is by an **inflection** of a pitch, making a brief microtonal dip or rise from the original pitch; this technique, similar to that of the "blue note" in jazz (see Chapter 56), makes possible a host of subtle pitch changes.

The musical system and the notes chosen in that system determine the sound and character of each work, whether classical, popular, or traditional. They are what make Western music sound familiar to us and why sometimes the music of other cultures may sound foreign.

The Major-Minor System

Just as melodies have inherent active and rest notes, so do the harmonies supporting them. The three-note chord, or triad, built on the first scale step is called the **Tonic (rest) chord (I)** **tonic**, or **I chord**, and serves as a point of rest. This **rest chord** is counterposed against other chords, which are active. The **active chords** in turn seek to be completed, or resolved, in the rest chord—the dynamic force in Western music, providing a forward direction and goal.

Dominant chord (V) The fifth scale step (*sol*), the **dominant**, forms the chief active chord (V), which brings a feeling of restlessness and seeks to resolve to the tonic. The triad built on **Subdominant chord (IV)** the fourth scale step (*fa*) is known as the **subdominant** (IV). The movement from the subdominant to the tonic (IV to I) is familiar from the "Amen" sung at the close of many hymns.

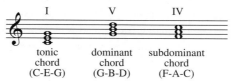

Rest chord and active chords in C major

These three basic triads are enough to harmonize many simple tunes. The Civil War song *Battle Hymn of the Republic* is a good example:

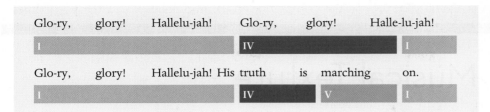

Glo-ry,	glory!	Hallelu-jah!	Glo-ry,	glory!	Halle-lu-jah!
I			IV		I

Glo-ry,	glory!	Hallelu-jah! His	truth	is	marching	on.
I			IV	V		I

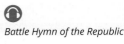

Battle Hymn of the Republic

The Key as a Form-Building Element

The three main chords of a musical work—tonic (I), dominant (V), and subdominant (IV)—are the foundations over which melodies and harmonic progressions unfold. Thus, a piece's key becomes a prime factor for musical unity.

At the same time, contrast between keys adds welcome variety. Composers begin by establishing the home key (for example, C major), then change to a related key, perhaps the dominant (G major), through a process known as **modulation**. In so doing, they create tension, because the dominant key is unstable compared with the tonic. This tension requires resolution, which is provided by the return to the home key.

Modulation

The progression, or movement, from home key to contrasting key and back outlines the basic musical pattern of statement-departure-return. The home key provides unity; the foreign key ensures variety and contrast.

The twelve major and twelve minor keys may be compared to rooms in a house, with the modulations equivalent to corridors leading from one to the other. A composer establishes the home key, then shapes the passage of modulation (the "corridor") into a key area that is not far away from the starting point. Alternately, composers may take an entire work and **transpose** it to a new key (making a transposition). This is convenient when a song's original key is too high or low to sing or play easily. You could begin on a different pitch and shift all the other pitches a uniform distance. In this way, the same song can be sung in various keys by differing voice ranges (soprano, alto, tenor, or bass).

Transposition

Although we are not always conscious of key centers and chord progressions while listening to music, these basic principles are deeply ingrained in our responses. We perceive and react to the tension and resolution provided by the movement of harmony, and we can sense how composers have used the harmonic system to give a coherent shape and meaning to their works.

Musical scales and key

YOUR TURN TO EXPLORE

Many classic rock songs are built on only three essential chords, I (tonic), IV (subdominant), and V (dominant)—the strong active and rest chords. Locate a recording of the Rolling Stones' *19th Nervous Breakdown,* and see if you can hear the fairly straightforward harmonic changes between these three chords. Now select a later rock-pop selection (alternative or heavy metal, for example) and listen to the chord structure. Do you perceive that it's more complex, with additional chords? Is the sense of a home base more ambiguous? How does the harmony affect the listener?

Chapter 5

Musical Texture

*"The composer . . . joins Heaven and Earth
with threads of sound."*

—Alan Hovhaness (1911–2000)

KEY POINTS

- **Texture** refers to the interweaving of the melodic lines with harmony.
- The simplest texture is **monophony**, a single voice or line without accompaniment.
- **Polyphony** describes a many-voiced texture with different melodic lines, based on **counterpoint**—one line set against another.

- **Homophony** occurs when one melodic voice is prominent over the accompanying lines or voices.
- **Imitation**—when a melodic idea is presented in one voice, then restated in another—is a common unifying technique in polyphony; **canons** and **rounds** are two types of strictly imitative works.

Types of Texture

Monophony

Melodic lines may be thought of as the various threads that make up the musical fabric, or the **texture**, of a piece. The simplest texture is **monophony**: a single voice. ("Voice" refers to an individual part or line, even in instrumental music.) Here, the melody is heard without any harmonic accompaniment or other melodic lines; it's you singing in the shower. It may be accompanied by rhythm and percussion instruments that embellish it, but interest is focused on the single melodic line rather than on any harmony. Until about a thousand years ago, the Western music we know about was monophonic, as some music of the Far and Middle East still is today.; we will hear an example of monophonic Islamic chant, sung throughout the Muslim world, in the Encounter on page 68.

Heterophony

Another common texture in non-Western cultures is **heterophony**, in which several musicians sing or play the same musical line (as in monophony), but each one varies some element—maybe a pitch or rhythm—so that they're "out of sync" with each other. These are usually subtle, nuanced variations that develop from individual expression. To Western ears, heterophony might sound as though the musicians are having trouble staying together (see the discussion of early American hymn singing in Chapter 24). Jazz (for example, the New Orleans jazz favorite *When the Saints Go Marching In*) and spirituals often depend on heterophonic texture—musicians' individual interpretations result in simultaneous elaborations of the same melody.

When the Saints Go Marching In

Polyphony

Polyphony ("many-voiced") describes a texture in which two or more different melodic lines are combined, thus distributing melodic interest among all the parts. Polyphonic texture is based on **counterpoint**; that is, one musical line set against another.

Examples of Musical Texture

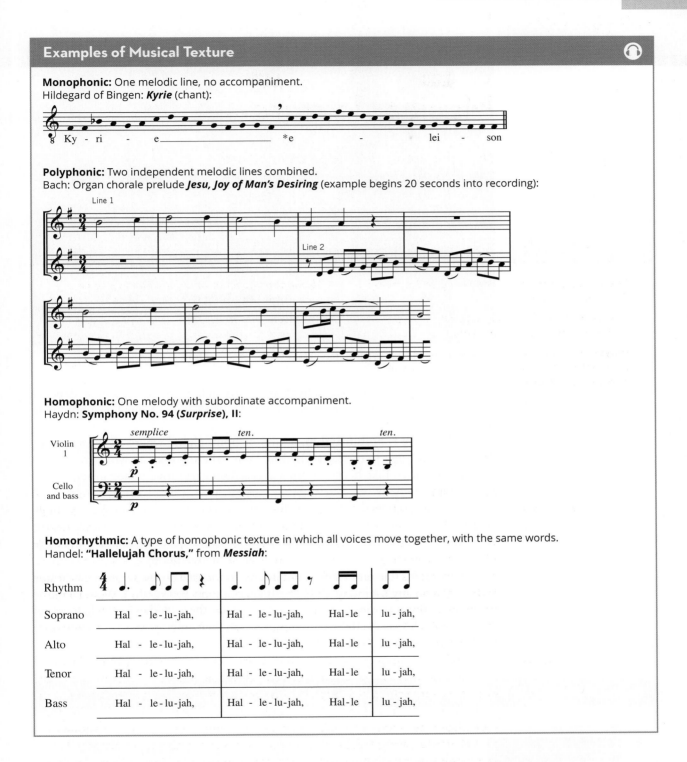

Monophonic: One melodic line, no accompaniment.
Hildegard of Bingen: ***Kyrie*** (chant):

Polyphonic: Two independent melodic lines combined.
Bach: Organ chorale prelude ***Jesu, Joy of Man's Desiring*** (example begins 20 seconds into recording):

Homophonic: One melody with subordinate accompaniment.
Haydn: **Symphony No. 94 (*Surprise*), II**:

Homorhythmic: A type of homophonic texture in which all voices move together, with the same words.
Handel: **"Hallelujah Chorus,"** from ***Messiah***:

In perhaps the most commonly heard texture, **homophony**, a single voice takes over the melodic interest, while the accompanying lines are subordinate. Normally, the accompanying lines become blocks of harmony, the chords that support, color, and enhance the principal line. Homophonic texture is heard when a pianist plays a melody in the right hand while the left sounds the chords, or when a singer or violinist carries the tune against a harmonic accompaniment on the piano. Homophonic texture, then, is based on harmony, just as polyphonic texture

Homophony

As in music, line and texture are the focus of this Kente cloth from Ghana, in Africa.

is based on counterpoint. The differences between the two can be subtle, depending on whether a listener perceives additional musical lines as equal or subordinate to a primary melody.

Homorhythm   Finally, there is **homorhythm**, a kind of homophony where all the voices or lines move together in the same rhythm. When there is text, all words are clearly sounded together. Like homophony, it is based on harmony moving in synchronization with a melody.

A composition need not use one texture exclusively throughout. For example, a large-scale work may begin by presenting a melody with accompanying chords (homophony), after which the interaction of the parts becomes increasingly complex as more independent melodies enter (creating polyphony).

We have noted that melody is the horizontal aspect of music, while harmony is the vertical. Comparing musical texture to the cross weave of a fabric makes the interplay of the parts clear. The horizontal threads, the melodies, are held together by the vertical threads, the harmonies. Out of their interaction comes a texture that may be light or heavy, coarse or fine.

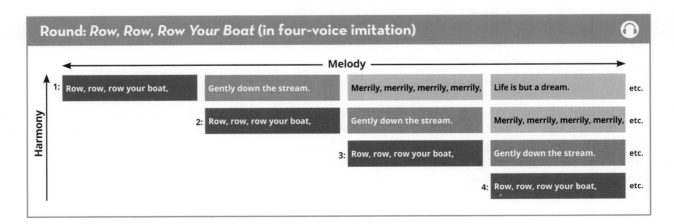

Contrapuntal Devices

When several independent lines are combined (in polyphony), one method that composers use to give unity and shape to the texture is **imitation**, in which a melodic idea is presented in one voice and then restated in another. While the imitating voice restates the melody, the first voice continues with new material. Thus, in addition to the vertical and horizontal threads in musical texture, a third, diagonal line results from imitation (see example opposite).

Imitation

The duration of the imitation may be brief or it may last the entire work. A strictly imitative work is known as a **canon**; and the simplest and most familiar form of canon is a **round**, in which each voice enters in succession with the same melody that can be repeated endlessly. Well-known examples include *Row, Row, Row Your Boat* and *Frère Jacques (Are You Sleeping?)*. In the example opposite, the round begins with one voice singing "Row, row, row your boat," then another voice joins it in imitation, followed by a third voice and finally a fourth, creating a four-part polyphonic texture.

Canon and round

Musical Texture and the Listener

Different textures require different kinds of listening. Monophonic music has only one focus—the single line of melody unfolding in real time. In homophonic music, the primary focus is on the main melody with subordinate harmonies as accompaniment. Indeed, much of the music we have heard since childhood—including traditional and popular styles—consists of melody and accompanying chords. Homorhythmic texture is easily recognizable as well, in its simple, vertical conception and hymnlike movement; the melody is still the most obvious line. Polyphonic music, with several independent melodies woven together, requires more experienced listening, but a good place to start is the round, the simplest polyphonic texture. With practice, you can hear the roles of individual voices and determine how they relate to each other, providing texture throughout a musical work.

Texture

YOUR TURN TO EXPLORE

Consider the textures used in Dylan's *Mr. Tambourine Man* and the Rolling Stones' *19th Nervous Breakdown*. In *Mr. Tambourine Man*, Dylan's vocal line predominates over the guitar accompaniment, making a homophonic texture; and in *19th Nervous Breakdown*, when the second voice enters to accompany Mick Jagger, it's homorhythmic (in the same rhythm). But some works feature more complex textures—where an ostinato (repeated bass), for example, presents some contrapuntal interest (listen for this in Public Enemy's *Don't Believe the Hype*). Select a favorite song and describe its texture. Do you hear multiple lines or a single, predominant one? Does complexity of lines make the listener's job more challenging?

Chapter 6

Musical Form

"The principal function of form is to advance our understanding. It is the organization of a piece that helps the listener to keep the idea in mind, to follow its development, its growth, its elaboration, its fate."

—Arnold Schoenberg

KEY POINTS

- **Form** is the organizing principle in music; its basic elements are repetition, contrast, and variation.
- **Strophic form**, common in songs, features repeated music for each stanza of text. In **through-composed form**, there are no large repeated sections.
- **Binary form (A-B)** and **ternary form (A-B-A)** are basic structures in music.
- A **theme**, a melodic idea in a large-scale work, can be broken into small, component fragments (**motives**). A **sequence** results when a motive is repeated at a different pitch.
- Many cultures use **call-and-response** (or **responsorial**) music, a repetitive style involving a soloist and a group. Some music is created spontaneously in performance, through **improvisation**.
- An **ostinato** is the repetition of a short melodic, rhythmic, or harmonic pattern.
- Large-scale compositions, such as symphonies and sonatas, are divided into sections, or **movements**.

F orm refers to a work's structure or shape, the way the elements of a composition have been combined by the composer to make it understandable to the listener. In all the arts, a balance is required between unity and variety, symmetry and asymmetry, activity and rest. Nature too has embodied this balance in the forms of plant and animal life and in what is perhaps the supreme achievement—the human form.

In His Own Words

❝ Improvisation is not the expression of accident but rather of the accumulated yearnings, dreams, and wisdom of our very soul."

—*Yehudi Menuhin*

Structure and Design in Music

Music of all cultures mirrors life in its basic elements of **repetition** and **contrast**, the familiar and the new. Repetition fixes the material in our minds and satisfies our need for the familiar, while contrast stimulates our interest and feeds our desire for change. Every kind of musical work, from a nursery rhyme to a symphony, has a conscious structure. One of the most common in vocal music, both popular and classical, is **strophic form**, in which the same melody is repeated with each stanza of the text, as for a folk song or carol (*Silent Night*). In this structure, while the music within a stanza offers some contrast, its repetition binds the song together. The direct opposite of strophic form in a song would be **through-composed** form, where no main section of the music or text is repeated.

Variation

One kind of form that falls *between* repetition and contrast is **variation**, where some aspects of the music are altered but the original is still recognizable. You hear this formal technique when you listen to a new arrangement of a well-known popular song: the tune is recognizable, but many features of the known version are changed.

This famous painting by **Andy Warhol** (1928–1987), *32 Campbell's Soup Cans*, illustrates the reliance of artists on the basic elements of repetition and variation.

While all musical structures are based in one way or another on repetition and contrast, the forms are not fixed molds into which composers pour their material. What makes each piece of music unique is the way the composer adapts a general plan to create a wholly individual combination. And performers sometimes participate in shaping a composition. In works based mostly on **improvisation** (pieces created spontaneously in performance—typical of jazz, rock, and certain non-Western styles), repetition, contrast, and variation all play a role. We will see that in jazz, musicians organize their improvised melodies within a pre-established harmonic pattern, time frame, and melodic outline that is understood by all the performers. And in Indian sitar music (see p. 172), improvisation is a refined and classical art, where the seemingly free and rhapsodic spinning out of the music is tied to a prescribed musical process that results in a lacework of variations. Thus, even pieces created on the spot are balanced by structural principles.

Binary and Ternary Form

Two basic structures are widespread in art and in music. **Binary** (two-part) **form** is based on a statement and a departure, without a return to the opening section. **Ternary** (three-part) **form** extends the idea of statement and departure by bringing back the first section. Formal patterns are generally outlined with letters: binary form as **A-B** and ternary form as **A-B-A** (illustrated in the chart on p. 28).

Both two-part and three-part forms are found in short pieces such as songs and dances. The longer ternary form, with its logical symmetry and its balance of the outer sections against the contrasting middle one, constitutes a clear-cut formation that is favored by architects and painters as well as composers.

The Building Blocks of Form

When a melodic idea is used as a building block in the construction of a larger work, we call it a **theme**. The introduction of a theme and its elaboration are the essence of musical thinking. This process of growth has its parallel in writing, when an idea, a topic sentence, is stated at the beginning of a paragraph and enlarged upon and developed by the author. Just as each sentence leads logically from one to the next, every musical idea takes up where the one before left off and continues convincingly to the next. The expansion of a theme, achieved by varying its melody, rhythm, or harmony, is considered **thematic development**. This is one of the most important techniques in music and requires both imagination and craft on the part of the creator.

Theme

Thematic development

Thematic development is generally too complex a process for short pieces, where a simple contrast between sections and modest expansion of material usually supply the necessary continuity. But it's necessary in larger forms of music, where it provides clarity, coherence, and logic.

	Certain procedures help the music flow logically. The simplest is repetition, which may be either exact or varied. Or the idea may be restated at a higher or
Sequence	lower pitch level; this restatement is known as a **sequence**. Within a theme, a small
Motive	fragment that forms a melodic-rhythmic unit is called a **motive**. Motives are the

cells of musical growth, which, when repeated, varied, and combined into new patterns, impart the qualities of evolution and expansion. These musical building blocks can be seen even in simple songs, like the national tune *America* (p. 29). The opening three-note motive ("My country") is repeated in sequence (at a different pitch level) on the words "Sweet land of." A longer melodic idea is treated sequentially in the third line, where the musical phrase "Land where my fathers died" is repeated one note lower on the words "Land of the pilgrim's pride."

Whatever the length or style of a composition, it will show the principles of repetition and contrast, of unity and variety. One formal practice based on repeti-

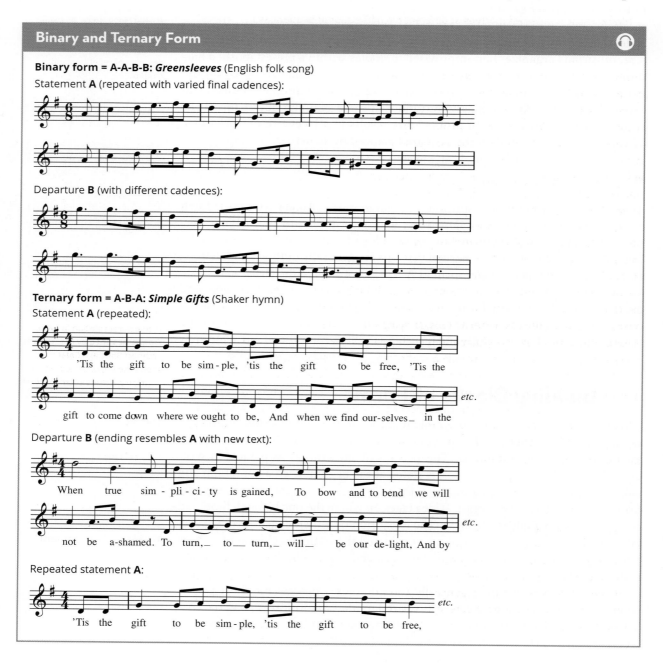

Binary and Ternary Form

Binary form = A-A-B-B: *Greensleeves* (English folk song)
Statement **A** (repeated with varied final cadences):

Departure **B** (with different cadences):

Ternary form = A-B-A: *Simple Gifts* (Shaker hymn)
Statement **A** (repeated):

'Tis the gift to be sim-ple, 'tis the gift to be free, 'Tis the
gift to come down where we ought to be, And when we find our-selves_ in the   *etc.*

Departure **B** (ending resembles **A** with new text):

When true sim-pli-ci-ty is gained, To bow and to bend we will
not be a-shamed. To turn,_ to_ turn,_ will_ be our de-light, And by   *etc.*

Repeated statement **A**:

'Tis the gift to be sim-ple, 'tis the gift to be free,   *etc.*

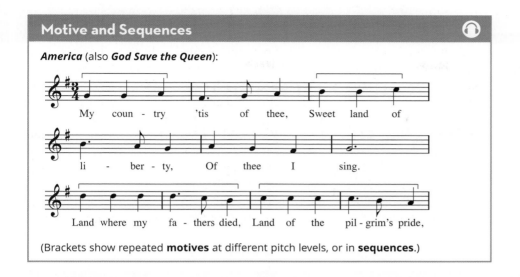

Motive and Sequences

America (also *God Save the Queen*):

My coun - try 'tis of thee, Sweet land of

li - ber - ty, Of thee I sing.

Land where my fa - thers died, Land of the pil - grim's pride,

(Brackets show repeated **motives** at different pitch levels, or in **sequences**.)

tion and heard throughout the world is **call and response**, or **responsorial** music. In this style of performance, predominant in early Western church music and also in the music of African, Native American, and African American cultures, a singing leader is imitated or answered by a chorus of followers. This is a typical singing style for spirituals and gospel music, as you will hear in a performance of one of the most famous spirituals of all time, *Swing Low, Sweet Chariot* (Chapter 50).

Another widely used procedure linked to the principle of repetition is **ostinato**, a short musical pattern—melodic, rhythmic, or harmonic—that is repeated throughout a work or a major section of a piece. One well-known work that uses this technique is the Pachelbel *Canon in D*, in which rich string lines unfold gradually over an ever-present bass pattern. This unifying technique is especially prevalent in popular styles such as blues, jazz, rock, and rap, which rely on repeated harmonies that provide a scaffolding for musical development.

Music composition is an organic form in which the individual notes are bound together within a phrase, the phrases within a theme, the themes within a section, the sections within a **movement** (a complete, comparatively independent division of a large-scale work), and the movements within the work as a whole (like a symphony)—just as a novel binds together the individual words, phrases, sentences, paragraphs, and chapters into a cohesive whole.

The Gare de Saint-Exupéry, a modern train station in Lyon, France, designed by the Spanish architect **Santiago Calatrava**, shows the importance of symmetrical patterns in architecture.

Musical form

YOUR TURN TO EXPLORE

Many popular songs are strophic, with repeated music for each new verse. Locate a recording of Madonna's *Like a Virgin,* and listen to it all the way through. There are three verses, each followed by the chorus, "Like a virgin." But after the second verse and chorus, there's a brief interlude of new, contrasting music sung to wordless text. Pick another song, and consider how the basic formal elements of repetition, contrast, and variation figure in its structure. How do these elements affect the listener's experience?

Chapter 7

Musical Expression: Tempo and Dynamics

"Ah, music . . . a magic beyond all we do here!"

—Albus Dumbledore, Headmaster,
Hogwarts School of Witchcraft and Wizardry

KEY POINTS

- **Tempo** is the rate of speed, or pace, of the music.
- We use Italian terms to designate musical tempo: some of the most familiar are *allegro* (fast), *moderato* (moderate), *adagio* (quite slow), *accelerando* (speeding up), and *ritardando* (slowing down).

- **Dynamics** describe the volume, or how loud or soft the music is played; Italian terms for dynamics include *forte* (loud) and *piano* (soft).
- Composers indicate tempo and dynamics as a means of expression.

The Pace of Music

Most Western music has steady beats underlying the movement; whether these occur slowly or rapidly determines the **tempo**, or rate of speed, of the music. Consequently, the flow of music in time involves meter patterns (the grouping and emphasis of the beats) and tempo.

Tempo also carries emotional implications. We hurry our speech in moments of agitation or eagerness. Vigor and gaiety are associated with a brisk speed, just as despair usually demands a slow one. Since music moves in time, its pace is of prime importance, drawing from listeners responses that are both physical and psychological.

Because of the close connection between tempo and mood, tempo markings indicate the character of the music as well as the pace. The markings, along with other indications of expression, are traditionally given in Italian. This practice reflects the domination of Italian music in Europe from around 1600 to 1750, when performance directions were established. Here are some of the most common tempo markings:

In His Own Words

" Any composition must necessarily possess its unique tempo. . . . A piece of mine can survive almost anything but a wrong or uncertain tempo."

—Igor Stravinsky

grave: solemn (very, very slow)	*moderato*: moderate
largo: broad (very slow)	*allegro*: fast (cheerful)
adagio: quite slow	*vivace*: lively
andante: a walking pace	*presto*: very fast

You frequently encounter modifiers such as *molto* (very), *meno* (less), *poco* (a little), and *non troppo* (not too much). Also important are terms indicating a change

Speed and movement are easily perceived in this photograph of the 2002 Tour de France. Here, the cyclists are racing toward the finish on Paris's famous Avenue des Champs-Élysées.

of tempo, among them *accelerando* (getting faster), *ritardando* (holding back, getting slower), and *a tempo* (in time, or returning to the original pace).

Loudness and Softness

Dynamics denote the volume (degree of loudness or softness) at which music is played. Like tempo, dynamics can affect our emotional response. The main dynamic indications, listed below, are based on the Italian words for soft *(piano)* and loud *(forte)*.

pianissimo (***pp***): very soft	*mezzo forte* (***mf***): moderately loud
piano (***p***): soft	*forte* (***f***): loud
mezzo piano (***mp***): moderately soft	*fortissimo* (***ff***): very loud

Directions to change the dynamics, either suddenly or gradually, are also indicated by words or signs:

crescendo (<): growing louder
decrescendo or *diminuendo* (>): growing softer

Tempo and Dynamics as Elements of Expression

The composer adds markings for tempo and dynamics to help shape the expressive content of a work. These expression marks increased in number during the late eighteenth and nineteenth centuries, when composers tried to make their intentions known ever more precisely; by the early twentieth century, few decisions were left to the performer at all.

In His Own Words

" Voices, instruments, and all possible sounds—even silence itself—must tend toward one goal, which is expression."
—C. W. Gluck (1714–1787)

Dynamics in music may be compared to the light and shade in this photograph of the sun shining through a forest of trees.

Tempo and Dynamics in a Music Score

Beethoven: **Symphony No. 5**, opening:

Tempo: Fast (*Allegro*), with vigor (*con brio*)
Dynamics: Very loud (*fortissimo*), then soft (*piano*)

Tempo and dynamics

If tempo and dynamics are the domain of the composer, what is the role of performers and conductors in interpreting a musical work? Performance directions can be somewhat imprecise—what is loud or fast to one performer may be moderate in volume and tempo to another. Even when composers give precise tempo markings in their scores (the exact number of beats per minute), performers have the final say in choosing a tempo that best delivers the message of the music.

YOUR TURN TO EXPLORE

Find a recording of Nirvana's *Smells Like Teen Spirit,* and listen to how it is built on shifting dynamic levels—alternating throughout between soft (*piano*) and loud (*forte*). How does this feature help organize the song? How do changing dynamics contribute to your interest? Choose another song you know, and describe how the musicians make use of dynamics. Are there different volume levels, even levels, gradual increases (*crescendos*), or decreases (*decrescendos*)? How do dynamics affect your experience in this song?

Chapter 8

Music and Words

"Let the words be the mistress of the melody, not its slave."

–Claudio Monteverdi

KEY POINTS

- A song's text can convey the meaning of the words or simply sounds. Some composers use the voice as an instrument, as in **vocalise** (melodies sung on a neutral sound like "ah") or **scat-singing** in jazz (to made-up syllables).

- **Secular** (nonreligious) music is generally sung in the language of the people (the **vernacular**). Much Western **sacred** (religious) music is in **Latin**, the language of the Roman Catholic Church.

- Composers may set an already-written text to music, or, as in opera and musical theater, work together with lyricists as a songwriting team.

- Each syllable of a song text may get one note (**syllabic** setting); one syllable may get a few notes (**neumatic** setting); or one syllable may get many notes (**melismatic** setting).

- Composers use **word-painting** to emphasize the text, perhaps with a drawn-out word over many notes (**melisma**) or with a melody that pictorializes a word.

Today, thanks largely to iTunes, many people consider "song" synonymous with any musical selection, with or without words. Though the term correctly refers to a union of music and words—something that is sung—the original Greek word for "music," *mousikas,* implied a union of melody, language, *and* movement. The Greek philosopher Plato considered music without words to be lacking in artistic taste, and it was through language that Greek listeners reacted to the mood of a composition.

There are many facets of text and music we can consider here. For starters, does the text communicate something that can be understood, or are the syllables **nonlexical** (nonsensical)? Examples of nonlexical syllables are "Na na na na, na na na na, na na na na, hey Jude"(from the Beatles' *Hey Jude*) and "Zip-a-dee-doo-dah, zip-a-dee-ay" (from Disney's *Song of the South*). Jazz singers often launch into **scat-singing**, a vocal improvisation using wordless vocables, like "Shoo-be-doo-be doo-wop" (Louis Armstrong famously invented this technique), and in English madrigals and Christmas carols you'll sometimes hear syllables like "fa la la la la" as a refrain. In all these cases, the sounds and rhythms of the "text" contribute to the music and its broad meaning. The voice can even be used for its timbral characteristics, like any other instrument—as in the technique called **vocalise**, or wordless melody (singing on a neutral vowel like "ah").

Singing without words

Throughout this book, you will encounter music with texts in a variety of languages other than English. Music for worship has been set for centuries in Hebrew, Greek, and Latin. Not only was **Latin** the language of the Roman Empire, it was also the language of learning at medieval and Renaissance universities and of the Roman Catholic Church until the Second Vatican Council of 1962, when the church

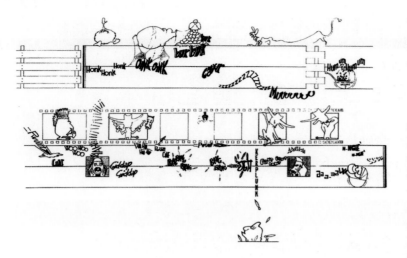

This humorous score of *Stripsody*, by soprano Cathy Berberian, features comic-book images that ask the vocalist to make sounds matching the pictures.

approved the use of the **vernacular** (the language of the people) for the Mass. **Secular** (nonreligious) music has traditionally been in vernacular languages. You will hear most selections sung in their original language (although we provide an English translation), since a sung translation will never fit the musical line as well as the original words. In the case of a famous lullaby by Brahms, though, you probably know the English version better than the original German words:

Brahms, *Lullaby*

Gu - ten   A - bend, gut'   Nacht,   mit__   Ro - sen   be -
Lul - la - by   and good   night,   with__   ro - ses   be -

dacht,__   mit__   Näg' - lein   be - steckt,   schlupf'.   un - ter   die   Deck',
dight,__   with__   li - lies   o'er__   spread,   is__   ba - by's   wee   bed,

In addition to modern European languages (Italian, French, Spanish, and German), you will also hear texts in Arabic, Chinese, and even Nahuatl, a language of the Aztec peoples. As we encounter words in other languages, their translations often have meanings that are slightly different from the original; if you have studied (or grown up with) a language other than English, you know that some terms or concepts really don't translate perfectly from language to language or culture to culture. This is another reason why it's important to consider the texts of songs in their original language even as we also try to grasp the meaning through the translation.

Which comes first in a song, the melody or the words? As we will see, many composers select an already existing poem or prose text to set to music, so clearly those words precede the tune. But great teams of lyricists / composers have worked together to come up with enduring songs, and there is no clear formula for their creations. When George Gershwin composed the tune that became *I Got Rhythm*, his partner / brother Ira set out to write lyrics that fit the syncopated rhythms. It took him several tries, and the famous ones they settled on do not rhyme ("I got rhythm, I got music, I got my girl, who could ask for anything more"). Likewise, the lyrics for the Talking Heads' famous song *Burning Down the House* were added after the band had found a set of rhythmic and melodic ideas that they liked.

The text of a song may help organize the tune. Words flow in phrases, just as melodies do, and both are punctuated (by cadences, in the case of music). Poems are often written in rhymed **stanzas**, or **strophes**. As mentioned earlier, the most common type of musical setting, in both popular and art music, is **strophic form**, in which the same music is repeated for each stanza. Or the song might feature a **refrain**, or **chorus**, words and music that recur after each stanza. In sung dramas (like operas), the text may be free (unrhymed, metrical) verse or even prose, as

Stanza/strophe

Refrain/chorus

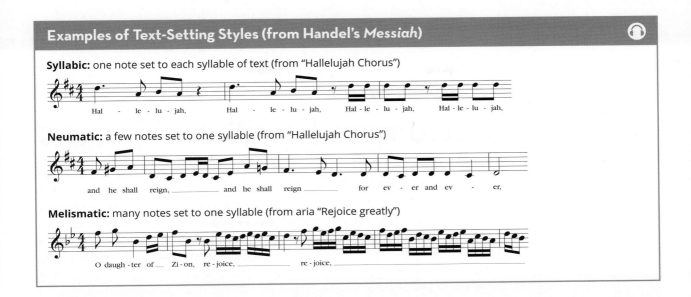

Examples of Text-Setting Styles (from Handel's *Messiah*)

Syllabic: one note set to each syllable of text (from "Hallelujah Chorus")

Hal - le - lu - jah, Hal - le - lu - jah, Hal - le - lu - jah, Hal - le - lu - jah,

Neumatic: a few notes set to one syllable (from "Hallelujah Chorus")

and he shall reign, _____ and he shall reign for ev - er and ev - er,

Melismatic: many notes set to one syllable (from aria "Rejoice greatly")

O daugh - ter of __ Zi - on, re - joice, re - joice, _____

people speak to each other. We will hear a variety of melodic styles in opera: some song-like passages (called arias) are very lyrical, while others are more speech-like.

How the words fit into the flow—both melodic and rhythmic—of a song makes the difference between a memorable song and an easily forgotten one. The simplest way that words and melody can fit together is a one-to-one match called **syllabic**: each syllable gets one note, as in "Happy Birthday." The opposite style of syllabic is **melismatic**, in which a single syllable is elongated by many notes, thereby giving a particular word more emphasis. Both styles, and a middle ground called **neumatic** (with a few notes to each syllable), are represented in the examples above from Handel's *Messiah*. In the last example, you can see how "rejoice" is drawn out in a long **melisma**, not only emphasizing the word, but capturing its joyful meaning through music. This technique is called **word-painting**, and you will hear it frequently in vocal music. Gospel, as well as some pop singers—such as Mariah Carey, Christina Aguilera, and Beyoncé Knowles—use melismas as part of their signature style.

The words of a song offer a way for all of us to understand the music, no matter what our cultural or aesthetic backgrounds. But keep in mind that often, especially when the text is a poem, the words themselves have purposefully vague or multiple implications, or are chosen by the poet (or the musician) for their sound and rhythm as much as for their specific meaning. One thing is sure: when words are sung, their power and effect always go well beyond their literal meaning on the page.

Text-setting styles

Music and words

YOUR TURN TO EXPLORE

Listen again to *Like a Virgin*, concentrating on the text and how it is delivered. You will hear that it is mostly syllabic, making the text clear, but in the choruses there is a short melisma on the important word "virgin." Madonna also makes use of syllables that don't contribute to the song's meaning ("whoa," "hey," "ooo"). In another song of your choice, listen for how the text is set (syllabic or melismatic) and whether there are examples of wordless singing. How do these text devices affect your understanding and enjoyment of the song? Why do you think a song may contain wordless singing?

Chapter 9

Voices and Instrument Families

"It was my idea to make my voice work in the same way as a trombone or violin—not sounding like them but 'playing' the voice like those instruments."

—Frank Sinatra (1915–1998)

KEY POINTS

- Properties of sound include pitch, duration, volume, and **timbre**, or **tone color**.

- An **instrument** generates vibrations and transmits them into the air.

- The human voice can be categorized into various ranges, including **soprano** and **alto** for female voices, and **tenor** and **bass** for male voices.

- The world instrument classification system divides into **aerophones** (such as flutes or horns), **chordophones** (violins or guitars), **idiophones** (bells or cymbals), and **membranophones** (drums).

Musical Timbre

Instruments

A fourth property of sound besides pitch, duration, and volume—**timbre**, or **tone color**—accounts for the striking differences in the sound quality of musical **instruments**, mechanisms that generate vibrations and launch them into the air. It's what makes a trumpet sound altogether different from a guitar or a clarinet. Timbre is influenced by a number of factors, such as the size, shape, and proportions of the instrument, the material from which it is made, and the manner in which the vibration is produced. A string, for example, may be bowed, plucked, or struck.

Each voice type and instrument has a limited melodic range (the distance from the lowest to the highest note) and dynamic range. We describe a specific area in the range of an instrument or voice, such as low, middle, or high, as its **register**.

In His Own Words

" If you can walk, you can dance. If you can talk, you can sing."

—*Zimbabwean proverb*

The Voice as Instrument

The human voice is the most natural of all musical instruments; it is also one of the most universal—all cultures enjoy some form of vocal music. Each person's voice displays a particular quality (or character) and range. The standard designations for

Voice types

vocal ranges, from highest to lowest, are **soprano**, **mezzo-soprano**, and **alto** (short for "contralto") for female voices; and **tenor**, **baritone**, and **bass** for male voices.

In earlier eras, Western social and religious customs severely restricted women's participation in public musical events. Thus, young boys, and occasionally

LEFT: Luciano Pavarotti (1935–2007), one of the greatest operatic tenors of all time.

RIGHT: E. J. Jones plays folk songs and dances on Scottish small pipes (aerophone), a quieter version of bagpipe.

men with soprano- or alto-range voices, sang female parts in church music and on the stage. In the sixteenth century, women singers came into prominence in secular (nonreligious) music. Tenors were most often featured as soloists in early opera, while baritones and basses became popular soloists later, in the eighteenth century. In other cultures, the sound of women's voices has always been preferred for certain styles of music, such as lullabies.

Throughout the ages, the human voice has served as a model for instrument builders, composers, and players who have sought to duplicate its lyric beauty, expressiveness, and ability to produce **vibrato** (a throbbing effect) on their instruments.

The World of Musical Instruments

LEFT: A steel drum band playing steelpans (idiophones) competes in the famous Panorama competition in Trinidad.

RIGHT: A drum (membranophone) ensemble from Burundi in Central Africa.

The diversity of musical instruments played around the world defies description. Since every conceivable method of sound production is used, and every possible raw material, it would be impossible to list them all here. However, specialists have devised a method of classifying instruments based solely on the way their sound

Wu Man plays the Chinese pipa, a plucked-string instrument (chordophone).

is generated. The system designates four basic categories. **Aerophones** produce sound by using air. Instruments in this category include flutes, whistles, and horns—in short, any wind instrument. One of the most common aerophones around the world is the **bagpipe**, with a somewhat raucous tone and built-in drones for harmony (listen to *Go to Berwick, Johnny* to hear typical bagpipe dance music). **Chordophones** produce sound from a vibrating string stretched between two points. The string may be set in motion by bowing, as on a violin; by plucking, as on a guitar or an Indian sitar (*Bhimpalasi*); or by striking, as for the Chinese hammered dulcimer, or yangqin (in *The Moon Reflected on the Second Springs*, the yangqin accompanies the Chinese bowed erhu).

Idiophones produce sound from the substance itself. They may be struck, as are steel drums from Trinidad (*Dougla Dance*); scraped or shaken, as are African rattles (*Gota*); or plucked, as is the mbira, or African "thumb piano" (*Mbira*). The variety of idiophones around the world is staggering. **Membranophones** are drum-type instruments that are sounded from tightly stretched membranes. They too can be struck, plucked, rubbed, or even sung into, to set the skin in vibration. You can hear traditional Indian tuned drums called tabla in *Bhimpalasi*, and untuned drums from Ghana in *Gota*.

In the next chapter, we will review the instruments used most frequently in Western music. Throughout the book, however, you will learn about other instruments associated with popular and art music cultures around the world that have influenced the Western tradition.

YOUR TURN TO EXPLORE

Listen again to Dylan's *Mr. Tambourine Man*, focusing on his different vocal timbres. Dylan has a unique and very recognizable vocal timbre that has been described as nasal, rough, or even like sandpaper. You don't hear this voice type in classical singing (opera, for example) or in other styles of pop music. The song offers two different instrument timbres as well: a chordophone (acoustic guitar) and an aerophone (harmonica), both played by Dylan. Select another song, and listen for the character of the singer's voice and any instrumental timbres. How do the different timbres affect your experience? Why do you think certain timbres are associated with certain sections of the song?

Voices

Chapter 10

Western Musical Instruments

*"In music, instruments perform the function
of the colors employed in painting."*

—Honoré de Balzac (1799–1850)

KEY POINTS

- The four families of Western instruments are **strings**, **woodwinds**, **brass**, and **percussion**.
- String instruments (chordophones) are sounded by **bowing** and **plucking**. Bowed strings include the violin, viola, cello, and double bass; plucked strings include the harp and guitar.
- Woodwind instruments (aerophones) include the flute, oboe, clarinet, bassoon, and saxophone.
- Brass instruments (aerophones) include the trumpet, French horn, trombone, and tuba.
- Percussion instruments include idiophones (xylophone, cymbals, triangle) and membranophones (timpani, bass drum); some are pitched (chimes), while others are unpitched (tambourine).
- Keyboard instruments, such as the piano and organ, do not fit neatly into the Western classification system.

The instruments of the Western world, and especially those of the orchestra, may be categorized into four groups of their own: strings, woodwinds, brass, and percussion. Not all woodwinds, however, are made of wood, nor do they share a common means of sound production. Furthermore, certain instruments do not fit neatly into any of these convenient categories (the piano, for example, is both a string and a percussion instrument).

String Instruments

The string family, all chordophones, includes two types of instruments: those that are **bowed** and those that are **plucked**. In the bowed-string family, there are four principal members: violin, viola, violoncello, and double bass, each with four strings (double basses sometimes have five) that are set vibrating by drawing a bow across them. The bow is held in the right hand, while the left hand is used to "stop" the string by pressing a finger down at a particular point, thereby leaving a certain portion of the string free to vibrate. By stopping the string at another point, the performer changes the length of the vibrating portion, and with it the rate of vibration and the pitch.

The **violin** evolved to its present form at the hands of the master instrument makers who flourished in Italy from around 1600 to 1750. It is capable of brilliance and dramatic effect, subtle nuances from soft to loud, and great agility in rapid passages throughout its extremely wide range.

The **viola** is somewhat larger than the violin and thus has a lower range. Its

Violin

Viola

LEFT: Grammy-Award-winning violinist Hilary Hahn (b. 1979) enjoys a prominent career as a soloist.

RIGHT: Yo-Yo Ma (b. 1955), the revered and wide-ranging virtuoso cellist.

strings are longer, thicker, and heavier. The tone is husky in the low register, somber and penetrating in the high. It often fills in the harmony, or it may **double** another part—that is, reinforce another part when it plays the same notes an octave higher or lower.

Cello

The **violoncello**, popularly known as **cello**, is lower in range than the viola and is notable for its singing quality and its dark resonance in the low register. Cellos often play the melody, and they enrich the sound with their full timbre.

The **double bass**, known also as a **contrabass** or **bass viol**, is the lowest of the orchestral string instruments. Accordingly, it plays the bass part—the foundation of the harmony. Its deep tones support the cello part an octave lower. These four string instruments constitute the core or "heart" of the orchestra, a designation that indicates the section's versatility and importance.

Harpist Julie Spring performs as a soloist and with orchestras.

String instruments can be played in many styles and can produce striking special effects. They excel at playing **legato** (smoothly, connecting the notes) as well as the opposite, **staccato** (with notes short and detached). A different effect, **pizzicato** (plucked), is created when a performer plucks the string with a finger instead of using the bow. **Vibrato**, a slight throbbing, is achieved by a rapid wrist-and-finger movement on the string that slightly alters the pitch. For a **glissando**, a finger of the left hand slides along the string while the right hand draws the bow, gathering all the pitches under the left-hand finger in one swooping sound. **Tremolo**, the rapid repetition of a tone through a quick up-and-down movement of the bow, is associated with suspense and excitement. No less important is the **trill**, a rapid alternation between a note and one adjacent to it.

String instruments are capable of playing several notes simultaneously, thereby producing harmony: **double-stopping** means playing two strings at once; playing three or four strings

LEFT: Milt Hinton (1910–2000), the "dean of jazz bass players," playing the double bass.

RIGHT: Bass guitarist Ricardo Winandy performs in the Brazilian progressive band Mindflow.

together is called **triple-** or **quadruple-stopping**. Another effect is created by the **mute**, a small attachment that fits over the bridge, muffling the sound. **Harmonics** are eerie, crystalline tones in a very high register that are produced by lightly touching the string at certain points while the bow is drawn across the string.

Two popular plucked-string instruments are the harp and the guitar. The **harp** is one of the oldest of musical instruments, with a home in many cultures outside Europe. Its plucked strings, whose pitches are changed by means of pedals, produce an ethereal tone. Chords on the harp are frequently played in broken form—that is, the notes are sounded one after another instead of simultaneously. From this technique comes the term **arpeggio**, which means "broken chord" (*arpa* is Italian for "harp"). Arpeggios can be created in a variety of ways on many instruments.

Harp

The **guitar**, another old instrument, dating back at least to the Middle Ages, probably originated in the Middle East. A favorite solo instrument, it is associated today with folk and popular music as well as classical styles. The standard **acoustic** (as opposed to electric) **guitar** is made of wood and has a fretted fingerboard and six nylon strings, which are plucked with the fingers of the right hand or with a pick. The electronically amplified **electric guitar**, capable of many specialized techniques, comes in two main types: the hollow-bodied (or electro-acoustic), favored by jazz and popular musicians; and the solid-bodied, used more by rock musicians. Related to the guitar are such traditional instruments as the **banjo** and **mandolin**.

Guitar

Woodwind Instruments

Woodwind instruments (aerophones) produce sound with a column of air vibrating within a pipe that has fingerholes along its length. When one or another of these holes is opened or closed, the length of the vibrating air column is changed. Woodwind players are capable of remarkable agility on their instruments by means of an intricate mechanism of keys arranged to suit the natural position of the fingers.

Nowadays woodwinds are not necessarily made of wood, and they employ several different methods of setting up vibration: blowing across a mouth hole (flute), blowing into a mouthpiece that has a single reed (clarinet and saxophone), or blow-

Flutist James Galway (b. 1939), the "man with the golden flute."

ing into a mouthpiece fitted with a double reed (oboe and bassoon). They do, however, have one important feature in common: the holes in their pipes. In addition, their timbres are such that composers think of them and write for them as a group.

The **flute** is the soprano voice of the woodwind family. Its tone is cool and velvety in the expressive low register, and often brilliant in the upper part of its range. The present-day flute, made of a metal alloy rather than wood, is a cylindrical tube, closed at one end, that is held horizontally. The player blows across a mouth hole cut in the side of the pipe near the closed end. The flute is used frequently as a melody instrument—its timbre stands out against the orchestra—and offers the performer great versatility in playing rapid repeated notes, scales, and trills. The **piccolo** (from the Italian *flauto piccolo,* "little flute") is the highest pitched instrument in the orchestra. In its upper register, it takes on a shrillness that is easily heard even when the orchestra is playing *fortissimo.*

The **oboe** continues to be made of wood. The player blows directly into a double reed, which consists of two thin strips of cane bound together with a narrow passage for air. The oboe's timbre, generally described as nasal and reedy, is often associated with pastoral effects and nostalgic moods. The oboe traditionally sounds the tuning note (A) for the other instruments of the orchestra. The **English horn** is an alto oboe. Its wooden tube is wider and longer than that of the oboe and ends in a pear-shaped opening called a **bell**, which largely accounts for its soft, expressive timbre.

The **clarinet** uses a single reed, a small, thin piece of cane fastened against its chisel-shaped mouthpiece. The instrument's tone is smooth and liquid, and its range remarkably wide in both pitch and volume. It too displays an easy command of rapid scales, trills, and repeated notes. The **bass clarinet**, one octave lower in range than the clarinet, has a rich dark tone and a wide dynamic range.

The **bassoon**, another double-reed instrument, sounds weighty in the low reg-

Oboe players in an orchestra.

LEFT: Bassoon players in an orchestra.

RIGHT: Richard Stoltzman (b. 1942) playing the clarinet in Carnegie Hall.

ister and reedy and intense in the upper. Capable of a hollow-like staccato and wide leaps that can sound humorous, it is at the same time a highly expressive instrument. The **contrabassoon** produces the lowest tone of the woodwinds. Its function in the woodwind section of supplying a foundation for the harmony may be likened to that of the double bass among the strings.

The **saxophone**, invented by the Belgian Adolphe Sax in 1840, is the most recent of the woodwind instruments. It was created by combining the single reed of the clarinet with a conical bore and the metal body of the brass instruments. There are various sizes of saxophone: the most common are soprano, alto, tenor, and baritone. Used only occasionally in the orchestra, the saxophone had become the characteristic instrument of the jazz band by the 1920s, and it remains a favorite sound in popular music today.

Brass Instruments

The main instruments of the brass family (aerophones) are the trumpet, French horn (or horn), trombone, and tuba. All these instruments consist of cup-shaped mouthpieces attached to a length of metal tubing that flares at the end into a

Trumpet soloist Alison Balsom plays with an orchestra.

bell. The column of air within the tube is set vibrating by the tightly stretched lips of the player, which are buzzed together. Going from one pitch to another involves not only mechanical means, such as a slide or valves, but also muscular control to vary the pressure of the lips and breath. Brass and woodwind instrument players often refer to their **embouchure**, the entire oral mechanism of lips, lower facial muscles, and jaw.

Trumpets and horns were prevalent in the ancient world. At first, they were fashioned from animal horns and tusks and were used chiefly for religious ceremonies and military signals. The **trumpet**, highest in pitch of the brass family, asserts itself with a brilliant, clear timbre. It is often associated with ceremonial display. The trumpet can also be

LEFT: Joshua Redman (b. 1969) playing tenor saxophone.

RIGHT: The French horn section of an orchestra.

muted, with a pear-shaped, metal or cardboard device that is inserted in the bell to achieve a muffled, buzzy sound.

French horn

The **French horn** is descended from the ancient hunting horn. Its mellow resonance can be mysteriously remote in soft passages and sonorous in loud ones; muted, it sounds distant. The horn is played with the right hand, cupped slightly, inserted in the bell and is sometimes "stopped" by plugging the bell tightly with the hand, producing an eerie and rasping quality. The timbre of the horn blends well with woodwinds, brasses, and strings.

Trombone and tuba

The **trombone**—the Italian word means "large trumpet"—offers a full and rich sound in the tenor range. In place of valves, it features a movable U-shaped slide that alters the length of the vibrating air column in the tube. The **tuba,** the bass instrument of the brass family, furnishes the foundation for the harmony, like the double bass and contrabassoon. The tuba adds depth to the orchestral tone, and a dark resonance ranging from velvety softness to a rumbling growl.

Other brass instruments are used in concert and marching bands. Among these is the **cornet**, similar to the trumpet and very popular in concert bands in the early twentieth century. The **bugle**, which evolved from the military (or field) trumpet of early times, sends out a powerful tone that carries well in the open

air. Since it has no valves, it is able to sound only certain pitches of the scale, which accounts for the familiar pattern of duty calls (and "Taps") in the army. The **fluegelhorn**, often used in jazz bands, is really a valved bugle with

LEFT: Carol Jantsch is the principal tubist with the Philadelphia Orchestra.

RIGHT: Trombonist Isrea Butler is active as a teacher and freelance musician.

a wide bell. The **euphonium** is a tenor-range instrument whose shape resembles the tuba. And the **sousaphone**, an adaptation of the tuba designed by the American bandmaster John Philip Sousa (see Chapter 51), features a forward bell and is coiled to rest over the shoulder of the marching player.

Percussion Instruments

The percussion instruments of the orchestra accentuate the rhythm, generate excitement at the climaxes, and inject splashes of color into the orchestral sound. This family (encompassing a vast array of idiophones and membranophones) is divided into two categories: instruments capable of producing definite pitches, and those that produce an indefinite pitch. In the former group are the **timpani**, or **kettledrums**, which are generally played in sets of two or four. The timpani has a hemispheric copper shell across which is stretched a "head" of plastic or calfskin held in place by a metal ring. A pedal mechanism enables the player to change the tension of the head, and with it the pitch. The instrument is played with two padded sticks. Its dynamic range extends from a mysterious rumble to a thunderous roll. The timpani first arrived in Western Europe from the Middle East, where Turks on horseback used them in combination with trumpets (see p. 75).

Timpani

Also among the pitched percussion instruments is the **xylophone** family; instruments of this general type are used in Africa, Southeast Asia, and throughout the Americas. The xylophone consists of tuned blocks of wood laid out in the shape of a keyboard. Struck with mallets with hard heads, the instrument produces a dry, crisp sound. The **marimba** is a more mellow xylophone of African origin. The **vibraphone**, used in jazz as well as art music, combines the principle of the xylophone with resonators, each containing revolving disks operated by electric motors that produce an exaggerated vibrato.

Xylophone

The **glockenspiel** (German for "set of bells") consists of a series of horizontal tuned steel bars of various sizes, which when struck produce a bright, metallic, bell-like sound. The **celesta**, a kind of glockenspiel that is operated by means of a keyboard, resembles a miniature upright piano. Its steel plates are struck by small hammers to produce a sound like a music box. **Chimes**, or **tubular bells**, a set of tuned metal tubes of various lengths suspended from a frame and struck with a hammer, are frequently called on to simulate church bells.

Evelyn Glennie (b. 1965) is a virtuoso solo percussionist in spite of being profoundly deaf.

Percussion instruments that do not produce a definite pitch include the **snare drum** (or **side drum**), a small cylindrical drum with two heads (top and bottom) stretched over a shell of wood or metal and played with two drumsticks. This instrument owes its brilliant tone to the vibrations of the lower head against taut snares (strings). The **bass drum** is played with a large, soft-headed stick and produces a low, heavy sound. The **tom-tom** is a colloquial name given to Native American or African drums of indefinite pitch. The **tambourine** is a round, hand-held drum with "jingles"—little metal plates—inserted in its rim. The player can strike the drum with the fingers or knee, shake it, or pass a hand over the jingles. Of Middle Eastern origin, it is particularly associated with music of Spain, as are **castanets**, little wood clappers mounted on wooden boards or, for Spanish dancing, moved by the player's fingers.

The **triangle** is a slender rod of steel bent into a three-cornered

Cymbals

shape; when struck with a steel beater, it gives off a bright, tinkling sound. **Cymbals**, which arrived in the West from central Asia during the Middle Ages, consist of two large circular brass plates of equal size; when struck against each other, they produce a shattering sound. The **gong** and the **tam-tam** are both broad circular disks of metal, suspended to a frame so as to hang freely. The tam-tam is a flat gong of indefinite pitch; the gong, however, with a raised metal center, has a definite pitch and when struck with a heavy drumstick produces a deep roar. In the Far East and Southeast Asia, the gong is central to the ensemble known as the gamelan (see p. 48).

Keyboard Instruments

Piano and organ

The **piano** was originally known as the *fortepiano*, Italian for "loud-soft," which suggests its wide dynamic range and capacity for nuance. Its strings are struck with hammers controlled by a keyboard mechanism. The piano cannot sustain a tone as well as the string and wind instruments, but in the hands of a fine performer, it is capable of producing a singing melody.

The piano boasts a notable capacity for brilliant scales, arpeggios, trills, rapid passages, and octaves, as well as chords. Its range from lowest to highest pitch spans more than seven octaves, or eighty-eight semitones. Its several foot pedals govern the length of time a string vibrates as well as its volume.

The **organ**, one of the earliest keyboard instruments, is also a type of wind instrument. The air flow to each of its many pipes is controlled by the organist from a console containing two or more keyboards and a pedal keyboard played by the feet. The organ's multicolored sonority can easily fill a huge space. Electronic keyboards, or synthesizers, capable of imitating pipe organs and other timbres, have become commonplace. Another early keyboard instrument, much used in the Baroque era, is the **harpsichord**. Its sound is produced by quills that pluck its metal strings.

The instruments described in this and the previous chapter form a vivid and diversified group, which can be heard and viewed with your book's online materials. To composers, performers, and listeners alike, they offer an endless variety of colors and shades of expression.

Pianist Lang Lang is one of the most sought-after soloists today.

YOUR TURN TO EXPLORE

Western instruments

Although the rock songs featured in this part employ the "standard" instrumentation of guitars and drums, there are many rock selections (especially in art or progressive rock) that use instruments drawn from the colorful palette of the orchestra, including brass and woodwinds. Find a song that adds some of these instruments, and describe how they contribute to the overall expressive nature of the music.

Chapter 11

Musical Ensembles

*"Conductors must give unmistakable and suggestive signals
to the orchestra—not choreography to the audience."*

—George Szell (1897-1970)

KEY POINTS

- Choral groups often feature **a cappella** singing, with no accompaniment.
- **Chamber music** is ensemble music for small groups, with one player per part.
- Standard chamber ensembles include **string quartets**, **piano trios**, and **brass quintets**.
- The modern **orchestra** can feature over one hundred players.
- Most **bands**—**wind**, **marching**, **jazz**, **rock**—feature a core of winds and percussion.
- Large ensembles are generally led by a **conductor** who beats patterns with a baton to help performers keep the same tempo.

The great variety in musical instruments is matched by a wide assortment of ensembles, or performance groups. Some are homogeneous—for example, choral groups using only voices or perhaps only men's voices. Others are more heterogeneous—for example, the orchestra, which features instruments from the different families. Across the world, any combination is possible.

Choral Groups

Choral music is sung around the world, both for religious purposes (sacred music) and for nonspiritual (secular) occasions. Loosely defined, a **chorus** is a fairly large body of singers who perform together; their music is usually sung in several voice parts. Many groups include both men and women, but choruses can also be restricted to women's or men's voices only. A **choir,** traditionally a smaller group, is often connected with a church or with the performance of sacred music. The standard voice parts in both chorus and choir correspond to the voice ranges described earlier: soprano, alto, tenor, and bass (abbreviated **SATB**). In early times, choral music was often performed without accompaniment, a style of singing known as *a cappella* (meaning "in the chapel"). Smaller, specialized vocal ensembles include the madrigal choir and chamber choir.

The Washington National Cathedral Girls Choir sings an evening church service.

Standard Chamber Ensembles

Duos	Quartets	Quintets	
Solo instrument (e.g., violin or clarinet) Piano	String quartet Violin 1 Violin 2 Viola Cello	String quintet Violin 1 Violin 2 Viola 1 Viola 2 Cello	Woodwind quintet Flute Oboe Clarinet Bassoon French horn (a brass instrument)
Trios	Piano quartet Piano Violin Viola Cello	Piano quintet Piano String quartet (violin 1, violin 2, viola, cello)	Brass quintet Trumpet 1 Trumpet 2 French horn Trombone Tuba
String trio Violin 1 Viola or violin 2 Cello Piano trio Piano Violin Cello			

Chamber Ensembles

Chamber music is ensemble music for a group of two to about a dozen players, with only one player to a part—as distinct from orchestral music, in which a single instrumental part may be performed by as many as eighteen players or more. The essential trait of chamber music is its intimacy.

The Ying String Quartet, founded in 1988 by four siblings.

Several of the standard chamber music ensembles consist of string players. The most well-known combination is probably the **string quartet**, made up of two violins, viola, and cello. Other popular combinations are the **duo sonata** (soloist with piano); the **piano trio**, **piano quartet**, and **piano quintet**, each made up of a piano and string instruments; the **string quintet**; as well as larger groups—the **sextet**, **septet**, and **octet**. Winds too form standard combinations, especially **woodwind** and **brass quintets**. Some of these ensembles are listed above.

Contemporary composers have experimented with new groupings that combine the voice with small groups of instruments and electronic elements with live performers. In some cultures, chamber groups mix what might seem to be unlikely timbres to the Western listener—in India, for example, plucked strings and percussion are standard.

The Orchestra

In its most general sense, the term "orchestra" may be applied to any performing body of diverse instruments—this would include the **gamelan** orchestras of Bali and Java, made up largely of gongs, xylophone-like instruments, and drums (you will hear this ensemble in an Encounter about the Javanese gamelan, p. 374). In the West, the term is now synonymous with **symphony orchestra**, an ensemble of strings coupled with an assortment of woodwinds, brass, and percussion instruments.

Typical Distribution of Orchestral Instruments				
Strings	16–18	first violins	10–12	cellos
	16–18	second violins	8–10	double basses
	12	violas	1–2	harps, when needed
Woodwinds	2–3	flutes, 1 piccolo	3	clarinets, 1 bass clarinet
	2–3	oboes, 1 English horn	3	bassoons, 1 contrabassoon
Brass	4–6	French horns	3	trombones
	4	trumpets	1	tuba
Percussion	3–5	players	1	timpani player (2–5 timpani)

The symphony orchestra has varied in size and makeup throughout its history but has always featured string instruments at its core. From its origins as a small group, the orchestra has grown into an ensemble of more than a hundred musicians, approximately two-thirds of whom are string players. The chart above shows the distribution of instruments typical of a large orchestra today.

The instruments are arranged to achieve the best balance of tone: most of the strings are near the front, as are the gentle woodwinds, with the louder brass and percussion at the back. A characteristic seating plan is shown on page 51.

Wind, Jazz, and Rock Bands

Band is a generic name applied to a variety of ensembles, most of which rely on winds and percussion. The band is a much-loved American institution. One American bandmaster, John Philip Sousa, achieved worldwide fame with his **wind**, or **concert**, **band** and the repertory of marches he wrote for it.

In the United States today, the wind band, ranging in size from forty to eighty or so players, is an established institution in most secondary schools, colleges, and universities and in many communities as well. Modern composers like to write for this ensemble, since it is usually willing to play new compositions. The familiar **marching band** usually entertains at sports events and parades. Besides

The University of Texas Longhorn Marching Band in the 2006 Rose Parade in Pasadena, California.

its core of winds and percussion, this group often features remnants from its military origins, including a display of drum majors (or majorettes), flags, and rifles. The repertory of marching bands is extensive, but almost always includes marches by John Philip Sousa, such as the well-known *Stars and Stripes Forever*.

The precise instrumentation of **jazz bands** depends on the particular music being played but usually includes a reed section made up of saxophones and an occasional clarinet, a brass section of trumpets and trombones, and a rhythm section of percussion, piano, double bass, and electric guitar. **Rock bands** often supplement amplified guitars and percussion with synthesizers, and may also feature other winds and brass.

Cincinnati Symphony Orchestra, with music director Paavo Järvi, in 2005.

The Role of the Conductor

Large ensembles, such as an orchestra, concert band, or chorus, generally need a conductor, who serves as the group's leader. Conductors beat time in standard metric patterns to help the performers keep the same tempo; many conductors use a thin stick known as a **baton**, which is easy to see. These conducting patterns, shown in the diagrams on page 51, further emphasize the strong and weak beats of the measure. Beat 1, the strongest in any meter, is always given a downbeat, or a downward motion of the hand; a secondary accent is shown by a change of direction; and the last beat of each measure, a weak beat, is always an upbeat or upward motion, thereby leaving the hand ready for the downbeat of the next measure.

Baton

Equally important is the conductor's role in interpreting the music for the group. He or she decides the precise tempo (how fast or slow) and the dynamics (how soft or loud) all the way through the piece. In most cases, the composer's markings are relative (how loud is *forte*?) and thus open to interpretive differences. Conductors also rehearse ensembles in practice sessions, helping the musicians to learn their individual parts. String players depend on the conductor, or sometimes the **concertmaster** (the first-chair violinist), to standardize their bowing strokes so that the musical emphasis, and therefore the interpretation, is uniform.

Concertmaster

The Orchestra in Action

A thrilling introduction to the infinite range of the modern orchestra is Benjamin Britten's *Young Person's Guide to the Orchestra,* written expressly to illustrate the timbre of each instrument. The work, composed in 1946 and subtitled

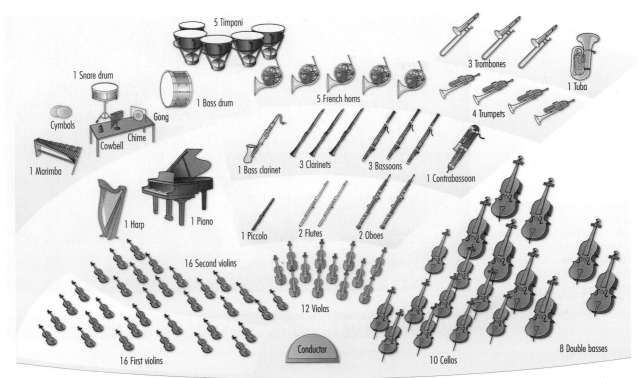

A typical seating plan for an orchestra.

Purcell, *Rondeau*

Variations and Fugue on a Theme of Purcell, is based on a dance tune by the great seventeenth-century English composer Henry Purcell. You can hear Purcell's original tune—in a broad triple meter and a minor key—in the online Listening Examples.

In *The Young Person's Guide*, Britten introduces the sound of the entire orchestra playing together, then the sonorities of each instrument family as a group—woodwinds, brasses, strings, percussion—and finally repeats the statement by the full orchestra. With the theme, or principal melody, well in mind, we hear every instrument in order from highest to lowest within each family. Next we encounter variations of the theme, each played by a new instrument (see Listening Guide 1). The work closes with a grand **fugue**, a polyphonic form popular in the Baroque era (1600–1750), which is also based on Purcell's theme. The fugue, like the variations, presents its subject, or theme, in rapid order in each instrument. (For a general discussion of the fugue, see Chapter 27.)

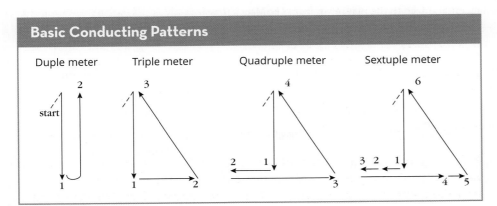

Basic Conducting Patterns

Duple meter   Triple meter   Quadruple meter   Sextuple meter

Gustavo Dudamel (b. 1981), a graduate of the Venezuelan music education system called El Sistema, was appointed conductor of the Los Angeles Philharmonic in 2009 at the age of twenty-seven.

YOUR TURN TO EXPLORE

Countless rock/pop songs are performed by an ensemble consisting of voice(s), guitar, bass guitar, and drums. This is the case with both *19th Nervous Breakdown* (Rolling Stones) and *Smells Like Teen Spirit* (Nirvana), although their styles are different. Compare the performances of these two songs, considering which ensemble members (voices, guitar, bass, drums) are featured, especially in any solo passages. Then select one of your favorite songs, and describe its ensemble. Are there any added instruments? Which are the prevalent members heard in the ensemble? How does this performance affect your enjoyment of the song? Find a version of the same song performed by a different band or ensemble (a "cover" version). How does the different instrumentation or timbre change your experience of the song?

LISTENING GUIDE 1

 16:36

Britten: *The Young Person's Guide to the Orchestra*
(*Variations and Fugue on a Theme of Purcell*)

DATE: 1946

BASIS: Dance from Purcell's incidental music to the play *Abdelazar* (*The Moor's Revenge*)

What to Listen For

Melody	Stately theme, based on tune by Baroque composer Henry Purcell.	**Texture**	Homophonic at the beginning; closing fugue is polyphonic.
Rhythm/ meter	Slow, triple meter for opening statement of theme, then changing to duple and compound.	**Form**	Theme with many variations.
		Performing forces	Full orchestra, statements by instrument families, then individual instruments.
Harmony	Begins in minor tonality; shifts between major and minor.		

0:00   **I. Theme:** Eight measures in D minor, stated six times to illustrate the orchestral families.

    1. Entire orchestra   4. Strings

    2. Woodwinds   5. Percussion

    3. Brass   6. Entire orchestra

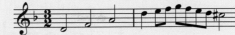

    II. Variations: 13 short variations, each illustrating a different instrument.

VARIATION	FAMILY	SOLO INSTRUMENT	ACCOMPANYING INSTRUMENTS
1:57 1	woodwinds	piccolo, flutes	violins, harp, and triangle
2		oboes	strings and timpani
3		clarinets	strings and tuba
4		bassoons	strings and snare drum
5:00 5	strings	violins	brass and bass drum
6		violas	woodwinds and brass
7		cellos	clarinets, violas, and harp
8		double basses	woodwinds and tambourine
9		harp	strings, gong, and cymbal
9:34 10	brass	French horns	strings, harp, and timpani
11		trumpets	strings and snare drum
12		trombones, tuba	woodwinds and high brass
11:53 13	percussion	various	strings

    (Order in which percussion instruments are introduced: timpani, bass drum, and cymbals; timpani, tambourine, and triangle; timpani, snare drum, and wood block; timpani and xylophone; timpani, castanets, and gong; timpani and whip; whole percussion section; xylophone.)

13:47   **III. Fugue:** Subject is based on a fragment of the Purcell theme, played in imitation by each instrument in the same order as the variations.

Woodwinds: (highest to lowest)	piccolo flutes oboes clarinets bassoons

Strings: (highest to lowest)	first violins second violins violas cellos double basses harp

Brass: (highest to lowest)	French horns trumpets trombones, tuba

Percussion:	various

15:39   Full orchestra at the end with Purcell's theme heard over the fugue.

Chapter 12

Style and Function of Music in Society

"A real musical culture should not be a museum culture based on music of past ages. . . . It should be the active embodiment in sound of the life of a community—of the everyday demands of people's work and play and of their deepest spiritual needs."

—*Wilfrid Mellers (1914-2008)*

KEY POINTS

- Most cultures around the world employ **sacred music** for religious functions, and **secular music** for entertainment and other nonreligious activities.

- There are many **genres**, or categories, of music; some works **cross over** categories, borrowing elements of one genre for use in another.

- The **medium** is the specific group (e.g., orchestra, chorus) that performs a piece.

- Some music is not written down, but is known through **oral transmission**.

- The distinctive features of any artwork make up its **style**. A musical style is created through individual treatment of the basic musical elements.

- We organize styles of artworks into historical periods, each with its own characteristics.

In Japanese *Noh* drama, performers often wear symbolic masks.

In every culture, music is intricately interwoven with the lives and beliefs of its people. Music serves different functions in different societies, though some basic roles are universal. In some cultures, such as in the Western classical tradition, only a few people are involved with the actual performance of music; in others, cooperative work is so much a part of society that the people sing as a group, with each person contributing a separate part to build a complex whole.

There is music for every conceivable occasion, but the specific occasions vary from one culture to another. Thus, musical genres, or categories of repertory, do not necessarily transfer from one society to another, though they may be similar. For example, Japanese *Noh* drama and a Beijing opera like *The Legend of the Red Lantern* (Encounter, p. 254) serve essentially the same role as Western opera does. And we can distinguish in most cultures between **sacred music**, for religious purposes (like the Islamic chant on p. 68), and **secular music**, for entertainment (such as the Mariachi band in the Encounter on p. 350).

It's important to differentiate between genre and form. A **genre** is a more general term that suggests something of the overall character of the work as well as its function. For example, song is a genre, as is **symphony**—usually designating a four-movement orchestral work. As we will see later, each movement of a symphony has a specific internal **form**, or structure. "Symphony" also implies the **medium**, or the specific group that performs the piece—in this case, an orchestra.

Titles for musical compositions occasionally indicate the genre and key: Symphony No. 94 in G Major, by Joseph Haydn, for example. Another way works are identified is through a cataloguing system, often described by **opus number** (*opus* is Latin for "work"; an example is Nocturne, Op. 48, a piano work by Frédéric Chopin). Other titles are more descriptive, such as *The Nutcracker* (a ballet by the Russian composer Peter Ilyich Tchaikovsky) and *The Trout* (a song by Franz Schubert, an Austrian composer).

Just as the context for music—when, why, and by whom a piece is performed—varies from culture to culture, so do aesthetic judgments. For example, the Chinese consider a thin, tense vocal tone desirable in their operas, while the Italians prefer a full-throated, robust sound in theirs.

Not all music is written down. Music of most cultures of the world, including some styles of Western music, is transmitted by example or by imitation and is performed from memory. The preservation of music without the aid of written notation is referred to as **oral transmission**. We will see that in modern times, music scholars known as ethnomusicologists, who study music in its cultural context, have attempted to "capture" music that had never previously been written down through field recordings (an example from East Africa is on p. 388).

Oral transmission

While we will consider how music operates in several different traditions, our Listening Guides focus primarily on Western art music—that is the notated and **cultivated** music of European and Euro-American society. We often label art music as "classical" or "serious," for lack of better terms. However, the lines that distinguish art music from other kinds can be blurred. **Vernacular** musics (often called "popular" or "traditional," wrongly understood as spontaneously

Note the stylistic differences between paintings of similar subject matter. LEFT: *The Guitar Player*, by **Jan Vermeer** (1632–1675). RIGHT: *The Old Guitar Player*, by **Pablo Picasso** (1881–1973).

TOP: An Afghan music master teaches his pupil to play traditional instruments.

BOTTOM: Famed cellist Pablo Casals working with a student.

generated by untrained musicians) are essential traditions in their own right, and both rock and especially jazz are believed by many to be new art forms, having already stood the test of time.

The Concept of Style

Style may be defined as the characteristic way an artwork is presented. The word may also indicate the creator's personal manner of expression—the distinctive flavor that sets one artist apart from all others. Thus, we speak of the literary style of Dickens or Hemingway, the painting style of Picasso or Rembrandt, or the musical style of Bach or Mozart (compare the paintings on p. 55).

What makes one musical work sound similar to or different from another? It's the style, or individualized treatment of the elements of music. We have seen that Western music is largely a melody-oriented art based on a particular musical system from which the underlying harmonies are also built. Musics of other cultures may sound foreign to our ears, because they are based on entirely different systems, and many do not involve harmony to any great extent. Complex rhythmic procedures and textures set some world musics apart from Western styles, while basic formal considerations—such as repetition, contrast, and variation—bring musics of disparate cultures closer. In short, a style is made up of pitch, time, timbre, and expression, creating a sound that each culture recognizes as its own.

Musical Styles in History

Each historical period has its own stylistic characteristics; although the artists, writers, and composers of a particular era may vary in outlook, they all share certain qualities. Because of this, we can tell at once that a work of art—whether music, poetry, painting, sculpture, or architecture—dates from the Middle Ages or the eighteenth century. The style of a period, then, is the total language of all its artists as they react to the political, economic, religious, and philosophical forces that shape their environment. A knowledge of historical styles will help you place a musical work within the context (time and place) in which it was created.

The timeline opposite shows the generally accepted style periods in the history of Western music. Each represents a conception of form and technique, an ideal of beauty, a manner of expression and performance attuned to the cultural climate of the period—in a word, a style!

Comparing styles I: Historical periods

YOUR TURN TO EXPLORE

Rock songs often convey a deeper meaning that goes beyond the words, some with sexual innuendo or drug references, others with social commentary. Listen again to the rap song *Don't Believe the Hype* (Public Enemy), which describes rampant racism and the reality of African American ghetto life. Pick another song that you believe comments on a social issue. What is the issue, and to what audience does the song appeal? What, in your opinion, is the function of such songs in our society? How do the various musical elements that we have considered contribute to the effect of a particular social-commentary song?

Musical Styles in History

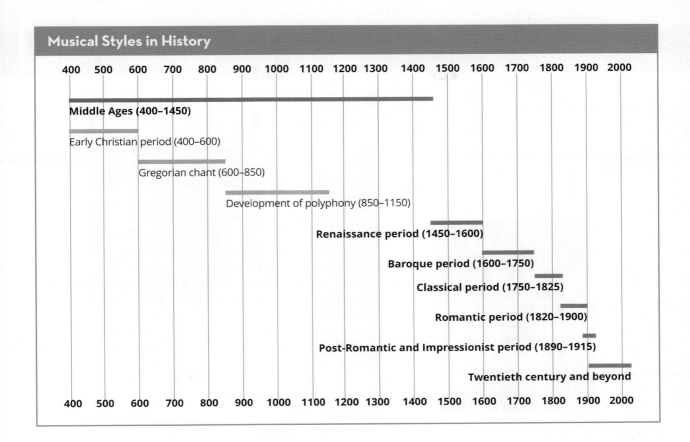

| 400 | 500 | 600 | 700 | 800 | 900 | 1000 | 1100 | 1200 | 1300 | 1400 | 1500 | 1600 | 1700 | 1800 | 1900 | 2000 |

Middle Ages (400–1450)

Early Christian period (400–600)

Gregorian chant (600–850)

Development of polyphony (850–1150)

Renaissance period (1450–1600)

Baroque period (1600–1750)

Classical period (1750–1825)

Romantic period (1820–1900)

Post-Romantic and Impressionist period (1890–1915)

Twentieth century and beyond

| 400 | 500 | 600 | 700 | 800 | 900 | 1000 | 1100 | 1200 | 1300 | 1400 | 1500 | 1600 | 1700 | 1800 | 1900 | 2000 |

Listening Examples

Understanding Historical Style Periods

Medieval: *Kyrie* (Hildegard)

Renaissance: *Inviolata, integra et casta es Maria* (Josquin)

Baroque: **Minuet in D** (Bach, *Anna Magdalena Bach Notebook*) • **Concerto in C Major for Two Trumpets, I** (Vivaldi)

Classical: **Symphony No. 94 (*Surprise*), II** (Haydn) • *Pathétique* **Sonata, I** (Beethoven)

Romantic: *Åse's Death*, from *Peer Gynt Suite* (Grieg) • **Prelude in E Minor, Op. 28, No. 4** (Chopin)

Twentieth century: *Jeux de vagues*, from *La mer* (Debussy) • *The Rite of Spring* (Stravinsky) • *Lux aeterna* (Ligeti)

Understanding Categories of Music

Sacred (religious) music: **"Hallelujah Chorus,"** from *Messiah* (Handel)

Secular (nonreligious) music: *Moonlight* **Sonata, I** (Beethoven)

Popular music: *When the Saints Go Marching In* (jazz band) • *If I Had a Hammer* (Pete Seeger)

Traditional music: *Swing Low, Sweet Chariot* (African American spiritual) • *Los Jilicatas* (Peru)

MIDDLE AGES AND RENAISSANCE

Events		Composers and Works

500

Fall of the Roman Empire. **476**
Charlemagne crowned first Holy Roman Emperor. **800**

1000

Construction begins on Gothic church of Notre Dame in Paris. **1163**

1098–1179 Hildegard of Bingen (*Alleluia, O virga mediatrix*)
1100–1300 Notre Dame School (*Gaude Maria virgo*)

1200

Marco Polo travels to China. **1271**
Last Crusade to the Holy Land. **1291**
Dante Alighieri begins writing *The Divine Comedy*. **1308**
Black Death strikes in Europe. **1348**

c. 1300–1377 Guillaume de Machaut
(*Ma fin est mon commencement*)

1400

Gutenberg Bible printed. **c. 1455**
Columbus discovers the New World. **1492**
First music book printed in Italy. **1501**
Michelangelo completes the sculpture *David*. **1504**
Council of Trent begins. **1545**
Elizabeth I crowned in England. **1559**

c. 1450–1521 Josquin des Prez (*Ave Maria . . . virgo serena*)
c. 1507–1568 Jacques Arcadelt (*Il bianco e dolce cigno*)
c. 1515–c. 1571 Tielman Susato (Three Dances)
c. 1525–1594 Giovanni Pierluigi da Palestrina
(*Pope Marcellus* Mass)
c. 1570–1603 John Farmer (*Fair Phyllis*)

1600

Shakespeare's **1602**
Hamlet
produced.

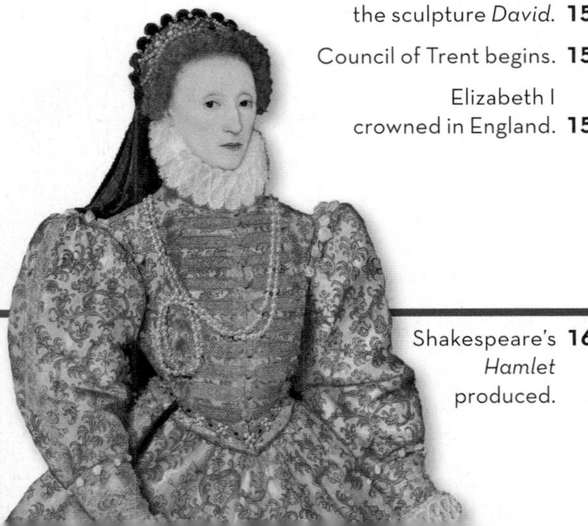

Part 2

The Middle Ages and Renaissance

Music as Commodity and Social Activity

"Nothing exists without music, for the universe is said to have been framed by a kind of harmony of sounds, and heaven itself revolves under the tones of that harmony."

—Isidore of Seville (c. 560–636)

Humans have been using sound to enhance their communication for thousands of years—in fact, some scholars argue that what we call "song" may have been the earliest form of speech. But our story begins when Europeans came up with the idea of putting sound to paper—the concept of musical **notation**, which is not unique to Western culture (musical notation from China dates back at least 2,500 years) but has defined the development of Western music and allowed for its astonishing variety, diffusion, and staying power.

Musical styles that stem from the European tradition are at the core of music-making throughout the world today, a level of influence that surpasses any language or religion. And this is because of notation, which allows us to think of a song or other musical work as a product or commodity to be preserved, taught and learned, bought and sold. Still, in Western culture as in all world cultures, making music is also a social activity that allows individuals to feel closely connected to a group, and to express their feelings both recreationally and spiritually.

Music notation was invented to further the goals of Christian worship, and social music-making was essential to the early Christian church. Therefore, much of the music we still have from the Middle Ages and Renaissance was intended for **sacred** purposes: sounds designed to inspire the faithful to worship. We will be exploring various ways in which these early worship-music traditions expanded and shifted to meet the needs of a changing society.

Despite the predominance of sacred music, more and more through this period we have evidence of **secular** music, social music-making for entertainment and personal expression. It's especially in the secular context that the idea of music as a social activity intersects with the economics of music as a commodity item—already in these early centuries of the Western tradition.

Angel musicians abound in the famous Linaiuoli Altarpiece, an early masterpiece by **Fra Angelico** (c. 1395–1455).

From Antiquity to the Middle of Things

While we believe that many ancient civilizations enjoyed flourishing musical cultures, only a few fragments of their music survive today. We do know that ancient Mediterranean cultures provided the foundation of the Western musical heritage, as well as the traditions that it shares with the Middle East.

The fall of the Roman Empire, commonly set in the year 476 CE, marked the beginning of a thousand-year period usually described as the Middle Ages. The first half of this millennium, from around 500 to 1000, was a period of political and cultural consolidation. During this era, all power flowed from kings, with the approval of the Roman Catholic Church. The struggle between these two centers of power, church and state, is at the core of European history and has resonances to this day. The modern concept of a strong, centralized government as the guardian of law and order is generally credited to Charlemagne (742–814), the celebrated emperor of the Franks. A progressive monarch, Charlemagne encouraged education and left behind him an extensive system of social justice. It was during his reign that Europeans started to make systematic use of musical notation.

During the later Middle Ages, from around 1000 to 1450, universities were founded throughout Europe, and cities emerged as centers of art and culture. Literary landmarks such as the *Chanson de Roland* (c. 1100) in France, Dante's *Divine Comedy* (1307) in Italy, and Chaucer's *Canterbury Tales* (1386; see illustration on p. 62) in England helped shape their respective languages. This time also witnessed the construction of the great cathedrals, including Notre Dame in Paris, one of the first centers in which **polyphony** (multivoiced music) was notated and integrated into musical worship.

Among the first named composers of the Western tradition, Léonin (who lived in the second half of the 1100s) and Pérotin (who worked around 1200) developed a style known as **organum**, in which plainchant—single-line melodies of the early Christian church—was "decorated" with one or more simultaneous musical lines. The effect was described at the time as astonishing, the same way that the Cathedral of Notre Dame, for which this music was composed, was considered an awe-inspiring tribute to divine power.

Reliquary of the emperor Charlemagne in the form of a portrait bust, c. 1350.

Markets and Courts

In the later Middle Ages, a merchant class that drew its wealth from trade and commerce arose outside of feudal society. Although travel was perilous—the roads were plagued by robbers and the seas by pirates—each region of Europe exchanged its natural resources for those it lacked: the plentiful timber and furs of Scandinavia were traded for English wool and cloth manufactured in Flanders; England wanted German silver and, above all, French and Italian wine; and European goods of all kinds flowed through the seaport of Venice to Constantinople in exchange for Eastern luxuries. Musicians and their works also moved along the trade routes: music became both a necessity (for worship activities) and a desirable recreational ornament, a crucial commodity in the economies of Europe.

In an era of violence brought on by deep-set religious beliefs, knights embarked on holy—and bloody—Crusades to capture the Holy Land from the Muslims. Although feudal society was male-dominated and idealized the figure of the fearless warrior, the status of women was raised by the universal cult of Mary, mother of Christ (see illustrations on p. 86), and by the concepts of chivalry that arose among the knights. In the songs of the court minstrels, women were adored with a fervor that laid the foundation for our concept of romantic love. This poetic attitude found its perfect symbol in the faithful knight who worshipped his lady from afar and was inspired by her to deeds of great daring and self-sacrifice, and led to the first great flowering of secular music writtten in the **vernacular** (the language of the people, as opposed to **Latin**, the formal language of the church and the sacred tradition).

In His Own Words

" We may compare the best form of government to the most harmonious piece of music; the oligarchic and despotic to the most violent tunes; and the democratic to the soft and gentle airs."

—*Aristotle (384–322 BCE)*

Two characters—the Miller, playing a bagpipe (top), and the Prioress (bottom)—from the Ellesmere manuscript of Geoffrey Chaucer's *Canterbury Tales* (c. 1400–10).

Most prominent in this secular tradition were the **troubadours** of Languedoc (what is now southern France) and the **trouvères** of northern France, who not only left us the first extensive notated tradition of love song, but also helped to introduce increasingly complex instruments into the Western tradition. Many instruments and song styles were adapted from the highly sophisticated Middle Eastern traditions of the time (see illustration below): a number of European courts (notably the court of Alfonso the Wise in what is now Spain) maintained good private relations with Muslim princes, despite their public rejection of Islam.

Looking Out and Looking In

Though there was significant cultural continuity from the 1400s into the 1500s, a number of important new concerns arose in the early part (1450–1520) of the time frame we now call the Renaissance. Europeans embarked (with the help of the newly developed compass) on voyages of discovery that opened up new horizons, both external and internal. Explorers of this age, in search of a new trade route to the riches of China and the Indies, stumbled on North and South America. During the course of the sixteenth and seventeenth centuries, these new lands became increasingly important to European treasuries and society.

After the fall of Constantinople to the Turks (1453), ancient Greek and Roman writings, many of which had been tightly guarded by the church during the Middle Ages, were brought to Europe in increasing numbers. They were distributed ever more widely through the medium of print, the European introduction of which (c. 1455) is generally credited to the German goldsmith and inventor Johannes Gutenberg. These writings from classical antiquity encouraged a tendency for individuals to look within, at their personal thoughts, beliefs, and reactions. While this led to increasing interest in human (secular) rather than divine (sacred) concerns, far-reaching religious reformations of the 1500s, both Protestant and Catholic, also gave this inward exploration a religious grounding.

The ideals that the ancient writings exemplified began to have a great influence in architecture, painting, and sculpture. Instead of the Gothic cathedrals and

In this miniature from the *Prayer Book* of Alfonso the Wise, King David is playing a rebec, in the manner of the Middle Eastern rabab.

fortified castles of the medieval world, lavish Renaissance palaces and spacious villas were built according to the harmonious proportions of the classical style, which strove for order and balance. This phenomenon first came to flower in Italy, the nation that stood closest to the classical Roman culture. As a result, the great names we associate with its painting and sculpture are predominantly Italian: Botticelli, Leonardo da Vinci, Michelangelo, and Titian. The nude human form, denied or covered for centuries, was revealed as a thing of beauty and used for anatomical study. Painters also began exploring the beauties of nature and conforming to the laws of perspective and composition.

Musicians in Medieval and Renaissance Society

Musicians were supported by the chief institutions of their society—the church, city, and state, as well as royal and aristocratic courts. They found employment as choirmasters, singers, organists, instrumentalists, copyists, composers, teachers, instrument builders, and, by the sixteenth century, music printers. There was a corresponding growth in a number of supporting musical institutions: church choirs and schools, music-publishing houses, civic wind bands. And there were increased opportunities for apprentices to study with master singers, players, and instrument builders. A few women can be identified as professional musicians in the Renaissance era, earning their living as court singers.

In *The Concert* (c. 1530–40), three ladies perform a French secular song with voice, flute, and lute. The Flemish artist is known only as the Master of the Female Half-Lengths.

The rise of the merchant class in the later Middle Ages brought with it a new group of music patrons. This development was paralleled by the emergence, among the cultivated middle and upper classes, of amateur musicians—men and women alike—who sang secular songs (chansons and madrigals) and played simple dances on instruments. When the system for printing from movable type was successfully adapted to music in the early sixteenth century, printed music books became available and affordable. As a result, musical literacy spread dramatically.

The concerns of musicians surrounding worship and play, individuality and community, and music both as commodity and as social activity were grounded in the historical circumstances in which they lived. But such issues also resonate with ways in which music is still enmeshed in culture to this day. In the next few chapters, we will examine how these long-standing concerns became rooted in Western society.

CRITICAL THINKING

1. How did society and musical institutions change from the Middle Ages to the Renaissance?

2. How was music-making similar and different in sacred (church) versus secular (court, marketplace) contexts in this period?

Chapter 13

Voice and Worship: Tradition and Individuality in Medieval Chant

"When God saw that many men were lazy, and gave themselves only with difficulty to spiritual reading, He wished to make it easy for them, and added the melody to the Prophet's words, that all being rejoiced by the charm of the music, should sing hymns to Him with gladness."

—St. John Chrysostom (c. 347–407)

KEY POINTS

- Sung worship is a shared feature among many world cultures, allowing for a more intense personal and collective connection with the divine.

- Religious communities (monasteries) fostered the extensive development of worship music, starting in the Middle Ages.

- The music of the early Christian church, called **plainchant** (or just **chant**), features monophonic, nonmetric melodies set in one of the church **modes**, or scales.

- Chant melodies fall into three categories (**syllabic**, **neumatic**, **melismatic**), based on how many notes are set to each syllable of text.

- The expressive music of Hildegard of Bingen exemplifies the tension between an individual, creative response to divine inspiration and community expectations of worship.

Voices raised in song as people connect to a spiritual power: wherever you are from, you may have encountered this in your own community, whether it's a church choir, an Islamic call to prayer, or a cantor addressing a synagogue. This is one of the most widespread purposes of music throughout world cultures—and in medieval Europe, communities of men and women dedicated themselves fully to sung prayer, seeking the salvation of humanity through music.

Monasteries   The culture of this period was shaped in large part by the rise of **monasteries**. It was the members of these religious communities who preserved the learning of the ancient world and transmitted it, through their manuscripts, to later European scholars. Because music was at the core of Christian prayer and could effectively enhance the church service, the religious communities supported it extensively. Women as well as men played a role in preserving knowledge and cultivating music for the church, since nuns figured prominently in church society.

Life in the Medieval Monastery

Both men and women in the Middle Ages withdrew from secular society into the shelter of monasteries, where they devoted themselves to prayer, scholarship, preaching, charity, or healing the sick, depending on the religious order they joined. Parents might choose a religious life for a child if they had no land holdings to give a son or no dowry for a daughter's wedding. Others might take this spiritual path as an adult—a widow who did not wish to remarry or a young woman who longed for the education that cloistered life provided.

In this fourteenth-century manuscript illumination, the monks sing during the celebration of Mass, and an altar boy (left) pulls a bell rope.

A life devoted to the church was not an easy one; the discipline was arduous. A typical day began at 2:00 or 3:00 a.m. with the celebration of the first of the daily services, the reading of lessons, and the singing of psalms. Each day in the church calendar had its own ritual and its own order of prayers. The members of the community interspersed their religious duties with work in the fields or the library, or producing items that could be sold—wine, beer, or cheese—thus bringing in revenue to the order. Many in religious life dedicated themselves to writing and preserving knowledge from earlier times. Such a person was Hildegard of Bingen, one of the most remarkable women of the Middle Ages, who was renowned in her day as a poet and prophet and whose serenely beautiful music has regained popularity in recent years.

Plainchant: Music of the Church

The early music of the Christian church is testimony to the highly spiritual nature of the Middle Ages. **Plainchant** consists of a single-line melody; it is thus monophonic in texture, lacking either harmony or counterpoint. Its freely flowing vocal line subtly follows the inflections of the Latin text and is generally free from regular accent. These beautiful melodies, shaped in part by Greek, Hebrew, and Syrian influences, represent the starting point of artistic creativity in Western music. In time, it became necessary to assemble the ever-growing body of music into an organized **liturgy**, a term that refers to the set order of church services and the structure of each service. The task extended over several generations, though tradition often credits Pope Gregory the Great (r. 590–604) with codifying these melodies, known today as **Gregorian chant**.

The Gregorian melodies, numbering more than three thousand, form an immense body of music, nearly all of it anonymous. In fact, tradition held that Pope Gregory had received the melodies of "true prayer" directly from the Holy Spirit in the form of a dove whispering into his ear—therefore, in a very real sense, those who sang Gregorian plainchant in the Middle Ages believed it to have been composed by a divine and not human mind.

Gregorian chant avoids wide leaps, allowing its gentle contours to create a kind of musical speech. Chant melodies fall into three main classes, according to the way they are set to the text: **syllabic**, with one note sung to each

In Her Own Words

  ❝The words I speak come from no human mouth; I saw and heard them in visions sent to me. . . . I have no confidence in my own capacities—I reach out my hand to God that He may carry me along as a feather borne weightlessly by the wind."

—Hildegard of Bingen

Manuscript illumination of Pope Gregory the Great dictating to his scribe Peter. A dove, representing the Holy Spirit, sits on his shoulder.

syllable of text; **neumatic**, generally with small groups of up to five or six notes sung to a syllable; and **melismatic**, with many notes set to a single syllable (see chart on p. 35). The melismatic style, which descended from the elaborate improvisations heard in Middle Eastern music, became an expressive feature of Gregorian chant and exerted a strong influence on subsequent Western music.

From Gregorian chant through music of the Renaissance, Western music used a variety of scale patterns, or **modes**. These preceded major and minor scales (scales are also types of modes), which are characterized by a strong pull toward a tonic note; the earlier modes lacked this sense of attraction. You may find that the melodic shapes of medieval modal music (and the example we will consider by Hildegard) seem unfamilar. This is because for those of us in Western culture, **tonal** melody and harmony are deeply ingrained in our musical experience. In fact, you may hear similarities between Hildegard's modal melodies and the melodies and scales used by Middle Eastern sacred traditions (see Encounter, p. 68); this makes sense, since both developed from the same Eastern Mediterranean religious heritage centuries ago.

A Song for Worship by Hildegard

Hildegard set many of her own texts to music; her poetry is characterized by brilliant imagery and creative language. Some of her songs celebrate the lives of local saints such as Saint Rupert, the patron of her monastery, while others praise the Virgin Mary, comparing her to a blossoming flower or branch and celebrating her purity. Our example is an *Alleluia* (LG 2), derived from the Hebrew words for "Praise [be] to God"; to this day, some version of the "Alleluia" is used in most Christian communities to express joyful celebration. Hildegard wrote this chant for a specific occasion—a feast day for the Virgin Mary. Might Hildegard have found particular inspiration as a woman writing in honor of a woman?

Hildegard of Bingen (1098–1179)

Hildegard of Bingen was the daughter of a noble German couple who promised her, as their tenth child, to the service of the church as a tithe (the practice of giving one-tenth of what one owns). Raised by a religious recluse from age eight, she lived in a stone cell with one window and took her vows at the age of fourteen. From childhood, Hildegard experienced visions, which intensified in later life. She was reportedly able to foretell the future.

Around the year 1150, Hildegard founded a monastery in Rupertsberg (near Bingen), in Germany. Her reported miracles and prophecies made her famous throughout Europe: popes, kings, and priests sought her advice on political and religious issues. Although never officially canonized, Hildegard is regarded as a saint by the church. Her highly original compositional style resembles Gregorian chant but is full of expressive leaps and melismas that clearly convey the meaning of the words.

MAJOR WORKS: A collection of poetry and visions entitled *Scivias* (*Know the Ways*) • A volume of religious poetry set to music (*Symphony of the Harmony of Celestial Revelations*) • A sung morality play (*The Play of the Virtues*) • Scientific and medical writings.

 Kyrie

Hildegard of Bingen: *Alleluia, O virga mediatrix* (*Alleluia, O mediating branch*)

DATE: Late 12th century

GENRE: *Alleluia* plainchant, from the Proper of the Mass on feasts for the Virgin Mary

What to Listen For

Melody	Unaccompanied, conjunct line with some expressive leaps and melismas.	**Expression**	Dramatic leaps of a fifth; high-range climaxes on important words.
Rhythm	Free and nonmetric, following the flow of words.	**Performing forces**	*A cappella* choir (voices alone), alternating soloist and choir.
Texture	Monophonic (single line).	**Text**	Prayer to the Virgin Mary, written by Hildegard.
Form	Three-part structure ("Alleluia"-verse-"Alleluia"), performed responsorially.		

	TEXT	TRANSLATION	PERFORMANCE
0:00	Alleluia.	Alleluia.	Solo intonation, then choral response; very melismatic.
0:45	O virga mediatrix sancta viscera tua mortem superaverunt, et venter tuus omnes creaturas illuminavit in pulchro flore de suavissima integritate clausi pudoris tui orto.	O mediating branch Your holy flesh has overcome death, and your womb has illuminated all creatures through the beautiful flower of your tender purity that sprang from your chastity.	Solo verse, with several melismas. Higher range, neumatic text setting.
2:56	Alleluia.	Alleluia.	Melismatic at the end. Choir returns to the opening.

Expressive leap of rising fifth and melisma on "mortem" (death):

The chant is in three parts, beginning and ending with the word "Alleluia" (meant to be sung by the entire worship community) and featuring a **verse** in the middle, sung by a single leader. The leader first sings the opening "Alleluia" phrase of the chant, and then that same phrase is repeated and extended in **unison** by the full ensemble. This **responsorial** practice of group repetition of a leader's text-music phrase has its roots in ancient Jewish practice. It differs from call and response (which we will encounter in a later chapter) because in this case

Islamic Chant

Many world cultures employ a kind of "intoned speech" in their worship or religious rituals, which is distinct from "music" for entertainment or other purposes. We have heard through the plainchant by Hildegard how this relatively simple style of song enhances Christian prayer. Among other religions that feature chanted prayers is Islam, which is centered on the Quran, the sacred text presenting the word of God as transmitted to the Prophet Muhammad by the Archangel Gabriel. The practice of chanting the Quran is governed by established oral traditions that specify the vocal timbre, rhythmic treatment of texts, pronunciation, and a special vibrato (a wavering fluctuation of the pitch). While different branches of Islam view other kinds of music more or less favorably—"haram" (sinful according to Quranic teaching) or "maqruh" (problematic but not explicitly forbidden)—they are united in considering properly chanted recitation of the Quran essential to daily devotion.

One of the most familiar sounds in Islamic culture is the call to prayer, or *Adhan,* which is sounded publicly five times daily—morning, noon, afternoon, sunset, and evening—and helps regulate Muslim life. (You may notice a similarity with the specifically regulated prayer times of medieval Christianity discussed above.) The Prophet Muhammad is credited with instituting the practice of the call to prayer, given from the minaret (a tower on the mosque) by the muezzin: a prayer leader chosen for his vocal ability to recite the *Adhan* melodiously and clearly for all to hear. Originally the muezzin began the call without amplification from the top of the tower, but today his voice is broadcast from the minaret via speakers.

The text of the *Adhan* reiterates the Islamic statement of faith: "There is no God but Allah and Muhammad is the Messenger of God." There are seven invocations in this recited prayer, and all but the last is repeated. You will hear the careful balance between repetition and contrast in the musical structure, as the first statement of each phrase is presented quite simply, and then followed by a more ornate, melismatic variation. The *Adhan* is usually performed freely, in a slow tempo, except at sunset, when it is chanted more quickly. The melody is based on an Arabic mode, or scale type, called a *maqam,* which defines not only the pitches in the melody but also patterns of embellishments. The *maqam* is different from modes in Western music.

The call to prayer is followed by the Blessings on the Prop het, a text from the Quran (chapter 33, verse 56) ending with the words "the opening"— an invitation to all to recite silently the opening chapter of the Quran. We hear a quite different musical style from the call in this blessing, which is delivered in a syllabic, speech-like rendition.

Archangel Gabriel giving the Quran to Muhammad (sixteenth century), from the *Siyer-i Nebi,* a Turkish epic by fourteenth-century writer Mustafa.

A muezzin, or crier, sounds the Muslim call to prayer from the minaret of a mosque.

Adhan: Call to Prayer 🎧

What to listen for:

- Repetitive structure of the text and music, with its subtle variations and rich melismas.
- Free, rhapsodic delivery.

Text	Translation	Performance
Allahu Akbar	God is most great.	Sung four times.
Ash-hadu an-la ilaha illa llah	I witness that there is no god but Allah.	Sung twice.
Ash-hadu anna Muhammadarn Rasulullah	I witness that Muhammad is the Messenger of God.	Sung twice.
Hayya ala s-salah	Come to prayer.	Sung twice.
Hayya ʻala ʻl-falah	Come to salvation.	Sung twice.
Allahu Akbar	God is most great.	Sung twice.
La ilaha illa-Allah	There is no god but Allah.	Sung once.

Adhan: Blessings on the Prophet (Quran 33:56) 🎧

What to listen for: faster, speechlike delivery of text.

Text	Translation
Inna Allaha wamala-ikatahu yusalloona AAala alnnabiyyi ya ayyuha allatheena amanoo salloo AAalayhi wasallimoo tasleeman. Assalatu was sal-amu alayka ya sayyidi ya liabiba Liah. Al Fatihah.	Verily God raineth blessings, and his angels pray for blessings, upon Muhammad. O ye who believe, pray for blessings and peace upon him. Blessings and Peace upon thee, O my liege-Lord. O beloved of God. The opening.

The priest Volmar records
Hildegard of Bingen's visions, in
this miniature from her poetry
collection *Scivias*.

the people are expected to repeat the leader's words and melody precisely, rather than changing the idea. Hildegard elaborates some words with melismas, especially in the last line of the verse, describing the Virgin's purity.

Because we know that Hildegard composed this praise song, it is *not* "Gregorian" chant—it is not part of the established repertory of praise song that was sanctioned in her day. The notion that *new* praise song could be used in the liturgy was very controversial at the time. How could a mere human come up with prayer melodies that would be appropriate for communication with God? This was all the more complicated for Hildegard, since many in the church held that women were unworthy to aspire to connection with the divine. She had to strike a balance between claiming divine inspiration and not appearing to be heretical or even devilish.

CRITICAL THINKING

1. Why was it a problem for medieval individuals to "claim credit" for composing plainchant?
2. How did Hildegard of Bingen instill her music with emotional expression?

YOUR TURN TO EXPLORE

Consider the way worship music is used in other communities around the world (for example, in Chinese or Vietnamese Buddhism, native traditions in both North and South America, Hindu practices in South Asia). How do other experiences of singing to communicate with the divine compare with the example considered in this chapter?

Chapter 14

Layering Lines:
Polyphony at Notre Dame

"When you hear the soft harmonies of the various singers . . . it drives away care from the soul, . . . confers joy and peace and exultation in God, and transports the soul to the society of angels."

—John of Salisbury (1120–1180)

KEY POINTS

- **Polyphony** (multivoiced music), originally improvised and eventually notated, is an essential feature of the Western musical tradition.

- In the Middle Ages, Paris's Cathedral of Notre Dame was a center for **organum,** the earliest

type of polyphony: two-, three-, or four-voice parts sung in fixed rhythmic patterns (**rhythmic modes**).

- Preexisting chants formed the basis for early polyphony, including organum.

Monophonic music is the most straightforward kind, and many world traditions focus on a single melodic line in their songs. But other traditions also cultivate greater complexity through the simultaneous sounding of multiple musical lines. This is the case of the Western tradition, which has become distinctive—and popular throughout the globe—because of its potential for layered complexity. From the symphonic hall to the mixing studio, the ability to create and coordinate simultaneous lines—call them melodies, layers, or "tracks"—is the mark of supreme musical craft and professional training.

Early polyphony, including organum, served to praise the Virgin Mary. French school, thirteenth century.

Early Polyphony

Polyphony, or the combination of two or more simultaneous melodic lines, is the single most important feature in the development of Western music. While improvised polyphony likely goes back many centuries, European polyphony is distinctive because it was notated, allowing for more detail and control over the musical texture. Notated polyphony began to emerge toward the end of the Romanesque era (c. 850–1150)—interestingly, around the same time that music notation itself became increasingly sophisticated on the European Continent. Because polyphonic music had to be written down in a way that would indicate precise rhythm and pitch, a more exact notational system developed, the direct ancestor of the one in use today.

With the development of notation, music expanded from an art of improvisation and oral tradition to one that was carefully planned and preserved. During the Gothic era (c. 1150–1450), which saw the rise of magnificent cathedrals, individual composers came to be recognized. These learned musicians, mostly clerics in religious communities, mastered the art of writing extended musical works in varied textures and forms.

Organum

The earliest polyphonic music, called **organum**, grew out of the improvisatory custom of adding a second voice to a Gregorian melody at the interval of a fifth or fourth. Soon a polyphonic art blossomed in which the individual voices moved with ever greater independence. In the forefront of this evolution were the com-

---

LISTENING GUIDE 3 1:26

Notre Dame School: *Gaude Maria virgo (Rejoice, Virgin Mary)*

DATE: Early 13th century
GENRE: Organum

What to Listen For

Melody	Short, repeated ideas exchanged between the upper voices.	**Texture**	Three-part polyphony, alternating with monophonic chant.
Rhythm/ meter	Simple pattern of long-short-long-short in upper voices over the slow-moving bottom voice (Tenor).	**Expression**	The opening words "Gaude Maria" drawn out in a long melismatic setting.
Harmony	Open, hollow-sounding cadences on the intervals of fifths and octaves.	**Performing forces**	*A cappella*; soloists sing organum; choir sings chant.
		Text	Prayer in praise of the Virgin Mary.

	TEXT	TRANSLATION	PERFORMANCE
0:00	Gaude Maria	Rejoice, Mary,	Organum style; upper two voices moving rhythmically over a sustained third voice (Tenor).
1:07	virgo cunctas hereses sola interemisti.	O Virgin, you alone have destroyed all heresies.	Monophonic chant, melismatic, then continuing in a neumatic setting.

Opening of organum, with two rhythmic upper voices over a long chant note:

posers centered at Paris's Cathedral of Notre Dame during the twelfth and thirteenth centuries. Their leader, Léonin (fl. 1150–c. 1201), is the first composer of polyphonic music whose name we know. He is credited with compiling the *Great Book of Organum* (*Magnus liber organi*), music for the entire church year, in this new musical style. His successor, Pérotin (fl. c. 1200), expanded the dimensions of organum by increasing the number of voice parts, first to three and then to four.

To the medieval mind, the new had to be founded on the old. Therefore composers of organum based their pieces on preexisting Gregorian chants. While the lower voice sang the fixed melody in extremely long notes, the upper voice or voices sang a freely composed part that moved rapidly above it. In such a setting, the chant was no longer recognizable as a melody by human ears; but, medieval singers reasoned, divine ears could still hear the prescribed prayer.

The Cathedral of Notre Dame in Paris, viewed from the Left Bank, with its prominent flying buttresses, was a major composition center for organum.

Gaude Maria virgo (Rejoice, Virgin Mary)

In the organum *Gaude Maria virgo* (LG 3), the opening polyphonic section features two voices singing in a **rhythmic mode**, a fixed pattern of long and short notes that is repeated or varied, over a sustained bottom voice taken from the chant of the same name. The setting, in the style of Pérotin (and possibly by him), is highly melismatic, with many notes sung to each syllable of text, a prayer in praise of the Virgin Mary. The form of this organum is typical in that it alternates polyphony, sung by soloists, and monophonic chant, sung by the choir.

A choir of monks in a detail from a fresco on the life of San Nicola, by the fourteenth-century Master of Tolentino.

Not all religious communities welcomed polyphony: some saw it as a distraction from the simplicity and equality of communal singing of plainchant, since it required specialized singers and composers who were sometimes characterized as overly vain about their musical skills. However, the magnificence and complexity of polyphonic music became increasingly sought after, since it was seen to enhance worship on the highest feast days, like Easter. Polyphony became a mark of distinction, both for the musicians who practiced it and for those who sponsored its innovations and expressive potential: and thus set the stage for the entire unfolding of the Western musical tradition.

CRITICAL THINKING

1. Why did composers of early polyphony use chant as the basis for their works?

2. What were considered the advantages and disadvantages of polyphony?

YOUR TURN TO EXPLORE

Many hip-hop songs are especially multilayered, but most other traditions that feature multiple performers (jazz and heavy-metal bands, for example, as well as several ensemble-based world traditions) are carefully layered as well. Consider a song that has several distinct lines or layers of voice or instrument. How are the voices/instruments/layers kept distinct, and how are they combined? Is one layer the most prominent throughout, or do different ones emerge in turn as leaders?

Chapter 15

Symbols and Puzzles: Machaut and the Medieval Mind

"Able was I ere I saw Elba."

—English palindrome referring to Napoleon's exile

KEY POINTS

- Religious wars (the Crusades) and medieval explorations enabled an exchange of musical instruments and theoretical ideas about music with Middle Eastern and Far Eastern cultures.

- Guillaume de Machaut was a poet-composer of the French **Ars nova** (new art) who wrote sacred music and polyphonic **chansons** (secular songs) set to fixed text forms (**rondeau, ballade, virelai).**

- Machaut's chanson *Ma fin est mon commencement* employs a palindromic form and an enigmatic text to display compositional craft and challenge the listener to careful listening and thinking.

The Sphinx's riddle, Fermat's last theorem, cryptography, the "Da Vinci Code": we humans are fascinated by riddles and puzzles, maybe because they challenge us to think of possibilities beyond our current understanding. In the Western tradition, music has been linked with mathematics and geometry since antiquity. Ancient Greek mathematician Pythagoras was renowned for his musical experiments, In medieval times, the four topics (Quadrivium) considered essential to education were music, mathematics, geometry, and astronomy. Since then, musicians have remained involved in exploring the mathematical or geometrical implications of their art and conveying puzzles through sound.

In Her Own Words

❝ Which creature walks on four legs in the morning, two legs in the afternoon, and three legs in the evening?"

—*The Sphinx of Thebes*

Medieval Minstrels and Court Musicians

Alongside the learned music of the cathedrals and choir schools grew a popular repertory of songs and dances that reflected every aspect of medieval life. Some musicians lived on the fringe of society, wandering among the courts and towns and entertaining audiences with their songs, dancing, juggling, and tricks. On a higher social level were the poet-musicians who flourished at the various courts of Europe. Those in the south of France were known as *troubadours*, while those in northern France were *trouvères*—both terms mean "finders" or "inventors." These aristocratic musicians wrote poetry-with-music that ranged from love songs and laments to political and moral ditties and chronicles of the Crusades.

Troubadours, trouvères

Opening Doors to the East: The Crusades

Extending over some two hundred years, from 1095 to 1291, the Crusades were a series of religious wars waged by Western Europeans to win back the Holy Land of Palestine from the Muslims, and were at once among the most violent episodes in recorded history and one of the most influential forces on medieval Europe. The movement of vast armies across the European Continent created increased trade along the routes, and allowed Westerners to gain a much broader knowledge of the world and other ways of life through their contact, albeit hostile, with Islam. Despite the pillaging and destruction, the interaction of distant cultures had positive results. The crusading knights learned from the expert military skills of the Turkish and Moorish warriors, and the advanced medical and scientific knowledge of the Arab world was imported to Europe. It was at this time too that the Arab number system was adopted in the West (until then, Europeans had used Roman numerals—I, II, III, IV, V—rather than the Arabic numerals 1, 2, 3, 4, 5). With this came a growing interest in numerology, which allowed for mathematics and other pattern-related disciplines to flourish in the West.

Musicians who traveled eastward with the crusading armies brought music, theoretical ideas, and instruments of all types back to their homeland. The medieval rebec, a small bowed-string instrument that was a forerunner of the modern violin, derived from the Arab rabab (see p. 62), and the loud, double-reed shawm (pp. 96, 98), the predecessor of the modern

A Turkish military (Janissary) band, with mounted players of trumpets, cymbals, and drums. Miniature from Vehbi's *Imperial Festival Book* (c. 1720).

oboe, was a military instrument used by Turkish armies. Many of our orchestral percussion instruments stem from Turkish models as well, including the cymbals, bells, and bass drum. Crusaders heard the sounds of the Saracen (Muslim) military trumpets and drums and soon adopted these as their call to battle. The foundation of our Western system of early scales (modes) also came from Eastern theoretical systems.

Despite the long-standing intolerance these wars fostered between the Western and Islamic worlds, an aura of romance and mystery hovers over the Crusades. Medieval poets, composers of opera, modern filmmakers, and even video game inventors have drawn on epic stories of knightly courage and chivalric love, keeping these historic episodes alive and exciting for us today.

Manuscript illumination of the crusading Christians defeating the Muslim leader Saladin, from the *Chronique des Empereurs* (c. 1460).

A polyphonic chanson is performed with voices and lute in this miniature representing the Garden of Love, from a Flemish manuscript of *Le Roman de la Rose* (c. 1500).

As in many songs today, medieval lyrics dealt with unrequited, or unconsummated, passion, idealizing the unobtainable object. At first these songs were monophonic, but the polyphonic developments in sacred music soon carried over to the secular realm, as we will hear in the works of Guillaume de Machaut, whose music bridges the tradition of the *trouvères* and a new creative sensibility.

Machaut and the French *Ars nova*

European contacts with Eastern cultures, along with developments in feudal social structure, inspired new concepts of life, art, and beauty. These changes were reflected in the musical style known as *Ars nova* (new art), which appeared in the early 1300s in France, and soon thereafter in Italy. The music of the French *Ars nova,* more refined and complex than music of the *Ars antiqua* (old art), which it displaced, ushered in developments in rhythm, meter, harmony, and counterpoint that transformed the art of music.

At the same time, writers such as Petrarch, Boccaccio, and Chaucer were turning from otherworldly ideals to human subjects; painters soon discovered the beauty of nature and the attractiveness of the human form. Similarly, composers like the French master Machaut turned increasingly from religious to secular themes. The influence of this last great poet-composer was far-reaching, his music and poetry admired long after his death. He was also the first composer to self-consciously collect his works and leave them for posterity.

Machaut's music introduced a new freedom of rhythm characterized by gentle syncopations and the interplay of duple and triple meters. In his secular works, he favored the **chanson**, which was generally set to a French courtly love poem written in one of several fixed text forms. These poetic forms—the **rondeau**, **ballade**, and **virelai**—established the musical repetition scheme of the chansons.

Chanson

We will consider a rondeau by Machaut (LG 4) that presents us with both an enigmatic text and a hidden musical structure involving palindromes, words or

Guillaume de Machaut (c. 1300–1377)

Machaut was the foremost poet-composer of the *Ars nova.* He took holy orders at an early age but worked much of his life at various French courts, including that of Charles, duke of Normandy, who subsequently became king of France. Machaut's double career as cleric and courtier inspired him to write both religious and secular music. His own poetry embraces the ideals of medieval chivalry. One of his writings, a long autobiographical poem of more than 9,000 lines in rhymed couplets, tells the platonic love story of the aging Machaut and a young girl named Peronne. The two exchanged poems and letters, some of which the composer set to music. Machaut spent his final years as a priest and canon at the Cathedral of Reims, admired as the greatest musician and poet of the time.

MAJOR WORKS: Motets, chansons (both monophonic and polyphonic) • A polyphonic Mass (*Messe de Notre Dame*), one of the earliest complete settings of the Ordinary of the Mass.

LISTENING GUIDE 4

🎧 5:39

Machaut: *Ma fin est mon commencement* (*My end is my beginning*)

DATE: Mid-14th century

GENRE: Polyphonic chanson (rondeau)

What to Listen For

Melody	Wavelike, with long melismas.
Rhythm/meter	Duple meter, syncopated.
Harmony	Open, hollow cadences.
Texture	Non-imitative polyphony.
Form	Two sections, A and B, repeated ABaAabAB (uppercase = refrain; lowercase = verses); palindromes in voices.
Performing forces	Three voices.
Text	Rondeau by the composer; puzzle text.

	A SECTION	B SECTION
Triplum		
Cantus		
Tenor		
	1, 4, 7 Ma fin est mon . . .	2, 8 Et mon commencement . . .
	3 Est teneüre . . .	
	5 Mes tiers . . .	6 Se retrograde . . .

			TEXT		TRANSLATION
0:00	Refrain	1.	Ma fin est mon commencement	A	My end is my beginning
0:42		2.	Et mon commencement ma fin	B	and my beginning my end
1:23	Partial verse	3.	Est teneüre vraiement.	a	and my true tenor.
2:05	Partial refrain	4.	Ma fin est mon commencement.	A	My end is my beginning.
2:47	Verse	5.	Mes tiers chans trois fois seulement	a	My third part three times only
		6.	Se retrograde et einsi fin.	b	moves backward and so ends.
4:10	Refrain	7.	Ma fin est mon commencement	A	My end is my beginning
		8.	Et mon commencement ma fin.	B	and my beginning my end.

phrases that read the same backward or forward (in music, this is referred to as retrograde movement). Machaut's text reiterates the refrain "My end is my beginning and my beginning is my end," a sentiment found in several biblical passages (e.g., Ecclesiastes 1:9–10: "The thing that hath been is that which shall be, and that which is done is that which shall be done. There is nothing new under the sun"), and one taken up by various rulers. Two centuries later, for example, while Mary, Queen of Scots, was imprisoned by Elizabeth I, she spent hours embroidering in French "En ma fin est mon commencement," or "In my end is my beginning." Thus, when we investigate the puzzles in Machaut's chanson, we must consider that their purpose was not merely to amuse but to carry a religious connotation as well.

The octagonal maze in the marble floor of the Cathedral of Amiens in France (1288) is similar to the one Machaut knew in Reims, which is now destroyed.

As a priest and a canon at the Reims Cathedral, Machaut was certainly familiar with the famous octagonal labyrinth or maze built into the floor of this church, and with the ritual processions held on Easter and other holy days that traversed the maze, moving to the center and back, with retrograde motion in each direction symbolic of Christ's path through hell to resurrection. With this insight, we can appreciate all the more the palindromic structure of *Ma fin est mon commencement*, in which the two upper voices trade parts in retrograde at the center of the work (the cantus B section is the triplum A section in retrograde; the triplum B section is the cantus A section in retrograde), while the bottom voice, the Tenor, is a retrograde of itself at the midpoint. Although this musical puzzle cannot be easily heard, Machaut provides clues to its structure in his text.

Similar elements of balance and symmetry can be found in his other works as well. Indeed, the secular works of Machaut and his contemporaries in the *Ars nova* reflect a growing interest in both regularity and complexity of musical patterns. These sonic puzzles often require the listener to focus carefully, and listen several times to understand the nuances of both craft and expression. Like all puzzles, they engage the brain in novel ways, and feed our human desire for subtlety and complexity.

CRITICAL THINKING

1. What ideas did Western European medieval society borrow from the Middle East?
2. How does Machaut use the palindromic process in *Ma fin est mon commencement*? Why do you think he does this?

YOUR TURN TO EXPLORE

Many composers have created music that uses symbols, ciphers, or puzzles in either its construction or its text. Find a couple of examples (you might search for "canon," "palindrome," or "puzzle" together with a composer's name) and compare them. Can you hear the different elements come together? If a listener can't readily hear the construction of the puzzle, what might be its expressive purpose in the composer's mind?

Chapter 16

Singing in Friendship:
The Renaissance Madrigal

"Come sing to me a bawdy song, make me merry."
—William Shakespeare, <u>Henry IV, Part 1</u>

KEY POINTS

- Both professional and amateur music-making expanded in the Renaissance through secular vocal and instrumental genres.
- Jacques Arcadelt was an early master of the **Italian madrigal**, a sixteenth-century tradition that linked music and lyric poetry. Madrigals usually feature expressive text setting, word-painting, and multiple meanings.
- **English madrigals**, such as those by John Farmer, were often simpler and lighter in style than their Italian counterparts.

When friends get together to celebrate, singing can't be far behind. Spontaneous social song is often monophonic throughout world cultures: everyone sings the same melody (think of "Happy Birthday"). Western culture has also developed a complex and widespread tradition of social **part song**, in which separate musical lines are combined into a harmonious whole—a fitting sonic image for friendship.

Social Music-Making in the Renaissance

In the Renaissance, while professional musicians entertained noble guests at court and civic festivities, more and more amateurs began making music in their homes. The music could be vocal—both unaccompanied and supported by instruments—or purely instrumental; indeed, in most prosperous homes you would find a lute (see illustration, p. 80) or a keyboard instrument. The study of music was considered part of the proper upbringing for a young girl or, to a lesser degree, boy. Partly as a result, women began to play prominent roles in the performance of music both in the home and at court. During the later sixteenth century in Italy, a number of professional women singers achieved great fame.

Two important secular genres arose from the union of poetry and music: the **French chanson** (an outgrowth of the medieval version we heard by Machaut) and the **Italian madrigal**. The intricate verse structures of French and Italian poetry helped shape these musical forms. The madrigal is known for the expressive device of **word-painting**—that is, making the music directly reflect the meaning of the words. An unexpected harsh dissonance, for example, might coincide with the word

In His Own Words

66 And we will sit upon the rocks, / Seeing the shepherds feed their flocks, / By shallow rivers to whose falls / Melodious birds sing madrigals."
—Christopher Marlowe (1564-1593)

Word-painting

A stylized sixteenth-century painting of four singers performing from music "part books." The couple in back are beating time. *Concert in the Open Air* (Italian School).

The Lute Player, by **Caravaggio** (1571–1610), performs an Arcadelt madrigal.

"death," or an ascending line might lead up to the word "heaven" or "stars." We will see how these so-called **madrigalisms** enhanced the emotional content of the music.

The Madrigal: Linking Music and Poetry

The sixteenth-century **madrigal**, the most important secular genre of the era, was an aristocratic form of poetry and music that flourished at the Italian courts as a favorite diversion of cultivated amateurs. The text consisted of a short poem of lyric or reflective character, often including emotional words for weeping, sighing, trembling, and dying, which the Italian madrigalists set suggestively. Love and unsatisfied desire were popular topics, but so were humor and satire, politics, and scenes of city and country life. The madrigal literature therefore presents a vivid panorama of Renaissance thought and feeling.

From the beginning, the Italian madrigal was an art form in which words and music were clearly linked. During its early period (c. 1525–50), the composer's chief concern was to give pleasure to amateur performers. As the genre grew in complexity and expanded to five or six voices, professionals were often hired to join the amateurs or even sing on their own. The final phase of the madrigal (1580–1620) extended beyond the late Renaissance into the world of the Baroque. The form became the direct expression of the composer's musical personality and feelings. One of the most artful and influential composers of this later Italian madrigal tradition was Claudio Monteverdi (1567–1643), who famously declared that his music was designed to serve the expressive power of his texts. Certain traits were carried to an extreme: rich chromatic harmony, dramatic declamation, vocal virtuosity, and vivid depiction of emotional words in music all lead us to the new Baroque style.

Jacques Arcadelt (c. 1507–1568)

The northern composer Arcadelt was highly influential in the development of the Italian madrigal. He moved from present-day Belgium to Italy in the 1520s, working first in Florence—the birthplace of the madrigal—and later in Rome, as a singer in the Sistine Chapel choir. His earliest madrigal publications were issued during the years in Rome: his first book of madrigals (published in 1538 and including the famous *Il bianco e dolce cigno*) became the most widely reprinted collection of the time. In 1551, Arcadelt moved north to take a post in France at the court of the cardinal of Lorraine, where he continued to write and publish both sacred and secular music. His musical style is simpler and more lyrical than that of earlier composers, and he gives careful attention to the text. Arcadelt set poems by many different writers, ranging from Petrarch to the Italian military commander Alfonso d'Avalos, who penned *Il bianco e dolce cigno*.

MAJOR WORKS: Some 250 madrigals, mostly for four voices • About 125 French chansons • Sacred music, including Masses and motets.

Arcadelt and the Early Madrigal

Arcadelt's lovely madrigal *Il bianco e dolce cigno* (*The White and Sweet Swan*, LG 5) was a huge hit in his lifetime and for some years to follow, perhaps because its intended audience was amateur performers. The composer delivers the words clearly, in a mostly homophonic setting, with subtle moments of word-painting—emphasizing certain words with melismas and others with chromaticism. Madrigal

---

LISTENING GUIDE 5   2:05

Arcadelt: *Il bianco e dolce cigno*
(*The White and Sweet Swan*)

DATE: Published 1538

GENRE: Italian madrigal

What to Listen For

Melody	Lyrical, conjunct; focus is on top line.	**Form**	Through-composed until the last line (which is repeated several times).
Rhythm/meter	Simple movement in duple meter.	**Expression**	Emotional words set with dissonance, chromaticism, melisma, and repetition.
Harmony	Consonant, full sound, with some dissonance and chromaticism for expression.	**Performing forces**	Four voices, *a cappella*.
Texture	Mostly homophonic; imitative entries on the last line.	**Text**	10-line poem by Alfonso d'Avalos.

	TEXT	**TRANSLATION**
0:00	Il bianco e dolce cigno	The white and sweet swan
	cantando more. Et io	dies singing. And I,
	piangendo giung' al fin del viver mio.	weeping, come to the end of my life.
	Stran' e diversa sorte,	Strange and different fate,
	ch'ei more sconsolato,	that it dies disconsolate,
	et io moro beato.	and I die happy—
	Morte che nel morire,	a death that in dying
	m'empie di gioia tutt'e di desire.	fills me fully with joy and desire.
	Se nel morir' altro dolor non sento,	If when I die no other pain I feel,
1:24	di mille mort' il dì sarei contento.	with a thousand deaths a day I would be content.

Last line is repeated several times to emphasize "di mille morte" ("a thousand deaths"):

Meter	1	2	3	4		1	2	3	4		1	2	3	4		1	2	3
Soprano																di mil-	le mort'il	dì
Alto		di mil-	le	mort'il dì,		di mil-					le	mort'il	dì					
Tenor			di mil-	le mort' il dì,		di mil-	le	mort' il dì										
Bass				di mil-	le mort'	il dì____												

Interface

Printing and Literacy

In an age when anyone can publish a message on the Internet for all the world to see, it's hard to imagine a time when the printed word was not how information was dispersed. Throughout the Middle Ages, information was transmitted orally, and only a tiny percentage of the population knew how to read and write. If a wealthy person or a religious institution (the only ones who could afford it) wanted a copy of a book, it had to be painstakingly made by hand. Knowledge was therefore in the hands of the very few, until the arrival of the printed book in the mid-1400s.

Although we credit the German craftsman Johannes Gutenberg (1397?–1468) with the invention of the printing press and the art of printing books, it's actually more accurate to say that he adapted the age-old wine press to the job. Moreover, the recipe for ink was well known from the manuscript era, and paper-making had already been introduced from the Far East, where the Chinese had been printing woodcuts for centuries. So Guten-

berg's task was to adapt these technologies and to develop a strong metal alloy for casting pieces of type, allowing him to print the first Western book: the Gutenberg Bible (c. 1455). This development was a major agent for social change: as books became available, education and literacy spread from the nobility and clergy to the merchant and middle classes.

As books for worship began to be printed, plainchant notation found its way into those books. It took, though, another fifty years for these skills to be applied successfully to printing polyphonic music, where notes and clefs had to be placed onto music staves and notes had to be aligned with text. The first person to master these problems was an Italian musician named Ottaviano Petrucci, who produced elegantly printed music books beginning in 1501 (see illustration below); unfortunately, these books were also very expensive to produce and cost Petrucci much business in several bankruptcies. But the technology was here to stay: other printers soon found cheaper means

to print music in quantity, making it possible for amateur musicians to purchase books and to learn to read music. These developments furthered the cause of secular music—anyone could now learn and perform chansons, madrigals, and dances.

Fast-forward some five hundred years to the Internet era: some consider the age of the printed book, and music, to be nearly over. But from another perspective, there are more paper books (and music!) available today than ever before, and the format of the Gutenberg book continues to be the model for the e-book. Recording may have largely replaced printing as our primary way of consuming music, but even prominent pop musicians continue to experiment with the power of the printed text. For example, singer-songwriter Beck released his 2012 *Song Reader* "album" as sheet music rather than recording, and coupled it with a website (www.songreader.net) where amateur and professional musicians alike can share their interpretations of his compositions.

A nineteenth-century rendering of Johannes Gutenberg at his printing press.

Music for a setting of *Ave Maria* from Petrucci's *Odhecaton*, the first printed music book (1501).

texts typically offer various levels of meaning, and this one is no different. Literally, the text refers to swans singing—which, according to ancient belief, they do only before they die. But references to death in madrigal poetry were usually understood as erotic, death being a conceit for sexual climax, which gives the text a whole new slant. Madrigals were sung as chamber music, with one singer on a line, reading from a **part book** (see illustration, p. 80). You can imagine what the double meaning of "death" could offer in mixed-company social singing!

The Madrigal in England

Just as Shakespeare adapted the Italian sonnet, so English composers developed the Italian madrigal into a native art form during the late sixteenth century and the reign of Elizabeth I (1558–1603). In their own madrigals, some English composers followed the late Italian model, setting dramatic love poetry in serious, weighty works, while others favored simpler texts in more accessible settings. New humorous madrigal types were cultivated, some with refrain syllables such as "fa la la." One of the most important English madrigal composers was John Farmer.

John Farmer (c. 1570–1603)

The English composer Farmer was active in Dublin, Ireland, as an organist and master of the choirboys at Christ Church. In 1599, he moved to London and published his only collection of four-voice madrigals. Farmer used clever word painting in these lighthearted works and helped shape the madrigal into a truly native art form.

MAJOR WORKS: English songs and madrigals (for four and six voices).

Farmer's *Fair Phyllis*

The pastoral text, lively rhythms, and good humor of *Fair Phyllis* (LG 6) make it a perfect example of the English madrigal. The poem tells of a shepherdess (Phyllis) being pursued by her lover, Amyntas (their names are stock ones for such rustic characters). The narrative brings their story to a happy conclusion with their amorous love play. English composers adopted the Italian practice of word painting, allowing us to "hear" this charming story. While it's fun to listen to these madrigals, more fun is to "tell" the story in interactive social song—remember, this music was designed for friends to sing with each other, rather than for professionals to perform to an audience. The melodies are simple enough that you might be able to sing them yourself after you've heard them a few times. How does your connection to the story change when you tell it, rather than hearing it?

A typical pastoral scene of a shepherd and sheperdess, by **Januarius Zick** (1730–1797).

CRITICAL THINKING

1. How did the madrigal tradition change from the early 1500s into the early 1600s?
2. What aspects of *Il bianco e dolce cigno* and *Fair Phyllis* make them suitable for amateur performance?

LISTENING GUIDE 6

 1:21

Farmer: *Fair Phyllis*

DATE: Published 1599

GENRE: English madrigal

What to Listen For

Melody	Dancelike, diatonic melody.
Rhythm/ meter	Lively rhythms; begins in duple meter, shifts to triple and back.
Texture	Varied: first monophonic, then some imitation; homorhythmic for last line.
Form	Short, repeated sections.

Expression	Word painting on opening line ("all alone") and on "up and down."
Performing forces	Four voices (SATB), *a cappella*.
Text	Lighthearted pastoral English poem.

TEXT

0:00   Fair Phyllis I saw sitting all alone,
Feeding her flock near to the mountain side.
The shepherds knew not whither she was gone,
But after her [her] lover Amyntas hied.

0:24   Up and down he wandered, whilst she was missing;
When he found her, oh, then they fell a-kissing.

0:48   Up and down . . .

Examples of word painting

"Fair Phyllis I saw sitting all alone"—sung by soprano alone:

"Up and down"—descending line, repeated in all parts imitatively; shown in soprano and alto:

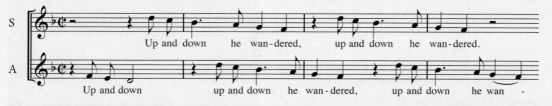

YOUR TURN TO EXPLORE

Can you find examples of twenty-first-century part songs (whether in North America or elsewhere) that are designed for social singing rather than concert performance? Does the number of singers in a group affect the performance, in terms of hearing the words clearly or being able to follow the interaction of the voices? Is the effect different if the musical story is sung by a mixed-gender rather than single-gender group?

Chapter 17

Remember Me: Personalizing the Motet in the Renaissance

"We know by experience that song has great force and vigor to move and inflame the hearts of men to invoke and praise God with a more vehement and ardent zeal."

—John Calvin

KEY POINTS

- Renaissance sacred music was generally performed **a cappella** (for unaccompanied voices) and features a fuller, more consonant sound (with "sweet" thirds and sixths) than medieval music. Some works are built on a fixed, preexisting melody (**cantus firmus**).

- Josquin des Prez's *Ave Maria . . . virgo serena* is a **motet** to the Virgin Mary set in varied textural styles, which are designed to convey the changing meanings in the text.

R eligious belief continued as a core aspect of identity in the Renaissance, even as the nature of that belief shifted to a more personal connection to the divine. This shift is perhaps most clearly reflected in the different artistic renditions of the Virgin Mary, on whom worshippers began to focus at this time.

Medieval painting presented life through symbolism; the Renaissance preferred realism. Medieval painters posed their idealized figures impersonally, facing frontally; Renaissance artists developed profile portraiture and humanized their

Visual arts

Leonardo da Vinci (1452–1519), whose remarkable *Last Supper* is the most reproduced religious painting of all time, was a contemporary of composer Josquin des Prez.

Medieval and Renaissance artistic approaches. LEFT: **Cimabue** (c. 1240–1302) aims to create an ideal effect, using magnificent colors, and there is an emotional distance between the characters that is in keeping with their distance from the worldly. RIGHT: **Raphael** (1483–1520) shapes a more realistic environment, and the emotional bond between mother and child resonates with the faithful's trust that the Virgin will care for those who believe in her.

subjects. Space in medieval works was organized in a succession of planes that the eye perceived as a series of episodes, but Renaissance painters made it possible to see the whole simultaneously. They discovered the landscape, created the illusion of distance, and focused on the physical loveliness of the world. Echoing the visual arts, musicians helped to reinforce and intensify this newly personal approach to praise-through-beauty.

Renaissance Sacred Music

The Renaissance marks the passing of European society from a predominantly religious orientation to a more secular one, and from an age of unquestioning faith and mysticism to one of growing reliance on reason and scientific inquiry. A new way of thinking centered on human issues and the individual. People gained confidence in their ability to solve their own problems and to order their world rationally, without relying exclusively on tradition or religion. This awakening, called **humanism**, was inspired by the ancient cultures of Greece and Rome, its writers and artworks.

Humanism

In attempting to reconcile the needs of the individual with the primacy of the divine, musicians expanded their approaches to sung worship. In addition to the monophonic Gregorian chant that defined Catholic prayer, music for church services included hymns, motets, and polyphonic settings of the Mass. These were normally multivoiced and, especially in the early Renaissance era, based on preexisting music. They were sung by professional male singers trained from childhood in cathedral choir schools.

The vocal forms of Renaissance music were marked by smoothly gliding melodies conceived specially for the voice. In fact, the sixteenth century has come to be regarded as the golden age of the *a cappella* style (for voices alone, without instrumental accompaniment). Polyphony in such works was based on the principle of

***A cappella* style**

imitation: musical ideas are exchanged between vocal lines, the voices imitating one another so that a similar phrase is heard in different registers. (Imitation is different from round in that the phrases sung by different voices in imitation are *similar* but not *identical*.) The result is a close-knit musical fabric capable of subtle and varied effects, in which each voice participates equally in the polyphonic prayer—a way to combine individual action with collaborative worship. In the matter of harmony, composers of the Renaissance leaned toward fuller chords. They turned away from the open fifths (missing the third of a triad) and octaves preferred in medieval times to the "sweeter" thirds and sixths. The use of dissonance in sacred music was carefully controlled.

Imitation

Polyphonic writing offered the composer many possibilities, such as the use of a fixed melody (**cantus firmus**) in one voice as the basis for elaborate ornamentation in the other voices. Triple meter had been especially attractive to the medieval mind because it symbolized the perfection of the Trinity. Renaissance composers, much less preoccupied with religious symbolism, showed a greater interest in duple meter.

Cantus firmus

Josquin des Prez and the Motet

"[Josquin] is the master of the notes. They have to do as he bids them; other composers have to do as the notes will."

—Martin Luther

In the Renaissance, one of the most popular genres was the **motet**—a sacred work with a Latin text, for use in the Mass and other religious services. The ability to combine newly written texts of praise with prescribed prayers was part of the appeal of the motet for composers, who were able to demonstrate their individual creativity through choice of text as well as musical invention. Motets in praise of the Virgin Mary were extremely popular because of the many religious groups all over Europe devoted to her, and also because of the potential for the faithful to identify with the powerful intimacy of the mother-child relationship.

The preeminent composers of motets from the early Renaissance (1450–1520) were from northern Europe, in particular present-day Belgium and northern France. Among these composers, we will consider Josquin des Prez, one of the great masters of sacred music.

Josquin des Prez (c. 1450–1521)

Josquin (as he is known) exerted a powerful influence on generations of composers to follow. After spending his youth in northern Europe, Josquin was employed for much of his varied career in Italy, at courts in Milan and Ferrara and in the papal choir in Rome. In Italy, he absorbed the classical virtues of balance and moderation, the sense of harmonious proportion and clear form, visible in the paintings of the era. Toward the end of his life, he returned to his native France, where he served as a provost at the collegiate church of Condé.

Josquin appeared at a time when the humanizing influences of the Renaissance were being felt throughout Europe. His music is rich in feeling, characterized by serenely beautiful melodies and expressive harmony.

MAJOR WORKS: Over 100 motets • At least 17 Masses • Many French chansons and Italian secular songs.

 Inviolata, integra et casta es Maria

LISTENING GUIDE 7 4:38

Josquin: *Ave Maria . . . virgo serena*
(*Hail Mary . . . gentle Virgin*)

DATE: 1480s?

GENRE: Latin motet

What to Listen For

Melody	High vs. low voices, singing in pairs; opening phrase quotes a chant.
Rhythm/ meter	Duple meter, with shift to triple, then back.
Harmony	Consonant; hollow-sounding cadences.
Texture	Imitative polyphony, with moments of homorhythm.

Form	Sectional according to strophes of the poem (each begins "Ave").
Expression	Personal plea from composer at the end.
Performing forces	Four-voice choir; *a cappella*.
Text	Rhymed, strophic prayer to the Virgin Mary.

	TEXT	TRANSLATION	DESCRIPTION
0:00	Ave Maria, gratia plena, Dominus tecum, virgo serena.	Hail Mary, full of grace, The Lord is with you, gentle Virgin.	Four voices in imitation (SATB) quote a chant; duple meter.
0:45	Ave cujus conceptio Solemni plena gaudio Caelestia, terrestria, Nova replet laetitia.	Hail, whose conception, Full of solemn joy, Fills the heaven, the earth, With new rejoicing.	Two and three voices, later four voices; more homorhythmic texture.
1:21	Ave cujus nativitas Nostra fuit solemnitas, Ut lucifer lux oriens, Verum solem praeveniens.	Hail, whose birth Was our festival, As our luminous rising light Coming before the true sun.	Voice pairs (SA/TB) in close imitation, then four voices in imitation.
1:59	Ave pia humilitas, Sine viro fecunditas, Cujus annuntiatio, Nostra fuit salvatio.	Hail, pious humility, Fertility without a man, Whose annunciation Was our salvation.	Voice pairs (SA/TB); a more homorhythmic texture.
2:27	Ave vera virginitas, Immaculata castitas, Cujus purificatio Nostra fuit purgatio.	Hail, true virginity, Unspotted chastity, Whose purification Was our cleansing.	Triple meter; clear text declamation; homorhythmic texture.
3:04	Ave praeclara omnibus Angelicis virtutibus, Cujus fuit assumptio Nostra glorificatio.	Hail, famous with all Angelic virtues, Whose assumption was Our glorification.	Imitative voice pairs; return to duple meter.
3:59	O Mater Dei, Memento mei. Amen.	O Mother of God, Remember me. Amen.	Completely homorhythmic; text declamation in long notes, separated by rests.

Ave Maria . . . virgo serena (LG 7) is a prime example of how Josquin experimented with varied combinations of voices and textures to highlight different emotional aspects of the text. In this four-voice composition dedicated to the Virgin Mary, high voices engage in a dialogue with low ones, and imitative textures alternate with **homorhythmic** settings (in which all voices move together rhythmically). Josquin opens the piece with a musical reference to a preexisting chant for the Virgin, but soon drops this melody in favor of a freely composed form that is highly sensitive to the text. Notice that the equality and interdependence of the voices is highlighted by the frequent changes in the way voices are grouped, and that smaller groupings of two or three voices tend to build to the full ensemble at the ends of phrases.

The final two lines of text, a personal plea to the Virgin ("O Mother of God, remember me"), is set in a simple texture that emphasizes the words, proclaiming the humanistic spirit of a new age. How do you think this direct appeal relates to the change in the depictions of the Virgin shown in the images on page 86? How does the full-chord sound that opens this section compare with the sound of the final "Amen," which is instead an open fifth?

Homorhythm

In His Own Words

66 The better the voice is, the meeter it is to honor and serve God."
—*William Byrd (c. 1540–1623)*

CRITICAL THINKING

1. In what way does the "humanist" approach differ from ways of thinking in the Middle Ages?
2. How does Josquin bring his own creativity to the text? Does this combination of individuality and tradition also connect to other examples we have examined?

YOUR TURN TO EXPLORE

The recording associated with our Listening Guide features a mixed-gender chorus of several voices to a part, but in the Renaissance, sacred music of this sort was almost exclusively sung by small all-male ensembles. Find a recording of this work (or another Josquin motet) by an all-male group (for example: the Hilliard Ensemble, The King's Singers, Chanticleer). How is the effect different from the version on your recording? Which do you find more expressive, and why?

Chapter 18

Glory Be: Music for the Renaissance Mass

"Our wisest mortals have decided that music should give zest to divine worship. If people take great pains to compose beautiful music for secular songs, they should devote at least as much thought to sacred song."

—Giovanni Pierluigi da Palestrina

KEY POINTS

- The most solemn ritual of the Catholic Church is the **Mass**, a daily service with two categories of prayers: the **Ordinary** (texts that remain the same for every Mass) and the **Proper** (texts that vary according to the day).

- Renaissance composers set texts from the Ordinary of the Mass (Kyrie, Gloria, Credo, Sanctus, Agnus Dei) for their polyphonic Masses.

- Reformers such as Luther and Calvin believed that monophonic congregational singing in the vernacular should define Christian worship, while the Catholic establishment preferred trained singers and polyphony.

- Giovanni Pierluigi da Palestrina's *Pope Marcellus Mass* met the Council of Trent's demands for a *cappella* singing with clearly declaimed text.

D oes elaborate music in church distract worshippers from their focus on the scriptural text? Or does the sublime power of sound convey ultimate praise, and help the faithful envision the blessings of heaven? To this day, many consider unison song essential for building collective purpose, whether in worship or in other group activity—while others rely on the grandeur of polyphony to convey magnificence and glory, whether in church or in other places of celebration.

The Renaissance Mass

A similar debate was at the core of Christian reform in the 1500s: while Protestants argued for the simple unity of congregational singing, Catholics affirmed the power of professional choirs and complex textures, especially in polyphonic settings of the Mass.

A reenactment of Christ's Last Supper with his disciples (see p. 85), the **Mass** is the most solemn ritual of the Catholic Church, and the one generally attended by public worshippers. The collection of prayers that makes up the Mass (its liturgy) falls into two categories: the **Ordinary**, texts that remain the same in every Mass; and the **Proper**, texts that vary from day to day throughout the church year, depending on the feast being celebrated. Aside from the Kyrie, which is a Greek

Ordinary and Proper

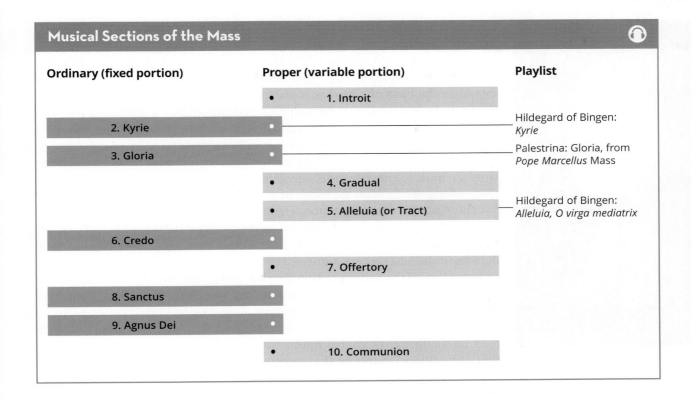

Musical Sections of the Mass

Ordinary (fixed portion)	Proper (variable portion)	Playlist
	• 1. Introit	
2. Kyrie	•	Hildegard of Bingen: *Kyrie*
3. Gloria	•	Palestrina: Gloria, from *Pope Marcellus* Mass
	• 4. Gradual	
	• 5. Alleluia (or Tract)	Hildegard of Bingen: *Alleluia, O virga mediatrix*
6. Credo	•	
	• 7. Offertory	
8. Sanctus	•	
9. Agnus Dei	•	
	• 10. Communion	

text, the rest of the Mass was in Latin, the language of the ancient Romans and the language of learning throughout the Middle Ages and Renaissance. You might be surprised to know that the Catholic Church continued to celebrate the Mass in Latin until the middle of the twentieth century.

With the rise of Renaissance polyphony, composers concentrated their musical settings on the Ordinary, the fixed portion that was sung daily. Its five prayers are the Kyrie, Gloria, Credo, Sanctus, and Agnus Dei. (Today, these sections are recited or sung in the vernacular, the language of the country, rather than in Latin—although in recent years there has been a resurgence of interest in the Latin Mass throughout the world.) The **Kyrie** is a prayer for mercy that dates from the early centuries of Christianity, as its Greek text attests. This prayer is followed by the **Gloria** ("Glory be to God on high"), a joyful hymn of praise. The third section, the **Credo** ("I believe in one God, the Father Almighty"), is the confession of faith and the longest of the Mass texts. Fourth is the **Sanctus** ("Holy, holy, holy"), a song of praise, which concludes with "Hosanna in the highest." The fifth and last part of the Ordinary, the **Agnus Dei** ("Lamb of God, Who takes away the sins of the world"), is sung three times, with different words for its conclusion. The order of the Mass, with its Ordinary and Proper prayers, appears above. (Recall the *Alleluia* from the Proper of the Mass in Chapter 13.)

Ordinary of the Mass

In His Own Words

66 The Credo is the longest movement. There is much to believe."

— *Igor Stravinsky*

The Reformation and Counter-Reformation

Around the time of Josquin's death (1521), major religious reforms were spreading across northern Europe. In 1517, the Augustinian monk Martin Luther (1483–1546) launched the Protestant movement known as the **Reformation** with his Ninety-Five Theses—a list of reforms he proposed for the practices of the Catholic

Portrait of the Protestant reformer Martin Luther, painted by **Lucas Cranach** (1472–1553).

Church. Rather than adopt these new ideas, the church excommunicated him, and the rest is history.

Both Luther and another important reformer, John Calvin (1509–1564), believed that simple, monophonic **congregational singing** in the vernacular should be the basis of Christian worship. Calvin rejected polyphony as distracting from the essential focus on scriptural text: his followers (including the early Pilgrim / Puritan colonists who came to North America from England) embraced the idea that worship song should be monophonic and shared by all congregants. But Luther, an admirer of Josquin, encouraged *his* followers to add polyphonic worship music to enhance the congregational unison singing; we will examine the result of his idea through the music of J. S. Bach in a later chapter.

The Catholic Church was undergoing its own reform movement, focused on a return to Christian piety, known as the Catholic Reformation or **Counter-Reformation**. This movement, which extended from the 1530s into the early decades of the next century, witnessed sweeping changes in the church as religious orders increased their efforts to help the poor and combat heresy. The church organized what some view as the longest committee meeting in history: the **Council of Trent**, which met, with some interruptions, from 1545 to 1563.

In its desire to regulate every aspect of religious discipline, the Council of Trent took up the matter of church music. The attending cardinals noted the corruption of traditional chants by the singers, who added extravagant embellishments to the Gregorian melodies. They also objected to the use of certain instruments in religious services, the practice of incorporating popular songs in Masses, the secular spirit that had invaded sacred music, and the generally irreverent attitude of church musicians. In polyphonic settings of the Mass, the cardinals claimed, the sacred text was made unintelligible by the elaborate texture. Some advocated abolishing polyphony altogether and returning to Gregorian chant, but there were many music lovers among them who opposed so drastic a step.

The committee assigned to deal with the music problem issued only general recommendations in favor of a pure vocal style that would respect the integrity of the sacred texts, avoid virtuosity, and encourage piety. We will hear some of these traits in the glorious polyphony by the Italian master Giovanni Pierluigi da Palestrina.

Palestrina and the *Pope Marcellus* Mass

Palestrina's *Pope Marcellus* Mass was once thought to have been written to satisfy the Council of Trent's recommendations for polyphonic church music, but this is

Giovanni Pierluigi da Palestrina (c. 1525–1594)

Palestrina (named for the town where he was born) worked as an organist and choirmaster at various Italian churches, including St. Peter's in Rome, where he spent the last twenty-three years of his life. He wrote largely sacred music—his output of Masses exceeds that of any other composer—and his music represents the pure *a cappella* style of vocal polyphony typical of the late Renaissance. He strove to make the words understood by properly accentuating them, thereby meeting the guidelines of the Catholic reform.

MAJOR WORKS: Over 100 Masses (including the *Pope Marcellus* Mass) • Madrigals and motets.

LISTENING GUIDE 8 5:50

Palestrina: Gloria, from *Pope Marcellus* Mass

DATE: Published 1567

GENRE: Gloria, from his setting of the Mass Ordinary

What to Listen For

Melody	Shifts between high- and low-range voices.	**Form**	Through-composed (no major section repeated), with some short ideas exchanged between voices.
Rhythm/ meter	Slow duple meter, weak pulse.		
Harmony	Full, consonant harmony.	**Expression**	Focus on the clarity of the words.
Texture	Monophonic opening; then homorhythmic, with some polyphony; frequent changes in the density of voices.	**Performing forces**	Six-part choir, *a cappella*.
		Text	Hymn of praise; second movement of the Ordinary of the Mass.

	TEXT	NO. OF VOICES	TRANSLATION
0:00	Gloria in excelsis Deo	1	Glory be to God on high,
	et in terra pax hominibus	4	and on earth peace to men
	bonae voluntatis.	4	of good will.
	Laudamus te. Benedicimus te.	4	We praise Thee. We bless Thee.
	Adoramus te.	3	We adore Thee.
	Glorificamus te.	4	We glorify Thee.
	Gratias agimus tibi propter	5/4	We give Thee thanks for
	magnam gloriam tuam.	3/4	Thy great glory.
	Domine Deus, Rex caelestis,	4	Lord God, heavenly King,
	Deus Pater omnipotens.	3	God, the Father Almighty.
	Domine Fili	4	O Lord, the only-begotten Son,
	unigenite, Jesu Christe.	6/5	Jesus Christ.
	Domine Deus, Agnus Dei,	3/4	Lord God, Lamb of God,
	Filius Patris.	6	Son of the Father.
2:44	Qui tollis peccata mundi,	4	Thou that takest away the sins of the world,
	miserere nobis.	4	have mercy on us.
	Qui tollis peccata mundi,	4/5	Thou that takest away the sins of the world,
	suscipe deprecationem nostram.	6/4	receive our prayer.
	Qui sedes ad dexteram Patris,	3	Thou that sittest at the right hand of the Father,
	miserere nobis.	3	have mercy on us.
	Quoniam tu solus sanctus.	4	For Thou alone art holy.
	Tu solus Dominus.	4	Thou only art the Lord.
	Tu solus Altissimus.	4	Thou alone art most high.
	Jesu Christe, cum Sancto Spiritu	6/3/4	Jesus Christ, along with the Holy Spirit
	in gloria Dei Patris.	4/5	in the glory of God the Father.
	Amen.	6	Amen.

Palestrina worked at the Vatican in Rome, where **Michelangelo** (1475–1564) painted the famous Sistine Chapel ceiling. *The Creation of Adam* (c. 1511).

In His Own Words

66 Among the various things which are suitable for man's recreation and pleasure, music is the first and leads us to the belief that it is a gift of God set apart for this purpose."

—*John Calvin*

probably not true. Since the papal choir sang without instrumental accompaniment, this Mass was most likely performed *a cappella*. It was written for six voice parts—soprano, alto, two tenors, and two basses, a typical setting for the all-male church choirs of the era. The highest voice was sung by boy sopranos or male falsettists (singing in falsetto, or head voice), and the alto part by male altos, or countertenors (tenors with very high voices).

The Gloria from the *Pope Marcellus* Mass (LG 8) exhibits Palestrina's hallmark style— restrained, serene, and celestial. The opening line, "Gloria in excelsis Deo" ("Glory be to God on high"), is chanted by the officiating priest. For the remaining text, Palestrina constructed a polyphonic setting, balancing the harmonic and polyphonic elements so that the words are clearly audible, an effect that foreshadows the recommendations of the Council of Trent. His music is representative of the pure *a cappella* style of vocal polyphony of the later Renaissance. It reflects the Catholic Church's belief that heavenly sounds produced by trained professionals would be more spiritually powerful than the rough song of an untrained congregation—the precise opposite of Calvin's concept of a "musical priesthood of all the faithful."

CRITICAL THINKING

1. What were some differences and similarities between Protestant and Catholic approaches to musical worship?
2. How did the Council of Trent influence the performance and style of sacred music?

YOUR TURN TO EXPLORE

Consider public events that involve "community spirit"—sports, political rallies, church services, etc. How is music used to foster that spirit? How do songs that are sung by the entire gathering differ from music played by professional musicians to "create the mood" at the event? Have you attended community events in which you were particularly inspired by the music? Was it participatory or listener-directed, or a combination of both?

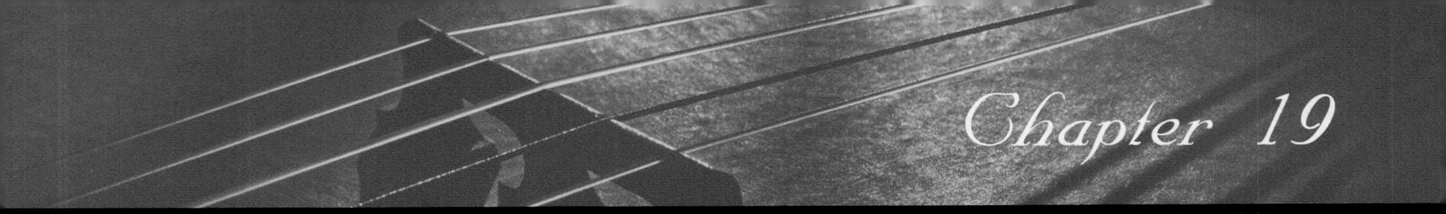

Chapter 19

Instrumental Movements: Medieval and Renaissance Dance Music

"A time to weep, and a time to laugh; a time to mourn, and a time to dance."

—*Ecclesiastes 3:4*

KEY POINTS

- Dance music has often been both groundbreaking and provocative in the Western tradition.
- Musical instruments in medieval and Renaissance Europe were categorized as soft (**bas**) or loud (**haut**) according to their purpose.
- Both professional and amateur musicians played instrumental dance music, often adding **embellishments**.

Throughout the Western tradition, dance music has both driven expressive change and been accused of fostering social disruption. While we might consider dance music from earlier times odd and stilted, our grandchildren will likewise be appalled at what we find provocative or sensuous in dances today. Instrumental music first flourished in conjunction with dance, since the varied layers of wordless sound gave the opportunity for creative interpretation through movement, just as they do in the hands of spinning DJs in the twenty-first century.

In His Own Words

❝ I hope his tune will be worthy of the instrument."
—*Cicero (106–43 BCE)*

Instrumental Music in the Middle Ages and Renaissance

In early times, instrumental music was largely an oral tradition that relied on the improvisation skills of players. Much of our knowledge of the instruments and performing practices comes, then, from artworks and historical documents rather than notated music. We know that early instruments were grouped into the same general families as modern ones—strings, woodwinds, brass, percussion, and keyboard—but unlike today, they were also categorized as soft (*bas*, or indoor) and loud (*haut*, or outdoor), according to their use.

Among the most common soft instruments were the **recorder**, an end-blown flute with a breathy tone; the **lute**, a plucked-string instrument of Middle Eastern

Soft vs. loud instruments

A city wind band, with bassoon, shawms, cornetto, and sackbut. Detail from *Procession in Honor of Our Lady of Sablon in Brussels* (1616), by **Denis van Alsloot** (c. 1570–1626).

origin; and various bowed-string instruments, including the **rebec** (see illustration, p. 62). The loud instruments, which played mainly for tournaments or outdoor processions, included the **shawm**, a nasal-sounding ancestor of the oboe (also of Middle Eastern origin); the **sackbut**, an early version of the trombone; and the **cornetto**, a wooden instrument with fingerholes like a recorder but a cup-shaped mouthpiece. These loud instruments made up the civic wind band, a group of three to five players found in most urban centers; this band was often accompanied by percussion instruments, including the **tabor** (a cylindrical drum) and **nakers** (small hand drums played in pairs).

Other brass instruments such as trumpets were used to heighten the grandeur during ceremonial processions and were also sounded in warfare, to frighten or confuse the enemy or to signal across the battlefield. Because of their construction and the fact that they played fanfares and other simple combinations of sounds rather than melodies, trumpets served mostly as sonic reinforcement at public events, and were integrated into the orchestra only from the later 1600s.

Our first notated record of instrumental music comes from a mere handful of dances in late medieval manuscripts, but with the advent of music printing in the sixteenth century, books of dance music became readily available for amateur and professional players alike. These publications included a wide variety of dance **Dance types** types, ranging from the slow and stately **pavane** to the showy, fast-paced **saltarello** to the group-oriented **ronde**, a circle or line dance. Because instruments were not yet specified, there was much flexibility in performance, based on the occasion and what was on hand. Since this was also the time when books describing the latest and most fashionable dances were published, we have a fairly good idea of what patterns of movement were considered most attractive and "trendy" for young Europeans to try out while the musicians played.

Susato and His *Danserye*

In His Own Words

❝ Music is a science that would have us laugh and sing and dance."

—Guillaume de Machaut

One of the most popular dance collections of the sixteenth century was published in Antwerp (in modern-day Belgium) in 1551 by Tielman Susato (c. 1515–c. 1571), a well-known printer and musician. Susato was a musical jack-of-all-trades: he composed and arranged different styles of secular and sacred works, and unlike modern musicians who generally specialize on a particular instrument, he played virtually all the brass and woodwind instruments of his day. This last talent gained him a position as a member of the Antwerp city band—an esteemed group of five instrumentalists who performed regular town concerts as well as for processions (or parades) held on religious occasions and for the entertainment of visiting dignitaries (see illustration of a civic band above). The music this group played is less clear, but we know they did not rely exclusively on notated music; rather, they were expert improvisers, able to turn a simple dance into an intricate, masterful work, much as a modern jazz band can build from a few standards to keep an audience moving and cheering for hours on end.

LISTENING GUIDE 9

⏱ 2:29

Susato: Three Dances

DATE: Published 1551

GENRE: Ronde

What to Listen For

Melody	Prominent tunes; short phrases.	**Form**	Three binary-form dances (each **A-A-B-B**).
Rhythm/ meter	Lively duple meter.	**Expression**	Occasional embellishments.
Harmony	Full chords, consonant; ronde 2 is modal.	**Performing forces**	Four-part instrumental group: loud wind band (shawm, cornetto, sackbut, tabor, tambourine).
Texture	Mostly homophonic.		

Ronde 1

0:00	A	Shawm solo
0:06	A	Tabor joins.
0:11	B	Loud band.
0:22	B	Repeat of **B**.

Opening phrase (**A**) of ronde 1:

Ronde 2

0:33	C	Cornetto with instruments.
0:38	C	Repeat of **C**.
0:44	D	Contrapuntal section.
0:55	D	Embellished repeat of **D**.

Opening phrase (**C**) of ronde 2::

Ronde 1 (transition)

l1:12	A	Played four times.

Ronde 3

1:23	E	Shawm with loud band.
1:34	E	Repeat of **E**.
1:45	F	New short section.
1:51	F	Repeat of **F**.

Opening phrase (**E**) of ronde 3::

Ronde 1

1:57	B	Played twice.
2:20		Final bow chord.

Susato's collection, called *Danserye,* features a variety of popular dance types, including the set of three rondes we will hear (LG 9). Although originally a country dance, the ronde made its way to the city and to the courts of the nobility. Our recording features the loud, civic-style wind band. The repeated dance sections allowed the musicians to improvise **embellishments**, or melodic decorations, as they saw fit, and the performers in our modern recording follow that custom, making sure that the sound is enriched and varied through the different combinations of instruments. The dances flow from one to another—you can imagine that once this high-spirited dance gets going, no one will want to stop. A final chord brings

Embellishments

Shawm players accompany an aristocratic group dancing a ronde. From a fifteenth-century French manuscript.

the gaiety to a close with all the players bowing to each other. It was through such dance pieces that Renaissance composers began to explore the possibilities of purely instrumental forms, beginning a tradition of finding new ways sound can move us—both physically and emotionally—when words don't "get in the way."

CRITICAL THINKING

Comparing styles 2: Medieval, Renaissance, and Baroque

1. What were the main categories of instruments in the Renaissance? How do they compare with modern Western instrument categories?
2. Who do you think might have performed dances in the Renaissance? Where would they have taken place?

YOUR TURN TO EXPLORE

Find video recordings of dances from past and/or non-Western traditions. How do the dancers' movements follow the patterns set out by the musicians? What kinds of variation, elaboration, or improvisation do the musicians employ on the basic patterns, whether through melody, texture, or timbre? What do you find most expressive about the union of movement and sound in these dances?

A Comparison of
Medieval, Renaissance, and Baroque Styles

	Medieval (c. 400–1450)	Renaissance (c. 1450–1600)	Baroque (c. 1600–1750)
Composers	Hildegard, Notre Dame composers, Machaut.	Josquin des Prez, Arcadelt, Susato, Palestrina, Farmer.	Monteverdi, Cozzolani, Purcell, Vivaldi, Bach, Handel, Billings.
Melody	Conjunct, small range.	Arched, smooth, asymmetrical melodies.	Lyrical and chromatic; continuous flow (late).
Rhythm/ meter	Nonmetric (early); triple meter.	Regular, gentle pulse; duple meter.	Strongly rhythmic (late).
Harmony	Modal.	Modal, moving toward tonality.	Major and minor tonality.
Texture	Monophonic (early); non-imitative polyphony (late).	Imitative polyphony.	Mixed textures; polyphonic (late).
Medium	*A cappella* vocal music.	*A cappella* vocal music.	Voices with instruments.
Vocal genres	Chant, organum, chanson, motet, Mass.	Mass, motet, madrigal, chanson.	Opera, cantata, oratorio.
Instrumental genres	Dance music.	Dance music.	Sonata, concerto, suite.
Use of pre-existent music	Sacred music based on chant.	Sacred music using cantus firmus (early); move toward freely composed.	Freely composed.
Performance sites	Church, court.	Church, court, home.	Public theaters, court, church.

BAROQUE ERA

Events		Composers and Works

1600

Death of Elizabeth I. **1603**

Gaspar Fernandes appointed choirmaster at Puebla Cathedral. **1606**

King James Version of the Bible printed. **1611**

Dr. William Harvey explains the circulatory system. **1628**

Bay Psalm Book printed in Massachusetts. **1628**

Period of Commonwealth begins in England. **1649**

1567–1643 Claudio Monteverdi (operas and madrigals)

1602–c. 1676 Chiara Margarita Cozzolani (*Magnificat*)

1650

John Milton's *Paradise Lost* published. **1667**

French court of Louis XIV established at Versailles. **1682**

Sir Isaac Newton's theory of gravitation published. **1687**

1659–1695 Henry Purcell (*Dido and Aeneas*)

1678–1741 Antonio Vivaldi (*The Four Seasons*)

1685–1750 Johann Sebastian Bach (Cantata *Wachet auf*; *The Art of Fugue*)

1685–1759 George Frideric Handel (*Water Music*; *Messiah*)

1700

1746–1800 William Billings (*David's Lamentation*)

Reign of Louis XV begins. **1715**

John Gay's *Beggar's Opera* performed. **1728**

George Washington born. **1732**

J. S. Bach's *Art of Fugue* published. **1751**

1750

Part 3

The Baroque Era

Music as Exploration and Drama

"These harmonic notes are the language of the soul and the instruments of the heart."

—*Barbara Strozzi (1619–1677)*

Music intensifies emotion. This may seem self-evident to us in the twenty-first century, but it was in the period that we are about to explore — the 1600s and early 1700s—that Europeans set out to develop musical approaches designed to "ramp up" various emotional states and help listeners experience their diversity more deeply.

Composers and performers became increasingly interested in how music could enhance the expression of words—most prominently through the development of a kind of musical theater called opera, but also through the training of specialized **Virtuosity** singers whose **virtuosity** (remarkable technical skill) made the amateur singing tradition of the Renaissance seem outdated and bland. Even more novel was a significant focus on the expressive power of musical instruments—not only in conjunction with voices, but on their own. While purely instrumental music existed before the 1600s, in the Baroque era it became much more prominent with the development of several new genres and the refinement of instrumental building and performance techniques.

During the early part of this period, musicians seemed almost giddy with the possibilities for intense expression, creating works that appear designed to swing

The Flemish painter **Peter Paul Rubens** (1577–1640) instills his paintings with high energy and drama. His voluptuous nudes, as in *Diana and Her Nymphs*, established the seventeenth-century ideal of feminine beauty.

Renaissance and Baroque sculptural approaches. LEFT: **Michelangelo** shows us David in contemplation (1501–04). RIGHT: In contrast, **Bernini** captures David in mid-slingshot (1623).

between musical extremes. As time passed, such experimentation gave way to a more standardized approach: the later Baroque is characterized by a greater interest in predictable musical forms and procedures.

"Baroque" Art and Culture

The years between 1600 and 1750 represent a period of change, adventure, and discovery. The conquest of the New World stirred the imagination and filled the treasuries of Western Europe. The ideas of Galileo and Copernicus in physics and astronomy, of René Descartes in mathematics, and of Spinoza in philosophy were milestones in the intellectual history of Europe. The English physician William Harvey explained the circulation of the blood, and Sir Isaac Newton formulated the theory of gravity. Empires clashed for control of the globe.

There was appalling poverty and wasteful luxury, magnificent idealism and savage oppression. Baroque art—with its vigor, elaborate decoration, and grandeur—projected the pomp and splendor of the era. Indeed, the term "baroque" (applied in retrospect by later writers who saw this period as excessively extravagant) derives from a Portuguese word that originally meant "misshapen" or "distorted."

A comparison between the two depictions of the biblical figure David above, one by Renaissance artist Michelangelo (1475–1564) and the other by Bernini (1598–1680), clearly reveals the Baroque love of the dramatic. The earlier sculpture is balanced, calm, reflective; on his shoulder is the sling with which he has just slain the giant Goliath, but the overall effect is static, poised. The Baroque David shows the young man in motion, every muscle in his body tensed in the act that will save his people. In like fashion, the Venetian school of painters and Northern masters such as Flemish artist Peter Paul Rubens captured the dynamic spirit of the new age, producing canvases ablaze in color and movement (see illustration opposite).

The Baroque was an era of absolute monarchy. Rulers throughout Europe modeled their courts on Versailles, a sumptuous palace on the outskirts of Paris. Louis

In His Own Words

❝ I do not know what I may appear to the world; but to myself I seem to have been only like a boy playing on the seashore . . . whilst the great ocean of truth lay all undiscovered before me."
—*Isaac Newton (1643–1727)*

Jan Vermeer is well known for his painting of bourgeois (middle-class) Dutch women playing keyboard instruments. *A Young Lady Seated at a Virginal,* c. 1670.

In His Own Words

❝ Music must be supported by the King and the princes."

—*Martin Luther*

XIV's famous statement "I am the State" summed up a way of life in which all art and culture served the ruler. Courts large and small maintained elaborate musical establishments, including opera troupes, chapel choirs, and orchestras. Baroque opera, the favorite diversion of the aristocracy, told stories of the gods and heroes of antiquity, in whom the nobility and courtiers saw flattering likenesses of themselves.

The middle classes, excluded from the salons of the aristocracy, created a culture of their own. Their music-making took place in the home. It was for the middle classes that the comic opera and the novel, both genres filled with keen and witty observations on life, came into being. For them, painting abandoned its grandiose themes and turned to intimate scenes of bourgeois life. The Dutch School, embodying the vitality of a new middle-class art, reached its high point with Rembrandt and Jan Vermeer (see illustration at left).

The Baroque was also an intensely devout period, with religion a rallying cry on some of the bloodiest battlefields in history. Protestants were centered in England, Scandinavia, Holland, and northern Germany, all strongholds of the rising middle class. On the Catholic side were two powerful dynasties: the French Bourbons and the Austrian-Spanish Hapsburgs, who fought one another as fiercely as they did their Protestant foes. Religion was an equally important part of life in the New World as well, both in the colonies of Protestant refugees who settled on the East Coast of North America and in the fervently Catholic Spanish and French colonies (Spanish in what is now Mexico, Central America, and the southwestern United States; French in Canada, the Mississippi valley, and the Gulf Coast).

England's John Milton produced the poetic epic of Protestantism (*Paradise Lost*), just as Dante had expressed the Catholic point of view in *The Divine Comedy* three and a half centuries earlier. The Catholic world answered Martin Luther's call for reforms with the Counter-Reformation (see Chapter 18), whose rapturous mysticism found expression in the canvases of El Greco (see illustration, p. 106). These paintings were the creations of a visionary mind that distorted the real in its search for a reality beyond.

Creative artists played a variety of roles in Baroque society. Rubens was not only a famous painter but also an ambassador and friend of princes. The composer Antonio Vivaldi was also a priest, and George Frideric Handel an opera impresario. Artists usually functioned under royal or princely patronage, or, like Johann Sebastian Bach, they might be employed by a church or city administration. In all cases, artists were in direct contact with their public. Many musical works were created for specific occasions—an opera for a royal wedding, a dance suite for a court festivity, a cantata for a religious service—and for immediate use.

Main Currents in Baroque Music

"The end of all good music is to affect the soul."

—*Claudio Monteverdi*

One of the most significant characteristics of the early Baroque style was a shift from a texture of several independent parts (polyphony) to one in which a single melody stood out (homophony).

A group of Florentine writers, artists, and musicians known as the Camerata (a name derived from the Italian word for "salon") first cultivated this approach, which they called "the new style," around 1600. The members of the Camerata were aristocratic humanists who aimed to resurrect the musical-dramatic art of ancient Greece. Although little was known of ancient music, the Camerata deduced that it must have heightened the emotional power of the text. Thus their "new style" consisted of a melody that moved freely over a foundation of simple chords.

Florentine Camerata

A new kind of notation accompanied the "new style": since musicians were familiar with the basic harmonies, the composer put a numeral above or below the bass note, indicating the chord required (a kind of notation called **figured bass**), and the performer filled in the necessary harmony. This system, known as **basso continuo**, provided a foundation over which a vocal or instrumental melody could unfold. It led to one of the most significant changes in all music history: the establishment of **major-minor tonality** (see Chapter 4). With this development, the thrust to the key note, or tonic, became the most powerful force in music. Each chord could assume its function in relation to the key center; and the movement between keys, governed by tonality, helped shape a musical structure. Composers were able to develop forms of instrumental music larger than had ever before been known.

Basso continuo

Major-minor tonality

The transition to major-minor tonality was marked by a significant technical advance: a new tuning system that allowed instruments to play in any key. Called **equal temperament**, this tuning adjusted (or tempered) the mathematically "pure" intervals within the octave to equalize the distance between adjacent tones, making it possible to play in every major and minor key without producing

The Hall of Mirrors in the French Royal Palace of Versailles exemplifies the Baroque love for elaborate decorations.

The rapturous mysticism of the Counter-Reformation found expression in this eerie landscape of **El Greco** (1541–1614), *View of Toledo*.

unpleasant sounds, and greatly increasing the range of harmonic possibilities available to the composer. J. S. Bach demonstrated this range in his two-volume keyboard collection *The Well-Tempered Clavier*: each volume contains twenty-four preludes and fugues, one in every possible major and minor key. Today, our ears are conditioned to the equal tempered system, since this is how pianos are now tuned.

The Camerata's members engaged in excited discussions about their new homophonic music, which they also proudly named the "expressive style." The group soon realized that their approach could be applied not only to a short poem but also to an entire drama, fostering the most notable Baroque innovation: "drama through music," or what we now call **opera**.

The elaborate scrollwork of Baroque architecture found its musical equivalent in the principle of continuous expansion of melody. A movement might start with a striking musical figure that would then be repeated and varied with seemingly infinite modifications, driven by rhythms that helped capture the movement of this dynamic age. In vocal music, wide leaps and chromatic tones helped create melodies that were highly expressive of the text.

Expressive devices

Baroque musicians used dissonant chords more freely, for emotional intensity and color. In setting poetry, for example, a composer might choose a dissonance to heighten the impact of a particularly meaningful word. The dynamic contrasts achieved in Renaissance music through varied imitative voicings gave way to a more nuanced treatment in the Baroque, allowing for a more precise expression of emotions, especially of the text. Dramatic *forte/piano* contrasts and echo effects were also typical of the era.

Finally, the Baroque inherited from the Renaissance an impressive technique of text painting, in which the music vividly mirrored the words. It was generally accepted that music ought to arouse the emotions, or "affections"—joy, anger, love, fear. By the late seventeenth century, an entire piece or movement was normally built on a single affection: the opening musical idea established the mood of the piece, which prevailed until the end. This procedure differs markedly from the practice of later eras, when music was based on two or more contrasting emotions.

The Rise of the Virtuoso Musician

As the great musical instrument builders in Italy and Germany improved and refined their instruments, Baroque performers responded with more virtuosic (remarkably skilled) playing. Composers in turn wrote works demanding even more advanced playing techniques. Out of these developments came the virtuosic violin works of Antonio Vivaldi (see Chapter 26).

Instrumental virtuosity had its counterpart in the vocal sphere. The rise of opera brought with it the development of a phenomenal vocal technique, exem-

Castrato

plified in the early eighteenth century by the **castrato**, a male singer who was castrated during boyhood in order to preserve the soprano or alto register of his voice for the rest of his life. What resulted, after years of training, was an incredibly agile voice of enormous range, powered by breath control unrivaled by most singers today. The castrato's voice combined the lung power of the male with the brilliance of the female upper register. Strange as it may seem to us, Baroque audiences associated this voice with heroic male roles. When castrato roles are performed today, they are usually sung in a lower register by a tenor or baritone, or in the original register by a countertenor or a woman singer in male costume.

Women, particularly singers, began to expand their role in music. Two early seventeenth-century Italian singers, Francesca Caccini and Barbara Strozzi, were among the earliest female composers to publish their works. Caccini stands out as the first woman to write an opera, and Strozzi was a prolific composer of both secular and sacred music. Some opera singers reached the level of superstars, such as the Italian sopranos Faustina Bordoni and Francesca Cuzzoni, who engaged in a bitter rivalry. As we will see, another, perhaps less expected venue for women was the cloister, or convent.

Improvisation played a significant role in Baroque music. In addition to elaborating on the simple harmonic foundation that was part of almost every musical work, musicians were expected to be able to improvise and add embellishments to what was written on the score, much like jazz or pop musicians today. Baroque music sounded quite different in performance from what was on the page.

Women in music

Improvisation

An All-European Art

As great voyages of exploration opened up unknown regions of the globe, exoticism became a discernible element of Baroque music. A number of operas looked to faraway lands for their settings—Persia, India, Turkey, the Near East, Peru, and the Americas—offering picturesque scenes and dances that may not have been authentic but that delighted audiences through their appeal to the imagination.

Paradoxically, alongside the interest in exotic locales and regional traditions, the Baroque was a period in which there was significant exchange among national cultures. The sensuous beauty of Italian melody, the pointed precision of French dance rhythm, the luxuriance of German polyphony, the freshness of English choral song—these characteristic local traditions eventually blended into an all-European art that absorbed the best of each national style. For example, we will see how Handel, a German, wrote Italian opera for English audiences and gave England the oratorio. And it was precisely through this internationalization that, in the end, the Baroque gave way to a new set of stylistic priorities. An era of discovery and experimentation in which diversity and variety of musical expression was the ultimate goal eventually resulted in commonality of purpose and style, as Europeans became more and more interested in the elements that made humans equal rather than different.

In His Own Words

66 Music is the universal language of mankind."

—*Henry Wadsworth Longfellow (1807–1882)*

CRITICAL THINKING

1. How did Baroque artists and composers bring drama to their works?
2. What was new about the so-called new music at the beginning of the Baroque period?

Chapter 20

Voicing the Virgin: Cozzolani and Italian Baroque Sacred Music

"Servants [of the Lord], collect your flowers, cover the ground with flowers; servants, strike up your song, sing to the citharas; virgins, strike the cymbals with your fingers."

—Chiara Margarita Cozzolani motet (<u>Colligite, pueri, flores</u>)

KEY POINTS

- Music has often been a means through which marginalized individuals and groups can express their perspective to the broader society.

- Women in seventeenth-century Italian convents were dedicated to singing as an integral part of their role as spiritual servants and advocates.

- Nuns adapted standard vocal music scorings to their needs by transposing parts and adding instruments.

- Chiara Margarita Cozzolani, a Benedictine nun who was a musician and composer, was one of a few whose works were published and circulated beyond the convent. Her *Magnificat* exemplifies both a common genre and an individual approach to text setting.

In Her Own Words

❝ Loving shepherds, while they feed their beloved flocks, often entertain them with the harmony of instruments and the melody of songs. . . . In the same way, so as to imitate the talents shared by the best shepherds . . . I wanted to compose and dedicate this *armonia* to your extraordinary taste and merit."

—*Chiara Margarita Cozzolani, dedication of a work to the Bishop of Crema*

In twenty-first-century America, we try to acknowledge the importance of diverse voices and perspectives within our communities. This can be difficult, since prejudice of all sorts (based on gender, race, ethnicity, disability, sexuality, and many other categories) can result from our human tendency to misunderstand those who are different from us, despite what may be the best of intentions. Artists and other creative people have often been shaped by their own experiences as members of a marginal group. And during times when certain groups are excluded from equal opportunity, those creative voices can be extremely powerful. A striking example comes from the experience of religious women in seventeenth-century Italy.

Nuns and Music in Baroque Italy

In comparison with modern times, when an individual can express her- or himself through various artistic means, the Baroque era offered few possibilities for creative women. While it is true that a handful of women singers made a name for themselves as professionals, their character and morality were often in question. In recent years, scholars have unearthed sheaves of documents and music that reveal a "secret" musical world within the confines of convents. Though convents were generally considered to be private places for spiritual retreat from outside influences, this was far from the case in seventeenth-century Italy, where they played a major societal role for women and allowed those who desired one a public voice through music.

Music-making at the Benedictine convent of St. Radegonda in Milan was, by all accounts, famous. Dignitaries and other visitors filled the church on special occasions to hear the nuns' angelic voices. In 1670, the Augustinian priest Filippo Picinelli lavished praise on the convent and on one nun in particular:

> The nuns of St. Radegonda of Milan are gifted with such rare and exquisite talents in music that they are acknowledged to be the best singers in Italy . . . they seem to any listener to be white and melodious swans, who fill hearts with wonder, and spirit away tongues in their praise. Among these sisters, Donna Chiara Margarita Cozzolani merits the highest praise. Chiara [her chosen name, meaning "clear"] in name but even more so in merit, and Margarita ["daisy"] for her unusual and excellent nobility of [musical] invention.

At a time when women's roles in the Catholic Church were extremely limited, this was extraordinary acknowledgment indeed of the power of female spirituality.

A chorus of nuns sings in the French Abbey of Port-Royal-des-Champs, as depicted by **Louise-Magdeleine Hortemels** (1688–1767).

Cozzolani's *Magnificat*

It is not surprising that feast days dedicated to the Virgin Mary were important occasions at St. Radegonda, celebrated with polyphonic singing. But Cozzolani must have felt a personal devotion to the Virgin. Among the many works she wrote in her honor are two settings of the Magnificat, or canticle of Mary, the concluding and climactic part of the evening office of Vespers. Both are large-scale, polychoral settings for two choirs of four voices each, accompanied by organ continuo. One mystery surrounding settings like these, which feature soprano, alto, tenor, and bass parts, is who sang the lower voices. Evidence suggests that some nuns could sing the tenor part without difficulty, but that the bass part was either sung up an octave or simply sounded by the basso continuo instrument rather than sung (our recording combines both these approaches). What is clear is that men, even priests, did not sing polyphony with the nuns in their services.

We can imagine that the Magnificat text—the Virgin's song of praise, from the biblical Gospel of Luke, upon learning that she would bear the son of God—was particularly attractive to women. Cozzolani's setting (LG 10) is dramatic and mystical, intended to intensify the nuns' experience of the Virgin's Annunciation and to help them reach a heightened level of religious ecstasy. A similar effect can be seen in Bernini's dynamic sculpture *Ecstasy of St. Teresa* (illustration at right), created around 1650, the same time as our *Magnificat*. Here, St. Teresa is resting on a cloud, confirming her divine experience. Dramatic gilded rays illuminate her, as she suffers both intense pleasure and pain at the hand of an angel who stabs her repeatedly with a golden spear. In Cozzolani's inspired work, virtuosic duets interrupt the larger choral forces that sing in homophony, and text and music are freely repeated in a highly expressive setting rich in word painting that is at once spiritual and sensual, like the sculpture.

In the *Ecstasy of Saint Teresa* (1652), sculpted by **Gian Lorenzo Bernini** (1598–1680), the nun experiences both extreme pain from the sword of the angel and, through divine intervention, a great love of God.

The Musical World of the Convent

In early times, when women had few choices in their lives, entering a convent was the only honorable alternative to marriage. We saw that a young Hildegard was placed in a German convent by her parents, in part for financial reasons but also because she showed an aptitude for the spiritual life. Records from sixteenth- and seventeenth-century convents in Italy reveal much about the women and their lives within the cloistered walls. In Bologna, something like one in seven females joined a convent, sometimes as a young novice placed there by her parents, other times to avoid an unwanted marriage or to seek asylum after being widowed. In Milan, where Chiara Margarita Cozzolani was cloistered, the statistics were even higher among upper-class women. The convent provided a basic education for its members, and music was an important part of the training.

Music was also the primary vehicle by which nuns had contact with the outside world. Throughout Italy and elsewhere in Europe, certain convents were renowned for their gifted singers, instrumentalists, and even composers.

It was not unusual for nobility, and the public in general, to visit convents to hear the music for Vespers, and some convents offered concerts in a parlor outside the cloister for friends and relatives. Church authorities took issue with these public performances, and attempted—with little success—to stop them; they even tried to ban the singing of polyphony, but the women, finding spiritual well-being in their music, willfully disobeyed the church orders.

It was in this nurturing atmosphere of the cloister that religious women were allowed to realize their musical talents, and some, like Cozzolani in Milan and Lucrezia Vizzana in Bologna, were able to publish their compositions, allowing the outside world a glimpse of the creative minds inside the convent walls. This phenomenon of extraordinary musical performances by cloistered girls and women reached a pinnacle in early eighteenth-century Venice, where

Music played an important role in the cloister, as shown in this detail of a nun playing the organ, by **August von Baye**r (1803–1875).

four religious institutions—called *ospedali*—for orphan girls gained fame for the girls' abilities in singing and orchestral playing. We will read in a later chapter about the composer/violinist Antonio Vivaldi, who nurtured the talents of the girls at the Venetian Ospedale della Pietà so successfully that the school's all-women orchestra was revered throughout Europe.

Several text lines recur as refrains, including the first, "My soul glorifies the Lord," and "He has done great things for me"; the latter often signals a shift from the free, rhapsodic motion to a lilting triple meter. These are lines that describe the personal experience of the Virgin Mary: through their repetition, the nuns would have had the opportunity to reflect on this all-too-rare female voice in Christian scripture. The **Doxology** *Magnificat* closes with a prayer of praise to God called the **doxology**; its words may be familiar to you, as they are frequently sung in Christian services today.

In its combination of ritual text and innovative musical expression, Cozzolani's *Magnificat* is a striking example of the tension between individuality and tradition that has characterized Western sacred music throughout the centuries. And it is one of many examples of artists from marginalized groups attempting to help their community build pride and positive identity despite society's prevailing prejudices.

Chiara Margarita Cozzolani (1602–c. 1676)

The youngest daughter of a wealthy Milanese merchant, Margarita Cozzolani entered the convent of St. Radegonda, taking the religious name Chiara and professing her final vows at age eighteen. One of her sisters and two of her aunts were also members of the convent; such networks of relatives in religious houses were common at the time. Soon Chiara took up an active role in music, serving as the director of one of the convent's two choirs and composing music. These talents were clearly encouraged: she published three collections of music, ranging from solo motets with accompaniment to large-scale Magnificat settings for double choir. Notable are her musical "dialogues" elucidating famous religious scenes, like that between Mary Magdalene and the angels at Christ's tomb on Easter morning. Her collection of 1650 contains a complete set of Vespers psalms for the major feasts of the year.

While some of Cozzolani's music is conservative in style, her larger works in particular mark her as one of the leading composers of the day. Later in her life, she served as abbess and prioress at St. Radegonda through years of conflict both within the convent (between rival choirs) and from outside, when religious authorities attempted to ban the performance of polyphony by the sisters, an order they blatantly disobeyed.

MAJOR WORKS: Several collections (1640 [now lost], 1642, 1648) that include motets for one to four voices with continuo and a four-voice mass • One collection of Vespers music (1650), including two *Magnificats* and dialogues for eight-voice choir as well as other motets, some accompanied by violins and continuo.

LISTENING GUIDE 10 9:15

Cozzolani: *Magnificat*

DATE: Published 1650

GENRE: Music for Vespers

What to Listen For

Melody	Lyrical, small-range duets; static choral lines.	**Form**	Refrains bring back several lines of text/music.
Rhythm/ meter	Shifts between duple and triple meter.	**Expression**	Varied tempos; some sections move freely.
Harmony	Consonant; some dissonance in solo passages.	**Performing forces**	Two soprano soloists and two double choirs (SATB) with organ and strings.
Texture	Shifts between homophonic ensembles and two-voiced duets; some imitation.	**Text**	Luke 1:46-55. ★= repeated text/music.

	TEXT	TRANSLATION

0:00	Magnificat anima mea magnificat Dominum, ★
	et exsultavit spiritus meus in Deo salvatore meo,
	quia respexit humilitatem ancillae suae.★
	    anima mea magnificat Domino
		My soul glorifies the Lord★
		and my spirit rejoices in God my Savior,
		who looks on His servant in her lowliness;★
		    my soul glorifies the Lord

1:43	Ecce enim ex hoc beatam me dicent omnes generationes,
	quia fecit mihi magna,
	qui potens est,
	et sanctum nomen eius,
	    anima mea magnificat
		henceforth all ages will call me blessed.
		He has done great things for me,
		He who is mighty,
		and holy is His name.
		    my soul glorifies the Lord

Continued on next page

2:57	et misericordia eius in progenies et progenies* timentibus eum.	And His mercy is from age to age,* on those who fear Him.
	Fecit potentiam in brachio suo,*	He puts forth His arm in strength*
	quia fecit mihi magna	*He has done great things for me*
4:10	dispersit superbos mente cordis sui;	and scatters the proud-hearted.
	deposuit potentes de sede*	He casts the mighty from their thrones,*
	et exaltavit humiles;	and raises the lowly.
	esurientes implevit bonis*	He fills the starving with good things,*
	mihi magna fecit	*He has done great things for me*
5:11	et divites dimisit inanes.	sends the rich away empty.
	Suscepit Israel puerum suum,*	He protects Israel his servant,*
	recordatus misericordiae suae,	remembering his mercy:
	magna mihi fecit	*He has done great things for me*
5:55	sicut locutus est ad patres nostros,* Abraham et semini eius in saecula.	The mercy promised to our fathers,* to Abraham and to his sons forever.

Doxology closing

7:16	Gloria Patri	Glory be to the Father
	anima mea magnificat Dominum	*my soul glorifies the Lord*
	et Filio	and to the Son
	anima mea magnificat Dominum	*my soul glorifies the Lord*
	et in spiriti sancto	and to the Holy Ghost,
	anima mea magnificat Dominum	*my soul glorifies the Lord*
8:09	Sicut erat in principio et nunc et simper et in secula saeculorum.	As it was in the beginning, now and ever shall be world without end.
	anima mea magnificat Dominum	*my soul glorifies the Lord*
8:42	Amen.	Amen.

CRITICAL THINKING

1. What role did women play in sacred music in seventeenth-century Italy?
2. In what ways might the Magnificat text and Cozzolani's setting have been significant to seventeenth-century nuns?

YOUR TURN TO EXPLORE

Find examples of music used for spiritual devotion in contemporary traditions, whether in North America (e.g., gospel, Christian rock, Jewish renewal) or beyond (Sufi traditions of the Middle East, Hindu worship in South Asia, Tibetan Buddhist chanting, Yoruba traditions in Africa and the Caribbean). How is the intensity of the religious experience translated into sound? (Think about vocal quality, texture, repetition and variation of musical ideas.) How do individuals interact with a larger group? How are your chosen examples similar to and different from the Cozzolani *Magnificat* in these respects?

Chapter 21

Performing Grief:
Purcell and Early Opera

"Opera is the delight of Princes."

    —Marco da Gagliano (Italian composer, 1582–1643)

KEY POINTS

- The most important new genre of the Baroque era was **opera**, a large-scale music drama that combines poetry, acting, scenery, and costumes with singing and instrumental music.
- The principal components of opera include the orchestral **overture**, solo **arias** (lyrical songs) and **recitatives** (speechlike declamations of the text), and ensemble numbers, including **choruses**.

- The text of an opera is called a **libretto**. The earliest opera libretti were base on mythology, epic poetry, and ancient history.
- Henry Purcell wrote *Dido and Aeneas*, based on *The Aeneid*, a Roman epic by Virgil. The closing Lament by Dido is a powerful expression of grief that reflects contemporary ideals about womanhood.

D ramatists and musicians who developed the tradition of sung drama—what we now call opera—understood music's power to intensify events; their aim was not realistic depiction but "hyper-reality." Both then and now, audiences knew that people don't sing to each other in real life. But characters in opera could convey strong emotions through music, making the experience of those emotions all the more compelling for the listener. The intense hyper-reality of sung drama has guaranteed its appeal and staying power for more than four centuries, and accounts for the use of music to enhance narrative multimedia (musical theater, film, video games) up to the present day.

The Components of Opera

An **opera** is a large-scale drama that is sung. It combines the resources of vocal and instrumental music—soloists, ensembles, chorus, orchestra, and sometimes ballet—with poetry and drama, acting and pantomime, scenery and costumes. To unify these diverse elements is a challenge that has attracted some of the most creative minds in the history of music. The plot and action are generally advanced through a kind of musical declamation, or speech, known as **recitative**. This vocal style is designed to imitate and emphasize the natural inflections of speech; its movement is shaped to the rhythm of the language.

    Recitative gives way from time to time to the **aria** (Italian for "air" or "tune"), which releases through melody the tension accumulated in the course of the action. The aria is a song, usually of a highly emotional nature. It is what audiences wait for, what they cheer, what they remember. An aria, because of its tunefulness,

Recitative

Aria

113

An opera performance at the Teatro Argentina in Rome, 1729, as portrayed by **Giovanni Paolo Pannini** (1691–1765).

can be effective even when sung out of context—for example, in a concert or on a CD. Arias can be "detached" in this way because they take place in "stop time"—the action is frozen and the character has the opportunity to dwell on a particular intense emotion. Words or groups of words, as well as musical phrases or even whole sections, are often repeated, as if the character were mulling them over in her or his mind. Once the aria ends, the action "un-freezes" and the drama returns to the "clock time" of recitative.

An opera may contain ensemble numbers—duets, trios, quartets, and so on—in which the characters pour out their respective feelings. The chorus may be used to back up the solo voices or may function independently. Sometimes it comments on the action, like the chorus of a Greek tragedy, and at other times is integrated into the action.

The orchestra sets the appropriate mood for the different scenes. It also performs the **overture**, heard at the beginning of most operas, which may introduce melodies from the arias. Each act of the opera normally opens with an orchestral introduction, and between scenes we may find interludes, or **sinfonias**.

The composer works with a librettist, who creates the characters and the story line, with its main threads and subplots. The **libretto**, the text or script of the opera, must be devised to give the composer an opportunity to write music for the diverse numbers—recitatives and arias, ensembles, choruses, interludes—that have become the traditional features of this art form.

Early Opera in Italy

An outgrowth of Renaissance theatrical traditions, early opera lent itself to the lavish spectacles and scenic displays that graced royal weddings and similar ceremonial occasions. A striking example of this tradition that is still performed and **Claudio Monteverdi** recorded to this day is *Orfeo* (1607), composed by Claudio Monteverdi, who even in his own day was recognized for having solidified early experiments with drama-through-music (as it was called) into a mature and powerful new genre.

Spread of opera By the time of Monteverdi's last opera, *The Coronation of Poppea* (1642), the first public opera houses had opened in Venice; opera was moving out of the palace and becoming a public and widespread entertainment. The accompanying orchestra, a string group with wind or brass instruments occasionally added for variety in timbre, became standard as Italian-style opera spread throughout Europe.

By the turn of the eighteenth century, Italian opera had gained wide popularity in the rest of Western Europe. Only in France was the Italian genre rejected; here, composers set out to fashion a French national style, in keeping with their strong traditions of court ballet and classical tragedy.

Opera in England

In early seventeenth-century England, the **masque**, a type of entertainment that combined vocal and instrumental music with poetry and dance, became popular among the aristocracy. Later, in the period of the Commonwealth (1649–60), stage plays were forbidden because the Puritans regarded the theater as an invention of the devil. A play set to music, however, could be passed off as a "concert," and this is the tradition behind one of the earliest English operas (and certainly the most famous), Henry Purcell's *Dido and Aeneas* (LG 11).

Dido and Aeneas

Purcell's opera, first performed at the girls' school in London where he taught, is based on an episode in Virgil's *Aeneid*, the ancient Roman epic that traces the adventures of the hero Aeneas after the fall of Troy. Since his contemporary audiences knew this Virgil classic, librettist Nahum Tate could compress the plot and suggest rather than fill in the details. Aeneas and his men are shipwrecked at Carthage on the northern shore of Africa. Dido, the Carthaginian queen, falls in love with him, and he returns her affection. But Aeneas cannot forget that the gods have commanded him to continue his journey until he reaches Italy, since he is destined to be the founder of Rome. Much as he hates to hurt the queen, he knows that he must depart.

The Aeneid

In the last act, the crew is ready to leave Carthage, although Aeneas has not yet told Dido of his imminent departure. Purcell begins the act with a sprightly tune in the style of a **hornpipe** (see Chapter 25), a dance form often associated with sailors, and characterized by a reversed dotted figure called a **Scotch snap** (short-long rhythm). This lively tune, introduced by the orchestra, is sung responsorially: one sailor sings the verse, answered by the male chorus. Underlying this festive mood, the growing chromaticism of the bass line foreshadows Dido's Lament.

Hornpipe

Upon hearing of Aeneas's mission, a grief-stricken Dido decides her fate—death—in the moving recitative "Thy hand, Belinda," and the heartrending Lament that is the culminating point of the opera, "When I am laid in earth." In Virgil's poem, Dido mounts the funeral pyre, whose flames light the way for Aeneas's ships as they sail out of the harbor. Dido's Lament unfolds over a five-measure **ground bass**, a repeated phrase that descends along the chromatic scale, often symbolic of grief in Baroque music. The repetitions of the text and music encourage the listener to dwell in the timelessness of the emotions performed through this scene. The scene also provides a powerful model for female grief, one considered appropriate by Purcell's society; but keep in mind that this was a model

Ground bass

Henry Purcell (1659–1695)

Purcell's standing as a composer gave England a leading position in the world of Baroque music. The London-born composer's career began at the court of Charles II (r. 1660–85) and extended through the turbulent reign of James II (r. 1685–88)—both Stuart kings—and into the period of William and Mary (r. 1689–1702). At these courts, Purcell held various posts as singer, organist, and composer. He wrote masques and operas for several venues, including the boarding school where *Dido and Aeneas* was performed. His incidental music for plays includes *Abdelazar (The Moor's Revenge)*, from which Benjamin Britten borrowed a dance as the basis for his *Young Person's Guide to the Orchestra* (see Chapter 11).

A truly international figure, Purcell wrote in many genres, assimilating the Italian operatic style along with the majesty of French music, all while adding his own lyrical gift for setting the English language to music.

MAJOR WORKS: Dramatic music, including *Dido and Aeneas* (1689), *The Fairy Queen* (1692), and incidental music for plays (including *Abdelazar*, 1695) • Sacred and secular vocal music • Instrumental music, including fantasias, suites, and overtures.

 Rondeau, from *Abdelazar*

created by men based on male notions of suitable female behavior. This is another feature of opera, in common with all popular multimedia: it provides a reflection of what the librettist and composer wished their society to think about human character and interaction.

CRITICAL THINKING

1. How was the distinction between "clock time" and "stop time" achieved in early opera? Why was this distinction important?
2. What musical elements change in the course of Dido's recitative and Lament? What aspects stay the same? How do these aspects convey grief?

Dido stabs herself with Aeneas's sword as he and his men sail out of the harbor. *The Death of Dido*, by **Andrea Sacchi** (1559–1661).

YOUR TURN TO EXPLORE

Consider an example of one of your favorite "hyper-real" forms of narrative/dramatic entertainment—science fiction/fantasy movie, TV show, video game. How is the more-than-real aspect conveyed? What role does music play in making the emotions more intense than "ordinary"? How does the music reinforce images and models of "ideal" (or "bad") character or behavior?

LISTENING GUIDE 11   5:32

Purcell: *Dido and Aeneas*, Act III, Opening and Lament

DATE:	1689
GENRE:	Opera, English
BASIS:	Virgil's *Aeneid*
CHARACTERS:	Dido, queen of Carthage (soprano) Belinda, Dido's serving maid (soprano)
	Aeneas, adventuring hero (baritone) Sorceress, Spirit, Witches

Act III, Opening   1:32

What to Listen For

Melody	Jaunty, playful tune.		**Form**	Strophic form, with instruments, solo voice, then chorus.
Rhythm/ meter	Sprightly tempo, in triple meter; use of Scotch-snap dotted figures.		**Performing forces**	String orchestra, with solo voice and chorus.
Harmony	Major key, with chromatic foreshadowing of Lament.			

Opening of hornpipe as solo verse:

Come a - way,   fel-low sai - lors, come a - way,

0:00   **Orchestral prelude**

0:32   **Solo verse** (first sailor):
Come away fellow sailors, come away,
Your anchors be weighing;
Time and tide will admit no delaying;
Take a boosey short leave of your nymphs on the shore,
And silence their mourning with vows of returning,
Tho' never intending to visit them more.

1:02   **Chorus:** repeats verse.

Recitative and Lament

What to Listen For

Melody	Recitative with half-step movement; more lyrical aria.
Rhythm/ meter	Free recitative; slow aria in triple meter.
Harmony	Based on repeated chromatic ground bass.

Form	Aria in two sections, each repeated (**A-A-B-B**), over ground bass.
Performing forces	Baroque-period instruments with solo voice.

Recitative: "Thy hand, Belinda," sung by Dido (accompanied by basso continuo only)   0:57

0:00   Thy hand, Belinda; darkness shades me.
On thy bosom let me rest;
More I would, but Death invades me;
Death is now a welcome guest.

Aria: "When I am laid in earth," Dido's Lament   3:03

Basis: Ground bass, five-measure pattern in slow triple meter, descending chromatic scale, repeated eleven times:

	SECTION	GROUND BASS STATEMENT NO.
0:57 Instrumental introduction.		1
1:09 When I am laid in earth, may my wrongs create	A	2
no trouble in thy breast.		3
When I am laid . . .	A	4
no trouble . . .		5
2:17 Remember me, remember me, but ah, forget	B	6
my fate, remember me, but ah, forget my fate.		7
Remember me . . .	B	8
forget my fate . . .		9
Instrumental closing.		10
		11

Chapter 22

Musical Sermons: Bach and the Lutheran Cantata

"I wish to make German psalms for the people, that is to say sacred hymns, so that the word of God may dwell among the people also by means of song."

—Martin Luther

One of the most important and lasting contributions that Martin Luther made to Western culture was the idea that musical worship belongs to the congregation. Both he and his fellow reformer John Calvin, as noted in Chapter 18, believed that the faithful should sing their praise collectively during the church service, rather than leaving song entirely to the priest and the choir. Unlike Calvin, however, Luther also believed that professional musicians—both singers and instrumentalists—had an important role in creating beautiful polyphony for the congregation to hear and reflect upon, much as the leader of the congregation played an important role in helping the faithful understand Scripture through sermons. As a sermon is an elaboration of a reading from the Bible, updating it for the congregation's contemporary concerns, the Lutheran cantata was an elaboration of the weekly hymn, allowing the congregation to understand the hymn from a new perspective.

Bach worked for many years at Leipzig's St. Thomas Church and its famous choir school, seen in the background. Colored engraving from c. 1749.

The Lutheran Chorale and Cantata

Luther and his followers created weekly hymns (known as **chorales**) for their congregations to sing by composing (or sometimes recycling) simple and memorable melodies, and then writing German poetry in multiple stanzas that translated and/or interpreted passages in the Bible. Congregational singing of a specific chorale was (and still is) integrated into each weekly Lutheran service, along with the Gospel reading, prayers, and a sermon.

In these hymns, sung in unison by the congregation and in four-part harmony by the professional choir, the melody was in the soprano, where all could hear it and join in the singing. In this way, the chorales greatly strengthened the trend toward clear-cut melody supported by chords (homophonic texture).

Arrangements of chorales gradually expanded, so that instead of using every stanza of the chorale the same way, musicians and poets began to substitute some inner stanzas with new poetry, further elaborating their message. The resulting elaboration-of-chorale, a sort of musical sermon on the original hymn, is what we now call the **Lutheran cantata**.

Bach and the Lutheran Cantata

Raised to serve Lutheran worship in his role as a professional musician, Johann Sebastian Bach was deeply familiar both with chorales and with the ways they could be elaborated. In his time, the cantata was an integral part of the church service, related, along with the sermon and prayers that followed it, to the Gospel reading for the day. Most Sundays of the church year required their own cantata, as did holidays and special occasions. Bach composed four or five such yearly cycles, from which only about two hundred works survive.

Bach's cantatas typically include five to eight movements, of which the first, last, and usually one middle movement are full-ensemble numbers—normally fashioned from the chorale tune—ranging from simple hymnlike settings to

In His Own Words

" As Cantor of the St. Thomas School . . . I shall set the boys a shining example . . . serve the school industriously . . . bring the music in both the principal churches of this town into good estate . . . faithfully instruct the boys not only in vocal but also in instrumental music . . . arrange the music so that it shall not last too long, and shall . . . not make an operatic impression, but rather incite the listeners to devotion."

—J. S. Bach

Johann Sebastian Bach (1685–1750)

Bach is the culminating figure of the Baroque style and one of the giants in the history of music. Born at Eisenach, Germany, he was raised a Lutheran and followed the family vocation of organist. At the age of twenty-three, he was appointed to his first important position: court organist and chamber musician to the duke of Weimar. During his Weimar period (1708–17), Bach's fame as organ virtuoso spread, and he wrote many of his most important works for that instrument.

From 1717 to 1723, he served as composer for the prince of Anhalt-Cöthen, where he produced suites, concertos, sonatas for various instruments, and a wealth of keyboard music. Bach's two marriages produced at least nineteen offspring, many of whom did not survive infancy; four of his sons became leading composers of the next generation.

Bach was thirty-eight when he was appointed to one of the most important music positions in Germany: cantor at St. Thomas Church in Leipzig. His duties were formidable (see quote above). He supervised the music for the city's four main churches, selected and trained their choristers, and wrote music for the daily services. He also served as director of the **collegium musicum**, a group of university students and musicians that gave regular concerts. In the midst of all this activity, Bach managed to produce truly magnificent works during his twenty-seven years in Leipzig (1723–50).

Two hundred or so church cantatas, the *St. John* and *St. Matthew Passions,* and the epic *Mass in B Minor* form the centerpiece of Bach's religious music, constituting a personal document of spirituality. Best known in his lifetime as an organist, Bach wrote organ compositions in both improvisatory and strict forms. His most important keyboard works are *The Well-Tempered Clavier,* forty-eight preludes and fugues in two volumes, and his last masterwork, *The Art of Fugue.* His orchestral music includes four suites of dance movements and the often-performed *Brandenburg Concertos.* Bach raised existing forms to the highest level rather than originating new forms. His mastery of contrapuntal composition, especially fugal writing, has never been equaled.

MAJOR WORKS: Sacred vocal music (over 200 church cantatas, four Passions, and the *Mass in B Minor,* 1749) • Orchestral music (four suites) • Concertos (including six *Brandenburg Concertos*) • Solo sonatas and keyboard music (*The Well-Tempered Clavier, The Art of Fugue*) • Organ works, including the *Toccata and Fugue in D Minor.*

 The Art of Fugue, Contrapunctus I; Sarabande, from Cello Suite No. 2; *Brandenburg Concerto* No. 1, I; *Toccata in D Minor; Jesu, Joy of Man's Desiring;* "Endlich, endlich wird mein Joch," from Cantata 56; *Minuet in D Minor*

intricate fugues. Interspersed with the ensembles are solo or duet arias and recitatives, some of which may also retain the chorale melody or its text, or set new poetry that expands on the theme of the chorale.

Wachet auf (Sleepers, Awake)

Bach wrote his cantata *Wachet auf* (LG 12) in 1731, for the end of the church year. The reading of the Gospel for this church feast is the parable of the Wise and Foolish Virgins, in which the watchmen sound a call on the city wall above Jerusalem to the wise virgins to meet the arriving bridegroom (Christ). The biblical text (Matthew 25:1–3) clearly urges all Lutherans to prepare themselves spiritually for the second coming of Christ.

Bach builds his "musical sermon" on a hymn by Philipp Nicolai (1599), using its tune in three of the cantata's seven movements. The chorale is in a standard three-part structure known as **bar form** (**A-A-B**), in which the first section (**A**) is repeated with new words, and the second section (**B**) is rounded off with the same closing phrase as the first. The first movement is a grand choral fantasia that features a majestic, marchlike motive signaling the arrival of Christ and an instrumental refrain that recurs between the vocal statements of the chorale. The fourth movement presents a unison chorale sung by the tenors against the watchman's memorable countermelody.

Bar form

The whole cantata reveals Bach's deep-rooted faith and his ability to communicate a meaningful spiritual message. The tune would still be resonating in the ears of the congregation as they sang the unison hymn later in the service, thereby deepening their appreciation for the words of the day's sermon.

CRITICAL THINKING

1. How does Bach's cantata portray the biblical story of the Wise and Foolish Virgins?

2. How is polyphony used in contrasting ways in the first and middle movements of the work?

YOUR TURN TO EXPLORE

Find recordings of a sacred song or hymn that has been reused/elaborated by musicians from different traditions (African American spirituals might be a good resource; for example, *Motherless Child*, *Swing Low, Sweet Chariot*, or *Amazing Grace*). How are different meanings of the song highlighted through different performances? Which ones do you think are more effective, and why?

LISTENING GUIDE 12   10:19

Bach: Cantata No. 140, *Wachet auf* (*Sleepers, Awake*), Nos. 1 and 4

DATE: 1731, performed in Leipzig

BASIS: Chorale (three stanzas) by Philipp Nicolai, in movements 1, 4, and 7

OVERVIEW: **1. Chorale fantasia** (stanza 1), E-flat major
      2. Tenor recitative (freely composed), C minor

3. Aria: Soprano/bass duet (freely composed), C minor
4. **Unison chorale** (stanza 2), E-flat major
5. Bass recitative (freely composed), E-flat to B-flat major
6. Aria: Soprano/bass duet (freely composed), B-flat major
7. Chorale (stanza 3), E-flat major

Chorale tune
(**A** section)

Wa-chet auf, ruft uns die Stim - me   der Wäch-ter sehr_ hoch auf der
Mit - ter - nacht heißt die - se Stun - de;   sie ru - fen uns_ mit hel - lem

Zin - ne,   wach auf, du Stadt Je - ru - sa - lem!
Mun - de: wo seid ihr klu - gen Jung-frau - en?

1. Chorale fantasia (chorus and orchestra)   6:06

What to Listen For

Melody	Sopranos have slow-moving chorale melody; opening rising line = watchmen's motive; long melisma on "Alleluja."	**Texture**	Alternation between instrument groups; complex, imitative polyphony in lower voices.
Rhythm/ meter	Insistent dotted rhythm in orchestra, begun in ritornello 1.	**Performing forces**	Four-part choir (SATB), with strings, double reeds, horn, bassoon, organ, violino piccolo.
Harmony	Uplifting major key (E-flat).		
Form	Three-part bar form (**A-A-B**), based on chorale tune structure.	**Text**	Music depicts the text (watchmen, wake-up call).

0:00   Ritornello 1, march-like dotted rhythm, alternating between violins and oboes:

A section

0:29   Wachet auf, ruft uns die Stimme   Awake! The voice of the
      der Wächter sehr hoch auf der Zinne,   watchmen calls us from high
      auf der Zinne,   on the tower,
      wach auf, du Stadt Jerusalem!   Awake, town of Jerusalem!

1:32   Ritornello 2.

      A section repeated (new text)

2:00   Mitternacht heisst diese Stunde,   Midnight is this very hour;
      sie rufen uns mit hellem Munde: they call to us with bright voices:
      Wo seid ihr klugen Jungfrauen?   where are you, wise virgins?

3:04   Ritornello 3.

      B section

3:24   Wohl auf, der Bräut'gam kommt,   Take cheer, the bridegroom comes,
      steht auf, die Lampen nehmt!   Arise, take up your lamps!
      Alleluja!   Alleluia!

Continued on next page

Macht euch bereit,	Prepare yourselves
zu der Hochzeit,	for the wedding,
Ihr müsset ihm entgegengehn!	You must go forth to meet him.

5:32   Ritornello 4.

4. Unison chorale   4:13

> ### What to Listen For
>
> | | | | |
> |---|---|---|---|
> | **Melody** | Tenors sing chorale melody in unison, set against moving countermelody in strings. | **Form** | Three-part bar form (**A-A-B**), with instrument ritornellos between vocal sections. |
> | **Harmony** | Bright major key (E-flat). | **Texture** | Slow-moving vocal line; faster strings and "walking" bass line. |

0:00   Ritornello 1.

0:41   **A section**

Zion hört die Wächter singen,	Zion hears the watchmen singing,
das Herz tut ihr vor Freuden springen,	for joy her very heart is springing,
sie wachet und steht eilend auf.	she wakes and rises hastily.

1:11   Ritornello 2.

1:50   **A section** (new text)

Ihr Freund kommt vom Himmel prächtig,	From resplendent heaven comes her friend,
von Gnaden stark, von Wahrheit mächtig,	strong in grace, mighty in truth,
ihr Licht wird hell, ihr Stern geht auf.	her light shines bright, her star ascends.

2:20   Ritornello 3.

2:47   **B section**

Nun komm du werte Kron,	Now come, you worthy crown,
Herr Jesu, Gottes Sohn.	Lord Jesus, God's own son.
Hosiana!	Hosanna!

3:08   Ritornello 4 (in minor).

3:29   **B section** (continues)

Wir folgen all	We follow all
zum Freudensaal	to the joyful hall
und halten mit das Abendmahl.	and share the Lord's supper.

Chorale tune in tenors set against countermelody in strings:

Chapter 23

Textures of Worship: Handel and the English Oratorio

"What the English like is something they can beat time to, something that hits them straight on the drum of the ear."

—George Frideric Handel

KEY POINTS

- The **oratorio** is a large-scale dramatic genre with a sacred text performed by solo voices, chorus, and orchestra; it is not staged or costumed.

- Originally conceived to put forth the message of the Catholic Church, the oratorio bears many similarities to opera.

- George Frideric Handel built his career as a composer of Italian-style opera; later in life, he invented the English oratorio, combining elements of Italian and English musical style.

- Handel's oratorios (including *Messiah*) have remained popular up to the present day.

Most of the music composed in Europe before the later 1700s enjoyed only a short arc of success: even the most highly esteemed works and composers fell into obscurity within one or two generations. George Frideric Handel's oratorios, and in particular *Messiah*, broke that trend: from their beginnings more than two and a half centuries ago, they have been performed continuously. Today, even small North American towns will feature a performance of *Messiah* every year as a staple of Christmastime celebrations; and larger urban centers often offer several performances, some incorporating audience sing-along during the most-loved choruses. The success of these works comes in part from their fitting the national mood during a time of British self-confidence, and in part from Handel's ingenuity in combining some of the most effective musical resources of his day as he invented an entirely new genre, the English oratorio. From their beginnings, Handel's oratorios have marked the meeting place of community worship with the grandeur and glory of power—political, sacred, and musical.

Saint Philip Neri (1515–1595) promoted lay singing in the oratory (prayer room) of the church.

The Oratorio

The **oratorio**, one of the great Baroque sacred vocal forms, descended from the religious play-with-music of the Counter-Reformation. It took its name from the Italian word for "place of prayer," and early oratorios were sponsored by the Catholic Church in public meeting places as ways to convey its messages about faith to as wide an audience as possible. A large-scale musical work for solo voices, chorus, and orchestra, the oratorio was generally based on a biblical story and

George Frideric Handel (1685–1759)

If Bach represents the spirituality of the late Baroque, Handel embodies its worldliness. Born in the same year, the two giants of the age never met.

Handel was born in Halle, Germany, and attended the University of Halle. He then moved to Hamburg, where he played violin in the opera house orchestra and absorbed the Italian operatic style popular at the time. In 1706, he traveled to Italy, where he composed his first sacred works and Italian operas. Six years later, he settled permanently in London, where his opera *Rinaldo* had conquered the English public the year before.

Handel's great opportunity came in 1720 with the founding of the Royal Academy of Music, launched for the purpose of presenting Italian opera. For the next eight years, he was active in producing and directing his operas as well as writing them. When the Italian style fell out of favor, he turned from opera to oratorio, quickly realizing the advantages offered by a genre that dispensed with costly foreign singers and lavish scenery. Among his greatest achievements in this new genre were *Messiah* and *Judas Maccabaeus*. Shortly after his seventy-fourth birthday, Handel collapsed in the theater at the end of a performance of

Messiah and died some days later. The nation he had served for half a century accorded him its highest honor: a burial at Westminster Abbey.

Handel's rhythm has the powerful drive of the late Baroque. His melodies, rich in expression, rise and fall in great majestic arches. And with his roots in the world of the theater, Handel knew how to use tone color for atmosphere and dramatic expression. His more than forty operas tell stories of heroes and adventurers in ingenious musical settings, with arias that run the gamut from brilliant virtuosic displays to poignant love songs. His most important instrumental works are the concertos and two memorable orchestral suites, the *Water Music* (1717) and *Music for the Royal Fireworks* (1749).

MAJOR WORKS: Over 40 Italian operas (including *Rinaldo* and *Julius Caesar*) • English oratorios (including *Israel in Egypt*, *Judas Maccabeus*, and *Messiah*) • Other vocal music • Orchestral suites, including *Music for the Royal Fireworks* and *Water Music* • Keyboard and chamber music.

 Alla hornpipe, from *Water Music*; "Hallelujah Chorus," Rejoice greatly," "O thou that tellest," from *Messiah*

In His Own Words

“ My Lord, I should be sorry if I only entertained them; I wished to make them better."

— *Remark made by Handel after a performance of Messiah*

performed without scenery, costumes, or acting. The action was sometimes depicted with the help of a narrator, but in other ways oratorio was very much like opera on a religious theme—on purpose, since the Catholic Church wanted to propose oratorio as a more moral alternative to opera. Like operas, oratorios unfolded as a series of recitatives and arias, with duets, trios, and choruses.

Handel had become familiar with the Catholic oratorio during his musical study in Italy. After successfully becoming the leading producer of Italian opera in England, he decided to diversify his musical efforts. Unlike most musical genres, the first English oratorios can actually be determined, since Handel invented the genre by combining elements of Italian opera (and Catholic oratorio) with a grand choral style that had been associated with the English monarchy. And unlike the Catholic oratorio, the text (called **libretto**, as in opera) was written by trusted poets rather than by religious leaders. Just as important, English oratorios were not sponsored officially by the church: they were an entrepreneurial venture by Handel and his collaborators, designed to turn a profit.

Handel's oratorios quickly became popular: not only was the music grand and inspiring while still being memorable and singable, but the religious stories about a "chosen people" (most Handel oratorios tell Old Testament stories) were very appealing to an English public that saw economic expansion into its colonies as an indication of divine blessing. By a few decades after Handel's death, oratorio performances featuring hundreds of singers and instrumentalists (see illustration opposite)—many times more than the composer would ever have envisioned—had become common. As the British Empire grew, and with it an increasing interest in choral singing throughout the English-speaking world, Handel's oratorios followed the empire's expansion.

Messiah

In the spring of 1742, the city of Dublin witnessed the premiere of what became one of the English-speaking world's best-loved works, Handel's *Messiah* (LG 13). The composer was reputed to have written down the oratorio in only twenty-four days, working as if possessed. The story circulated of his servant finding him, after the completion of the "Hallelujah Chorus," with tears in his eyes. "I did think I did see all Heaven before me, and the Great God Himself!" he reportedly said. Such stories about divine inspiration and the genius composer's ability to create in an almost superhuman fashion helped to build the reputation of *Messiah* and oratorios like it.

The libretto is a compilation of biblical verses from the Old and New Testaments, set in three parts. The first part (the Christmas section) relates the prophecy of the coming of Christ and his birth; the second (the Easter section), his suffering, death, and the spread of his doctrine; and the third, the redemption of the world through faith. The orchestration features mainly strings; oboes and bassoons strengthen the choral parts, and trumpets and drums are reserved for special numbers.

The lovely soprano aria "Rejoice greatly, O daughter of Zion" is in three-part, or **A-B-A′**, form. In this type of **da capo aria**, the composer usually did not write out the third part (**A′**), since it duplicated the first, allowing the star singer the opportunity to ornament or elaborate the third part on the fly, a crowd-pleasing device in both opera and oratorio. For "Rejoice greatly," though, Handel did write out the last section, varying it considerably from the first. This may have been partly because he liked having as much control as possible over the expressive shape of the music, rather than leaving too many choices up to his performers. It may also have had to do with the fact that some of the first English oratorio performers were less skilled (especially in improvisation) than their Italian operatic counterparts, so Handel may have thought it prudent to give his singer as detailed a set of instructions as possible.

At the beginning of this aria, violins introduce an energetic figure that will soon be taken up by the voice. Notable are the melismatic passages on the word "rejoice." Throughout, the instruments exchange motives with the voice and help provide an element of unity with the **ritornellos**, or instrumental refrains, that bring back certain passages.

The climax of *Messiah* comes at the close of the second part, the Easter section, with the familiar "Hallelujah Chorus." In this movement, we hear shifting textures in which the voices and text overlap and then come together to clearly declaim the text.

London's Westminster Abbey is packed for this Handel performance on the centenary of the composer's birth, as depicted by **Edward Edwards** (1738–1806).

Giovanni Battista Cipriani's (1727–1785) allegorical study for a Handel memorial reflects how revered the composer was after his death.

Handel's extraordinary ability to combine tuneful melodies and intriguing textures with striking homorhythmic passages is most evident in this beloved chorus.

CRITICAL THINKING

Reviewing Baroque vocal genres

1. What are the contrasting ways Handel sets individual words to music in "Rejoice greatly"? in the "Hallelujah Chorus"?
2. What religious or inspirational story do you think might lend itself to a modern approach to the oratorio? Why?

YOUR TURN TO EXPLORE

Find a recording of a contemporary setting of a sacred text. How have the composer and performers chosen to use texture and other musical devices to bring out the spiritual aspects of the words that they, or their communities, find most important? Is the music designed to encourage participation by the community for which it has been designed, or is the expressive power left up to trained specialists?

LISTENING GUIDE 13 7:48

Handel: *Messiah*, Nos. 18 and 44

DATE: 1742

GENRE: Oratorio, in three parts

PARTS: I: Christmas section
    II: Easter section
    III: Redemption section

Part I: Christmas Section / 18. Soprano aria, "Rejoice greatly"   4:15

What to Listen For			
Melody	Lyrical lines, with long melisma on "rejoice"; slower second part in a minor key.	**Form**	Three part (da capo, **A-B-A′**), with shortened last section; instrumental introduction (ritornello).

0:00	Instrumental ritornello.	Vocal theme presented in violins in B-flat major.
	A section	
0:16	Rejoice greatly, O daughter of Zion shout, O daughter of Jerusalem, behold, thy King cometh unto thee. Instrumental ritornello.	Disjunct rising line, melismas on "rejoice"; melody exchanged between soprano and violin. Syncopated, choppy melody, ends in F major.
	B section	
1:30	He is the righteous Saviour and he shall speak peace unto the heathen.	Begins in G minor, slower and lyrical; modulates to B-flat major.

A′ section

2:33   Rejoice greatly . . .

After an abridged ritornello, new melodic elaborations; longer melismas on "rejoice."

Extended melisma on "rejoice" from **A′** section:

re-joice   great-ly,

Part II: Easter Section / 44. "Hallelujah Chorus"

3:33

What to Listen For

Texture	Varies from homorhythmic (all voices together) to imitative polyphony; fugal treatment, with overlapping voices.
Performing forces	SATB chorus, with voices in alternation, accompanied by orchestra.
Expression	Varied dynamics for dramatic effect.

0:00   Short instrumental introduction.
       Hallelujah!

Four voices, homorhythmic at opening.

0:24   For the Lord God omnipotent reigneth.

Textural reductions, leading to imitation and overlapping of text; builds in complexity, imitative entries.

1:12   The kingdom of this world
       is become the Kingdom of our Lord
       and of His Christ;

Homorhythmic treatment, simple accompaniment.

1:29   and He shall reign for ever and ever.

Imitative polyphony, voices build from lowest to highest.

1:51   King of Kings and Lord of Lords.
       Hallelujah!

Women's voices introduce the text, punctuated by "Hallelujah"; closes in homorhythmic setting with trumpets and timpani.

Opening of chorus, in homorhythmic style:

Chapter 24

Independent Study: Billings and the North American Sacred Tradition

"I don't think myself confined to any Rules for Composition laid down by any that went before me . . . in fact I think it best for every composer to be his own carver."

—William Billings

KEY POINTS

- Colonists in New England took part in congregational hymn singing, which often involved a call-and-response practice called **lining-out**.

- Some congregations later fostered choirs that developed more elaborate, notation-based singing traditions.

- By the end of the 1700s, a tradition of singing schools had developed in North America: William Billings's **anthem** *David's Lamentation* is an example of a work composed for congregational singing.

Even as we've come to rely more and more on sound recordings rather than live performance for our musical entertainment, the opportunities and resources for studying music have multiplied. Most towns have at least one community music school, hundreds of books and CDs are available to provide music lessons, and thousands of YouTube videos offer demonstrations (some more skillful than others) of performance on every imaginable instrument. Basic musical literacy in North America is comparatively high, thanks to a long tradition of both formal and informal music teaching (especially self-study).

From "Lining-Out" to Singing Schools

Lining-out

The Calvinist-inspired Pilgrims and Puritans in seventeenth-century New England used a system called **lining-out** for their psalm singing in church: a leader sang each line of a psalm, and the congregation repeated it in turn. In communities that could not afford a psalm book for each church member, everyone could learn the melody and text this way, and could participate equally in the musical worship. The intent of lining-out was to create monophonic, unison singing by the repeating congregation; more often than not, however, individuals modified the melody slightly when sing-

Heterophony

ing it back, to suit their interpretation of the text. This resulted in a **heterophonic** effect—many people singing slight variants of the same melody simultaneously.

Interface

Shape-Note Singing and Worship in North America

The Pilgrims and Puritans who settled New England in the early decades of the 1600s were Calvinists for whom psalm singing was an identity-defining practice. The first book published in North America was a book of psalms—the *Bay Psalm Book* (1628)—designed for singing both in congregation and at home. The first edition did not include music notation, since the standard melodies were well known and the English poetic translations were designed to fit those melodies. By the time singing schools had taken hold in New England in the late 1700s, music literacy was widespread in the North American colonies. A booming musical print industry arose as a result, helping to keep the literary level in the United States high from that point on.

Since the earliest days of Western notation, music had been taught with a sytem called **solfège**, in which syllables were used to memorize intervals between notes in a standard scale pattern. The original system had six syllables, which were eventually expanded to seven in order to account for the full seven-note scale: *do–re–mi–fa–sol–la–ti–do* (see Chapter 3). However, teachers realized that it was possible to simplify the system and account for all seven notes by using only four syllables, *mi–fa–sol–la*; that method was the one used in the New England colonies. As the singing schools became more widespread, teachers in search of additional ways to improve solfège instruction came up with the idea of changing the shape of the note head depending on the syllable. The result, what we now call **shape-note notation** (see example below), was invented around 1790 in Philadelphia and contributed to the explosion of musical worship in the young and expanding United States. Some congregations still sing from shape notes today: listen to the Original Sacred Harp Singers' interpretation of *David's Lamentation*, and consider how it differs from the LG recording.

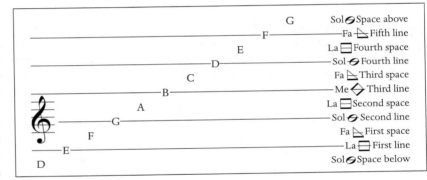

Church leaders, unhappy with the rather "sloppy" musical effects of this oral tradition, also complained that the approach had discouraged congregants from learning to read music, which they considered to be an important part of literacy for a good Christian. By the 1720s, leaders were encouraging people to read actual music notation rather than repeat a leader's melodies. While many congregations continued the practice of lining-out, others sponsored "singing schools" that were designed to teach a congregation the basics of notation and theory. Along with these schools came the need for both printed instructional materials and local individuals able to lead them. Thus, the first opportunities arose for musicians born in North America to teach music at least semi-professionally. And a growing musically literate public began to express an interest in singing music that was more complex than monophonic psalms, which meant that some choirs embraced polyphonic singing in church—a move considered scandalous by more conservative Puritan leaders. By the time of the Revolutionary War, some of the polyphonic repertory was composed by American composers—the most famous of whom was a friend of Paul Revere, William Billings.

The frontispiece to Billings's *New England Psalm-Singer* (1770), depicting singers around a table performing a canon for six voices, with a ground-bass part.

Billings and *The New England Psalm-Singer*

Billings's *New England Psalm-Singer* (1770) was a collection of his own compositions, a significant departure from the reliance on British arrangements previously published in the colonies. In the introduction to the book, Billings discussed the basics of music notation and theory (especially useful for singing schools) and his own method of composition—which was original and not bound by the rules of the European tradition he had inherited (see the quote that begins this chapter). This style consisted mostly of simple homophonic textures, often with the melody in the tenor line rather than the soprano, and an occasional simple passage of imitation to give the singers an opportunity to interact in a slightly more complex way.

David's Lamentation

One of Billings's most famous works is *David's Lamentation* (LG 14), first published in 1778. The text is a paraphrase of the biblical passage describing the sorrow of King David when he discovered that his son Absalom had been killed (2 Samuel 18:33). It is a poignant moment—Absalom had rebelled against his father, and yet David could not bring himself to punish him. This **anthem** was designed for sacred congregational singing; its text is a single stanza, though the second section is repeated, resulting in an **A-B-B** form. The first section features homophony in all voices; the second begins with a short solo by the bass before a return to the full ensemble in homophony; and then a quasi-imitative passage passes a short musical idea among voice pairs before a final homophonic close. There is enough variety in this short setting to make things interesting for each voice part, but not so much textural complexity that amateur singers would be overly challenged.

Billings's music helped to cement a nationwide commitment to musical literacy that made it possible for the North American music industry to find a steady market as it blossomed in the 1800s. We have him to thank, in part, for the institutional importance of music in our lives today, as well as for the model of musical self-reliance that we can find in every town and every corner of the Internet.

In His Own Words

" [My new compositions have] more than twenty times the power of the old slow tunes."

—William Billings

William Billings (1746–1800)

Billings, likely a self-taught musician, practiced a number of other trades, especially leather tanning; he also held some minor public posts in the city of Boston. He taught at singing schools in the Boston area for most of his life, and his musical publications quickly became popular partly because they rode the wave of the movement for independence from England: a number of his songs mixed sacred texts with political references. Billings had close connections to the radical elements of the independence movement in Boston: not only did Paul Revere engrave the frontispiece for the composer's *New England Psalm-Singer*, but one of the movement's foremost leaders, Samuel Adams, was a good friend. While Billings was less financially successful in his later years and died in poverty, he was viewed in his own lifetime and in the early years of the Republic as an iconic figure, embodying in his musical approach the scrappy self-sufficiency of an emerging nation.

MAJOR WORKS: Over 340 works for use in singing schools and churches • Six primary collections: *The New England Psalm-Singer* (Boston, 1770); *The Singing Master's Assistant* (Boston, 1778); *Music in Miniature* (Boston, 1779); *The Psalm-Singer's Amusement* (Boston, 1781); *The Suffolk Harmony* (Boston, 1786); *The Continental Harmony* (Boston, 1794).

CRITICAL THINKING

1. How did lining-out differ from regular singing?
2. What are the most noteworthy features of Billings's career and music?

YOUR TURN TO EXPLORE

Consider how a person might learn to read music today. Look online for free sites that offer basic music-reading lessons, and choose a couple to compare. If you can already read music, consider the differences between online methods and the way you learned. Are there aspects of notation that you think they discuss more or less clearly? If you don't yet read music, try a couple of basic lessons from each site. How are the approaches similar and different, what makes them more or less helpful?

LISTENING GUIDE 14

🎧 1:48

Billings: *David's Lamentation*

DATE: Published 1778

GENRE: Anthem

What to Listen For

Melody	Mostly stepwise, moving through various voices.	**Form**	**A-B-B**.
Rhythm/ meter	Duple meter, regular rhythmic patterns.	**Expression**	Simple declamation of spiritualism.
Harmony	Consonant.	**Performing forces**	SATB voices.
Texture	Homorhythmic, four-part chorus, with solos and duets.	**Text**	Paraphrase of 2 Samuel 18:33.

	TEXT	DESCRIPTION
0:00	David, the king, was grieved and moved,	Homorhythmic, four voices, mostly syllabic, a little text repetition.
0:09	He went to his chamber and wept;	
0:18	And as he went, he wept, and said:	Bass solo, monophonic, syllabic.
0:26	"O my son! O my son!	Homorhythmic, four voices.
0:36	Would to God I had died	Text repeated three times: tenor-bass duet, soprano-bass duet, four voices in homorhythm.
0:49	For thee, O Absalom, my son!"	Ending is homorhythmic.
1:01	And as he went . . .	Choir repeats text.

First two lines in the soprano part, with shape-note notation:

Da - vid, the king,   was griev - ed and mov - ed, He went to his cham-ber, his cham-ber, and wept;

Blending Worship Traditions in Colonial Latin America

Sixteenth-century Spanish settlers came to the New World in search of gold and other goods to take back to Europe; in the Americas, they were surprised to find complex societies with long-standing traditions, which included elaborate ceremonies that incorporated singing and musical instruments. We have found no evidence of music notation in the complex pictographs (image-based narratives) that native societies developed, and the Spaniards were not concerned with preserving any "pagan" customs, so we have little idea of what indigenous American musical traditions sounded like before the Europeans arrived. Spaniards *were* concerned, however, with bringing Catholic religious practice to the conquered peoples, and as we have seen, Christian worship was closely tied with music.

Catholics in New Spain (as the European settlements were called) actively worked to assimilate the local peoples into their religious communities. The philosophy of the Jesuit religious order, the main Catholic teaching branch at the time, held that most beliefs could be reconciled with the message of their One True Church. And the reforms of the Council of Trent had stated that while prayers and songs for the church service needed to be in Latin, other devotional texts and songs could be in the local languages of the worshippers. Thus, the missionaries who came to spread the word of God to the American natives taught them plainchant in Latin, but also worked with them to develop worship songs in their native language that incorporated imagery from their own religious traditions, so that

The impressive façade of the Puebla Cathedral, noted for its mix of Renaissance and Baroque styles (completed 1690).

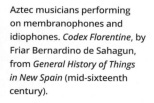

Aztec musicians performing on membranophones and idiophones. *Codex Florentine*, by Friar Bernardino de Sahagun, from *General History of Things in New Spain* (mid-sixteenth century).

the local people could embrace the new religion at least partly on their own terms.

A few of these mixed-language and mixed-imagery devotional songs (**villancicos**) have survived: some were composed by Gaspar Fernandes (1566–1629), a native of Portugal who moved to Mexico to become choirmaster at the splendid Puebla Cathedral in the early 1600s. His duties there included teaching both chant and polyphony to the choirboys (children of Native Americans or of Spaniards who had married local women), and playing the organ. He also assembled a large manuscript collection of ritual, devotional, and secular music that was being used (and in part composed) in Mexico at the time.

The villancico by Fernandes that we will consider uses the Nahuatl language of the indigenous Nahua people (in italic below) in alternation with Spanish—and the Spanish spelling may reflect the pronunciation of Nahua contemporaries of Fernandes. The text mixes traditional Christian nativity imagery (the mule and the ox next to the Christ child) alongside other images more typical of Aztec culture (pearls, gems, flowers). While the manuscript only includes vocal lines, modern performances often incorporate the kinds of percussion instruments that are documented in both Aztec and Christian images from New Spain. Some scholars think that the rhythmic patterns of the song, unusual for European music of the time, are an attempt by Fernandes to convey the unique sonic flavor brought to musical worship by his Native American collaborators.

A Nahua ceremonial Deer Dance mask. The Deer Dance, generally accompanied by percussion instruments, remains popular in Mexico today.

What to listen for: 🎧

- A short-long rhythm unusual for European music of this time, possibly derived from Aztec practices.
- Solo/ensemble refrain alternating with solo/duet verse.
- Varied instrumental accompaniment, including percussion, elaborated by modern performers on the basis of images and accounts of the time (but not present in the original score).

Text	Translation	Description
Tleycantimo choquiliya Mis prasedes, mi apisión. Aleloya.	Why now do you cry, my pleasures, my passion. Alleluia.	Refrain: Soloist alone, then five voices mostly in slightly staggered homophony with some imitation toward the end of phrases.
Dejalto el llando crecida, miral to el mulo y el buey. *Ximoyollali,* mi rey. *Tlein mitztolinia,* mi vida?	Stop your growing tears, look at the mule and the ox. Take comfort, my king. What disturbs you, my beloved?	Verse, section 1: Two solo voices alternate phrases.
No sé por qué deneis pena, tan lindo cara de rosa. *Nocpiholotzin,* niño hermosa, *nochalchiuh, naxoquena.*	I know not why you are pained, such beautiful rosy face, precious noble child, lovely child, my green jade, my lily.	Verse, section 2: Same melody and texture for the verse's second section.
Jesós de mi goraçón, no lloreis, mi pantasía.	Jesus of my heart, do not cry, my fantasy.	Verse, section 3: Voices join and provide rhythmic emphasis on "Jesus"; imitation and word repetition as the verse ends.
Tleycantimo choquiliya Mis prasedes, mi apisión. Aleloya	Why now do you cry, my pleasures, my passion. Alleluia.	Refrain: Repeats exactly as in the beginning.

Chapter 25

Grace and Grandeur:
The Baroque Dance Suite

"To enjoy the effects of music fully, we must completely lose ourselves in it."

—Jean-Philippe Rameau (1683-1764)

Technology has always played a crucial role in the development of music. We have already encountered notational technologies (handwriting and print) that were essential to preserving and transmitting musical ideas. We now consider more closely the technologies of sound production: how musicians and craftspeople collaborated to imagine and manufacture increasingly sophisticated musical instruments.

St. Cecilia, patroness of musicians, plays a Baroque violin in this painting by **Guido Reni** (1575–1642). There is no chin rest, so she plays it braced against her shoulder; her grip on the bow also differs from that of modern players.

Though humans have been involved in this creative practice since before recorded history, it was during the Baroque era that the Western tradition developed a remarkable focus on instruments and music written for them—a focus that eventually became the central feature of Western concert music in the following century. This flowering of instrumental music was encouraged by wealthy patrons who were eager to invest money and resources in magnificent displays. Since that time, elaborate instrumental music has often been used to convey grandeur on special occasions; most likely every time you have witnessed a grand celebration, it has been enhanced by graceful and powerful soundscapes made possible by the evolving technology of musical instruments.

Baroque Instruments

The seventeenth century saw a dramatic improvement in the construction of string instruments. Some of the finest violins ever built came from the North Italian workshops of Stradivarius, Guarneri, and Amati: to this day musicians seek them out, and pay millions of dollars for the best-made exemplars. The strings were made of gut rather than the steel used today. Gut, produced from animal intestines, yielded a softer yet more penetrating sound. In general, the string instruments of the Baroque resemble their modern descendants except for certain details of construction. Playing techniques, though, have changed somewhat, especially bowing.

While woodwind instruments were used primarily for loud outdoor events through the 1600s, in the late Baroque composers prized such instruments increasingly for color as builders expanded their range and subtlety. The penetrating timbres of the recorder, flute, and oboe, all made of wood at the time, were especially effective in suggesting pastoral scenes, while the bassoon cast a somber tone.

An evening outdoor concert in 1744 by the Collegium Musicum of Jena, Germany, featuring an orchestra of strings, woodwinds, trumpets, and drums gathered around a harpsichord.

The trumpet developed from an instrument used for military signals to one with a solo role in the orchestra. It was still a "natural instrument"—that is, without the valves that would enable it to play in all keys—demanding real virtuosity on the part of the player. Trumpets contributed a bright sonority to the orchestral palette, to which the French horns, also natural instruments, added a mellow, huntlike sound. Timpani were occasionally added, furnishing a bass to the trumpets.

In recent years, a new drive for authenticity has made the sounds of eighteenth-century instruments familiar to us. Recorders and wooden flutes, restored violins with gut strings, and mellow-toned, valveless brass instruments are being played again, so that the Baroque orchestra has recovered not only its smaller scale but also its transparent tone quality.

The Baroque Suite

One of the most important instrumental genres of the Baroque was the **suite**, a group of short dances performed by the diverse array of instruments just described. It was a natural outgrowth of earlier traditions, which paired dances of contrasting tempos and character.

Dance types

The suite's galaxy of dance types, providing contrasting moods but all in the same key, could include the German **allemande**, the French **courante**, the Spanish **sarabande**, and the English **jig** (**gigue**), as well as a **minuet**, **gavotte**, lively **bourrée**, **passepied**, or jaunty **hornpipe**. Some dances were of peasant origin, bringing a touch of earthiness to their more formal surroundings. The suite sometimes opened with an overture, and might include other brief pieces with descriptive titles reflecting their origin in choreographed theatrical dance.

Binary and ternary form

Each piece in the Baroque suite was set either in **binary** form, consisting of two sections of approximately equal length, each rounded off by a cadence and each repeated (**A-A-B-B**); or in **ternary** form (**A-B-A**), which we will hear in the selection from Handel's *Water Music*. In both structures, the **A** part usually moves from the home key (tonic) to a contrasting key (dominant), while the **B** part makes the corresponding move back. The two sections often share closely related melodic material. The form is easy to hear because of the modulation and the full stop at the end of each part.

The principle of combining dances into a suite could be applied to solo instrumental music (notably for harpsichord or solo violin) and to chamber ensembles,

A royal sortie on the Thames River in London, similar to the *Water Music* party, as depicted by **Giovanni Antonio Canal (Canaletto)** (1697–1768).

as well as to orchestral forces. It was an important precedent to the multimovement cycle that later became standard in Classical instrumental music.

Handel and the Orchestral Suite

Two orchestral suites by Handel, the *Water Music* and *Music for the Royal Fireworks*, are memorable contributions to the genre. The *Water Music* was played (although probably not first composed) for a royal party on the Thames River in London on July 17, 1717. Two days later, the *Daily Courant* reported:

> On Wednesday Evening, at about 8, the King took Water at Whitehall in an open Barge, . . . and went up the River towards Chelsea. Many other Barges with Persons of Quality attended, and so great a Number of Boats, that the whole River in a manner was cover'd; a City Company's Barge was employ'd for the Musick, wherein were 50 Instruments of all sorts, who play'd all the Way from Lambeth . . . the finest Symphonies, compos'd express for this Occasion, by Mr. Handel; which his Majesty liked so well, that he caus'd it to be plaid over three times in going and returning.

The conditions of an outdoor performance, in which the music would have to contend with the breeze on the river, birdcalls, and similar noises, prompted Handel to create music that was marked by lively rhythms and catchy melodies.

Hornpipe   The *Water Music*'s Suite in D Major opens with a majestic three-part Allegro that sounds a fanfare in the trumpets, answered by the French horns and strings. One of the most recognized dances from the *Water Music* is the **hornpipe** from this suite (LG 15). Its sprightly opening theme features decorative trills in the strings and woodwinds, answered by regal brass and timpani; this is followed by a more reflective **B** section set in a minor key. The return of **A** completes the ternary form.

More than two and a half centuries after it was written, Handel's *Water Music* is still a favorite with the public, indoors or out. We need to hear only a few measures to understand why, since it is a perfect example of using technology (the latest instruments) for the most marvelous result possible.

CRITICAL THINKING

1. How would you describe the sound of Baroque-era instruments compared with modern ones?

2. How is the suite an international musical genre?

YOUR TURN TO EXPLORE

Find a performance of a band playing a march—the marches by John Philip Sousa are a great example of the genre. How do the changing timbres of the various instrument combinations compare with the timbres of Handel's hornpipe? How does the structure of the march resemble and differ from the ternary form of the hornpipe? Why do you think these similarities and differences exist?

LISTENING GUIDE 15   🎧 2:50

Handel: *Water Music*, Suite in D Major, Alla hornpipe

DATE: 1717 (first performance)

GENRE: Dance suite

MOVEMENTS: Allegro   Lentement
               Alla hornpipe   Bourrée
               Minuet

Second movement: Alla hornpipe, D major

What to Listen For			
Melody	Ascending line with leaps and trills; second section has descending minor-scale melody.	**Form**	Three-part (**A-B-A**).
Rhythm/ meter	Triple meter in a quick tempo.	**Timbre**	Instrument groups exchange motivic ideas.

0:00   **A section**—disjunct theme in strings and double reeds, with trills, later answered by trumpets and French horns; in D major, at a moderate, spritely tempo:

Continued alternation of motives between brass and strings.

0:55   **B section**—strings and woodwinds only (no brass); fast-moving string part with syncopated winds; in B minor:

1:46   **A section**—repeat of entire first section; ends in D major.

Chapter 26

Sounding Spring: Vivaldi and the Baroque Concerto

"[His playing] terrified me . . . he came with his fingers within a mere grass-stalk's breadth of the bridge, so that the bow had no room—and this on all four strings with imitations and at incredible speed."

—A contemporary musician (describing Vivaldi's violin technique)

KEY POINTS

- Baroque musicians developed the **concerto**, a genre that generally featured either a solo instrument or a small group of soloists set against a larger ensemble.

- First and last movements of concertos tended to follow a refrain-based structure known as **ritornello form**.

- Antonio Vivaldi, a virtuoso violinist, composed *The Four Seasons*, a well-loved set of solo violin concertos that exemplify **program music**.

How can sound mean something independently of words? Many of us today automatically refer to musical works as "songs," but as we know, the term is really only accurate when lyrics are involved. And one of the characteristics of the Western tradition is the complexity of its independent instrumental music. Separated from the need to follow the meanings and patterns of text, instrumental music can create meaning just through patterns of sound. However, even as they explored purely musical ways of fashioning "sound stories," composers frequently called on written language to help them, as well as their listeners, explore the possibilities for what music could mean. These explorations played out in especially interesting ways through a new genre: the concerto.

The Baroque Concerto

Contrast was as basic an element of Baroque music as unity. This twofold principle found expression in the **concerto**, an instrumental form based on the opposition between two dissimilar bodies of sound. The concerto contrasted one or more "featured" instruments with a larger orchestral ensemble, an approach that lent itself to experiments in sonority and virtuoso playing. A concerto usually consisted of three movements, in the sequence Allegro–Adagio–Allegro. The first and last movements tended to follow a loosely structured form based on the alternation between orchestral refrains and virtuosic outbursts by the soloist(s), which

Ritornello form

Antonio Vivaldi (1678–1741)

The son of a violinist, Vivaldi grew up in his native Venice. He was ordained in the church while in his twenties and became known as "the red priest," a reference to the color of his hair. For the greater part of his career, Vivaldi was *maestro de' concerti,* or music master, at the most important of the four music schools for which Venice was famous, the Conservatorio dell'Ospedale della Pietà. These schools were attached to charitable institutions established for the upbringing of orphaned children—mostly girls—and played a vital role in the musical life of Venetians. Much of Vivaldi's output was written for concerts at the school, which attracted visitors from all over Europe.

One of the most prolific composers of his era, Vivaldi also wrote, in addition to his many concertos, chamber music and operas as well as cantatas, an oratorio, and an extended setting of the *Gloria,* which is today one of his most performed works. His life came to a mysterious end: a contemporary Venetian account notes that the composer, who had once earned 50,000 ducats in his day (about $4 million today), died in poverty as a result of his extravagance.

MAJOR WORKS: Over 230 violin concertos, including *Le quattro stagioni* (*The Four Seasons,* c. 1725) • Other solo, double, triple, and orchestral concertos • Sinfonias • Vocal music, including operas and oratorios, Mass movements, and a *Magnificat.*

 Concerto in C Major for Two Trumpets, I; *The Seasons,* I

---

has taken on the Italian name for "refrain," **ritornello form**. This flexible form prepared the way for the more systematic structures in the concerto of the Classical and Romantic periods.

The concerto was first developed in the Italian peninsula in the late 1600s, but quickly spread north and was eagerly embraced by performers and patrons alike. J. S. Bach took the concerto to a new and almost encyclopedic level in his six *Brandenburg Concertos.* But of all the composers in the Baroque concerto tradition, Antonio Vivaldi was the most famous and the most prolific.

Program Music: Vivaldi's *The Four Seasons*

Vivaldi is in fact best remembered for his more than 500 concertos, about 230 of which are for solo violin, some with descriptive titles. He was active during a period that was crucially important to a new style in which instruments were liberated from their earlier dependence on vocal music. His novel use of rapid scale passages, extended arpeggios, and contrasting registers contributed decisively to the development of violin style and technique. And he played a leading part in the history of the concerto, effectively exploiting the contrast in sonority between large and small groups of players.

Vivaldi's best-known work is *The Four Seasons,* a group of four solo violin concertos, each named for a season. We have observed the fondness for word painting in Renaissance and Baroque vocal works, where the music is meant to portray the action and emotion described by the text. In *The Four Seasons,* Vivaldi applies this principle to instrumental music. While each concerto has an independent musical logic, it is also accompanied by a poem, describing the joys of that particular

A concert by the girls of one of Venice's famous *ospedali,* or orphanages, by **Gabriele Bella** (1730–1799). Vivaldi taught music at the most prestigious of these institutions.

In *A Concert*, by **Leonello Spada** (1576–1622), musicians play the theorbo (a long-necked lute) and Baroque violin. A guitar sits on the table.

season. Each line of the poem is printed above a certain passage in the score; the music at that point mirrors graphically the action described. This literary link is called **program music**.

In the first movement of *Spring* (*La primavera*; LG 16), an Allegro in E major, both poem and music evoke the birds' joyous welcome to spring and the gentle murmur of streams, followed by thunder and lightning. The image of birdcalls takes shape in staccato notes, trills, and running scales; a storm is portrayed by agitated repeated notes answered by quickly ascending minor-key scales. Throughout, an orchestral ritornello (refrain) returns again and again (representing the general mood of spring) in alternation with the **episodes**, which often feature the solo violin. Ultimately, "the little birds take up again their melodious song" as we return to the home key. A florid passage for the violin soloist leads to the final ritornello.

In the second movement, a Largo in 3/4, Vivaldi evokes the poetic image of a goatherd who sleeps in a "pleasant, flowery meadow" with his faithful dog by his side. Over the bass line played by the violas, which sound an ostinato rhythm, he writes, "The dog who barks." In the finale, an Allegro marked "Rustic Dance," we can visualize nymphs and shepherds cavorting in the fields as the music suggests the drone of bagpipes. Ritornellos and solo passages alternate in bringing the work to a happy conclusion.

Like Bach, Vivaldi was renowned in his day as a performer rather than a composer. Today, he is recognized both as the "father of the concerto," having established ritornello form as its basic procedure, and as a herald of musical Romanticism in his use of pictorial imagery. In his compositions, we encounter an early attempt to empower instrumental music to create independent meanings apart from words and beyond the enhancement of dance.

CRITICAL THINKING

1. How did composers achieve both unity and contrast in the concerto?

2. What musical techniques did Vivaldi employ in *Spring* to depict the imagery of that season?

YOUR TURN TO EXPLORE

With a classmate or two, find an example of instrumental music with a title that describes some place or mood or activity. What specific elements of the music do you think were designed to convey that image? Did you and your classmate come up with the same correspondences? What might account for similarities and differences in your interpretation? Can you think of ways that the composer or performers might have made the image even more compelling or clear?

3:33

Vivaldi: *Spring,* from *The Four Seasons* (*La primavera,* from *Le quattro stagioni*), Op. 8, No. 1, I

DATE: Published 1725

GENRE: Programmatic concerto for solo violin, based on an Italian sonnet:

No. 1: *Spring (La primavera)*   No. 3: *Autumn (L'autunno)*
No. 2: *Summer (L'estate)*   No. 4: *Winter (L'inverno)*

I. **Allegro**
Joyful spring has arrived,
the birds greet it with their cheerful song,
and the brooks in the gentle breezes
flow with a sweet murmur.

The sky is covered with a black mantle,
and thunder and lightning announce a storm.
When they fall silent, the little birds
take up again their melodious song.

II. **Largo**
And in the pleasant, flowery meadow,
to the gentle murmur of bushes and trees,
the goatherd sleeps, his faithful dog at his side.

III. Allegro (Rustic Dance)
To the festive sounds of a rustic bagpipe
nymphs and shepherds dance in their favorite spot
when spring appears in its brilliance.

First movement: Allegro, E major

What to Listen For

Melody	Flashy solo violin; fast scales and trills.	**Performing forces**	Solo violin with string orchestra and basso continuo (keyboard).
Form	Ritornello as unifying theme; alternates with contrasting episodes.	**Expression**	Musical images from poem (birds, brooks, breeze, storm).
Timbre	Distinctive sound of Baroque instruments.		

Ritornello theme:

	DESCRIPTION	PROGRAM
0:00	Ritornello 1, in E major.	Spring
0:32	Episode 1; solo violin with birdlike trills and high running scales, accompanied by violins.	Birds
1:07	Ritornello 2.	Spring
1:15	Episode 2; whispering figures like water flowing, played by orchestra.	Murmuring brooks
1:39	Ritornello 3.	Spring
1:47	Episode 3 modulates; solo violin with repeated notes, fast ascending minor-key scales, accompanied by orchestra.	Thunder, lightning
2:15	Ritornello 4, in the relative minor (C-sharp).	Spring
2:24	Episode 4; trills and repeated notes in solo violin.	Birds
2:43	Ritornello 5, returns to E major; brief solo passage interrupts.	
3:12	Closing tutti (whole ensemble).	

Chapter 27

Process as Meaning: Bach and the Fugue

"He, who possessed the most profound knowledge of all the contrapuntal arts, understood how to make art subservient to beauty."

—Carl Philipp Emanuel Bach (1714–1788),
about his father, J. S. Bach

KEY POINTS

- The **organ** and **harpsichord** were the main keyboard instruments of the Baroque era.
- Keyboard players improvised and created freeform pieces called **preludes** or **toccatas**, followed by more structured works, such as **fugues**.
- *The Art of Fugue* is J. S. Bach's last and most comprehensive example of contrapuntal writing.

Instrumental music, in several contemporary traditions, often includes a component of improvisation: musicians will elaborate counterpoint on the spot, drawing on established conventions as well as their own creative imagination. Without the distraction of words, the listener's ear can focus on the shape and interaction of musical lines: this interaction provides the music's expressive resources and meaning. Thus, while some counterpoint-based music can be understood as individual "pieces" (which are always played the same way), counterpoint is also a process. And just like today's rock and jazz stars, the great composers of the past frequently *improvised* their polyphonic processes, so that the performer-composer and listener were more equal participants in the unfolding of meaning through sound.

Keyboard Instruments in the Baroque Era

Keyboard instruments, which are inherently suited to polyphonic performance, have been featured in Western music since the Middle Ages; in the 1600s, however, instruments such as the **organ** and **harpsichord** reached a new level of refinement. These technological advances encouraged musicians to broaden their technique, and musicians' experiments likewise spurred instrument builders to new heights.

The harpsichord differs from the modern piano in two important ways. First, its strings are plucked by quills rather than struck with hammers, and its tone cannot be sustained like that of the piano, a product of the early Classical era. Second, the pressure of the fingers on the keys can produce subtle dynamic nuances but not the piano's extremes of loud and soft (see illustration on p. 145).

German builders of the 1600s and 1700s created organs with various sets of pipes, each with a sharply contrasting tone color, so that the ear could pick out the separate lines of counterpoint. The organ's multiple keyboards made it possible to achieve terraced levels of soft and loud. J. S. Bach was a sought-after consultant to church-organ builders, since he was renowned as an outstanding keyboard player. He was also famous for his ability to improvise at the organ or harpsichord—and his improvisations ranged from relatively free-form approaches with highly contrasting musical ideas and tempos (in what was often called a **toccata** or **prelude**) to a much more systematic working-out of a single musical thought (generally labeled fugue). Bach wrote out a number of his most successful improvisations, usually to serve as models for his students.

The toccata and prelude were designed to showcase the performer's dexterity and were often paired/contrasted with more systematically organized forms—you may know Bach's famous *Toccata and Fugue in D Minor*, which was the opening music for Disney's 1940 film *Fantasia* and has been heard in many films since. We will focus on the more tightly structured form, the fugue, since it illustrates the Baroque ideal of systematic elaboration of short musical ideas.

A spectacular Baroque organ (1738) in St. Bavo's Cathedral, Haarlem, The Netherlands.

The Fugue and Its Devices

A **fugue** is a contrapuntal composition in which a single theme pervades the entire fabric, entering in one voice (or instrumental line) and then in another. The fugue, then, is based on the principle of **imitation**. Its main theme, the **subject**, constitutes the unifying idea, the focal point of interest in the contrapuntal web.

We have already encountered the fugue or fugal style in a number of works: in *The Young Person's Guide to the Orchestra*, by Britten; in Handel's choruses in *Messiah*; and in the opening movement of Bach's cantata *Wachet auf*. Though a fugue may be written for a group of instruments or voices, as in these works, Bach was most renowned for writing—and improvising—fugues for a solo keyboard instrument.

The subject of the fugue is stated alone at the beginning in one of the voices—referred to by the range in which it sounds: soprano, alto, tenor, or bass. It is then imitated in another voice—this is the **answer**—while the first can continue with a **countersubject** (a different theme heard against the subject) or new material. When the subject has been presented in each voice once, the first section of the fugue, the **exposition**, is at an end. From then on, the fugue alternates between sections that feature entrances of the subject and **episodes**—interludes (lacking the subject) that serve as areas of relaxation.

Subject and answer

Countersubject

Exposition
Episodes

In **Josef Albers's** (1888–1976) *Fugue* (1925), the interlocking and parallel lines resemble the polyphonic textures of the fugue.

Contrapuntal Devices

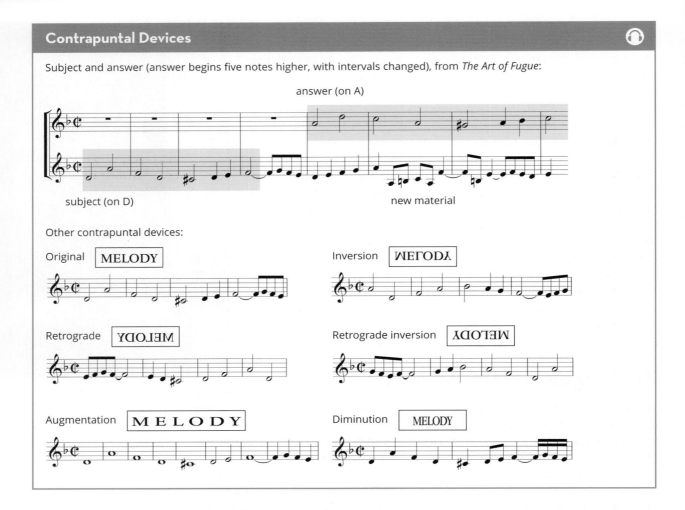

Subject and answer (answer begins five notes higher, with intervals changed), from *The Art of Fugue*:

answer (on A)

subject (on D)

new material

Other contrapuntal devices:

Original   MELODY

Inversion

Retrograde

Retrograde inversion

Augmentation   MELODY

Diminution   MELODY

Contrapuntal devices   Contrapuntal writing is marked by a number of devices used since the earliest days of polyphony. A subject can be presented in longer time values, often twice as slow as the original, called **augmentation** (see box above), or in shorter time values that go by faster, called **diminution**. The pitches can be stated backward (starting from the last note and preceding to the first), known as **retrograde**, or turned upside down (in mirror image), moving by the same intervals but in the opposite direction, a technique called **inversion**. Overlapping statements of the subject, called **stretto**, heighten the tension.

Bach's Keyboard Fugues

Bach worked his entire life to refine his fugal technique, combining mastery of craft with creativity and beauty. Although every fugue follows the same principle, with an exposition that presents the subject in at least two (and usually three or more) voices, and then an alternation between returns of the subject and contrasting musical ideas, no two fugues are alike in detail. Indeed, the process of combining predictable material with fresh ideas is at the core of musical composition, and *The Well-Tempered Clavier*   Bach was a master. *The Well-Tempered Clavier*, a collection of forty-eight preludes and fugues issued in two volumes and demonstrating a new system for tuning keyboard instruments that approaches our contemporary equal-semitone norm, is a testament to his skill. Bach intended the collection as a teaching aid, with each individual prelude and fugue demonstrating a different set of expressive and technical challenges for the aspiring keyboard player.

Contrapunctus I, from *The Art of Fugue*

Bach's last demonstration of contrapuntal mastery was *The Art of Fugue*, a collection of fourteen fugues and four canons that systematically explores all the wizardry of fugal devices. Because it is unclear for which instrument(s) Bach intended this work, it has been recorded by orchestras, chamber ensembles, and even brass groups—among them the well-known Canadian Brass. The collection is viewed today as keyboard music, probably meant for organ or harpsichord.

This two-manual harpsichord was built by the Flemish maker **Jan Couchet** (c. 1650).

We will consider the opening fugue, called Contrapunctus I. Its four voices introduce the subject successively, in the order alto-soprano-bass-tenor; this constitutes the exposition. (See chart below and LG 17.) After the first episode, a contrasting set of musical ideas, the extended middle section features several false entries and an overlapping of subjects (in stretto). At the end, the tonic (D minor) is reestablished by a bold statement of the answer in the bass, heard on the organ pedals. The final chord, a major triad, jolts us from the contemplative minor-key setting; this practice of shifting from minor to major at the end was a common feature in Baroque keyboard music.

Bach increases the complexity of the counterpoint with each fugue in this collection, as if he were challenging his performer to ever greater dexterity and mental engagement. Since all of his keyboard music was designed to teach prospective students to refine their technique, this "capstone" work can be understood as the ultimate achievement for both fingers and brain. Bach would have expected his advanced students to go on to improvise these kinds of processes on their own, as they demonstrated their professional independence.

Comparing styles 3: Baroque to Classsical

CRITICAL THINKING

1. What are some of the contrasting ways a subject can be modified in a fugue while still being recognizable to the listener?

2. How does Bach indicate to the listener that he is about to conclude his "process of elaboration" in Contrapunctus I?

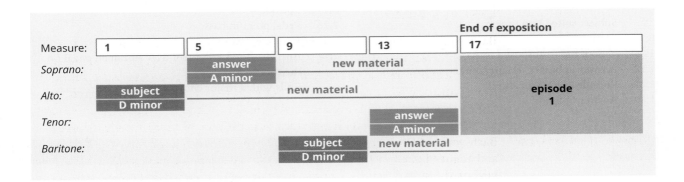

					End of exposition	
Measure:	1	5	9	13	17	
Soprano:		answer / A minor		new material		episode 1
Alto:	subject / D minor		new material			
Tenor:				answer / A minor		
Baritone:			subject / D minor	new material		

YOUR TURN TO EXPLORE

Seek out a recording (or better yet, a live performance) of an improvisation-oriented musician such as a rock guitarist or a jazz pianist. Listen for how the melody/harmony of each "standard tune" is first presented relatively straightforwardly, and then varied through several repetitions. How does the performer weave aspects of a recognizable melody through the texture as he/she improvises? Are there particular portions of the melody that are featured more prominently, and if so, why do you think this is?

LISTENING GUIDE 17 3:12

Bach: Contrapunctus 1, from *The Art of Fugue*

DATE: 1749, published 1751

GENRE: Fugue (from a collection of canons and fugues on a single theme)

What to Listen For

Melody	Tune (the subject) outlines a minor chord.	**Form**	Four-voice fugue, with exposition, middle, and closing sections; episodes separate fugue statements.
Harmony	Minor throughout, but closes on a major chord; last fugue statement is over a sustained pitch.	**Performing forces**	Solo keyboard (organ or harpsichord).
Texture	Imitative entries of same melody: subject (on D) alternates with answer (on A).		

EXPOSITION (see chart on p. 145)

Four entries of the subject (answer) in alternation:

0:00	Alto (subject).
0:10	Soprano (answer).
0:19	Bass (subject).
0:28	Tenor (answer).
0:38	Episode 1 (six measures) ends the exposition.

MIDDLE ENTRIES

Subject stated two times:

0:52	Alto.
1:05	Soprano (transposed to A).
1:12	Answer in bass (overlaps soprano in stretto).
1:21	Episode 2 (four measures).
1:30	Answer in tenor.

1:40	Episode 3 (five measures).
1:52	Answer anticipated in alto, then full statement in soprano.

CLOSING SECTION

2:10	Subject in bass (but anticipated in soprano).
2:19	Episode 4.
2:26	Pedal point in bass.
2:44	Rhetorical pauses.
2:52	Answer—final statement over sustained pedal on the tonic.
	Ends with a major chord.

A Comparison of
Baroque and Classical Styles

	Baroque (c. 1600–1750)	Classical (c. 1750–1825)
Composers	Monteverdi, Cozzolani, Purcell, Vivaldi, Bach, Handel, Billings.	Haydn, Mozart, Beethoven.
Melody	Continuous melody with wide leaps, chromatic tones for emotional effect; speechlike melody in recitative.	Symmetrical melody in balanced phrases and cadences; tuneful, diatonic, with narrow leaps.
Rhythm	Single rhythm predominant; steady, energetic pulse; freer in vocal music.	Dance rhythms favored; regularly recurring accents.
Harmony	Chromatic harmony for expressive effect; major-minor system established with brief excursions from the tonic to other keys.	Diatonic harmony favored; tonic-dominant relationship expanded, becomes the basis for large-scale form.
Texture	Homophonic texture (early Baroque); polyphonic texture (late Baroque); linear-horizontal dimension.	Homophonic texture; chordal-vertical dimension.
Instrumental genres	Trio sonata, concerto, suite, prelude, fugue	Symphony, concerto, solo sonata, string quartet, other chamber music genres.
Vocal genres	Opera, Mass, Magnificat, oratorio, cantata, anthem.	Opera, Mass, oratorio.
Form	Binary and ternary forms predominant.	Larger forms, including sonata-allegro form, developed.
Dynamics	Subtle dynamic nuances; *forte/piano* contrasts; echo effects.	Continuously changing dynamics through *crescendo* and *decrescendo.*
Timbre	Continuous tone color throughout one movement.	Changing tone colors between sections of works.
Performing forces	String orchestra, with added woodwinds; organ and harpsichord prevalent.	Orchestra standardized into four families; introduction of clarinet, trombone; rise of piano to prominence.
Improvisation	Improvisation expected; harmonies realized from figured bass.	Improvisation largely limited to cadenzas in concertos.
Emotion	Emotional exuberance and theatricality.	Emotional balance and restraint.

CLASSICAL ERA

Events		Composers and Works

Reign of Louis XV begins. **1715**

1700

1725

George Washington born. **1732**

1732–1809 Joseph Haydn (*Emperor* Quartet; Symphony No. 100)

Benjamin Franklin experiments with electricity. **1752**

1750

1756–1791 Wolfgang Amadeus Mozart (*Eine kleine Nachtmusik*; Piano Concerto in G Major; *Don Giovanni*; *Requiem*)

Catherine the Great crowned empress of Russia. **1762**

1770–1827 Ludwig van Beethoven (*Moonlight* Sonata; Symphony No. 5)

First edition of *Encyclopaedia Britannica*. **1771**

1775

American Revolution begins. **1775**

Friedrich von Schiller writes "Ode to Joy." **1785**

French Revolution begins. **1789**

Edward Jenner discovers vaccination for smallpox. **1796**

Napoleon crowned emperor of France. **1804**

1800

Napoleon defeated at Battle of Waterloo. **1815**

1825

Part 4

Eighteenth-Century Classicism

Music as Order and Logic

"Music [is] the favorite passion of my soul."
—*Thomas Jefferson (1743-1826)*

Some artistic movements can easily be pinpointed in time, those whose leaders make strong statements about the need for radical change. Classicism is not such a movement: in fact, in some ways classicism is a constant concern in Western culture, since its roots are in the values of order and reason expressed by the ancient Greeks and Romans, who laid the foundations for the very notion of European identity. Ideals of classicism have repeatedly resurfaced through the centuries, and in some cases have coexisted with other stylistic concerns. For example, French artists and musicians in the early 1700s never thought of their work as "baroque": they were the ones who introduced the term to disparage others who didn't share their "classical" sensibility.

The Enlightenment

The later 1700s were a time when classical ideals were especially strong in Europe, combined with a philosophical and intellectual movement known as the **Enlightenment**, which stressed the centrality of reason in human experience. Artists and musicians strove to join the social push toward order and reason, developing works characterized by clarity and regularity of structure, and by an ideal of "natural simplicity." This tendency led to the development of an international musical style that was held up by subsequent generations as timeless, embodying the most perfect manifestations of musical logic. While previous styles had risen and fallen with fashion, the music of the Classical style was preserved and treasured even as later styles developed in contrast to its ideals—and this music continues to form the core of the Western concert tradition to this day.

The Parthenon, Athens (447–432 BCE). The architecture of ancient Greece embodied the ideals of order and harmonious proportions.

Classicism and Enlightenment Culture

The Classical era in music encompasses the last half of the eighteenth century and the early decades of the nineteenth (c. 1750–1825). During this era, the rule of strong aristocratic sovereigns continued throughout Europe. Louis XV presided over extravagant celebrations in Versailles, and Frederick the Great ruled in Prussia, Maria Theresa in Austria, and Catherine the Great in Russia. In such societies, the ruling class enjoyed its power through hereditary right. At the same time, a new economic power was growing through the Industrial Revolution, which gathered momentum in the mid-eighteenth century through a series of important inventions—from James Watt's improved steam engine and James Hargreaves's spinning jenny in the 1760s to Eli Whitney's cotton gin in the 1790s. These decades saw significant advances in science—Benjamin Franklin harnessed electricity, Joseph Priestley discovered oxygen, and Edward Jenner perfected vaccination—and intellectual life, with the publication of the French *Encyclopédie* and the first edition of the *Encyclopaedia Britannica*. (See Interface, p. 152.)

The eighteenth century has been called the Age of Reason as well as the Enlightenment. Philosophers considered social and political issues in the light of reason and science, but they were also advocates for the rising middle class. The intellectual climate, then, was nourished by two opposing streams. While Classical art captured the exquisite refinement of a way of life that was drawing to a close, it also caught the first wave of a new social structure that would emerge with the revolutionary upheavals at the end of the century.

Just as eighteenth-century thinkers idealized the civilization of the Greeks and Romans, artists revered the unity and proportions of ancient architecture and fine arts. In this spirit, Thomas Jefferson patterned the nation's Capitol, the University of Virginia (see illustration above), and his home at Monticello after Greek and Roman temples. His example spurred on a classical revival in the United States, which made Ionic, Doric, and Corinthian columns indispensable features of public buildings well into the twentieth century.

By the 1760s, though, a Romantic point of view was emerging in literature. The French philosopher Jean-Jacques Rousseau, sometimes called the "father of Romanticism," produced some of his most significant writings in these years. One celebrated declaration, "Man is born free, and everywhere he is in chains," epitomizes the temper of the time. The first manifestation of the Romantic spirit in Germany was a literary movement known as *Sturm und Drang* (storm and stress). Two characteristic works appeared in the 1770s by the era's most significant young writers: *The Sorrows of Young Werther,* a novel by Johann Wolfgang von Goethe, and *The Robbers,* a play by Friedrich von Schiller. The famous poem "Ode to Joy," set by Beethoven in his Ninth Symphony, was Schiller's proclamation of universal brotherhood; and Goethe would become the favorite lyric poet of the Romantic composers.

By the end of the century, the old world of the aristocracy was beginning to give way to a new society of the people and to an era that produced some of the greatest artworks of Western culture. Thus, backward-looking classicism itself contained the seeds of what would become the most significant and self-conscious progressive redefinition of European culture.

Classicism in Music

The Classical period in music is characterized best by the masters of the so-called Viennese School—Haydn, Mozart, Beethoven, and their successor Franz Schubert. These composers worked in an age of great musical experimentation and discovery, when musicians took on new challenges: first, to explore thoroughly the possibilities offered by the major-minor

Thomas Jefferson's design for the Rotunda of the University of Virginia at Charlottesville, completed in 1826, reflects his admiration for classical architecture.

Romanticism in literature

Edited by Denis Diderot and with contributions from many specialists, the great French *Encyclopédie* (1751–72) sought to bring together knowledge from all over the world.

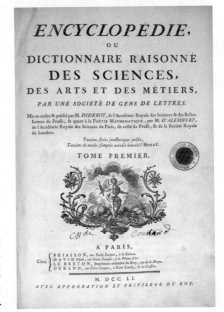

Interface

Science, Philosophy, and Music in the Age of Enlightenment

In a major intellectual and cultural shift, the eighteenth century looked toward the advancement of knowledge through reason and science. Among those who spearheaded change were the philosopher Voltaire and the physicist who developed the laws of gravity, Isaac Newton. These thinkers embraced a new philosophy that sought to understand all things according to nature and mathematics rather than religion. Scholars arduously collected information to increase the overall body of knowledge, and society in general embraced a focus on learning. One result was the great French *Encyclopédie*, a thirty-five-volume reference source purporting to systematize all knowledge, written by the leading intellectuals of the day, including Voltaire and Jean-Jacques Rousseau. Musicians took part in this effort to amass learning: Rousseau (also a composer) published a comprehensive dictionary of musical terms; Jean-Philippe Rameau wrote an important music theory treatise; and in 1776, the Englishman Charles Burney penned the first music history text (the ancestor of your textbook), which sought to record all knowledge about musicians and their works.

Some of the most celebrated technological achievements were connected to music: for example, "music boxes" with rotating cylinders and other mechanical means of plucking strings or striking metal plates when wound up. (Many of these musical machines were created by clock makers, who were making tremendous technological strides in miniaturizing time-keeping devices in the 1700s.) Some musical machines, known as automata, were made to resemble humans: a life-size human flute player played twelve separate melodies, and there's a famous automaton, now in the museum of Art and History in Neuchâtel, Switzerland, of a woman playing an organ, pressing the keys of the instrument with her fingers. While the "robotic" performer's bodily movements may seem less convincing to us in an age of sophisticated CGI animation, they were certainly among the most humanlike mechanical actions that had ever been seen at the time, and they demonstrated the power of human ingenuity.

Across the Atlantic, the statesman and scientist Benjamin Franklin was central to the American Enlightenment through his scientific experi-

A glass armonica from Boston, c. 1830.

ments with electricity and his diverse inventions, including the lightning rod, bifocal glasses, the Franklin stove, and the glass armonica—a musical instrument made of tuned water glasses, for which both Mozart and Beethoven composed works. Franklin was a musician himself (he played harp and guitar), and he wrote a treatise on musical aesthetics, in which he espoused a philosophy of simplicity in melody and harmony.

We can easily relate the Enlightenment's goals of reasoned thought and simplicity to the music we are studying from this period. Both the individual musical elements—melody, rhythm, and harmony—and the overall structures are designed to embody a clarity, balance, and logic new to composition. This was truly intended as a "universally understandable" language of sound, and it is partly because of this quasi-scientific clarity that many still point to the music of the Classical era as the most straightforward pathway into understanding the musical logic of the European tradition.

An automaton of a mandolin player, built by P. Gaultier (eighteenth century).

system; and second, to perfect a large-scale form of instrumental music—known as sonata form—that exploited those possibilities to the fullest degree. Having found this ideal structure, composers then developed it into the solo and duo sonata, the trio and quartet (especially the string quartet), the concerto, and the symphony.

"Classicism" did not imply a strict adherence to traditional forms; as we will see, the composers of the Viennese School experimented boldly and ceaselessly with the materials at their disposal. And it should not surprise us to find that Romantic elements appear as well in the music of Haydn, Mozart, and Beethoven, especially in their late works. These composers dealt with musical challenges so brilliantly that their works have remained unsurpassed models for all who followed.

Elements of Classical Style

The music of the Viennese masters is notable for its elegant, lyrical melodies. Classical melodies "sing," even those intended for instruments. They are usually based on symmetrical four-bar phrases marked by clear-cut cadences, and they often move stepwise or by small leaps within a narrow range. Clarity is further provided by repetition and the frequent use of sequence (a pattern repeated at a higher or lower pitch). These devices make for balanced structures that are readily accessible to the listener.

The harmonies that sustain the melodies are equally clear. Chords are built from the seven tones of the major or minor scale (meaning they are diatonic) and therefore are firmly rooted in the key. The chords underline the balanced symmetry of phrases and cadences, and they form vertical columns of sound over which the melody unfolds freely, generally in a homophonic texture (a melody with accompanying harmony).

Much of the music is in one of the four basic meters—2/4, 3/4, 4/4, or 6/8—and moves at a steady tempo. If a piece or movement begins in a certain meter, it is apt to stay there until the end. Rhythm works closely with melody and harmony to make clear the symmetrical phrase-and-cadence structure of the piece. Well-defined sections establish the home (tonic) key, move to contrasting but closely related keys, and return to the home key. The result is the beautifully molded architectural forms of the Classical style, fulfilling the listener's need for both unity and variety.

Despite its aristocratic elegance, music of the Classical era absorbed a variety of folk and popular elements. This influence made itself felt not only in the German dances, minuets, and waltzes of the Viennese masters but also in their songs, symphonies, concertos, string quartets, and sonatas.

The Patronage System

The culture of the eighteenth century thrived under the **patronage**, or sponsorship, of an aristocracy that viewed the arts as a necessary adornment of life. Music was part of the elaborate lifestyle of the nobility, and the center of musical life was the palace.

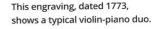

The minuet was one of the most popular dances in the eighteenth century. *The Minuet under an Oak Tree* (1787), by **François Louis Joseph Watteau** (1758–1823).

This engraving, dated 1773, shows a typical violin-piano duo.

The social events at court created a steady demand for new works from composers, who had to supply whatever their patrons wanted. Although musicians ranked little better than servants, their situation was not quite as depressing as it sounds. The patronage system actually gave musicians economic security and provided a social framework within which they could function. It offered important advantages to those who successfully adjusted to its requirements, as the career of Joseph Haydn clearly shows (see p. 159).

Opportunities for Women

While aristocratic women like Marie Antoinette, archduchess of Austria and wife of French king Louis XVI, continued their regular music studies, middle-class women also found a place as musicians under the patronage system. In Italy and France, professional female singers achieved prominence in opera and in court ballets. Others found a place within aristocratic circles as court instrumentalists and music teachers, offering private lessons to members of the nobility.

Maria Anna Mozart

Two women in particular, both associated with Wolfgang Amadeus Mozart, stand out as impressive keyboard players of the late eighteenth century. His sister, Maria Anna Mozart (1751–1829), known as Nannerl, was an accomplished pianist who as a child toured widely with Wolfgang, performing concertos and four-hand piano works. Their father noted that Nannerl, at age twelve, played "so beautifully that everyone is talking about her and admiring her execution." A friend of

Maria Theresia von Paradis

Mozart's, the blind composer Maria Theresia von Paradis (1759–1824), was an excellent pianist and organist, renowned for her remarkable musical memory, which retained some sixty different concertos that she prepared for an extended European tour.

The public prominence achieved by these women was unusual for the era. However, the many engravings and paintings of the time illustrating music-mak-

Map of Europe, 1763–89, showing major musical centers.

ing scenes make it clear that women participated frequently in performances at home, in aristocratic salons, and at court. Ultimately, with the growth of the music trades, especially music printing and publishing, women found more professional opportunities open to them. And as more amateurs participated in music-making, women of the middle as well as upper classes found an outlet for their talents.

From Palace to Concert Hall

At this time, musical performances were beginning to move from the palace to the concert hall. The rise of the public concert gave composers a new venue (site) in which to perform their works. Haydn and Beethoven conducted their own symphonies at concerts, and Mozart and Beethoven played their own piano concertos. The public flocked to hear the latest works—unlike modern (classical music) concertgoers who are interested mainly in music of the past. The eagerness of eighteenth-century audiences for new music surely stimulated composers to greater productivity.

An aristocratic concert. Oil and wood panel, attributed to **Jean-Honoré Fragonard** (1732–1806).

While great virtuoso performers continued to be highly prized, the clarity and simplicity of the Classical style made it increasingly accessible to the informed amateur—whether through performance or through careful listening. More and more instrumental music was described in terms of dialogue and communication—whether between performers or between the composer and the public. As the idea of communication through instrumental storytelling became ingrained, the notion of using that communication to build a deep and intimate connection between the uniquely inspired composer-genius and the receptive listener grew more appealing to musicians and their audiences. This too was an essential element in the emerging Romantic sensibility, as we will see in the work of Beethoven and in the public response to Mozart's late compositions.

CRITICAL THINKING

1. What were the primary characteristics of Classicism?

2. How are Classical ideals reflected in eighteenth-century music?

Chapter 28

Musical Conversations: Haydn and Classical Chamber Music

"You listen to four sensible persons conversing, you profit from their discourse, and you get to know their several instruments."

—Johann Wolfgang von Goethe (writing about string quartets)

KEY POINTS

- Form is the most important organizing element in **absolute music**, which has no specific pictorial or literary program.
- Melodic ideas, or **themes**, are used as building blocks in a composition; these themes are made up of short melodic or rhythmic fragments known as **motives**.
- Themes can be expanded by varying the melody, rhythm, or harmony through **thematic development**; this usually happens in large-scale works.
- The Classical era is the golden age of **chamber music** (ensemble music for two to about ten performers, with one player per part). The **string quartet** (two violins, viola, and cello) was the most important chamber-music genre of the era.
- Joseph Haydn's *Emperor* Quartet features a famous set of variations on a hymn he wrote for the Austrian emperor.

You get together with some friends and begin a conversation on a topic of common interest. Members of your group will agree or disagree with each other, expand on others' perspectives, interrupt each other as things get more heated, all while keeping a friendly spirit going, with the goal of reaching a satisfactory conclusion. This is how eighteenth-century Europeans understood chamber music, and in particular the string quartet: the equal participation of various instruments was an essential aspect of a new sensibility. These were conversations without words, but they were just as purposeful, and just as structured, as real conversations might be. The way composers achieved this was through an emphasis on predictable musical forms, which would allow musicians and listeners alike to "follow the discussion" to its logical conclusion, and to profit, as Goethe's quote above suggests, from its artistic expression.

Expanding Musical Ideas

As noted in Chapter 6, a musical idea that is used as a building block in the construction of a composition is called a **theme**. Varying a theme's melodic outline,

A modern-day photograph of the Eszterháza Palace in Fertöd, Hungary, where Haydn was employed.

rhythm, or harmony is considered **thematic development**. This is one of the most important techniques in composition and requires both imagination and craft on the part of the creator. In addition to its capacity for growth, a theme can be fragmented by dividing it into its constituent motives, a **motive** being its smallest melodic or rhythmic unit. A motive can grow into an expansive melody, or it can be treated in **sequence**—that is, repeated at a higher or lower level. Thematic development is generally too complex for short pieces, where repetition, a simple contrast between sections, and a modest expansion of material usually supply the necessary continuity. But thematic development is necessary in larger forms, where it provides clarity, coherence, and logic.

Motive and sequence

The development of thematic material—through extension, contraction, and repetition—occurs in music from all corners of the world (see Encounter, p. 172). In considering the fugue by Bach, we have already seen that musical structure and logic can unfold through a partly planned, partly improvised process. Other traditions reflect this approach: in jazz, for example, musicians organize their improvised melodies within a highly structured, preestablished harmonic pattern, time frame, and melodic outline that is understood by all the performers.

The most prominent musicians of the Classical era were also excellent improvisers—both Mozart and Beethoven, for example, drew crowds when they improvised at the keyboard. However, the forms of the Classical style are composed-out and fixed: they indicate a fully worked-out rational argument, rather than a flexible process-in-motion like the one we encountered in Bach's fugue. Because this music is so dependent on the listener's expectation of recognizable structures, it's crucial for us to understand the conventions on which composers and listeners based musical meaning.

Thematic development

Classical Forms

Every musical work has a form; it is sometimes simple, other times complex. In **absolute music**, where there is no prescribed story or text to hold the music together, form is especially important. The story is the music itself, so its shape is of primary concern for the composer, the performer, and the listener. Most instrumental works of the Classical era—symphonies, sonatas, concertos, string quartets, and other types of chamber music—follow a sequence of sections or movements that is known as a **multimovement cycle**. We will briefly consider the overall characteristics of that cycle, and then dwell in turn (in this and the following chapters) on the formal conventions of each movement.

Absolute music

Multimovement cycle

Multimovement Cycle: General Scheme

Movement	Character/Tempo	Form	Playlist
First	Long, dramatic Allegro	Sonata-allegro	Mozart, *Eine kleine Nachtmusik*, I Beethoven, Symphony No. 5, I
Second	Slow, lyrical Andante or Adagio	Theme and variations or **A-B-A**	Haydn, *Emperor* Quartet, II Symphony No. 100 (*Military*), II
Third (optional)	Dancelike Allegro or Allegretto	Minuet and trio (18th c.) Scherzo and trio (19th c.)	Mozart, *Eine kleine Nachtmusik*, III Beethoven, Symphony No. 5, III
Fourth (last)	Lively, spirited Allegro or Vivace	Sonata-allegro (or rondo or sonata-rondo)	Beethoven, Symphony No. 5, IV

The outline of the multimovement cycle above sums up the common practice of both the Classical and Romantic eras. It can help you build expectations and listening strategies, provided you remember that it is no more than a general scheme.

Each individual movement has an internal form that binds its different sections into one artistic whole. You have already learned two of the simplest forms: two-part, or binary (**A-B**), and three-part, or ternary (**A-B-A**). Rather than start with the customary form of the first movement of the cycle (sonata-allegro form), which is more intricate and will be the subject of a later chapter, we will begin with a less complex form, as exemplified by the second movement of a string quartet by Haydn.

The Second Movement: Theme and Variations

The second is usually the slow movement of the cycle, offering a contrast to the first movement—usually a spirited Allegro—and characterized by lyrical, songful melodies. Typically, it is an Andante or Adagio in **A-B-A** or theme-and-variations form.

We have already noted that variation is an important procedure in music, but in one form—**theme and variations**—it is the ruling principle. Here, the theme is clearly stated at the outset and serves as the point of departure; it may be newly invented or borrowed (like the theme in Britten's *Young Person's Guide to the Orchestra*; see LG 1). The theme is likely to be

This anonymous watercolor depicts a performance of a string quartet, the most influential chamber-music genre of the era.

a small two- or three-part idea, simple in character to allow room for elaboration. It is followed by a series of variations in which certain features of the original idea are retained while others are altered. Each variation sets forth the idea with some new modification—you might say in a new disguise—through which the listener glimpses something of the original theme.

Any musical element may be developed in the variation process. The melody may be varied by adding or omitting notes or by shifting the theme to another key—a favorite procedure in jazz, where the solo player embellishes a popular tune with a series of decorative flourishes. The chords that accompany a melody may be replaced by others; the shape of the accompaniment may be changed;

note lengths, meter, or tempo can also be altered through rhythmic variation, and the texture may be enriched by interweaving the melody with new themes or countermelodies.

Chamber music, as we have seen, is music for a small ensemble—two to about ten players—with one player to a part. In this intimate genre, each instrument is expected to assert itself fully, but function as part of a team rather than as a soloist. The central position in Classical chamber music was held by the **string quartet**, which consists of two violins (a first and a second), a viola, and a cello. Other favored combinations were the duo sonata (violin and piano, or cello and piano; see illustration, p. 153); the piano trio (violin, cello, and piano); and the quintet, usually a combination of string or wind instruments, or a string quartet with solo instrument such as the piano or clarinet. (See chart in Chapter 11.) Because the string quartet was intended to be enjoyed by a small group of cultivated music lovers, composers did not need expansive gestures here. They could present their most private thoughts, and indeed, the final string quartets of Haydn, Mozart, and Beethoven contain some of their most profound music. Joseph Haydn, with his sixty-eight string quartets, played a central role in the evolution of this genre.

In His Own Words

> I learned from Haydn how to write quartets. No one else can do everything—be flirtatious and be unsettling, move to laughter and move to tears—as well as Joseph Haydn."
>
> —*Wolfgang Amadeus Mozart*

Haydn's *Emperor* Quartet

Haydn wrote most of his string quartets in sets of six, and his Op. 76 quartets are no exception. The third in the set is known as the *Emperor* because the second movement is based on a hymn Haydn wrote for the Austrian emperor Franz II. The invasion of Vienna by Napoleonic armies in 1796 raised a spirit of patriotism across Austria, to which Haydn responded with a musical tribute that became the country's national anthem, *Gott erhalte Franz den Kaiser* (*God Keep the Emperor Franz*). The hymn was sung in all the theaters of Vienna for the emperor's birthday on

Joseph Haydn (1732–1809)

Haydn was one of the most prolific composers of the Classical period. Born in the small Austrian village of Rohrau, he absorbed the folk songs and dances of his homeland. The beauty of his voice secured him a place as a choirboy at St. Stephen's Cathedral in Vienna.

In 1761, when he was twenty-nine, Haydn entered the service of the Esterházys, a family of enormously wealthy Hungarian princes famous for their patronage of the arts, with whom he remained for almost thirty years. The family palace of Eszterháza was one of the most splendid in Europe (see illustration, p. 157), and music played a central role in the constant round of festivities there. The musical establishment under Haydn's direction included an orchestra, an opera company, a marionette theater, and a chapel. His life exemplifies the patronage system at its best.

By the time Haydn reached middle age, his music had brought him much fame. After his prince's death, he made two visits to England in the 1790s, where he conducted his works with phenomenal success. He died in 1809, revered throughout Europe.

It was Haydn's historic role to help perfect the new instrumental music of the late eighteenth century, as well as expand the orchestra's size and resources through greater emphasis on the brass, clarinets (new to the orchestra), and percussion. His expressive harmony, structural logic, and endlessly varied moods embodied the mature Classical style.

MAJOR WORKS: Chamber music, including 68 string quartets (*Emperor*, Op. 76, No. 3) • Over 100 symphonies (including the 12 *London* symphonies, Nos. 93–104) • Concertos for violin, cello, harpsichord, and trumpet • Sacred vocal music (Masses, motets, and two oratorios, including *The Creation*) • 14 operas • Keyboard music (including 40 sonatas).

 Emperor Quartet, Op. 76, No. 3, II; Symphony No. 94 (*Surprise*), II; Symphony No. 100 (*Military*), II

LISTENING GUIDE 18

Haydn: String Quartet, Op. 76, No. 3 (*Emperor*), II

DATE: 1797

MOVEMENTS: I. Allegro; sonata-allegro form
II. Poco adagio, cantabile; theme and variations
III. Menuetto, Allegro; minuet and trio
IV. Finale, Presto; sonata-allegro form

What to Listen For

Melody	Lyrical melody in five phrases of four measures each, several of which are repeated: **a-a-b-c-c**.	**Form**	Theme (**a-a-b-c-c**) and four variations, each in the same structure; closing four-measure coda.
Rhythm/ meter	Simple rhythms in quadruple meter; some syncopation in later variations.	**Expression**	Tempo is rather slow, in a singing style; subtle and contrasting dynamics.
Harmony	In G major, some chromaticism in variation 3.	**Performing forces**	Two violins, viola, and cello.
Texture	Homophonic opening; becomes more polyphonic.		

Structure of the theme:

Phrase **a** (repeated):

Phrase **b**:

Phrase **c** (repeated):

0:00 **Theme:** played by violin 1, with a simple chordal accompaniment.

1:19 **Variation 1:** theme played by violin 2 in a duet with high-range decorative figurations in violin 1.

2:28 **Variation 2:** theme played by the cello, accompanied by other instruments; grows more polyphonic.

3:46 **Variation 3:** theme played by the viola; syncopated accompaniment in violin 1; some chromaticism.

5:04 **Variation 4:** theme returns to violin 1, set in a polyphonic texture.

6:18 **Coda:** short closing with sustained cello note, over which the other instruments fade out softly.

February 12, 1797; thanks to Haydn, Austria now had a moving anthem comparable to those of England (*God Save the King*) and France (*La Marseillaise*).

Haydn wrote his Op. 76, No. 3, quartet a few months later, in the summer of 1797, using the imperial hymn as a basis for a majestic theme and variations in the slow movement (LG 18). Haydn gives each player an equal chance to participate in the "conversation" about the hymn tune. After the tune is introduced by the first violin in a simple setting, each instrument takes its turn with the theme: the second violin, with an embroidered accompanying line played by its violin partner; the cello, with its deep and dignified tone; then the dark viola—Haydn's own instrument—with rich chromatic color. The fourth and final variation brings back the melody in a more complex polyphonic texture. This lyrical tune, thought to be based on a Croatian folk song, was a favorite of Haydn's and reportedly the last music played before his death.

As you listen to the variations that Haydn builds on the hymn to the emperor, think about the kinds of expectations that he would like you, as the listener, to have about this conversation—which is not only an interaction between four string-instrument-playing friends but also an interaction between Haydn and you.

Austrian emperor Franz II, for whom Haydn wrote a birthday hymn. Anonymous, early nineteenth century.

CRITICAL THINKING

1. What are some ways composers unify their compositions?

2. How can musical elements be modified to achieve variation? How is this different from using *new* musical elements to create contrast?

YOUR TURN TO EXPLORE

Look for videos of performers from different chamber-music traditions—from the Classical era, but also jazz, country, rock, hip-hop, and maybe Indian or Chinese classical/traditional repertories. In what way do these performers appear to be "performing friendship" through their music-making? What differences are there in the interactions or conversations between performers and between performers and audience, in these various traditions?

Chapter 29

The Ultimate Instrument: Haydn and the Symphony

"My Prince was always satisfied with my works. I not only had the encouragement of constant approval but as conductor of an orchestra I could make experiments, observe what produced an effect and what weakened it, and . . . improve, alter, make additions or omissions, and be as bold as I pleased."

—Joseph Haydn

KEY POINTS

- The **symphony**, a genre designed to demonstrate the expressive capabilities of a full orchestra, arose as one of the principal instrumental traditions during the Classical era.

- The heart of the Classical orchestra (about thirty to forty players) was the strings, assisted by woodwinds, brass, and percussion.

- Joseph Haydn wrote over 100 symphonies; among these, his last 12—the so-called *London* Symphonies—are his masterpieces in the genre.

In His Own Words

❝ A symphony must be like the world; it must embrace everything."
—*Gustav Mahler (1860–1911)*

The palette of tone colors available to a symphony composer is remarkable. Even the most complex synthesizers cannot match the nuance of live instruments, especially when they are combined by the dozens into a carefully coordinated unit—the orchestra. It was during the Classical era that the notion of the orchestra as the "ultimate instrument" began to develop, and composers sought to realize their greatest expressive potential through this medium, which remains to this day (even as it has changed over the centuries) probably the most versatile and powerful musical resource of the Western tradition. While you can hear orchestral sounds (often electronically manipulated) in television and film, experiencing a symphony orchestra in person is so much more compelling than hearing it on a recording. Witnessing the sonic and physical coordination and interaction between dozens of musicians is something you owe to yourself, now that you have learned (through LG 1 in Chapter 11) how to distinguish between instrumental timbres in an orchestra.

Early History of the Symphony

Overture

The **symphony**, which held the central place in Classical instrumental music, had its roots in the Italian opera **overture** of the early eighteenth century, an orchestral piece in three sections: fast-slow-fast. First played to introduce an opera, these three sections eventually became separate movements, to which the early German symphonists added a number of innovations. One was the use of a quick, aggressively rhythmic theme rising from low to high register with such speed that it became known as a "rocket theme." Equally important was the use of drawn-out *crescendos* (sometimes referred to as a steamroller effect), slowly gathering force as they built to a climax. Finally, composers added a dance movement, an elegant minuet.

The Classical Orchestra

The Classical masters established the orchestra as we know it today: an ensemble of the four instrumental families. The heart of the orchestra was the string family. Woodwinds provided varying colors and assisted the strings, often doubling them. The brass sustained the harmonies and contributed body to the sound, while the timpani supplied rhythmic life and vitality. The eighteenth-century orchestra numbered from thirty to forty players; thus, the volume of sound was still more appropriate for the salon than the concert hall. (We will hear a movement from Haydn's Symphony No. 100 on eighteenth-century period instruments.)

Classical composers created a dynamic style of orchestral writing in which all the instruments participated actively and each timbre could be heard. The interchange of themes between the various instrumental groups assumed the excitement of a witty conversation; in this, the Classical symphony also resembled the string quartet.

In His Own Words

66 Can you see the notes behave like waves? Up and down they go! Look, you can also see the mountains. You have to amuse yourself sometimes after being serious so long."

—Joseph Haydn

Haydn's Symphony No. 100 (*Military*)

Joseph Haydn contributed well over 100 symphonies to the genre, establishing the four-movement structure and earning himself the nickname "father of the symphony." His masterworks in the genre are his last set of 12, the so-called

Natural horns (without valves) and woodwinds are seen in this painting of a small orchestra performing in an eighteenth-century Venetian palace.

LISTENING GUIDE 19   🎧 5:33

Haydn: Symphony No. 100 in G Major (*Military*), II

DATE: 1794

MOVEMENTS: I. Adagio-Allegro; sonata-allegro form, G major
I. Allegretto; A-B-A′ form, C major
III. Moderato; minuet and trio, G major
IV. Presto; sonata-allegro form, G major

Second movement: Allegretto

What to Listen For

Melody	Simple, graceful theme, in regular phrases.	**Form**	Three-part form, with varied return (**A-B-A′**); **A** is in binary form.
Rhythm/ meter	Marchlike, regular duple meter.	**Expression**	Sudden dynamic contrasts.
Harmony	Change from C major to C minor, then back to C major.	**Performing forces**	Large orchestra, including woodwinds, trumpets, French horns, and many percussion instruments.
Texture	Homophonic.		

0:00   **A section**—C major, rounded binary form ‖: a :‖: b a :‖

   a = elegant, arched theme with grace notes; eight measures, with string and flute:

Repeated with oboes, clarinets, and bassoons.

0:29   **b** = eight+ four measures, theme developed from **a,** with strings and flute:

   b + **a** phrases repeated with oboes, clarinets, and bassoons.

1:40   **B section**—C minor, "military" sound, with added percussion (triangle, cymbals, bass drum); begins with loud, C minor statement of **a;** mixes **a** and **b** themes with sudden dynamic changes:

2:45   **A section**—returns to C major, later adds percussion section; varied statements feature different instruments.

4:33   **Coda**—solo trumpet fanfare, followed by drum roll, leads to *fortissimo* chord in A-flat major; motive from theme **a** is repeated until full orchestra closing.

London Symphonies, commissioned for a concert series in London. These late works abound in expressive effects, including syncopation, sudden *crescendos* and accents, dramatic contrasts of soft and loud, daring modulations, and an imaginative plan in which each family of instruments plays its own part.

Haydn's Symphony No. 100, the *Military*, was first presented in 1794 during his second London visit and was received enthusiastically by the British public. Its nickname comes from the composer's use of percussion instruments associated with Turkish military music—namely the triangle, cymbals, bass drum, and bell tree (see p. 75). The work also features a solo trumpet fanfare, another colorful military effect. Haydn, as well as Mozart and Beethoven, knew of these new instruments from the Turkish Janissary bands that performed in Vienna; after many centuries of wars between the Austrian Hapsburg Empire and the powerful Ottoman Empire, cultural exchanges between these political domains allowed Western Europeans the opportunity to hear, and adopt, these exotic sounds.

The Main Hall of the Eszterházy Palace in Hungary, where the music master Haydn spent his summer months along with the court (eighteenth century).

The Second Movement: A-B-A′

Haydn's *Military* Symphony features a memorable second movement (LG 19) that combines the concept of variations with a simple three-part, or ternary, structure that can be diagrammed as **A-B-A′**. The graceful opening theme is heard in various guises that alter the timbre and harmony throughout. We are startled by the sudden change to the minor mode in the middle section, and also struck by the trumpet fanfare and drum roll that introduce the closing coda. The movement ends with a victorious *fortissimo* climax.

As you listen to the contrasting melodies and timbres of this movement, think again about the notion of conversation that we explored in Chapter 28. What can Haydn "tell" you when he has so many more sonic resources at his disposal?

CRITICAL THINKING

1. What contributions did Haydn make to the genre of the symphony?
2. How is this second movement similar to the second movement of the Haydn quartet examined in Chapter 28? How is it different?

YOUR TURN TO EXPLORE

Look for (ideally video) recordings of large instrumental ensembles from several varied traditions—Western orchestras, but also (for example) gamelan ensembles from Indonesia, a Vietnamese Nha Nhac performance, a big-band jazz group. How does the range/variety of timbres differ from ensemble to ensemble? How is each similar to and different from a Western orchestra?

Chapter 30

Expanding the Conversation: Mozart, Chamber Music, and Larger Forms

"People make a mistake who think that my art has come easily to me. Nobody has devoted so much time and thought to composition as I. There is not a famous master whose music I have not studied over and over."

—*Wolfgang Amadeus Mozart*

KEY POINTS

- The first movement of the Classical multimovement cycle is usually in a fast tempo and in **sonata-allegro form**, with three main sections: **exposition**, **development**, and **recapitulation**.

- The third movement is a triple-meter pair of dances, usually a **minuet and trio**.

- Wolfgang Amadeus Mozart, a child prodigy who started to write music before the age of five, contributed to nearly all musical genres of the Classical era, including the symphony, sonata, concerto, chamber music, sacred music, and opera.

- One of Mozart's best-known chamber works is *Eine kleine Nachtmusik (A Little Night Music)*, a serenade for strings.

In His Own Words

" Only when the form grows clear to you will the spirit become so too."

—*Robert Schumann*

All narrative and interactive genres—novels, plays, movies, video games—rely on a structural framework. Those engaging with the narrative learn to understand the conventions of the genre, and the creators engage in a "conversation" with the reader/spectator/player through fulfilling or challenging their expectations. Your enjoyment of such genres hinges on your willingness to learn the structural conventions and understand the subtlety with which the creators are manipulating them. "Sonata-allegro form," which we begin exploring in this chapter, quickly became a favorite resource for instrumental composers, since the musical story it can tell is significantly more dynamic than the one available through simpler forms (like, for example, theme and variations). Comprehending its principles and being able to follow its unfolding are essential for a deeper understanding of all instrumental music from this period onward: the form opens up opportunities for a profound conversation between composers, performers, and listeners. And if the string quartet can be understood as a conversation between four close friends, other genres of chamber music reveal a more wide-ranging discussion among a more diverse cohort; we will examine one such expanded conversation composed by Mozart.

Mozart's *Eine kleine Nachtmusik*

Two popular expanded chamber genres in Mozart's day were the **divertimento** and the **serenade**. Both are lighter genres that were performed in the evening or at social functions. Mozart wrote a large variety of social music of this sort, the most famous of which is *Eine kleine Nachtmusik* (1787), a serenade for strings whose title means literally *A Little Night Music*. The work was most likely written for a string quartet supported by a double bass and was meant for public entertainment, in outdoor performance. The four movements of the version we know (originally there were five) are compact, intimate, and beautifully proportioned.

The First Movement: Sonata-Allegro Form

The most highly organized and often the longest movement in the multimovement cycle is the opening one, which is usually in a fast tempo such as Allegro and is written in **sonata-allegro form** (also known as **sonata form**). This movement establishes a home (tonic) key, then moves, or **modulates**, to another key, and ultimately returns to the home key. We may therefore regard sonata-allegro form as a drama between two contrasting key areas. In most cases, each key area is associated with a theme, which has the potential for development. The themes are stated, or "exposed," in the first section; developed in the second; and restated, or "recapitulated," in the third.

(1) The opening section of sonata-allegro form—the **exposition**, or statement—generally presents the two opposing keys and their respective themes. (In some cases, a theme may consist of several related ideas, in which case we speak of a theme group.) The first theme establishes the home key, or tonic. A **bridge**, or transitional passage, leads to a second theme in a contrasting key; in other words, the function of the bridge is to modulate. After the second theme, a closing section, sometimes with a new closing theme, rounds off the exposition in the contrasting key. In eighteenth-century sonata-allegro form, the exposition is repeated.

(2) Conflict and action, the essence of drama, characterize the **development.** This section may wander through a series of foreign keys, building up tension against the inevitable return home. The frequent modulations contribute to a sense of activity and restlessness. Here, the composer reveals the potential of the themes by varying, expanding, or contracting them, breaking them into their component motives, or combining them with other motives or with new material. When the development has run its course, the tension lets up and a bridge passage leads back to the key of the tonic.

(3) The beginning of the third section, the **recapitulation**, or restatement, is the psychological climax of sonata-allegro form. The return of the first theme in the tonic satisfies the listener's need for unity. The recapitulation restates the first and second themes more or less in their original form, but with one important difference from the exposition: both themes now remain in the tonic, thereby asserting the dominance of the home key. The movement often ends with a **coda**, an extension of the closing idea that leads to the final cadence in the home key.

Leopold Mozart with his two young children, Nannerl and Wolfgang, performing in Paris (1763–64), a watercolor by **Louis de Carmontelle** (1717–1806).

Summary of Sonata-Allegro Form

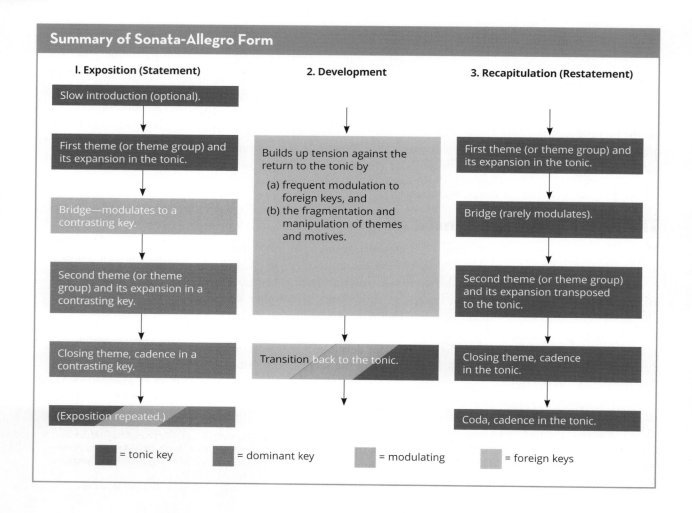

I. Exposition (Statement)	2. Development	3. Recapitulation (Restatement)
Slow introduction (optional).		
First theme (or theme group) and its expansion in the tonic.	Builds up tension against the return to the tonic by	First theme (or theme group) and its expansion in the tonic.
Bridge—modulates to a contrasting key.	(a) frequent modulation to foreign keys, and (b) the fragmentation and manipulation of themes and motives.	Bridge (rarely modulates).
Second theme (or theme group) and its expansion in a contrasting key.		Second theme (or theme group) and its expansion transposed to the tonic.
Closing theme, cadence in a contrasting key.	Transition back to the tonic.	Closing theme, cadence in the tonic.
(Exposition repeated.)		Coda, cadence in the tonic.

■ = tonic key   ■ = dominant key   ■ = modulating   ■ = foreign keys

The features of sonata-allegro form, summed up in the chart above, are present in one shape or another in many movements, yet no two pieces are exactly alike. What might at first appear to be a fixed plan actually provides a supple framework for infinite variety in the hands of the composer.

Let us examine how Mozart deploys sonata-allegro form in the first movement of *Eine kleine Nachtmusik* (LG 20). The movement opens with a strong, marchlike theme that rapidly ascends to its peak (an example of a "rocket theme"), then turns downward at the same rate. Mozart balances this idea with an elegant descending second theme. The closing theme exudes a high energy level, moving the work into its short development; and the recapitulation brings back all the themes, ending with a vigorous coda.

The Third Movement: Minuet-and-Trio Form

In the Classical instrumental cycle, the third movement is almost invariably a **minuet and trio**. The minuet was originally a Baroque court dance whose stately triple (3/4) meter embodied the ideal of an aristocratic age. Since dance music lends itself to symmetrical construction, you often find in a minuet a clear-cut structure based on phrases of four and eight measures. The tempo ranges from stately to lively and whimsical.

Wolfgang Amadeus Mozart (1756–1791)

Mozart was born in Salzburg, Austria, the son of Leopold Mozart, an esteemed court composer-violinist. The most extraordinarily gifted child in the history of music, he started to compose before he was five; by age thirteen, he had written sonatas, concertos, symphonies, religious works, and several operas. The young artist rebelled against the social restrictions imposed by the patronage system, and at twenty-five established himself in Vienna as a struggling freelance musician.

Mozart reached the peak of his career in the late 1780s with his three comic operas (*The Marriage of Figaro, Don Giovanni,* and *Così fan tutte*) on librettos by Lorenzo da Ponte. Although in poor health, he continued to produce masterpieces for the Viennese public, including his Clarinet Concerto (he was one of the first to compose for this new instrument) and his final opera, *The Magic Flute* (1791). With a kind of fevered desperation, he then turned to the *Requiem,* commissioned by a music-loving count, which he left unfinished. He died on December 4, 1791, shortly before his thirty-sixth birthday.

Mozart is revered for the inexhaustible wealth of his elegant and songful melodies. His instrumental music combines a sense of drama with contrasts of mood ranging from lively and playful to solemn and tragic. His symphonic masterpieces are the six written in the final decade of his life, and the last ten string quartets are some of the finest in the literature. One of the outstanding pianists of his time, Mozart also wrote many works for his own instrument. His piano concertos elevated this genre to one of prime importance in the Classical era.

MAJOR WORKS: Chamber music, including 23 string quartets • Divertimentos and serenades (*Eine kleine Nachtmusik,* K. 525) • Keyboard music, including 17 piano sonatas • Sets of variations (*Ah! vous dirai-je Maman*) • Orchestral music, including some 40 symphonies • Concertos, including 27 for piano, 5 for violin, others for solo wind instruments • Comic (*buffa*) operas, including *Le nozze di Figaro* (*The Marriage of Figaro,* 1786) and *Don Giovanni* (1787) • Serious (*seria*) operas, including *Idomeneo* (1791) • German *Singspiel,* including *Die Zauberflöte* (*The Magic Flute,* 1791) • Sacred choral music, including *Requiem* (incomplete, 1791).

 Eine kleine Nachtmusik, I, III; *Ah! vous dirai-je Maman;* Clarinet Concerto, II; *Confutatis,* from *Requiem;* Piano Concerto, K. 467, II; Piano Sonata, K. 331, III; Symphony No. 35, II; Symphony No. 40, III

The movement's name results from the custom of presenting two different dances as a group, the first repeated after the second (resulting in **A-B-A**). The dance in the middle was originally arranged for only three instruments, hence the name "trio," which persisted even after the customary setting for three had long been abandoned. At the end of the trio, you find the words **da capo** ("from the beginning"), signifying that the first section is to be played over again (as it was in the Baroque aria; see Chapter 21).

Each part of the minuet-trio-minuet in turn subdivides into two-part, or binary, form. The second section of the minuet (**b**) or trio (**d**) may bring back the opening theme, making a rounded binary form (see chart below). The composer indicates the repetition of the subsections within repeat signs (| | : : | |). However, when the minuet returns after the trio, it is customarily played straight through, without repeats (**a b**).

Minuet (**A**)	Trio (**B**)	Minuet (**A**)
‖ :a: ‖ :b: ‖	‖ :c: ‖ :d: ‖	a b

The minuet and trio that makes up the third movement of *Eine kleine Nachtmusik* is marked by regular four-bar phrases set in rounded binary form. The

A couple performing a minuet-quadrille, an eighteenth-century court dance.

minuet opens brightly and decisively. The trio, with its polished, soaring melody, presents a lyrical contrast. The opening music then returns, satisfying the Classical desire for balance and symmetry.

While sonata-allegro and minuet-and-trio are different forms, they both rely on predictable principles of statement, contrast, and return that are at the core of the Classical style. Each movement of *Eine kleine Nachtmusik* provides a different perspective in a balanced, rational, yet inventive musical argument—the hallmark of Mozart's artistry.

CRITICAL THINKING

1. How does Mozart's serenade fit the model for multimovement instrumental works in this era?

2. How might musical structures from the Classical era be compared to a play, novel, movie, or video game?

Hearing larger forms

YOUR TURN TO EXPLORE

Find video examples of dancing in contrasting traditions—for example, modern ballroom dance, country or square dancing, ballet, break-dancing or other hip-hop styles, Thai or Indian or Balinese classical dance, Native American ceremonial dance, or a TV dance program. Can you notice patterns of statement, repetition, contrast, and return in the music that accompanies the dance? How is the musical logic of those formal elements reflected in the dancers' movements?

LISTENING GUIDE 20   🎧 📹 7:39

Mozart: *Eine kleine Nachtmusik* (*A Little Night Music*), K. 525, I and III

DATE: 1787

MOVEMENTS: I. Allegro; sonata-allegro form, G major   III. Allegretto; minuet and trio form, G major
       II. Romanza, Andante; sectional rondo form, C major   IV. Allegro; sonata-rondo form, G major

First movement: Allegro   5:30

What to Listen For			
Melody	Marchlike; disjunct, ascending (rocket) theme; then graceful descending tune.	**Form**	Sonata-allegro form in three sections: exposition-development-recapitulation.
Rhythm/meter	Quick duple meter.	**Expression**	Sudden dynamic contrasts.
Harmony	Consonant, in G major (tonic key).	**Performing forces**	String quartet with double bass (or string orchestra).
Texture	Homophonic.		

EXPOSITION

0:00   Theme 1—aggressive, ascending "rocket" theme, symmetrical phrasing, in G major:

Transitional passage, modulating.

0:46   Theme 2—graceful, contrasting theme, less hurried, in the key of the dominant, D major:

0:58   Closing theme—insistent, repetitive, ends in D major.
       Repeat of exposition.

DEVELOPMENT

3:07   Short, begins in D major, manipulates theme 1 and closing theme; modulates, and prepares for recapitulation in G major.

RECAPITULATION

3:40   Theme 1, in G major.
4:22   Theme 2, in G major.
4:34   Closing theme, in G major.
5:05   Coda—extends closing, in G major.

Third movement: Allegretto

2:09

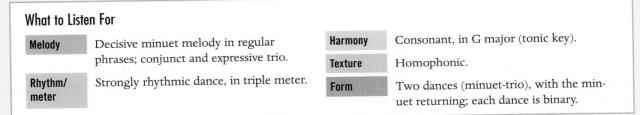

What to Listen For

Melody	Decisive minuet melody in regular phrases; conjunct and expressive trio.
Rhythm/ meter	Strongly rhythmic dance, in triple meter.

Harmony	Consonant, in G major (tonic key).
Texture	Homophonic.
Form	Two dances (minuet-trio), with the minuet returning; each dance is binary.

0:00   Minuet theme—in accented triple meter, decisive character, in two sections (eight measures each), both repeated:

0:44   Trio theme—more lyrical and connected, in two sections (8 + 12 measures), both repeated:

1:41   Minuet returns, without repeats.

North Indian Classical Music

We have seen how musical structures were expanded and developed in the Classical era, so that a single movement of a symphony or a concerto might take fifteen minutes or more to perform. Still, we can expect that its sections will be marked by predictable patterns of either repetition (or variation) or new material. Similar processes take place in the music of other cultures, although the end result is quite different. A case in point is North Indian classical music, a centuries-old performance tradition linked to Hinduism and its deities. This musical style is based not on entirely fixed musical works, but rather on long-standing traditional repertories of motives and themes elaborated by expert performers. Rather than featuring a key center, each semi-improvised elaboration introduces a **raga**, a series of pitches that also projects a particular mood and an association with a certain time of day.

We will consider *Raga Bhimpalasi*, performed by the venerable Indian musician Ravi Shankar (1920–2012), who plays a **sitar**, a long-necked plucked string instrument with metal strings and gourd resonators. He is often accompanied by a performer who plays a complex rhythmic cycle (**tala**, meaning "clap") with a small set of hand drums called **tabla**. A typical Indian classical piece can take up to several hours to play; our selection, however, is a mere twelve minutes. Indian audiences understand that *Raga Bhimpalsi* is performed in the afternoon—at the height of the day's heat—and it projects a mood of tenderness and longing.

The raga provides the pitches for the highly ornamented melody, and its tala is an additive rhythmic cycle of fourteen; you can hear Shankar explain both the raga and tala in a brief demonstration at the beginning. Harmony is not really a part of this music, except for what's produced by the striking of strings that sound **drones** (sustained pitches). As in a sonata-allegro form, we can expect the work to play out in sections; but while there is a general outline to the overall structure, improvisation plays a key role throughout. As the performance progresses, the tempo gradually accelerates to an extended climax, with dazzling passagework on the sitar accompanied by animated rhythms on the tabla.

Indian musicians learn to play this music by apprenticing to master players, who pass their performance techniques down to the next generation via an oral tradition. Ravi Shankar taught his daughter Anoushka this way, and she has herself become a great sitar artist. Shankar in fact introduced Indian classical music to the Western world, inspiring a genre of "raga-rock" in the 1960s and 70s. He gave a memorable performance at the original Woodstock Festival in August 1969, and the Beatles employed sitar on their recordings. Beatle George Harrison even studied sitar with Shankar and collaborated on projects with him, thus ensuring broad international visibility for the Indian master. A fortuitous example of the Eastern and Western worlds of music colliding.

Raga Bhimpalasi

What to listen for:

- Improvised melodic elaborations by the sitar on a series of pitches.
- Raga in its ascending and descending form.
- Complex rhythmic accompaniment on the tabla (2 + 4 + 4 + 4).

The introductory section (*alap*) is slow and unmetered, played by the sitar alone; the pitches of the raga are established in this improvisatory section. The second section (*gat*) begins with the entrance of the tabla, which sets up the rhythmic cycle (tala). With the third section (*jhala*), the tempo speeds up and the interplay between the instruments becomes more complex.

Composer and sitar player Ravi Shankar, performing here with his daughter Anoushka, was the most renowned and honored figure in Indian classical music of the twentieth century.

Chapter 31

Conversation with a Leader: The Classical Concerto

"Give me the best instrument in Europe, but listeners who understand nothing or do not wish to understand and who do not feel with me in what I am playing, and all my pleasure is spoilt."

—W. A. Mozart

KEY POINTS

- The Classical concerto form has three movements, alternating fast-slow-fast.
- The first movement, the longest and most complex, is called **first-movement concerto form**.
- Mozart's Piano Concerto in G Major, K. 453—with its graceful melodies, brilliant piano passagework, and virtuosic **cadenzas** (improvised solo passages)—is a notable example of the genre.

I f chamber music in the Classical period was designed to convey a musical conversation among equals, the Classical **concerto** was closer to a political rally—an inspiring leader helping to advance a larger group to a common purpose. While the genre continued to display some of the traits of the Baroque concerto, it was also influenced by the logic of the multimovement principle that governed other Classical genres such as the string quartet and symphony. In the concerto, composers relied on outstanding performers to provide the soloist's vitality, and sought to balance that energy with the complex collaboration of many unified voices.

Movements of the Classical Concerto

During the Baroque era, "concerto" could refer to a solo group and orchestra or to a solo instrument and orchestra. The Classical era shifted the emphasis to the latter combination, while keeping the fast-slow-fast pattern established by Vivaldi for the three movements. One unique feature of the solo concerto is the **cadenza**, a virtuosic solo passage in the manner of an improvisation that comes toward the end of a movement. It creates a dramatic effect: the orchestra falls silent, and the soloist (for example, the pianist or violinist) launches into a free play of fantasy on one or more themes of the movement.

The first movement adapts the principles of the Baroque concerto's ritornello procedure (based on a recurring theme) to those of sonata-allegro form. **First-movement concerto form** is sometimes described as a sonata-allegro form with a double exposition: the movement opens with an orchestral exposition (or ritornello) in the tonic key, presenting several themes, followed by the soloist playing elaborated versions of these themes. The solo cadenza appears near the end of the

Engraving of a concerto performance (1777), with a woman soloist, by **Johann Rudolf Holzhalb** (1723–1806).

movement, and a coda brings it to a close with a strong affirmation of the tonic key. We will examine how this form unfolds in one of Mozart's most beloved concertos.

Mozart's fortepiano, now in the Mozarteum in Salzburg, Austria. Notice how the colors of the white and black keys are the reverse of today's piano. (Listen to Mozart's Piano Sonata, K. 331, in Listening Examples.)

Mozart and the concerto

Mozart and the Piano Concerto

Mozart played a crucial role in the development of the genre. His twenty-seven piano concertos, written primarily as display pieces for his own public performances, abound in the brilliant flourishes and elegant gestures characteristic of eighteenth-century music. Five of his most impressive were written in just one year, 1784; one of these, the G Major Concerto, K. 453, Mozart wrote for his young student Babette (Barbara) von Ployer. Proud of his talented student, he invited the composer Giovanni Paisiello to the premiere performance, writing to his father, "I am fetching Paisiello in my carriage, as I want him to hear both my pupil and my compositions."

This work beautifully illustrates the richness of Mozart's creativity and his formal clarity. In the first movement (LG 21), the orchestral exposition sets up the main themes, after which the soloist weaves figurations around these melodies—including a new, lighthearted one as well—in its own exposition. An orchestral tutti leads to the development section, which makes virtuosic demands on the soloist. This concerto, notable also for its graceful writing for woodwinds, is usually performed today with a cadenza that Mozart wrote for it. The lyrical slow movement is followed by an Allegretto in theme and variations form; Mozart was so fond of its charming, dancelike tune that he taught it to his pet starling, who consistently missed one note and got the rhythm wrong.

The interaction of a virtuoso soloist with a larger and more varied ensemble allowed Mozart and his contemporaries to expand the Classical ideal of musical conversation to embrace a strong conversation leader—a "heroic" figure in keeping with an emerging ideal that we will explore in the next chapter.

CRITICAL THINKING

1. How is the Classical concerto like the Baroque concerto? How does it differ?

2. How is the virtuosic ability of the performer displayed in the Classical concerto?

YOUR TURN TO EXPLORE

Seek out videos of performances from different traditions that feature a soloist-leader: concertos from the Western orchestral tradition, but also (for example) rock bands, large jazz ensembles, or gospel groups. In what ways does the soloist interact with the larger ensemble? What are the respective roles of soloist and ensemble?

LISTENING GUIDE 21   11:29

Mozart: Piano Concerto in G Major, K. 453, I

DATE: 1784

MOVEMENTS: I. **Allegro; first-movement concerto form, G major**
　　　　　　　　II. Andante; first-movement concerto form, C major
　　　　　　　　III. Allegretto, Presto; theme-and-variations form, G major

First movement: Allegro

What to Listen For

Melody	Lilting first theme; quiet and lyrical second theme; new, graceful piano theme in second exposition.	**Texture**	Mostly homophonic.
		Form	First-movement concerto form, with orchestral and solo expositions, then development, recapitulation, and coda.
Rhythm/ meter	Lively, marchlike rhythm and tempo.		
		Expression	Elegant and refined, with decorative turns.
Harmony	Major key; shift to key of the dominant (D) in piano exposition.	**Performing forces**	Solo piano and orchestra (pairs of woodwinds, horns, and strings).

ORCHESTRAL EXPOSITION (RITORNELLO), in G major

0:00   Theme 1—refined theme in violins, with woodwind figurations:

0:27   Transitional theme—forceful, in full orchestra.

1:01   Theme 2—gently undulating theme in violins, answered in woodwinds:

1:40   Closing theme—stated quietly in orchestra.

SOLO EXPOSITION

2:10   Theme 1—piano enters with a sweep into the main theme, decorated, in G major; woodwind accompaniment; scales and arpeggio figurations in piano.

2:45   Transitional theme—orchestral ritornello; piano has decorative part; modulates to key of the dominant.

3:11   Piano theme—introduced by piano alone in D major, then presented in woodwinds:

4:01   Theme 2—in piano, with string accompaniment.

4:55   Closing—decisive, in D major.

DEVELOPMENT

5:16   Virtuosic piano part, with references to the piano theme, runs and arpeggios against woodwinds; various modulations, leading back to the tonic.

RECAPITULATION

6:34   Theme 1—returns in strings, with woodwind accompaniment; piano plays a decorated version of theme.

7:01   Transitional theme—forceful, in full orchestra.

7:32   Piano theme, solo, in G major, more decorated, with a light orchestral accompaniment.

8:23   Theme 2—in piano, then in woodwinds, now in G major.

9:28   Cadenza—solo piano, variations on earlier themes; ends on the dominant.

10:44   Closing—final ritornello, in G major.

Chapter 32

Personalizing the Conversation: Beethoven and the Classical Sonata

"To play without passion is inexcusable." —*Ludwig van Beethoven*

KEY POINTS

- Classical **sonatas** were set either for one solo instrument (usually the piano) or for duos (violin and piano, for example).

- Sonatas were sometimes designed for amateur performance in the home, but were also used by composer-performers as show pieces.

- The solo sonatas of Mozart and especially Ludwig van Beethoven are among the most significant in the keyboard literature.

- The *Moonlight* Sonata, perhaps Beethoven's best-known piano work, evokes the new Romantic style in its expressive manipulation of Classical conventions.

W hile group conversations can be heated, our most intense interactions with friends tend to be one on one: this is where we reveal most about ourselves, and build the deepest emotional connections. Similarly, while quartets and other chamber music highlighted the group-conversational possibilities of the Classical style, the sonata was designed for a more intimate expressive space. Featuring one or two performers, it either gave amateurs the opportunity for one-to-one musical interactions or allowed a skilled professional the opportunity to communicate directly with the listener. It was especially through the sonata that Ludwig van Beethoven developed a style that has been continuously valued as strikingly individual and meaningful from the time of his first performances. Beethoven's individuality, however, is evident because he developed it within a set of formal conventions against which he could "push"; if we do not understand these formal expectations, which his contemporaries had internalized, his intimate musical conversations with us cannot have the power and the passion that he envisioned.

A young Beethoven performs for Mozart. Engraving from the German School (early nineteenth century).

The Sonata in the Classical Era

Haydn, Mozart, and their successors understood the term **sonata** as an instrumental work for one or two instruments, consisting of three or four contrasting movements. The movements followed the basic order of the multimovement cycle that we have been exploring (see chart on p. 158).

In the Classical era, the sonata—for piano alone or for two instruments (violin or cello and piano)—became an important genre for amateurs in the home, as well as for composers like Mozart and Beethoven performing their own music at concerts. Beethoven's thirty-two piano sonatas, which span his entire compositional output, are among his most important works. The so-called *Moonlight* Sonata (LG 22) dates from his formative years but looks forward to the emotional expressiveness of the Romantic era.

Beethoven's *Moonlight* Sonata

Shortly after Beethoven's death, the *Moonlight* Sonata was given its title by German poet Ludwig Rellstab, who likened the work to the moonlit scenery along Lake Lucerne in Switzerland. (Note that in this case the "program music" aspect of the piece was added by a listener, rather than the composer.) When Beethoven composed the sonata in 1801 (early in his career), he was enamored of a young pupil, Countess Giulietta Guicciardi. The sonata is dedicated to her, but since this dedication seems to have been a last-minute decision, the work is probably not a programmatic statement of his love.

This work, one of a pair from Op. 27, breaks the formal molds—Beethoven called it a "fantasy sonata" (*sonata quasi una fantasia*), although he retained the

Countess Giulietta Guicciardi, the dedicatee of the *Moonlight* Sonata.

Ludwig van Beethoven (1770–1827)

Beethoven was born in Bonn, Germany. From age eleven, he supported his mother and two younger brothers by performing as an organist and harpsichordist. At twenty-two he moved to Vienna, where, although he was not attached to the court of a prince, the music-loving aristocrats helped him in various ways—by paying him handsomely for lessons or presenting him with gifts. He was also aided by the emergence of a middle-class public and the growth of concert life and music publishing.

When he was still in his twenties, Beethoven began to lose his hearing. His helplessness in the face of this affliction dealt a shattering blow to his pride: "How could I possibly admit an infirmity in the one sense that should have been more perfect in me than in others," he wrote to his brothers. Although he never regained his hearing and struggled with a sense of isolation, the remainder of his career was spent in ceaseless effort to achieve his artistic goals. He died at age fifty-six, famous and revered.

Beethoven is the supreme architect in music, a master in large-scale forms like the sonata and the symphony. His compositional activity fell into three periods. The first reflected the Classical elements he inherited from Haydn and Mozart. The middle period saw the appearance of characteristics more closely associated with the nineteenth century: strong dynamic contrasts, explosive accents, and longer movements. In his third period, Beethoven used more chromatic harmonies and developed a skeletal language from which all nonessentials were rigidly pared away. It was a language that transcended his time.

Beethoven's nine symphonies, five piano concertos and violin concerto, thirty-two piano sonatas, seventeen string quartets, opera *Fidelio*, and the *Missa solemnis* are indispensable to their respective repertories.

MAJOR WORKS: Orchestral music, including nine symphonies (the "Ode to Joy" is featured in Symphony No. 9), overtures • Concertos, including five for piano and one for violin • Chamber music, including string quartets, piano trios, sonatas for violin and cello, wind chamber music • 32 piano sonatas, including Op. 13 (*Pathétique*) and Op. 27, No. 2 (*Moonlight*) • Other piano music (*Für Elise*) • One opera (*Fidelio*) • Choral music, including *Missa solemnis* • Songs and one song cycle.

 Für Elise; Moonlight Sonata, I; *Pathétique* Sonata, II; Symphony No. 5, I; "Ode to Joy," from Symphony No. 9

In His Own Words

❝ The pianoforte is the most important of all musical instruments; its invention was to music what the invention of printing was to poetry.❞

—George Bernard Shaw
(1856–1950)

typical three-movement format. In the dreamy first movement, one of the most famous of all his works, the melody sings continuously, moving through various keys and registers. A short contrasting idea intervenes between two statements of the melody. While the form of this movement displays elements of development and recapitulation, it does not present the opposition of themes or keys typical of a first movement. Instead, it looks ahead to song forms favored by Romantic composers—indeed, it is almost a "song without words," a genre that arose in the generation following Beethoven.

The second movement is a gentle **scherzo** (quick-paced dance, a variant of the minuet) and trio set in a major key, providing necessary psychological relief between the emotionally charged opening movement and the stormy finale. The full force of Beethoven's dramatic writing is reserved for this closing movement, which he set in a full-blown sonata-allegro form.

Although Beethoven himself was not particularly won over by this sonata —"Surely I have written better things," he argued—it was an immediate success with audiences and remains one of the most beloved works in the Classical repertory. This may be partly because of a perception that Beethoven's musical ideas are "breaking out" of the conventions of the genre, making the intimacy of his message even more compelling. But again, if we were not expecting a particular set of structural milestones in the first movement, Beethoven's choice to reject those milestones would not be nearly as powerful. His intimate musical message would reveal less about his passionate convictions.

CRITICAL THINKING

1. What are the types of sonata composed in the Classical era?
2. What is unusual about the form of Beethoven's *Moonlight* Sonata?

LISTENING GUIDE 22

 5:45

Beethoven: Piano Sonata in C-sharp Minor, Op. 27, No. 2 (*Moonlight*), I

DATE: 1801

MOVEMENTS: I. **Adagio sostenuto; modified song form, C-sharp minor**
II. Allegretto; scherzo and trio, D-flat major
III. Presto agitato; sonata-allegro form, C-sharp minor

First movement: Adagio sostenuto

What to Listen For

Melody	Delicate, singing melody, moves slowly; heard in various ranges; then short ideas are passed between hands.
Rhythm/ meter	Continuous triplet pattern of accompaniment under slow, duple melody.
Harmony	Expressive minor key; modulations.
Texture	Homophonic, with active accompaniment; then contrapuntal.
Form	Modified song form; strophic with two strophes separated by a developmental section.
Expression	Ethereal mood; soft dynamic.

INTRODUCTION

0:00   Four-measure arpeggiated chords.

STROPHE 1

0:23   Melody in the right hand (shaded), with dotted figure on repeated note, accompanied by left-hand arpeggios, C-sharp minor; four-measure phrases:

0:48   Melody in a new key, expands and modulates.

1:12   New idea in dialogue between the two hands.

1:51   Melody returns, in a higher range.

MIDDLE SECTION

2:14   Motivic development of the dialogue, exchanged between the hands over a pedal on the dominant (G-sharp):

STROPHE 2

3:20   Returns to the opening melody and key center (C-sharp minor), followed by a short dialogue idea.

CODA

4:52   Closes with the melody stated in the bass on a repeated pitch (left hand).
        Resolution on a tonic cadence, with arpeggios and chords.

YOUR TURN TO EXPLORE

Find video examples of solo piano performances, and contrast them with the ensemble conversations you have examined in other explorations. How are the performer's behavior, the setting, and the interaction with the audience different? Contrast solo performances of similar repertory by amateurs and professionals: besides the skill of the performer, what other aspects of the performance (self-presentation, connection with others, expressive gestures, and so on) are different?

Chapter 33

Disrupting the Conversation: Beethoven and the Symphony in Transition

"I carry my thoughts about with me for a long time . . . before writing them down. I change many things, discard others, and try again and again until I am satisfied. . . . I turn my ideas into tones that resound, roar, and rage until at last they stand before me in the form of notes."

—*Ludwig van Beethoven*

KEY POINTS

- Beethoven's music is grounded in the Classical tradition but pushes its limits in a way that helped define the emerging Romantic sensibility.

- Beethoven's nine symphonies exemplify his experiments with Classical conventions. Best known is his Fifth, built on a famous four-note motive that permeates all four movements.

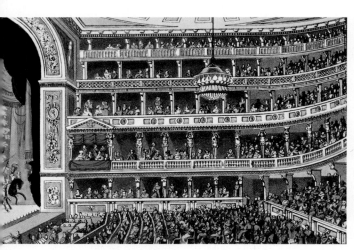

The Theater an der Wien in Vienna, where (in 1808) Beethoven presented a concert that included his Fifth and Sixth Symphonies.

Even during his own lifetime, Beethoven was hailed as a genius, and his influence on the orchestral tradition that followed can be felt to the present day. His ability to disrupt the elegant, balanced musical conversation of the Classical era is seen as evidence of supreme inspiration, the mark of an artist who will say what he needs to say regardless of the effect on the social order. Indeed, the presence of "Beethoven the hero" in the imagination of Western culture has extended far beyond the concert hall—even if you had not encountered the name of any composer considered so far, you likely had heard of Beethoven. Yet this composer was also working carefully to balance the formal expectations of the tradition within which he had been trained with "strategic disruptions." His unique approaches do not entail rejecting the conventions of Classical form: in fact, formal considerations are absolutely essential to the meaning and power of his music. This transitional place between convention and disruption is one major element that keeps Beethoven's music so compelling more than two centuries after it was written.

Beethoven's Symphonies

The symphony provided Beethoven with the ideal medium through which to address his public. His first two symphonies are closest in style to the two Classical masters who preceded him, but with his third, the *Eroica*, Beethoven began to expand the possibilities of the genre—the work was originally dedicated to Napoleon, and it was quickly interpreted as a personal narrative of individual heroism. The Fifth Symphony, which we consider here, is popularly viewed as a model of the genre. The finale of the Ninth, or *Choral,* Symphony, in which vocal soloists and chorus join the orchestra, is a setting of Friedrich von Schiller's "Ode to Joy," a ringing prophecy of the time when "all people will be brothers" (for more on the Ninth, see Interface, p. 182).

The Fifth Symphony

Perhaps the best-known of all symphonies, Beethoven's Symphony No. 5 can be heard not just as a standard four-movement cycle but as a unified whole that progresses from conflict and struggle to victorious ending. Now that we have examined individual movements in the cycle, we can tackle an entire symphony and consider both how it fits the parameters of the Classical cycle and how it pushes beyond them (LG 23).

The first movement, in a sonata-allegro form marked "Allegro con brio" (lively, with vigor), springs out of the rhythmic idea of "three shorts and a long" that dominates the entire symphony. This idea, perhaps the most commanding and recognizable gesture in the whole symphonic literature, is pursued with an almost terrifying single-mindedness in this dramatic movement. In an extended coda, the basic rhythm reveals a new fount of explosive energy. Beethoven described the motive as "Fate knocking at the door."

The second movement is a serene theme and variations, with two melodic ideas. Beethoven exploits his two themes with all the procedures of variation—changes in melodic outline, harmony, rhythm, tempo, dynamics, register, key, mode, and timbre. The familiar four-note rhythm (short-short-short-long) is sounded in the second theme, relating this movement to the first.

Third in the cycle is the scherzo, which opens with a rocket theme introduced by cellos and double basses. After a gruff, humorous trio in C major, the scherzo returns in a modified version, followed by a transitional passage to the final movement, in which the timpani sounds the memorable four-note motive.

The monumental fourth movement bursts forth without pause, once again bringing back the unifying rhythmic motive. This unification makes the symphony an early example of **cyclical form**, in which a theme or musical idea from one movement returns in a later one. Here, Beethoven unleashes not only a new energy and passion but also new instruments not yet part of the standard orchestra: piccolo, contrabassoon, and trombones all expand the ensemble's range and intensity. This last movement, in sonata-allegro form with an extended coda, closes with the tonic chord proclaimed triumphantly by the orchestra again and again.

Beethoven's hearing aid, an ear trumpet, resting on a copy of his Third Symphony (the *Eroica*).

Beethoven's career bridged the transition from the old society to the new. His commanding musical voice and an all-conquering will forged a link to the coming Romantic age.

Interface

Beethoven and the Politics of Music

Composers have produced some of their most powerful music in response to the political climate in which they lived. This is especially true of Beethoven, who was born in Germany but adopted Austria as his homeland during a time of great tumult and change.

An advocate for democracy and the underprivileged in his youth, Beethoven watched with interest as the French general Napoleon Bonaparte rose to power after the French Revolution (1789–99). At first, he greatly admired Napoleon: his Third Symphony (*Eroica*) was originally called *Bonaparte*, but when the ruler declared himself emperor in 1804, Beethoven tore up the title page bearing the dedication. "So he too is nothing more than an ordinary man," the composer wrote.

Besides Austria, Beethoven also claimed a kinship with Great Britain— for the people and their democratic parliamentary system, and possibly also because the British were allies of Austria against the French in the Napoleonic Wars. Heartfelt nationalistic sentiments found expression in his

Battle Symphony (1813), also known as *Wellington's Victory*, celebrating the recent British victory over the Napoleonic army at the Battle of Vitoria, in Spain. The work (replete with muskets and cannons) is programmatic in its vivid retelling of the battle through fanfares and patriotic tunes associated with both the French and the British (*Rule, Britannia* and *God Save the King*). Today, *Wellington's Victory* is heard most frequently at Fourth of July celebrations in the United States to accompany fireworks and ceremonial pageantry—an interesting "translation" of Beethoven's anti-French sentiments into American patriotism.

One of Beethoven's most famous works is the last movement of his Symphony No. 9 (1822–24), which features a choral setting of Friedrich von Schiller's poem "Ode to Joy." The text is an expression of universal brotherhood inspired by the powerful social forces behind the French Revolution. This great symphony has become a rallying cry for widely divergent philosophies ever since. At one extreme, the Ger-

man dictator Adolf Hitler demanded that Beethoven's work be played for his birthday in 1941. At another, the last movement was selected to celebrate the fall of the Berlin Wall in 1989, and today it is played on official occasions of both the Council of Europe and the European Union. The ideology behind the "Ode to Joy" is valued outside Western culture as well: in 1971, it was named the national anthem of Rhodesia (now Zimbabwe) in Africa; in 1989, student protestors at China's Tiananmen Square revolt chose it as their freedom statement; and each year, the symphony is performed in Japan with a colossal choir to ring in the New Year.

More recently, Beethoven's music took on yet another political role: to help build a musical bridge between North and South Korea. After a 2008 concert by the New York Philharmonic in Pyongyang, North Korea, the orchestra performed two days later in Seoul, South Korea, ending with the uplifting strains of Beethoven's Symphony No. 5; earlier that week, the "Ode to Joy" was played at the swearing-in ceremony of South Korean president Lee Myung-Bak.

Beethoven and his music have thus acquired a strong association with intense, collective endeavor toward a common purpose, one that goes far beyond what he might have envisioned even in his more explicitly political works. This association may be partly influenced by the forces required to perform the Ninth Symphony— especially its last, choral movement— which are truly massive, embodying through sound the cooperation of vastly disparate elements into a powerful singularity of expression.

LEFT: German crowds at the fall of the Berlin Wall in November 1989. RIGHT: The emperor Napoleon in his coronation robe (c. 1804), as painted by **Baron François Simon Gerard** (1770–1837).

LISTENING GUIDE 23   31:34

Beethoven: Symphony No. 5 in C Minor, Op. 67

DATE: 1807–8

MOVEMENTS: I. Allegro con brio; sonata-allegro form, C minor
        II. Andante con moto; theme and variations (two themes), A-flat major
      III. Allegro; scherzo and trio, C minor
      IV. Allegro; sonata-allegro form, C major

First movement: Allegro con brio   7:31

What to Listen For

Melody	Fiery four-note motive, the basis for thematic development; contrasting, lyrical second theme.
Rhythm/meter	Four-note rhythmic idea (short-short-short-long) shapes the movement.
Harmony	C minor, with dramatic shifts between minor and major tonality.
Texture	Mostly homophonic.
Form	Concise sonata-allegro form, with extended coda; repetition, sequence, and variation techniques.
Expression	Wide dynamic contrasts; forceful, energetic tempo.

EXPOSITION

0:00   Theme 1—based on the famous four-note motive (short-short-short-long), in C minor:

0:06   Motive is expanded sequentially:

0:43   Expansion from four-note motive; horns modulate to the key of the second theme.

0:46   Theme 2—lyrical, in woodwinds, in E-flat major; heard against relentless rhythm of the four-note motive:

1:07   Closing theme—rousing melody in a descending staccato passage, then the four-note motive.

1:26   Repeat of the exposition.

DEVELOPMENT

2:54   The beginning of the development is announced by a horn call.

3:05   Manipulation of the four-note motive through a descending sequence:

Continued on next page

3:16   Melodic variation, interval of a third filled in and inverted:

4:12   Expansion through repetition leads into the recapitulation; music is saturated with the four-note motive.

RECAPITULATION

4:18   Theme 1—explosive statement in C minor begins the recapitulation.
4:38   Brief oboe cadenza.
5:15   Theme 2—returns in C major, not in the expected key of C minor.
5:41   Closing theme.
5:58   Coda—extended treatment of the four-note motive; ends in C minor.

Second movement: Andante con moto

10:01

What to Listen For

Melody	Two contrasting themes: smooth first theme; rising second theme built on four-note idea.
Rhythm/meter	Flowing triple meter.
Harmony	Related key: A-flat major.

Texture	Mostly homophonic.
Form	Variations, with two themes; varied rhythms, melodies, harmony (major and minor).
Timbre	Warm strings, brilliant woodwinds, powerful brass.

0:00   Theme 1—broad, flowing melody, heard in low strings:

0:52   Theme 2—upward-thrusting four-note (short-short-short-long) motive heard first in clarinets:

Brass fanfare follows.

Examples of variations on theme 1

1:57   Embellished with running 16th notes, low strings:

3:52   Embellished with faster (32nd) notes in violas and cellos.
5:04   Melody exchanged between woodwind instruments (fragments of theme 1):

6:36   Melody shifted to minor, played staccato (detached version of theme 1):

8:10   Coda—*Più mosso* (faster), in the bassoon.

Third movement: Scherzo, Allegro   5:27

What to Listen For

Melody	Wide-ranging, ascending scherzo theme; more conjunct, quick trio theme.	**Form**	**A-B-A′** (scherzo-trio-scherzo); plus a link to the final movement.
Rhythm/ meter	Quick triple meter throughout; insistent focus on four-note rhythm.	**Expression**	Wide-ranging dynamic contrasts; fast tempo.
Harmony	Dramatic C-minor scherzo; trio in C major.	**Timbre**	Themes in low strings; plucked (pizzicato) strings at the return of the scherzo; timpani in transition to the last movement.
Texture	Homophonic; some fugal treatment in the trio.		

0:00   Scherzo theme—a rising, rocket theme in low strings, sounds hushed and mysterious:

0:19   Rhythmic motive (from movement I) explodes in the horns, *fortissimo*:

1:59   Trio theme—in C major, in double basses, set fugally, played twice; contrast with C-minor scherzo:

2:30   Trio theme is broken up and expanded through sequences.

3:29   Scherzo returns, with varied orchestration, including pizzicato strings.

4:46   Transition to the next movement, with timpani rhythm from the opening four-note motive:

Tension mounts, orchestra swells to the heroic opening of the fourth movement.

Fourth movement: Allegro (without pause from movement III)   8:32

What to Listen For

Melody	Triumphant theme outlining C-major triad; energetic second theme.	**Form**	Sonata-allegro form, with long coda; cyclic (return of material from earlier movements).
Rhythm/ meter	Very fast duple meter; four-note rhythmic idea.	**Expression**	Forceful dynamics; *fp* (*forte/piano*) effects; intense and spirited.
Harmony	C major; remains in major throughout.	**Performing forces**	Added instruments (piccolo, contrabassoon, trombones).
Texture	Mostly homophonic.		

Continued on next page

EXPOSITION

5:30   Theme 1—in C major, a powerful melody whose opening outlines a triumphant C-major chord:

6:03   Lyrical transition theme in French horns, modulating from C to G major.

6:29   Theme 2—in G major, vigorous melody with rhythm from the four-note motive, in triplets:

6:55   Closing theme—featuring clarinet and violas, decisive.

DEVELOPMENT

7:30   Much modulation and free rhythmic treatment; brings back the four-note motive (short-short-short-long) from the first movement.

9:04   Brief recurrence, like a whisper, of the scherzo.

RECAPITULATION

9:39   Theme 1—in C major; full orchestra, *fortissimo*.

10:43   Theme 2—in C major, played by strings.

11:10   Closing theme, played by woodwinds.

11:38   Coda—long extension; tension is resolved over and over again until the final, emphatic tonic.

CRITICAL THINKING

1. Why was Beethoven's music considered "transitional" to a new artistic perspective?

2. Which Romantic qualities are heard in Beethoven's Fifth Symphony? Which are Classical-era traits?

YOUR TURN TO EXPLORE

Find several references to Beethoven or his music (visual, literary, or sonic) in popular culture or commercial contexts. What is being said or shown or implied about the composer and his work? Can you determine how truthful/accurate or invented/mythical those claims or images might be? Why do you think those aspects of Beethoven are being highlighted? How is the mythology of Beethoven being used, and to whose advantage?

Chapter 34

Making It Real: Mozart and Classical Opera

"I like an aria to fit a singer as perfectly as a well-tailored suit of clothes."

—W. A. Mozart

KEY POINTS

- In the Classical era, two types of Italian opera prevailed: **opera seria** (serious opera) and **opera buffa** (comic opera).
- While serious opera continued a tradition of idealized characters and plots, comic opera aimed at a more realistic depiction of human concerns and emotions.
- Mozart's *Don Giovanni* combines elements of serious and comic opera in a powerful dramatic work that is performed all over the world.

Musical theater has never been, and never will be, about full-out realism: after all, people don't converse by singing. However, certain traditions of opera (just like certain traditions of film) have tried to convey realistic nuances in human interactions and emotions. And while some operas (and movies) reflect specific historical or cultural priorities (consider the 1939 film *Gone with the Wind*, for example), and thus may seem dated or old-fashioned to following generations, other works convey aspects of the human condition that easily cross boundaries of time and location. Mozart's comic operas fall in this latter category: more than two centuries after their premieres, they still rank high with modern producers and performers (sometimes with creative choices of staging, costumes, or casting) and always succeed with audiences. The characters are often not entirely "comic"—they are fleshed-out human beings, with contradictory emotions that shift and develop through the drama. The persuasive power of musical characterization is what makes Classical opera, especially in the hands of Mozart, truly the first "modern" tradition of musical theater.

In His Own Words

❝ I should say that in opera the poetry must be the obedient daughter of music."

—W. A. Mozart

Classical Opera

Operas of the early eighteenth century accurately reflected the society from which they sprang. The prevalent form was *opera seria*: "serious," or tragic, Italian opera, a highly formalized genre inherited from the Baroque that consisted mainly of recitatives and arias specifically designed to display the virtuosity of star singers to the aristocracy. Its rigid conventions were shaped largely by the poet Pietro Metastasio (1698–1782), whose librettos, featuring stories of kings and heroes drawn from classical antiquity, were set again and again throughout the century.

Opera seria

The Burgtheater in Vienna, where Mozart's opera *The Marriage of Figaro* was first performed.

Increasingly, however, audiences and artists moved toward a simpler style that reflected human emotions more realistically. One result was the comic opera that flourished in every country of Europe. Known in England as **ballad** (or dialogue) **opera**, in Germany as *Singspiel*, in France as *opéra comique*, and in Italy as *opera buffa*, these lighter genres were initially seen merely as a less important counterpart to the more "socially elevated" serious tradition. Eventually, however, the support of a rising merchant class with an increasing disposable income helped bring the comic tradition into the limelight.

While serious opera was almost invariably in Italian, comic opera was generally in the local language of the audience (the vernacular), although Italian *opera buffa* was popular thoughout much of Europe. *Opera buffa* presented lively, down-to-earth plots rather than the remote concerns of gods and mythological heroes. It featured an exciting ensemble at the end of each act in which all the characters participated, instead of the succession of solo arias heard in the older style. And it abounded in farcical situations, humorous dialogue, and popular tunes. As the Age of Revolution approached, comic opera became an important social force whose lively wit delighted even the aristocrats it satirized. *Opera buffa* spread quickly, steadily expanding its scope until it culminated in the works of Mozart.

Mozart's *Don Giovanni*

Don Giovanni combines elements of *opera buffa* with those of more intense *opera seria*. Set to a libretto by Lorenzo da Ponte, with whom Mozart collaborated on two other comic masterworks—*Le nozze di Figaro* (*The Marriage of Figaro*) and *Così fan tutte* (*Women Are Like That*)—*Don Giovanni* recounts the tale of the aristocratic Don Juan, an amoral womanizer who has seduced and abandoned women across Europe, and who is finally doomed to hell by the ghost of a man he has murdered. It is ironic that the most notorious womanizer of the time, the Venetian nobleman Giacomo Casanova, attended the 1787 premiere of the opera in Prague and, as a friend of da Ponte, may even have contributed to the libretto.

After an instrumental overture, the first act begins with a comic aria by the servant Leporello (whose name means "little rabbit"). Leporello is keeping guard impatiently outside the house of Donna Anna (Lady Anna) while his master Don Giovanni, in disguise, is inside trying to seduce her. But something goes awry and the masked culprit runs out of the house (and onto the stage) with Donna Anna in pursuit, intent not only on catching the offender but on learning his true identity. Her cries for help wake her father, the Commendatore (commandant), who rushes out to protect his daughter but is killed in a duel with Don Giovanni. The opening scene thus juxtaposes comic posturing with sexual violence and murder, demonstrating to us that this will be no ordinary lighthearted drama. Grief-stricken, Donna Anna makes her fiancé, Don Ottavio, swear to avenge her father's death. Both Anna and the Commendatore are characters suited to *opera seria*, as is the opening murder scene.

In the next scene, we meet another woman, Donna Elvira, who is in a rage over a man who has abandoned her. In her aria "Ah, chi mi dice mai" ("Ah, who can tell me where that cruel one is"), she recounts with sweeping lines, accompanied by bold orchestral gestures, how she was spurned by the man she loved and vows to rip his heart out (LG 24). As the aria concludes and the style shifts to recitative, Don

Costume design for *Don Giovanni* as sung by Adolphe Nourrit (1802–1839).

Giovanni steps forward to comfort her, and she recognizes him as the very man who spurned her. Don Giovanni quickly deploys Leporello to distract her and makes a speedy exit, as he frequently does throughout the drama when things get "too complicated."

What follows is the famous Catalogue Aria, "Madamina, il catalogo è questo" ("My dear little lady, this is the catalogue"), in which Leporello—first in a rapid, speechlike patter and then in comforting, lyrical tones—regales Elvira with a list of Giovanni's conquests: 640 in Italy, 231 in Germany, 100 in France, 91 in Turkey, but in Spain . . . 1,003. In a lilting minuet, he comically describes the blondes, brunettes, plump ones, thin ones, old ones, and young ones that make up the list.

The confident Don Juan orders Leporello to invite the statue of the Commendatore, father of one of his many conquests, to dinner. Watercolor by **Giuseppe Bernardino Bison** (1762–1844).

While Leporello's aria is written for comic effect, the context is not at all lighthearted: he is brutally spelling out to Donna Elvira that she is but one of thousands of women his master has seduced, implicitly recommending her to "get over it." Much as we might find this scene offensive today, some—even many—of Mozart's male contemporaries would have been amused to see a noblewoman humiliated by a servant in public. But throughout *Don Giovanni*, the paradox of class difference and the hypocrisy that allowed men to boast of "conquests" and women to be shamed for "giving in" is treated with a great deal of ambiguity.

In the next scene, the peasants Zerlina and Maseppo are about to marry. Attracted to the bride, Giovanni begins his seduction by flattering Zerlina with his own marriage proposal in the lovely duet "Là ci darem la mano" ("There we will be, hand in hand"). Although not sung between real lovers, this is the main love duet in the opera. Giovanni continues to pursue numerous women until his final nocturnal adventure. After escaping trouble by leaping over a wall into a graveyard, he comes face-to-face with the statue of the Commendatore and orders the cowering Leporello to invite the statue to dinner. To everyone's amazement and horror, the statue shows up at the dinner, only to drag the evildoer down to his death.

We cannot claim that Mozart held entirely progressive views overall, but in this and other comic operas he holds his society up to a mirror and emphasizes the contradictions inherent in separating people based on class and gender. This is another reason why Mozart's comic operas still speak so strongly to modern audiences: they can easily be understood to contain messages about social unfairness and the rights of individuals, ideas that appeal to enlightened audiences to this day.

CRITICAL THINKING

1. What are the prevailing types of opera in the Classical era, and how do these differ from one another?
2. How is the subject matter of *Don Giovanni* timeless?

YOUR TURN TO EXPLORE

Don Giovanni has been produced countless times. Find productions of this opera that emphasize a particular aspect of the design, characters, or plot. (One example that you might seek out is a 1990 production by Peter Sellars set in Spanish Harlem in the late twentieth century, introducing issues of race into the casting and the dramatic interaction.) How do the singers' vocal qualities, their interaction with each other and the orchestra, and staging choices create different dramatic nuances?

LISTENING GUIDE 24
 11:54

Mozart, *Don Giovanni*, Act I, scene 2

DATE: 1787

GENRE: *Opera buffa*

LIBRETTIST: Lorenzo da Ponte

CHARACTERS: Don Giovanni, a licentious young nobleman (baritone)
Leporello, Giovanni's servant (bass)
Donna Anna, a noblewoman (soprano)
Commendatore, the commandant; father of Donna Anna (bass)

Don Ottavio, fiancé of Donna Anna (tenor)
Donna Elvira, a lady deserted by Giovanni (soprano)
Zerlina, a peasant girl (soprano)
Masetto, a peasant, fiancé to Zerlina (bass)

Aria (Donna Elvira, with Don Giovanni and Leporello)
3:34

What to Listen For

Melody	Short orchestral introduction, then disjunct aria outlining triads, with many leaps; wide-ranging cadenza near the end.
Rhythm/ meter	Accented duple meter.
Form	Two main sections, each repeated with variation (**A-B-A′-B′**).

Performing forces	Short orchestral introduction, then alternates between soprano aria, orchestra, and interjections from Don Giovanni and Leporello.
Expression	Anger is emphasized by sudden dynamic shifts, quick tempo, and changes in range.

Donna Elvira

A section

0:00   Orchestral introduction.

0:22   Ah, chi mi dice mai,
quel barbaro dov'è?
Che per mio scorno amai,
che mi mancò di fè.

Ah, who can tell me
where that cruel one is?
I loved him, to my shame,
and he broke his pledge to me.

B section

0:42   Ah, se ritrovo l'empio,
e a me non torna ancor,

0:54   vo' farne orrendo scempio,
gli vo' cavar il cor!

Ah, if I find that evil one,
and he doesn't return to me,
I'll make a horrible scene,
I'll rip his heart out!

Don Giovanni (to Leporello)

1:06   Udisti? Qualche bella dal vago
abbandonata. Poverina!
Cerchiam di consolare il suo tormento.

You hear? A lovely one
abandoned by her lover. Poor girl!
Let's try to ease her pain.

Leporello

Così ne consolò mille e ottocento.

Just as he consoled 1,800 of them.

Donna Elvira

A section repeated, with variations

1:44   Ah, chi mi dice mai . . .

Ah, who can tell me . . .

B section repeated, with variations

2:06   Ah, se ritrovo l'empio . . .

Ah, if I find that evil one,

Don Giovanni

Signorina!   Signorina!

Donna Elvira's anger, shown with wide-ranging, disjunct line (**B section**):

Consoling interjection of "poverina" ("poor girl") by Don Giovanni:

Recitative (Donna Elvira, Don Giovanni, Leporello)   2:47

What to Listen For			
Melody	More static lines, speechlike.	**Performing forces**	Accompanied by continuo instrument only.
Rhythm	Quick notes, delivered freely.		

Donna Elvira

0:00   Chi è là?   Who's there?

Don Giovanni

Stelle! che vedo?   What the devil! Who do I see?

Leporello (aside)

O bella! Donna Elvira!   Oh, lovely! Donna Elvira!

(In this quick-paced recitative, the outraged Donna Elvira recognizes Don Giovanni as the man who seduced her. Unable to calm her, Don Giovanni suggests that Leporello tell her everything and takes his leave. Leporello attempts to console Donna Elvira by pulling out a list of his master's many conquests, which he proceeds to read in the famous Catalogue Aria that follows.)

Catalogue Aria (Leporello)   5:37

What to Listen For			
Melody	Opening section, fast and patter-like (syllabic text setting); second section is more lyrical.	**Rhythm/ meter**	Opening Allegro in duple meter; then slower, minuet-like Andante in 3/4.
		Form	Two main sections (Allegro, Andante), some repeated text with varied music.

A section: Allegro

0:00   Madamina!   My dear lady,
Il catalogo è questo,   this is the catalogue
delle belle, che amò il padron mio!   of the beauties my master made love to!
Un catalogo egli è ch'ho fatto io: It's a catalogue I made myself:
osservate, leggete con me!   look at it, read it with me!

Continued on next page

0:23	In Italia, sei cento e quaranta;	In Italy, six hundred and forty;
	In Alemagna, due cento trent'una;	in Germany, two hundred and thirty-one;
	Cento in Francia, in Turchia novant'una;	a hundred in France, in Turkey ninety-one;
	ma, ma in Ispagna, son già mille e tre!	but in Spain there are already a thousand and three!
0:54	V'han fra queste contadine,	Among these are country girls,
	cameriere, cittadine;	chambermaids, and city girls;
	v'han Contesse, Baronesse,	there are countesses, baronesses,
	Marchesane, Principesse,	marchionesses, princesses,
	e v'han donne d'ogi grado,	there are women of every class,
	d'ogni forma d'ogni età.	of every form and every age.
1:11	In Italia, sei cento e quaranta . . .	[Repeated text, varied music.]

B section: Andante con moto

2:04	Nella bionda, egli ha l'usanza	With blondes, he likes to
	di lodar la gentilezza;	praise their charm;
	nella bruna la costanza,	with brunettes, their constancy,
	nella bianca la dolcezza!	with the white haired [or the old ones], their sweetness!
2:47	Vuol d'inverno la grassotta,	In the winter he prefers the plump ones,
	vuol d'estate la magrotta;	in the summer, the thin ones;
	E la grande, maestosa;	and the large ones, the majestic ones,
	la piccina, ognor vezzosa.	the small ones, are always welcome.

B section: music repeated with variations

3:40	Delle vecchie fa conquista	He seduces the old ones just
	per piacer di porle in lista.	for the pleasure of adding them to the list.
	Sua passion predominante	But his main passion is for
	è la giovin principiante.	the young beginners.
	Non si picca, se sia ricca,	He doesn't mind whether she's rich,
	se sia brutta, se sia bella;	whether she's ugly, whether she's pretty;
4:26	purché porti la gonella,	as long as she wears a skirt,
	voi sapete quel che fa.	you know what he does.

Syllabic, patter quality in **A section**:

Soothing, lyrical quality in **B section**, in lilting 3/4:

Chapter 35

Mourning a Hero: Mozart and the Requiem

"I am writing a Requiem for myself."
—W. A. Mozart? (as quoted after his death
in a contemporary newspaper)

KEY POINTS

- Classical composers continued the tradition of writing worship music for their communities.
- Sacred music genres of the later 1700s included the **oratorio** and the **Mass**.
- Mozart's *Requiem* Mass, left unfinished at the composer's death, exemplifies the grand style of Catholic music in Vienna.

The stereotype of a great artist dying tragically young is nowhere more evident than in the popular image of Mozart, whose passing at age thirty-five was understood even by his contemporaries as a huge loss. The fact that during his final illness Mozart was working on a powerful memorial work—music to accompany a funeral Mass—has compounded the opportunity to view his last composing moments as symbolic of the tragedy of his premature death. Yet while his *Requiem* has been recognized as a deeply moving work from its first performances, it can also provide us with a cautionary tale about mythologies of genius.

From shortly after his death came accounts of a mysterious stranger knocking on Mozart's door with a commission for a Mass that the composer understood as a premonition, along with rumors of Mozart believing himself poisoned rather than diseased in his final days. But Mozart's own letters in the months preceding his death show him in a cheerful mood, and he was working on a number of other projects alongside the *Requiem* during his last few weeks. Ultimately myths surrounding a remarkable composer's early death continue to shape our culture's notions of creative genius (think of more recent musicians who died prematurely, like Jimi Hendrix, Janis Joplin, Kurt Cobain, or Notorious B.I.G.) .

In Her Own Words

❝Among all the arts, music alone can be purely religious."
—Madame de Staël
(1766-1817)

Sacred Music in the Classical Era

In this era, the principal genres of sacred choral music were the Mass, the Requiem Mass, and the oratorio. A **Mass,** you will recall, is a musical setting of the most solemn service of the Roman Catholic Church, and a **Requiem** is a musical setting of the Mass for the Dead. The **oratorio,** of which Handel's *Messiah* is a prime example, is generally focused on a biblical story. All these genres were originally intended to be performed in church, although by the nineteenth century they

Requiem

Frontispiece from an 1802 edition of Mozart's *Requiem*.

Nineteenth-century print of the choir of St. Stephen's Cathedral in Vienna, where Mozart was offered the post of Kapellmeister shortly before he died.

would find a much larger audience in the concert hall. We will consider the Classical sacred tradition through one of the era's most beloved masterpieces, Mozart's *Requiem*.

Mozart's *Requiem*

Mozart's last large-scale composition was quickly hailed as one of the masterpieces of the Classical era. The composer left only sketches for the later movements of this work, which were eventually completed by his favorite pupil, Franz Xaver Süssmayr. We can, however, attribute to Mozart himself the dramatic *Dies irae* ("Day of Wrath"), a vision of Judgment Day. The text for this movement, a rhymed Latin poem by a thirteenth-century friar, is designed to emphasize the terrible power of divine intervention, beginning with the words "Day of wrath, day that will dissolve the world into burning coals, as David bore witness with the Sibyl" (LG 25).

The score calls for four soloists (soprano, alto, tenor, bass) and four-part chorus, accompanied by an orchestra that includes basset horns and bassoons. The extended use of low wind and brass timbres was a relative novelty in the later 1700s, and its effect is stunning to this day. The power of Mozart's *Dies irae* unfurls against headlong running notes and shattering accents. On the words *Quantus tremor est futurus* ("How great a tremor there will be"), the wavering lines paint the text vividly. An abrupt cadence leads to the *Tuba mirum* ("A trumpet with an astonishing sound"), featuring a memorable trombone solo and bass singer who together summon souls before the throne of God. The other soloists enter one by one: first the tenor, who sings a slower Andante on *Mors stupebit et natura* ("Death will be stunned, as will Nature"), followed by the alto and soprano, all four ending in a solo quartet.

The final chorus, *Rex tremendae majestatis!* ("King of tremendous majesty"), fiercely projects the sense of the words. Dotted rhythms and syncopated chords in the orchestra impart an overwhelming urgency, leading up to the final plea—*Salva me, fons pietatis!* ("Save me, fount of piety")—which is sung softly.

A relative recounted that on December 4, 1791, as the composer lay feverishly weak on his bed, several singers from the theater sang through the completed portions of the *Requiem* with Mozart on the alto line. At the *Lacrimosa* ("Weeping") verse, he put the music aside and wept—and then he died that same night. It is likely that stories like this one were embellished by those who wanted to highlight the almost supernatural expressive palette of the work, and to raise Mozart's reputation to an even more remarkable level after his death.

And remarkable it is. Over the centuries since its composition, the expressive power of the *Requiem* has been widely recognized by audiences from many cultures. This moving work was chosen for the funeral of President John F. Kennedy, who was assassinated in 1963; and in 2002, on the one-year anniversary of the September 11 attack on the World Trade Center in New York, a rolling performance of Mozart's *Requiem* was given in all corners of the globe (in Europe, Asia, Central America, and the United States), each beginning at 8:46 a.m., the time of the first attack. Mozart could never have imagined how much his work would ultimately mean to the world.

LISTENING GUIDE 25   6:29

Mozart: *Dies irae*, from *Requiem*

DATE: 1791

GENRE: Requiem Mass

What to Listen For

Melody	Dramatic choral opening, then operatic solo verses; final verse has choral outcry.
Rhythm/meter	Forceful, accented duple meter; closing has strong dotted-rhythmic idea.
Harmony	Alternation between minor (opening and closing) and major; some harsh combinations.
Texture	Largely homophonic.
Form	Set in eight verses, each treated with different performing forces.

Expression	Mood shifts from fear (loud, accented) to wonderment to a quiet plea for salvation.
Performing forces	Chorus, solo voices, and orchestra; choral opening and closing; verses 3–7 focus on solo voices.
Timbre	Trumpets and timpani prominent; bass voice/trombone duet (verse 3).
Text	Rhymed Latin poem with eight three-line verses; clear text declamation with some word painting.

VERSE	LATIN	TRANSLATION	DESCRIPTION
0:00 **1.**	Dies irae, dies illa Solvet saeclum in favilla: Teste David cum Sibylla.	Day of wrath, day that will dissolve the world into burning coals, as David bore witness with the Sibyl.	Full chorus and orchestra; dramatic homophonic setting; clear text declamation.
0:13 **2.**	Quantus tremor est futurus, Quando judex est venturus, Cuncta stricte discussurus!	How great a tremor there will be, when the judge is to come briskly shattering every [grave].	Chorus and orchestra; more polyphonic texture. Verses 1 and 2 repeated.
1:47 **3.**	Tuba mirum spargens sonum Per sepulchra regionum, Coget omnes ante thronum.	A trumpet with an astonishing sound through the tombs of the region drives all [men] before the throne.	Trombone solo, echoed by bass solo; trombone continues with countermelody; homophonic orchestral accompaniment.
2:36 **4.**	Mors stupebit et natura, Cum resurget creatura, Iudicanti responsura.	Death will be stunned, as will Nature, when arises [man] the creature responding to the One judging.	Tenor solo, with homophonic orchestral accompaniment.
2:51 **5.**	Liber scriptus proferetur, In quo totum continetur, Unde mundus judicetur.	The written book will be brought forth, in which the whole [record of evidence] is contained whence the world is to be judged.	Tenor solo continues.
3:15 **6.**	Iudex ergo cum sedebit, Quidquid latet apparebit, Nil inultum remanebit.	Therefore when the Judge shall sit, whatever lay hidden will appear; nothing unavenged will remain.	Alto solo with orchestra.
3:30 **7.**	Quid sum miser tunc dicturus? Quem patronum rogaturus?	What am I the wretch, then, to say? what patron I to beseech?	Soprano solo with orchestra.

Continued on next page

Cum vix justus sit securus?	when scarcely the just [man] will be secure.	Last line repeated by all soloists.
4:37 **8.** Rex tremendae majestatis! Qui salvandos salvas gratis! Salve me, fons pietatis!	King of tremendous majesty, who saves those to be saved, save me, fount of piety!	Dramatic full chorus setting.

Verse 1 opening; full chorus with clearly declaimed text:

Verse 3 duet, with trombone and bass solo:

CRITICAL THINKING

Comparing styles 4: Classical to Romantic

1. How does Mozart use various vocal and instrumental textures and timbres to convey the changing emotions of the "Day of Judgment" prayer?
2. What similarities and differences are there between this sacred choral work and the two Baroque sacred works we've considered (Bach's cantata and Handel's oratorio)?

YOUR TURN TO EXPLORE

Find examples of music designed to pay tribute to or memorialize tragic events (for example the 9/11 terrorist attacks, the AIDS epidemic, war or natural disasters). Is the music meant to soothe pain or rekindle grief, or for yet other purposes—and how do the composers make musical choices to achieve those purposes?

A Comparison of
Classical and Romantic Styles

	Classical (c. 1750–1825)	Romantic (c. 1820–1900)
Composers	Haydn, Mozart, Beethoven.	Schubert, Berlioz, Hensel, Chopin, Schumann, Verdi, Wagner, Foster, Gottschalk, Brahms, Tchaikovsky, Grieg, Fauré, Puccini, Debussy, Joplin.
Melody	Symmetrical melody in balanced phrases and cadences; tuneful; diatonic, with narrow leaps.	Expansive, singing melodies; wide ranging; more varied, with chromatic inflections.
Rhythm	Clear rhythmically, with regularly recurring accents; dance rhythms favored.	Rhythmic diversity and elasticity; tempo rubato.
Harmony	Diatonic harmony favored; tonic-dominant relationships expanded, become basis for large-scale forms.	Increasing chromaticism; expanded concepts of tonality.
Texture	Homophonic textures; chordal-vertical perspective.	Homophony, turning to increased polyphony in later years of era.
Instrumental genres	Symphony, solo concerto, solo sonata, string quartet, other chamber-music genres.	Same large genres, adding one-movement symphonic poem; solo piano works.
Vocal genres	Opera, Mass, Requiem Mass, oratorio.	Same vocal forms, adding works for solo voice and piano/orchestra.
Form	Ternary form predominant; sonata-allegro form developed; absolute forms preferred.	Expansion of forms and interest in continuous as well as miniature programmatic forms.
Audience	Secular music predominant; aristocratic audience.	Secular music predominant; middle-class audience.
Dynamics	Continuously changing dynamics through *crescendo* and *decrescendo*.	Widely ranging dynamics for expressive purposes.
Timbre	Changing tone colors between sections of works.	Continual change and blend of tone colors; experiments with new instruments and unusual ranges.
Performing forces	String orchestra with woodwinds and some brass and timpani; thirty-to-forty-member orchestra; piano becomes prominent.	Introduction of new instruments (tuba, English horn, valved brass, harp, piccolo); much larger orchestras; piano predominant as solo instrument.
Virtuosity	Improvisation largely limited to cadenzas in concertos.	Increased virtuosity; composers specify more in scores.
Expression	Emotional balance and restraint.	Emotions, mood, atmosphere emphasized; interest in the bizarre and macabre.

ROMANTIC ERA

Events		Composers and Works

Part 5

The Nineteenth Century

Music as Passion and Individualism

"Music, of all the liberal arts, has the greatest influence over the passions."

—Napoleon Bonaparte (1769–1821)

In His Own Words

❝ Our sweetest songs are those that tell of saddest thoughts."

— *Percy Bysshe Shelley (1792–1822)*

If the time frame of Classicism is hard to pin down, Romanticism is one of the artistic trends for which beginnings can be most readily identified, since it was a self-conscious break from the ideals of the Enlightenment. The artistic movement really comes into its own through music in the early decades of the 1800s. Indeed, it is a musician—Ludwig van Beethoven—who is often identified as the first great creative Romantic, and whose influence looms to the present day as an embodiment of passionate individual expression. Many of the common tenets of Romanticism are still very much with us: the artist struggling against rather than working within society and convention; the need for art to unsettle rather than soothe; the belief that works display their creator's distinctive originality and self-expression.

An Age of Revolutions

The Romantic era grew out of the social and political upheavals that followed the French Revolution in the last decade of the 1700s. The revolution signaled the transfer of power from a hereditary landholding aristocracy to the middle class. This change, firmly rooted in urban commerce and industry, emerged from the Industrial Revolution, which brought millions of people from the country into the cities. The new society, based on free enterprise, celebrated the individual as never before. The slogan of the French Revolution—"Liberty, Equality, Fraternity"—inspired hopes and visions to which artists responded with zeal. Sympathy for the oppressed, interest in peasants, workers, and children, faith in humankind and its destiny, all formed part of the increasingly democratic character of the Romantic period, and inspired a series of revolutions and rebellions that gradually led to the modern political landscape of Europe.

The spirit of the French Revolution is captured in *Liberty Leading the People*, by **Eugène Delacroix** (1798–1863).

Romantic Writers and Artists

Romantic poets and artists rebelled against the conventional concerns of their Classical predecessors and were drawn instead to the fanciful, the picturesque, and the passionate. These men and women emphasized intense emotional expression and were highly aware of themselves as individuals apart from all others. "I am different from all the men I have seen," proclaimed philosopher Jean-Jacques Rousseau. "If I am not better, at least I am different." In Germany, a group of young writers created a new kind of lyric poetry that culminated in the art of Heinrich Heine, who became a favorite poet of Romantic composers. A similar movement in France was led by Victor Hugo, the country's greatest prose writer. In England, the revolt against the formalism of the Classical age produced an outpouring of emotional lyric poetry that reached its peak in the works of Lord Byron, Percy Bysshe Shelley, and John Keats.

The newly won freedom of the artist proved to be a mixed blessing. Confronted by a world indifferent to artistic and cultural values, artists felt more and more cut off from society. A new type emerged: the bohemian, a rejected dreamer who starved in an attic and shocked the establishment through peculiar dress and behavior. Eternal longing, regret for the lost happiness of childhood, an indefinable discontent that gnawed at the soul—these were the ingredients of the Romantic mood. Yet the artist's pessimism was based in reality. It became apparent that the high hopes fostered by the French Revolution were not to be realized overnight. Despite the brave slogans, all people were not yet equal or free. The short-lived optimism gave way to doubt and disenchantment, a state of mind that was reflected in the arts and in literature.

The nineteenth-century novel found one of its great themes in the conflict between the individual and society. Hugo dedicated *Les misérables* "to the unhappy ones of the earth." His novel's hero, Jean Valjean, is among the era's memorable discontented (well known from the 1985 musical and 2012 film of the same name). Some writers sought escape by glamorizing the past, as Walter Scott did in *Ivanhoe* and Alexandre Dumas *père* in *The Three Musketeers*. A longing for far-off lands inspired the exotic scenes that glow on the canvases of Jean-Auguste Dominique Ingres and Eugène Delacroix. The Romantic world was one of "strangeness and wonder": the eerie landscape we meet in Samuel Taylor Coleridge's poem *Kubla Khan*, the isolation we feel in Nathaniel Hawthorne's novel *The Scarlet Letter*, and the supernatural atmosphere we encounter in Edgar Allan Poe's poem *The Raven*.

The French conquest of Algeria, in northern Africa, inspired **Delacroix** to paint an exotic harem: *The Women of Algiers* (1834).

Sympathy for the oppressed underscored the dramatic character of the Romantic movement. **Honoré Daumier** (1808–1879), *The Burden*.

Romanticism in Music

The Industrial Revolution brought with it the means to create more affordable and responsive musical instruments, as well as the technical improvements that strongly influenced the sound of Romantic music (see Interface, p. 232).

As music moved from palace and church to the public concert hall, orchestras increased in size. Naturally, this directly influenced the sound. New instruments such as the piccolo, English horn, tuba, and contrabassoon added varied timbres and extended the high and low ranges of the orchestra (see table on

The rallying cry of the French people, as depicted in a 1993 performance in Madrid of the stirring musical *Les misérables*; the show is adapted from Victor Hugo's 1862 novel of the same name.

An engraving for Edgar Allan Poe's *The Raven* (1845), published in a poetry collection illustrated by **Charles Joseph Staniland** (1838–1916).

p. 203). The dynamic range also expanded—sweeping contrasts of very loud (***fff***) and very soft (***ppp***) lent new drama to the music of the Romantics. And as orchestral music developed, so did the technique of writing for instruments. **Orchestration** became an art in itself. Composers now had a palette as broad as those of painters, and they used it to create mood and atmosphere and to evoke profound emotional responses. With all these developments, it was no longer feasible to direct an orchestra from the keyboard or the first violin desk, as had been the tradition in the eighteenth century, and thus a central figure—the conductor—was needed to guide the performance.

In order to communicate their intentions as precisely as possible, composers developed a vocabulary of highly expressive terms. Among the directions frequently encountered in nineteenth-century scores are *dolce* (sweetly), *cantabile* (songful), *dolente* (sorrowful), *maestoso* (majestic), *gioioso* (joyous), and *con amore* (with love, tenderly). A new interest in folklore and a rising tide of nationalism inspired composers to make increased use of the folk songs and dances from their native lands. As a result, a number of national styles—Hungarian, Polish, Russian, Bohemian, Scandinavian, and eventually American—flourished, greatly enriching the melodic, harmonic, and rhythmic language of music.

The exotic attracted composers as well as artists and writers. Russian, German, and French composers turned for inspiration to the warmth and color of Italy and Spain and to the glamour of Asia and the Far East. French and Italian opera composers also drew on exotic themes, notably Giuseppe Verdi in *Aida*, set in Egypt; and Giacomo Puccini in the Japanese-inspired *Madame Butterfly,* which we will hear.

Romantic Style Traits

Above all, nineteenth-century musicians tried to make their instruments "sing." Melody was marked by a lyricism that gave it an immediate appeal, and it is no accident that themes from Romantic symphonies and concertos have been transformed into popular songs, and that tunes by composers such as Frédéric Chopin, Verdi, and Peter Ilyich Tchaikovsky have enjoyed an enduring popularity with the public.

The Romantic Orchestra

Berlioz's Orchestra (*Symphonie fantastique*, 1830)	Brahms's Orchestra (Symphony No. 3, 1883)	Tchaikovsky's Orchestra (*The Nutcracker*, 1892)
STRINGS Violins 1 Violins 2 Violas Cellos Double basses 2 harps	**STRINGS** Violins 1 Violins 2 Violas Cellos Double basses	**STRINGS** Violins 1 Violins 2 Violas Cellos Double basses 2 harps
WOODWINDS 2 flutes (1 on piccolo) 2 oboes 2 clarinets (1 on E-flat clarinet) English horn 4 bassoons	**WOODWINDS** 2 flutes 2 oboes 2 clarinets 2 bassoons, contrabassoon	**WOODWINDS** 2 flutes and piccolo 2 oboes, 1 English horn 2 clarinets, bass clarinet 2 bassoons
BRASS 4 French horns 2 cornets, 2 trumpets 3 trombones (1 bass trombone) 2 ophicleides	**BRASS** 4 French horns 2 trumpets 3 trombones	**BRASS** 4 French horns 2 trumpets 2 trombones, bass trombone Tuba
PERCUSSION Timpani Cymbals Snare drum Bass drum Tubular bells (chimes)	**PERCUSSION** Timpani	**PERCUSSION** Timpani Cymbals, gong, triangle Tambourine, castanets Bass drum Tubular bells (chimes) Keyboard Celesta Other special effects (including toy instruments)

Romantic harmony and form

Composers employed combinations of pitches that were more chromatic and dissonant than those of their predecessors, allowing for emotionally charged and highly expressive harmony. They expanded the instrumental forms they had inherited from the Classical masters to give their ideas more time to play out. A symphony by Haydn or Mozart takes about twenty minutes to perform; one by Johannes Brahms lasts at least twice that long. Where Haydn wrote more than a hundred symphonies and Mozart more than forty, Franz Schubert (following the example of Beethoven) wrote nine, and Brahms four.

New orchestral forms emerged as well, including the one-movement symphonic poem, the choral symphony, and works for solo voice with orchestra. In many of these works, we can see how music in the nineteenth century drew steadily closer to the other arts. Even in their purely orchestral music, Romantic composers captured with remarkable vividness the emotional atmosphere that surrounded poetry and painting.

This chromolithograph from around 1865 shows the Royal Pavilion at Brighton, England, with its Islamic domes and minarets reflecting the nineteenth-century fascination with Eastern culture. Designed by **John Nash** (1752–1835).

Nineteenth-century music was linked to dreams and passions—to profound meditations on life and death, human destiny, God and nature, pride in one's country, desire for freedom, the political struggles of the age, and the ultimate triumph of good over evil. These intellectual and emotional associations brought music into a commanding position as a link between the artist's most personal thoughts and the realities of the outside world.

The Musician in Society

Virtuoso violinist Niccolò Paganini, painted in 1832 by **Delacroix**.

The newly democratic societies liberated composers and performers. Musical life now reached the general populace, since performances took place in the public concert hall as well as in the salons of the aristocracy. Where eighteenth-century musicians had belonged to a glorified servant class and relied on aristocratic patronage and the favor of royal courts, nineteenth-century musicians, supported by the new middle class, met their audience as equals; they could make a living in their profession. Indeed, as solo performers began to dominate the concert hall, whether as pianists, violinists (Niccolò Paganini, at left), or conductors (Franz Liszt, both pianist *and* conductor; see opposite), they became "stars" who were idolized by the public.

Although composition remained largely a man's province, a few women broke away from tradition and overcame social stereotypes to become successful composers. Among them are Clara Wieck Schumann, a talented performer and composer of piano, vocal, and chamber music, and Fanny Mendelssohn Hensel, known for her songs and piano music and also for the salon concerts she hosted in her home (see Chapter 39). We will see too that women exerted significant influence as patrons of music or through their friendships with composers. Novelist George Sand played a key role in Chopin's career, as did Princess Carolyne Sayn-Wittgenstein in Liszt's. Nedezhda von Meck is remembered as the mysterious woman who supported Tchaikovsky in the early years of his career

The Hungarian pianist and composer Franz Liszt conducting one of his oratorios in Budapest.

and made it financially possible for him to compose. These activities highlight the crucial, but largely private, contributions of women to music in this era.

With the creation of a lucrative musical market for both the home and the concert hall, debates arose about the relationship between art and commerce. While some composers (such as songwriter Stephen Foster) were exploited by the growing publishing industry, others (such as opera composer Giuseppe Verdi) were savvy businessmen and helped to establish economic models that benefit musicians to this day.

In the later 1800s, distinctions widened between "light music" for entertainment and "art music" for serious listening, a separation that gradually led to categories of "popular" and "classical" music in the century to come. So paradoxically, while access to music became much more democratic, there arose a distinction between "highbrow" and "lowbrow" in musical repertories. But this only happened later in the century: the early and middle Romantic period was a time of expansion for all aspects of music, and musicians became more important to the imagination of society than they had ever been before.

A salon concert (c. 1855) hosted by the Berlin composer Bettina von Arnim, seated in the black dress. Watercolor by **Carl Johann Arnold** (1829–1916).

CRITICAL THINKING

1. What are the principal ideas of Romanticism? How are these reflected in art and literature?

2. How did changing roles of musicians in society affect the development of Romantic music?

Chapter 36

Musical Reading: Schubert, Schumann, and the Early Romantic Lied

"Out of my great sorrows I make my little songs."

—Heinrich Heine

The immense appeal of the Romantic art song was due in part to the increased popularity and availability of the piano. A lithograph by **Achille Devéria** (1800–1857), *In the Salon*.

I f a song is meaningful to us, we may have a tendency to identify the words as carrying that meaning. But those words are sung, not spoken, and if someone were to read them, we would likely not find the effect nearly as compelling. This is the power and paradox of song: while it's easy to focus on the text, the music carries the subtle intensity. Some songs rely on simple musical elements, highlighting the predominance of the voice; others employ greater complexity of melody, texture, and timbre, providing multiple resources for the expression of emotion. Within the music you listen to on a regular basis, you can probably identify a wide range of approaches to the interaction between text and music. Becoming aware of these different approaches will increase your understanding of the expressive potential of song.

The Lied

Though songs have existed throughout the ages, the **art song** as we know it today was a product of the Romantic era. The **Lied** (plural, **Lieder**), as the new genre was called, is a German-texted solo song, generally with piano accompaniment.

Prominent composers in this tradition were Franz Schubert, Robert Schumann, and Johannes Brahms, as well as Fanny Mendelssohn Hensel and Clara Wieck Schumann.

In some repertories, the words for a song are newly written; in others, composers choose preexisting poetry for their musical settings. Composers of the Lied were especially dedicated to the latter approach, often releasing "competing" musical settings from the outpouring of poetry that marked German Romanticism. Johann Wolfgang von Goethe (1749–1832) and Heinrich Heine (1797–1856) were the two leading figures among a group of poets who, like Wordsworth, Byron, Shelley, and Keats in England, favored short, personal, "lyric" poems. Overall, Romantic poems range from tender sentiment to dramatic balladry; common themes are love, longing, and the beauty of nature. Some composers, like Schubert and Schumann, wrote groups of Lieder that were unified by a narrative thread or descriptive theme, known as a **song cycle**.

Schubert (walking at left) on an outing in the Austrian countryside with his friends (known as Schubertians), painted by one of them (also at left), **Leopold Kupelwieser** (1796–1862).

Another circumstance that made the art song popular was the emergence of the piano as the preferred household instrument of the nineteenth century. Voice and piano together infused the short lyric form with feeling and made it suitable for amateurs and artists alike, in both the home and the concert hall.

Types of Song Structure

In the nineteenth century, two main song structures prevailed. One was **strophic** form, in which the same melody is repeated with every stanza, or strophe, of the poem; hymns, carols, as well as most folk and popular songs are strophic. This form sets up a general atmosphere that accommodates all the stanzas, all sung to the same tune.

The other song type, **through-composed**, proceeds from beginning to end without repetitions of whole sections. Here the music follows the story line, changing according to the text. This makes it possible for the composer to mirror every shade of meaning in the words.

There is also an intermediate type that combines features of the other two. The same melody may be repeated for two or three stanzas, with new material introduced when the poem requires it. This is considered a **modified-strophic** form, similar to what we heard in the lovely first movement of Beethoven's *Moonlight* Sonata.

Schubert and the Lied

Franz Schubert was a young songwriting prodigy who composed more than six hundred Lieder in his short life. While some of his songs (like *Elfking*, examined below) were performed in concert settings, most of his career was built on intimate musical performances in friends' and sponsors' homes, for which Schubert would write not only Lieder but also dances and chamber works. His gift for melodic writing and the subtle interactions he created between vocal part and accompaniment have made his Lieder a staple of the art-song repertory for both amateurs and professionals to the present day.

In His Own Words

❝ [With a good poem] you immediately get a good idea; melodies pour in so that it is a real joy. With a bad poem you can't get anywhere; you torment yourself over it, and nothing comes of it but boring rubbish.❞

— *Franz Schubert*

Franz Schubert (1797–1828)

Schubert was born in Vienna and educated at the Imperial Chapel, where he sang in the choir that later became the famous Vienna Boys' Choir. Although his father hoped he would pursue a career in teaching, Schubert fell in with a small group of writers, artists, and fellow musicians who organized a series of concerts, called Schubertiads, where the young composer's newest works could be heard. One of his friends claimed that "everything he touched turned to song."

He wrote *Elfking*, as well as other great songs, when he was still a teenager. This work won him swift public recognition; still, he had difficulty finding a publisher for his instrumental works, and he was often pressed for money, selling his music for much less than it was worth. His later works, including the song cycle *Winter's Journey*, sound a somber lyricism that parallels his struggle with life, made worse by being afflicted with syphilis. Schubert's dying wish, at age thirty-one, was to be buried near the master he worshipped—Beethoven; his wish was granted.

Schubert's music marks the confluence of the Classical and Romantic eras. His symphonies and chamber music are Classical in their clear forms. In his songs, though, he was wholly the Romantic, writing beautiful melodies that match the tone of the poetry he set. To his earlier masterpieces he added, in the final year of his life, a group of profound works that includes the String Quintet in C, three piano sonatas, and thirteen of his finest songs.

MAJOR WORKS: More than 600 Lieder, including *Erlkönig* (*Elfking*, 1815), *Die Forelle* (*The Trout*, 1817), and the song cycles *Die schöne Mullerin* (*The Lovely Maid of the Mill*, 1823) and *Winterreise* (*Winter's Journey*, 1827) • Nine symphonies, including the *Unfinished* (No. 8, 1822) • Chamber music, including quintets, string quartets, piano trios • Piano sonatas • Seven Masses • Other choral music • Operas and incidental music.

 Trout **Quintet, IV;** *The Miller and the Brook,* **from** *The Lovely Maid of the Mill*

Elfking (Erlkönig)

This masterpiece of Schubert's youth (LG 26) captures the Romantic "strangeness and wonder" of the poem, a celebrated ballad by Goethe, in which a father and his sick child are riding through a forest on a windy night. *Elfking* is based on a legend that whoever is touched by the king of the elves must die.

The eerie atmosphere of the poem is first established by the piano. Galloping triplets are heard against a rumbling figure in the bass. This motive, perhaps suggesting a horse's pounding hooves (or maybe a child's fast heartbeat?), pervades the song, helping to unify it. The poem's four characters—the narrator, father, child, and seductive elf—are all sung by one soloist but vividly differentiated through changes in the melody, register, harmony, rhythm, and accompaniment.

The legend of *The Elfking* (c. 1860), as portrayed by **Moritz von Schwind** (1804–1871), a good friend of Schubert's.

The child's terror is suggested by clashing dissonance and a high vocal range. The father calms his son's fears with a more rounded vocal line, sung in a low register. And the Elfking cajoles the child in suavely melodious phrases set in a major key.

The song is through-composed; Schubert chose to avoid stanza-based repetition, instead changing the accompaniment for each stanza of Goethe's poem, shaping his music to follow the action of the story with a steady rise in tension—and pitch—that builds almost to the end. The work of an eighteen-year-old, *Elfking* was a milestone in the history of musical Romanticism: Schubert chose it as his first work to be published (though he had written many other songs), and it quickly became one of the most popular songs of the nineteenth century.

LISTENING GUIDE 26 4:00

Schubert: *Elfking* (*Erlkönig*)

DATE: 1815

GENRE: Lied

What to Listen For

Melody	Wide-ranging; each character sings in a different range.
	    Narrator: middle register, minor key.
	    Father: low register, minor key.
	    Son: high register, minor key.
	    Elfking: middle register, major key.

Rhythm/ meter	Almost constant triplets in the piano; duple meter; more lilting feel for Elfking.
Harmony	Shifts from minor to major (for Elfking); dissonance projects the boy's terror.

Form	Through-composed.
Expression	Fast, with a mood of urgency in the accompaniment and dramatic dialogue.
Performing forces	Solo voice and piano.
Text	Narrative poem in eight stanzas by Johann Wolfgang von Goethe.

0:00   Piano introduction—minor key and rapid repeated octaves in triplets set the mood, simulating horse's hooves:

TEXT	**TRANSLATION**
	Narrator (minor mode, middle range)
0:23 Wer reitet so spät durch Nacht und Wind? Es ist der Vater mit seinem Kind; Er hat den Knaben wohl in dem Arm, Er fasst ihn sicher, er hält ihn warm.	Who rides so late through night and wind? It is the father with his child; he has the boy close in his arm, he holds him safely, he keeps him warm.
	Father (low range)
"Mein Sohn, was birgst du so bang dein Gesicht?"	"My son, why do you hide your face in fear?"
	Son (high range)
"Siehst, Vater, du den Erlkönig nicht? Den Erlenkönig mit Kron' und Schweif?"	"Father, don't you see the Elfking? The Elfking with his crown and train?"
	Father (low range)
"Mein Sohn, es ist ein Nebelstreif."	"My son, it is a streak of mist."
	Elfking (major mode, melodic)
1:29 "Du liebes Kind, komm, geh mit mir! Gar schöne Spiele spiel' ich mit dir; Manch' bunte Blumen sind an dem Strand; Meine Mutter hat manch' gülden Gewand."	"You dear child, come with me! I'll play very lovely games with you. There are lots of colorful flowers by the shore; my mother has some golden robes."
	Son (high range, frightened)
1:51 "Mein Vater, mein Vater, und hörest du nicht, Was Erlenkönig mir leise verspricht?"	"My father, my father, don't you hear the Elfking whispering promises to me?"

Continued on next page

Father (low range, calming)

"Sei ruhig, bleibe ruhig, mein Kind;	"Be still, stay calm, my child;
In dürren Blättern säuselt der Wind."	it's the wind rustling in the dry leaves."

Elfking (major mode, cajoling)

2:13
"Willst, feiner Knabe, du mit mir geh'n?	"My fine lad, do you want to come with me?
Meine Töchter sollen dich warten schön;	My daughters will take care of you;
Meine Töchter führen den nächtlichen Reih'n	my daughters lead the nightly dance,
Und wiegen und tanzen und singen dich ein."	and they'll rock and dance and sing you to sleep."

Son (high range, dissonant outcry)

2:31
"Mein Vater, mein Vater, und siehst du nicht dort,	"My father, my father, don't you see
Erlkönigs Töchter am düstern Ort?"	the Elfking's daughters over there in the shadows?"

Father (low range, reassuring)

"Mein Sohn, mein Sohn, ich seh' es genau,	"My son, my son, I see it clearly,
Es scheinen die alten Weiden so grau."	it's the gray sheen of the old willows."

Elfking (loving, then insistent)

3:00
"Ich liebe dich, mich reizt deine schöne Gestalt,	"I love you, your beautiful form delights me!
Und bist du nicht willig, so brauch' ich Gewalt."	And if you're not willing, then I'll use force."

Son (high range, terrified)

3:12
"Mein Vater, mein Vater, jetzt fasst er mich an!	"My father, my father, now he's touching me!
Erlkönig hat mir ein Leids gethan!"	The Elfking has done me harm!"

Narrator (middle register, speechlike)

3:26
Dem Vater grausets, er reitet geschwind,	The father shudders, he rides swiftly,
Er hält in Armen das ächzende Kind,	he holds the moaning child in his arms;
Erreicht den Hof mit Müh und Noth:	with effort and urgency he reaches the courtyard:
In seinen Armen das Kind war todt.	in his arms the child was dead.

Melody of son's dissonant outcry on "My father, my father":

Schumann and the Song Cycle

"Music is to me the perfect expression of the soul."

The turbulence of early German Romanticism, its fantasy and subjective emotion, found its voice in Robert Schumann. Like Schubert, Schumann showed his lyric gifts in his songs, many of which appear in unified song cycles with texts from a single poet.

A Poet's Love (Dichterliebe)

Schumann wrote his great cycle *A Poet's Love*, sixteen songs to poems by Heinrich Heine, in 1840. While the texts come from the same poetry collection, they tell no real story; rather, they follow a psychological progression that spirals downward from the freshness of love through a growing disappointment to complete despair.

We will consider the first song in the cycle, *In the Lovely Month of May* (LG 27), which consists of two strophes (verses, or stanzas). The piano's introduction to the first strophe sets a wistful rather than joyous mood, and the song proceeds to

Robert Schumann [1810–1856]

Schumann was born in Zwickau, Germany, and studied law at the University of Leipzig and at Heidelberg. But he soon surrendered to his passion for music—it was his ambition to become a pianist and to study with Friedrich Wieck, one of the foremost teachers of his day. When an injury to his right hand dashed his dream of being a pianist, Schumann turned his efforts to composition. While still in his twenties, he created many of his most important piano works. Meanwhile, his literary talent found expression through a publication he established, *Neue Zeitschrift für Musik* (*The New Journal of Music*); this soon became the leading journal of music criticism in Europe.

Throughout the 1830s, Robert carried on an intense courtship with the gifted pianist and composer Clara Wieck, daughter of his former teacher. Friedrich, who viewed his daughter as his supreme achievement, refused to allow them to marry; but they did finally, in 1840, when Clara was twenty-one and Robert thirty. The two settled in Leipzig, pursuing their careers side by side. Clara furthered her husband's music as the foremost interpreter of his piano works, but her devotion could not ward off Robert's increasing withdrawal from the world and auditory hallucinations. After he threw himself into the Rhine River, Clara was forced to place him in an asylum, where his psychotic behavior gave way to advanced dementia, the result of syphilis. He died in 1856, at the age of forty-six.

Schumann's music is imbued with impassioned melodies, novel changes of harmonies, and driving rhythms that reveal him as a true Romantic. His four symphonies exude a lyric freshness and Romantic approach to harmony. He often attached literary meanings to his piano music and was fond of cycles of short pieces connected by a literary theme or musical motto. In his songs, he stands alongside Schubert. Just as Schubert had an affinity for the poetry of Goethe, Schumann favored the texts of Heine, whose poems make up his song cycle *A Poet's Love* (*Dichterliebe*).

MAJOR WORKS: More than 200 Lieder, some in song cycles, including *Dichterliebe* (*A Poet's Love*, 1840) • Orchestral music, including four symphonies and a piano concerto • Chamber music, including string quartets, piano trios, a piano quintet, and a piano quartet • Piano music, including sonatas and numerous miniatures • One opera • Choral music • Incidental music.

evoke the fragility of a new love—through its harmonic meandering between two key centers and by its lack of a final resolution. We are left suspended at the end, knowing there is much more to this story in the songs that follow.

There is lovely text-painting at the end of the first verse, as the melody rises to a climax on "did love rise up." The piano's introduction, interlude, and postlude frame the two text strophes and provide a circular shape to the song. We might wonder if this Lied is really about a new relationship, or rather expresses the longing and desire of a lost or unrequited love.

Both Schubert and Schumann created a unity of expression between text and music (and voice and piano) that enhanced the words of the poems they chose, giving them meanings beyond what their poets had envisioned. This is the nature of song, and the reason why we still thrill at its power.

CRITICAL THINKING

1. What are the respective roles of the singer and pianist in a Lied?
2. What is Romantic about these two songs of Schubert and Schumann?

Clara Schumann at age thirty-one, with her husband Robert. Anonymous lithograph (1850).

YOUR TURN TO EXPLORE

Consider a couple of your favorite songs. Are they strophic, through-composed, or modified strophic? Why do you think the songwriters have chosen those particular forms? Do they differentiate the stanzas? How are instruments used to reinforce musical repetitions and to help underline key moments?

LISTENING GUIDE 27

 1:38

Schumann: *In the Lovely Month of May, from A Poet's Love (Dichterliebe)*

DATE: 1840

GENRE: Lied, from a song cycle

What to Listen For

Melody	Winding melodic line, set syllabically; both verses rise to a climax.
Rhythm/ meter	Piano part moves somewhat freely in rising lines.
Harmony	Meandering, with a lack of resolution to the tonic.

Form	Strophic (two verses); with a piano prelude, interlude, and postlude.
Expression	Melancholic mood portrays unrequited love.
Performing forces	Solo voice and piano.
Text	Heinrich Heine poem, with text-painting in the music.

	TEXT	TRANSLATION
0:00	Piano introduction.	
	Strophe 1	
0:13	Im wunderschönen Monat Mai als alle Knospen sprangen, da ist in meinem Herzen die Liebe aufgegangen.	In the lovely month of May, as all the buds were blossoming, then in my heart did love rise up.
0:45	Piano interlude.	
	Strophe 2	
0:52	Im wunderschönen Monat Mai als alle Vögel sangen, da hab ich ihr gestanden mein Sehnen und Verlangen.	In the lovely month of May, as all the birds were singing, then did I confess to her my longing and desire.
1:18	Piano postlude, ending on a dissonance with no final resolution of the harmony.	

Opening of vocal line:

Im wun - der-schö-nen Mo - nat Mai,

Chapter 37

Marketing Music: Foster and Early "Popular" Song

"Weep no more my lady,
Oh! Weep no more today;
We will sing one song for the old Kentucky home,
For the old Kentucky home far away."

—Stephen Foster

KEY POINTS

- Nineteenth-century songwriters in the United States combined elements of European art song and opera with other traditions to create commercially successful "popular" music.

- Songs often were popularized through **minstrel shows**, which were racially charged theatrical variety shows.

- The minstrel and **parlor songs** of Stephen Foster (including *Jeanie with the Light Brown Hair*) were very successful during his lifetime and remain so today.

What makes a song successful? Some melodies have become so beloved and familiar that we no longer associate them with an individual composer—for example, "Happy Birthday," which you probably have sung countless times without compensating the copyright holder, Warner Chappell Publishing Company. This is one meaning of "popular"—we think of "Happy Birthday" as belonging to "the people." Another meaning connects to the idea of success: some music has brought great financial profit, partly because it has been carefully marketed. These two meanings of "popular" intersect in the songs of Stephen Foster, whose music has long saturated North American culture. Foster helped build a powerful musical industry in the nineteenth-century United States, while earning very little profit from the skyrocketing sales of his sheet music. The accessibility of his songs laid the foundation for the enormous international influence of North American musical culture in the following century.

Music in Early North America: Cultivated and Vernacular

European immigrants to the Americas brought with them cultivated repertories such as operas, chamber music, and symphonies. Along with this imported "high art," they also began to develop traditions of lighter music—for dancing, singing at home, and public events such as parades. These traditions were thought of as

Posters advertising minstrel shows often used images of performers both in blackface costume (below) and in more formal poses (above), perhaps to reassure audiences of the "proper" nature of the show.

Camptown Races

vernacular, more connected to new notions of "American popular identity." However, there was not yet a clear split between "classical" and "popular" music in the nineteenth century; the various traditions were mutually influential, and audiences would often encounter them in the same spaces and even performed by the same ensembles.

Stephen Foster, Parlor Song, and Minstrelsy

The songs of Stephen Foster exemplify the intersection between the vernacular American spirit and the European art tradition. Foster was familiar with the Italian operas that were popular among the upper classes, and was also aware of the great financial success of nostalgic "folk songs" that helped second- and third-generation Anglo immigrants fantasize about an ideal Old Country their grandparents had left. He blended the two traditions in his **parlor songs**, which are often sweet, sentimental, and nostalgic; we will consider one, *Jeanie with the Light Brown Hair*. Though many of Foster's songs were designed for amateur performance in the parlor (a reception or gathering place) of a middle-class home, several became popular through a very prominent and uniquely North American nineteenth-century musical tradition: the minstrel show.

Minstrelsy can be unpleasant for modern audiences to face: the shows featured white performers in blackface, acting out idealized "scenes from the plantation" that were vastly different from the realities of slave life. Minstrelsy is one of the first traditions that revealed white Americans' fascination with—and misunderstanding of—African Americans, and because of its widespread popularity in the 1800s, it shaped stereotyping of African American culture well into the twentieth century.

Two examples of Foster's songs written for or incorporated into minstrel shows are *Camptown Races*, in which a slave sings of his happy time betting on horses, and *Old Folks at Home* ("Way down upon the Swanee River"). While Foster himself was sympathetic toward the Abolitionist cause and wanted his "plantation songs" to inspire compassion for the plight of slaves, it was they rather than his parlor songs that earned him most of his income.

A Song by Foster

Foster's *Jeanie with the Light Brown Hair* (LG 28) was written in 1853–54, just after the composer separated from his wife. In his sketchbook, the original title was not "Jeanie" but "Jennie," from Jane Denny McDowell's name. The tone is bittersweet, wishing for days gone by, and draws on the then-popular tradition of Anglo-Irish folk song. The song, like most of Foster's, is strophic and set for solo voice and piano, thereby meeting the growing need for parlor music appropriate for amateurs. The brief cadenza before the return of the opening music marks a moment of free interpretation for the performer. Though we might be tempted to read this as a personal narrative expressing Foster's own nostalgia, we must also keep in mind that Foster was not a singer and would have expected the song to be

Stephen Foster (1826–1864)

Foster grew up outside Pittsburgh, where he spent much of his life, and attended Jefferson College (now Washington & Jefferson College). Rather than completing his degree, he moved to Cincinnati, where he wrote his first hit song, *Oh! Susanna*. Many of Foster's early songs were for the blackface minstrel shows that were popular during this era. From 1847 on, he was under contract with the Christy Minstrels, who specialized in performing blackface shows. For them, he wrote some of his most enduring songs, including *Camptown Races* and *Old Folks at Home*. Later he turned to ballads and love songs, like *Jeanie with the Light Brown Hair*. These songs, evoking themes of lost youth and happiness, reflect his desire to write more

serious music. Although Foster did not spend much time in the South, it is thought that *My Old Kentucky Home*, today the state song of Kentucky, was inspired by Harriet Beecher Stowe's antislavery novel *Uncle Tom's Cabin*.

Foster was perhaps the first American to make a living as a professional songwriter, but composers in this era made little profit from their publications. After he and his wife separated, Foster moved to New York, where he wrote his famous song *Beautiful Dreamer*, conceived in the style of an Italian air. He died there at age thirty-seven, a penniless alcoholic, victim to a fall in a cheap New York hotel room. Today, Foster's songs are much better known than he is.

 Camptown Races; Oh! Susanna; Massa's in the Cold, Cold Ground

performed primarily by amateurs in their homes, each of whom would bring her or his own interpretation of the object of the melancholy "dreaming."

Unlike some other Foster songs, *Jeanie* was not a huge success during his lifetime. However, it reached millions nearly a century later when, in 1941, a dispute broke out over licensing fees charged by companies that owned the rights to newly composed music, and some radio broadcasters chose to air older music that would cost them less to play. Thus, economic considerations once again helped to make this song even more "popular."

The title page to *Jeanie with the Light Brown Hair* (1854).

CRITICAL THINKING

1. How did ideas about "high" and "low" culture come together in nineteenth-century North American music?

2. What makes the lyrics and music of Stephen Foster "popular" today?

YOUR TURN TO EXPLORE

What can you find out about the economic networks that support musicians or bands? How do you suppose the musicians' creative choices (country, rap, folk-rock) have influenced their commercial distribution? Do you think technologies have influenced these creative choices, and if so, how?

LISTENING GUIDE 28

 1:27

Foster: *Jeanie with the Light Brown Hair*

DATE: 1854

GENRE: Parlor song

What to Listen For

Melody	Wavelike (descending, then ascending); syllabic setting.	**Texture**	Homophonic.
Rhythm/ meter	Moderate tempo in broad quadruple meter.	**Form**	Strophic, in **A-A′-B-A** song form.
		Performing forces	Tenor and pianoforte.
Harmony	Major key, simple block- and broken-chord accompaniment.	**Text**	Strophic poem by Foster (verse 1 only).

0:00   **Piano introduction**

0:12   **Verse**

I dream of Jeanie with the light brown hair,   **A section**
Borne, like a vapor, on the summer air!
I see her tripping where the bright streams play,   **A′ section** (varied)
Happy as the daisies that dance on her way.
Many were the wild notes her merry voice would pour,   **B section**
Many were the blithe birds that warbled them o'er;
Oh! I dream of Jeanie with the light brown hair,   **A section** returns.
Floating like a vapor, on the soft summer air.

1:13   **Piano postlude**

Opening of verse, with descending melodic line:

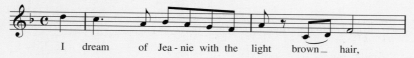

I   dream   of   Jea - nie with the   light   brown — hair,

B section, with wavelike line:

Ma - ny   were the wild   notes   her mer - ry voice would pour.

Chapter 38

Dancing at the Keyboard: Chopin and Romantic Piano Music

"To be a great composer, one needs an enormous amount of knowledge, which . . . one does not acquire from listening only to other people's works, but even more from listening to one's own."

—Frédéric Chopin

KEY POINTS

- Technical improvements to the nineteenth-century piano led to the development of the modern concert grand piano.
- Polish composer Frédéric Chopin dedicated his entire compositional output to the piano; he is said to have originated the modern piano style.
- Chopin's works include études (highly virtuosic study pieces), meditative nocturnes, preludes, and dances (including **Polish mazurkas** and polonaises), as well as sonatas and concertos for piano. His music calls for the use of **rubato**, or "robbed time."

Of all musical instruments, the piano is the most central to the Western musical tradition. From the nineteenth century onward, the instrument was increasingly hailed as equally suited to amateurs and professionals, to the home and to the concert hall. Before the arrival of recorded sound, families and communities alike gathered around the piano to make and hear music. Learning to play was long a staple of refined education, and you may have taken at least a few lessons yourself. One of the most valued aspects of the piano is its suitability for polyphonic and homophonic textures, whether on its own or by accompanying voices or instruments. It can also create a variety of dynamic and resonant effects. Today the piano is still considered the most expressive instrument available to most musicians, and we owe this to the skilled individuals who refined the technologies of construction and performance in the early nineteenth century.

The Nineteenth-Century Piano

The rise in popularity of the piano helped shape the musical culture of the Romantic era. It proved especially attractive to amateurs because melody and harmony could be performed on one instrument, as they couldn't on strings or winds. The piano thus played a crucial role in the taste and experience of the new mass public.

Hardly less important was the rise of the virtuoso pianist. At first, the per-

A Parisian salon concert depicted by **James Tissot** (1836–1902).

former was also the composer; Mozart and Beethoven introduced their own piano concertos to the public. With the developing concert industry, however, a class of virtuoso performers arose whose only function was to dazzle audiences by playing music composed by others.

The nineteenth century saw a series of crucial technical improvements that led to the development of the modern concert grand, mandated by Romantic composers' quest for greater power and dynamic range. Piano manufacturing eventually moved from the craft shop to the factory, allowing a huge increase in production at a significantly reduced cost. A standardized instrument was developed that had a metal frame supporting increased string tension, as well as an improved mechanical action and extended range of notes—from five octaves to seven or more. At the Paris Exhibition of 1867, two American manufacturers took the top awards, among them Steinway, maker of some of today's finest pianos. By the early twentieth century, the piano had become a universal fixture in the homes of middle-class and upper-class families.

In His Own Words

" The pianoforte is the most important of all musical instruments; its invention was to music what the invention of printing was to poetry."

—*George Bernard Shaw*

The Short Lyric Piano Piece

With its ability to project melodious and dramatic moods within a compact form, the short lyric piano piece, or **character piece**, was the equivalent to the song. Composers adopted new and sometimes fanciful terms for such works. Some titles—"Prelude," "Intermezzo" (interlude), "Impromptu" (on the spur of the moment), and "Nocturne" (a night piece), for example—suggest free, almost improvisational forms. Many composers produced keyboard versions of dances like the Polish mazurka and polonaise and the Viennese waltz, as well as the lively scherzo. They sometimes chose more descriptive titles for character pieces that depict a mood or scene, such as "Wild Hunt," "The Little Bell," and "Forest Murmurs" (all by Franz Liszt).

Nineteenth-century composers who refined the short piano piece—Schubert, Chopin, Liszt, Felix Mendelssohn, Fanny Mendelssohn Hensel, Robert and Clara

Frédéric Chopin (1810–1849)

Chopin was born outside Warsaw to a French father and a Polish mother. He studied at the Conservatory of Warsaw, but in 1831 left for Paris, where he spent the remainder of his career. Paris in the 1830s was the center of the new Romanticism, and the circle in which Chopin moved included the most famous composers, writers, and artists in France.

Through the virtuoso pianist Franz Liszt, Chopin met the novelist George Sand, with whom he had a long relationship. He spent his summers at Sand's estate in Nohant, where she entertained prominent artists and writers. These were productive years for the composer, although his health grew progressively worse and his relationship with Sand ran its course from love to conflict, jealousy, and hostility. He died of tuberculosis in Paris at the age of thirty-nine.

Chopin's works, central to the pianist's repertory, include four epic ballades, the thoroughly Romantic Sonatas in B-flat Minor and B Minor, and two piano concertos. The nocturnes are melancholic and meditative. The preludes are visionary fragments, and in the études, which crown the literature of the study piece, Chopin's piano technique is transformed into poetry. The mazurkas, derived from a Polish peasant dance, evoke the idealized landscape of his youth, and the polonaises revive the stately processional dance in which Poland's nobles hailed their kings.

MAJOR WORKS: Two piano concertos • Piano music, including four ballades, three sonatas, preludes, études, mazurkas, polonaises, scherzos, waltzes, impromptus, and nocturnes • Chamber music, all with piano • Songs.

 Prelude in E Minor, Op. 28, No. 2; Prelude in B-flat Minor, Op. 28, No. 4

Schumann, and Brahms—showed inexhaustible ingenuity in exploring the technical resources of the instrument and its potential for expression.

A Mazurka by Chopin

"My life [is] an episode without a beginning and with a sad end."

Frédéric Chopin's music, rooted in the heart of Romanticism, made this era the piano's golden age. His style was entirely his own—there is no mistaking it for any other—and he remains one of the most original artists of the nineteenth century.

Chopin's entire creative life revolved around the piano, and he is credited with originating the modern piano style. The delicate ornaments in his melodies—trills, grace notes, runs—seem magically to prolong a single tone, and widely spaced chords in the bass line, sustained by the pedal, set up masses of sound that encircle the melody. All this generally lies so well for the trained hand that the music seems almost to play itself. "Everything must be made to sing," he told his pupils.

Much of Chopin's piano music looks back to his Polish roots, including his polonaises and mazurkas, both native dance forms. The **mazurka** originated in Mazovia, Chopin's home district in Poland, as a lively triple-meter dance with the accent on the second or third beat of the measure. In his hands, the genre was transformed from a heroic folk dance to a true art form. The Mazurka in B-flat Minor, Op. 24, No. 4, one of a set of four written in 1833, is an exquisite example of the genre (LG 29). We are drawn into a sinuous melody that is rich in chromaticism and elusive in mood. While most mazurkas have a simple ternary (**A-B-A**) form, this one is longer, with clearly defined sections, each colored with new emotional content.

Chopin's music calls for the use of **rubato**, or "robbed time," in which certain

Portrait of George Sand (Aurore Dupin, Baroness Dudevant, 1804–1876), famous novelist and Chopin's lover.

liberties are taken with the rhythm without upsetting the basic beat. Chopin taught his students that the left hand should remain steady while the right-hand melody might hesitate a little here and hurry forward there. The subtle harmonic shifts between major, minor, and modal scales typical of folk music, and the spirited rhythms as well as the large-scale structure, make this one of Chopin's most ambitious works. Schumann praised the expressive depth of Chopin's music, suggesting he was a "poet." And to this day, his music is revisited around the world by pianists of all abilities, each finding a unique way to revitalize the composer's extraordinary connection with this most technologically versatile of instruments.

CRITICAL THINKING

1. What genres of piano compositions were new to the Romantic period? Which continued from the Classical era?

2. Why is Chopin considered "the poet of the piano"?

YOUR TURN TO EXPLORE

Compare videos of different keyboard players, ideally performing the same Chopin piece. Do the performers choose the same tempo, both overall and at specific "rubato" moments? How do different performers' choices reveal different notions of expressiveness? How do pianists' physical movements differ, and how does this movement create different ideas of "singing through the piano"?

LISTENING GUIDE 29

 5:06

Chopin: Mazurka in B-flat Minor, Op. 24, No. 4

DATE: 1833

GENRE: Mazurka for solo piano

What to Listen For

Melody	Chromatic lines, wide-ranging, disjunct.	**Texture**	Largely homophonic, with regular left-hand accompaniment in quarter notes.
Rhythm/ meter	Moderate triple meter; dancelike dotted and double-dotted rhythms; frequent accents on third beat, later on second beat.	**Form**	A-B-A'-B-A'-C-C-D-A; long coda.
Harmony	Shifts between major and minor; modal harmonies; much chromaticism.	**Expression**	Much rubato; many accents.

Introduction

0:00   Melodic octave, decreases chromatically:

Moderato ♩ = 132

etc.

A section

0:09   Short, syncopated, dotted-note idea, rises sequentially and in a *crescendo*; beat 3 is accented in alternate measures:

B section

0:35   More disjunct, with rising line, answered by falling double-dotted pattern; marked *dolce* (sweetly); accents now on third beat of each measure:

0:57   Section closes with a reminiscence of **A.**

1:21   **B section** repeated, with a hint of **A.**

C section

2:10   Simpler texture in octaves, more lyrical (legato, or smooth); octaves at opening of section are answered by block chords:

2:22   **C section** repeated.

D section

2:33   Triplet pattern in melody; animated, with accents now on second beat of alternate measures:

3:24   **A section** returns, introduced by falling chromatic intervals reminiscent of **B section.**

Coda

3:50   Simpler, more static melody; accents on second beat; slows into final cadence on F; accompaniment drops out for a lingering last melodic idea.

Chapter 39

Musical Diaries: Hensel and Programmatic Piano Music

"I have called my piano pieces after the names of my favorite haunts . . . they will form a delightful souvenir, a kind of second diary."

—*Fanny Mendelssohn Hensel*

KEY POINTS

- While women in the nineteenth century were discouraged from composing by social convention, they played an essential role as patrons, sponsors, and teachers, as well as coordinating musical activity in the home.

- Fanny Mendelssohn Hensel, sister of Felix Mendelssohn and an important sponsor of his music, was also was a talented pianist and composer, known today for her Lieder and piano music, including the autobiographical cycle *The Year* (*Das Jahr*).

I n telling our story about the musical past, we've been focusing on composers, largely because written-down compositions constitute the most precise evidence we have of musical activity before the invention of sound recording at the end of the 1800s. But other types of individuals have been essential to music from even before the beginnings of notation: for example, performers have brought written compositions to life, teachers have passed on both performance skills and compositional savvy, and patrons have provided musicians with career-promoting opportunities. While social assumptions about women long discouraged them from composing (and limited their public performances), they were crucial teachers and sponsors of music from the earliest days of the European tradition. Considering their roles is important, since it can help us remember that composition and performance are only two aspects of musical activity, and that teaching—and active sponsorship—are still just as crucial to the success of both new and established musical works.

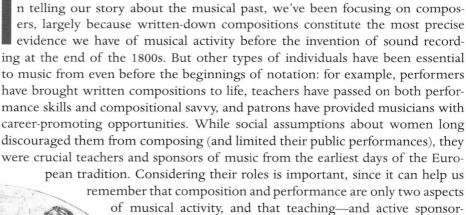

German artist **Ludwig Richter** (1803–1884) portrays a typical family music-making scene in his woodcut *Hausmusik* (1851).

Women and Music in Nineteenth-Century Society

In this era, women made great strides in establishing careers as professional musicians and public advocates for musical innovation. This path was now possible through the broadening of educational opportunities: in

Music, Gender, and Domesticity

A young woman enjoys the solitary diversion of the piano in *A Sonata of Beethoven*, painted by **Alfred Edward Emslie** (1848–1918).

In the nineteenth century, young women in Europe and in America alike were expected to have certain accomplishments, and primary among these was music. Though Fanny Mendelssohn Hensel received excellent music training—equivalent to that of her famous composer/brother Felix—she was strongly advised by both her father and brother to exhibit these skills only in the private world of the parlor, where friends gathered for informal conversation and entertainment, rather than in a public venue, and to focus her life entirely on home and family. Such was the burden of upper-class women: societal expectations were rigid, and few challenged these attitudes.

If you have read Jane Austen's novel *Pride and Prejudice* (or seen one of the several film adaptations), you may recall Mr. Darcy's high standard for the women of his day: "A woman must have a thorough knowledge of music, singing, drawing, dancing, and the modern languages." Notice that music comes first; indeed, in this and other Austen novels, women are frequently called upon to play the piano, sometimes accompanying themselves while singing. The purpose of this demonstration is not only for the entertainment of family and friends; an accomplished performance by a woman of marriageable age could attract—and seduce—a possible suitor at home, all within the bounds of socially acceptable behavior.

In *Pride and Prejudice*, Mary Bennet is devoted to practicing her music skills in an effort to compensate for her less-than-beautiful appearance. The scenes presented here mirrored Austen's own life; according to one family memoir, Jane "began her day with music," choosing to practice before breakfast, in solitude. Beyond the written word, the image of the young woman at the keyboard is strongly reinforced by artists, whose scenes of domestic music-making, ranging from the Baroque era (see the Vermeer painting on p. 104) through the nineteenth century (see Emslie painting, at left), confirm not only the importance of music in the life of women, but also the increasing popularity of the piano and the secure place it won in middle- and upper-class homes.

Miss Elizabeth Bennet plays the pianoforte for Mr. Darcy and a friend, from an 1895 edition of Jane Austen's *Pride and Prejudice* (originally published 1813), illustrated by **Charles Edmond Brock** (1870–1938).

public conservatories, women could receive training as singers, instrumentalists, and even composers. Likewise, the rise of the piano as the favored chamber instrument, both solo and with voice or other instruments, provided women of the middle and upper classes with a performance outlet that was socially acceptable. Indeed, as music for the home increased in importance with the mass-marketing of instruments and sheet music, such music-making was increasingly associated with female social graces. This made instruction on the piano and other

Hensel's music room in her Berlin residence (1849) features her grand piano at right. Watercolor by **Julius Eduard Wilhelm Helfft** (1818–1894).

amateur-friendly instruments more and more desirable; and increasingly women became piano teachers as well as students, since it was considered a little scandalous for a man to be in close proximity—let alone physical contact—with an unrelated woman.

Although composition remained largely a man's province, some women broke away from tradition and overcame social stereotypes to become successful composers. Among them were Fanny Mendelssohn Hensel, known for her songs, piano music, and chamber works; and Clara Wieck Schumann, a talented performer and composer of piano, vocal, and chamber music. Both, however, were only tentatively encouraged by their male relatives. Women also exerted a significant influence as patrons of music or through their friendship with composers. We noted earlier that novelist George Sand enabled Chopin to focus on his creative work during their sometimes stormy relationship. Several women of the upper class, including Fanny Mendelssohn and Bettina von Arnim (see p. 205), presided over musical salons where composers could gather to perform and discuss their music.

Fanny Mendelssohn Hensel and the Piano Miniature

The music of Fanny Hensel has been neglected until recent years, when she was lifted from the shadow of her famous brother to reveal her genuine talents. Well educated in music and recognized in her lifetime as a gifted composer, she remained reluctant to make her compositions public. Her story enhances our modern-day understanding of the challenges faced by women musicians in the Romantic era.

A Piano Cycle: *The Year (Das Jahr)*

Hensel's cycle of piano works entitled *The Year* shows her at the pinnacle of her artistry. This set of twelve pieces, each named for a month of the year, and one postlude was once thought to be a kind of travel diary, documenting her year-long trip to Italy in 1839–40. But with the discovery in 1989 of a lost manuscript in her hand, missing for nearly 150 years, scholars have found a deeper meaning in the works. Each miniature piece is prefaced by a poetic epigram and a painting by her husband, Wilhelm Hensel, and is written on different-colored paper. The poems and artwork seem to suggest the passage of time or the seasons of one's life, perhaps her own. The cycle is unified through recurring motives, tonal schemes, and references to the works of other composers, including her brother Felix.

We will consider the character piece entitled *September: At the River* (LG 30), which is accompanied by a drawing of a bare-footed woman by the stream and several poetic lines from Goethe: "Flow, flow, dear river, / Never will I be happy." This melancholic idea is captured in the haunting, meandering melody, sounded

In Her Own Words

" I want to admit how terribly uppity I've been and announce that six 4-part Lieder . . . are coming out next. . . . My choir has enjoyed singing them . . . and I've made every effort to make them as good as possible."

—*Fanny Mendelssohn Hensel*

Fanny Mendelssohn Hensel (1805–1847)

Fanny Mendelssohn was born into a highly cultured family (her grandfather, Moses Mendelssohn, was a leading Jewish scholar/philosopher). She was especially close to her younger brother Felix, a renowned composer and conductor.

Raised in Berlin, Fanny learned piano from her mother and studied theory and composition with the well-known composer Carl Friedrich Zelter. Because of her gender, however, she was actively discouraged from pursuing music as a career. Her father cautioned her to focus on "the only calling for a young woman—that of a housewife." In 1829, Fanny married the court artist Wilhelm Hensel. She remained active during the following years as a composer, pianist, and participant in the regular salon concerts held each Sunday at the Mendelssohn residence, which she eventually organized. She died suddenly of a stroke on May 13, 1847, while preparing to conduct a cantata written by her brother. Having lost his dearest companion, Felix died just six months later.

Although she wrote several large-scale works, including a piano trio and a string quartet, Hensel's output was dominated by Lieder, choral part songs, and piano music, notably *The Year* (*Das Jahr*), a set of twelve character pieces. Most of her compositions were intended for performance at the family's Sunday musical gatherings. Her solo vocal music is highly lyrical, and her choice of Romantic poets and complex piano writing place her in the mainstream of the Lieder tradition. Her piano music reflects a strong interest in Bach's contrapuntal procedures.

MAJOR WORKS: Instrumental music, including an orchestral overture, a string quartet, and a piano trio • Over 125 piano works: sonatas, preludes and fugues, and character pieces, including *Das Jahr* (*The Year*, 1841) • Vocal music, including four cantatas and part songs for chorus, and over 250 Lieder.

---

below a stream of notes signifying the flowing river. The piece takes us on a daring journey through distant key centers, unfolding in a typical three-part form of statement-departure-return, framed by a brief introduction and coda. *The Year* was never published in its entirety; indeed, only *September* was included in Fanny's collection of piano works and without its literary and visual details. The musical and extra-musical links in this set make it a significant large-scale venture for the composer, who reached a new level of achievement that even her brother had not yet attained in his piano works.

CRITICAL THINKING

1. Why was the piano considered such an important domestic instrument?
2. What difficulties did a woman composer face in this era? What other important roles did women play in music, and why?

Romantic miniatures

YOUR TURN TO EXPLORE

In contemporary society, are certain musical styles, traditions/genres, and/or instruments associated more with women than with men, or vice versa? If so, why? How do different ideals of gender in your community play out in the way music is performed, created, or supported?

LISTENING GUIDE 30

Hensel: *September: At the River*, from *The Year (Das Jahr)*

DATE: 1841

GENRE: Character piece, from a programmatic cycle of 12

What to Listen For

Melody	Slow-paced melody in piano's middle range, set against fast-moving, churning notes; much chromaticism.
Rhythm/ meter	Lilting 6/8 meter; constant running 16th notes; some rubato.
Harmony	Begins and ends in B minor; modulates through various distant keys in the middle; very chromatic.

Texture	Polyphonic, with slow-moving melodies accompanied by fast-moving lines and chords.
Form	Ternary (**A-B-A′**), with a short introduction and coda.
Expression	Free push and pull of the beat (rubato); swelling and *decrescendo* in dynamics; movement evokes the flow of the river.

Introduction

0:00   Gentle, flowing 16th notes, punctuated by chords and octaves; slows down before the next section.

A section

0:12   Wistful, slow-moving melody in the middle register, in B minor, accompanied by constantly flowing fast notes and bass chords (melody notes are circled):

More movement in the main melody; grows chromatic and modulates; slows into next section, growing louder.

B section

1:23   Melody moves more quickly, in a new key, with more emphasis under a churning accompaniment. Grows louder and more chromatic, with high-range octaves exchanging a three-note idea with the main melody; builds in a swirling *crescendo*.

A′ section

1:56   Returns to the main melody, in B minor, but with more chromaticism; octave chords make a long descent to the tonic.

Coda

2:38   Introduction returns; fast-moving notes with chords; dies away *pianissimo*.

Chapter 40

Piano Triumphant: Gottschalk and Romantic Virtuosity

"Syncopation is in the soul of every true American."
—Irving Berlin (1888–1989)

KEY POINTS

- In addition to its crucial role in the home and salon, the piano became the most important solo instrument in the concert hall starting in the mid-1800s.

- Hungarian composer Franz Liszt pioneered modern piano technique, with his virtuoso performance style and flashy, technically difficult compositions.

- The pianist Louis Moreau Gottschalk was the first internationally acclaimed American composer of classical music. His piano piece *The Banjo* evokes banjo-playing styles and quotes popular songs of the time.

A compelling aspect of live musical performance is the extraordinary energy on display, especially when a single performer takes center stage. Our attention can be riveted to the remarkable physical dexterity, elegance, and stamina of the featured soloist—whose outwardly effortless delivery of emotionally gripping music can seem almost supernatural. Those who invented this kind of concert for the halls of the 1800s left a legacy that remains in the large arenas that fill with thousands of cheering fans to this day.

Ladies swoon at a performance by Franz Liszt in Berlin.

Pianos in Public: Virtuosity and the Recital

As we have seen, the piano was an essential resource for the home and the salon. But public performers were exploring the more dramatic potential of the "instrument that can play soft and loud." Most influential of these was the theatrically inclined Hungarian pianist/composer Franz Liszt (1811–1886), who created a new kind of musical event—the solo piano recital—that remains a vital part of contemporary concert life.

From the beginning of his career, Liszt was fascinated by the technical possibilities of the piano. As a twenty-year-old, he heard the celebrated violin virtuoso Niccolò Paganini perform (see p. 204), and decided to follow Paganini's lead and play solo recitals entirely from memory, with the piano parallel to the front of the stage so the audience could see his every movement. At the same time, he enriched the piano repertory with his own dazzling, difficult pieces. Audiences went wild, triggering a "Lisztomania" (see image on p. 227) that made him famous and scandalized those who saw his performances as empty show-off displays of dexterity and strength. Other skilled solo pianists entered the fray. One, Louis Moreau Gottschalk, came to Europe from the young United States.

Gottschalk: Composer for the Americas

A native of New Orleans who traveled widely, Gottschalk was the first American to achieve international fame as a classical composer. As a young child prodigy, he listened to the West Indian and African American dances and songs performed at Congo Square, the sanctioned gathering-place for slaves in New Orleans, where African traditions were both maintained and updated for a new land. In the 1840s, Gottschalk traveled to France to continue his musical studies. Although his application was rejected by the Paris Conservatory, he managed to study privately nevertheless, and drew rave reviews for his recitals. Following his success abroad, Gottschalk returned to the United States in 1853 and concertized extensively, spreading his blend of European-classical and novel music throughout the Americas.

In his own piano compositions, Gottschalk liked to take popular or folk melodies and elaborate them with increasingly complex accompaniment, astonishing audiences with his performing dexterity. He drew from Caribbean and South American as well as North American traditions, and like his contemporaries also chose favorite moments from operatic works as starting-points for improvisations. In this respect, Gottschalk both represented and fostered the overlap between "high" and

Louis Moreau Gottschalk (1829–1869)

The son of an English-born Jewish father and a French-Creole mother, Gottschalk was a child prodigy on the piano: at age eleven, he made his formal concert debut. His father sent him to study in Paris, where he charmed the likes of Chopin and Berlioz with his pianistic talents and highly original compositions.

After returning to America in the early 1850s, Gottschalk began writing in a new "Western" idiom: *Tournament Galop,* for example, is a dance form named after the fastest gait of a horse. He sailed to Cuba, where he wrote and conducted operas in Havana, and also to Puerto Rico and other Caribbean islands, absorbing their music and rhythms and producing some of his finest piano works.

With the onset of the Civil War in 1861, Gottschalk returned to the United States to perform in support of the Northern army, at which time he wrote *Union,* an extended paraphrase on national tunes (including *The Star-Spangled Banner, Yankee Doodle,* and *Hail, Columbia!*). Over the next three years, he traveled thousands of miles across the entire North American continent, giving more than a thousand recitals and promoting both classical and popular music as well as education. He spent his last four years in South America, where he encouraged classical music and organized "monster" concerts in Rio de Janeiro that involved some 650 musicians. He contracted malaria in Brazil and died there in 1869. Although Gottschalk wrote a handful of operas, songs, and symphonic works, he is remembered today almost exclusively for his piano music—which exploits all manner of dance forms and song forms from South America and the Caribbean.

MAJOR WORKS: Orchestral works, including *Symphony romantique: A Night in the Tropics* • Solo piano music: polkas, mazurkas, scherzos, galops (*Tournament Galop*), contradances, Creole and African American–inspired works (*The Banjo*), musical "souvenirs" (from Cuba and Puerto Rico), variations (on *Home, Sweet Home*), and a paraphrase on national airs (*Union*).

"low" traditions that characterized concert life in the Americas in the mid-1800s. In the generation after his death, musicians and audiences began drawing a sharper distinction between "art" and "popular" culture, and the highly syncopated style that he developed has been said to anticipate ragtime, an African American piano style that peaked in popularity around 1900 (see Chapter 51).

Piano Minstrelsy: *The Banjo*

Gottschalk's music, with its lively, folk-rooted melodies and rhythms, has enjoyed a recent surge in popularity with pianists and audiences. The jaunty piano work we will consider, *The Banjo* (LG 31), features highly syncopated rhythms and jagged melodic lines that simulate banjo strumming and picking techniques. The banjo was the most popular African American instrument in the mid-nineteenth century, and Gottschalk certainly heard it played in his native New Orleans; audiences would also have appreciated its association with the highly popular minstrel shows of the time (see Chapter 37). *The Banjo,* subtitled *Grotesque Fantasy: An American Sketch,* presents two varied sections, the first largely rhythmic, set in the low range of the piano, and the second a high-range, banjo-style tune. The coda sounds the familiar strains of Foster's *Camptown Races* and evokes the spiritual *Roll, Jordan, Roll* as well. This brilliant, virtuosic work illustrates Gottschalk's innovative techniques and ideas as well as his sparkling originality.

Both the work and the composer's career reflect the ways that North American musicians in the nineteenth century were endeavoring to create a new style from a blend of European-influenced "high art" traditions and soundscapes understood as "American," and seeking to bring that style to increasingly large and enthusiastic audiences throughout the United States.

In His Own Words

"Generally speaking, my style is very bold . . . the prevailing characteristics of my music are passionate expression, intense ardor, rhythmical animations, and unexpected turns."

—Louis Moreau Gottschalk

CRITICAL THINKING

1. How was the nineteenth-century concert artist's approach to the piano different from the domestic piano music we have examined in previous chapters?
2. How did Gottschalk incorporate American themes in *The Banjo*?

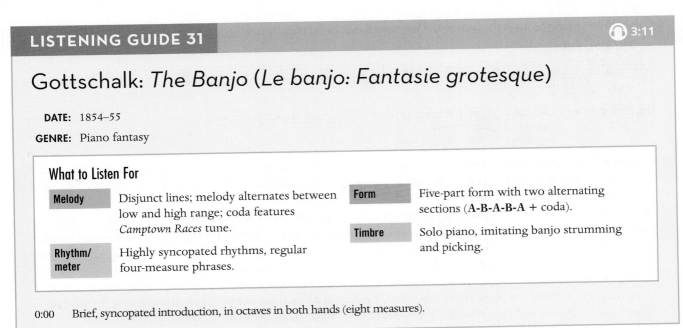

LISTENING GUIDE 31   3:11

Gottschalk: *The Banjo (Le banjo: Fantasie grotesque)*

DATE: 1854–55

GENRE: Piano fantasy

What to Listen For

Melody	Disjunct lines; melody alternates between low and high range; coda features *Camptown Races* tune.	**Form**	Five-part form with two alternating sections (**A-B-A-B-A** + coda).
Rhythm/ meter	Highly syncopated rhythms, regular four-measure phrases.	**Timbre**	Solo piano, imitating banjo strumming and picking.

0:00   Brief, syncopated introduction, in octaves in both hands (eight measures).

Continued on next page

A section

0:07   Rhythmic idea, in bass range of piano; repeated in four-measure phrases, decorated with flourishes:

0:30   A simple rocking-bass melody is heard, then repeated.

B section

0:44   Fast-paced, high-range melody, marked "brilliant"; syncopated against the regular bass:

A four-note descending pattern is repeated, followed by a glissando.

A section

1:07   Return to the **A section**.

1:27   Slow, rocking-bass melody.

B section

1:40   Fast, high-range melody returns. Four-note descending idea, followed by glissando.

A section

2:03   Opening rhythmic idea.

2:14   Rocking-bass melody.

Coda

2:24   *Camptown Races* tune, in simplified rhythm.

2:38   Tune is heard an octave higher and faster. Speed increases to a high flourish, then a final *fortissimo* chord.

Comparison of tune heard in the coda with *Camptown Races*, by Stephen Foster:

Camptown Races

YOUR TURN TO EXPLORE

Compare video recordings of solo performers from different traditions—for example, rock/metal guitarists, concert pianists, jazz saxophonists, R&B vocalists, bluegrass fiddlers. How does the performer put her or his physical dexterity on display, and balance it with the goal of musical expression? If other musicians are present, what is the balance/interaction between the soloist and the other musicians?

Chapter 41

Personal Soundtracks: Berlioz and the Program Symphony

*"The painter turns a poem into a painting;
the musician sets a picture to music."*

—Robert Schumann

KEY POINTS

- Many Romantic composers cultivated **program music**—instrumental music with a literary or pictorial association supplied by the composer—over **absolute music**.

- Hector Berlioz's *Symphonie fantastique* is a five-movement **program symphony** unified by a recurring theme (*idée fixe*) that represents the composer's beloved.

A s we walk through campus wearing our headphones or earbuds, we might think of the music playing on our portable player as a personal soundtrack, a musical accompaniment to our everyday life. Of course, when we choose our playlists, we pick from favorite songs we have purchased, rather than creating our own soundscapes from scratch. In an era before recording technology, those who wanted a "soundtrack" for their lives had to compose it themselves. One extraordinary example comes from the work of Hector Berlioz, who combined his musical creativity with the idea of personal storytelling and raised program music to a new level.

Shakespeare's play *A Midsummer Night's Dream* inspired this fanciful canvas by **Henry Fuseli** (1741–1825), *Titania and Bottom* (c. 1790).

Romantic Program Music

Music often evokes specific ideas or visual images. Sometimes these are the products of the listener's imagination, but other times they are intended by the composer. Schumann's quote above aptly suggests how a composer might think when creating such a work. The genre that evokes images and ideas became known as **program music**, or instrumental music with literary or pictorial associations. The program is supplied by the composer, either in the title or in an explanatory note. A title such as *King Lear* (by Berlioz), for example, suggests specific characters and events, while *Pièces fugitives* (*Fleeting Pieces*, by Clara Schumann) merely labels the mood or character of the work. Program music is distinguished from **absolute**, or pure, **music**, which consists of musical patterns that are designed

Musical Instruments and New Technologies

By the early nineteenth century, the Industrial Revolution was affecting virtually every aspect of daily life, including music-making. The increased availability of raw materials, improvements in the production of metal alloys, and the ability to cast metal parts with machines powered by steam engines made refinements possible in all

The trombone multipavilions was one of the many new, and unusual, instruments created by the Belgian instrument maker **Adolphe Sax**, inventor of the saxophone.

types of instruments. The piano, as the preferred household instrument, acquired a new key action that made it easier to repeat a single note quickly, and a cast-iron frame that allowed for heavier strings. This new frame lent both stability of pitch (the old wooden frame was prone to warping) and the potential for much louder dynamics. The American manufacturers Chickering (in Boston) and Steinway (in New York) led the way in developing the modern grand piano.

Although the violin had undergone improvements in the Baroque era (see p. 134), it reached its modern form in the nineteenth century with a secure chin rest and a newly designed bow with which players could achieve more playing power. Harpists and timpanists could change pitches more quickly with their new foot pedals, developed from mechanical automata devices (see p. 152). While trumpets and horns had previously been limited to the pitches available on a natural instrument (the overtone series), new technology offered the possibility of valves—both rotary and piston—that diverted the air flow to longer and

shorter segments of tubing, thereby increasing the pitch range to the full chromatic scale.

One of the first valved instruments was the *cornet à pistons*, a mellow and agile brass instrument that was promptly adopted into military bands. Hector Berlioz pronounced it vulgar at first, but soon realized its potential, adding two to his large orchestra for an 1833 performance of the *Symphonie fantastique*. (Listen for them in the *March to the Scaffold*.) Woodwind instruments gained increased flexibility with the advent of new key mechanisms. Bavarian inventor Theobold Boehm provided flutists with the means to cover sound holes their fingers could not reach, and he eventually developed a metal flute that replaced the standard wooden model. Similar innovations carried over to other instruments, such as the clarinet, oboe, and bassoon.

This period of technological innovation also encouraged inventors to dream up new-fangled instruments. Around the mid-century, Belgian inventor Adophe Sax developed the saxophone, along with various saxhorns, some with bells. The saxophone has never been fully established as an orchestral instrument (although French composers like Maurice Ravel gave it a fleeting chance to be heard), yet it found a solid niche in military bands and, from the early twentieth century, in jazz. What is clear is that modern concert bands, jazz bands, and orchestras would be quite different today without the sweeping changes and developing technologies of the nineteenth-century industrial world.

The Chickering piano, made in Boston, was a focal point for entertainment in many nineteenth-century homes.

without intended literary or pictorial meanings, like Beethoven's Fifth Symphony.

Program music was especially important during the nineteenth century, when musicians became sharply conscious of the connection between their art and the world around them. Adding a programmatic title brought music closer to poetry and painting, and helped composers relate their own work to the moral and political issues of their time. The passion for program music was so strong that it invaded even the most revered form of absolute music, the symphony. We will consider Berlioz's monumental program symphony, the *Symphonie fantastique*.

Berlioz and the *Symphonie fantastique*

"To render my works properly requires a combination of extreme precision and irresistible verve, a regulated vehemence, a dreamy tenderness, and an almost morbid melancholy."

The flamboyance of Victor Hugo's poetry and the dramatic intensity of Eugène Delacroix's painting found their musical counterpart in the works of Hector Berlioz, whose music is intense, bold, and passionate. He was the first great proponent of musical Romanticism in France.

Berlioz wrote his best-known program symphony when he was twenty-seven, basing its story on his personal life. His score describes "a young musician of morbid sensibility and ardent imagination, in . . . lovesick despair, [who] has poisoned himself with opium. The drug, too weak to kill, plunges him into a heavy sleep accompanied by strange visions. . . . The beloved one herself becomes for him a melody, a recurrent theme that haunts him everywhere."

The symphony's recurrent theme, called an *idée fixe* (fixed idea), acts as a musical thread unifying the five diverse movements, though its appearances are varied in harmony, rhythm, meter, tempo, dynamics, register, and instrumental color. This type of unification, called **thematic transformation**, serves the huge, expansive form of Berlioz's symphony. These transformations take on literary as well as musical significance, as the following description by Berlioz shows.

The Program

I. *Reveries, Passions*. "[The musician] remembers the weariness of soul, the indefinable yearning he knew before meeting his beloved. Then, the volcanic love with which she at once inspired him, his delirious suffering . . . his religious consolation." The Allegro section introduces a soaring melody, the fixed idea.

II. *A Ball*. "Amid the tumult and excitement of a brilliant ball he glimpses the loved one again." This dance movement is in ternary (three-part) form. In the middle section, the fixed idea reappears in waltz time.

III. *Scene in the Fields*. "On a summer evening in the country he hears two shepherds piping. The pastoral duet, the quiet surroundings . . . all unite to fill his heart with a long-absent feeling of calm. But she appears again [*idée fixe*]. His heart contracts. Painful forebodings fill his soul." The composer said that his aim in this pastoral movement was to establish a mood of "sorrowful loneliness."

IV. *March to the Scaffold*. "He dreams that he has killed his beloved, that he has been condemned to die and is being led to the scaffold. . . . At the very end the

Listeners flee Berlioz's bombastic orchestra in this satirical engraving from 1846.

Berlioz's *idée fixe* was inspired by the Shakespearean actress Harriet Smithson (1800–1854).

Hector Berlioz (1803–1869)

Berlioz was born in southern France. His father, a well-to-do physician, expected the boy to follow in his footsteps, but the Romantic revolution was brewing in Paris, and Berlioz, under the spell of such artists as Victor Hugo and Eugène Delacroix, followed his dream to study music. He became a huge fan of Beethoven and of Shakespeare, to whose plays he was introduced by a visiting English troupe. Berlioz fell madly in love with an actress in this troupe, Harriet Smithson: "I became obsessed by an intense, overpowering sense of sadness," he wrote. "I could not sleep, I could not work, and I spent my time wandering aimlessly about Paris and its environs."

In 1830, Berlioz won the coveted Prix de Rome, which gave him an opportunity to work in Italy. That same year, he composed the *Symphonie fantastique*, his most celebrated work. After returning from Rome, he began a hectic court-ship of Harriet Smithson, whom he married, only to realize it was Shakespeare he had loved rather than Harriet.

Berlioz's works, showing the favorite literary influences of the Romantic period, draw on Goethe, Lord Byron, and especially Shakespeare, the source for his overture *King Lear,* his opera *Béatrice et Bénédict*, and his dramatic symphony *Romeo and Juliet*. It was in the domain of orchestration that Berlioz's genius asserted itself most fully. His scores, calling for the largest orchestra that had ever been used, abound in novel effects and discoveries, revealing him as one of the boldest innovators of the nineteenth century.

MAJOR WORKS: Orchestral music, including overtures (*King Lear*) and program symphonies (*Symphonie fantastique* and *Romeo et Juliette*) • Choral music, including a *Requiem Mass* • Three operas, including *Les Troyens* (*The Trojans*) • Nine works for solo voice and orchestra • Writings about music, including an orchestration treatise.

fixed idea reappears for an instant, like a last thought of love interrupted by the fall of the blade."

V. *Dream of a Witches' Sabbath.* "He sees himself at a witches' sabbath surrounded by a host of fearsome spirits who have gathered for his funeral. Unearthly sounds, groans, shrieks of laughter. The melody of his beloved is heard, but it has lost its noble and reserved character. It has become a vulgar tune, trivial and grotesque. It is she who comes to the infernal orgy. A howl of joy greets her arrival. She joins the diabolical dance. Bells toll for the dead. A burlesque of the *Dies irae*. Dance of the witches. The dance and the *Dies irae* combined."

The last two movements are perfect examples of the Romantic era's preoccu-pation with the grotesque and the supernatural. In the fourth (LG 32), a diabolical march in minor, the theme of the beloved appears at the end in the clarinet, and

Francisco Goya (1746–1828) anticipated the passionate intensity of Berlioz's music in this painting of the *Witches' Sabbath,* c. 1819–23.

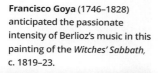

LISTENING GUIDE 32

 4:37

Berlioz: *Symphonie fantastique*, IV

DATE: 1830

GENRE: Program symphony with five movements

PROGRAM: A lovesick artist in an opium trance is haunted by a vision of his beloved, which becomes an *idée fixe* (fixed idea).

Idée fixe

MOVEMENTS: I. *Reveries, Passions*: Largo; Allegro agitato e appassionato assai (lively, agitated, and impassioned)
  II. *A Ball*: Valse, Allegro non troppo
  III. *Scene in the Fields*: Adagio
  IV. *March to the Scaffold*: Allegretto non troppo
  V. *Dream of a Witches' Sabbath*: Larghetto, Allegro assa**i**

IV. *March to the Scaffold*

What to Listen For

Melody	Two main march themes (**A** and **B**), both strongly accented.	**Expression**	Diabolical mood; sudden dynamic changes, idea of the beloved at the end as a clarinet solo, then a sudden chord (beheading).
Rhythm/ meter	Duple-meter march.	**Timbre**	Prominent timpani; instruments in unusual ranges.
Harmony	Set in minor mode.		
Form	Sonata-like, with two themes introduced, developed, then recapped.		

0:00   Opening motive: muted horns, timpani, and pizzicato low strings; forecasts syncopated rhythm of a march (theme **B**):

0:24   Theme **A**—an energetic, downward minor scale in low strings, then violins (with bassoon countermelody):

1:31   Theme **B**—diabolical march tune, played by brass and woodwinds:

1:56   Developmental section:
        Theme **B**—in brass, accompanied by strings and woodwinds.
        Theme **A**—soft, with pizzicato strings.
        Theme **B**—brass, with woodwinds added.
        Theme **A**—soft, pizzicato strings, then loud in brass.

3:02   Theme **A**—full orchestra statement in original form, then inverted (now an ascending scale).

Continued on next page

4:05　Fixed idea in clarinet ("a last thought of love"), marked "as sweetly and passionately as possible," followed by a loud chord that cuts off the melody ("the fall of the blade"):

Pizzicato bass notes, possibly depicting the fall of the head, are followed by loud, triumphant chords that close the movement.

is cut off by a grim *fortissimo* chord. In this vivid portrayal of the story, we clearly hear the final blow of the guillotine blade, the head rolling, and the resounding cheers of the crowd.

In the final movement, Berlioz sounds an infernal spirit that nourished a century of satanic operas, ballets, and symphonic poems. The mood is heightened by the introduction of the traditional religious chant *Dies irae* ("Day of Wrath") from the ancient Mass for the Dead, scored for the bassoons and tubas.

This composition is an extraordinary example of the Romantic desire to reflect the intensity of personal experience through music, but it also opens up the essential paradox of program music: if you heard the *March to the Scaffold* without knowing its title or its descriptive program, would you understand the story it's supposed to tell? Can the music convey meaning without the story?

CRITICAL THINKING

1. What musical effects did Berlioz use to "paint" the image/story of a march to the scaffold?
2. What is Romantic about the program and music of *Symphonie fantastique*?

YOUR TURN TO EXPLORE

What excerpts from your favorite music might you use to tell a story about yourself and your emotional life? List the songs or pieces. How might you want to modify the music (its tempo, instrumentation, texture, etc.) to convey your emotions more precisely? How would you try to make sure a listener would understand your story accurately?

Chapter 42

Sounding a Nation: Grieg and Orchestral Nationalism

"I dipped into the rich treasures of native folk song and sought to create a national art out of this hitherto unexploited expression of the folk soul of Norway."

—Edvard Grieg

KEY POINTS

- Prominent types of Romantic program music include the **concert overture**, **incidental music** to a play, and the **symphonic poem** (a one-movement work).

- Political unrest throughout Europe stimulated schools of nationalistic composers in Russia, Scandinavia, Spain, England, and Bohemia.

- Edvard Grieg looked to the folklore of his native Norway in many of his works. His incidental music for *Peer Gynt* was written to accompany a play by Henrik Ibsen about this folk legend, then was excerpted into an independent suite.

One of the most important roles that music plays in all human societies is building community cohesion. Since the nineteenth century, the notion of community has been strongly tied to the concept of nationality: a distinctive culture and heritage shared by people who live in a common territory. But although individuals are associated with a nation by birth or immigration, they can choose whether or not—and how—to highlight that association through their music. While this concern was especially important in nineteenth-century Europe, aspects of musical nationalism still play a role in building communities today; for example, compositions are often commissioned for presidential inaugurations, such as the variations on the Shaker tune *Simple Gifts* written by film composer John Williams for Barack Obama's inauguration in 2009.

Varieties of Orchestral Program Music

One type of program music came out of the opera house, where the overture, a rousing orchestral piece in one movement, served as an introduction to an opera (or a play). Some operatic overtures became popular as separate concert pieces, which in turn pointed the way to a new type of **overture** not associated with opera: a single-movement concert piece for orchestra that might evoke a land- or seascape, or embody a patriotic or literary idea, like Tchaikovsky's *Romeo and Juliet*.

Program overture

Another type of program music, **incidental music**, usually consists of an overture and a series of pieces performed between the acts of a play and during

Playwright Henrik Ibsen frequented the Grand Café in Oslo daily; this rendering is by fellow Norwegian **Edvard Munch** (1863–1944), best known for *The Scream.*

important scenes. The most successful pieces of incidental music were arranged into suites (such as Felix Mendelssohn's *A Midsummer Night's Dream*). This use of music to enhance spoken drama was influential in the development of musical accompaniment to silent film at the very end of the 1800s, and in the tradition of film soundtracks after the 1920s.

Eventually, composers felt the need for a large orchestral form that would serve the Romantic era as the symphony had served the Classical. Franz Liszt created the **symphonic poem**, the nineteenth century's most original contribution to large forms. A symphonic poem is program music for orchestra in one movement, with contrasting sections that develop a poetic idea (like Debussy's *Prelude to "The Afternoon of the Faun,"* Chapter 49), suggest a scene, or create a mood. It differs from the concert overture, which usually retains a traditional Classical form, by having a much freer structure. The symphonic poem (also called **tone poem**) gave composers the flexibility they needed for a big single-movement work. It became the most common type of orchestral program music through the second half of the century.

Musical Nationalism

"I grew up in a quiet spot and was saturated from earliest childhood with the wonderful beauty of Russian popular song. I am therefore passionately devoted to every expression of the Russian spirit. In short, I am a Russian through and through!"

—Peter Ilyich Tchaikovsky

In nineteenth-century Europe, political conditions so encouraged the growth of nationalism that it became a decisive force within the Romantic movement. The pride of conquering nations and the struggle for freedom of suppressed ones gave rise to strong emotions that inspired the works of many creative artists.

Romantic composers expressed their nationalism in a variety of ways. Some based their music on the songs and dances of their people, others wrote dramatic works based on folklore or peasant life—for example, the Russian fairy-tale operas and ballets of Tchaikovsky. And some wrote symphonic poems and operas celebrating the exploits of a national hero, a historic event, or the scenic beauty of their country: Bedřich Smetana's *The Moldau* is a popular tone poem depicting the river that was the lifeblood of the emerging state of Bohemia.

In associating music with the love of homeland, composers sought to give expression to the hopes of millions of people. The political implications were not lost on the authorities. Some of Giuseppe Verdi's operas, for example, had to be altered again and again to suit the censor (his plots often portrayed rulers as unjust or suggested "dangerous" ideas). During the Second World War, the Nazis outlawed the playing of Chopin's polonaises in Warsaw and Smetana's descriptive symphonic poems in Prague because of the powerful symbolism behind these works.

Several regions throughout Europe gave rise to a national voice through music. In particular, the Russian school produced a circle of young musicians called "The Mighty Five" (or "The Mighty Handful"), whose members sought to free themselves from the older sounds of the German symphony, French ballet, and Italian opera and express a true Russian spirit. England and Spain produced nationalistic composers as well whose music was intended to echo the souls of their countries (see map below).

Schools of Musical Nationalism in Europe

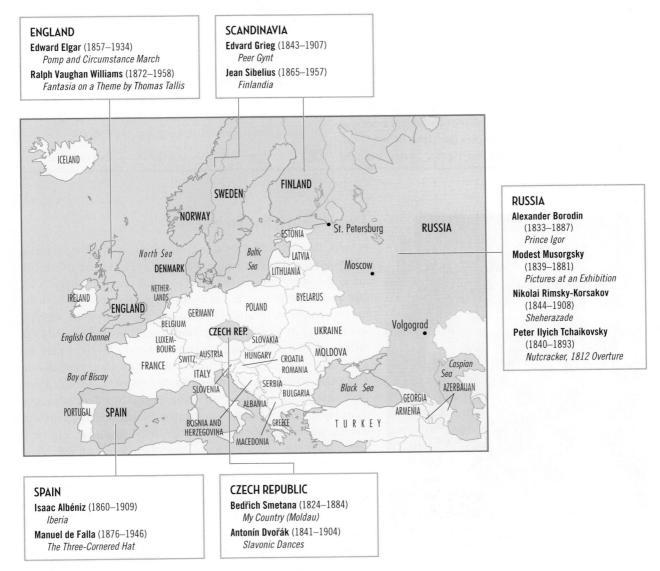

ENGLAND
Edward Elgar (1857–1934)
  Pomp and Circumstance March
Ralph Vaughan Williams (1872–1958)
  Fantasia on a Theme by Thomas Tallis

SCANDINAVIA
Edvard Grieg (1843–1907)
  Peer Gynt
Jean Sibelius (1865–1957)
  Finlandia

RUSSIA
Alexander Borodin
  (1833–1887)
  Prince Igor
Modest Musorgsky
  (1839–1881)
  Pictures at an Exhibition
Nikolai Rimsky-Korsakov
  (1844–1908)
  Sheherazade
Peter Ilyich Tchaikovsky
  (1840–1893)
  Nutcracker, 1812 Overture

SPAIN
Isaac Albéniz (1860–1909)
  Iberia
Manuel de Falla (1876–1946)
  The Three-Cornered Hat

CZECH REPUBLIC
Bedřich Smetana (1824–1884)
  My Country (Moldau)
Antonín Dvořák (1841–1904)
  Slavonic Dances

A Scandinavian Nationalist: Edvard Grieg

Among nationalist composers of the nineteenth century, the Norwegian master Edvard Grieg stands out for his ability to capture the essence of his country's folklore and dance through music. It was his goal to create an art that was accessible to all the public.

Edvard Grieg (1843–1907)

Born in Bergen, Norway, Grieg attended the famous Leipzig Conservatory in Germany, where he fell under the spell of Felix Mendelssohn and Robert Schumann. After returning to Norway, Grieg worked to promote Scandinavian music through an academy he helped found. Though he tried his hand at larger musical forms—the symphony and the sonata—he felt more at home with smaller-scale works, including songs, for which he had a lyric gift. He also wrote many piano works, including arrangements of Norwegian folk tunes. His growing stature brought him a stipend from the Norwegian government that allowed him to focus on composition and an invitation to collaborate with the famous playwright Henrik Ibsen on his play *Peer Gynt*. By the 1880s, Grieg was truly an international figure, having brought much visibility to his homeland through music. He died suddenly in 1907, just as he was to embark on a concert tour to England.

Grieg's music is notable for its lyricism and for his nationalistic use of folk music and dances, leading the way for early twentieth-century composers like Béla Bartók (see Chapter 61). His well-crafted piano miniatures are among his best works, as is his popular Piano Concerto in A Minor, which was admired and performed by virtuoso Franz Liszt and is often played today.

MAJOR WORKS: Orchestral works, including incidental music and suites (*Peer Gynt*, Nos. 1 and 2), overtures, symphonic dances • Piano music, including a concerto, a sonata, many small-scale pieces and dances • Chamber music, including violin sonatas, a string quartet • Songs.

 Åse's Death, Hall of the Mountain King, from *Peer Gynt*

The King of the Trolls, from Ibsen's *Peer Gynt* as illustrated by **Arthur Rackham** (1867–1939).

Peer Gynt, Suite No. 1

Henrik Ibsen's play *Peer Gynt,* based on a Norwegian folk tale, premiered in Christiana, Norway, in 1876. Like most folk tales, the story presents a strong moral message. Peer is an idle and boastful youth; his mother Åse reprimands him for his laziness, which caused him to lose his bride-to-be, Ingrid, to another. At her wedding, however, Peer abducts Ingrid, only to abandon her later. He runs away to a forest, where he seduces a young girl who turns out to be a daughter of the Mountain King, ruler of the trolls. When her sisters find out she is pregnant, they vow to revenge her, but Peer manages to escape them. Now an outlaw, he builds a cottage in the woods, where Solveig, a girl he once loved, comes to live with him. Life seems safe for a while, but when Peer's mother dies, he sets off on a series of fantastical adventures; on the shores of North Africa, he cavorts with the Arabian girl Anitra, who performs a sultry dance for him. Peer finally returns home many years later to find Solveig, now a middle-aged woman, still faithful to him.

At Ibsen's invitation, Grieg composed some twenty-two pieces, including preludes and dances, as incidental music for the play. Not altogether happy with the result, he later extracted eight of the movements and combined them—in a different order—into two orchestral suites, of four movements each.

Two of the most endearing and popular pieces—*Morning Mood* and *In the Hall of the Mountain King* (LG 33)—are from Grieg's first suite, which also includes *Åse's Death* and *Anitra's Dance. Morning Mood,* an atmospheric depiction of the sunrise, opens the suite. It features a lyrical theme that is passed between instruments,

Grieg: *Peer Gynt*, Suite No. 1 (Op. 46), excerpts

DATE: 1874–75 (play); 1888 (suite)

GENRE: Incidental music to a play by Henrik Ibsen

MOVEMENTS: *Morning Mood*
Åse's Death
Anitra's Dance
In the Hall of the Mountain King

What to Listen For

Morning Mood

Melody	Dreamy melody in an inverted arch shape, with decorative grace notes.
Rhythm/meter	Lilting 6/8 meter.
Harmony	E major, with many harmonic inflections; static chords.
Texture	Homophonic.
Form	Three-part (**A-B-A′**).
Expression	Grows to a loud climax; swells in dynamics, then dies away.
Performing forces	Pastoral instruments (flute, oboe, horn) are prominent.

In the Hall of the Mountain King

Melody	Ghostly melody in two phrases, with a rising accented line.
Rhythm/meter	Duple-meter march; short, staccato notes and offbeat accents.
Harmony	B minor.
Texture	Homophonic.
Form	A single theme repeated over and over; closing coda.
Expression	Huge *crescendo* and *accelerando* to a dramatic ending.
Performing forces	Pizzicato strings and staccato woodwind effects; offbeats in brass and percussion.

Morning Mood

3:50

A section

0:00   A flowing melody is exchanged between flute and oboe, with sustained string chords; builds in a *crescendo*:

0:49   Full orchestral statement, marked *forte*; continues to build, then dies down;
cello motive leads to a new *crescendo*.

B section

1:29   Reaches a climax, then cellos alternate with higher strings in sudden dynamic changes; builds in a
crescendo, then *decrescendo*; a brief shift to the minor.

A′ section

1:59   French horn has the main theme, accompanied by wavering woodwinds.
2:12   Louder statement in low strings and woodwinds.
2:32   Horn introduces a slower statement of the theme in violins, answered by clarinet.

Coda

2:45   A quiet mood, with trills in woodwinds; solo French horn.

Continued on next page

3:17   Flute has the theme, slowing, then bassoon; tranquil chords in strings; closing chords in full orchestra with a soft timpani roll.

In the Hall of the Mountain King

2:31

0:00   An eerie theme is heard six times, played softly in low pizzicato strings and bassoons:

0:55   Theme continues in violins, answered by woodwinds, with strong offbeat accents.
1:11   Pizzicato theme moves to a higher range in violins, grows louder and a little faster; answered by oboes and clarinets.
1:26   Louder statement accompanied by a bowed-string spinning figure.
1:40   Full orchestra at *fortissimo*, with strong accents.
1:52   Brass is prominent as the music speeds up and is more accented.

Coda

2:12   Sudden chords, alternating with running passages; a timpani roll leads to the final chord.

building to a long climax. Grieg wrote that he imagined "the sun breaking through the clouds at the first *forte*."

In the Hall of the Mountain King was conceived as grotesque ballet music—a march for the wild troll daughters of the Mountain King. The girls taunt and threaten Peer for seducing one of them, with the insistent theme growing louder and faster as they chase him. The crashing final chords signify the collapse of the mountain on top of the trolls.

Though these excerpts from the *Peer Gynt* Suite share the common orchestral language of the nineteenth century, this strikingly expressive work, like other nationalist program music, draws on the unique imagery and folk traditions of the composer's homeland. Can you "hear" the imagery of Norway that Grieg means to convey?

CRITICAL THINKING

1. What are the various genres of program music that developed in the nineteenth century, and how do they differ from each other?
2. What are some ways that nationalism is reflected in nineteenth-century music?

YOUR TURN TO EXPLORE

What kinds of musical repertories do you think best represent the communities with which you identify? Are those communities shaped by regional or ethnic identity, and does their music reflect those identities? If you are a fan of a particular musician or group, what characteristics do your fellow fans share, and how does the music reinforce those common elements?

Chapter 43

Absolutely Classic: Brahms and the Nineteenth-Century Symphony

"It is not hard to compose, but it is wonderfully hard to let the superfluous notes fall under the table."

—Johannes Brahms

KEY POINTS

- Composers continued writing instrumental music without a program (**absolute music**) throughout the nineteenth century, including symphonies, concertos, and chamber music.

- Romantic symphonies were characterized by lyrical themes, colorful harmonies, expanded proportions, and larger orchestras featuring new instruments.

- German composer Johannes Brahms continued the Classical traditions of the Viennese masters in his four symphonies. His Third Symphony is Classical in structure but Romantic in tone.

Music may not be a truly universal language, but it is certainly more flexible in meaning than any communication based on words. Sound can seem to dig deeper into our emotions than the logic of words—and this aspect of music made it especially appealing to the Romantics, as we have seen. Yet many thought that program music, linking sound to a narrative or an image, was a step backward from the potential of music to express things beyond words. These were (and are) the proponents of **absolute music**: without a program, relying entirely on structures of sound for its expressive power. This repertory continues to dominate in orchestral concerts, since audiences enjoy the opportunity for individual interpretation that is opened up when music is not explicitly linked to anything else. And indeed, in most Western traditions, even when a voice is ostensibly the primary focus of a song, there is often an instrumental "break" in which the expressive potential of music is allowed to float freely and expand the listener's experience.

In His Own Words

66 Without craftsmanship, inspiration is a mere reed shaken in the wind."

—Johannes Brahms

Absolute Music in the Romantic Era

In addition to new programmatic genres such as the symphonic poem and program symphony, Romantic composers continued writing in the multimovement genres established in the Classical era, which included the symphony, the concerto,

The nineteenth-century orchestra offered the composer new instruments and a larger ensemble. Engraving of an orchestral concert at the Covent Garden Theatre, London, 1846.

and chamber music (string quartets and quintets, piano trios and quartets). As we have seen, the most important organizing element in absolute music is form, since there is no prescribed story or extramusical literary program provided by the composer. Though the basic components of the three- or four-movement cycle covered in Chapters 28–32 were retained, nineteenth-century composers did not always follow the "traditional rules."

Form and Expression in the Romantic Symphony

In the course of its development beyond the Classical-period tradition of Haydn, Mozart, and Beethoven, the symphony gained weight and importance. Nineteenth-century composers found the symphony a suitable framework for their lyrical ("singing") themes, harmonic experiments, and individual expressions. By the Romantic era, music had moved from palace to public concert hall, the orchestra had vastly increased in size, and the symphonic structure was growing steadily longer and more expansive (see chart on p. 203).

The first movement, the most dramatic of the Romantic symphony, generally retains the basic elements of sonata-allegro form. It might have a drawn-out, slow introduction, and it often features a long and expressive development section. The second movement, often in a loose three-part form, may retain its slow and lyri-

Johannes Brahms (1833–1897)

Born in Hamburg, Germany, Brahms gave his first performance on piano at age ten. He soon developed what would be a lifelong affection for folk music, collecting songs and folk sayings throughout his life. Brahms had the good fortune to study with Robert Schumann at Düsseldorf, who recognized in his pupil a future leader of the circle dedicated to absolute music. Robert and his wife Clara took the young musician into their home, and their friendship opened up new horizons for him.

The death of Brahms's mother in 1865 inspired him to write his *German Requiem,* with biblical texts that he selected himself, in her memory. He ultimately settled in Vienna, where, at age forty, he began writing his great symphonic works. During these years, he became enormously successful, the acknowledged heir of the Viennese masters. Robert Schumann had died of syphilis in 1856, and Brahms had tenderly supported Clara through the ordeal of his mental collapse. Forty years later, Clara's declining health gave rise to his *Four Serious Songs.* Her death deeply affected the com-

poser, already ill with cancer. He died ten months later and was buried in Vienna, near Beethoven and Schubert.

Brahms's four symphonies are unsurpassed in the late Romantic period for their breadth of conception and design. In his two piano concertos and violin concerto, the solo instrument is integrated into a full-scale symphonic structure. Brahms gorgeously captured the intimacy of chamber-music style, and is an important figure in piano music as well. As a song writer, he stands in the direct succession from Schubert and Schumann, with about two hundred solo songs.

MAJOR WORKS: Orchestral music, including four symphonies, variations, overtures • Four concertos (two for piano, one for violin, one double concerto for piano/violin • Chamber music, including piano trios and quartets • Duo sonatas • Piano music, including sonatas, character pieces, dances, variations • Choral music, including the *German Requiem* (1868) and part songs • Lieder, including *Wiegenlied* (*Lullaby*).

 Wiegenlied (Lullaby); Symphony No. 4, IV

LISTENING GUIDE 34 6:20

Brahms: Symphony No. 3 in F Major, III

DATE: 1883

GENRE: Symphony

MOVEMENTS: I. Allegro con brio; sonata-allegro, F major
III. Poco allegretto; A-B-A′ form, C minor
II. Andante; modified sonata form, C major
IV. Allegro; sonata-allegro; F major

Third movement: Poco allegretto

What to Listen For

Melody	Lyrical, melancholic melody with waltz-like feeling; arched, regular phrases.
Rhythm/ meter	Moderate triple meter; rhythmic complexity with three-against-two patterns (contrasting rhythms sounded together) and syncopation.
Harmony	Alternates minor-major-minor keys; chromatic in middle section.
Form	Three-part structure (**A-B-A′**).
Expression	Arched dynamics and subtle rubato.
Timbre	Woodwinds featured in middle section; French horns bring a return to **A**.

0:00   **A section**—yearning cello melody, accompanied by rustling string figures; symmetrical phrasing:

0:27   Violins repeat the cello theme, extending the range and dynamics.
0:52   Theme 2, played by violins, "leans" over the bar line above a moving cello line; violins and cellos in duet.
1:27   Return of opening theme in flutes and oboes, with broader accompaniment.
1:57   **B section**—a connected three-note figure in woodwinds, in A-flat major, accompanied by offbeat 16th notes in the cellos:

3:27   Woodwinds hint at a return to the main theme, accompanied by sustained strings.
3:46   **A′ section**—French horns announce the opening theme in C minor, with richer orchestration.
4:14   Oboes take up the haunting melody as the accompaniment builds.
4:41   Theme 2, now heard in the clarinets and bassoons.
5:17   Violins and cellos take up the main theme, played in octaves for greater intensity; generally thicker and more contrapuntal accompaniment.
5:44   **Brief coda**—reminiscent of **B section**; the last chord is punctuated by pizzicato strings.

cal nature but can also range in mood from whimsical and playful to tragic and passionate. Third in the cycle is a strongly rhythmic dance or scherzo, with overtones of humor, surprise, caprice, or folk dance. The fourth and final movement has a dimension and character designed to balance the first. Often it also follows

Brahms's study and personal library in Vienna, in a nineteenth-century painting.

sonata-allegro form and may close the symphony on a note of triumph or pathos.

Brahms's Symphony No. 3 in F Major

Johannes Brahms was a traditionalist; his aim was to show that new and important things could still be said in the tradition of the Classical masters. The Third Symphony, written in 1883 when he was fifty years old, is the shortest of his four symphonies and the most Romantic in tone. In form, however, the work looks back to the Classical structures of the eighteenth century. The first movement, a conventional sonata-allegro, opens with a dramatic figure: a three-note motive (F–A♭–F) that could be related to the composer's personal motto, "Frei aber froh" ("Free but happy," perhaps referring to his bachelorhood). This idea permeates the entire symphony. The slow movement, a haunting Andante in sonata-allegro form, evokes the peacefulness of nature with its simple, hymnlike theme in the woodwinds.

Rather than following with a scherzo, Brahms wrote a melancholy waltz in C minor, set in ternary form (LG 34). The opening theme, a poignant cello melody, is heard throughout this impassioned orchestral "song without words," accompanied by restless string figures. First the violins, then the woodwinds take up the melody, whose arched rise and fall suggests a huge orchestral sigh. The middle section, now in a major key, presents two themes set against an expressive, chromatic accompaniment. The return of the opening theme is newly orchestrated, then closes with an emotional statement by the violins and cellos playing in octaves. A short coda brings back the mood of the middle section, closing with two soft pizzicato chords. The finale, a dramatic sonata-allegro, features concise themes and abrupt changes of mood. Throughout, the listener is challenged by shifting moods, timbres, and melodies that affirm the technical command and the creative invention of a great Romantic master.

Later generations of orchestral composers have often tried to find a middle way between fully absolute and explicitly program music. Certainly, however, the appeal of Classical forms continues to the present day, thanks in no small measure to their revitalization through the music of Brahms and his followers.

CRITICAL THINKING

Romantic era orchestral music

1. What remains "Classical" about the treatment of absolute music in the Romantic era? What is "Romantic" about these structures?

2. How would you describe the expressive devices (melody and harmony, for example) of the Romantic symphony in comparison with those of the Classical symphony?

YOUR TURN TO EXPLORE

Choose a pop song that includes one or more extended instrumental passages, and focus on the sections when the voice is silent. What do the instruments express beyond the meaning of the words? What specific elements (melody, harmony, timbre) does the composer employ to emphasize those wordless meanings? How do those meanings influence the overall effect of the song?

Chapter 44

Multimedia Hits: Verdi and Italian Romantic Opera

"The box office is the proper thermometer of success."

—Giuseppe Verdi

KEY POINTS

- Romantic opera developed distinct national styles in Italy, Germany, and France, and women singers excelled in all styles.

- Both **opera seria** (serious opera) and **opera buffa** (comic opera) were favored in Italy; they marked the peak of the **bel canto** (beautiful singing) style.

- Giuseppe Verdi is best known for his operas, which embody the spirit of Romantic drama and passion. His *Rigoletto*, based on a play by Victor Hugo, is one of the most performed operas today.

Music is an essential component of contemporary multimedia, whether films, television shows, or video games. Hit songs are often associated with them—and so it was from the beginning of what we might call commercially sucessful multimedia, which arose in the Italian theatrical tradition in the 1800s. Before the age of recording, catchy excerpts from operas were marketed in arrangements, whether for the home (piano four-hands, voice and guitar) or for public places (wind band medleys). This allowed the music to saturate its culture, becoming popular in both the economic and the social sense. In the process, it became connected to the social aspirations of its audiences, providing emotional reinforcement to political messages—another important role played by music to this day.

A portrait of Swedish soprano Jenny Lind (1820–1887).

Women and Nineteenth-Century Opera

Successful multimedia has always relied on the draw of star performers, and this was true of the Italian musical-theatrical tradition—opera—from its early days. By the time of Mozart, fashion had shifted from the castrati toward the more "natural" voices of female sopranos, and from that point on, women opera singers were among the most prominent performers of their day, in demand throughout Europe and the Americas. One international star was Jenny Lind, famous for her roles in operas by the Italians Gaetano Donizetti and Vincenzo Bellini, among others. A concert artist as well, Lind made her American debut in 1850 in a tour managed with immense hoopla by circus impresario P. T. Barnum. During her tour, Lind sang both Italian operatic excerpts and American parlor ballads, emphasizing the flexibility between art and popular music in nineteenth-century North America.

One of the most celebrated Italian singing stars, Giuseppina Strepponi, helped to launch the career of Giuseppe Verdi, who later became her husband. While

Milan's famous opera house La Scala (c. 1850), where some of Verdi's operas premiered.

Strepponi's own singing career faded as Verdi's career rose, she continued to provide suggestions and artistic support—underlining the important role many women played not only as singers and composers, but also as "teammates" to their musical partners.

Verdi and Italian Opera

"Success is impossible for me if I cannot write as my heart dictates!"

In His Own Words

  It seems to me that the best material I have yet put to music is *Rigoletto*. It has the most powerful situations, it has variety, vitality, pathos; all the dramatic developments result from the frivolous, licentious character of the Duke. Hence Rigoletto's fears, Gilda's passion, etc., which give rise to many dramatic situations, including the scene of the quartet."

—*Giuseppe Verdi*

Italy in the nineteenth century still recognized the opposing genres of *opera seria* (serious opera) and *opera buffa* (the Italian version of comic opera), legacies of an earlier period. One of the most important composers of this era was Gioachino Rossini (1792–1868), whose masterpieces include *Il barbiere di Siviglia* (*The Barber of Seville*, 1816) and *Guillaume Tell* (*William Tell*, 1829). These operas marked the high point of a **bel canto** (beautiful singing) style, characterized by florid melodic lines delivered by voices of great agility and purity of tone.

Verdi was the consummate master of nineteenth-century Italian opera. In his case, time, place, and personality were happily merged. He inherited a rich musical tradition, his capacity for growth was matched by extraordinary energy, and he was granted a long life in which to engage fully his creative gifts. He also came into his professional peak at a time when music publishers were helping to build markets for composers who were willing to work closely with them on licensing and other commercial ventures.

Verdi's music was adopted by those who supported political independence for Italy, which was then under Austrian rule. The intensity of his compositions and the potential for some of the stories to be read as calls for liberation made him a figurehead for the Italian unification movement—though Verdi himself was only mildly political: he agreed to serve in the senate of newly unified Italy, but retired after only one term. The combination of appealing melodies, intense dramatic situations, and savvy marketing by his publisher Ricordi made Verdi's music a national soundtrack for the new Italian spirit. Every town in Italy, no matter how small, has a street bearing Verdi's name, and his operas are still the most frequently performed around the world.

Giuseppe Verdi (1813–1901)

Born in a small town in northern Italy, Verdi got off to an early start by writing operas for Milan's La Scala opera house. After the tragic deaths of his daughter, baby son, and young wife in 1838–40, the distraught composer wrote no music for months. Then one night he met the director of La Scala, who insisted he take home a libretto about Nebuchadnezzar, king of Babylon. Verdi returned to work, and the resulting opera, *Nabucco,* launched him on a spectacular career.

Italy at the time was liberating itself from Austrian Hapsburg rule, and Verdi identified himself with the national cause. His works took on special meaning for his compatriots; the chorus of exiled Jews from *Nabucco* became an Italian patriotic song that is still sung today. In 1848, Verdi began an association with soprano Giuseppina Strepponi, whom he later married, and proceeded to produce one masterpiece after another. At seventy-three, he completed *Otello,* his greatest lyric tragedy. And in 1893, on the threshold of eighty, he astonished the world with *Falstaff* (a comic opera based on *The Merry Wives of Windsor*). In all, he wrote twenty-eight operas.

Verdi's favorite literary source was Shakespeare, whose plays inspired *Macbeth, Otello,* and *Falstaff. La traviata* is based on *La dame aux camellias* by Alexandre Dumas, and *Il trovatore* on a fanciful Spanish play. *Aida,* a monumental work commissioned in 1870 by the ruler of Egypt to mark the opening of the Suez Canal, premiered in Cairo. On his death, Verdi left his fortune to a home for aged musicians (Casa Verdi) that he founded in Milan and that still exists today.

MAJOR WORKS: 28 operas, including *Macbeth* (1847), *Rigoletto* (1851), *Il trovatore* (*The Troubadour,* 1853), *La traviata* (*The Lost One,* 1853), *Un ballo in maschera* (*The Masked Ball,* 1859), *Don Carlos* (1867), *Aida* (1871), *Otello* (1887), and *Falstaff* (1893) • Vocal music, including a *Requiem* Mass.

 Dies irae, from *Requiem*

Rigoletto

The epitome of Romantic drama and passion, Verdi's music for *Rigoletto* communicates each dramatic situation with profound emotion. A play by Victor Hugo, an acknowledged leader of French Romanticism, was Verdi's source of inspiration.

The setting is a Renaissance-era ducal court in northern Italy. The plot revolves around lechery, deceit, and treachery. At a ball in the Duke's palace, the hunchbacked jester Rigoletto taunts a nobleman, whose wife is the object of the Duke's wandering eye, while another nobleman places a curse on the Duke for compromising his daughter's honor and on Rigoletto for making a joke of it. Unbeknown to Rigoletto, his daughter Gilda will be the Duke's next conquest, despite the fact that the jester has kept her in seclusion. Through complicated trickery involving the Duke and some conspirators, Gilda is carried off from Rigoletto's house. The jester then plots his revenge—to kill the Duke—with the assassin Sparafucile and his sister Maddalena. In the last act, Maddalena lures the Duke to a lonely tavern where Rigoletto forces Gilda to watch through a window as the man she loves woos Maddalena. The jester arranges to send Gilda away, dressed as a man, but she deceives her father and sacrifices herself for the unworthy man she loves. About to dispose of the sack containing what he believes is the Duke's body, Rigoletto is horrified to find Gilda in the sack instead. He recalls the curse one last time, as Gilda dies in his arms.

In Act III, the Duke sings the best known of

Lithograph depicting the quartet scene from *Rigoletto,* from an 1863 performance in Paris. Rigoletto and his daughter Gilda, on the left, watch the Duke and Maddalena inside the tavern.

Verdi's tunes, "La donna è mobile" ("Woman is fickle"), a simple but rousing song accompanied by a guitarlike orchestral strumming (LG 35). The orchestra previews the catchy melody, which is heard numerous times in a strophic setting that brings back the opening text as a refrain.

The quartet that follows shortly is a masterpiece of operatic ensemble writing, as Verdi himself noted ("In His Own Words," p. 248). Each character presents a different point of view: the Duke woos Maddalena in a lovely bel canto–style melody; Maddalena answers with a laughing line in short notes; Gilda, watching from outside, is heartbroken as she laments her lost love; and Rigoletto swears vengeance for his beloved daughter.

These two show-stopping numbers ensured the immediate success of *Rigoletto*. It remains one of the most frequently performed operas of the international repertory—and every Italian singer can belt out "La donna è mobile." Verdi's music is simultaneously great art and powerful pop.

Costumes for the first production of Verdi's *Rigoletto* at Teatro la Fenice, Venice, March 11, 1851.

LISTENING GUIDE 35
 8:13

Verdi: *Rigoletto*, Act III, excerpts

FIRST PERFORMANCE: 1851, Venice

LIBRETTIST: Francesco Maria Piave

BASIS: *Le roi s'amuse*, a play by Victor Hugo

MAJOR CHARACTERS: The Duke of Mantua (tenor)
Rigoletto, the Duke's jester, a hunchback (baritone)
Gilda, Rigoletto's daughter (soprano)
Sparafucile, an assassin (bass)
Maddalena, Sparafucile's sister (contralto)

What to Listen For

Aria

Melody	Soaring tenor line, with accented notes.
Rhythm/ meter	Lilting triple-meter, "oom-pah-pah" accompaniment; some rubato.
Form	Two strophes, framed by orchestral ritornello that unifies the aria.
Expression	Stirring music, with broadly contrasting dynamics.

Quartet

Melody	Dialogue between characters; then simpler, square melody, "Bella figlia."
Rhythm/ meter	Allegro, with agitated movement.
Expression	Each character reveals his/her emotion.
Performing forces	Quartet (Duke, Maddalena, Gilda, Rigoletto).

Aria: "La donna è mobile" (Duke)
2:43

0:00   Orchestral ritornello previews the Duke's solo; opening melody of aria:

La don - na è   mo - bi - le   qual pium - a al   ven - to,   mut - a d'ac - cen - to

*(The Duke, in a simple cavalry officer's uniform, sings in the inn;
Sparafucile, Gilda, and Rigoletto listen outside.)*

Duke

0:12	La donna è mobile	Woman is fickle
	qual piuma al vento,	like a feather in the wind,
	muta d'accento,	she changes her words
	e di pensiero.	and her thoughts.
	sempre un amabile	Always lovable,
	leggiadro viso,	and a lovely face,
	in pianto o in riso,	weeping or laughing,
	è menzognero.	is lying.
	La donna è mobile, etc.	Woman is fickle, etc.
1:01	Orchestral ritornello.	
1:11	È sempre misero	The man's always wretched
	chi a le s'affida,	who believes in her,
	chi lei confida	who recklessly entrusts
	mal cauto il core!	his heart to her!
	pur mai non sentesi	And yet one who never
	felice appieno	drinks love on that breast
	chi su quel seno	never feels
	non liba amore!	entirely happy!
	La donna è mobile, etc.	Woman is fickle, etc.

(Sparafucile comes back in with a bottle of wine and two glasses, which he sets on the table; then he strikes the ceiling twice with the hilt of his long sword. At this signal, a laughing young woman in Gypsy dress leaps down the stairs: the Duke runs to embrace her, but she escapes him. Meanwhile Sparafucile has gone into the street, where he speaks softly to Rigoletto.)

Quartet (first part): "Un dì" (Duke, Maddalena, Gilda, Rigoletto)   5:29

Duke

2:44	Un dì, se ben rammentomi,	One day, if I remember right,
	o bella, t'incontrai . . .	I met you, O beauty . . .
	Mi piacque di te chiedere,	I was pleased to ask about you,
	e intesi che qui stai.	and I learned that you live here.
	Or sappi, che d'allora	Know then, that since that time
	sol te quest'alma adora!	my soul adores only you!

Gilda

Iniquo!	Villain!

Maddalena

Ah, ah! . . . e vent'altre appresso	Ha, ha! . . . And perhaps now
le scorda forse adesso?	twenty others are forgotten?
Ha un'aria il signorino	The young gentleman looks like
da vero libertino . . .	a true libertine . . .

Duke (starting to embrace her)

Sí . . . un mostro son . . .	Yes . . . I'm a monster . . .

Gilda

Ah padre mio!	Ah, Father!

Maddalena

Lasciatemi, stordito.	Let me go, foolish man!

Duke

Ih che fracasso!	Ah, what a fuss!

Continued on next page

Maddalena	
Stia saggio.	Be good.
Duke	
E tu sii docile,	And you, be yielding,
non fare tanto chiasso.	don't make so much noise.
Ogni saggezza chiudesi	All wisdom concludes
nel gaudio e nell'amore.	in pleasure and in love.

(He takes her hand, vowing his love for her. Outside, Rigoletto reveals the unfaithful lover to Gilda as the dialogue continues, leading to the famous quartet below.)

Quartet (second part): "Bella figlia"

Overall form: **A-B-A′-C**

How characters interact in the ensemble and how they fit into the musical structure:

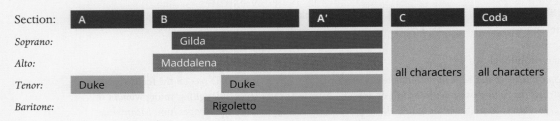

Opening melody of "Bella figlia," sung by the Duke:

Bel - la fi - glia dell' a - mo - re,   schia - vo son de' vez - zi tuo - i,

	Duke		Section
4:15	Bella figlia dell'amore,	Beautiful daughter of love,	**A**
	schiavo son de' vezzi tuoi;	I am the slave of your charms;	
	con un detto sol tu puoi	with a single word you can	
	le mie pene consolar.	console my sufferings.	
	Vieni, e senti del mio core	Come, and feel the quick beating	
	il frequente palpitar . . .	of my heart . . .	
	Con un detto sol tuo puoi	With a single word you can	
	le mie pene consolar.	console my sufferings.	

(Many text lines repeated.)

	Maddalena		
5:19	Ah! ah! rido ben di core,	Ha! Ha! I laugh heartily,	**B**
	chè tai baie costan poco.	for such tales cost little.	
	Gilda		
	Ah! cosí parlar d'amore . . .	Ah! To speak thus of love . . .	
	Maddalena		
	Quanto valga il vostro gioco,	Believe me, I can judge	
	mel credete, sò apprezzar.	how much your game is worth.	
	Gilda		
	. . . a me pur l'infame ho udito!	. . . I too have heard the villain so!	

		Section
Rigoletto (to Gilda)		
Taci, il piangere non vale.	Hush, weeping is of no avail.	
Gilda		
Infelice cor tradito,	Unhappy, betrayed heart,	
per angoscia non scoppiar. No, no!	do not burst with anguish. Ah, no!	
Maddalena		
Son avvezza, bel signore,	I'm accustomed, handsome sir,	
ad un simile scherzare.	to similar joking.	
Mio bel signor!	My handsome sir!	
Duke		
6:01 Bella figlia dell'amore, etc.	Beautiful daughter of love, etc.	A′
Vieni!	Come!	
Rigoletto		
Ch'ei mentiva sei sicura.	You are sure that he was lying.	
Taci, e mia sarà la cura	Hush, and I will take care	
la vendetta d'affrettar.	to hasten vengeance.	
sì, pronta fia, sarà fatale,	Yes, it will be swift and fatal,	
io saprollo fulminar.	I will know how to strike him down.	
taci, taci . . .	Hush, hush . . .	
All characters		
Repeated text from above.		C
7:27 Coda, featuring all characters.		Coda

CRITICAL THINKING

1. How does the drama in the quartet from *Rigoletto* work differently from an ensemble scene in a spoken play?
2. Why was opera a good vehicle for nationalism?

YOUR TURN TO EXPLORE

Identify a song or instrumental track made popular through films, TV, or video games. Search online to determine how the music has been circulated or "remixed" outside the film/show/video itself. How well does the music work in a new context—does its expressive quality change without the framework of the original story?

Chinese Opera

The costumes in Beijing opera are often colorful and elaborate.

Musical theater has been one of the leading forms of entertainment in China for centuries, and Beijing (or Peking) opera is perhaps the most prestigious of the many regional styles. Beijing opera is a blend of music, mime, and dance, with stylized gestures and movements as well as colorful costumes and masks. Its repertory is large, with many works based on novels about the country's political and military struggles.

After flourishing in the early 1900s, both in China and internationally, the genre suffered during the decade-long period known as the Cultural Revolution, a movement begun by the chairman of the Communist Party, Mao Zedong, in 1966 to purge China of a class-structured society. No person or institution was safe during this decade of social upheaval; anyone "elitist" or influenced by the capitalist West was considered an enemy. Operas that did not present communist themes were considered subversive and therefore banned. They were replaced by eight approved "model plays" that fostered the ideals of communism: one of these was *The Story* (or *Legend*) *of the Red Lantern*.

This drama concerns communist underground activities during the Japanese occupation of China in 1939. We saw that the libretto for Verdi's *Rigoletto* was based on a contemporaneous play by Victor Hugo; *The Story*

of the Red Lantern likewise draws on a contemporary (1958) novel, *There Will be Followers of Revolution*, by Qian Daoyuan. And as Verdi's operas, written during a time of political turmoil in Italy, became rallying cries in the nationalistic movement for his country's liberation from oppressive regimes, so too was this Chinese opera written as a political manifesto against the Japanese occupation of China in the 1920s and 30s.

The protagonist Li Tiemei learns from her adoptive grandmother of the sacrifices her parents made during the communist revolution, and of the work of Li Yuhu, who then took up the cause of the communist martyrs and was taken prisoner. Li Tiemei vows that she will follow the example of her father, determined "to do such a thing and to be such a person." Her anger toward the Japanese enemy grows increasingly intense as the opera progresses.

Dramatic works of all genres and cultures rely on powerful human passions to engage the audience. The title character of *Rigoletto* is an ambiguous one, only partly sympathetic: bitter and revengeful toward his noble employer, the Duke, desperately possessive of his only child, the jester lets his emotions bring about his downfall through the death of his beloved daughter. The death of her parents is the starting point for Li Tiemei's quest; she too demonstrates extreme anger and hatred toward her enemies, but her determination to carry on the work of her father makes her a more

likable character. Unlike Western operas, there is no tale of romance in *The Story of the Red Lantern*; rather, it presents an ideological family—not blood-related—drawn together by revolutionary martyrs.

The so-called model plays were heard often on the radio and seen in stage and film versions (including a widely circulated 1963 film). Indeed, this was a political art form well known to all the Chinese people. Beijing opera enjoyed a revival after the "lost decade" of the Cultural Revolution and remains a popular form of entertainment today; new works are being premiered, and traditional works updated, for modern audiences in China and abroad.

You will hear that the singing styles and accompanying instruments are vastly different in the Western and Chinese operatic traditions; this is the result of differing aesthetics of vocal timbre as well as divergent conceptions of melodic and harmonic movement. But both styles rely on acting, particular gestures, and other body movements (as well as a focused use of instruments) to communicate the story behind the words being sung. Our selection, "To be such a person," is for a soprano soloist accompanied by traditional Chinese instruments, including the erhu, an ethereal-sounding bowed-string instrument; the yang qin, a kind of hammered dulcimer; and the pipa, a plucked lute (see photo below). The opera is sung in Mandarin, one of the main Chinese languages.

What to listen for:

- Singing lines in the erhu.
- Hammering, repeated notes on the yang qin.
- Percussive plucking on the pipa.
- The penetrating vocal timbre.

After an instrumental introduction, the voice begins, singing melismatically, wavering between pitches and with a wide vocal vibrato. The instruments drop out occasionally, then rejoin the voice, weaving heterophonic lines around the melody and punctuating the voice with percussive sounds rather than harmony. The vocal range and pace of the song pick up several times, reaching a loud climax near the end, when Li Tiemei resolves to carry on the work of her father.

The Story of the Red Lantern

"To be such a person" text:

My grandma told me the tale of the red light,
She used few words but expressed them deeply.
Why should my father and uncle dare to take risks?
All for the sake of saving China and saving the poor
As well as defeating Japanese invaders.
Encouraged by what they have been doing,
I am determined to follow their example,
To do such a thing and to be such a person.

I am seventeen years old this year,
Old enough to share my father's burdens.
If my father is carrying a load weighing one thousand jin
  [about 1,100 pounds]
I should carry eight hundred for him.

A young Chinese woman in traditional dress plays the pipa, a plucked-string instrument.

Chapter 45

Total Art: Wagner and German Romantic Opera

"The whole [Ring] will then become—out with it! I am not ashamed to say so—the greatest work of poetry ever written."

—*Richard Wagner*

KEY POINTS

- In Germany, the genre *Singspiel* (light, comic drama with spoken dialogue) gave way to more serious works, including Richard Wagner's **music dramas**, which integrated music, poetry, drama, and spectacle.

- Wagner's music dramas are not sectional (with arias, ensembles, and the like) but are continuous, unified by **leitmotifs**, or recurring themes, that represent a person, place, or idea. His most famous work is the four-opera cycle *The Ring of the Nibelung*.

In His Own Words

" True drama can be conceived only as resulting from the collective impulse of all the arts to communicate in the most immediate way with a collective public.... Thus the art of tone ... will realize in the collective artwork its richest potential.... For in its isolation music has formed itself an organ capable of the most immeasurable expression—the orchestra."

—*Richard Wagner*

Through Hollywood blockbusters, we have become accustomed to being "told" by the movie soundtrack when a character is in danger from an evildoer or monster, or when we should start crying. Films and TV shows have also taught us to associate musical ideas with specific characters, so that we can be made aware that someone on screen is thinking about an absent character through the appearance of that character's music in the soundtrack. We owe this supremely effective resource to the work of Richard Wagner, who established the idea that multimedia can convey multiple meanings at once: words may be telling us one thing, and the music may be adding something else that is more subtle. Contemporary composers have repeatedly credited Wagner's concept of "leitmotif," which we will explore in this chapter, with opening up opportunities to create powerful musical reinforcement in film, TV, and computer gaming.

Wagner and German Musical Theater

Nineteenth-century Germany had no long-established opera tradition, as Italy and France did. The immediate predecessor of German Romantic opera was the *Singspiel*, a light or comic drama with spoken dialogue like Mozart's *The Magic Flute* (*Die Zauberflöte*). One element that characterized German musical theater of the early 1800s was **melodrama**: scenes with spoken dialogue or minimal singing, but striking orchestral accompaniment to intensify the dramatic effect of the words.

The greatest figure in German opera, and one of the most significant in the history of the Romantic era, was Richard Wagner. Historians often divide the period into "before" and "after Wagner." The course of post-Romantic music is unimag-

Richard Wagner (1813–1883)

Wagner was born in Leipzig, Germany. Atfter studying briefly at the University of Leipzig, he gained practical experience conducting in provincial theaters. At twenty-three, he married the actress Minna Planer, and began to produce his first operas. He wrote the librettos himself, as he did for all his later works, unifying music and drama more than anyone had before.

Wagner's early opera *Rienzi* won a huge success in Dresden. With his next three works, *The Flying Dutchman, Tannhäuser,* and *Lohengrin,* Wagner chose subjects derived from medieval German epics. In them, he displayed a profound feeling for nature, employed the supernatural as an element of the drama, and glorified the German land and people. In 1849, after a failed revolution in Dresden, Wagner fled to Switzerland, where he set forth his theories of the music drama, the name he gave his complete integration of theater and music. He proceeded to put theory into practice in the cycle of four music dramas called *The Ring of the Nibelung,* and two more—*Tristan and Isolde* and *Die Meistersinger von Nürnberg.*

Wagner soon won the support and admiration of the young monarch Ludwig II of Bavaria, who commissioned him to complete the *Ring* and helped him build a theater to present his music dramas, which ultimately became the Festival Theater at Bayreuth. And the composer (now separated from Minna) found a woman he considered his equal in will and courage—Cosima, the daughter of his old friend Franz Liszt. She left her husband and children in order to join him.

The Wagnerian gospel spread across Europe as a new art-religion. The *Ring* cycle was completed in 1874 and presented to worshipful audiences at the first Bayreuth Festival two years later. Wagner's final work was *Parsifal* (1877–82), based on the legend of the Holy Grail.

MAJOR WORKS: 13 operas (music dramas), including *Rienzi* (1842), *Der fliegende Holländer* (*The Flying Dutchman,* 1843), *Tannhäuser* (1845), *Lohengrin* (1850), *Tristan und Isolde* (1865), *Die Meistersinger von Nürnberg* (*The Mastersingers of Nuremberg,* 1868), and *Parsifal* (1882) • Cycle of music dramas: *Der Ring des Nibelung* (*The Ring of the Nibelung*), consisting of *Das Rheingold* (*The Rhine Gold,* 1869), *Die Walküre* (*The Valkyrie,* 1870), *Siegfried* (1876), and *Götterdämmerung* (*The Twilight of the Gods,* 1876) • Orchestral music • Piano music • Vocal and choral music • Writings: *Art and Revolution; The Art Work of the Future.*

 Ride of the Valkyries

inable without the impact of this complex and fascinating figure. We will consider his music drama *Die Walküre* (*The Valkyrie,* which includes the famous *Ride of the Valkyries*), part of his cycle *The Ring of the Nibelung.*

The Ring of the Nibelung

Wagner did away with the concept of separate arias, duets, ensembles, choruses, and ballets, developing an "endless melody" that was molded to the natural inflections of the German language, more melodious than the traditional recitative but freer and more flexible than the traditional aria. He conceived of opera as a total artwork (in German, *Gesamtkunstwerk*) in which the arts of music, poetry, drama, and visual spectacle were fused together, each element created and controlled by his creative genius: a **music drama**.

Music drama

The orchestra became its focal point and unifying element, fashioned out of concise themes—the **leitmotifs**, or "leading motives," that recur throughout a work, undergoing variation and development like the themes and motives of a symphony. The leitmotifs carry specific meanings, suggesting in a few notes a person, an emotion, an idea, an object. Through a process of continual transformation, they trace the course of the drama, the changes in the characters, their experiences and memories, and their thoughts and hidden desires.

Leitmotif

Wagner based his musical language on chromatic harmony, which he pushed

Chromatic harmony

A Valkyrie on her winged horse, in a design (c. 1876) by **Carl Emil Doepler**.

to its then farthermost limits. Chromatic dissonance gives his music its restless, intensely emotional quality. Never before had unstable pitch combinations been used so eloquently to portray states of the soul.

The story of *The Ring of the Nibelung* centers on the treasure of gold that lies hidden in the depths of the Rhine River, guarded by three Rhine Maidens. Alberich the Nibelung, who comes from a hideous race of dwarfs that inhabit the dark regions below the earth, tries to make love to the maidens. When they repulse him, he steals the treasure and makes it into a ring that will bring unlimited power to its owner. Wotan, father of the gods (for whom Wednesday, or Wotan's Day, is named), tricks Alberich out of the ring, whereupon the dwarf pronounces a terrible curse: may the ring destroy the peace of mind of all who gain possession of it, may it bring them misfortune and death.

Thus begins the cycle of four dramas that ends only when the curse-bearing ring is returned to the Rhine Maidens. Gods and heroes, mortals and Nibelungs, intermingle freely in this tale of betrayed love, broken promises, magic spells, and general corruption brought on by the lust for power. Wagner freely adapted the story from the myths of the Norse sagas and the legends associated with a medieval German epic poem, the *Nibelungenlied*. (Norse mythology and Wagner's *Ring* were also the inspiration for J. R. R. Tolkien's epic *Lord of the Rings* and for the three popular movies based on that literary work, as well as for many role-playing games.)

Die Walküre (The Valkyrie)

Die Walküre, the second work in the cycle, revolves around the twin brother and sister Siegmund and Sieglinde, the offspring of Wotan by a mortal. Their love is not only incestuous but also adulterous, for she has been forced into a loveless marriage with the grim chieftain Hunding, who challenges Siegmund to battle. The second act opens with a scene between Wotan and Brünnhilde, one of his nine daughters, called Valkyries. The Valkyries' perpetual task is to circle the battlefield on their winged horses and swoop down to gather up the fallen heroes, whom they bear away to the great hall of Valhalla, where they will sit forever feasting with the gods. At the insistence of Wotan's wife Fricka (the goddess of marriage), Wotan acknowledges that Siegmund has violated the holiest law of the universe and sadly realizes that he must die in combat with Hunding. Brünnhilde decides to disobey her father's command to let Hunding win the duel by shielding Siegmund. But Wotan appears and holds out his spear, upon which Siegmund's sword is shattered. Hunding then buries his own spear in Siegmund's breast. Wotan, overcome by his son's death, turns a ferocious look upon Hunding, who falls dead. Then the god hurries off in pursuit of the daughter who dared to defy his command.

Ride of the Valkyries

Act III opens with the famous *Ride of the Valkyries*, a vivid orchestral picture of the nine warrior maidens on their way from the battlefield back to Valhalla, carrying fallen heroes slung across the saddles of their winged horses (LG 36). This prelude features some of Wagner's most brilliant scoring. The rustling strings and woodwinds give way to the memorable "Ride" theme (familiar from movie soundtracks and even commercials), which is sounded repeatedly by a huge and varied brass section through a dense orchestral texture that builds to several climaxes beneath the warriors' voices.

Brünnhilde is the last Valkyrie to arrive, carrying Sieglinde and several fragments of Siegmund's sword. Sieglinde wants to die, but Brünnhilde tells her she must live to bear his son, who will become the world's mightiest hero. Brünnhilde remains to face her father's wrath. Her punishment is severe: she is to be deprived of her godhood, Wotan tells her, to become a mortal. He will put her to sleep on a rock, and she will fall prey to the first mortal who finds her. Brünnhilde begs him to soften her punishment: let him at least surround the rock with flames so that only a fearless hero will be able to penetrate the wall of fire. Wotan relents and grants her request. He kisses her on both eyes, which close at once. Striking the rock three times, he invokes Loge, the god of Fire. Flames spring up around the rock, and the "magic fire" leitmotif is heard, followed by the "magic sleep" and "slumber" motives. "Whosoever fears the tip of my spear shall never pass through the fire," he sings, as the orchestra announces the theme of Siegfried, the fearless, yet-unborn son of Sieglinde who in the third music drama will force his way through the flames and awaken Brünnhilde with a kiss.

While the action in this final scene is fairly static, Wagner brings together several strands of meaning through the interaction of the leitmotifs, even introducing us to a character (Siegfried) who has not even been born. Wotan does not name Siegfried, but the striking brass motive names him through music, and prepares us to meet him on the following night (Wagner conceived the *Ring* to be performed on four consecutive evenings). Contemporary film composers such as John Williams also have used this foreshadowing device (in the *Star Wars* films, for example; see Chapter 67), introducing early in the film subtle musical references that prepare us for a full "reveal" later on.

Arthur Rackham's drawing portrays Brünnhilde asleep in a ring of fire.

LISTENING GUIDE 36   5:51

Wagner: *Die Walküre (The Valkyrie)*, Act III, Opening and Finale

DATE: 1856; first performed 1870, in Munich

GENRE: Music drama: second in a cycle of four (*The Ring of the Nibelung*)

CHARACTERS: Wotan, father of the gods (bass-baritone)
Brünnhilde, his favorite daughter (soprano)
Valkyries, the nine daughters of Wotan

Act III, scene 1: *Ride of the Valkyries*   1:17

What to Listen For			
Melody	Swirling strings and woodwinds, then famous "Ride" leitmotif ascends, repeated many times.	**Expression**	Excited mood; huge dynamic contrasts; evokes battle cries and flying warriors.
Rhythm/ meter	Lively dotted rhythm in 9/8 for the "Ride" leitmotif.	**Performing forces**	Huge orchestra featuring brass (including eight French horns, bass trumpet, various sized trombones, Wagner tubas and contrabass tuba); woodwinds (piccolos, English horn, and bass clarinet); large percussion section (cymbals, triangle, glockenspiel, gong); and strings (including six harps).
Harmony	Leitmotif heard in minor and major.		
Texture	Polyphonic, combines main theme and swirling idea.		

Continued on next page

0:00   Orchestral prelude, marked *Lebhaft* (Lively), in 9/8 meter.
         Rushing string figure alternates with fast wavering in woodwinds, then
0:08   insistent dotted figure begins in horns and low strings.
         Swirling string and woodwind lines, accompanied by dotted figure.
0:22   Famous "Ride" motive, heard first in a minor key in the horns:

0:34   "Ride" motive is now heard in a major key in the trumpets.
         Four-note dotted motive exchanged between low and high brass instruments, heard above swirling idea.
1:04   "Ride" motive heard *fortissimo*, as curtain opens.

   (Four Valkyries, in full armor, have settled on the highest peak above a cave.)

Act III, closing of scene 3: Wotan and Brünnhilde

4:34

What to Listen For			
Melody	Three recurring themes (leitmotifs); endless melody; forceful descending trombone melody.	**Expression**	Melodies signify magic fire, magic sleep, slumber, Siegfried; dramatic invocation of Loge, god of Fire; long closing, *ff* to *ppp*.
Rhythm/ meter	Broad, duple meter; majestic.	**Performing forces**	Bass (Wotan) with orchestra; focus on trombones (calling Loge); woodwinds and French horns (in magic fire music); harps (in magic sleep music) and brass (Siegfried theme).
Harmony	Rich, chromatic harmony.		
Texture	Continuous orchestral sound.		

(Wotan clasps Brünnhilde's head in his hands. He kisses her long on the eyes. She sinks back with closed eyes, unconscious in his arms. He gently bears her to a low mossy mound . . . and lays her upon it. He looks upon her and closes her helmet; his eyes rest on the form of the sleeper, whom he covers with the great shield of the Valkyrie. He turns slowly away, then again turns around with a sorrowful look.)

(He strides with solemn decision to the middle of the stage and directs the point of his spear toward a large rock.)

0:00   A forceful trombone passage precedes Wotan's invocation of Loge, god of Fire:

Wotan's evocation of Loge:

Lo- ge, hör!   Lau - sche hie-her!

Wotan

0:08   Loge, hör'! Lausche hieher!   Loge, listen! Harken here!
         Wie zuerst ich dich fand, als feurige Gluth,   As I found you first, a fiery blaze,
         wie dann einst du mir schwandest,   as once you vanished from me,
         als schweifende Lohe;   a random fire;
         wie ich dich band, bann' ich dich heut'!   as I allied with you, so today I conjure you!
         Herauf, wabernde Lohe,   Arise, magic flame,
         umlod're mir feurig den Fels!   girdle the rock with fire for me!

(He strikes the rock thrice with his spear.)

Loge! Loge! Hieher!   Loge! Loge! Come here!

(A flash of flames issues from the rock, which swells to an ever-brightening fiery glow. Bright shooting flames surround Wotan. With his spear he directs the sea of fire to encircle the rock; it presently spreads toward the background, where it encloses the mountain in flames.)

1:03   "Magic fire" music, heard in full orchestra:

1:40   "Magic sleep" motive, evoked in descending chromatic line in woodwinds:

1:53   "Slumber" motive, heard in woodwinds:

Wotan (singing to "Siegfried" motive)

2:03   Wer meines Speeres Spitze fürchtet,   Whosoever fears the tip of my spear
      durchreite das Feuer nie!   shall never pass through the fire!

(He stretches out the spear as a spell. He gazes sadly on Brünnhilde. Slowly he turns to depart. He turns his head again and looks back. He disappears through the fire.)

2:34   Brass in *fortissimo* announce the "Siegfried" motive; long orchestral closing:

CRITICAL THINKING

1. What innovations did Wagner bring to the world of opera?

2. In what ways do leitmotifs contribute to the shaping of drama?

YOUR TURN TO EXPLORE

Consider an instance of epic-scale multimedia—the *Star Wars* or *Lord of the Rings* movie "cycles," or an MMORPG like World of Warcraft or RuneScape. Can you identify leitmotifs associated with situations, characters, key objects? Do they evolve along with the characters as the drama progresses, and if so, how? How do you think the use of leitmotifs helps shape the dramatic/gaming experience?

Chapter 46

Poetry in Motion:
Tchaikovsky and the Ballet

"Dance is the hidden language of the soul."
—Martha Graham

O ut of movement, dance weaves an enchantment all its own. We watch with amazement as dancers synchronize their actions to the music, performing pirouettes and intricate footwork with the utmost grace, and leaps that seem to triumph over the laws of gravity. A special glamour attaches to the great dancers—Mikhail Baryshnikov, Fred Astaire, Martha Graham, Lil Buck, and their peers—yet theirs is an art based on an inhumanly demanding discipline. Their bodies are their instruments, which they must keep in excellent shape in order to perform the gymnastics required of them. They create moments of elusive beauty, made possible only by total control of their muscles. It is this combination of physical and emotional factors, blended with the expressive resources of music, that marks the distinctive power of choreographed dance.

A French court dancer from the era of Louis XIV.

The Ballet

Beginning in the Renaissance, the choreographed dance known as **ballet** was central to lavish festivals and theatrical entertainments presented at the courts of kings and dukes. Royal weddings and other celebrations were accompanied by spectacles with scenery, costumes, and staged dancing known as *intermedio* in Italy, **masque** in England, and *ballet de cour* in France. Louis XIV himself took part in one, as the Sun King. Elaborate ballets were also featured in the operas by French composers.

The eighteenth century saw the rise of ballet as an independent art form. French ballet was preeminent in the early nineteenth century, then Russian ballet came into its own—helped along considerably by the arrival in 1847 of French-born Marius Petipa, the great choreographer at St. Petersburg. Petipa created the dances for more than a hundred works, invented the structure of the classic *pas de deux* (dance for two), and brought the art of staging ballets to unprecedented heights.

Peter Ilyich Tchaikovsky (1840–1893)

The son of a Russian government official, Tchaikovsky entered the newly founded Conservatory of St. Petersburg at the age of twenty-three. He was immediately recommended by Anton Rubinstein, director of the school, for a teaching post in the new Moscow Conservatory, and his twelve years in Moscow saw the production of some of his most successful works.

Extremely sensitive by nature, Tchaikovsky was subject to attacks of depression. The social stigma associated with being a homosexual may have led him to marry a student at the conservatory, but they soon separated. Good fortune followed when in 1877 Nadezhda von Meck, the wealthy widow of an industrialist, sent Tchaikovsky money to go abroad, and launched him on the most productive period of his career. Bound by the rigid conventions of her time and class, von Meck had to be certain that her enthusiasm was for the artist, not the man; hence she stipulated that she never meet the recipient of her patronage.

Tchaikovsky was the first Russian whose music appealed to Western tastes—it was performed in Vienna, Berlin, and Paris—and in 1891 he was invited to participate in the inaugural concert of Carnegie Hall in New York. Two years later, he conducted his *Pathétique* Symphony in St. Petersburg, where the work met with a lukewarm reception. He died within several weeks, at the age of fifty-three, and the tragic tone of his last work led to rumors that he had committed suicide. More likely he contracted cholera from tainted water.

Although Tchaikovsky declared, "I am Russian through and through!," he also came under the spell of Italian opera, French ballet, and German symphony and song. These he joined to the strain of folk melody that was his heritage as a Russian, imposing on this mixture his sharply defined personality.

MAJOR WORKS: Eight operas, including *Eugene Onegin* (1878) • Three ballets: *Swan Lake* (1877), *The Sleeping Beauty* (1890), and *The Nutcracker* (1892) • Orchestral music, including seven symphonies (one unfinished), three piano concertos, a violin concerto, symphonic poems (*Romeo and Juliet*), and overtures (*1812 Overture*) • Chamber and keyboard music • Choral music • Songs.

 March and *Waltz of the Flowers*, from *The Nutcracker*

Tchaikovsky and *The Nutcracker*

The giant of Russian ballet in the later nineteenth century was Peter Ilyich Tchaikovsky, who also composed well-loved works in other instrumental genres. Tchaikovsky belonged to a generation that saw its truths crumbling and found none to replace them; his music typifies the end-of-the-century mood of pessimism that engulfed the late Romantic movement.

Tchaikovsky had a natural affinity for the theater. His three ballets—*Swan Lake, The Sleeping Beauty,* and *The Nutcracker*, all choreographed by Petipa— were quickly established as basic works of the Russian repertory. We will hear excerpts from the popular ballet that's performed every Christmas all over the world, *The Nutcracker.*

Act I takes place at a Christmas party during which two children, Clara and Fritz, receive a nutcracker from their godfather. After the children have gone to bed, Clara returns to gaze at her gift, falls asleep, and begins to dream. First she is terrified to see mice scampering around the tree. Then the dolls she has received come alive and fight a battle with the mice, which reaches a climax in the combat between the Nutcracker and the Mouse King. Clara helps her beloved Nutcracker by throwing a slipper at the Mouse King, who is vanquished. The Nutcracker then becomes a handsome Prince, who sweeps Clara away with him.

Act II finds them in Confiturembourg, the land of sweets, ruled by the Sugar Plum Fairy (LG 37). The Prince presents Clara to his family, and a celebration

A traditional Russian nutcracker—a toy soldier who comes alive in Tchaikovsky's ballet.

A performance of the *Trepak* from *The Nutcracker*, by the Royal Ballet at Covent Garden, London, in 2008.

follows, with a series of dances that reveal all the attractions of this magic realm. The dances are accompanied by colorful instruments; Tchaikovsky wrote to his publisher that he had discovered a new one in Paris, "something between a piano and a glockenspiel, with a divinely beautiful tone, and I want to introduce it into the ballet." The instrument was the **celesta,** whose timbre perfectly suits the Sugar Plum Fairy's dance. In the *Trepak* (Russian Dance, featuring the famous Cossack squat-kick; see illustration at left), the orchestral sound is enlivened by a tambourine. Other exotic dances follow, from Arabia and China, climaxing with the *Waltz of the Flowers.*

This engaging work conjures up everything we have come to associate with the Romantic ballet. It is an example of the way music has been combined with movement in the Western tradition to tell stories that are both more precise than instrumental program music and more subtle and nuanced than opera and song.

CRITICAL THINKING

1. How does Tchaikovsky use instruments to portray characters in his dances?

2. How does *The Nutcracker* embrace and depart from musical nationalism and exoticism?

YOUR TURN TO EXPLORE

Find two videos of dancers from separate traditions (for example, classical ballet, modern dance, tap, jazz and/or Broadway dance, hip-hop)—some extraordinary performers you might look for are Rudolf Nureyev, Savion Glover, Bob Fosse, Katherine Dunham, Lil Buck. Note how the dancer varies and repeats movements, the variety of melodic ideas in the music, and the way the music and movement are synchronized. Do you think the dancer is conveying a story through her/his moves, and if so, how would you describe it? If not, what do you think the dancer is conveying?

LISTENING GUIDE 37

 2:56

Tchaikovsky: *The Nutcracker,* Two Dances

DATE:	1892
GENRE:	Ballet (from which an orchestral suite was made)
BASIS:	E. T. A. Hoffmann story, expanded by Alexandre Dumas *père*
CHOREOGRAPHER:	Marius Petipa

SEQUENCE OF DANCES:	*March*	*Chinese Dance*
	Dance of the Sugar Plum Fairy	*Dance of the Toy Flutes*
	Trepak	*Waltz of the Flowers*
	Arab Dance	

Dance of the Sugar Plum Fairy: Andante non troppo

1:44

What to Listen For

Melody	Staccato melody, somewhat chromatic.
Rhythm/meter	Bouncy duple meter.
Form	Three-part (**A-B-A**).

Expression	Quiet and mysterious mood.
Performing forces	Bell-like timbre of celesta, accompanied by bass clarinet and pizzicato strings.

A section

0:00   Short introduction (four measures) of pizzicato strings.

0:08   Main theme introduced by celesta, staccato in a high range (in dialogue with bass clarinet):

B section

0:39   Brief section with arched lines in woodwinds and celesta, answered by strings.

A section

1:11   Solo celesta leads back to the main theme, accompanied by staccato strings. Closes with a loud pizzicato chord.

Trepak (Russian Dance): Tempo di trepak, molto vivace (very lively)

1:12

What to Listen For

Melody	Short, staccato melody, descending, with *sforzandos* (accents).
Rhythm/meter	Lively peasant dance, heavy accents; *accelerando* (getting faster).
Texture	Homophonic; contrapuntal **B** section.

Form	Three-part (**A-B-A**).
Expression	Vivacious mood; builds to a frenzy at the end.
Performing forces	Tambourine featured with strings and woodwinds; trumpet fanfare.

A section

0:00   Lively dance tune in strings, repeated in full orchestra:

B section

0:27   Brief diversion in the same rhythmic style, melody in the low strings.

A section

0:47   Return of the dance tune; quickens at the end, with trumpet fanfare and syncopations.

Chapter 47

Exotic Allure: Puccini and the Italian Verismo Tradition

"It may be a good thing to copy reality; but to invent reality is much, much better."

—Giuseppe Verdi

KEY POINTS

- At the turn of the twentieth century, an important movement called **post-Romanticism** reflected an expansion and intensification of late Romantic trends, especially in Germany, Austria, and Italy.

- Italian composer Giacomo Puccini wrote some of the best-loved operas of all time, including *Madame Butterfly*, which combines two end-of-the-century trends: **verismo** (realism) and **exoticism** (Japanese culture and music).

The intensity that musical accompaniment brings to words can generate meanings that surpass those of the poetry or lyrics being set. This is why musical multimedia always produces an effect that is at least a little unreal, or "hyper-real." However, realism is also an effective artistic choice: a way to make a message more powerful because the characters delivering it are recognizable to an audience. And a way to spice up realism is to mix it with elements of a foreign or fantastic setting, so that familiar perspectives are filtered through unfamiliar contexts. This tactic is what makes many science fiction and fantasy movies and video games so compelling; and we can see it too in the exotic realism that characterizes post-Romantic musical trends at the turn of the twentieth century.

The geisha Cio-Cio-San on the cover of the earliest English vocal score of *Madame Butterfly*, published by Ricordi. Design by **Leopoldo Metlicovitz** (1868–1944).

Post-Romanticism

The late Romantic ideals were carried into the **post-Romantic** era through the Italian operatic tradition—in particular, by Giacomo Puccini—and by German composers such as Richard Strauss (1864–1949) and Gustav Mahler (1860–1911), both notable for inspired orchestral writing infused with sensuous lyricism. Mahler, like many of his contemporaries, also had a strong fascination with Eastern culture. So did Puccini: his enduring opera *Madame Butterfly* radiates an **exoticism** that was gaining popularity in the arts at the time (see p. 268).

Giacomo Puccini (1858–1924)

Puccini was born in Lucca, Italy, the son of a church organist. He entered the conservatory in Milan in 1880, and thirteen years later had his first operatic success with *Manon Lescaut*. His partners were librettists Luigi Illica and Giuseppe Giacosa, both of whom also collaborated with him on the three most successful operas of the early twentieth century: *La bohème*, *Tosca*, and *Madame Butterfly*.

Puccini's travels to oversee the international premieres of several of his works were demanding. In 1903, a serious car crash left him bedridden for six months, and in 1908 an extramarital affair caused a public scandal. "I am always falling in love," he once declared. "When I no longer am, make my funeral." In 1910, *The Girl of the Golden West* received its world premiere at the Metropolitan Opera in New York; this was followed by a trio of three one-act works that included *Gianni Schicchi*, one of his best-loved masterpieces.

Puccini's last opera, *Turandot*, is based on a Chinese fairy tale about a beautiful but cruel princess. Struggling with cancer, Puccini died in 1924 before finishing the final scene. His friend Franco Alfano completed the opera, using Puccini's sketches. The first performance took place in 1926 at La Scala, and was conducted by Arturo Toscanini, Puccini's greatest interpreter. The opera ended as Puccini had left it, without the final scene—Toscanini laid down his baton after the Lament over the death of one of the main characters, turned to the audience, and said in a choking voice, "Here ends the master's work."

MAJOR WORKS: 12 operas, including *Manon Lescaut* (1893), *La bohème* (1896), *Tosca* (1900), *Madame Butterfly* (1904), *La fanciulla del west* (*The Girl of the Golden West*, 1910), *Gianni Schicchi* (1918), and *Turandot* (1926) • Choral works • Solo songs • Orchestral, chamber, and solo piano works.

Puccini and Verismo Opera

"God touched me with His little finger and said, 'Write for the theater, only for the theater.' And I obeyed the supreme command."

Giacomo Puccini was the main voice among a group of opera composers associated with a movement known as **verismo**, or realism. The advocates of this trend tried to bring into the theater the naturalness of writers such as Emile Zola and Henrik Ibsen. Instead of choosing historical or mythological themes, they picked subjects from everyday life and treated them in down-to-earth fashion. The most famous verismo operas include Puccini's *La bohème* (*Bohemian Life*, 1896) and *Tosca* (1900), and Ruggero Leoncavallo's *I Pagliacci* (*The Clowns*, 1892). Although it was a short-lived movement, verismo had counterparts in Germany and France, and arguably was influential in the rising multimedia tradition of film. And it produced some of the best-loved works in the operatic repertory.

Madame Butterfly

Puccini's style emphasizes soaring melodies and rich orchestral timbres and colors, as well as elements borrowed from Wagner, notably leitmotifs (recurring melodies). His style is thoroughly accessible, yet his operas are complex mechanisms built from many different influences.

Puccini's inspiration for *Madame Butterfly* came in 1900 during a visit to London, where he attended a performance of David Belasco's play of the same name. Like his other operas, this one tells the story of a tragic-heroic female protagonist, a young geisha named Cio-Cio-San (Madame Butterfly) from Nagasaki who

In His Own Words

" I have had a visit today from Mme. Ohyama, wife of the Japanese ambassador. . . . She has promised to send me native Japanese music. I sketched the story of the libretto for her, and she liked it, especially as just such a story as Butterfly's is known to her as having happened in real life."

—*Giacomo Puccini*

Geisha

renounces her profession and religion in order to marry an American naval officer called Pinkerton. (A **geisha** is most closely equivalent to a courtesan in Western culture; these women were highly trained in the arts of classical music, poetry, and dancing, and were easily recognizable by their black, laquered hair, distinctive makeup, and ornate silk kimono.) Butterfly and Pinkerton are married in a house promised to the couple by the marriage broker, and Pinkerton departs soon thereafter. When he returns several years later—with a new American wife in tow—he learns that Butterfly has given birth to their son and decides to take the child back with him to America. Butterfly accepts his decision with dignity, but rather than return to her life as a geisha, she commits suicide (the samurai warrior's ritual *seppuku*, also known as *hara-kiri*).

Exoticism

Madame Butterfly marks a turn-of-the-century interest in exoticism. The entire score is tinged with Japanese color: traditional Japanese melodies are juxtaposed with **pentatonic** and **whole-tone** passages, and you can hear instrument combinations evoking the timbres of a *gagaku* orchestra (with harp, flute, piccolo, and bells). Simple moments in the score—a single, unaccompanied melody, for example—have their visual equivalent in the clear lines of Japanese prints. Another exotic touch comes in the opening of Act I, where Puccini makes a brief reference to *The Star-Spangled Banner*.

La Japonaise (1876), by **Claude Monet** (1840–1926), depicting the nineteenth-century Paris fad for all things Japanese.

Our selection is from Act II, which takes place three years after the marriage (LG 38). Butterfly has heard nothing from her husband, leading her maid Suzuki to doubt that Pinkerton will ever return. She is quickly rebuked, however, in Butterfly's soaring aria "Un bel dì" ("One beautiful day"), in which the young bride pictures their happy reunion and recalls Pinkerton's promise to return "when the robins build their nests." This aria is one of the most memorable in all opera. At first, Butterfly sings with a distant, ethereal quality, accompanied by solo violin, while she dreams of Pinkerton's return. The intensity rises when she imagines seeing his ship in the harbor. Her speechlike melody peaks on the word "morire" ("die"), as she explains how she will playfully hide from him at first in order not to die from happiness at their reunion. The emotional level builds—along with the dynamics—and her final soaring line climaxes on "l'aspetto" ("I wait for him"), with the orchestra now playing the heartrending music at *fff*.

While Butterfly may be an idealized rather than a believable character, her naivety and vulnerability make her a beloved heroine. Puccini's ability to combine realistic references to Japanese culture with memorable melodies of the bel canto tradition of his predecessor Verdi, along with his own unique orchestral language, cemented his position in the operatic repertory. After him, the Italian tradition lost its predominance, and indeed opera gradually became displaced in the popular imagination by other musical-theatrical traditions and eventually by film—which took on the values of multimedia intensity and hyper-reality that draw us to the movies in droves.

CRITICAL THINKING

1. How does Puccini evoke exoticism in *Madame Butterfly?*
2. Do you find the character of Butterfly realistic? Explain why or why not.

YOUR TURN TO EXPLORE

Find an example of contemporary music (for example, a popular song) that is intended to evoke an "exotic" quality. What exotic topic does the work engage? How is that quality reflected in the music—melody, choice of instruments, unusual rhythms, and so on? Why do you think the musicians have chosen this exotic topic? How might it reflect our society's understanding (stereotypes?) of the culture that is being depicted?

LISTENING GUIDE 38

 4:35

Puccini: *Madame Butterfly,* "Un bel dì"

DATE: 1904

LIBRETTISTS: Giuseppe Giacosa and Luigi Illica

BASIS: Play by David Belasco, from a short story by John Luther Long, derived from Pierre Loti's tale *Madame Chrysanthème*

SETTING: Nagasaki, Japan, at the beginning of the 20th century

PRINCIPAL CHARACTERS: Cio-Cio-San, or Madame Butterfly (soprano)
Suzuki, her maid (mezzo-soprano)
B. F. Pinkerton, lieutenant in the U.S. Navy (tenor)
Sharpless, U.S. consul at Nagasaki (baritone)
Goro, marriage broker (tenor)
Prince Yamadori (tenor)
Kate Pinkerton, American wife of Pinkerton (mezzo-soprano)

What to Listen For

Melody	Soaring line, alternating with speechlike section; reaches several climaxes.
Rhythm/ meter	Slow and dreamy, then more agitated rhythmically.
Harmony	Rich accompaniment; some unison writing.
Expression	Dreamlike, then passionate and emotional; rising dynamic lines.
Performing forces	Sparse accompaniment at opening by solo violin.

Opening, ethereal vocal line:

Un ____ bel dì, ve - dre - mo   le - var - si un fil di fu - mo

Continued on next page

Final climactic moment on "l'aspetto" ("I wait for him"):

Tien - ti   la tua   pa - u - ra, io con si - cu - ra   fe - de   l'a - spet - to.

TEXT	TRANSLATION
0:00	Un bel dì, vedremo	One lovely day we'll see
	levarsi un fil di fumo	a thread of smoke rise
	sull'estremo confin del mare.	at the distant edge of the sea.
	E poi la nave appare—	And then the ship appears—
	poi la nave bianca entra nel porto,	then the white ship enters the harbor,
	romba il suo saluto.	thunders its salute.
	Vedi? E venuto!	You see? He's come!
	Io non gli scendo incontro. Io no.	I don't go down to meet him. Not I.
	Mi metto là sul cieglio del colle	I place myself at the brow of the hill
	e aspetto gran tempo e non mi pesa,	and wait a long time, but the long
	la lunga attesa.	wait doesn't oppress me.
	E uscito dalla folla cittadina	And coming out of the city's crowd
	un uomo, un picciol punto	a man, a tiny speck
	s'avvia per la collina.	starts toward the hill.
2:14	Chi sarà? Chi sarà?	Who will it be? Who?
	E come sarà giunto	And when he arrives
	che dirà? Che dirà?	what will he say? What?
	Chiamerà Butterfly dalla lontana.	He'll call Butterfly from the distance.
	Io senza dar risposta me ne starò nascosta	I'll stay hidden, partly to tease him
	un po' per celia	and partly not to die
	e un po' per non morire al primo incontro,	at our first meeting,
	ed egli alquanto in pena chiamerà:	and a little worried he'll call
	piccina mogliettina olezzo di verbena,	little wife, verbena blossom,
	i nomi che mi dava al suo venire	the names he gave me when he came here.
	tutto questo avverrà, te lo prometto.	All this will happen, I promise you.
	Tienti la tua paura,	Keep your fear to yourself,
	io con sicura fede l'aspetto.	with certain faith I wait for him.

Japanese Music

From around 1600 to the mid-nineteenth century, Japan had limited contact with the West. Its rulers, fearing the strength of the European powers and the disruptive effects of their influence on Japanese society, banned traders and Christian missionaries, and built an elaborate but self-contained artistic culture. Then in 1854, the U.S. Navy, under the command of Commodore Matthew Perry, forced the country to open its doors to world commerce, ending two hundred years of isolation. Japan quickly adopted some Western ways and institutions, while the United States and Europe experienced a "craze" for all things Japanese—fans, bronzes, woodblock art prints, and music. England also experienced this *japonisme* fever, inspiring W. S. Gilbert and Arthur Sullivan's much-loved operetta *The Mikado* (1885), which satirizes British society but is set in Japan.

When Giacomo Puccini visited London and saw the play *Madame Butterfly*, he too was hooked, and began studying Japanese melodies—some of which appear, if only fleetingly, in his opera. We know that Puccini was particularly fond of a melody titled *Echigo Jishi*, or *The Lion of Echigo*, composed around 1811. This melody accompanies a dance from a **kabuki** play, a type of dance-drama that is highly stylized, with elaborate costumes and makeup. The dance tells the story of a traveling entertainer named Kakubei, who hawks products from the Echigo district while performing a lion's dance, complete with elaborate headgear, and waving long strips of cloth in dif-

Geishas play the shamisen and drum for a theatrical performance in Kyoto, Japan.

ferent patterns. There was a long folk tradition of lions' dances in Japan, and today there are many versions of *Echigo Jishi*.

Japanese folk melodies are often built on a pentatonic, or five-note, "gapped" scale. We will hear two versions of *Echigo Jishi*: the first is the melody in its simplest form—probably as Puccini knew it—played on a shamisen, a banjo-like lute with three twisted silk strings (see photo above); the second is a dance performance that starts off with a drum, followed by a shamisen playing variations on the melody. You'll notice there is no real supporting harmony, and the rhythmic movement of the longer, dance version is rather free. Puccini's knowledge of tunes like *Echigo Jishi* allowed him to infuse his opera with authentic hints of Japanese culture.

Echigo Jishi 🎧

What to listen for:

- *Tune:* The basic five-note scale, with gaps; the tune is played with a pulse.
- *Dance version:* Varied plucking and strumming techniques on the shamisen, the drum punctuating the dance, and the changing tempos.

The drum begins, then the shamisen enters with an elaboration of the tune. The sections alternate between shamisen solo and drum/shamisen together. At around two minutes, the main tune is heard more clearly, alternating with rapid, repeated notes on shamisen and irregular drumbeats.

The tune undergoes variations in different ranges and tempos. The dance builds to a fast-paced climax, then the music slows, with a regular drumbeat and closing vocal interjections.

Chapter 48

Accepting Death:
Fauré and the Requiem

*"To express that which is within you with sincerity,
in the clearest and most perfect manner, would
seem to me always the ultimate goal of art."*

—Gabriel Fauré

KEY POINTS

- In French Romantic music, the **mélodie** song tradition paralleled the German Lied tradition.

- Composer Gabriel Fauré had a complex career as both church musician and conservatory leader; his music exemplifies a nineteenth-century French interest in small and intimate musical forms.

- Fauré's *Requiem* is a unique contribution to the genre, reflecting the freedom with which late-Romantic composers addressed sacred music.

We often turn to music for comfort in times of trouble. "When all hope is gone," sings Elton John, "sad songs say so much." Many also seek spiritual sustenance—and the two strands combine in the Requiem, or Mass for the Dead, a genre long cultivated by musicians in the Western tradition (see Chapter 35). Although the Catholic Church specifies certain texts and prayers for the Requiem Mass, composers have often taken liberties with them, customizing the tradition for their own spiritual tendencies and expressive goals. Several musicians of the nineteenth century wrote unique *Requiems*; we will consider the one by French composer Gabriel Fauré. Why Fauré decided to write his *Requiem* is a matter of speculation, but having spent his entire life as a church musician, his own explanation makes sense: to show death as "a happy deliverance, a yearning for the happiness of the beyond, rather than a painful experience."

Fauré and Late French Romanticism

Romantic music in France followed several streams. We have examined the grand orchestral music of Berlioz, and the stirring exploits of pianists in salons (Chopin) and concert halls (Liszt, Gottschalk). Also grand were the theatrical productions at the French Opéra—not just the sung dramas, but the choreographed dances as well (see a brief discussion of French ballet in Chapter 46). Art song was very *Mélodie* important in French salons and homes, and composers developed the **mélodie**, a tradition self-consciously separate from the German Lied, to accommodate the unique features of the French language while drawing musical inspiration from

Gabriel Fauré (1845–1924)

Born in southwestern France, Fauré showed musical ability at an early age; he played the harmonium (a type of chamber organ) at his school chapel, and was sent to Paris to attend the École Niedermeyer. There he trained to become a church musician, studying chant and Renaissance polyphony. He took composition lessons from Camille Saint-Saëns, a well-known composer at the Paris Conservatory. After serving in the military during the Franco-Prussian Wars, Fauré was appointed assistant organist at the Church of St. Sulpice in Paris (famous today from *The Da Vinci Code*, a best-selling novel by Dan Brown made into a blockbuster movie in 2006), but he soon landed the position of choirmaster at the Church of La Madeleine, a splendid neo-Classical structure (see illustration below).

Fauré's fame as a composer grew during the 1890s, which led to his appointment as a composition teacher at his alma mater, the École Niedermeyer, and then to a position as director of the prestigious Paris Conservatory. He was highly influential as a critic for *Le Figaro*, a major Paris newspaper, and as president of the Société Musicale Indépendente, which he helped found to further the cause of French music. A growing deafness forced him to resign from the conservatory in 1920, but his influence was far-reaching: he counted both Maurice Ravel and the famous composition teacher Nadia Boulanger (see Chapter 54) among his students, and he was a major proponent of French Impressionism. His restrained musical writing was in direct contrast to German Romanticism, notably that of Wagner; he deliberately wished to distance himself from this style. Fauré is considered a master of French song, but his *Requiem* Mass is his most performed work.

MAJOR WORKS: Dramatic works, including three operas (*Prométhée*) and incidental music to six plays • Sacred vocal music, including *Messe basse*, *Requiem*, and *Cantique de Jean Racine* • Secular choruses • More than 100 songs, six song cyles (including *La bonne chanson*, 1892–94) • Instrumental music, including orchestral suites from stage works • Many chamber works (piano quintets, piano quartets, a piano trio, a string quartet) • Many piano works (nocturnes, preludes, impromptus).

---

the songs of Schubert. Especially in the last quarter of the 1800s, the Symbolist poetry of Charles Baudelaire, Stéphane Mallarmé, and Paul Verlaine gave French song composers golden opportunities to explore subtlety and ambiguity in the relationship between words and music.

Sacred music also continued to play an important role in France, and the early career of Gabriel Fauré (like that of so many other musicians before and since) was grounded in playing and creating music for the Catholic Church. Fauré is remembered for the intimate and personal sentiment his music exudes. He favored writing in small forms—songs, piano miniatures, and chamber music—but his most famous work today remains the *Requiem*.

Fauré's *Requiem*

Fauré wrote his *Requiem* over a span of more than twenty years, and its structure is far from standard. He used Latin liturgical texts (along with texts from the Burial Service and Office of the Dead), but he edited them freely, and left out phrases when it suited him; the word "requiem" (meaning "rest") pervades the entire work. The *Requiem* was premiered in 1888 at the Church of La Madeleine in Paris, for the funeral of a well-known architect. Although it is most often heard today in the full orchestra arrangement, Fauré's original concept was small in scale, comprising a chamber orchestra (minus violins) and organ, with brass added later

The Church of La Madeleine, where Fauré worked, was first conceived as a temple to glorify Napoleon's army.

LISTENING GUIDE 39

 4:30

Fauré: *Libera me*, from *Requiem*, Op. 48

DATE: 1887–89 (revised 1893, 1900)

GENRE: Mass for the Dead

MOVEMENTS:
1. *Introit* and *Kyrie*
2. *Offertoire*
3. *Sanctus*
4. *Pie Jesu*
5. *Agnus Dei* and *Lux aeterna*
6. **Libera me**
7. *In Paradisum*

What to Listen For

Melody	Baritone solo is lyrical, wide-ranging; chorus has melody in unison.
Rhythm/ meter	Pulsating ostinato accompanies opening and closing; shift to 6/4 meter in the middle (*Dies irae*).
Harmony	D minor; some expressive chromaticism.
Texture	Homophonic solo and choral writing.

Form	Three-part, **A-B-A′**.
Expression	Sensitive dynamics; serene mood.
Text	Roman Catholic Mass for the Dead, Office for the Dead, and Burial Service.
Performing forces	Baritone solo, SATB chorus, chamber orchestra (brass, strings, harp, timpani, organ).

	TEXT	TRANSLATION	PERFORMANCE
0:00	Libera me, Domine, de morte aeterna in die illa tremenda: quando coeli movendi sunt et terra dum veneris judicare saeculum per ignem.	Deliver me, O Lord, from eternal death on that fearful day when the heavens and earth shall be moved, when you shall come to judge the world by fire.	Baritone solo.
1:10	Tremens factus sum ego et timeo dum discussio venerit atque ventura ira.	I am made to tremble, and I fear when destruction shall come and also the coming wrath.	SATB choir; homophonic.
1:43	Dies irae, dies illa, calamitatis et miseriae dies magna et amara valde	That day, that day of wrath, calamity, and misery, that terrible and very bitter day.	
2:12	Requiem aeternam dona eis, Domine, et lux perpetua luceat eis.	Grant them eternal rest, O Lord, and let perpetual light shine on them.	
2:55	Libera me Domine . . .	Deliver me, O Lord . . . choir, with soloist.	AB unison. SATB unison

Opening melody (returns at closing), with underlying pulsations (shown in pizzicato cellos):

Do - mi - ne,_____ de mor - te ae - ter - na

to brighten the sound. We will hear this more intimate setting—actually the second version of the work, first performed in early 1893.

This *Requiem* has seven movements, some of which feature less familiar texts. Throughout, there are moments that sound funereal, including hollow chords in the choir that are reminiscent of chant. Fauré uses the organ, brass, and harp colors effectively throughout, and he creates memorable celestial sounds in the solo soprano *Pie Jesu* ("Pious Jesus," originally sung by a boy soprano) and the closing *In Paradisum* ("In Paradise"), during which the casket is "carried" from the church by angels.

The *Libera me* ("Deliver me, O Lord") movement (LG 39) was actually composed some years earlier as a work for baritone and organ. The low strings set up a marchlike pulse to accompany the lyrical baritone solo. Although he sings of "that fearful day" ("die illa tremenda"), his air is altogether reassuring. The homophonic choir's declamation of fear is equally comforting, until we are startled by the forceful French horn's introduction to the terrifying *Dies irae* text, sung *fortissimo* by the choir. But this vision of the Judgment Day is fleeting, as the music softens for the uplifting *Requiem aeternam* ("Grant them eternal rest"). The mood becomes mysteriously chromatic as the choir calls for perpetual light ("lux perpetua") to shine on the deceased, after which we return to the opening *Libera me* march, now sung in unison by the full choir. The movement closes serenely with the soloist and choir reiterating the words "Deliver me, O Lord."

In some ways a modest work, Fauré's *Requiem* speaks volumes to the listener, projecting a mood and sound world that was unique to Requiem Masses. Fauré clearly sought to avoid the bombastic, overtly dramatic style of those by Berlioz and Verdi; his is a personal and compassionate work that offers hope to the dead and the living alike.

Fauré playing the organ at La Madeleine.

CRITICAL THINKING

1. What were some of the main genres and traditions in French Romantic music?
2. How do Fauré's choices of scoring and texture create variety and nuance in his *Requiem*?

In His Own Words

66 Just as Mozart's is the only *Ave verum corpus*, [Fauré's] is the only *Pie Jesu*."

—Camille Saint-Saëns

YOUR TURN TO EXPLORE

Find an example of a musical work designed to reflect on a tragic or sorrowful event and/or offer comfort or hope to those who have witnessed it. If words are incorporated, where are they from, and what kind of imagery do they evoke? How is music used to reinforce particular words or bring out specific meanings? What instrumental (and vocal) forces are used, and why do you think that particular instrumentation was chosen? What musical (as opposed to word-related) elements of the work might be intended to reflect the intensity of sorrow, or foster the lightness of hope?

Chapter 49

Mythical Impressions: Program Music at the End of the Nineteenth Century

"For we desire above all—nuance,
Not color but half-shades!
Ah! nuance alone unites
Dream with dream and flute with horn."

—Paul Verlaine (1844–1896)

KEY POINTS

- **Impressionism** in music is characterized by modal and exotic scales (chromatic, whole tone, and pentatonic), unresolved dissonances, tone combinations such as ninth chords, rich orchestral color, and free rhythm, all generally cast in small-scale programmatic forms.
- The most important French Impressionist composer was Claude Debussy. His orchestral work

Prelude to "The Afternoon of a Faun" was inspired by a Symbolist poem, and later choreographed by the great Russian dancer Vaslav Nijinsky.

- Debussy and his contemporaries were highly influenced by non-Western and traditional music styles heard at the Paris World Exhibition of 1889.

There is something about mythological characters that speaks both to essential human nature and to the mystery of the supernatural. They can serve as a resource for a musician, poet, or painter to pull us out of the ordinary, give us a glimpse into the possible. Mythological themes have been especially prominent in Western multimedia, from the sung plays of ancient Greece to contemporary film and role-playing games. A striking example is provided by one of the most famous works of the later 1800s, Claude Debussy's *Prelude to "The Afternoon of a Faun,"* which we will examine in this chapter. Looking backward to ancient mythology and forward to new sound worlds and expressions, it reflects the subtle perspectives of several creative minds through words, sounds, and movement.

Symbolism and Impressionism in Paris

In the 1860s, breaking with what they considered the static grandiosity of contemporary art, Impressionist painters tried to capture on canvas the freshness of their first impressions and the continuous change in the appearance of their subjects through varied treatment of light and color. A hazy painting by Claude Monet,

Impression: Sun Rising, completed in 1867, was rebuffed by the academic salons of Paris (see illustration below), and **Impressionism** quickly became a term of derision. However, Monet's luminous painting style was eagerly embraced by Parisian artists such as Edgar Degas and Auguste Renoir. We will see how composers like Debussy tried to emulate the use of color and iridescence that characterize this new style.

A parallel development in poetry was similarly influential to French composers: the Symbolist movement sought to evoke poetic images through suggestion rather than description, through symbol rather than statement. This literary revolt against tradition gained prominence in the works of French writers Stéphane Mallarmé and Paul Verlaine, both of whom were strongly influenced by the American poet Edgar Allan Poe. Through their experiments in free verse forms, the Symbolists were able to achieve in language an abstract quality that had once belonged to music alone.

This music scene is typical of the everyday activities captured by Impressionists. *Young Girls at the Piano* (1892), by **Pierre-Auguste Renoir** (1841–1919).

Translating Impressions into Sound

Inspired by the Impressionist and Symbolist movements, a number of French composers of the later 1800s also attempted to break from tradition in order to experiment with greater subtlety and expressive ambiguity. The major-minor system, as we saw, is based on the pull of the active tones to the tonic, or rest tone. Impressionist composers regarded this as a formula that had become too obvious. In their works, we do not hear the triumphal final cadence of the Classical-Romantic period, in which the dominant chord is resolved to the tonic chord with the greatest possible emphasis. Instead, more subtle harmonic relationships come into play. Rather than viewing dissonance as a momentary disturbance, composers began to use dissonance as a goal in itself, freeing it from the need to resolve. They taught their listeners to accept tone combinations that had formerly been regarded as inadmissible, just as the Impressionist painters taught people to see colors in sky, grass, and water they had never seen there before. Composers made use of the entire spectrum of notes in the chromatic scale, and also explored the whole-tone scale and others derived from various non-Western musics.

Freed from a strong tonal center and rigid harmonic guidelines, composers experimented with new tone combinations such as the **ninth chord**, a set of five notes in which the interval between the lowest and highest tones is a ninth. The effect was one of hovering between tonalities, creating elusive effects that evoke the misty outlines of Impressionist painting.

These floating harmonies demanded the most subtle colors, and here composers learned new techniques of blending timbres from their counterparts in art. Painters juxtaposed brush

The Impressionists took painting out of the studio and into the open air; their subject was light. **Claude Monet**, *Impression: Sun Rising*.

Interface

Music, World Colonization, and the Exotic

In 1889, France hosted a fair called the Paris World Exhibition, to mark the centenary of the French Revolution. The fair highlighted technological achievements, including the newly invented Edison phonograph—a huge attraction—and the Eiffel Tower, constructed specially for this event. In addition to displaying triumphs of human ingenuity, the exhibition was highly political, reflecting imperialist and nationalist trends throughout Europe.

France's colonial empire was immense at this time, including territories in northern and western Africa, parts of the Middle East, and Indochina, which today takes in Vietnam and Cambodia. The French sought to affirm their position as a world power by showcasing these far-reaching colonies and their cultures. Accordingly, spectators were treated to displays of antiphonal singing from sub-Saharan Gabon, belly dancers and whirling dervishes from the Middle East, dancers from Cambodia, and Annamite (Vietnamese) theatrical productions—all in an effort to upstage the great British Empire, whose vast imperial holdings had been represented just three years earlier at a London Colonial Exhibition. The Dutch for their part showcased their wealthy East Indian colonies with a gamelan orchestra and dancers from Java, the most populated island of modern-day Indonesia.

With the spread of nationalism across Europe, countries were eager to offer their native repertories of both classical and folk music. The French were introduced to contemporary Russian composers in concerts conducted by composer Nicolai Rimsky-Korsakoff, while Spanish national styles, including flamenco and Gypsy dance music, quickly became favorites. This international soundscape captured the ears of musicians, who responded with their own "exotic" music. It was here that French composers Claude Debussy and Maurice Ravel first heard the unique sound of the Javanese gamelan (an ensemble made up of gongs, chimes, and drums; see p. 374). Debussy later raved to a friend about "the Javanese music able to express every nuance of meaning, even unmentionable shades, and which makes our tonic and dominant seem like empty phantoms for the use of unwise infants." He attempted to capture something of this sound world—its pentatonic scale, unusual timbre, and texture—in compositions like the famous symphonic poem *La mer* (*The Sea*, 1905), the piano work *Pagodas* (from *Estampes*, 1903), and several piano preludes. We will see that twentieth-century composers, including the bold American innovator John Cage (Chapter 62), continued to explore the unique timbre of the gamelan.

This watercolor of a *Cambodian Dancer* (1906), by the French artist **Auguste Rodin** (1840–1917), reflects the artistic interest in exotic subjects.

Composers were also charmed by the folk and popular musics they heard at the fair. Debussy sought to recreate the rhythms of Spanish Gypsy and flamenco dancers in his piano music (*The Interrupted Serenade* and *Evening in Granada*). Ravel's roots in the Basque region of France (where the Pyrénées separate France and Spain) brought him even closer to Spanish folk traditions, which he emulated in his hypnotic *Boléro*, the *Spanish Rhapsody*, and the violin work *Tzigane* (*Gypsy*, 1924). But Ravel too looked to faraway cultures he first experienced at the fair, evoking Middle Eastern folk tales (from *Arabian Nights*) and Persian music in his orchestral song cycle *Sheherazade* (1903). What began as an exhibition of world power and national pride among industrialized nations thus had far-reaching effects; music, appropriated to deliver a political message, was also opening eyes and ears to the wonder of the exotic.

The central hall of the Paris World Exhibition, designed by **Jean Béraud** (1849–1935).

strokes of pure color on the canvas, leaving it to the eye of the viewer to do the mixing. Debussy similarly replaced the lush, full sonority of the Romantic orchestra with veiled sounds: flutes and clarinets in their dark, velvety registers, violins in their lustrous upper range, trumpets and horns discreetly muted; and over the whole, a shimmering gossamer of harp, celesta, triangle, glockenspiel, muffled drum, and brushed cymbal. One instrumental color flows into another close by, as from oboe to clarinet to flute, in the same way that Impressionist painting moves from one color to another in the spectrum, from yellow to green to blue.

Debussy's *Prelude to "The Afternoon of a Faun"*

Claude Debussy's best-known orchestral work was inspired by a pastoral poem by Symbolist writer Stéphane Mallarmé describing the faun, a mythological forest creature that is half man, half goat, and symbolizes raw sensuality. Debussy intended his music to be a series of "backdrops" that would illustrate the faun and his actions. We can thus consider this work a coming together of visual Impressionism and textual Symbolism through sound (LG 40).

The work follows the familiar pattern of statement-departure-return (**A-B-A′**), yet the progression is fluid and rhapsodic, with a relaxed rhythm. We first hear a flute solo in the lower register. The melody glides along the chromatic scale, narrow in range and languorous. Glissandos on the harp usher in a brief dialogue in the horns, a mixture of colors never heard before.

Next, a more decisive motive emerges, marked *en animant* (growing lively). This is followed by a third theme, an impassioned melody that carries the piece to

Claude Debussy (1862–1918)

The most important French composer of the late nineteenth–early twentieth century, Debussy was born near Paris and entered the Paris Conservatory when he was eleven. Within a few years, he was shocking his professors with bizarre harmonies that defied the rules. He was only twenty-two when his cantata *The Prodigal Son* won the coveted Prix de Rome. By this time, he had already realized his future style.

The 1890s, the most productive decade of Debussy's career, culminated in the opera *Pelléas and Mélisande*, based on the Symbolist drama by the Belgian poet Maurice Maeterlinck. At first, *Pelléas* was attacked as being decadent and lacking in melody and form, but this opera made Debussy famous. His energies sapped by the ravages of cancer, Debussy died in March 1918, during the bombardment of Paris.

Like artist Claude Monet and writer Paul Verlaine, Debussy considered art to be a sensuous experience. "French music," he declared, "is clearness, elegance, simple and natural declamation . . . aiming first of all to give pleasure." His fame rests on a comparatively small output;

Pelléas and Mélisande is viewed by many as his greatest achievement. Among his orchestral compositions, the *Prelude to "The Afternoon of a Faun"* became a favorite with the public early on, as did *The Sea (La mer)*.

Many of his piano pieces demonstrate an interest in non-Western scales and instruments (he regarded sonata-allegro form as an outmoded formula), which he first heard at the Paris Exhibition in 1889 (see Interface). Debussy also helped establish the French song (*mélodie*) as a national art form. His settings of the French Symbolist poets Verlaine and Mallarmé are exquisite and refined.

MAJOR WORKS: Orchestral music, including *Prélude à "L'après midi d'un faune"* (*Prelude to "The Afternoon of a Faun,"* 1894), *Nocturnes* (1899), *La mer* (*The Sea*, 1905) • Dramatic works, including the opera *Pelléas et Mélisande* (1902) and a ballet • Chamber music, including a string quartet and various sonatas • Piano music, including two books of preludes (1909–10, 1912–13) • Songs, choral music, and cantatas.

 Jeux de vagues, from *La mer*

LISTENING GUIDE 40

 9:45

Debussy: *Prelude to "The Afternoon of a Faun"* (*Prélude à "L'après-midi d'un faune"*)

DATE: 1894

GENRE: Symphonic poem

What to Listen For

Melody	Lyrical, sinuous melody; chromatic at opening and closing.	**Texture**	Homophonic; light and airy.
Rhythm/ meter	Free-flowing rhythms; sense of floating; lacks pulse; middle section is more animated.	**Form**	Loose **A-B-A′** structure.
		Expression	Evocative mood; sensual.
		Timbre	Rich colors, especially in the woodwinds.
Harmony	Use of "blue" chords, with lowered thirds.	**Performing forces**	Strings (with two harps), woodwinds, French horns, and antique cymbals.

Opening of poem:

Ces nymphes, je les veux perpétuer.
     Si clair
Leur incarnat léger, qu'il voltige dans l'air
Assoupi de sommeils touffus.
     Amais-je un rêve?

These nymphs I would perpetuate.
     So light
their gossamer embodiment, floating on the air
inert with heavy slumber.
     Was it a dream I loved?

A section

0:00   Opening chromatic melody in flute; passes from one instrument to another, accompanied by muted strings and a vague sense of pulse:

B section

2:48   Clarinet introduces a more animated idea, answered by a rhythmic figure in cellos.

3:16   New theme with livelier rhythm in solo oboe, builds in a *crescendo*:

4:34   Contrasting theme in woodwinds, then strings, with syncopated rhythms, builds to a climax:

A′ section

6:22   Abridged return, in a varied setting.

an emotional climax. The first theme then returns in an altered guise. At the close, antique cymbals (small disks of brass whose rims are struck together gently and allowed to vibrate) play pianissimo. "Blue" chords (with lowered thirds and sevenths) are heard on the muted horns and violins, sounding infinitely remote. The work dissolves into silence, leaving us, and the faun, in a dream-like state.

Debussy's symphonic poem was widely performed (as far away as Boston in 1902), but it gained even more prominence when it was choreographed by the great Russian dancer Vaslav Nijinsky (about whom we will learn more in Chapter 53). Nijinsky himself danced the role of the faun (see illustration at right), and his sensuous cavorting among the nymphs caused a scandal in Paris: this choreography is often viewed as a turning point in modern ballet. Nijinsky's choreography helped make Debussy's work all the more successful, but it also introduced a problem: to what extent does the meaning added by a dancer/choreographer "shape" the interpretation of a musical work? Does a storytelling choreography go against the subtlety and vagueness of Debussy's Symbolist/Impressionist approach?

The great Russian dancer Vaslav Nijinsky as the faun in the 1912 ballet version of *Prelude to "The Afternoon of a Faun."* Design by **Léon Bakst** (1866–1924).

CRITICAL THINKING

1. How did composers translate the literary devices of Symbolism and/or the innovative use of color in Impressionist painting into sound?
2. How did non-Western musical ideas affect Debussy and his contemporaries?

YOUR TURN TO EXPLORE

Pick a movie, TV show, or video game that includes music and draws on mythology. How are specific elements like timbre, melody, and harmony used to reinforce certain characters or dramatic moments? How do you think those musical choices contribute to the simultaneously real/unreal quality of mythology?

Music at the 1889 World's Fair

Chapter 50

Jubilees and Jubilation: The African American Spiritual Tradition

"In the Negro melodies of America I discover all that is needed for a great and noble school of music."

—Antonín Dvořák

KEY POINTS

- In the early 1800s, Americans of all backgrounds came together in **camp meetings** to sing songs of worship.

- In their own meetings, black slaves and freedmen developed a semi-improvised tradition of sacred songs known as **spirituals**.

- Spirituals such as *Swing Low, Sweet Chariot* were popularized by choral groups from African American colleges in the late 1800s and were arranged as art songs in the early 1900s. They have served as the basis for other elaborations ever since.

F rom the United States' earliest decades, immigrants from all lands (including the involuntary immigrants brought to North America through slavery) have intersected here, sharing their cultures and musical practices. While in some cases racial and ethnic segregation were obstacles to musicians' performing together, in others they were a starting point for musical exchange. The mixtures of traditions that characterize the American musical landscape today have direct parallels in past centuries, especially in the rise of sacred songs known as spirituals.

Spirituals and the Jubilee Tradition

Camp meeting

Ring shout

At the turn of the 1800s, a Christian movement known as the Second Great Awakening was sweeping the young United States. In **camp meetings**, lasting days or even weeks, African Americans (freedmen and slaves) and European Americans alike gathered to sing hymns of praise, to popular or folk tunes of the time. Blacks also brought the tradition of the **ring shout**, developed by the slaves from African traditions into an extended call and response that built to a religious fervor. White church leaders noted that some in their community were modifying their own worship after witnessing these inspirational practices.

In separate camp meetings organized by slaves, the tradition of the **spiritual** crystallized as both a way of worship and a subversive political endeavor, with coded messages about earthly escape concealed in texts that promised heavenly

A nineteenth-century depiction of a camp meeting during the Second Great Awakening (c. 1830).

deliverance. Spirituals offered slaves community and solidarity through the monophonic singing (plus some heterophonic elaboration) of their shared musical ideas. White Northerners who first documented this oral tradition around the time of the Civil War were struck by the "foreignness" of the spirituals, which tended to be full of rhythmic and melodic traits that did not fit European norms.

Spirituals gained a broader cultural presence immediately after the Civil War, when a group of students at Fisk University (a newly established college for freed slaves in Nashville, Tennessee) formed the Fisk Jubilee Singers, to raise funds for the institution. And this they did: the singers toured with great success throughout the northern United States and even Europe in the 1870s, eventually raising the amazing-for-the-time sum of $150,000, enough to construct a major building and endow the college's future. The choir built a repertory of sacred European choral masterworks, but it was the arrangements of spirituals from the singers' own tradition that most astounded audiences. When the original cohort disbanded after a few years, the university reconstituted the Fisk Jubilee Singers as a smaller ensemble, and they continued performing even as the popularity of the choral spiritual faded at the end of the 1800s. The group continues as a jewel of Fisk University to this day.

Spirituals and the Art-Song Tradition

In 1893, on the coattails of the European craze for "jubilee" spirituals, Czech composer Antonín Dvořák (1841–1904) made the claim that opens this chapter. Not many white American composers agreed, since black traditions were still widely considered inferior. But some African Americans took up Dvořák's challenge and began to create arrangements of spirituals for solo voice and piano. Perhaps the most influential was Harry T. Burleigh, who not only sang for and worked with Dvořák during the years the Czech composer

A nineteenth-century poster advertising a tour by the Fisk Jubilee Singers.

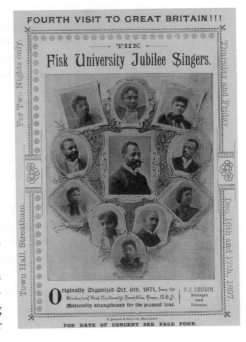

One of the earliest recording technologies was the wax cylinder, pioneered by Thomas Edison in the 1870s. This is the cylinder on which our recording by the Fisk Jubilee Quartet is stored.

taught in the United States, but also became editor for an important music publisher. Burleigh's many voice-and-piano settings of spirituals, first published in the 1910s, were quickly adopted as concert staples by black and white singers alike.

The trend toward "art-song" arrangements of spirituals overlapped with one of the most important cultural movements of the early twentieth century: the **Harlem Renaissance**, an attempt by African American artists and philosophers to claim a "high culture" space for their people, in order to counteract the systematic racism and marginalization they suffered in America. (See Chapter 57 for more on the Harlem Renaissance.) Presenting spirituals as art songs positioned the black tradition alongside the European American as a valid aspect of American art.

Swing Low, Sweet Chariot

One of the most famous of spirituals reflects the intersection between Native American, African American, and European American peoples in the American West. *Swing Low, Sweet Chariot* may or may not have been created by Wallace Willis, a slave who worked at a Choctaw boarding school in what is now southeastern Oklahoma; but it was from Willis and his wife Minerva that the school's director, Reverend Alexander Reid, heard the spiritual in the 1840s. Decades later, Reid attended a performance of the Fisk Jubilee Singers and suggested that they add *Swing Low* and other spirituals he and his wife had heard from Willis to their repertory. So, ironically, this iconic song was introduced to the African American ensemble that made it most famous by a white man who had first heard it at a Native American school.

Swing Low became one of the favorites of the Fisk Singers, who recorded it several times in the first decade of the 1900s (we will hear a recording the Fisk Jubilee Quartet made in 1910; LG 41). The spiritual was also arranged as an art song by several African American composers, including Burleigh in 1917 (we will also hear his version). In many arrangements and reworkings, it has since become a staple of American musical culture.

The text of the spiritual is loosely based on a passage from the biblical Second Book of Kings, in which the prophet Elijah is taken up to Heaven in a whirlwind and a chariot of fire. The melody uses a five-note (**pentatonic**) scale, and features several repetitions of both music and text. The Fisk recording provides harmonies that are in keeping with the Euro-American sacred choral tradition and sustain the melody as unobtrusive accompaniment. The piano part in Burleigh's arrangement establishes a more complex and blues-related harmony, and a more polyphonically independent interaction between voice and instrument. Burleigh also chooses to modify one of the notes of the melody the second time the text is sung, perhaps imitating the blue-note bending of pitch characteristic of the African American singing tradition.

From its origins in the Indian country of the West through its transmission by white Americans to the most celebrated African American vocal ensemble of the day, to its reconfiguration by black composers and singers into art song and then its spread throughout the American musical landscape, *Swing Low, Sweet Chariot* is a striking example of the cultural mixture and renewal that characterize the vernacular music of the United States. Many of our most loved "traditional" American songs have histories that are as complex as the country and the peoples that have created them, and some have also moved into the concert repertory, as examples of Amerian art song.

LISTENING GUIDE 41

Swing Low, Sweet Chariot

DATE: Composed in the 1840s, arrangements from 1911 (Fisk) and 1917 (Burleigh)

GENRE: Spiritual

What to Listen For

Melody	"Gapped" pentatonic, limited range, paired open and closed phrases.
Rhythm/meter	Duple meter, with some triplets; flowing, with flexible syncopations.
Harmony	Fisk: simple and mostly diatonic. Burleigh: harmonic ambiguity connected to blues and jazz traditions.
Texture	Fisk: homophonic, with clear lead singer. Burleigh: piano interacts polyphonically with voice.

Form	Fisk: strophic, with first stanza serving as a refrain. Burleigh: four-part, **A-B-C-A′**.
Expression	Fisk: straightforward delivery of lyrics and repetitive harmonization. Burleigh: several contrasting moods.
Text	Elaboration of II Kings 2, 11; multiple stanzas in Fisk, shorter version in Burleigh.
Performing forces	TTBB male quartet (Fisk); soprano and piano (Burleigh).

Fisk arrangement

4:25

0:00	*Swing low, sweet chariot,*	Tenor 1 alone.
	Coming for to carry me home,	TTBB.
	Swing low, sweet chariot,	Tenor 1 with words, others humming.
	Coming for to carry me home.	TTBB.
0:23	I'm sometimes up, and I'm sometimes down	
	(Coming for to carry me home),	
	But still my soul feels heavenly bound	
	(Coming for to carry me home).	Alternation of soloist/humming and TTBB response.
	Chorus	
0:46	If you get there before I do	
	(Coming for to carry me home),	
	Tell all my friends I'm coming too	
	(Coming for to carry me home).	
	Chorus	
1:35	I never shall forget that day	
	(Coming for to carry me home),	
	When Jesus washed my sins away	
	(Coming for to carry me home).	
	Chorus	
2:26	I looked over Jordan, and what did I see?	
	(Coming for to carry me home),	
	A band of angels coming after me,	
	(Coming for to carry me home).	
3:18	*Chorus sung twice more.*	

Continued on next page

Beginning of chorus:

Swing low,   sweet   char - i - ot,   Com-ing for to car - ry me   home,

Burleigh arrangement   2:43

0:00		Piano introduction sets up a "swinging/rocking" motion, subtly syncopated rhythms, and modified diatonic harmony ("added sixth" chords).
0:08	*Swing low, sweet chariot,* *Coming for to carry me home,* *Swing low, sweet chariot,* *Coming for to carry me home.*	Voice presents straightforward melody, piano continues rocking motion and added-sixth diatonic harmonies.
0:40		Melody is varied in piano, harmony more chromatic.
0:48	Swing low, sweet chariot, Coming for to carry me home,	First note of vocal melody is changed slightly (blue note); piano harmony more chromatic and rhythmically active/irregular.
1:04	Coming for to carry me home.	Eventually returns to diatonic opening harmony.
1:18	I looked over Jordan, what did I see? Coming for to carry me home, A band of angels coming after me, Coming for to carry me home.	Melody is repeated and a little more rhythmical, piano part more active and chromatic. Rising pentatonic scale in piano at end of stanza.
1:50	*Swing low, sweet chariot,* *Coming for to carry me home,* *Swing low, sweet chariot,* *Coming for to carry me home.*	Melody in voice, same as opening. Piano back to rocking diatonic accompaniment, eventually building chromaticism that intensifies under singer's last note; resolves with a pentatonic scale that spans the full sonic space of the piano.

CRITICAL THINKING

1. What was the significance of the Fisk Jubilee Singers to the spread of the spiritual?

2. What are some differences between the Fisk and Burleigh arrangements of *Swing Low, Sweet Chariot*?

YOUR TURN TO EXPLORE

Find two or three separate arrangements of a song from a folk tradition—like *Amazing Grace, Greensleeves,* or *Yankee Doodle*. How does each arrangement create a balance between the simple folk melody and the additional musical resources—is the arrangement homophonic or polyphonic? Is the original melody modified in any way, and if so, how? In what way do you think each arrangement is faithful to the traditional melody, or to the cultural tradition from which it is derived? Which one do you think is most musically expressive, and why?

Chapter 51

A Good Beat:
American Vernacular Music
at the Close of an Era

"Ragtime is the American Creation and the
Marvel of Musicians in all Civilized Countries."

—*John Stark (Scott Joplin's publisher)*

KEY POINTS

- The great bandmaster and composer John Philip Sousa fostered the American wind band tradition, an outgrowth of the British military band.

- **Ragtime** was an African American piano style characterized by syncopated rhythms and sectional forms, made famous by Scott Joplin, the "King of Ragtime."

- Joplin's *Maple Leaf Rag* is made up of four repeated **strains** in a form that resembles the marches of Sousa, whose band often played arrangements of Joplin's rags.

- The **piano roll** was an early form of musical playback technology.

We often show appreciation for music by saying it has "a good beat"—we like it because it makes us want to move to it. Musicians have been putting bodies into joyful motion from before recorded history, and our music-inspired movements help us come together on a wide variety of social occasions—such as marching and dancing. Although these may seem like separate endeavors, they both rely on music to structure their regular patterns of moving, and in late nineteenth-century America those patterns overlapped and reinforced each other in two very popular traditions: the ragtime piano dance and the wind-and-brass-band march. These two traditions were supported by the development of new technologies in both instrument-making and recording.

The U.S. Marine Band, with its director, John Philip Sousa, playing cornet (in right front) in the inaugural parade for President Grover Cleveland (1885).

John Philip Sousa and the Band Tradition

In addition to parlor ballads (like those of Stephen Foster) and piano music (including pieces by Louis Moreau Gottschalk), nineteenth-century America's vernacular traditions also encompassed music for brass bands. An outgrowth of the British military band, wind groups thrived throughout the United States, beginning with the regimental bands that played during the Revolutionary War (1775–83). The most famous eighteenth-century band was the U.S. Marine Band, originally just a small group of woodwinds, French horns, and percussion. By the Civil War era (1861–65), both Northern and Southern regiments marched to the sound of bands that included brass instruments as well as woodwinds, thanks to the pioneering efforts of such designers as the Belgian Adolphe Sax (inventor of the saxophone and several brass instruments; see p. 232). After the war, many bands reorganized as concert and dance ensembles. Such was the case with the Union Army group under the direction of virtuoso cornet player and bandmaster Patrick S. Gilmore, who wrote the lyrics for the rousing *When Johnny Comes Marching Home* to welcome back soldiers from North and South alike.

Patrick S. Gilmore

America's most famous bandmaster was John Philip Sousa (1854–1932), who conducted the U.S. Marine Band from 1880 to 1892, after which he formed his own group. Known as the "March King," Sousa wrote over 130 marches for band, along with dance music and operettas. He toured North America and Europe extensively with his group, delighting audiences with his *Semper Fidelis* (1888), *Washington Post* (1889), and the ever-popular *Stars and Stripes Forever* (1897), as well as arrangements of ragtime, the newest rage in dance music. Sousa's fame spread further through hundreds of thousands of sheet music copies of his marches and, early in the new century, through the new mass-marketing of recordings: he created, nearly single-handedly, a national music for America that continues to resonate in its concert halls, on its streets, in its sports stadiums, and in the hearts of its people.

Washington Post

Scott Joplin and Ragtime

While bands were sought after to accompany social dancing, often it was more practical to just hire a piano player (since you could count on a piano being present in every social hall and almost every living room, as sound systems are today). In the last decades of the 1800s, a style developed primarily among African American performers that took Euro-American traditions and modified them through rhythmic and melodic variation. It was called **ragtime**, and it became a vital precursor of jazz. Scott Joplin, known as the "King of Ragtime," was one of the first black Americans to gain widespread visibility as a composer.

Joplin is best remembered today for his piano "rags," which reflect his preoccupation with classical forms. They combine balanced phrasing and key structures with highly syncopated melodies. And like earlier dance forms, they are built in clear-cut sections, their patterns of repetition reminiscent of those heard in Sousa marches.

The popular Turkey Trot was danced to ragtime; the woman wears a feathered headdress typical of the early 1900s.

The *Maple Leaf Rag*, probably the best-known rag ever composed, is typical in its regular, sectional form (LG 42). Quite simply, the dance presents four sixteen-measure sections, called **strains**, in a moderate duple meter; each strain is repeated before the next one begins. As in most rags, the listener's interest is focused throughout on the syncopated rhythms of the melodies, played by the right hand, which are supported by a steady, duple-rhythm accompaniment in the left hand. Joplin's sophisticated piano rags brought him worldwide recognition.

This performance of the *Maple Leaf Rag* is also noteworthy because it is the first example we have encountered so far of music played by its own composer, rather than by more modern performers. This is achieved not through a sound recording but rather by a **piano roll**, a long strip of paper with holes punched in it, designed to be recorded and played back in a mechanically enhanced **player piano**. As Joplin played the rag, the player piano punched holes in the roll that corresponded to the notes he played as well as to their length and dynamics. You could then purchase a copy of the roll to recreate Joplin's performance on a similar machine. Only because some player pianos and piano rolls have survived the

Scott Joplin (1868–1917)

Joplin was born in Texarkana, Texas, to a musical family. His father, a former slave, played violin, and his mother sang and played banjo. He began musical instruction on the guitar and bugle and quickly showed such a gift that he was given free piano lessons. He left home when he was only fourteen and traveled throughout the Mississippi Valley, playing in honky-tonks and piano bars and arrivng in 1885 in St. Louis, the center of a growing ragtime movement.

Joplin helped ragtime gain public notice when he and a small orchestra he had formed performed at the 1893 World Exposition in Chicago. Around this time, he also sought more formal musical training at the George R. Smith College in Sedalia, Missouri. It was at a club in Sedalia that Joplin, surrounded by a circle of black entertainers, introduced his *Maple Leaf Rag*. Fame came to the composer in 1899 when the sheet music of the piece sold a million copies. Financial security came as well: he insisted on receiving royalties rather than a flat payment for this and other ragtime pieces. He eventually moved to New York, where he was active as a teacher, composer, and performer.

Joplin strove to elevate ragtime from a purely improvised style to a more serious art form that could stand on a level with European art music. Realizing that he must lead the way in this merger of styles, he began work on his opera *Treemonisha*, which he finished in 1911. But the opera was not well received, and Joplin fell into a severe depression from which he never fully recovered; he died in New York City on April 1, 1917. *Treemonisha* remained unknown until its successful revival in 1972 by the Houston Grand Opera. In 1976, nearly sixty years after his death, Joplin was awarded a Pulitzer Prize for his masterpiece.

MAJOR WORKS: Stage works, including two operas (*Treemonisha,* 1911) • Piano rags, including *Maple Leaf Rag* (1899) and *Pine Apple Rag* (1908) • Piano music • Songs.

 Pine Apple Rag

---

ever-changing process that makes technologies obsolete, we can hear Joplin's own rendition of his signature rag.

Some in Joplin's day were not enthusiastic about the emerging recording technologies. Sousa himself, though he benefited economically from the sales of recordings of his band, warned that reliance on recordings would not only take their livelihood away from musicians by reducing demand for live performances, but also create a population of Americans who could not play music for themselves. Every time we download an MP3 file because it has a good beat that we can dance to—especially if we obtain it for free—we help to confirm Sousa's worst fears.

CRITICAL THINKING

1. Why were bands and Sousa in particular so important to the musical culture of the United States?
2. How is piano roll technology similar to and different from modern MP3 recordings?

Title page of *Maple Leaf Rag* (1899).

Comparing styles 5: Romantic to twentieth century

YOUR TURN TO EXPLORE

Seek out examples of phonograph recordings online. Try to find a couple different examples—78-RPM discs, 45-RPM, 33 1/3-RPM (or even older cylinder technologies!). How are these playback technologies similar and different? What do you think of the sound quality—is the noise level distracting, can you ignore it to focus on the music? Why do you think each of these formats was considered groundbreaking in its day? Now compare a CD and an MP3 (or other digital format) recording of a favorite musical work. Again, how are the technologies similar and different, from each other and from phonograph recording? What advantages and disadvantages does each format provide?

LISTENING GUIDE 42

 3:21

Joplin: *Maple Leaf Rag*

DATE: Published 1899

GENRE: Piano rag

What to Listen For

Melody	Catchy, syncopated, disjunct melodies.
Rhythm/ meter	Marchlike duple meter; syncopated in right hand, steady beat in bass.
Harmony	Major key; shifts to a new key in **C** section (the trio); decorative rolled chords.
Texture	Homophonic; chordal accompaniment to the melody.

Form	Dance made up of four sections (strains), each 16 measures and repeated: **A-A-B-B-A-C-C-D-D**.
Performing forces	Joplin plays on a 1910 Steinway piano roll.

0:00 **A**, strain 1—syncopated, middle-range ascending melody, in A-flat major; accompanied by a steady bass; begins with an upbeat in bass; Joplin adds ornamental flourishes in left hand:

0:22 **A**—strain 1 repeated.

0:44 **B**, strain 2—similar syncopated pattern in melody; begins in a higher range and descends; steady bass accompaniment; in A-flat major:

1:06 **B**—strain 2 repeated.

1:28 **A**—return to strain 1.

1:50 **C**, strain 3, also called the trio—in D-flat major; more static melody; new rhythmic pattern with right hand playing on downbeats; bass accompaniment is more disjunct:

2:12 **C**—strain 3 repeated.

2:34 **D**, strain 4—returns to A-flat major, with a contrasting theme; its syncopated pattern is related to strain 1:

D—strain 4 repeated.

A Comparison of
Romantic, Impressionist, and Early Twentieth-Century Styles

	Romantic (c. 1820–1900)	Impressionist (c. 1890–1915)	Early twentieth century (c. 1900–40)
Representative composers	Schubert, Berlioz, Hensel, Chopin, Schumann, Verdi, Wagner, Foster, Gottschalk, Brahms, Tchaikovsky, Grieg, Fauré, Puccini, Debussy, Joplin.	Debussy, Ravel.	Stravinsky, Schoenberg, Copland, Still, Revueltas.
Melody	Expansive, singing melodies; wide-ranging; many chromatic inflections and dramatic leaps.	Built on chromatic, whole-tone, and non-Western scales.	Instrumental conception; disjunct, wide-ranging; interest in folk tunes.
Harmony	Increasing chromaticism, expanded concepts of tonality.	Weak tonal center; free treatment of dissonance.	Atonality; polychords and polyharmony; tone rows; extremes in dissonance.
Rhythm	Rhythmic diversity, tempo rubato.	Floating rhythm; obscured pulse; no sense of meter.	Changing meter, polyrhythm, syncopation.
Texture	Homophonic (early); increasingly polyphonic in later years.	Homophonic; chords moving in parallel motion.	Contrapuntal, linear movement.
Instrumental genres	Symphonic poem, program symphony, symphony, concerto, ballet, dances, incidental music, miniatures.	Programmatic genres, symphonic poem, preludes.	Neo-Classical genres (symphony, concerto), ballet suites.
Vocal genres	Lied (solo), part song, Mass, Requiem Mass, opera, spiritual.	Solo song with orchestra, opera.	Solo song with chamber ensemble, opera.
Form	Expansion of forms; interest in continuous as well as miniature programmatic forms.	Short, lyric forms.	Succinct, tight forms; revived older forms.
Audience	Secular music predominant; middle class and aristocratic salons.	Public theaters.	Public concerts, radio broadcasts.
Dynamics	Continuously changing dynamics through *crescendo* and *decrescendo*.		Widely ranging dynamics for expressive purposes.
Timbre	Continual change, blend of true colors; experiments with new instruments.	Veiled blending of timbres, muted instruments, shimmering colors.	Bright, lean sound; piano is part of orchestra; winds and percussion favored.
Performing forces	New instruments, including English horn, tuba, valved brass, harp, piccolo; larger orchestra; piano is predominant solo instrument.	Harps added; bell-like percussion.	Diverse percussion, non-Western instruments; unusual combinations and ranges of instruments.

THE MODERN ERA

Events		Composers and Works

Composers and Works

1880

1874–1951 Arnold Schoenberg (*Pierrot lunaire*)

1874–1954 Charles Ives (*Country Band March*)

1881–1945 Béla Bartók (*Concerto for Orchestra*)

1882–1971 Igor Stravinsky (*The Rite of Spring*)

1885–1935 Alban Berg (*Wozzeck*)

$E = m. C^2$

1890

1893–1918 Lili Boulanger (*Psalm 24*)

1895–1978 William Grant Still (*Suite for Violin and Piano*)

1898–1937 George Gershwin (*Porgy and Bess*)

1899–1940 Silvestre Revueltas (*Homage to Federico García Lo*

1899–1974 Edward Kennedy ("Duke") Ellington (*Take the A Tra*

Alfred Einstein presents his theory of relativity. **1905**

First World War begins. **1914**

U.S. enters war. **1917**

18th Amendment (Prohibition) passes. **1919**

19th Amendment (women's suffrage) passes. **1920**

1900

1900–1990 Aaron Copland (*Appalachian Spring*)

1915–1959 Billie Holiday (*Billie's Blues*)

1915–1967 Billy Strayhorn (*Take the A Train*)

Great Depression begins. **1929**

Spanish Civil War begins. **1936**

Second World War begins. **1939**

U.S. enters war. **1941**

1925

1950

Part 6

Twentieth-Century Modernism

Making Music Modern

*"The entire history of modern music may be said to be
a history of the gradual pull-away from the German
musical tradition of the past century."*

—Aaron Copland

Modernisms

Much of the twentieth century was characterized by artists' self-conscious attempts
to make their art "modern," not only expressing their own creative visions but
suggesting progressive directions for others to follow. This led to purposeful
departures from tradition, which have been labeled with a variety of "isms"—
Expressionism, futurism, Fauvism, serialism, neo-Classicism, and so on. What
these "isms" all have in common is a concern with "making art new." However,
the particular strategies through which individuals tried to make music modern
were often quite different from one another. This is why it can be useful to think of
multiple musical modernisms, each serving a different creative purpose. We will
examine several of them in the chapters to come.

Most modernists did share a wish to reject nineteenth-century models and
a suspicion of popular or mass culture. The twentieth century, however, was
also a time when sound recording made vernacular traditions ever more prominent, and modernist musicians often grappled with this powerful cultural
phenomenon—sometimes rejecting it, other times integrating some aspects of
popular music and culture into their search for the new.

LEFT: The powerful abstraction
of African sculpture strongly
influenced European art.

RIGHT: **Henri Rousseau** (1844–
1910) found his subject matter in
distant places. *The Sleeping Gypsy*
(1897).

LEFT: In *Girl Running on a Balcony* (1912), futurist painter **Giacomo Balla** (1871–1958) experiments with how art can portray movement.

RIGHT: **Pablo Picasso's** (1881–1973) use of vibrant colors and bold overlapping shapes in *Mandolin and Guitar* (1924) looks beyond Cubism toward the surrealist school.

Early Modernist Art

Just as European and American societies saw great changes in the era from 1890 to 1940, so did the arts witness a profound upheaval. A first wave of modernist attitudes took hold just before the First World War (1914–18), when European arts tried to break away from overrefinement and capture the spontaneity and freedom from inhibition that was associated with primitive life (though artists often had an idealized notion of "exotic" cultures outside Europe; see Rousseau illustration opposite). Likewise, some composers turned to what they perceived as the revitalizing energy of non-Western rhythm, seeking fresh concepts in the musics of Africa, Asia, and eastern Europe.

In the years surrounding the war, two influential arts movements arose: **futurism,** whose manifesto of 1909 declared an alienation from established institutions and a focus on the dynamism of twentieth-century life; and **Dadaism,** founded in Switzerland in 1916. The Dadaists, mainly writers and artists who reacted to the horrors of the war's bloodbath, rejected the concept of art as something to be reverently admired. To make their point, they produced works of absolute absurdity. They also reacted against the excessive complexity of Western art by trying to recapture the simplicity of a child's worldview. Following their example, the French composer Erik Satie (1866–1925) wrote music in a simple, "everyday" style.

The Dada group, with artists like Marcel Duchamp, merged into the school of **surrealism,** which included Salvador Dali and Joan Miró (see p. 296), both of whom explored the world of dreams. Other styles of modern art included **Cubism,** the Paris-based style of painting in geometric patterns embodied in the works of Pablo Picasso, Georges Braque, and Juan Gris; and **Expressionism,** which made a significant impact on music of the early twentieth century (as we will see in Chapter 52). The new styles in both art and music that flourished after the war are often referred to as **avant-garde,** a French term originally used to describe the part of an army that charged first into battle. Artists who identify as avant-garde distinguish themselves from traditional high culture and from mass-market taste, seeking to explore true creativity by breaking from social and artistic conventions, sometimes radically.

Futurism, Dadaism

Surrealism, Cubism, Expressionism

Avant-garde

Spanish artist **Joan Miró** (1893–1983) explores the surrealist world of dreams through the distortion of shapes. *Dutch Interior I.*

James Reese Europe

Musical Markets in the United States

We have seen how musicians in the young United States often blended high-art music with more vernacular styles in search of commercial success. This emphasis on the marketplace helped to create a set of distinctly American musical traditions and contributed to the international spread of those traditions in the twentieth century.

Throughout the United States, minstrel shows (see Chapter 37) expanded into the tradition of **vaudeville,** which combined all kinds of comedic theatrical and musical acts, many written by immigrant composers and often satirizing new immigrants in ways similar to the portrayal of African Americans in minstrelsy. New York City (especially the thoroughfare called Broadway) became the most vibrant center for vaudeville, and by the turn of the twentieth century it was the most prolific center of music publishing as well. The popular music written in the following decades, along with its writers and publishers, is known as **Tin Pan Alley** for the street in Manhattan where publishers had their business. Perhaps the most successful Tin Pan Alley composer was Irving Berlin, whose first hit song, *Alexander's Ragtime Band,* helped catapult the ragtime craze worldwide; he followed this with such timeless songs as *White Christmas* and *Easter Parade,* among many others.

In 1917, the United States officially entered the First World War, an act that spurred the composition of patriotic songs, marches, and love ballads. Songwriter George M. Cohan's inspirational *Over There* (see below), announcing that "the Yanks are coming," resounded across oceans and eventually won him the Congressional Gold Medal of Honor. The war facilitated the dissemination of American music abroad, in part through the efforts of James Reese Europe, an African

LEFT: The cover to the sheet music of George M. Cohan's famous First World War song *Over There* (1917).

RIGHT: A vaudeville show from 1917. Watercolor by **Charles Demuth** (1883–1935).

American musician and army bandleader who introduced ragtime and early jazz styles to France. Upon his return home in 1919, he declared that he was "more firmly convinced than ever that Negros should write Negro music. We have our own racial feeling and if we try to copy whites, we will make bad copies."

Between Two Wars: Music in the Great Depression

America came out of the "Great War" a changed country. The next decade, known as the Roaring 20s, witnessed the growth of radio—in 1920, a Detroit station aired the first news broadcast—and film, with the advent of the "talkies." The 1920s were relatively prosperous and brought many social changes, including the Eighteenth Amendment (Prohibition), which banned the manufacture and sale of alcohol; the ratification of the Nineteenth Amendment, granting women the right to vote; the Harlem Renaissance (see Chapter 57), celebrating African American literary and artistic culture; and the Jazz Age, which spread the ballroom culture across the United States (the seductive tango and the "kicky" Charleston were all the rage), as well as "flapper" fashions for women that discarded Victorian modes of dress in favor of shapeless straight shifts that stopped at the knees.

Otto Dix (1891–1969) captures the energy of the Charleston dance craze, in *Metropolis* (1928).

In 1929, the booming world economy suffered a catastrophic setback with the Wall Street crash, and the country settled into a decade-long Great Depression, the most serious economic collapse in the history of the United States. Tin Pan Alley faded, though the jazz club scene, as well as films and Broadway musical theater, allowed a brief escape from the difficulties of the era. Among the popular entertainments from the Depression was George Gershwin's musical *Girl Crazy* (1930), featuring the very popular *I Got Rhythm*. Big-band jazz (swing) dominated popular music, promoted by the dance craze, radio, and live concerts. One of the most well-known bands was the Duke Ellington Orchestra, which we will hear playing their signature tune, *Take the A Train*, in Chapter 56

The big-band phenomenon continued through the Second World War (1939–45), during which time many musicians toured with the USO (United States Organizations), performing for the soldiers serving their country. By now, radio had reached into most corners of the world; American troops abroad listened to Armed Forces Radio. Once again, songwriters capitalized on the patriotic spirit with such tunes as *Boogie Woogie Bugle Boy* (of Company B) and Irving Berlin's *God Bless America*, sung by singer Kate Smith in a famous and moving 1938 radio broadcast.

As Europeans rejected their own Romantic past, American modernist composers saw the opportunity to take the lead in defining the future in the new "American century." The cultural diversity of North America provided a wealth of resources to inspire modernist musicians, and their different backgrounds and goals—both creative and social-political—resulted in a variety of styles (some incorporating folk music, blues, and jazz) that we will explore. As in previous movements, modernism was both a reaction against the past and a distillation of it; the movement transformed a culture and allowed for endless experimentation.

With Europe on the brink of entering the Second World War, Kate Smith's 1938 radio broadcast of *God Bless America* stirred strong nationalist sentiments at home.

Features of Early Musical Modernism

"To study music, we must learn the rules.
To create music, we must break them."

—Nadia Boulanger

The New Rhythmic Complexity

Twentieth-century music enriched the standard patterns of duple, triple, and quadruple meter by exploring the possibilities of nonsymmetrical patterns based on odd numbers: five, seven, eleven, or thirteen beats to the measure. In nineteenth-century music, a single meter customarily prevailed through an entire movement or section. Now the metrical flow shifted constantly (**changing meter),** sometimes with each measure. Formerly, one rhythmic pattern was used at a time. Now composers turned to **polyrhythm,** the simultaneous use of several patterns. As a result of these innovations, Western music achieved something of the complexity and suppleness of Asian and African rhythms. This revitalization of rhythm is one of the major achievements of early twentieth-century music.

Composers also enlivened their music with materials drawn from popular styles. Ragtime, with its elaborate syncopations, traveled across the Atlantic to Europe. The rhythmic freedom of jazz captured the ears of a great many composers, who strove to achieve something of the spontaneity of that popular style.

The New Melody and Harmony

Nineteenth-century melody is fundamentally vocal in character: composers tried to make the instruments sing. In contrast, early twentieth-century melody is conceived in relation to instruments rather than the voice, abounding in wide leaps and dissonant intervals. Composers have greatly expanded our notion of what a melody is, rejecting the neatly balanced phrase repetitions of earlier music and creating tunes and patterns that would have been inconceivable before the early 1900s.

The infinite looping and interlacing of colorful circles in **Robert Delaunay's** (1885–1941) *Endless Rhythm* (1934) is suggestive of the new rhythmic energy of the modernist movement.

Irregular lines and sudden leaps, comparable to those found in early modernist melodies, characterize this vista from Arches National Park in Utah.

No single factor sets off early twentieth-century music from that of the past more decisively than the new conceptions of harmony. The triads of traditional harmony gave way to stacked chords with more and more notes added, eventually forming highly dissonant chords of six or seven notes; these created multiple streams of harmony, or **polyharmony**. The new sounds burst the confines of traditional tonality and called for new means of organization, extending or replacing the major-minor system. The most significant changes to harmonic organization came in the work of Arnold Schoenberg and his followers, who advocated for the elimination of harmonic centers altogether (what is generally described as **atonality**; see Chapter 52) and developed an entirely new and extremely influential principle known as **serialism**, or **twelve-tone composition** (Chapter 55).

Orchestration

The rich sonorities of nineteenth-century orchestration gave way to a leaner, brighter sound, played by a smaller orchestra. Instrumental color was used not so much for atmosphere as for bringing out the form and the lines of counterpoint. The string section, with its warm tone, lost its traditional role as the heart of the orchestra; attention was focused on the more penetrating winds. The emphasis on rhythm brought the percussion group into greater prominence, and the piano, which in the Romantic era was preeminently a solo instrument, found a place in the orchestral ensemble.

Modernist musical culture was above all individualistic: in seeking out the new, composers tried to distinguish their approach not just from the past but from other competing visions of the musical future. Musicians belonging to the high-art tradition were also keenly conscious of the growing presence of mass culture, and grappled with the extent to which vernacular styles could coexist with (or be assimilated into) their creative visions. And even as they rejected many facets of Romanticism, modernists shared concerns about national identity and artistic independence that had been founded by that revolutionary and deeply infuential nineteenth-century movement.

Intersecting lines and bold blocks of color mirror modernist orchestration in this work: *Composition in Red, Yellow, and Blue* (1937–42), by **Piet Mondrian** (1872–1944).

CRITICAL THINKING

1. How did the United States move past domination by European music in the nineteenth century toward its own musical voice in the early twentieth?
2. What are some of the most important features of musical modernism?

Previewing early twentieth-century styles

Chapter 52

Anything Goes: Schoenberg and Musical Expressionism

"I personally hate to be called a revolutionist, which I am not. What I did was neither revolution nor anarchy."

—Arnold Schoenberg

KEY POINTS

- Austrian composer Arnold Schoenberg was highly influential in the movement called **Expressionism**. He believed in making music new by freeing dissonance from having to resolve to consonance, and eventually rejected tonality altogether (**atonality**).

- Schoenberg's song cycle *Pierrot lunaire*, from his atonal-Expressionist period, incorporates ***Sprechstimme*** (speechlike melody) and ***Klangfarbenmelodie*** (tone-color melody).

Creativity involves finding a balance between innovation and tradition. Even a seemingly novel creation—for example, the iPad—depends on decades of experiments and earlier products that establish a context within which something can be defined as groundbreaking. Throughout the Western tradition, artists have sought to redefine the "new," and this was especially true for those who embraced the concept of modernism in the early 1900s. Some ways of making music new were perceived as more radical than others, and even today listeners react strongly to the expansion of musical parameters that took place at that time. But musicians whose experiments are still considered extreme did not necessarily consider their music revolutionary (see the epigraph above); rather, they believed they were taking the appropriate next steps in what they thought of as music's evolution into the present and future.

Arnold Schoenberg's Expressionist painting *The Red Gaze* (1910) is highly reminiscent of Edvard Munch's *The Scream*.

The Emancipation of Dissonance

Throughout the history of music, as listeners became increasingly tolerant of new sounds, one factor remained constant: a clear distinction was drawn between dissonance (the element of tension) and consonance (the element of rest). Consonance was the norm, dissonance the temporary disturbance. In many twentieth-century works, however, tension became the norm. A dissonance could serve even as a final cadence, provided it was less dissonant than the chord that came before; in relation to the greater dissonance, it was judged to be consonant. Twentieth-century composers emancipated dissonance by freeing it from the obligation to resolve to consonance. Their music taught listeners to accept tone combinations whose like had never been heard before.

Schoenberg and Atonality

While French artists explored radiant impressions of the outer world through Impressionism, their German counterparts preferred digging down to the depths of the psyche. As with Impressionism (Chapter 49), the impulse for the Expressionist movement came from painting. Artists such as Edvard Munch (famous for *The Scream*) influenced the composer Arnold Schoenberg and his disciples Alban Berg and Anton Webern (as well as writers like Franz Kafka), just as the Impressionist painters influenced Debussy.

The musical language of Expressionism favored hyper-expressive harmonies, extraordinarily wide leaps in the melody, and the use of instruments in their extreme registers. Expressionist music soon reached the boundaries of what was possible within the major-minor system. Inevitably, it had to push beyond. Schoenberg eventually advocated doing away with tonality altogether by giving the twelve tones of the chromatic scale equal importance—creating what is commonly known as **atonal** music, or music rejecting the framework of key. Consonance, according to Schoenberg, was no longer relevant to his expressive needs: he started writing music that moved from one level of dissonance to another, functioning always at maximum tension, without areas of relaxation. Schoenberg developed his atonal-Expressionist style for a number of years, before moving on to a more systematic "twelve-tone" method (to be discussed in Chapter 55). One work in which he explored this new approach most thoroughly was the song cycle *Pierrot lunaire*, composed in 1912.

In His Own Words

" Whether one calls oneself conservative or revolutionary, whether one composes in a conventional or progressive manner, whether one tries to imitate old styles or is destined to express new ideas . . . one must be convinced of the infallibility of one's own fantasy and one must believe in one's own inspiration."

—*Arnold Schoenberg*

Arnold Schoenberg (1874–1951)

Schoenberg was born in Vienna and took lessons in counterpoint with a young composer, Alexander von Zemlinsky. Through Zemlinsky, he was introduced to the advanced musical circles of Vienna, which at that time were under the spell of Wagner's operas.

Schoenberg became active as a teacher himself, and soon gathered about him a band of students that included Alban Berg and Anton Webern. With each new work, he moved closer to taking as bold a step as any composer ever has—the rejection of tonality. Military service in the First World War was followed by a compositional silence of eight years (1915–23), during which he evolved a set of structural procedures to replace tonality. His "method of composing with twelve tones" firmly established him as a leader of contemporary musical thought.

Schoenberg taught composition in Berlin until Hitler came to power in 1933. He emigrated to America and joined the faculty of the University of Southern California, then was appointed professor of composition at the University of California, Los Angeles. He became an American citizen in 1940, taught until his retirement at the age of seventy, and continued his musical activities until his death seven years later.

Schoenberg's early works exemplify post-Wagnerian Romanticism; they still used key signatures and remained within the boundaries of tonality. In his second period, the atonal-Expressionist, he abolished the distinction between consonance and dissonance and any sense of a home key. In his third style period, Schoenberg exploited the twelve-tone method, and in the last (American) phase of his career carried the twelve-tone technique to further stages of refinement. Several of the late works present the twelve-tone style in a manner markedly more accessible than earlier pieces, often with tonal implications, as in the cantata *A Survivor from Warsaw.*

MAJOR WORKS: Orchestral music, including *Five Pieces for Orchestra*, *Variations for Orchestra*, and two concertos • Operas • Choral music, including the cantata *A Survivor from Warsaw* (1947) • Chamber music, including four string quartets, string sextet *Verklärte Nacht* (*Transfigured Night*, 1899), and *Pierrot lunaire* (1912) • Piano music.

LISTENING GUIDE 43

 0:51

Schoenberg: *Pierrot lunaire*, Part III, No. 18

DATE: 1912

GENRE: Song cycle (21 songs, 7 each in three parts)

Part I: Pierrot, a sad clown figure, is obsessed with the moon, having drunk moonwine; his loves, fantasies, and frenzies are exposed.

Part II: He becomes ridden with guilt and wants to make atonement.

Part III: He climbs from the depths of depression to a more playful mood, but with fleeting thoughts of guilt; then he becomes sober.

18. *The Moonfleck (Der Mondfleck)*

What to Listen For

Melody	Disjunct line, quasi-speechlike (*Sprechstimme*).
Rhythm/meter	Very fast, sounds free-flowing.
Harmony	Harshly dissonant.
Texture	Complex counterpoint with canonic (strict imitative) treatment.

Form	Rondeau text with poetic/musical refrain.
Timbre	Pointillistic, flickering instrumental effects.
Performing forces	Voice with five instruments (piccolo, clarinet, violin, cello, piano).
Text	21 poems from Albert Giraud's *Pierrot lunaire*, all in rondeau form.

TEXT

0:00 *Einen weissen Fleck des hellen Mondes*
Auf dem Rücken seines schwarzen Rockes.
So spaziert Pierrot im lauen Abend,
Aufzusuchen Glück und Abenteuer.

Plötzlich stört ihn was an seinem Anzug,
Er besieht sich rings und findet richtig—

0:23 *Einen weissen Fleck des hellen Mondes*
Auf dem Rücken seines schwarzen Rockes.

Warte! denkt er: das ist so ein Gipsfleck!
Wischt und wischt, doch—bringt ihn
nicht herunter!
Und so geht er, giftgeschwollen, weiter,
Reibt und reibt bis an den frühen Morgen—
Einen weissen Fleck des hellen Mondes.

TRANSLATION

With a fleck of white from
the bright moon on the back of his black jacket.
Pierrot strolls about in the
mild evening seeking his fortune and adventure.

Suddenly something strikes
him as wrong, he checks his
clothes and sure enough finds

a fleck of white from the
bright moon on the back of his black jacket.

Damn! he thinks: that's a
spot of plaster! Wipes and
wipes, but—he can't get it off.
And so goes on his way,
his pleasure poisoned, rubs
and rubs till the early morning—
a fleck of white from the bright moon.

Opening of vocal line:

Pierrot lunaire

Schoenberg chose the texts for his song cycle from a collection of poems by Belgian writer Albert Giraud, a disciple of the French Symbolists. Giraud's Pierrot was a poet-rascal-clown (connected to a long tradition of improvised theater) whose chalk-white face, passing abruptly from laughter to tears, enlivened every puppet show and pantomime in Europe. The poems were liberally spiced with elements of the macabre and the bizarre that suited the end-of-century taste for decadence; with their abrupt changes of mood from guilt and depression to atonement and playfulness, they fired Schoenberg's imagination. He picked twenty-one texts (in German translation), arranged them in three groups of seven, and set them for a female vocalist and a chamber ensemble of five players on eight instruments: piano, flute/piccolo, clarinet/bass clarinet, violin/viola, and cello. No song in the cycle uses the same combination of instruments.

The Cubist painting *Pierrot* (1919) by Spanish artist **Juan Gris** (1887–1927) is one of many renderings of this character.

One of the composer's goals was to bring spoken word and music as close together as possible; he achieved this aim through ***Sprechstimme*** (speechlike melody), a new style in which the vocal melody is spoken rather than sung. The result is a weird but strangely effective vocal line. Schoenberg also experimented with what he called ***Klangfarbenmelodie*** (tone-color melody), where each note of a melody is played by a different instrument, creating a shifting effect that evokes the moonbeams mentioned in the text.

Each poem is a **rondeau,** a fifteenth-century verse form in which the opening lines of the poem return as a refrain in the middle and at the end (see the Machaut example in Chapter 15). We will focus on No. 18 from the cycle, *The Moonfleck* (*Der Mondfleck*; LG 43). Pierrot, out to have fun, is disturbed by a white spot—a patch of moonlight—on the collar of his jet-black jacket. He rubs and rubs but cannot get rid of it. The piano introduces a three-voice fugue, while the other instruments unfold devices such as strict canons in diminution (smaller note values) and retrograde (backward). Schoenberg was obviously fascinated by such constructions, which recall the wizardry of the Renaissance and Baroque contrapuntists.

The combination of atonality, *Sprechstimme*, and *Klangfarbenmelodie* in this work shocked many in Schoenberg's audience. Others found his experiments with sound entirely appropriate not only to Giraud's poems but to contemporary fascinations with the unconscious and the uncanny; they eagerly subscribed to the series of private concerts Schoenberg offered. Avant-garde music that pushes the boundaries of convention imay not be to everyone's taste, but there have always been listeners who have been intrigued by the inventiveness of modern composers.

CRITICAL THINKING

1. How did Schoenberg and his fellow Expressionists emancipate dissonance?

2. What are the most innovative aspects of *Pierrot lunaire*?

YOUR TURN TO EXPLORE

Seek out recordings of musicians who are currently attempting to expand the parameters of musical expression. How are they "making music new"? Which elements of the Western tradition (or other traditions) are they keeping, and which are they rejecting? What is their rationale for doing this? Who are their audiences, and how do their audiences respond to this new music?

Chapter 53

Calculated Shock: Stravinsky and Modernist Multimedia

"I hold that it was a mistake to consider me a revolutionary. If one only need break habit in order to be labeled a revolutionary, then every artist who has something to say and who in order to say it steps outside the bounds of established convention could be considered revolutionary."

—Igor Stravinsky

KEY POINTS

- Modernist approaches to art, music, and dance were combined by Paris's Ballet Russes under the leadership of impresario Serge Diaghilev.

- Russian composer Igor Stravinsky revitalized rhythm by increasing its complexity—using, for example, **polyrhythms** and **changing meters**.

- Stravinsky's early works, including his ballets *The Firebird*, *Petrushka*, and *The Rite of Spring*, are strongly nationalistic; the last evokes rites of ancient Russia through new instrumental combinations and the percussive use of dissonance, as well as polyrhythmic and polytonal writing.

I n every human society, dance plays important social, expressive, and/or religious roles. While dancing faded out of most Christian ritual during the Middle Ages, much Western music since has been designed for dancing, whether simple social types or more elaborate choreographies that tell a story. Much multimedia today involves dance (music videos are perhaps the most striking example), which helps to emphasize important aspects of the music and also provides complementary meanings.

The Rite of Spring: Collaborative Multimedia

Serge Diaghilev

The art of ballet was significantly revitalized with the career of the impresario Serge Diaghilev (1872–1929), whose Paris-based dance company, the Ballets Russes, opened up a new chapter in the cultural life of Europe. He surrounded his dancers—the greatest were Vaslav Nijinsky and Tamara Karsavina—with productions worthy of their talents. He invited artists such as Picasso and Braque to paint the scenery, and commissioned the three ballets—*The Firebird*, *Petrushka*, and *The Rite of Spring*—that catapulted Russian composer Igor Stravinsky to fame.

The Rite of Spring was designed as a fully integrated modernist multimedia spectacle, with an innovative choreography by Vaslav Nijinsky (whose provocative way with Debussy's music had helped build "buzz" for the Ballet Russes)

and experimental stage designs by renowned artist Nich-
olas Roerich. Nijinsky's choreography was considered as
groundbreaking as Stravinsky's music: it involved dancers
creating jerky and irregular movements with individual
limbs, jumping up and down in place, and forming rotating geometric patterns onstage (see illustrations at right
and on p. 306).

Audience members at the premiere, held on May 29,
1913, at the swanky Parisian Théâtre des Champs-Élysées,
had been primed for a work that would push the envelope
of dance and music. And reaction to the ballet was immediate that first night: mild protests as soon as the initial
dissonant notes sounded soon turned to an uproar. Cries
of "Shut up!" were heard around the theater from both
supporters and detractors, and one critic barked obscen-
ities at the elegantly dressed ladies who found the work
offensive: finally the dancers couldn't hear the music, and
the show had to be interrupted. When the dust settled,
the reactions ranged from "magnifique" to "abominable."

Yet several more performances were given that season,
none of which were greeted with such a hullabaloo. And
there is some evidence that the management of the Ballets
Russes "seeded" some of the individuals who disrupted
the premiere, trying to ensure press coverage. While
Stravinsky was publicly incensed with the disrespect that
had been shown his music, he must have been aware of
its shocking and unsettling quality. The very fact that the
work was received negatively by traditionalists made him
the darling of the avant-garde, providing crucial support
for his rise to prominence as a modernist composer.

Valentine Hugo's (1887–1968)
sketches of the *Sacrificial Dance*
from the ballet *The Rite of Spring*,
choreographed by Nijinsky.

Musical Innovation

For more than half a century, Stravinsky reflected several main currents in twentieth-century music. First through his ballets, he was a leader in the revitalization
of rhythm in European art music. He is also considered one of the great orches-
trators, his music's sonority marked by a polished brightness and a clear texture.
The Rite of Spring, subtitled "Scenes of Pagan Russia," not only embodies the cult
of primitivism that so startled its first-night audience, but also sets forth a new
musical language characterized by the percussive use of dissonance, as well as
polyrhythms and polytonality.

Though later modernist principles would call for more bare-bones ensembles,
here the size of the orchestra is monumental. Stravinsky often uses the full force
of the brass and percussion to create a barbaric, primeval sound and gives the
strings percussive material such as pizzicato and successive down-bow strokes.
The overall impact of the orchestration is harsh and loud, with constantly changing colors. Some of Stravinsky's melodies quote Russian folk songs, and the
remaining melodic material, often heard in short fragments, uses limited ranges
and extended repetition in a folk-song-like manner. Similarly, within each scene,
he minimizes harmonic changes through the use of ostinatos, pedal points, and
melodic repetition.

Igor Stravinsky (1882–1971)

Born in Russia, Stravinsky grew up in a musical environment and studied composition with Nikolai Rimsky-Korsakov. His music attracted the attention of impresario Serge Diaghilev, who commissioned him to write a series of ballets (*The Firebird, Petrushka, The Rite of Spring*) that launched the young composer to fame. The premiere of *The Rite of Spring* in 1913 was one of the most scandalous in music history. Just a year later, however, when presented at a symphony concert, it was received with enthusiasm and deemed a masterpiece. When war broke out in 1914, Stravinsky took refuge first in Switzerland and then in France. With the onset of the Second World War, he decided to settle his family in Los Angeles; he became an American citizen in 1945. His later concert tours around the world made him the most celebrated figure in twentieth-century music. He died in New York in 1971.

Stravinsky's musical style evolved throughout his career, from the post-Impressionism of *The Firebird* and the primitivism of *The Rite of Spring* to the controlled Classicism of his mature style (*Symphony of Psalms*), and finally to the twelve-tone method of his late works (*Agon*). In his ballets, which are strongly nationalistic, Stravinsky invigorated rhythm, creating a sense of furious and powerful movement. His lustrous orchestrations are so clear that, as Diaghilev remarked, "one can see through [them] with one's ears."

MAJOR WORKS: Orchestral music, including *Symphonies of Wind Instruments* (1920) and *Symphony in Three Movements* (1945) • Ballets, including *L'oiseau de feu* (*The Firebird*, 1910), *Petrushka* (1911), *Le sacre du printemps* (*The Rite of Spring*, 1913), *Agon* (1957) • Operas, including *Oedipus Rex* (1927) • Other theater works, including *L'histoire du soldat* (*The Soldier's Tale*, 1918) • Choral music, including *Symphony of Psalms* (1930) and *Threni: Lamentations of the Prophet Jeremiah* (1958) • Chamber music • Piano music • Songs.

 The Rite of Spring, Introduction

The most innovative and influential element of *The Rite of Spring* is the energetic interaction between rhythm and meter. In some scenes, a steady pulse is set up, only to serve as a backdrop for unpredictable accents or melodic entrances. In other passages, the concept of a regular metric pulse is totally abandoned as downbeats occur seemingly at random. With this ballet, Stravinsky freed Western music from the traditional constraints of metric regularity.

The *Introduction*'s writhing bassoon melody, played in its uppermost range, depicts the awakening of the Earth in spring (LG 44). The *Dance of the Youths and Maidens* then erupts with a series of violent chords, with unpredictable accents that veil any clear sense of meter. These dissonant chords alternate with folklike melodies, as the music builds to a loud, densely textured climax. We get a brief respite in the *Game of Abduction*, as another folk melody is introduced; but the level of activity quickly becomes chaotic, replete with seemingly random accents. The primitive atmosphere continues to the culminating *Sacrificial Dance* that closes Part II, during which the young girl—the "chosen one"—dances herself to death in a frenzy.

Stravinsky capitalized on the scandal-success of *The Rite of Spring* by having the work performed only orchestrally, detaching it from its original multimedia project. Indeed, he (deceptively) began to claim that the music had always been the driving reason behind the project: that choreography and staging had been afterthoughts. Today, *The Rite* stands as one of the landmarks in twentieth-century symphonic literature.

The Kirov Ballet performs "The Glorification of the Chosen One" from Stravinsky's *Rite of Spring,* with costumes and choreography reconstructed from the original production.

But it never would have come about had it not been for the Ballet Russes and the opportunity the group gave Stravinsky to collaborate on pathbreaking multimedia.

CRITICAL THINKING

1. What elements made *The Rite of Spring* shocking to its first audiences? Do you think it is still shocking today?

2. How did different media contribute to the expressive effect of *The Rite of Spring*?

YOUR TURN TO EXPLORE

Consider the music videos for one of your favorite songs, or any video of music you consider especially meaningful that adds a story line (not just images of musicians playing). How does the dancing or story line help bring out specific elements of the music? Are there aspects of the music/song that you think are obscured or made less effective by the addition of the video/dancing? How might you change the "video track" to bring out different aspects of the music, perhaps ones that you would find more significant?

LISTENING GUIDE 44 4:34

Stravinsky: *The Rite of Spring (Le sacre du printemps),* Part I, excerpts

DATE:	1913
GENRE:	Ballet (often performed as a concert piece for orchestra)
BASIS:	Scenes of pagan Russia
SCENARIO:	Nicholas Roerich and Igor Stravinsky
CHOREOGRAPHY:	Vaslav Nijinsky

SECTIONS:

Part I: *Adoration of the Earth*	Part II: *The Sacrifice*
Introduction	*Introduction*
Dance of the Youths and Maidens	*Mystic Circle of the Adolescents*
Game of Abduction	*Glorification of the Chosen One*
Spring Rounds	*Evocation of the Ancestors*
Games of the Rival Tribes	*Ritual Action of the Ancestors*
Procession of the Sage	*Sacrificial Dance*
Dance of the Earth	

Introduction (closing measures)

What to Listen For

Melody	Disjunct, floating, folk-song melody.	**Expression**	Haunting mood, represents awakening of the earth; very slow tempo (*Lento*).
Rhythm/ meter	Free shifting meter; the four-note rhythmic idea establishes a duple pulse.	**Timbre**	High-range bassoon with solo clarinets, pizzicato strings.

Continued on next page

0:00   Folk tune played by the bassoon, from the opening:

0:12   Pizzicato rhythmic figure in violins:

0:19   Clarinet flourish, followed by a sustained string chord.
0:22   Violin figure returns to establish the meter for the next section.

Dance of the Youths and Maidens

What to Listen For

Melody	Russian folk-song melodies alternate with nonmelodic sound blocks.		**Form**	Sectional, with opening section recurring several times (**A-B-A′-C-A-D-E-F-G-A″-F′**).
Rhythm/ meter	Basic duple pulse with irregular accents; constant eighth-note motion.		**Expression**	Forceful, with high energy and changing dynamics.
Harmony	Dissonant chord (polytonal) repeated over and over; sound blocks.		**Timbre**	Changing instrumental colors throughout.
Texture	Dense, complex polyphony.		**Performing forces**	Huge orchestra with expanded brass, woodwind, and percussion sections.

0:30   Strings play harsh, percussive chords (**A**), reinforced by eight horns, with unpredictable accents:

0:37   English horn (**B**) plays the pizzicato motive from the *Introduction*.
0:42   Brief return of the opening accented chords (**A′**).
0:45   Motives combine with new ideas (**C**). Strings continue their chords; English horn repeats its four-note motive; loud brass interruptions and a descending melodic fragment.
1:02   Return of opening accented chords (**A**).
1:10   Bassoon plays syncopated folk melody (**D**), over accented string chords:

1:38   Steady eighth-note pulse (**E**); four-note motive alternates between the English horn and trumpet; scurrying motives in the winds and strings, and sustained trills.
1:50   Four-note motive (English horn, then violins) and sustained trills; low string instruments hit the strings with the wood of their bows (*col legno*).

1:58   French horn and flute introduce a folklike melody (**F**); texture thickens with activity:

2:16   Flutes repeat the theme (from **F**).
2:29   New melody (**G**) appears in trumpets with parallel chords:

2:42   Texture is abruptly reduced; accents of the opening section (**A″**) return; frenetic activity continues.
2:50   Melody (**F′**) in piccolo, then in lutes and strings; unpredictable accents, scurrying activity, and an expanding texture lead to the climax.

Game of Abduction

What to Listen For

Melody	Scurrying melodic figures and horn calls, brief folk tune.
Rhythm/ meter	Fast tempo, meter not established; unpredictable accents.
Harmony	Harshly dissonant, crashing chords.

Texture	Dense, with shifting activity.
Expression	Frenetic and primitive mood.
Timbre	Quickly shifting instrumental colors.

3:16   Sustained chords, hurrying string sounds, and syncopated accents.
3:20   Woodwinds and piccolo trumpet introduce a folk theme; texture is dense with constantly changing activity and timbres:

3:29   Horns introduce a new motive, alternating the interval of a fourth:

3:48   New thematic idea, in a homorhythmic texture and changing meters:

3:56   Horn motive returns.
4:07   Timpani and full orchestra alternate strong beats; irregular accents.
4:24   Series of loud chords and a sustained trill end the movement.

Chapter 54

Still Sacred: Religious Music in the Twentieth Century

"The Church knew what the Psalmist knew: Music praises God. Music is well or better able to praise Him than the building of the church and all its decoration; it is the Church's greatest ornament."

—Igor Stravinsky

KEY POINTS

- Talented French artists and composers have long competed for a special prize, the Prix de Rome, that allows them the opportunity to live in Rome and explore their creativity.
- Lili Boulanger, the first woman to win the prize, combined Impressionist ideas with the emerging modernist approach to dissonance. Her

  sister Nadia was a highly respected teacher and composer.
- Boulanger's *Psalm 24* is an example of modernist sacred music written from the perspective of personal devotion rather than commissioned by a religious institution.

Religious institutions provided the primary employment and sponsorship for the Western musical tradition for centuries. From the 1800s, as secular music became more and more prominent, many musicians still continued to play and write for their worship communities and draw on religious themes, for works not necessarily designed to be performed in church but rather meant to convey their own spiritual convictions. Spiritual topics inspired expressive sounds even before the development of notation; it's not surprising that they have continued to do so into the modernist era and beyond.

Post-Impressionism, Lili Boulanger, and the Prix de Rome

Many composers of the early twentieth century fell under the spell of Impressionist music by Debussy and his followers; the influence of such post-Impressionist trends can be heard not only in France (in the music of Maurice Ravel, for example), but across Europe and in the United States. At the same time, however, new currents led to radical changes in music composition that assaulted the ears of listeners, as we saw in the previous two chapters. In France, composers could be found representing both camps; among the innovators in the developing French school was Lili Boulanger, who embraced not only Impressionism but an innovative harmonic language as well. Like several notable musicians before her, she was singled out for her talent in the prestigious French competition known as the Prix de Rome (Rome prize).

The coveted Prix de Rome, extending back as far as the seventeenth century, was open to young artists and musicians under the age of thirty; the winner received a monetary award and a three-year grant to study at the Villa Medici in Rome. Some of France's most renowned composers were awarded the prize, including Hector Berlioz, Georges Bizet, Claude Debussy, and, once women were allowed to enter (from 1903), Lili Boulanger. The prize meant instant fame for the winners, and it launched the careers of many great French artists and musicians. The recognition for Boulanger, though, the first woman to win, was bittersweet, as the celebrity status and hectic schedule associated with her position took a toll on her already fragile health.

French composer Nadia Boulanger, Lili's sister, poses with 1907 Prix de Rome contestants.

Psalm 24

Boulanger's setting of *Psalm 24* (LG 45), written in 1916, is one of three choral works she set to Psalm texts; these are largely recognized as some of her finest compositions. *Psalm 24* is the briefest of the three, but powerfully majestic, featuring forces typical for French sacred music. The dramatic introduction, a fanfare for brass, harp, organ, and timpani, sets a commanding tone, after which the tenors and basses sing the first three verses, punctuated with accented instrumental

Lili Boulanger (1893–1918)

Parisian composer Lili Boulanger, younger sister of the famous pedagogue Nadia Boulanger and the daughter of two musicians, showed an early affinity for music, but her training was hampered by chronic illness that resulted in her untimely death at the age of twenty-four. Her immune system had been damaged from having bronchial pneumonia at age two, and she suffered painful bouts of Crohn's disease throughout her short life. A precocious child, Lili learned to sing and play violin, cello, harp, and piano through private instruction, and she sat in on classes at the Paris Conservatory with her sister when her health permitted.

Both sisters set their sights on winning the famous Prix de Rome competition for composition, which their father had won in 1835. Nadia took second prize in 1908 (after almost being eliminated for writing an instrumental, rather than choral, fugue), and Lili, after withdrawing from the 1912 competition because of ill health, won first prize in 1913 for her cantata *Faust et Hélène*. She received a contract with the Ricordi music-publishing house, but her illness prevented her from fulfilling the three-year term in Rome, and the onset of the First World War directed her energies away from composition and toward an organization she founded that attempted to keep musicians in contact with their families during the war.

Although Boulanger focused on choral and chamber music, she was under contract to write two operas as well, and completed part of one, *La Princesse Maleine*, on a libretto by the well-known writer Maurice Maeterlinck. In 1917, she underwent an appendectomy that doctors hoped would relieve her pain, but she soon weakened. Her final composition, a poignant *Pie Jesu*, was dictated from her deathbed to her devoted sister Nadia. Lili's choral music—both secular and sacred—is among her most distinguished work, and her moving Psalm settings reflect the strength of her Catholicism. Her music is lyrical, with innovative harmonies and complex counterpoint.

MAJOR WORKS: An unfinished opera, *La Princesse Maleine* • Sacred and secular choral works, including settings of Psalms 24, 129, and 130 • Songs for voice and orchestra, including the song cycle *Clairières dans le ciel* (voice and piano/orchestra, 1915) and *Pie Jesu* (soprano, string quartet, and organ, 1918) • Cantata *Faust et Hélène* (1913) • Piano and chamber music.

LISTENING GUIDE 45 3:25

Boulanger: *Psalm 24*

DATE: 1916

GENRE: Choral Psalm setting

What to Listen For

Melody	Lyrical, small-ranging, and conjunct.
Rhythm/meter	Triple meter; highly accented in opening and closing.
Harmony	Vague harmonic direction.
Texture	Largely chordal, homophonic; parallel lines evoke Impressionism.

Form	Three-part (**A-B-A**).
Expression	Dramatic, martial tone, with ethereal middle section.
Performing forces	Tenor solo, SATB chorus, brass, harp, organ, timpani.
Text	Translation of Psalm 24 (English translation from New Revised Standard Bible).

0:00   Introduction: Short brass fanfare, sets dramatic tone.

0:06   1. La terre appartient à l'Éternel, et tout ce qui s'y trouve,
        la terre habitable et ceux qui l'habitent.
        The earth is the Lord's, and all that is in it;
        the world and those who live in it.

      2. Car Il l'a fondée sur les mers,
        et l'a établie sur les fleuves.
        For He has founded it on the seas,
        and established it on the rivers.

      3. Qui est-ce qui montera à la montagne de l'Éternel,
        et qui est-ce qui demeurera au lieu de sa sainteté?
        Who shall ascend the hill of the Lord,
        and who shall stand in His holy place?

(right column for 0:06) Tenors and basses only, highly accented. Voices alternate with fanfare in brass and organ.

0:45   4. Ce sera l'homme qui a les mains pures, et le coeur net,
        dont l'âme n'est point portée à la fausseté
        et qui ne jure point pour tromper.
        Those who have clean hands and pure hearts,
        who do not lift up their souls to what is false
        and who do not swear falsely.

(right column for 0:45) Men's voices and organ; more serene.

1:12   5. Il recevra la bénédiction de l'Éternel
        et la justice de Dieu son sauveur.
        They will receive the blessing from the Lord,
        and vindication from the God of their salvation.

(right column for 1:12) Tenor solo, with harp; ecstatic mood.

1:37   6. Telle est la génération de ceux qui Le cherchent,
        qui cherchent Ta face en Jacob.
        Such is the company of those who seek Him,
        who seek the face of the God of Jacob.

(right column for 1:37) Chant-like chorus; mystical mood.

2:03   7. Portes, Élevez vos têtes, portes éternelles,
        haussez-vous, et le Roi de gloire entrera.
        Lift up your heads, O gates, and be lifted up,
        O ancient doors! That the King of Glory may come in.

      8. Qui est ce Roi de gloire? C'est l'Éternel fort
        et puissant dans les combats.

(right column for 2:03) Full chorus, martial and triumphant.

> *Who is the King of Glory? He is the Eternal King of Glory,*
> *strong and mighty in battle.*
>
> 9. Portes, élevez vos têtes,
>   élevez-vous aussi, portes éternelles;
>   et le Roi de gloire entrera.
>   *Lift up your heads, O gates, and be lifted up, O ancient doors!*
>   *That the King of Glory may come in.*
>
> 2:53 10. Qui est ce Roi de gloire? C'est l'Éternel des armées,   Tempo picks up, piece closes on a
>   c'est Lui qui est le Roi de gloire, Éternel.   *fortissimo* chord.
>   *Who is the King of Glory? The Lord of Hosts,*
>   *He is the King of Glory.*

exchanges. The fourth verse, with men and organ alone, is calmer, projecting a Debussy-like air. The tranquillity continues with a rapturous tenor solo, which promises the benediction, and an ethereal, chant-like delivery of the sixth verse by unison men with harp. The last verses return to a triumphal tone, with full chorus and instruments, marching to a resplendent close—hardly the music one expects from a frail, dying woman. Her death silenced a highly individual voice, one of the most promising of the early twentieth century.

The French text of *Psalm 24* would have been incompatible with the Latin-only rule governing the services of the Catholic Church until 1963. Like many of her contemporaries, Boulanger composed sacred music that was not specifically designed for traditional worship: the *Psalm* is an expression of her personal devotion rather than a strictly functional religious work. This approach has become more common in the last century, as composers and musicians have responded to the increasingly flexible relationship between individual spirituality and the multitude of religious traditions that connect and intersect in the modern world.

CRITICAL THINKING

1. Why was the Prix de Rome important in French musical culture? What were the features of the competition?
2. How do the musical elements of *Psalm 24* reflect different aspects of turn-of-the-twentieth-century styles, as well as older traditions?

YOUR TURN TO EXPLORE

Find one or more musical works that set a spiritual or sacred text *not* connected with a specific religious service, or that are meant to reflect an individual or a community's connection with the divine using newly chosen words rather than a standard prayer text. For example, you might look at Christian rock, hip-hop affiliated with the Five Percenter Nation, or the Jewish Renewal movement. What are the musical resources (melody, harmony, instrumentation) that are used to convey those words? Are they the same resources that might be chosen for secular music, or are they different in some way? In what contexts is this music performed, and by whom? How do the musical features, text-setting, and context in which these works are performed compare with the Boulanger *Psalm*, and with other sacred examples you have encountered before, whether through this course or in your personal experience?

Interface

The Consummate Pedagogue

Are you fortunate enough to have had a great teacher at some point, someone with an exceptional ability to communicate and foster enthusiastic learning? If so, you are indeed lucky; if not yet, perhaps you have heard about such a teacher from a friend. Putting your finger on what makes a great pedagogue is difficult, and teaching techniques will not be the same from one person to the next. In music, however, one woman is universally recognized for her outstanding career as a teacher.

Like her younger sister Lili, Nadia Boulanger (1887–1979) showed special talent for music at an early age, but she decided she was not as gifted a composer as her sister and so dedicated her life to teaching. Although she eventually taught at the Paris Conservatory, it was not easy for a woman to be accepted there (or anywhere) as a professor, so she helped found a school for Americans at Fontainebleau, outside Paris. The list of her pupils is amazing, and includes many prominent performers, conductors, and composers. Aaron Copland (see Chapter 59), who attended the school in its first year, was in awe of his mentor: "Nadia Boulanger knew everything there was to know about music; she knew the oldest and the latest music, pre-Bach and post-Stravinsky."

Nadia could be a tough taskmaster, especially for her most gifted students. She had no patience for anyone who was not serious, asserting that "the art of music is so very deep and profound that to approach it very seriously *only* is not enough. One must approach music with a serious vigor, and at the same time, with a great, affectionate joy." And when a student dared to challenge her criticism of his composition, claiming that Bach had often used

Nadia Boulanger lecturing to music students in 1976.

the same technique, she reportedly quipped, "He can; you cannot." Nadia recognized talent immediately: she refused to teach George Gershwin (see Chapter 58) because she felt she had nothing to offer him, and when she attended the 1910 premiere of Stravinsky's ballet *The Firebird* in Paris, she recognized his genius right away, and she and Stravinsky became close friends for life.

The respect Nadia earned helped her forge new paths for women in music: for example, she was the first woman to be invited to conduct such major symphony orchestras as the London Philharmonic, the New York Philharmonic, and the Boston Symphony Orchestra and to conduct premieres of works by Copland and Stravinsky. The accolades and awards she received are impressive indeed, including honorary doctorates from Harvard, Yale, and Oxford.

Nadia Boulanger's career is a perfect example of the essential role played by teachers in the shaping of musical tradition. Performers are glamorous in the public eye, composers are credited with pioneering new styles, but teachers work systematically in the background to build, expand, and sustain the culture that underpins the entire enterprise.

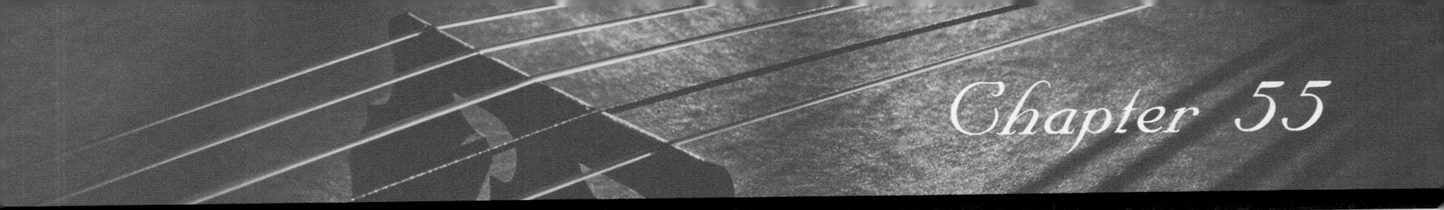

Chapter 55

War Is Hell: Berg and Expressionist Opera

"Boredom . . . is the last thing
one should experience in the theater."

—Alban Berg

KEY POINTS

- Arnold Schoenberg and his students Alban Berg and Anton Webern became known as a **Second Viennese School**, of modernist composition, in the first half of the 1900s.

- Berg's music is rooted in the post-Romantic tradition, but he also drew on the twelve-tone system devised by his teacher.

- Berg's most famous work is *Wozzeck*, an Expressionist opera based on a play about a disturbed man who moves between reality and hallucination in a society that has turned its back on him.

Art is sometimes designed to evoke ideal beauty, or to create a place of inspiration beyond the everyday. But other times the artist's goal is to shine a light on social problems and raise questions about inequality and the oppression of disenfranchised people. "Protest music" may be simple and easily performed as a resource to rally large groups in support of a cause, but it can also be extremely complex and experimental. Especially during the first half of the twentieth century, several composers combined social advocacy with their cutting-edge exploration of new musical techniques. Probably the most striking example comes from the theatrical work of Alban Berg, who was the most commercially successful Expressionist composer, finding a compelling path midway between the lushness of late Romanticism and the disconcerting atonality of his teacher Arnold Schoenberg.

The Second Viennese School and the Twelve-Tone Method

Having accepted the necessity of moving beyond the existing tonal system, Schoenberg sought a unifying principle that would take its place. He found this in a strict technique, worked out by the early 1920s, that he called "the method of composing with twelve tones"—that is, with the twelve chromatic pitches, each one carrying equal weight. Any composition that uses Schoenberg's method, also known as **serialism,** is based on a particular arrangement of the twelve tones called a **tone row**.

Serialism, tone row

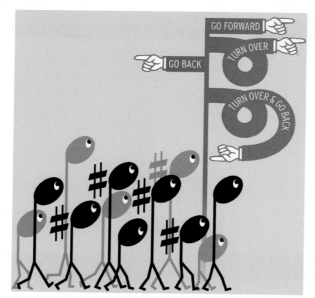

This *New Yorker* cartoon helps visualize the concept of a tone row and its permutations.

The composer can arrange the pitches in any order, and once the row is established, it becomes the basis for all the piece's themes, harmonies, and musical patterns.

Schoenberg provided flexibility and variety in this seemingly confining system through alternative forms of the tone row. A **transposed row** keeps the same order of intervals but begins on a different pitch. In **inversion,** the movement of the notes is in the opposite direction—up instead of down, and vice versa—so that the row appears upside down. **Retrograde** is an arrangement of the pitches in reverse order, so that the row comes out backward, and **retrograde inversion** turns the row upside down *and* backward. (The same techniques were used in the Baroque fugue; see diagram on p. 144.)

Schoenberg's pioneering efforts in the breakdown of the traditional tonal system and his development of the twelve-tone method revolutionized musical composition. His innovations were taken further by his most gifted students, Alban Berg and Anton Webern. These three composers are often referred to as the **Second Viennese School** (the first being the school of Haydn, Mozart, and Beethoven).

Alban Berg and *Wozzeck*

Berg brought great lyrical imagination to the abstract procedures of the Schoenbergian technique. In his operas, he was drawn to Expressionist themes focusing on human foibles and depravity, and on characters who were utterly powerless to control the world around them.

Berg's style was rooted in German Romanticism—the world of Brahms and Wagner, and especially the late-Romantic soundscapes of Gustav Mahler (1860–1911). The Romantic streak in his temperament tied him to this heritage even after he had adopted the twelve-tone style. Berg was a musical dramatist: for him, music was bound up with character and action, mood and atmosphere. Yet, like his teacher, he also leaned toward the formal patterns of the past—fugue and passacaglia, variations, sonata, and suite.

Expressionist painter **Wassily Kandinsky** (1886–1944) defied notions of beauty in order to define the artist's inner self. *Small Pleasures* (1913).

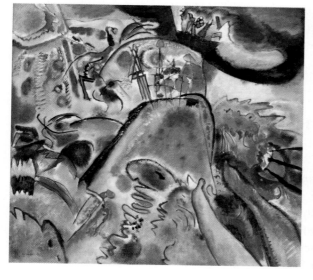

Berg's opera *Wozzeck* was inspired by an early Romantic play by German writer Georg Büchner that was based on gruesome, real-life events. In the title character of Wozzeck, a common soldier, Büchner created an archetype of the "insulted and injured" inhabitants of the earth.

Wozzeck is the victim of his sadistic Captain and the coldly scientific Doctor, who uses the soldier for his experiments—to which he submits because he needs the money. (Wozzeck is given to hallucinations; the Doctor is bent on proving his theory that mental disorder is related to diet.) The action centers on Wozzeck's unhappy love for Marie, by whom he has an illegitimate son. Marie, however, is infatuated with the handsome

Alban Berg (1885–1935)

Berg was born in Vienna into a well-to-do family and grew up in an environment that fostered his artistic interests. At nineteen, he began studying with Arnold Schoenberg, an exacting master and mentor who shaped his outlook on art.

At the outbreak of war in 1914, Berg was called up for military service despite his uncertain health (he suffered from asthma and a nerve ailment). After the war, with the premiere of his opera *Wozzeck* at the Berlin State Opera in 1925, Berg rose from obscurity to international fame. During his mature years, he was active as a teacher and also wrote about music, propagandizing tirelessly on behalf of Schoenberg and his school. But with the coming to power of Hitler, the works of the twelve-tone composers were banned in Germany as alien to the spirit of the Third Reich.

Exhausted and ailing after the completion of his Violin Concerto (1935), Berg went to the country for a short rest before resuming work on his second opera, *Lulu*. An insect bite brought on an abscess, then infection, and finally blood poisoning on his return to Vienna. He died on Christmas Eve that year, seven weeks before his fifty-first birthday.

Besides *Wozzeck*, Berg's most widely known composition is the *Lyric Suite*, an instrumental work in six movements, the first and last of which strictly follow the twelve-tone method. Berg spent the last seven years of his life working on *Lulu*, which is based on a single twelve-tone row. The opera remained unfinished at his death until the orchestration was completed by the Austrian composer Friedrich Cerha, and now *Lulu* has taken its place alongside *Wozzeck* as one of the more challenging and effective works of the modern lyric theater. Berg is probably the most widely admired master of the twelve-tone school. His premature death robbed contemporary music of a major figure.

MAJOR WORKS: Two operas: *Wozzeck* (1917–22) and *Lulu* (unfinished, 1935) • Orchestral music, including *Three Orchestral Pieces*, Op. 6 (1915), and the Violin Concerto (1935) • Chamber music, including *Lyric Suite* (1926) • Piano music • Songs.

 Wozzeck, Act 1, scene 1

Drum Major. Wozzeck slowly comes to the conclusion that she has been unfaithful to him. Ultimately he cuts her throat, then, driven back to the death scene by guilt and remorse, he drowns himself. The story ends when Marie's child is notified of the death of his mother, a traumatic event that implicitly begins the cycle of social alienation all over again.

Berg's libretto organized the play into three acts, each containing five scenes that are linked by brief orchestral interludes. Harmonically, the greater part of the opera is cast in an atonal-Expressionist idiom. Berg anticipates certain twelve-tone procedures, and generally organizes each scene and interlude as a systematic "study" on a particular musical idea. He also looks back to the tonal tradition, writing a number of passages in major and minor keys and using leitmotifs in the Wagnerian manner. Throughout, we hear moments of passionate lyricism that alternate with speechlike vocal lines (*Sprechstimme*).

In the next-to-last scene of the opera (LG 46), Wozzeck returns to the path near the pond where he has killed Marie and stumbles against her body. He asks, "Marie, what's that red cord around your neck?" He finds the knife with which he committed the murder, throws it into the pond, and, driven by his delusions, follows it into the water. His last words as he drowns are "I am washing myself in blood—the water is blood . . . blood!" The Doctor appears, followed by the Captain. We see the haunted scene through their eyes as they both ignore Wozzeck's drowning groans and respond to a general sense of dread.

The crazed Wozzeck stabs Marie in Act III of Berg's opera, in this 1952 production at the Théâter des Champs-Élysées, Paris.

In His Own Words

"When I decided to write an opera, my only intentions . . . were to give the theater what belongs to the theater. . . . The music was to be so formed as consciously to fulfill its duty of serving the action at every moment."

—*Alban Berg*

The final scene opens with a symphonic interlude in D minor, a passionate lament for the life and death of Wozzeck that shows how richly Berg's music was influenced by the final vestiges of Romanticism. The scene takes place in the morning in front of Marie's house, where children are playing. Marie's son rides a hobbyhorse. Other children rush in with news of the murder, but the little boy does not understand—or at least appears not to. The children run off as he continues to ride and sing. Then, noticing that he has been left alone, he calls "Hop, hop" and rides off after them on his hobbyhorse. This final scene—with the curtain closing on an empty stage—is utterly heartbreaking.

Wozzeck envelops the listener in a hallucinated world that could only have come from central Europe in the 1920s. But its characters reach out beyond time and place to become eternal symbols of the human condition, and especially of the struggle of disenfranchised people—poor, mentally disabled, and war-torn—within societies that turn their back on them.

LISTENING GUIDE 46 4:44

Berg: *Wozzeck*, Act III, scene 4

DATE: 1922

GENRE: Opera, in three acts

BASIS: Expressionist play by Georg Büchner

CHARACTERS: Wozzeck, a soldier (baritone)   Captain (tenor)
Marie, his common-law wife (soprano)   Doctor (bass)
Marie and Wozzeck's son (treble)   Drum Major (tenor)

Act III, scene 4: By the pond

What to Listen For

Melody	Use of *Sprechstimme* (speechlike melody); disjunct line.
Rhythm/ meter	Movement alternates between metric and free-flowing.
Harmony	Both tonal and atonal language; dissonant and chromatic.
Expression	Intensely emotional vocal line, supported by dissonance and surging dynamics.
Timbre	Eerie mood created by a celeste and unusual instrument combinations; colorful orchestral effects.

Wozzeck

0:00 Das Messer? Wo ist das Messer? Ich
hab's dagelassen. Näher, noch näher.
Mir graut's . . . da regt sich was.
Still! Alles still und tot.

The knife? Where is the knife?
I left it there. Around here somewhere.
I'm terrified . . . something's moving.
Silence. Everything silent and dead.

(shouting)

Mörder! Mörder!

Murderer! Murderer!

(whispering again)

Ha! Da ruft's. Nein, ich selbst.

Ah! Someone called. No, it was only me.

(Still looking, he staggers a few steps farther and stumbles against the corpse.)

0:54	Marie! Marie! Was hast du für eine rote Schnur um den Hals? Hast dir das rote Halsband verdient, wie die Ohrringlein, mit deiner Sünde! Was hängen dir die schwarzen Haare so wild? Mörder! Mörder! Sie werden nach mir suchen. Das Messer verrät mich!	Marie! Marie! What's that red cord around your neck? Was the red necklace payment for your sins, like the earrings? Why's your dark hair so wild about you? Murderer! Murderer! They will come and look for me. The knife will betray me!

(looks for it in a frenzy)

Da, da ist's.   Here! Here it is!

(at the pond)

So! Da hinunter!   There! Sink to the bottom!

(throws knife into the pond)

Es taucht ins dunkle Wasser wie ein Stein.   It plunges into the dark water like a stone.

(The moon appears, blood-red, from behind the clouds. Wozzeck looks up.)

2:03	Aber der Mond verrät mich, der Mond ist blutig. Will denn die ganze Welt es ausplaudern! Das Messer, es liegt zu weit vorn, sie finden's beim Baden oder wenn sie nach Muscheln tauchen.	But the moon will betray me: the moon is bloodstained. Is the whole world going to incriminate me? The knife is too near the edge: they'll find it when they're swimming or diving for snails.

(wades into the pond)

Ich find's nicht. Aber ich muss mich waschen. Ich bin blutig. Da ein Fleck— und noch einer. Weh! Weh! Ich wasche mich mit Blut— das Wasser ist Blut . . . Blut . . .

I can't find it. But I must wash myself. There's blood on me. There's a spot here— and another. Oh, God! I am washing myself in blood— the water is blood . . . blood . . .

(drowns)

Wozzeck's last words before drowning, accompanied by very soft ascending chromatic scales in strings:

(The Doctor appears, followed by the Captain.)

Captain

3:12	Halt!	Wait!

Doctor (stops)

Hören Sie? Dort!   Can you hear? There!

Captain (stops as well)

Jesus! Das war ein Ton!   Jesus! What a ghastly sound!

Doctor (pointing to the pond)

Ja, dort!   Yes, there!

Captain

Es ist das Wasser im Teich. Das Wasser ruft. Es ist schon lange niemand ertrunken.

It's the water in the pond. The water is calling. It's been a long time since

Continued on next page

Kommen Sie, Doktor! Es ist nicht gut zu hören.

anyone drowned Come away, Doctor. It's not good for us to be hearing it.

(tries to drag the Doctor away)

Doctor (resisting and continuing to listen)

3:50   Das stöhnt, als stürbe ein Mensch. Da ertrinkt Jemand!

There's a groan, as though someone were dying. Somebody's drowning!

Captain

Unheimlich! Der Mond rot, und die Nebel grau. Hören Sie? . . . Jetzt wieder das Ächzen.

It's eerie! The moon is red, and the mist is gray. Can you hear? . . . That moaning again.

Doctor

Stiller, . . . jetzt ganz still.

It's getting quieter . . . now it's stopped altogether.

Captain

Kommen Sie! Kommen Sie schnell!

Come! Come quickly!

(He rushes off, pulling the Doctor along with him.)

CRITICAL THINKING

1. What are the essential principles of twelve-tone composition?

2. How does Berg's Expressionism in *Wozzeck* relate to early Romantic ideals?

YOUR TURN TO EXPLORE

Find examples of musical works designed to bring attention to social problems or to protest against established political situations—protest songs against war or oppression, music associated with "pride" movements, and the like. If there are words, how does the music reinforce the meaning and impact of the words? What musical style and specific elements of melody, harmony, and instrumentation have the composer and/or performers chosen, and how do those musical elements represent "opposition"? What can you find out about the effect that those works have had on the political struggle or social debate with which they are associated?

Chapter 56

American Intersections: Jazz and Blues Traditions

"All riddles are blues,
And all blues are sad,
And I'm only mentioning
Some blues I've had."
    —Maya Angelou (b. 1928)

KEY POINTS

- The roots of **jazz** lie in African traditions, Western popular and art music, and African American ceremonial and work songs.
- **Blues,** a genre based on three-line stanzas set to a repeating harmonic pattern, was an essential factor in the rise of jazz.
- Louis Armstrong (trumpet player, singer) was associated with **New Orleans–style jazz,** characterized by a small ensemble improvising simultaneously.

- Armstrong's groundbreaking improvisatory style was a huge influence on jazz musicians, including singer Billie Holiday.
- The 1930s saw the advent of the **swing** (or **big-band**) **era** and the brilliantly composed jazz of Duke Ellington.
- By the late 1940s, big-band jazz gave way to smaller group styles, including bebop, cool jazz, and West Coast jazz; Latin American music also influenced later jazz styles.

S ome call jazz the "American classical music," and there's no question that the tradition has been associated with the United States for more than a century. Primary antecedents of jazz were West African musical traditions brought to this continent by slaves and developed (sometimes in secret) to both maintain continuity with a lost homeland and provide a creative distraction from hard labor. But jazz was also heavily influenced by Euro-American vernacular traditions, partly through the tradition of minstrelsy (see Chapter 37), and music from the Americas. Jazz bands played for the popular dances (such as ragtime) that swept the country from the 1890s into the 1940s. As the century wore on, many musicians attempted fruitful "cross-pollinations" between jazz and blues, another tradition rooted in black culture, as well as between jazz and Euro-American cultivated music (as we will see in the case of George Gershwin). Jazz has since taken many forms, and it remains one of the most vibrant and powerful musical traditions of our day, evolving along with the multifaceted culture of the United States.

In His Own Words

❝ It don't mean a thing if it ain't got that swing."
    —Duke Ellington

Painter **Romare Bearden** (1911–1988) captures the spirit of jazz performance in his colorful collage *Empress of the Blues* (1974).

Roots of Jazz and Blues

Eighteenth-century slaves from Africa's west coast, often called the Ivory or Gold Coast, brought to America such singing styles as call and response and distinctive vocal inflections. In the next century, black music also embraced dancing and the singing of **work songs** (communal songs that synchronized the rhythm of work), **ring shouts** (religious rituals that involved moving counterclockwise in a circle while praying, singing, and clapping hands), and **spirituals** (see Chapter 50). The art of storytelling through music and praise singing (glorifying deities or royalty) were other traditions retained by slaves that contributed to the rich African American repertories.

In the years after the Civil War, a new style of music arose in the South, especially in the Mississippi Delta: country, or rural, blues, performed by a male singer and, by the turn of the century, accompanied by a steel-string guitar. This music voiced the difficulties of everyday life. A blues text typically consists of a three-line stanza whose first two lines are identical. The vocal lines featured melodic **Blue notes** "pitch bending," or **blue notes**, sung over standard harmonic progressions (**chord changes**)—usually twelve (or occasionally sixteen) bars in length. Among the greatest blues singers were Charlie Patton (c. 1891–1934), Bessie Smith (1894 –1937), and, more recently, B.B. King ("King of the Blues," b. 1925). Blues style derives from the work songs of Southern blacks, but may also owe some elements to the folk songs of poor Euro-Americans in the Southern Appalachians—one example of the complexity of identifying purely African American musical traditions.

New Orleans Jazz

The sheet-music cover for the popular fox trot *La jazzbandette* (1921), published in Paris.

Blues was an essential factor in the development of the **New Orleans jazz** tradition. This city, which had long facilitated interaction across races and cultures, was where jazz gained momentum through the fusion of ragtime (see Chapter 51) and blues with other traditional styles—spirituals, work songs, and ring shouts, but also Caribbean and Euro-American styles. There, in Congo Square, slaves met in the pre–Civil War era to dance to the accompaniment of drums, gourds, mouth harps, and banjos. Their music featured a strong underlying pulse with syncopations and polyrhythm. Melodies incorporated African-derived techniques such as rhythmic interjections, vocal glides, and percussive sounds made with the tongue and throat, and were often set in a musical scale with the lowered third, fifth, or seventh of a major scale (blue notes).

New Orleans ensembles depended on the players' improvisation to create a polyphonic texture. One of the greats of New Orleans jazz was trumpet player and singer Louis "Satchmo" Armstrong (1901–1971), a brilliant improviser who transformed jazz into a solo art that presented improvised fantasias on chord changes. Armstrong's instrumental-like approach to singing (**scat-singing**), his distinctive inflections, and his improvisatory style were highly influential to jazz vocalists, including Billie Holiday, one of the leading singers in jazz history.

Billie Holiday (1915–1959)

Known as Lady Day, Holiday was born in Philadelphia and grew up in Baltimore. In 1928, with barely any formal education, she moved to New York, where she probably worked as a prostitute. Around 1930, Holiday began singing at clubs in Brooklyn and Harlem, and was discovered three years later by a talent scout who arranged for her to record with the white clarinetist Benny Goodman. This first break earned her $35.

By 1935, Holiday was recording with some of the best jazz musicians of her day. As her popularity increased, she was featured with several prominent big bands—making her one of the first black singers to break the color barrier and sing in public with a white orchestra. She recorded her most famous song in 1939—*Strange Fruit*, about a Southern lynching. With its horrible images of blacks dangling from trees, the song resonated with blacks and whites alike and became a powerful social commentary on black identity and equality.

By the 1940s, Holiday's life had deteriorated, the result of alcohol, drug abuse, and ill-chosen relationships with abusive men. She began using opium and heroin, and was jailed on drug charges in 1947. Her health—and her voice—suffered because of her addictions, although she still made a number of memorable recordings. She died of cirrhosis of the liver in 1959, at the age of forty-four.

SELECTED RECORDINGS: *God Bless the Child* and *Billie's Blues*, both on the album *Lady Day: The Best of Billie Holiday; Fine & Mellow* and *Strange Fruit*, on the album *Strange Fruit*.

The Jazz Singer Billie Holiday

Holiday had a unique talent that was immediately recognized by other musicians. "You never heard singing so slow, so lazy, with such a drawl," one bandleader reminisced. Although she had never received formal vocal training, she had a remarkable sense of pitch and a flawless delivery—a style she learned from listening to her two idols, Bessie Smith and Louis Armstrong. We will hear a song that Holiday wrote and recorded in 1936, *Billie's Blues* (LG 47), and performed regularly throughout her career. It's a twelve-bar blues, with a short introduction and six choruses—a **chorus** is a single statement of a melodic-harmonic pattern, like a twelve-bar blues or thirty-two-bar popular song—some of which are instrumental. The first verse (chorus 2) is a typical three-line strophe, but as the work progresses, the form becomes freer. In the vocal choruses, Holiday demonstrates her masterful rhythmic flexibility and talent for jazz embellishments (scoops and dips on notes). In this performance, we hear Artie Shaw's creative clarinet improvisations and Bunny Berigan's earthy, "gutbucket" trumpet playing (displaying an unrestrained, raspy quality of tone).

Holiday's song exemplifies the intersection between jazz and blues, and also the continuing connection between jazz and dance, since the regular musical phrases and repeating structure are perfectly suited to the popular dances of the time. Most jazz of the first half of the 1900s was performed in dance clubs, and patrons would be as likely to dance to Holiday's song as they would to listen.

Jazz chorus

Billie Holiday, with jazz trumpeter Louis Armstrong in the 1947 film *New Orleans*.

Duke Ellington and the Swing Era

"Somehow I suspect that if Shakespeare were alive today, he might be a jazz fan himself."

In the 1930s and 40s, early jazz gave way to the **swing,** or **big-band, era.** Bands needed arranged and composed music—that is, written down, rather than improvised—and one musician who played a major role in its development was

LISTENING GUIDE 47

Holiday: *Billie's Blues*

DATE: Recorded 1936

GENRE: 12-bar blues

What to Listen For

Melody	Syncopated melodies with pitch inflections; free improvisations.	**Form**	12-bar blues (introduction and six choruses; choruses 2, 3, 6 are vocal).
Rhythm/ meter	Slow tempo, 4/4 meter; steady rhythmic accompaniment under more complex, flexible solo lines.	**Expression**	Laid-back feeling, different moods in the solos.
Harmony	Repeated harmonic progressions for each chorus (I–IV–I–V–I).	**Performing forces**	Holiday, vocal, with trumpet, clarinet, piano, guitar, string bass, and drums.
Texture	Polyphonic, with countermelodies against a solo voice or instrument.	**Text**	Chorus 2 is a typical blues text; the others are more free.

0:00   **Introduction** (4 bars)—bass and piano.

0:07   **Chorus 1**—ensemble (12 bars).

0:32   **Chorus 2**—vocal (12 bars):   Lord, I love my man . . .
                                           [repeated text line]
                                           But when he mistreats me . . .

Opening of first vocal chorus, showing syncopated line, with upward slide at the end:

0:56   **Chorus 3**—vocal (12 bars):   My man wouldn' gimme . . .
                                           [new text without repeated lines]

1:21   **Chorus 4**—solo clarinet improvisation (12 bars).

1:45   **Chorus 5**—solo trumpet improvisation (12 bars).

2:11   **Chorus 6**—vocal (12 bars):   Some men like me . . .
                                           [new text without repeated lines]

Edward Kennedy "Duke" Ellington, whose group first went on the road in 1932 and remained popular until his death. His unique big-band style of jazz won over a wide audience, both black and white, who danced away their cares in clubs and hotel ballrooms across the country.

Billy Strayhorn   In 1939, Ellington began a collaboration with Billy Strayhorn (1915–1967), a classically trained pianist who served as an arranger and composer for the band; together they achieved an unparalleled success with their suites, tone poems, ballets, and even sacred music. Ellington and Strayhorn collaborated for many years, each man's work so complementary to the other that, in many cases, their individual efforts are difficult to determine. One of the few works solidly credited to Strayhorn, however, is *Take the A Train* (first recorded in 1941; LG 48), and it epitomizes the swing style. (The A train refers to one of the subway lines that run through Manhattan to Harlem.)

Take the A Train

Ellington's orchestral palette was much richer than that of the New Orleans band. It included two trumpets, one cornet, three trombones, four saxophones (some of the players doubling on clarinet), two string basses, guitar, drums, vibraphone, and piano. This piece is a thirty-two-bar song form, with four phrases (**A-A-B-A**) of eight measures each; each **A-A-B-A** iteration makes a chorus. The introduction features Ellington at piano, with a syncopated chromatic motive; this is followed by three choruses. In the first chorus, the saxophones present the memorable tune, answered by muted trumpets and trombones in call and response. The second chorus stars band member Ray Nance on muted trumpet, with an underlying conversation in the reeds. Nance's masterful improvisation, complete with bent notes, **shakes** (shaking the lips to fluctuate between pitches), and glissandos, has been imitated by trumpet players everywhere. An energetic four-measure interlude that feels like triple meter suddenly intervenes, followed by the third chorus—another trumpet solo (this one open, or unmuted). The coda is a big-band signature closing: it repeats the opening eight bars of the piece twice, each time more softly.

Duke Ellington, performing with a band at the 1966 Grammy Awards.

Like many jazz tunes, *Take the A Train* was built on the chord changes of an earlier song, but it is enhanced with playful tunes, complex harmonies, and rich orchestration. Its lush, composed-out style is quite different from the more sparse and apparently spontaneous approach we hear in Holiday's song, but both demonstrate the combination of pre-planned roadmap and in-the-moment elaboration that defines jazz as a tradition.

Edward Kennedy ("Duke") Ellington (1899–1974)

Ellington was born in Washington, D.C., and began to study piano at age seven. By the 1920s, he was playing in New York jazz clubs—including Harlem's Cotton Club—with his group The Washingtonians. He soon reached a leading position in the jazz world with his renowned orchestra, which toured America and Europe in the 1930s and 40s.

Ellington was also a highly talented pianist, but he rarely played extended solos with his group; rather, he was a facilitator and accompanist who shared rhythmic and melodic ideas with the entire ensemble. Largely a self-taught musician, Ellington learned how to orchestrate for his ensemble through experimentation, trying new effects with different timbres and voicings. Indeed, some consider the entire jazz orchestra to be his instrument.

His recordings feature mostly his compositions and arrangements, along with those by collaborator Billy Strayhorn. A concern for structure resulted in works with complex forms not usually associated with jazz. Among his most famous compositions are *Black and Tan Fantasy* (1927), *Mood Indigo* (1930), *Sophisticated Lady* (1933), *Ko-Ko* (1940), and *Black, Brown and Beige* (1943); his most famous recording is *Take the A Train*. He also scored music for film, including Otto Preminger's *Anatomy of a Murder* (in which he also acted, 1959). Today Ellington is remembered as a composer who brought the jazz art to new heights; as an arranger who served as a teacher and model to several generations of musicians; and as a major artistic figure in the Harlem Renaissance (see Chapter 57).

SELECTED RECORDINGS: *Best of the Duke Ellington Centennial Edition* (1999, available for download), which includes *Black and Tan Fantasy, East Saint Louis Toodle-O, Take the A Train,* and *Sophisticated Lady.*

Bebop, Cool, Latin Jazz

Dizzy Gillespie playing his custom-made trumpet, with raised bell.

By the end of the 1940s, musicians were rebelling against big-band jazz and developing new styles. **Bebop** (also known as **bop**) was an invented word mimicking the two-note trademark phrase of this new style of fast tempos and complex harmonies. Trumpeter Dizzy Gillespie, saxophonist Charlie Parker, and pianist Thelonious Monk were among the leaders of the bebop movement in the 1940s. Over the next two decades, the term "bebop" came to include a number of sub-styles such as cool jazz, West Coast jazz, hard bop, and soul jazz. Trumpeter Miles Davis was the principal exponent of **cool jazz**, a laid-back style characterized by dense harmonies, lowered levels of volume, moderate tempos, and a new lyricism. **West Coast jazz** was a small-group, cool-jazz style featuring mixed timbres (one instrument for each color, often without piano) and contrapuntal improvisations. Among the important West Coast ensembles that sprang up in the 1950s were the Dave Brubeck Quartet (with Paul Desmond on saxophone) and the Gerry Mulligan Quartet (with Chet Baker on trumpet). Since the 1970s, jazz has branched out in more directions than this short overview can name.

Latin American music has always been highly influential in the development of jazz, chiefly its dance rhythms and percussion instruments (for example, conga drum, bongos, and cowbells). In the 1930s and 40s, bandleaders such as Xavier Cugat brought Latin dance music—especially the rumba—into the mainstream. Duke Ellington's band recorded two hit Latin numbers: *Caravan* (1937, featuring Puerto Rican trombonist Juan Tizol) and *Conga Brava* (1940). Latin elements were integral to the bebop style of the late 1940s, and the next decades saw a strong Brazilian, as well as Cuban, influence on jazz. We will see that these influences were significant in musical theater as well, particularly in the shows of Leonard Bernstein (Chapter 63).

In the last century, many strands of jazz have developed, and there are controversies about whether some of them can legitimately be labeled jazz. There is no question, however, that jazz is among the most vibrant and original North American contributions to the modern musical landscape.

CRITICAL THINKING

1. What were some of the traditions that led to the development of jazz?

2. How does New Orleans jazz differ from big-band jazz? How do later jazz styles differ from big-band jazz?

YOUR TURN TO EXPLORE

Find an example of a jazz performance by one of the renowned singers of the twentieth century (like Ella Fitzgerald or Louis Armstrong) or a more recent jazz singer. How does the singer's approach to syncopation and blue notes and other elaborations compare with the one taken by Holiday in *Billie's Blues?* How do the instrumentalists interact with the singer? How do any extended instrumental solos compare with the ones on our recording? If you find a video recording, what is the venue for the performance (concert hall, dance club?), and how is the performer interacting with the audience (and what is the audience response)? How does this performance compare with those in other repertories we've been considering?

LISTENING GUIDE 48 2:54

Strayhorn: *Take the A Train*, by the Duke Ellington Orchestra

DATE: Recorded February 15, 1941

GENRE: Big-band jazz

What to Listen For

Melody	Disjunct, syncopated themes with call-and-response exchanges between instruments.
Rhythm/meter	Broad quadruple meter, at a moderate tempo; syncopated rhythms, short riffs (repeated phrases).
Harmony	Complex, advanced harmonies; chromatic; modulates to another key.
Form	32-bar song form (**A-A-B-A**) for each of three choruses, with introduction and coda.

Expression	Animated movement with special jazz effects (bent notes, shakes, glissandos).
Timbre	Big-band sound, with reed, brass, and percussion sections.
Performing forces	Jazz big band (trumpets, trombones, saxophones, piano, guitar, bass, drums); soloists: Duke Ellington (piano), Ray Nance (trumpet).

0:00 **Introduction**—four measures in piano (Ellington), with syncopated, chromatic motive.

Chorus 1 (A-A-B-A)

0:06 **A**—unison saxophones state the disjunct melody, in the key of C, with interjections from muted trumpets and trombones (eight bars), against a steady rhythm accompaniment:

0:17 **A**—repeated (eight bars).

0:28 **B**—contrasting episode in saxophones; syncopated melody with low brass and rhythm section.

0:39 **A**—saxophones restate main melody with a new rhythmic figure from the brass; rippling piano figures.

0:50 **Chorus 2 (A-A-B-A)**
Ray Nance on muted trumpet, accompanied by saxophones and rhythm section;
trumpet solo in second phrase, with bent pitches:

1:35 **Interlude**—four measures, sustained accents as though in triple rather than quadruple meter.

1:41 **Chorus 3 (A-A-B-A)**
A—saxophones play a version of main theme (four measures); followed by unmuted trumpet solo (Nance).

1:52 **A**—trumpet solo continues, with sustained chords in saxophones.

2:04 **B**—trumpet solo with countermelodies in saxophones and trombones; closes with fanfare without rhythm accompaniment; punctuated by cymbal crash.

2:14 **A**—original theme played by saxophones in new key (E-flat); brass interjects, alternating with muted and open notes.

2:26 **Coda**—two repetitions of **A** (eight bars each), first *mezzo piano*, then softer, with a final closing saxophone riff.

Chapter 57

Modern America: Still and Musical Modernism in the United States

"What are the qualities which must be inherent in the person who aspires to write music? First, and most important, is the ability to induce the flow of inspiration, that indefinable element which transforms lifeless intervals into throbbing, vital, and heartwarming music."

—William Grant Still

KEY POINTS

- American composers of the early twentieth century sought to define a unique tradition of American modernism.
- The **Harlem Renaissance** was a cultural movement in the 1920s and 30s that highlighted African American contributions to the country's cultural heritage.
- African American composer William Grant Still broke numerous racial barriers in the art-music tradition. His Suite for Violin and Piano looks to three black visual artists for inspiration.

How can or should music reflect the identity of a composer? Romanticism introduced the ideal of autobiographical expression by the creative individual, and nationalism added the question of group identity, leaving artists to struggle with striking a balance between those two mandates. The 1920s and 30s were a time when African American artists in many media banded together to identify creative outlets for blacks that would both pay tribute to their heritage and recognize individual excellence regardless of race or ethnicity. One of the most prominent and successful musicians who joined this effort, William Grant Still, is now regarded as a pioneer both in the search for a "modern American sound" and in opening a wider range of musical opportunities for African Americans.

The Harlem Renaissance

In the early 1900s, economic opportunity brought increasing numbers of African Americans to New York City, and specifically to the northern part of Manhattan called Harlem. By the beginning of the economic boom of the 1920s, a contemporary poet referred to Harlem proudly as "not merely a Negro colony or

Interface

Identity and the Arts in the Harlem Renaissance

Sculptor **Richmond Barthé** (1901–1989) focused on depicting African Americans at work in the fields and as ceremonial participants. *African Dancer* (1933).

You may know that the French term "renaissance" describes a rebirth or renewal of something from the past. The cultural movement known as the Harlem Renaissance, sometimes referred to as "the New Negro movement," was a literary, artistic, and sociological movement that highlighted African American intellectual life in the 1920s and 30s. It was a renewal of sorts in that African Americans looked to their historical and ethnic roots; centered in the predominantly black area of New York City known as Harlem, the movement was sparked in part by the craze for jazz that was sweeping the country. Among the artists associated with it was sculptor Richmond Barthé, whose sympathetic portrayals of blacks—field workers, men of recognition, victims of racial violence, and African dancers—emphasized their individuality and physicality (see image).

The most important literary figure was Langston Hughes, a highly innovative African American poet whose works, depicting the struggles of working-class blacks, radiated with black pride. A frequent visitor to the Harlem jazz clubs, Hughes wrote verse that imitated the rhythms and flow of jazz, thus creating a new kind of jazz poetry. His first collection, *The Weary Blues* (1926), included his most famous poem, "The Negro Speaks of Rivers," dedicated to W. E. B. DuBois, founder of the National Association for the Advancement of Colored People (NAACP), comparing the spirit of his people to the rivers of the world. Another literary figure central to this movement was Zora Neale Hurston, whose creative efforts explored what it meant to be black and female in a male-dominated society. Her essay "How It Feels to Be Colored Me" reveals a woman strengthened by the hardships she has endured. Yet Hurston rejected "the sobbing school of Negrohood" that promoted self-pride. She claimed to transcend her race: "I belong to no race nor time. I am the eternal feminine with its string of beads." Her famous essay colorfully describes moments when she feels racial differences, such as when she attends a jazz club with a white friend who does not experience the sense of the "jungle beyond" that she feels from the music.

Most jazz musicians, including Duke Ellington and Billie Holiday, gained early recognition performing in Harlem jazz clubs, including the famous Apollo Theater and the Cotton Club. A prolific composer as well, Ellington considered his works to be "tone parallels" to the lives of blacks. Like Hurston, African American musicians uniformly rejected the stereotyped images of blacks that had been popular in minstrel shows, and they worked to break down the long-standing prejudice against black musicians and artists. Among these crusaders was composer William Grant Still, whose creative efforts merge art and traditional musical genres: he held the view that "the Negro artist is important in American society because he demonstrates that achievement is possible in our democracy."

African American poet **Langston Hughes** (1902–1967) was an important Harlem Renaissance figure.

community, [but] a city within a city, the greatest Negro city in the world." Building on a growing sense of a new black cultural identity, a book of essays called *The New Negro* was published in 1925, edited by philosopher Alain Locke, a Harvard graduate who became the first African American Rhodes scholar. Locke and the other authors of *The New Negro* encouraged their fellow black artists to look to Africa for inspiration on how to shape their American future, and the essays spoke about racial equality and pride in black cultural heritage. The ideas from the essays in *The New Negro* are credited with sparking the so-called **Harlem Renaissance** (see Interface on p. 329).

Still's Suite for Violin and Piano

In choosing the genre of the suite, which had long been part of the European dance and programmatic tradition, Still was able to draw on an established genre (one that reflected the modernist neo-Classical trend) and also to evoke images that he felt exemplified the artistic efforts of black America in a progressive way. He based each movement on a different artwork by African American artists. The spirited first movement was inspired by the sculpture *African Dancer* by Richmond Barthé (p. 329), a noted Harlem Renaissance artist. The second movement evokes the expressive mood of *Mother and Child* by Sargent Johnson, one of the first Californian black artists to achieve fame. And the rhythmically charged closing movement draws on the impish humor of *Gamin* by Augusta Savage, the most prominent African American woman artist of her day. Her sculpture (p. 332) captures the confident image of a street-smart kid in Harlem ("gamin" suggests a street urchin).

The movements of the suite all employ modal harmonies and melodies featuring lowered thirds and sevenths, typical of the blues. Throughout his career,

William Grant Still (1895–1978)

Still grew up in Little Rock, Arkansas. His parents, both educators, encouraged his early music studies on violin. He left college to work as a professional musician in Memphis and then New York, earning a reputation as an arranger for radio and musical theater, while continuing his classical music studies with French-born composer Edgard Varèse. Still deliberately moved away from the avant-garde, however, to find his original voice in the music of his black cultural heritage.

His first symphony, the *Afro-American*, was premiered in 1931 by the Rochester Philharmonic Orchestra: the first symphony by an African American composer to be performed by a major American orchestra. The symphony brought him numerous commissions from major orchestras, including the New York Philharmonic. In 1934, he won a Guggenheim Fellowship and moved to Los Angeles, where he wrote film and television scores. An opera, *Trou-*

bled Island, was produced by New York's City Opera in 1949, marking another first for an African American composer. Still was recognized with many honorary degrees during his last years, and wrote theme music for such popular TV series as *Gunsmoke* and *Perry Mason*. He remained in Los Angeles until his death in 1978. In his music, Still looked to writers and artists of the Harlem Renaissance for inspiration, including the renowned poet Langston Hughes, whose libretto he set for *Troubled Island*, on the struggles of the Haitian people.

MAJOR WORKS: Orchestral music, including four symphonies (No. 1, *Afro-American* Symphony, 1930) • Orchestral suites • Film scores • Stage works, including four ballets (*La Guiablesse*, 1927; *Sahdji*, 1930) • Eight operas, including *Troubled Island* (1937–49) • Chamber music, including Suite for Violin and Piano (1943) • Vocal music, including *Songs of Separation* (1949) and spiritual arrangements • Piano music • Choral music.

LISTENING GUIDE 49

 2:07

Still: Suite for Violin and Piano, III

DATE: 1943

GENRE: Suite for violin and piano

MOVEMENTS: I. Majestically and vigorously (based on Richmond's Barthé's *African Dancer*)
II. Slowly and expressively (based on Sargent Johnson's *Mother and Child*)
III. Rhythmically and humorously (based on Augusta Savage's *Gamin*)

What to Listen For

Melody	Bluesy, short, syncopated ideas, with flatted third and seventh scale tones; ideas exchanged between violin and piano.
Rhythm/meter	Quick 2/4 meter; rhythmic and highly syncopated, with chords played on offbeats.
Harmony	Modal, with blues chords; stride bass; use of ostinatos.
Texture	Mostly homophonic.
Form	Sectional form, with four- and eight-measure ideas; opening returns frequently.
Timbre	Violin trills, glissandos, and double stops.
Expression	Playful and humorous; evokes image of cocky street kid depicted by sculpture.

0:00   Four-measure introduction in piano, with ostinato bass and offbeat chords.

0:05   Violin enters with syncopated line, four-measure idea in fragments, with stride piano accompaniment:

0:26   Rising line to a new syncopated violin idea, accompanied by a syncopated, more active piano part.

0:35   Low-range, repeated-note idea in violin, against moving piano line.

0:45   Piano takes over low-range melody, with violin playing double stops.

0:56   Opening motive returns, varied, in violin; piano is more syncopated.

1:06   Humorous repeated-note exchange between piano and violin.

1:17   Opening motive returns in violin, includes glissando and more active piano accompaniment.

1:27   Repeated-note idea is developed in violin.

1:38   Recapitulation of opening, including brief piano introduction.

1:59   Coda, with rising violin line, then triumphant double-stop chords and glissando to the last chord.

Still favored blues as source material for his music, explaining that "they, unlike spirituals, do not exhibit the influence of Caucasian music." The last movement of the suite (LG 49) zips along with a flashy and syncopated violin line accompanied by an insistent bass that resembles the jazz piano style known as **stride**. Sometimes   **Stride piano**

Gamin, a sculpture by **Augusta Savage** (1892–1962). Savage played a significant role in the Harlem Renaissance.

called "Harlem stride piano," this style evolved from ragtime and features a regular four-beat pulse with left-hand chords on the second and fourth beats. The movement unfolds in sections, sometimes engaging the piano and violin in a call-and-response exchange, but it keeps returning to the opening exuberant idea, varied with ornamentation and dazzling glissandos in the violin.

Not all members of the concert music establishment embraced blues and jazz as compositional resources. And while the Harlem Renaissance was a powerful cultural moment for the growth of black cultural prestige, its supporters were more interested in fostering musical traditions that they understood as more thoroughly African American—blues, jazz, and spirituals—than in encouraging the development of modernist art music. Today there are still too few African Americans involved in shaping the idea of an American art-music tradition; though as the twenty-first century progresses, a lively interaction of musical styles and repertories is helping to bring a wider range of voices into that dialogue.

CRITICAL THINKING

1. How does the music of William Grant Still fit the ideals of the Harlem Renaissance?
2. Why would the proponents of the Harlem Renaissance have been more interested in jazz and blues than in modernist art music?

YOUR TURN TO EXPLORE

Seek out works by African American art-music composers of the twentieth and twenty-first centuries. (Three examples are Will Marion Cook, Undine Smith Moore, and Olly Wilson; how might you go about finding more?) How have these individuals chosen to incorporate their heritage into their compositions? Are their approaches to racial/ethnic heritage different from Still's, or from the way European or Euro-American composers have used their own heritage as inspiration?

Chapter 58

Folk Opera? George Gershwin and Jazz as "Art"

"Jazz has contributed an enduring value to America in the sense that it has expressed ourselves."

—George Gershwin

KEY POINTS

- George Gershwin built international fame through his Tin Pan Alley songs, musical theater productions, and "jazzy" compositional and performance style.

- Seeking to unite elements of jazz and the European concert tradition, Gershwin composed several hybrid works, including the "folk opera" *Porgy and Bess*, widely considered his masterpiece.

Several musicians of the mid-1900s, both African American and Euro-American, attempted to bring the jazz tradition forward not only as a booming commercial enterprise but also as a distinctive kind of cultivated music. Their compositions were not only creatively outstanding but also financially successful and influential on other musicians; yet they were criticized both for "whitewashing" an African American tradition and for introducing commercial music into the lofty halls of art. In this, they joined a long line of artists who have been accused of "selling out" the purity of their musical heritage, a line that continues to this day. We will consider the case of one of the most beloved composers of the early twentieth century, George Gershwin, whose all-too-short life was dedicated to the proposition that jazz could be as expressive an art form as any European-derived tradition.

In His Own Words

"A song without music is a lot like H_2 without the O."

—Ira Gershwin

"Cultivated Jazz"

Gershwin was one of the most gifted American composers of the twentieth century. He first broke into the music business as a "song plugger" who demonstrated and sold sheet music on New York's Tin Pan Alley. From the early years of that industry, songwriters had capitalized on the rising fashion for ragtime and then jazz styles. Many of the most popular songs printed, performed onstage, and eventually recorded and broadcast made some reference to ragtime or jazz, though the songs themselves followed structural and melodic conventions similar to the Anglo-American parlor ballads of Foster and other nineteenth-century songwriters.

George Gershwin (1898–1937)

Gershwin grew up in Manhattan, where he worked for a Tin Pan Alley publisher, playing and singing new releases for customers. "This is American music," he told one of his teachers. "This is the kind of music I want to write." He had his first big hit in 1920, with the song *Swanee,* recorded by Al Jolson.

During the 1920s, Gershwin won international acclaim with *Rhapsody in Blue,* premiered in 1924 by the Paul Whiteman Orchestra. This was followed by his Concerto in F (1925) and the tone poem *An American in Paris* (1928). He also had a string of hit musicals, beginning with *Lady, Be Good* (1924), his first collaboration with his brother Ira, who wrote many of his song lyrics. Gershwin wrote enduring film scores, including *Shall We Dance* (1937, featuring the song *They Can't Take That Away from Me*), starring Fred Astaire and Ginger Rogers. His folk opera *Porgy and Bess* is perhaps his masterpiece. He died of a brain tumor in 1937, at not quite thirty-nine.

In his music, Gershwin achieves an appealing rhythmic vitality through the use of syncopation, blue notes, and an "oom-pah" accompaniment typical of jazz piano style. His harmonic language extends from diatonic to very chromatic, with sudden shifts in tonality. His melodies range from declamatory to highly lyrical, and his forms are typical blues and song structures. No master has achieved this union of styles—popular and classical, vernacular and art—more successfully than Gershwin.

MAJOR WORKS: Orchestral works, including *Rhapsody in Blue* (1924, for piano and jazz orchestra), Concerto in F (1925), and *An American in Paris* (1928) • Piano music • More than 30 stage works, including *Strike Up the Band* (1927), *Girl Crazy* (1930), *Of Thee I Sing* (1931), and *Porgy and Bess* (1935) • Songs for films, including *Shall We Dance* (1937) • Other songs (such as *Swanee, 'S Wonderful, Embraceable You, The Man I Love*).

Gershwin, a talented pianist, became familiar with techniques developed by African American jazz performers, and gained renown for his ability to play songs in a particularly effective and jazzy way—and this afforded opportunities to him as a white musician that black musicians could not enjoy in the 1920s. As Gershwin began writing his own Broadway / Tin Pan Alley songs, he incorporated syncopations and harmonic variations that closely resembled improvised jazz. As a result, his songs became among the most commercially and artistically successful in the entire Tin Pan Alley repertory (many are still used as "standards" by jazz performers today).

Not content with his commercial success, and also inspired by the goals of the Harlem Renaissance, Gershwin joined those who sought to expand jazz into the cultivated sphere. A number of his instrumental works were both groundbreaking and much loved from their premiere—most notably *Rhapsody in Blue* (for piano and orchestra), which Gershwin performed at a concert entitled "An Experiment in Modern Music," held on Lincoln's birthday, February 12, in 1924. The concert, conducted by Paul Whiteman, was billed as a radical new approach to a uniquely American art music, one that included jazz. It was attended by prominent critics and composers, and Gershwin's *Rhapsody* was immediately hailed as the highlight, though debates continue about whether the work can properly be understood as jazz.

Rhapsody in Blue

After the success of his *Rhapsody,* Gershwin traveled to Paris to study more deeply in the European art tradition, but was turned away by renowned teacher Nadia Boulanger (see Chapter 54), who was concerned that classical training would have a negative effect on his jazz-influenced style. During his brief stay in France, Gershwin wrote *An American in Paris,* another of his most successful orchestral-jazz works; it was later (1951) choreographed in a film featuring dance stars Gene Kelly and Leslie Caron.

Porgy and Bess

Gershwin's most ambitious attempt at bringing jazz into the art tradition is *Porgy and Bess*. The composer called it a folk opera, purposefully juxtaposing two concepts that had previously been understood as incompatible. The story is set in a South Carolina tenement, and puts an African American spin on long-standing operatic topics of love and betrayal. *Porgy and Bess* falls somewhere between opera and musical theater, featuring continuous music and recurring themes similar to Wagner's leitmotifs and a seriousness never before heard on the Broadway stage, but also a number of memorable and "excerptable" song-and-dance numbers. Gershwin insisted that the entire cast should consist of classically trained black singers—a controversial decision, but one that he felt would both provide opportunity for undervalued performers and ensure that the interpretation would be as authentic as possible.

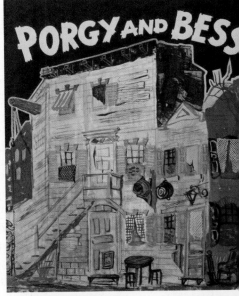

The famous opening aria, *Summertime* (LG 50), is a melancholy song that evokes an African American spiritual, with its relaxed tempo, swaying intervals, gentle syncopations, blue notes, and expressive microtonal dips in pitch. It unfolds in a straightforward strophic form, set in a poignant minor key that anticipates the tragedy to come. The song is reprised several times throughout the opera, most notably near the end, when Bess sings it before she leaves Porgy and heads to New York.

In *Porgy and Bess*, Gershwin realized his dream of transforming jazz into an art tradition. His success lit a beacon for composers like Leonard Bernstein (Chapter 63), who claimed that for later generations of composers, "jazz entered their bloodstream, became part of the air they breathed, so that it came out in their music. . . . [They] have written music that is American without even trying." On the other hand, some African Americans (including Duke Ellington, who later changed his mind) were suspicious of this Euro-American depiction of their culture (especially since the story features episodes of drugs and violence), fearing a continuation of racist stereotypes. Still, many black artists expressed high estimation for the opportunities the work provided, one going as far as calling Gershwin "the Abraham Lincoln of Negro Music." *Porgy and Bess* is not only a powerful artwork but in some ways a reflection of the complexity of race relations in the United States—as is Gershwin's iconic role as a white composer of jazz standards.

TOP: The cover to a souvenir program from *Porgy and Bess* showing the set for Catfish Row.

BOTTOM: The lullaby *Summertime* is heard in a scene from the 1959 movie version, starring Dorothy Dandridge as Bess and Sammy Davis Jr. as Sportin' Life.

CRITICAL THINKING

1. How did Gershwin contribute to different musical traditions of the early 1900s?
2. In what ways is *Porgy and Bess* like an opera? From what other genre(s) does it draw?

YOUR TURN TO EXPLORE

Find a recording of a Tin Pan Alley song by George Gershwin (*I Got Rhythm, 'S Wonderful, But Not for Me, The Man I Love,* or another) and compare it with the recording of *Billie's Blues*. What musical similiarities do you hear (in blue notes, syncopation, other melodic or rhythmic elements), and what differences? Do you think it's legitimate to think of Gershwin's compositions as jazz? Why or why not? Why might it matter whether this is jazz, and to whom?

LISTENING GUIDE 50

 2:26

Gershwin: *Summertime,* from *Porgy and Bess*

DATE: 1935

GENRE: Aria from folk opera

CHARACTERS:
Porgy, a crippled beggar (bass-baritone)   Clara, Jake's wife (soprano)
Bess, Crown's girl (soprano)   Jake, a fisherman (baritone)
Crown, a stevedore (baritone)   Sportin' Life, a dope peddler (baritone)

What to Listen For

Melody — Languid melody, plays on interval of a third; regular phrasing; high pitch on the last chord, then a downward slide.

Rhythm/ meter — Rhythmic subtleties and gentle syncopation.

Harmony — Minor key, with rich chromaticism.

Texture — Homophonic, with instrumental lines alternating with the voice.

Form — Strophic (two verses), with variations, brief introduction, interlude, and closing.

Expression — Vocal inflections (dips, slides, blue notes).

Performing forces — Soprano and orchestra; backup chorus on our recording.

Text — By librettist DuBose Heyward; lyrics by Heyward and Ira Gershwin.

0:00   Orchestral introduction.
Gently syncopated vocal line opens with the interval of a third:

0:21   Summertime an' the livin' is easy,
Fish are jumpin', an' the cotton is high.
Oh, yo' daddy's rich, an yo' mamma's good lookin',
So hush, little baby, don't you cry.

1:21   One of these mornin's you goin' to rise up singin';
Then you'll spread yo' wings an' you'll take to the sky
But till that mornin' there's a' nothin' can harm you
With Daddy and Mamma standin' by.

Chapter 59

Sounds American: Ives, Copland, and Musical Nationalism

"I no longer feel the need of seeking out conscious Americanism. Because we live here and work here, we can be certain that when our music is mature it will also be American in quality."

—Aaron Copland

KEY POINTS

- Several modernist composers in the United States attempted to craft a musical style that would reflect a truly "American" sound.

- Charles Ives drew on the music of his New England childhood—hymns, songs, marches—which he set using **polytonality** and **polyrhythms**.

- Aaron Copland used the early American song *Simple Gifts* in his famous ballet *Appalachian Spring*, commissioned by the great choreographer/dancer Martha Graham.

---

atriotism has been an essential part of national identity since democracies began to replace authoritarian states in the late 1700s. As a nation founded explicitly on ideals of democracy, the United States has rightly fostered pride in the principles that distinguish it from other countries. But as a nation of immigrants with diverse cultural heritages, part of a large continent that can equally legitimately claim the label "America," we have also struggled to define the shifting nature of American identity (understood as a quality that all U.S. citizens have in common). Music has always played a part in that definition, and some of the most compelling American sounds have emerged from attempts to integrate vernacular musical traditions with music that aims at a higher quality of the spirit.

Ives and New England Modernism

We have explored the vital roles that nonconcert traditions—especially parlor songs, brass band marches, and worship songs—played in North American musical life of the late

American Gothic, by **Grant Wood** (1891–1942), is an example of regionalism, celebrating rural life in the United States.

Charles Ives (1874–1954)

Ives was born in Danbury, Connecticut, the son of a U.S. Army bandleader in the Civil War. At thirteen he held a job as church organist, and at twenty he entered Yale, where he studied composition with Horatio Parker. Ives's talent for music was evident at Yale, yet he decided against a professional life in music, suspecting that society would not pay him for the kind of music he wanted to compose. He was right.

Ives entered the business world in 1899, and two decades later he was head of the largest insurance agency in the country. He composed at night, on weekends, and during vacations, concerned only to set down the sounds he heard in his head. As the conductors and performers he tried to interest in his compositions pronounced them unplayable, he hired a few musicians to play his works so he could hear them. When well-meaning friends suggested that he try to write music people would like, he could only respond, "I can't do it—I hear something else!"

Ives's double life as a business executive by day and composer by night finally took its toll. In 1918, when he was forty-four, he suffered a physical breakdown that left his heart damaged. Although he lived almost forty years longer, he produced very little music in those years.

When Ives recovered, he privately printed his Piano Sonata No. 2 (Concord)—and *Essays Before a Sonata*, a kind of elaborate program note that formulated his views on life and art. These were followed by the *114 Songs*. The three volumes, distributed free to libraries, music critics, and whoever else asked for them, gained Ives the support of other experimental composers who were also struggling to make their way in an indifferent music world. Beginning with a performance in 1939 of his *Concord* Sonata in New York City, Ives was finally "discovered" by the general public and proclaimed as the "grand old man" of American music. In 1947, his Third Symphony won a Pulitzer Prize. At age seventy-three, Ives found himself famous. He died in New York City at the age of seventy-nine.

The central position in Ives's orchestral music is held by the four symphonies. Among his other orchestral works are *Three Places in New England, The Unanswered Question,* and *A Symphony: New England Holidays* (a cycle of four symphonic poems). The Piano Sonata No. 2—"Concord, Mass., 1840–1860"—which occupied him from 1909 to 1915, reflects various aspects of New England culture. Ives was a master songwriter as well, penning over 100 songs, with familiar tunes—patriotic, religious, or popular—tinged with bittersweet harmonies.

MAJOR WORKS: Orchestral music, including four symphonies, *Three Places in New England* (1914), *The Unanswered Question* (1908), and *A Symphony: New England Holidays* (1913) • Chamber music, including string quartets and violin sonatas • Piano music, including sonatas (No. 2, *Concord*, 1915) • Choral music • Many songs.

In His Own Words

> Beauty in music is too often confused with something that lets the ear lie back in an easy chair. . . . Analytical and impersonal tests will show that when a new or unfamiliar work is accepted as beautiful on its first hearing, its fundamental quality is one that tends to put the mind to sleep."
>
> —*Charles Ives*

1800s. One New England musician born into this rich environment was Charles Ives. Since his father was a Civil War bandmaster, Ives was thoroughly steeped in the vernacular heritage of his country. His compositional voice, however, followed very modernist tendencies, making him one of the more innovative, and misunderstood, composers of the early twentieth century.

Ives's tonal imagery was drawn from music of his childhood—hymns, patriotic songs, marches, parlor ballads, and fiddling songs. Growing up in a small Connecticut town, he was accustomed to hearing the pungent clash of dissonance when two bands in a parade, each playing a different tune in a different key, came close together. He was familiar with the effect of quarter tones (an interval half the size of a half step) when fiddlers at country dances veered a bit off pitch. And as an adult, he remembered the sound of the wheezy harmonium (a reed organ) accompanying church hymns, both sung and played out of tune. All these dissonances, Ives realized, were not exceptions but rather the norm of American musical life. They naturally led him to such concepts as polytonality, polyharmony, and polyrhythm.

LISTENING GUIDE 51   🎧 4:20

Ives: *Country Band March*

DATE: c. 1903

GENRE: March, arranged for wind band

What to Listen For

Melody	Forceful march theme, over which many well-known tunes occur; main march returns throughout.
Rhythm/ meter	Mostly duple, but with syncopation and triplets that disguise the meter.
Harmony	Harshly dissonant, polytonal.
Form	Sectional (**A-B-A-B′-A′**).

Expression	Humorous; the realism of amateur bands; nostalgic American tunes.
Performing forces	Large wind ensemble, including woodwinds (piccolo, flutes, oboes, clarinets, bassoons, saxophones), brass (cornets, trumpets, French horns, trombones, baritones, tubas), and percussion (drums, cymbals, bells, triangle, xylophone).

A section

0:00   Short introduction, with a chromatic descending line in the full ensemble, syncopated and shifting meters; a repeated-note transition.

0:11   Main march tune in a regular duple meter, with on-beat and offbeat accents:

0:27   Fleeting reference to *London Bridge* in trumpets and oboe.

0:33   Slower passage in woodwinds and saxophones, followed by repeated-note transition.

0:45   *Arkansas Traveler* tune heard in trumpets and cornets, slightly offset rhythmically:

0:55   *Semper fidelis* march by Sousa (trio), as cornet solo:

    Battle Cry of Freedom heard simultaneously (followed by four-note hint of *Yankee Doodle*):

B section

1:05   Lyrical oboe solo, followed by *Marching Through Georgia* in flute and piccolos:

1:28   Clear statement of *London Bridge*:

1:44   *My Old Kentucky Home*, in slow triplets:

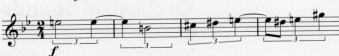

Continued on next page

A section repeated
1:51   Introduction.
2:03   March tune.
2:38   *Arkansas Traveler*, then *Semper fidelis* / *Battle Cry of Freedom*; hint of *Yankee Doodle*.

B′ section, with a new closing section
2:58   Oboe solo leads to new material.
3:05   Rhythmic, syncopated idea.

A′ section, with variations
3:19   March tune in a new key, with harsh "wrong note" dissonance in brass.
3:29   *British Grenadiers* march:

3:42   Brief transition, leads to return of march theme.

Country Band March

Ives took bold steps in his *Country Band March* (LG 51), an early work written around 1903, just after he graduated from Yale. Here he set his compositional path for the future by using well-known musical quotations—from children's songs, patriotic tunes, hymns, and even a march by John Philip Sousa (see Chapter 51). The main march theme we hear is most likely by Ives himself, but he weaves into it a highly complex mesh of other tunes, creating all manner of chaos. We hear polytonality and polyrhythms as tunes collide and overlap. The songs cited are nostalgic ones for Ives, from his Protestant New England upbringing, but we also catch the playful side of the composer—who simulates the realism of an amateur band's performance skills by having musicians play out of tune, make bad entrances, miscount, and hit wrong notes. You will recognize some of the tunes: *London Bridge* and *Yankee Doodle*; *My Old Kentucky Home* (by Stephen Foster); and the Sousa march *Semper fidelis*. The work is not actually in a march form, but is rather a five-part sectional form that brings back the opening march theme in various guises.

Yankee Doodle

Ives is now considered especially visionary and progressive for having embraced vernacular (including commercial) music in his work. But most of his contemporaries in the art-music sphere considered commercial music inadequate as a resource for artistic development. Rural folk traditions were thought to be more closely linked to the American spirit, and the composer who most successfully transformed these traditions into a national sound was Aaron Copland.

Copland and the American Orchestral Soundscape

Copland is one of America's greatest twentieth-century composers. Few have been able to capture the spirit of this country so successfully—his well-crafted and classically proportioned works have an immediate appeal. His ballet suites are

Aaron Copland (1900–1990)

Copland was born in Brooklyn, New York, and during his early twenties studied in Paris with the famous teacher Nadia Boulanger (p. 314). After his return from Paris, he wrote works in jazz and neo-Classical styles, but at the same time realized that a new public for contemporary music was being created by the radio and phonograph and film scores: "It made no sense to ignore them and to continue writing as if they did not exist."

The 1930s and 40s saw the creation of works that established Copland's popularity. *El Salón México* (1936) is an orchestral piece based on Mexican melodies and rhythms. His three ballets—*Billy the Kid, Rodeo,* and *Appalachian Spring*—continue to delight international audiences. Among his film scores are two on novels by John Steinbeck and William Wyler's *The Heiress,* which brought him an Academy Award. He wrote two important works during wartime: *A Lincoln Portrait,* for speaker and chorus, with

texts drawn from Lincoln's speeches, and the Third Symphony. Despite his evident nationalism, Copland was investigated in the 1950s as a supporter of the Communist Party, and in 1953 he was removed from the inaugural ceremonies for President Eisenhower as a result of his leftist politics. In the 1960s, Copland demonstrated that he could also handle twelve-tone techniques when he wrote his powerful *Connotations for Orchestra.*

MAJOR WORKS: Orchestral music, including three symphonies, a piano concerto, *El Salón México* (1936), *A Lincoln Portrait* (1942), *Fanfare for the Common Man* (1942) • Ballets, including *Billy the Kid* (1938), *Rodeo* (1942), and *Appalachian Spring* (1944) • Operas, including *The Tender Land* (1954) • Film scores, including *Of Mice and Men* (1939), *Our Town* (1940), *The Red Pony* (1948), and *The Heiress* (1948) • Piano music • Chamber music • Choral music • Songs.

 Simple Gifts

quintessentially American in their portrayal of rural life (*Appalachian Spring*) and the Far West (*Rodeo* and *Billy the Kid*).

Copland came self-consciously to an American sound: born in New York of Jewish immigrant parents, he trained in Europe with proponents of early twentieth-century modernism, then returned to the United States during the Great Depression of the 1930s and espoused the ideal that art should "serve the American people" during times of economic and social struggle. His new "American modernist" style was designed to have wide appeal and be "useful" in a variety of contexts (radio, film, theater). In keeping with this ideal, Copland wrote incidental music for plays and scores for significant films that spoke to the American condition during the Depression, such as *Of Mice and Men* (1939) and *Our Town* (1940).

Martha Graham dancing in the ballet *Appalachian Spring.*

While Copland admired jazz and incorporated it in his early works, his American style was rooted primarily in Appalachian and other Anglo-American folk melodies (as well as Mexican folk melodies). He also cited Stravinsky's startling approach to rhythm and orchestration as a basic influence. Like Stravinsky's early ballets, some of Copland's most successful compositions involved a collaboration with prominent dancers and choreographers, who were also seeking to establish a genuinely American tradition of modern dance.

Appalachian Spring

Among Copland's ballets, *Appalachian Spring* is perhaps his best known, written in collaboration with the celebrated

American Folk Traditions

You have undoubtedly heard the familiar song *Yankee Doodle*, but are probably not aware of its long and involved history. Although the tune is now thought to be American in origin, it was first printed in Great Britain, and British soldiers sang it during the Revolutionary War in derision of American troops (a "doodle" is a simpleton). The Brits even marched into the Battle of Lexington in 1775 with their fife-and-drum corps playing *Yankee Doodle*, only to be defeated by the militiamen. Soon, the Yankees took over the song to taunt the British with their own lyrics.

Yankee Doodle seems, however, to predate the war, first surfacing orally in the 1740s. There are many variations on the tune and different verses that changed with historical events. Most of the lyrics are humorous: the line in which Yankee Doodle "stuck a feather in his cap and called it macaroni" probably refers to a foppish young man, or "dandy," noted for his outlandish fashions, common in the 1770s. (You can find the origin of this word in the *Oxford English Dictionary*; today, we might call him a metrosexual.) The best-known lyrics during the late eighteenth and early nineteenth centuries were the "Visit to Camp" stanzas, giving a country bumpkin's view of what goes on in a military camp (see lyrics below). It was not unusual in this era to poke fun at the motley nature of the American militia, often dressed in homespun clothing or deerskins and carrying all manner of weapons.

Yankee Doodle came to be associated with New England (it remains the state song of Connecticut), and the word "Yankee" with northerners. It was a favorite song of the Northern soldiers during the Civil War (1861–65), although there were also Confederate lyrics. Soldiers often carried small song books with them, which might include such favorites as *Pop Goes the Weasel, Auld Lang Syne, Annie Laurie, Yankee Doodle,* and Stephen Foster's *My Old Kentucky Home*. And both sides had their brass bands with them at the front. One report claims that before the Battle of Murfreesboro, with the rival armies camped near each other, the two bands alternated songs, the Northern group playing *Yankee Doodle* and the Southern band playing a patriotic rebel tune (possibly *Dixie*); after several exchanges, they joined together to play *Home, Sweet Home*. The next morning, a bloody battle ensued, leaving thousands dead.

After the war, *Yankee Doodle,* though considered trite by some, remained a symbol of American pride and nationalism. Union General Ulysses S. Grant, who became the eighteenth president, allegedly once said, "I know only two tunes: one of them is *Yankee Doodle*, and the other isn't." Many people learned the song from medleys of patriotic tunes. With the growing popularity of the piano, there was great demand for

A Revolutionary War band marches into battle to the tune of *Yankee Doodle,* played on fife and drums. Painting by **Archibald M. Willard (1836–1918).**

The Americus Brass Band, a Civil War replica band, has been featured in numerous movies and television programs, providing source music and appearing onscreen as well.

this kind of musical potpourri; a Civil War–era favorite by Louis Gottschalk (see Chapter 40), called *L'Union* (1862), paraphrased *Yankee Doodle* along with *The Star-Spangled Banner* and *Hail, Columbia*.

The tune also remained popular with brass bands after the Civil War. Composer Charles Ives, the son of a Union Army bandleader, grew up listening to his father's band in Danbury, Connecticut, and likely heard these brass-band versions. As we have seen, numerous patriotic tunes and old hymns, including *Yankee Doodle*, are quoted in his instrumental compositions. Like generations before him, Ives valued these traditional songs as part of his American consciousness. In one of the composer's own songs, the text reflects his nostalgia for his musical heritage: "I think there must be a place in the soul all made of tunes of long ago. . . . They sing in my soul of the things our Fathers loved."

We will hear the song in two performances: the first is the U.S. Army Old Guard Fife and Drum Corps (Revolutionary War–era version); the second is the Americus Brass Band (1866 version for Civil War brass band, with lyrics).

Yankee Doodle 🎧

What to listen for:

First recording
- Fifes in unison, then two-part harmony.
- Strong rhythmic patterns in rope-tension drums.

Second recording
- Brass-band instrumental version of verse/chorus.
- Unison singing of three traditional verses (right).

Text

1. Father and I went down to camp,
   Along with Captain Goodwin;
   There we saw the men and boys
   As thick as hasty pudding.

   Chorus:
   Yankee Doodle keep it up,
   Yankee Doodle dandy;
   Mind the music and the step,
   And with the girls be handy.

2. And there was General Washington,
   Upon a snow white charger,
   He looked as big as all outdoors,
   Some thought he was much larger.

   Chorus: Yankee Doodle . . .

3. And there I see'd a little keg,
   All bound around with leather,
   They beat it with two little sticks,
   To call the men together.

   Chorus: Yankee Doodle . . .

Members of the Protestant Shaker sect in a dance. Lithograph by **Nathaniel Currier** (1813–1888).

choreographer Martha Graham (1894–1991), who also danced the lead. Copland noted that when he wrote the music, he took into account Graham's unique choreographic style: "She's unquestionably very American: there's something prim and restrained, simple yet strong, about her, which one tends to think of as American." The ballet portrays "a pioneer celebration in spring around a newly built farmhouse in the Pennsylvania hills in the early part of the nineteenth century. The bride-to-be and the young farmer-husband enact the emotions, joyful and apprehensive, their new partnership invites." The ballet, which premiered in 1944 in Washington, D.C., was given new life in Copland's popular 1945 orchestral suite, set in seven sections.

Simple Gifts

The opening section of the suite introduces the characters in the ballet with a serene, ascending motive that evokes the first hint of daybreak over the vast horizon (LG 52). In the most famous part of the work, we hear the well-known early American song *Simple Gifts* ("'Tis the gift to be simple"), a tune associated with the Shaker religious sect, known for rituals that included spinning around and dancing. This simple, folklike tune is designed to provide a quintessential American sound; Copland sets it in a clear-cut theme and variations, with a colorful orchestration tinged with gentle dissonance. The flowing tune takes on several guises, shaded by changing timbres, keys, and tempos.

Copland's music was quickly embraced as a truly American orchestral sound. It continues to be widely heard at events (or even in commercials!) that aim to emphasize national pride, as well as incorporated (and imitated) in movie scenes that illustrate the grandeur of the West. The America that his music envisions is a rural one, connected to the land and its traditions; it is also mostly an Anglo America, since the Appalachian tunes he employs have their roots in English folk music. Copland's goal was to create an inclusive soundscape for the United States; and his music, like Sousa's, is still a powerful presence in the cultural life of the nation.

CRITICAL THINKING

1. What elements make the music of Ives so experimental and modernist? What older traditions does he draw on?

2. What qualities in Copland's music have been understood as particularly American? What other kinds of American sounds and identities are not part of his music, and why might this matter?

YOUR TURN TO EXPLORE

Identify two musical works (songs or any other genre) that you consider to be self-consciously American: not only the text, but the music as well. What elements of each work project its American identity? What kind of America does each work suggest—what kinds of individuals or attitudes or backgrounds does it include, and what kinds does it leave out? What parallels and contradictions can you find between the two different versions of "musical American-ness"?

LISTENING GUIDE 52

Copland: *Appalachian Spring*, excerpts

DATE: 1945

GENRE: Ballet suite in seven sections

What to Listen For

Section 1

Melody	Rising motive quietly unfolds, outlining a triad.
Rhythm/ meter	Very slow, tranquil; changing meter is imperceptible.
Harmony	Overlapping of chords (polychordal) produces a gentle dissonance.
Texture	Individual instruments are featured.
Expression	Introduces the characters; evokes a broad landscape at daybreak.

Section 7

Melody	Theme with four phrases (**a-a′-b-a″**); later variations use only parts of the tune.
Rhythm/ meter	Flowing duple meter, then tune in augmentation (slower).
Harmony	Moves between various keys.
Form	Theme and five variations, on a traditional Shaker song.
Timbre	Each variation changes tone colors; individual instruments are featured.
Expression	Calm and flowing; majestic closing.

Section I: Very slowly

2:42

0:00   Low strings on a sustained pitch; solo clarinet, then flute with a rising motive:

0:16   Violin and flutes alternate the rising figure; harp punctuates; other instruments enter, creating dissonance.

0:52   Violin in high range, with more movement; the rising figure is heard in various instruments.

1:25   Solos in various woodwinds and trumpet.

1:54   Solo oboe, then bassoon; descending motive.

2:31   Clarinet with closing triad, over sustained harmony.

Section 7: Theme (*Simple Gifts*) and five variations

3:03

Theme

0:00   Solo clarinet with tune in four phrases (**a-a′-b-a″**), accompanied by harp (playing harmonics) and flute:

Continued on next page

0:28   Brief transition.

Variation 1

0:34   Oboe and bassoon present the tune; grows dissonant, with *sforzando* on third phrase played by all woodwinds.

0:56   Short, rhythmic transition.

Variation 2

0:59   Tune in violas in augmentation (steady rhythmic accompaniment continues); violins (in octaves) enter in second phrase, in canon with the violas (dissonance on the last note is marked with arrow):

1:35   Transition.

Variation 3

1:45   Trumpets and trombones, with swirling strings; loud brass section; then quieter in woodwinds.

Variation 4

2:10   Woodwinds with a slower version of the tune.

Variation 5

2:30   Full orchestra with majestic, homophonic statement; somewhat dissonant; *fortissimo,* then dies out.

Chapter 60

Also American: Revueltas and Mexican Musical Modernism

"From an early age I learned to love [the music of] Bach and Beethoven. . . . I can tolerate some of the classics and even some of my own works, but I prefer the music of my people that is heard in the provinces."

—Silvestre Revueltas

KEY POINTS

- The music of Mexican composer Silvestre Revueltas is expressively nationalistic, with folkloric rhythms and melodies set in a dissonant framework.

- Revueltas's orchestral work *Homage to Federico García Lorca* honors this Spanish writer, executed in 1936 during the Spanish Civil War.

- Revueltas and other American modernists were influenced by the **mariachi ensemble**, a vernacular Mexican tradition.

Latin American musical repertories have long been important to Anglo-American audiences and musicians, especially in the areas close to the southern U.S. border: the culture and history of the United States and Mexico have been intertwined since well before the two countries came into their modern borders. Like their counterparts in the United States, other American musicians have long worked to reconcile their connection to European traditions with crafting a uniquely American sound. And like Copland and Still, they have realized their nationalist approach largely through reference to vernacular traditions.

Musical Traditions of Mexico

The modern musical traditions of Mexico are rich and varied, embracing the indigenous Amerindian cultures as well as Hispanic culture. Mexico's ties to Spain began in 1519, when Spanish soldiers colonized the territory, and continued until 1821, when the country achieved its independence.

By the late nineteenth century, the goal of creating a nationally distinctive style lured musicians and artists alike to Amerindian and mestizo cultures. (Mestizos are people of mixed Spanish and Amerindian ancestry; today they are the majority in Latin American countries.) The Mexican Revolution of 1910 further changed the artistic life of the country, conjuring strong feelings of patriotism. In the post-revolutionary period, sometimes called the "Aztec Renaissance,"

Carlos Chávez

composers tried to evoke or suggest, rather than recreate, the character of this native music for a modern age. The works of Carlos Chávez (1899–1978), including seven symphonies and two Aztec ballets, are rich in Amerindian flavor. Chávez and Silvestre Revueltas were two of the most decisive influences on Mexican musical culture.

Silvestre Revueltas: "Mestizo Realist"

Revueltas is considered a representative of "mestizo realism," a nationalist modernist movement that drew on elements of Mexico's traditional culture. His music is highly flavored with folk elements, especially mariachi band traditions.

Homage to Federico García Lorca

In His Own Words

❝ There is in me a particular interpretation of nature. Everything is rhythm. . . . Everybody understands or feels it. . . . My rhythms are dynamic, sensual, vital; I think in images that meet in melodic lines, always moving dynamically."

—*Silvestre Revueltas*

Revueltas responded musically to one of the early tragedies of the Spanish Civil War: the execution in 1936 of the poet Federico García Lorca by a Fascist firing squad. The openly homosexual García Lorca had made anti-Fascist statements and had provoked the Spanish dictator Francisco Franco with his politically controversial plays. Revueltas's moving composition *Homenaje a Federico García Lorca* premiered in Madrid in 1937 during a Fascist bombing of the city. The review in the *Heraldo de Madrid* accorded the music a "revolutionary status."

With this *Homage*, Revueltas blends the traditions of Mexican-vernacular and European-modernist music. The work is written for a chamber ensemble, heavily balanced toward winds (the string section numbers only two violins and one bass) and includes piano. The first movement, *Baile* (*Dance*), features bitingly dissonant tunes over a frenzied ostinato. The second movement, *Duelo* (*Sorrow*), also makes

Silvestre Revueltas (1899–1940)

Born in the mountain state of Durango, Revueltas was a child prodigy on violin and later studied composition at the Conservatorio Nacional de Música in Mexico City. He continued his studies in the United States until 1929, when he was called home by his friend Carlos Chávez to serve as assistant conductor of the Orquesta Sinfónica de Mexico.

With the onset of the Spanish Civil War in the late 1930s, the intensely political Revueltas went to Spain, where he participated in the cultural activities of the Loyalist government. Upon his return home in late 1937, he produced a series of masterworks, including his best-known orchestral piece, *Sensemayá* (1938), inspired by the verses of Afro-Cuban poet Nicolás Guillén (another anti-Fascist), which imitate onomatopoetically the sounds and rhythm of Afro-Cuban music and speak against colonial imperialism. In 1939, Revueltas wrote

the film score for *La noche de los mayas* (*The Night of the Mayas*), which projects a modern primitivism not unlike Stravinsky's *Rite of Spring*. The composer died at age forty of alcohol-induced pneumonia.

Revueltas's love for Mexican provincial music is immediately obvious, voiced through lyrical, direct melodies that are driven by such rhythmic techniques as polyrhythms and ostinatos. Despite a modern harmonic language rich in dissonance and chromaticism, Revueltas's music is deeply emotional and Romantic in its inspiration. His skillful handling of the orchestral palette evokes the picturesque traditional orchestras of Mexico.

MAJOR WORKS: Orchestral music, including *Sensemayá* (1938) • Seven film scores, including *La noche de los mayas* (*The Night of the Mayas*, 1939) • Chamber music, including *Homenaje a Federico García Lorca* (*Homage to Federico García Lorca*, 1937) • Two ballets • Songs, including seven *Canciones* (1938, on texts by García Lorca).

LISTENING GUIDE 53

Revueltas: *Homage to Federico García Lorca*, III, *Son*

DATE: 1937

GENRE: Chamber orchestra suite

MOVEMENTS: I. *Baile (Dance)*   II. *Duelo (Sorrow)*   **III. *Son***

What to Listen For

Melody	Three themes, syncopated; colorful and folklike ideas.	**Form**	Sectional (**A-B-A-C-A-C-B-A-C**-coda).
Rhythm/ meter	Strongly rhythmic and syncopated; shifting meters; percussive accents.	**Expression**	Evokes a mariachi ensemble.
		Timbre	Unusual instrumentation, focused on winds; trumpets and violins in pairs; piano prominent.
Harmony	Dissonant, with mariachi-like idea played in thirds (**C section**).	**Performing forces**	Chamber orchestra (piccolo, E-flat clarinet, two trumpets, trombone, tuba, piano, percussion, two violins, and bass).
Texture	Polyphonic and complex.		

0:00   **A section**—rhythmic and highly syncopated, in shifting meter; seven-note
melodic turns in piano and violins, with glissandos in violins (violin 1 is shown):

0:15   **B section**—piano and string ostinato introduces chromatic solo trumpet melody (accompanied by trombone):

0:29   **A section**—rhythmic punctuations, as at beginning.

0:35   **C section**—Mexican dance theme *(son)* in alternating meter (6/8 and 2/4);
muted trumpets playing in parallel thirds:

Trumpets are answered by violins and woodwinds.

0:58   Development of rhythmic figure from **C section**, in low brass (tuba), answered by woodwinds,
then trumpets.

1:08   Brief return of **A section**.

1:21   Return of Mexican tune (**C section**), in full orchestra.

1:37   Rhythmic figure from **C** developed.

1:55   **B section**—return of slow trumpet melody, with trombone countermelody.

2:05   **A section**—return of opening section.

2:16   **C section**—mariachi melody in violins, trumpet offbeats. Grows dissonant.

2:34   **Coda**—cluster chord (adjacent notes played together) in piano, then fast, loud, frenetic.

Musical Traditions in Mexico

As Mexico began nurturing its own artistic traditions, drawn not only from the country's Hispanic culture but also from its rich indigenous Amerindian cultures, composer Carlos Chávez took a leadership role in this new musical movement. Paralleling the example of artists like Diego Rivera and José Orozco, who had already begun a nationalist school of painting, Chávez instigated a government-sponsored program to develop a national voice in music. His efforts caught the attention of Aaron Copland, who accepted Chávez's invitation to visit Mexico City in 1932; there, he was immediately captivated by the country's traditional music, noting that "Mexico possesses a very strong folk art . . .

which provides the artist with rich source material." This cultural interaction resulted in Copland's delightful orchestral work *El Sálon México,* subtitled *A Popular Type Dance Hall in Mexico City* and including at least four Mexican folk songs. Chávez premiered his friend's work in 1937 with the Mexico City Orchestra to great success. While in Mexico, Copland also befriended composer Silvestre Revueltas, whose colorful orchestral poems, he claimed, conjured up "the bustling life of a typical Mexican fiesta." Copland noted that Revueltas's music was derived from the "everyday side of Mexican life," and that he composed "organically tunes which are almost indistinguishable from the original folk material itself."

One strong voice of the growing Mexican nationalism was the mariachi ensemble. This group originated in the mid-nineteenth century near Guadalajara, as a string orchestra with both bowed and plucked instruments: violins, guitars (including a large acoustic bass guitar known as the guitarrón), and vihuelas (a kind of folk guitar). By the 1930s, the group as heard by Copland had taken on a distinctly urban sound, adding trumpets and other instruments. The mariachi ensembles we hear today were standardized during the 1950s. Modern players often wear the costumes of the charros—Mexican cowboys with wide-brimmed sombreros—or other, more regional dress. The band includes a melody group, with violins

The Mariachi Regio Internacional (playing violins, trumpets, guitarrón, and guitar) in Plaza Garibaldi, Mexico City.

and trumpets, and a rhythm section of vihuelas, guitar, guitarrón, and occasionally harp. Their repertory is largely dances, many set in triple meter but with shifting meters and strong accents.

We can hear this folk style in *El Cihualteco*, a famous dance piece in the mariachi tradition. The dance type *son* stands at the heart of the mariachi repertory, and this one is associated with the Spanish flamenco-style dance known as *zapateado*, characterized by strongly syncopated rhythms against which dancers drive their boots into the floor. Our selection falls into the standard verse/chorus structure, with witty four-line verses alternating with the chorus ("Ay, sí, sí; ay, no, no"). The melodic lines are often played in thirds, making the sound consonant, and the shifting accents give a sense of restlessness and unpredictability to the dance.

Muralist **José Clemente Orozco** (1883–1949) captures the spirit of the revolutionary movement in *Zapatistas* (1931).

El Cihualteco (The Man from Cihuatlán) 🎧

What to listen for:

- Strongly syncopated rhythms.
- Verse/chorus, alternating with instrumental interludes.
- Trumpets and violins playing the melody in parallel thirds.

	Text	Translation
Verse 1 (sung twice)	Arriba de Cihuatlán le nombran "la água escondida" donde se van a bañar Cihualtecas de mi vida.	Above Cihuatlán they call it "hidden waters," where the dear Cihualtecan girls go to bathe.
Chorus	Ay, sí, sí; ay, no, no. Ay, sí, sí; ay, no, no. Ay, sí; ay, no. Ay, sí; ay, no. De veras sí, de veras no. Lo que te dije se te olvidó y al cabo sí, y al cabo no.	Ay, yes, yes; ay, no, no. Ay, yes, yes; ay, no, no. Ay, yes; ay, no. Ay, yes; ay, no. Surely yes; surely no. You forgot what I told you and finally yes, and finally no.
Verse 2 (sung twice)	Cihualteco de mi vida, dime quién te bautizó. ¿Quién te puse "Cihualteco" para que te cante yo?	Dear Cihualteco, tell me who baptized you. Who named you "El Cihualteco" so that I can sing to you?
Chorus repeated (text slightly changed).		

The murals of the Mexican painter **Diego Rivera** (1886–1957) glorify his native culture and people in an elegant social and historical narrative. *Flower Festival* (1925).

use of an ostinato—this time a rocking accompaniment in pianos and strings—against a soulful melody.

The title of the last movement, *Son* (LG 53), refers to a type of traditional Mexican song/dance based on a mixture of indigenous, African, and Spanish traditions. *Sones* (the plural) are characterized by shifting meter, moving between simple triple (3/4) and compound (6/8) meter. Revueltas's writing here is highly evocative of a mariachi ensemble, one of the most common vernacular groups that perform *sones*. The typical mariachi consists of several trumpets, violins, and guitars. While Revueltas maintains the distinctive mariachi sound of paired trumpets and violins, he enriches the highest and lowest registers with woodwinds, brass, and bass, and replaces the guitars with piano.

This carefree movement may seem like a strange homage to a slain poet. But the traditional Mexican view of life (and death) is to experience each day to the fullest. In Mexico, the Day of the Dead is celebrated joyfully: houses are decorated with colorful skulls made from sugar, and tables are adorned with bread shaped like bones.

CRITICAL THINKING

1. How did Revueltas merge vernacular and art-music traditions?
2. What elements are distinctive in mariachi music, and how did composers emulate these in their compositions?

YOUR TURN TO EXPLORE

Find examples of music associated with Mexico (for example, mariachi ensembles), and compare it with music associated with South America (for example, Brazilian samba, Argentinian tango, or Chilean Andean traditions). What are the similarities and differences (in instrumentation, vocal quality, the use of solo voices versus ensembles, how featured voices or instruments are "backed up" by other voices/instruments, characteristic rhythmic patterns)?

Chapter 61

Classic Rethinking: Bartók and the "Neo-Classical" Turn

"Folk songs bind the nation, bind all nations and all people with one spirit, one happiness, one paradise."

—Leos Janáček

KEY POINTS

- Twentieth-century composers used more authentic folk and traditional elements in their nationalistic music than nineteenth-century composers did.
- Hungarian composer Béla Bartók collected traditional songs and dances from his native land and incorporated elements from them into his compositions.
- Bartók's music displays new scales and rhythmic ideas and a modern, polytonal harmonic language, all set in Classical forms. In his programmatic *Concerto for Orchestra*, the whole ensemble is the "soloist."

Increased access to recording technology and mass distribution of music through the Internet now make musical traditions across the planet available to us at the click of a mouse. In the last few decades, a "world music" recording industry has exposed contemporary listeners to more and more musical variety—often combining different traditions and modifying them to suit what producers think will appeal to a particular audience. So while the music that we hear may feature more elements from disparate cultures, sometimes the combination of those elements masks the uniqueness of each regional style. It's worthwhile to consider how musical characteristics meaningful in a particular cultural context may change meaning when taken outside of that context. Sometimes new musical meanings can arise from the integration of traditional and folk music into experimental art music, as a number of modern composers have found.

In His Own Words

"Everything old is new again."

—Songwriter Peter Allen (1944–1992)

Neo-Classicism

One way of rejecting the nineteenth century was to return to even earlier eras. Instead of revering Beethoven and Wagner, as the Romantics had done, composers began to emulate the great musicians of the early eighteenth century—Bach, Handel, and Vivaldi—and the detached, objective style often associated with their music. **Neo-Classical** composers turned away from the symphonic poem and the Romantic attempt to bring music closer to poetry and painting. They preferred absolute to program music, and they focused attention on craftsmanship and balance, an affirmation of the Classical virtues of objectivity and control but also of twentieth-century ideals of progress through science. These composers revived a

Painter **Marc Chagall** (1887–1985) fled occupied France for America in 1941, and painted *The War* just two years later.

number of older forms such as toccata, fugue, concerto grosso, and suite, while retaining the traditional symphony, sonata, and concerto. They valued the formal above the expressive; accordingly, the new Classicism, like the old, strove for purity of line and proportion.

Modernist Nationalism

Twentieth-century nationalism differed from its nineteenth-century counterpart in one important respect: composers approached traditional music with a scientific spirit, prizing the ancient tunes precisely because they departed from the conventional mold. By this time, the phonograph had been invented. The new students of folklore (**ethnomusicologists**, who study music in its cultural and global context; see Interface) took recording equipment into the field to preserve the songs exactly as the village folk sang them. And composers who were inspired by these folk elements tried to retain the original flavor of the songs and dances in their works.

Many of the Romantic-era national schools (see Chapter 42) continued into the twentieth century. The modern English school, for example, is best represented by Benjamin Britten (1913–1976), whose operas include *Peter Grimes* (1945), about an English fishing village, and *Billy Budd* (1951), based on a Herman Melville story; we heard his *Young Person's Guide to the Orchestra* in Chapter 11. The Russian school continued with two important figures: Sergei Prokofiev (1891–1953), known for his symphonies, operas, and piano concertos, as well as the popular, narrated *Peter and the Wolf* and the film score to *Lieutenant Kijé;* and Dmitri Shostakovich (1906–1975), whose symphonies and operas established his international reputation during the era of the Soviet Union (1917–91).

We will consider here the music of a composer who strongly evoked the folk traditions of his homeland while also embracing the clarity and sparseness of neo-Classicism: Béla Bartók, a major proponent of Hungarian nationalism and an avid collector of folk songs.

Bartók and the Eastern European Tradition

Béla Bartók reconciled the traditional songs of his native Hungary with the main currents of European music, thus creating an entirely personal language. His search for authentic folk music led him to collect, with his colleague Zoltán Kodály (1882–1967), more than 2,000 songs and dances representing various Eastern European cultures. In the characteristic rhythmic and melodic features of these folk traditions, Bartók found distinctive raw material for his neo-Classical style.

Concerto for Orchestra

Bartók rejected the late Romantic orchestral sound in favor of a palette of colors all his own. His orchestration ranges from brilliant mixtures to threads of pure color that bring out the intertwining melody lines. In the summer of 1943, two years before his death, Bartók was commissioned to write the *Concerto for Orchestra*, a work in five movements that treats "the single orchestral instruments in a concertante or soloistic manner." Here, the virtuoso is the entire orchestra.

We will hear the fourth movement, *Interrupted Intermezzo,* which opens with a plaintive tune in the oboe and flute; its pentatonic structure evokes a Hungarian folk song. The nonsymmetrical rhythm, alternating between 2/4 and 5/8 meter,

In His Own Words

❝ To handle [a] folk tune is one of the most difficult tasks.... We must penetrate it, feel it, and bring out its sharp contours.❞

—*Béla Bartók*

Interface

Anthropology and Traditional Music

Throughout history, musicians have been intrigued by new and unfamiliar sounds; a case in point is the 1889 Paris Exposition (see Interface on p. 278), where many types of world music reached European ears for the first time. In the second half of the nineteenth century, however, scholars were developing a new, systematic field of study known as ethnomusicology, which focused on understanding non-Western and traditional music within its unique cultural context, much like the research of cultural anthropologists. As in anthropology, this kind of research necessitated observation, or field work: scholars traveled to sometimes distant locales and immersed themselves in the culture they chose to study, interacting with the people, recording songs and dances on primitive recording devices, and transcribing them when they returned home. This research opened up a broader worldview of music, and transcription became a means of preserving disappearing traditions.

There were limitations to this process: some subtleties of the music could not easily be written in Western notation—traits like unique vocal timbres, microtonal ornamentation, or rhythmic nuances. Still, some scholars persisted, like Frances Densmore, who devoted her entire life to the study of American Indian music. Densmore found early inspiration in the performances she heard at the 1904 St. Louis World Exposition, where she notated a song of the famous Apache chief Geronimo. This interest soon led her to study the music of various Indian nations. She helped preserve these cultural treasures in her many recordings, today held at the Library of Congress, and in a book entitled *The American Indians and Their Music* (1926), directed at lay readers.

Composers Béla Bartók and Zoltán Kodály are notable for their field work in the villages and countryside of Eastern Europe, where they attempted to identify national musics of diverse cultural groups—Slovak, Romanian, Bulgarian, Serbian, Croatian, Hungarian, Roma (or Gypsy), and Arab. They took on this project not as composers but as folklorists; the thousands of songs they collected reflect the very essence of these peoples—their social rituals (weddings, matchmaking, and dancing) and their religious ceremonies. Bartók in particular borrowed heavily in his own compositions from the melodies, rhythms, and poetic structures of this rich body of traditional music. He was partial to modal scales, especially those of Slovak and Romanian melodies, and he tried to imitate the free speech-rhythms of Hungarian music, which follow the natural inflections of the language. He was also fascinated by the diversity of dance rhythms, often employing asymmetrical additive meters built from groupings of 2, 3, or 4, as you will hear in his *Concerto for Orchestra*.

Like these musician-scholars, you too may have the opportunity to expand your understanding of other cultures, peoples, and behaviors through a class in cultural or social anthropology. And like Bartók and Kodály, you may find these new insights not across the world but close to home, where you can explore the diversity of racial, religious, national, and cultural identities that surround you.

Béla Bartók recording a folk song during his travels to Transylvania, in Eastern Europe.

gives the movement an unpredictable charm. Then a memorable broad theme is heard in the strings, but the mood is disrupted by a harsh clarinet melody borrowed from Shostakovich's Symphony No. 7, a musical portrayal of the Nazi invasion of Russia in 1942. Bartók made an autobiographical statement in this movement: "The artist declares his love for his native land in a serenade, which is suddenly interrupted in a crude and violent manner; he is seized by rough, booted men who even break his instrument." The two opening themes eventually return in a sentimental declaration of the composer's love for his homeland.

Béla Bartók (1881–1945)

A native Hungarian, Bartók studied at the Royal Academy in Budapest. His interest in the nationalist movement and folklore led him to realize that what passed for Hungarian in the eyes of the world was really music of the Roma, or Gypsies. With his fellow composer Zoltán Kodály, he toured the remote villages of the country, determined to collect the native songs before they died out forever.

Although Bartók became a leading figure in his country's musical life, he was troubled by the alliance between the Hungarian government and Nazi Germany on the eve of the Second World War. So much so that he moved to New York City in 1940. Suffering from leukemia in his final years, he received a series of commissions that spurred him to compose his last works, which rank among his finest. He died in New York at the age of sixty-four.

Bartók discovered that Eastern European traditional music was based on ancient modes, unfamiliar scales, and nonsymmetrical rhythms. His study of this music brought him to new concepts of melody, harmony, and rhythm—his harmony can be bitingly dissonant, and polytonality abounds in his work. He is also one of the great rhythmic innovators of modern times. Like Stravinsky, Bartók fre-

quently used pounding, stabbing rhythms, syncopation, changing meters, and repeated patterns (ostinatos). In his middle years, he turned from thinking harmonically to thinking linearly. The resulting complex texture is a masterly example of modern dissonant counterpoint. But, again like Stravinsky, he carefully disclaimed the role of revolutionary. Despite the newness of his musical language, he adhered to the logic and beauty of Classical form.

A virtuoso pianist himself, Bartók was a master of modern piano writing; his works typify the twentieth-century use of the piano as an instrument of percussion and rhythm. His six string quartets rank among the finest in the twentieth century. He is best known to the public for the major works of his last period: the *Music for Strings, Percussion, and Celesta,* regarded by many as his masterpiece, and the *Concerto for Orchestra,* a favorite with American audiences.

MAJOR WORKS: Orchestral music, including *Music for Strings, Percussion, and Celesta* (1936) and *Concerto for Orchestra* (1943) • Concertos (two for violin; three for piano) • Stage works, including an opera (*Bluebeard's Castle,* 1918) and two ballets • Chamber music, including six string quartets, sonatas, duos • Piano music, including *Allegro barbaro* (1911) and *Mikrokosmos* (six books, 1926–39) • Choral music • Folk-song arrangements for solo voice and for choir.

In gathering musical material from Eastern European folk music, Bartók was going "back to his roots" and seeking to express an authentic and distinctive Hungarian sensibility. Much of our encounters with folk music nowadays are with cultures that are different from our own. And musicians often borrow freely from distant cultures, integrating foreign instruments or musical ideas for their intriguing or exotic sound qualities, not necessarily to convey a distant tradition accurately.

Comparing styles 6: Early to later twentieth century

CRITICAL THINKING

1. What are some of the main characteristics of neo-Classicism?

2. How does Bartók evoke nationalistic ideas in his music?

YOUR TURN TO EXPLORE

Find recordings of Western musicians who have incorporated folk or world music instruments and/or melodies into their compositions and performances; compare them with recordings of those instruments or melodies by ensembles from the original culture. (If you have a non-Western heritage and can find examples from that culture, all the better.) What musical elements have the Western musicians adopted from the other culture, and which elements have they maintained from Western tradition? Why do you think they have made those choices? Which versions do you find more expressive or compelling? Does hearing the original version change your perception of the "blended" version? What are the advantages and disadvantages of such blending?

LISTENING GUIDE 54   🎧 4:20

Bartók: *Interrupted Intermezzo*, from *Concerto for Orchestra*

DATE: 1943

GENRE: Orchestral concerto

MOVEMENTS: 1. Introduction, Allegro non troppo/Allegro vivace; sonata-allegro form
2. *Game of Pairs*, Allegretto scherzando; **A-B-A′** form
3. Elegia, Andante non troppo; in three episodes
4. ***Interrupted Intermezzo,*** **Allegretto; rondo-like form**
5. Pesante/Presto; sonata-allegro form

Fourth movement: *Interrupted Intermezzo*

What to Listen For	
Melody — Three contrasting themes: folklike and pentatonic (**A**); broad and lyrical (**B**); harsh descending line in clarinet (**C**).	**Form** — Rondo-like structure (**A-B-A′-C-B′-A″**).
Rhythm/ meter — Shifting meters (2/4, 5/8, 3/4, 5/8) and irregular rhythms.	**Expression** — Nostalgic and sentimental; violent interruption at idea of Nazi invasion.
	Timbre — Solo woodwinds featured (oboe, clarinet, flute); darkly colored (violas).
Harmony — Polytonal and atonal harmonies; dissonant.	

0:00   Dramatic four-note introduction, unison in strings.

0:05   **A section**—plaintive, folklike tune, played by oboe in a changing meter with asymmetrical rhythms:

Theme heard in flute and clarinets; dialogue continues in woodwinds and French horn.

1:00   **B section**—sweeping lyrical melody in violas, in shifting meter:

Violins take up lyrical theme an octave higher, with countermelody in violas; marked "calmo" (calm).

1:44   **A′ section**—dissonant woodwinds lead to a varied statement of opening theme; more chromatic.

2:04   **C section**—tempo picks up; clarinet introduces a new theme (from a Shostakovich symphony):

2:17   Dissonant punctuations in brass and woodwinds.

2:31   Theme is parodied in violins.

2:44   Theme is introduced by tubas in its original form, then heard in inversion in strings:

2:57   **B′ section**—flowing **B section** theme returns in muted strings.

3:31   **A″ section**—woodwinds play fragments of opening theme; flute cadenza; leads into gentle closing.

THE POSTMODERN ERA

Events		Composers and Works

1920

1912–1992 John Cage (*Sonatas and Interludes*)

1918–1990 Leonard Bernstein (*West Side Story*)

b. 1929 George Crumb (*Caballito negro*)

1930

b. 1932 John Williams (*The Empire Strikes Back*)

b. 1936 Steve Reich (*Electric Counterpoint*)

b. 1938 John Corigliano (*Prelude: Mr. Tambourine Man*)

Second World War begins. **1939**

U.S. enters the war. **1941**

First nuclear weapon tested. **1945**

Communists under Mao **1949** assume power in China.

1940

b. 1941 Bob Dylan (*Mr. Tambourine Man*)

1944–2013 John Tavener (*A Hymn to the Mother of God*)

b. 1947 John Adams (*Dr. Atomic*)

First mass-produced stereo recordings released. **1958**

President John F. Kennedy assassinated. **1963**

Martin Luther King Jr. assassinated. **1968**

First home computers produced. **1974**

1950

b. 1953 Tod Machover (*Jeux Deux*)

b. 1957 Tan Dun (*Crouching Tiger, Hidden Dragon*)

b. 1962 Jennifer Higdon (*blue cathedral*)

1975

Vietnam War ends. **1975**

Soviet Union is dissolved. **1991**

Terrorists attack the **2001** World Trade Center and Pentagon.

iPhone introduced. **2003**

Barack Obama elected **2003** first African American president.

2000

Part 7

Postmodernism: The Twentieth Century and Beyond

Beyond Modernism?

*"From Schoenberg I learned that tradition
is a home we must love and forgo."*

—Lukas Foss

The Postmodern Turn

No one agrees on how to define **postmodernism**, and perhaps, as with modernism, it makes more sense to talk about several different departures from tradition, as mid-twentieth-century artists strove to find new means of expression beyond the principles of modernism. With the increasing social turmoil that followed the Second World War, the arts passed through a period of violent experimentation with new media, new materials, and new techniques. Artists introduced popular elements into their work; emphasized combinative techniques like collage, pastiche, or quotation; and revived traditional and classical elements. Their ideas continue to open broad possibilities for artistic expression: all art—highbrow or lowbrow—is considered to have equal potential for greatness.

Art, Film, Literature

In architecture, for example, the trend is away from sleek glass skyscrapers and toward a more neo-eclectic look. While modernist designer Mies van der Rohe believed that "less is more," Robert Venturi, a leader in the postmodern movement in architecture, countered with "less is a bore," suggesting that buildings were more interesting if they had some decorative elements. One stunning example is Frank Gehry's design for the Walt Disney Concert Hall in Los Angeles, the interpretation of which has ranged from a blossoming flower to a sailing ship (see illustration at left).

A trend away from objective painting led to **abstract expressionism** in the United States during the 1950s and 60s. In the canvases of painters such as Robert Motherwell (see illustration opposite) and Jackson Pollock, space, mass, and color were freed from the need to imitate objects in the real world. The urge toward abstraction was felt equally in sculpture, as is evident in the work of such artists as Henry Moore and Barbara Hepworth (opposite). At the same time, however, a new kind of realism appeared in the art of Jasper Johns, Robert Rauschenberg, and others, who owed some of their inspiration to the Dadaists of four decades earlier. Rauschenberg's aim, as he put it, was to work the "gap between life and art." This trend culminated in **pop art**, which drew its themes from modern

The Walt Disney Concert Hall in Los Angeles, designed by **Frank Gehry** (b. 1929) and completed in 2003, is considered a masterpiece of postmodern architecture.

LEFT: In *The Red and Black #51*, by **Robert Motherwell** (1915–1991), abstract blocks of color adorn a musical score.

RIGHT: *Three Standing Forms* (1964), by English sculptor **Barbara Hepworth** (1903–1975), is an abstraction representing the relationship between nature and humankind.

TOP: **Roy Lichtenstein** (1923–1997), *The Melody Haunts My Reverie* (1965).

BOTTOM: Artists **Christo** (b. 1935) and **Jeanne-Claude** (1935–2009) were allowed to wrap the Pont Neuf Bridge in Paris with sand-colored fabric (1985).

urban life: machines, advertisements, comic strips, movies, commercial photography, and familiar objects connected with everyday living. A similar aim motivated Andy Warhol's pop art paintings (p. 27) and the comic-strip art of Roy Lichtenstein (right).

Other subcategories of postmodern art include **new classicism**, **minimalism**, and performance and multimedia art. Artists have explored ecological and natural issues through environmental art, or **earthworks**, which advocates an approach akin to that of minimalism (spare and simple). Bulgarian artists Christo and his wife Jeanne-Claude (both used only their first names) exploited installation art as a new way to view old landscapes and to draw attention to form by concealing it. Their projects included wrapping Paris's Pont Neuf Bridge (1985; below) and the Reichstag government building in Berlin (1995) in fabric; one of their largest installations, called *The Gates* (2005), placed 7,503 gates with orange-colored fabric over the paths of New York's Central Park.

Postmodernist art embraces a pluralistic attitude toward gender, sexual orientation, and ethnicity. One creative artist whose expression is distinctively feminist is Judy Chicago, best known for *The Dinner Table* (1979), a triangular table with thirty-nine place settings that pay tribute to important women throughout history. African American artist Faith Ringgold creates "storybook" quilts, narrative paintings with quilted borders; some of these make up a *Jazz Series*, depicting black musicians in the context of life in the 1920s and 30s (see p. 362).

Artists have also featured recognizable images in their work, sometimes employing the technique of collage or quotation from a literary, musical, or visual source. Jasper Johns's work incorporated common symbols—flags, numbers, letters. He wrote that using the flag "took care of a great deal for me because I didn't have to design it," allowing him to focus on the makeup of the work as a whole. Such techniques enabled artists to take something familiar and make it unique—just as Gottschalk did in *Le Banjo* and Ives in *Country Band March*.

Postmodern ideas were easily extended to the medium of film, beginning with the "new wave" movement of the 1950s and 60s, epitomized in the films of Jean-Luc Godard (*Breathless,* 1960), Federico Fellini (*La Strada,* 1954; 8½, 1963), and Michelangelo Antonioni (*Blowup,* 1966; *The Passenger,* 1975). More recent directors who explore post-modernism include Jane Campion (*Two Friends,* 1986; a saga of two schoolgirls that is arranged in reverse order) and Quentin Tarantino, in the *Kill Bill* films (2003–04)—which pay homage to the Italian spaghetti western, Kung Fu movies, and other familiar stereotypes—and the genre-bending *Inglourious Basterds* (2009). Visual collage is used in Godfrey Reggio's non-narrative *Koyaanisqatsi* (1982) and *Powaqqatsi* (1988), both of which set soundtracks by minimalist composer Philip Glass (b. 1937).

Among the postmodern novelists you might know are E. L. Doctorow, whose *Ragtime* (1975), weaving historical characters into the story, has received many awards and was made into a popular musical (1996; revival, 2009), and Gabriel García Márquez, whose *One Hundred Years of Solitude* explores the fluidity of time. The works of Kurt Vonnegut, a classic novelist on many required reading lists (*Cat's Cradle,* 1963; *Slaughterhouse Five,* 1969), create a chaotic, fictional universe. Some recent authors have explored their identity through their writings: among them African American writers Maya Angelou (*I Know Why the Caged Bird Sings,* 1969) and Toni Morrison (*The Bluest Eye,* 1970; *Beloved,* 1987), and Chinese American Amy Tan (*The Joy Luck Club,* 1989). Even popular works such as J. K. Rowling's Harry Potter books spin out postmodern themes that establish the mythic Harry among our contemporary superheroes.

TOP: African American artist **Faith Ringgold** (b. 1930) celebrates jazz in *Groovin High* (1986), with couples dancing at the Savoy Ballroom in Harlem.

MIDDLE: **Jasper Johns's** (b. 1930) collage *Three Flags* (1958) overlays three canvasses to skew how the viewer perceives a familiar image.

BOTTOM: A hyperkinetic scene of urban life, from **Godfrey Reggio's** film *Koyaanisqatsi* (1982), for which Philip Glass wrote the minimalist musical score.

Music in a Postmodern World

The definition of postmodernism in music is even more elusive than it is in other art forms. But we can start with a breaking away from the modernist stance that mass media was incompatible with art. Like Warhol and fellow proponents of pop art, mid-twentieth-century musicians could not ignore the cultural saturation of technology, especially as recordings became more readily available in the 1950s, both LP (long-playing 33-rpm) and 45-rpm records. Many consumers purchased hi-fi's (high-fidelity music systems) as well as the newly invented television for their homes.

TV shows like *Your Hit Parade* (1950–59) and *Dick Clark's American Bandstand* (1952–89) introduced the newest acts to the public, and the earliest early rock-and-roll performers. The boom of FM radio in the 1970s made listeners' choices increasingly vast and complex, and musical mass media took a further jump forward with the launch of MTV in 1981. In the past decade, the Internet has added yet another unfathomable resource to our musical landscape: many of us can't imagine living without the teeming media buffet that is YouTube, launched in 2005.

It was also in the prosperous 1950s that some of our most enduring musicals were first produced, including Alan Jan Lerner and Frederick Loewe's *My Fair Lady,* Richard Rodgers and Oscar Hammerstein's *The Sound of Music,* and Leonard Bernstein's *West Side Story,* which we will consider (Chapter 63). Musical theater and film have gone hand in hand since the invention of synchronized sound, and for much of the late twentieth century movies were an essential source of musical pleasure. Now video games have added a more customized touch to the multimedia experience.

Teenagers dance to the top 40 hits in a 1969 *American Bandstand* show, hosted by Dick Clark (rear).

While some composers continued the path set out by Schoenberg toward ever stricter organization in music, others looked toward freer forms and procedures. The anti-rational element in art—leaning on intuition, change, and improvisation—was favored by composers like John Cage, who wrote **chance,** or **aleatoric, music** that left decisions determining overall shape to the performer or to chance (Chapter 62). In music as in the visual arts, the distinctions between elite and popular are shrinking: we will hear, for example, how composer John Corigliano uses the popular poetry of folksinger Bob Dylan as the starting point for his own song cycle (Chapter 65), and how film and video game scores rely extensively on the conventions of art music (Chapter 67). And the globalization of society has hugely impacted musical composition, opening composers up to a vast world of non-Western music, as in the works of John Cage and Tan Dun (Chapter 67).

Chance music

Music as Protest

Political issues, a concern for musicians since the Middle Ages, have been especially so since the mid-1900s. The "Red scare" of communism during the 1950s and early 60s saw the blacklisting of many creative Americans—among them composers Aaron Copland (who wrote the very American *Appalachian Spring*) and Leonard Bernstein (*West Side Story*), clarinetist Artie Shaw (whom we heard performing with Billie Holiday in Chapter 56), and folksinger Pete Seeger, as well as writers Langston Hughes and W. E. B. DuBois. Even the physicist J. Robert Oppenheimer, the "father of the atomic bomb" and subject of the John Adams opera *Doctor Atomic,* was not exempt (Chapter 69).

Protest songs are a long-standing American tradition, and the last decades of the twentieth century provided causes worthy of musicians' creativity. Bob Dylan's voice was clearly heard with landmark protest songs (*Blowin' in the Wind* and *The Times They Are a-Changin'*) during the 1960s civil rights movement, and

LEFT: Folk-song writer/singer Pete Seeger, famous for his protest songs, accompanies himself on banjo in an outdoor concert in New York City.

RIGHT: The legendary guitarist/singer Jimi Hendrix at the Woodstock Festival (1969), flashing a peace sign to the audience.

Joan Baez sings at the Occupy Wall Street protest in New York, November 2011.

Pete Seeger's *If I Had a Hammer* became, along with *We Shall Overcome*, an anthem for civil rights causes.

America's involvement in the Vietnam War supplied more ammunition for musical protests, like those performed at the 1969 Woodstock Festival, a seminal event for such artists as guitarist Jimi Hendrix (see above). New musical styles that developed in the 1980s—punk rock and rap, in particular—protested strongly against discrimination, poverty, corruption, and government policies (Public Enemy's *Don't Believe the Hype,* 1988), while some pop singers, like Michael Jackson, worked to end the disastrous famine in Africa (*We Are the World,* 1985).

The intense drug culture and sexual revolution of the 1960s was reflected in songs of rock groups (including the Rolling Stones) and in the antiwar musical *Hair* (1967, revived 2008). Musical feminism took varied forms as well, from the folksy protest songs of Joan Baez (below left) to the "in-your-face" songs of the Dixie Chicks. Other significant social causes include protecting the environment and grappling with the atrocities of war, notably the Holocaust (the subject of Steven Spielberg's 1993 film *Schindler's List,* with a soundtrack by John Williams). Wars in Iraq and Afghanistan fueled a revival of musical commentaries, as have recent political campaigns. Barack Obama's 2008 campaign for the presidency attracted the talents of Black Eyed Peas' member will.i.am, who wrote the now famous collage-style video *Yes We Can.*

New Technologies

Probably the most important development that affected music during the mid-twentieth century was the refinement of recording and playback technologies, which heralded the advent of electronic music. Two trends emerged simultaneously in the late 1940s and early 50s. *Musique concrète,* based in Paris, relied on sounds made by any natural source, including musical instruments, that were recorded onto magnetic tape and then manipulated by various means. *Electronische Musik,* originating in Cologne, Germany, and explored by Karlheinz Stockhausen among others, used only electronically produced sounds. By the 1960s, compact and affordable synthesizers suited for mass production were being developed by Robert Moog and Donald Buchla, but it was a recording called *Switched-On Bach,* made in 1968 by Walter Carlos (a transgender musician now known as Wendy

Carlos) that catapulted the synthesizer and the genre of electronic music to instant fame. The Moog synthesizer was quickly adopted by musicians for a variety of commercial purposes, including film scores for Stanley Kubrick's *A Clockwork Orange* (1971) and *The Shining* (1980).

Moog synthesizer

In 1983, the Yamaha DX7, one of the best-selling synthesizers of all time, was unveiled. That same year saw the official adoption of a standardized protocol known as the Musical Instrument Digital Interface (MIDI), which allowed composers to record data such as pitch, duration, and volume on the computer for playback on one or more synthesizers. By the mid-1980s, digital-sampling synthesizers, capable of recreating a realistic-sounding grand piano, trumpet, violin, bird call, car crash, or any other sound that can be sampled, was accessible to the average musician. With the affordability of digital synthesizers and personal computers, and their ability to communicate with one another, the digital revolution took the world of electronic music by storm.

MIDI

Much of the music we hear today as movie and TV soundtracks is electronically generated, although some effects resemble the sounds of conventional instruments so closely that we are not always aware of the new technology. Popular-music groups have been "electrified" for years, but now most of them regularly feature synthesizers and samplers that both simulate conventional rock band instruments and produce altogether new sounds; electronic resources like Autotune help them manipulate vocal and instrumental pitch either in the studio or in performance.

Robert Moog, creator of the Moog synthesizer.

Collage, a major genre of art, has also found a place in music: composer Lukas Foss (b. 1922) juxtaposed or overlapped fragments of Bach, Handel, and Scarlatti in his *Baroque Variations*, just as John Lennon created a sound collage of special effects and vocals in *Revolution 9* (*The Beatles*, 1968). And the device of quotation has proved its significance to popular as well as art music, since the entire tradition of hip-hop hinges on the creative sampling and layering of musical excerpts in ways the composer feels are artistically striking and/or culturally significant. All these techniques and many more make up the palette of the modern composer. We will listen for the individuality of each musical voice as we try to comprehend the expressive and eclectic language of today's music.

CRITICAL THINKING

1. What makes postmodernism so difficult to define?
2. What are some of the most significant musical developments of the late twentieth century?

Music Technology

As early as 1955, composers set out to see how the computer could enhance the creative process of composition. Could the machine possibly compose by itself? Composer, record producer, and multimedia artist Brian Eno showed that it could in a way; he coined the term "generative music" for his compositions in which the computer grows "little seeds" that produce ever-changing music, thereby introducing the idea of chance music to audiences. Other composers have sought out ways for musicians and computers to interact in live performances.

One of the most creative minds in the world of music technology is Tod Machover, described in 1999 by the *Los Angeles Times* as "America's most wired composer." Machover's explorations into interactivity—between the audience and at-home listeners as well as between performers and computers—and his outreach to popular culture have made him a leader in the contemporary music scene. The composer admits that the 1967 release of the Beatles' *Sgt. Pepper's Lonely Hearts Club Band* album piqued his interest in manipulating sounds and creating entirely new ones. Now a professor at the Massachusetts Insti-

tute of Technology (MIT), he heads up the Media Lab there, where the popular video games *Guitar Hero* and *Rock Band* were developed by two of his students, Alex Rigopulos and Eran Egozy. In his effort to be inclusive in the music-making process, Machover oversaw the development of a program called Hyperscore, which allows anyone, even children, to "compose" music using just lines and colors; *Toy Symphony* (2003), which provided children with appealing high-tech "music toys," was one result. "Technology has paved the way for almost anyone to hit the right notes," he claims.

Machover also developed the new technology of "hyperinstruments," using the computer to expand the expressive ability of traditional instruments. His work for hypercello *Begin Again Again . . .* was written for the virtuoso Yo-Yo Ma and, in keeping with the postmodern idea of quotation, pays homage in its opening theme to the Sarabande from J. S. Bach's Cello Suite No. 2. Throughout, the cellist is in control of an array of devices that both produce and transform sound through the angle and pressure of the bow. This piece is so crazily virtuosic that the composer asked Yo-Yo Ma after one rehearsal, "Is there any hair left on your bow?"

Machover's interest in popular culture, another postmodern hallmark, extends to his recent compositions,

ComposerTod Machover experiments with the hypercello in his lab at MIT.

including *VinylCello* (2007), which calls for a DJ turntable artist to back up the amplified cello soloist. And his sci-fi operas are just as wired. *VALIS* (1987; acronym for Vast Active Living Intelligent System), based on the popular novel by Philip Dick and written for the tenth anniversary of the postmodern Pompidou Center in Paris, closes with a pounding rock finale, evoking the music that was formative to Machover; and *Death and the Powers* (2010) not only features a high-tech chorus of dancing robots, but also relies on over forty computers to run the production and 140 speakers to create an ultramodern sound world.

We will consider a hyperpiano concerto by Machover titled *Jeux Deux*, written in 2005 for the Boston Pops Orchestra and featuring an augmented percussion section. The work's title plays off Debussy's masterpiece *Jeux* (*Games*), a dance piece that begins with a tennis match in which the ball goes missing. Machover notes that *Jeux* was a "spiritual antecedent" to *Jeux Deux*, which builds on two matches (it translates loosely as "two-person game"): one between the piano soloist and the orchestra (as in most concertos) and another between the human and the hyperpiano, which can do amazing "nonhuman" things. The pianist plays an electronic piano (a Yamaha Disklavier Grand), which is augmented by software that analyzes what the soloist is playing and signals the computer to trigger a sequence of notes or multiply and speed up notes to exceed what any human hand can do—at times, it sounds as if ghosts are playing along on the keyboard. The work is traditional in its three-section, fast-slow-fast structure, but the movements are played without pause.

Machover's *Jeux Deux* performed by the Boston Pops Orchestra, with pianist Michael Chertock, conductor Keith Lockhart, and live computer graphics.

We will hear the third movement, labeled "Bouyant and Precise"; it starts off with a spritely tune that seems straightforward enough until it hiccups with rhythmic displacements, building in dense, dissonant polyphony. A slower middle section featuring the piano and flute offers a brief respite. Short piano cadenzas intercede, leading to a frenzied, bombastic coda. Machover's groundbreaking musical technologies are as fun as they are innovative: a *Boston Globe* reviewer found the playful *Jeux Deux* to be "a wild, lovely, and utterly modern collision of art and science."

Jeux Deux

What to listen for:

- The unsettling metric shifts of the main theme.
- The Disklavier going crazy, in a fast and furious flurry of notes.

"Bouyant and Precise": A suspended cymbal roll leads to a bouncy duple-meter tune in the piano. The strings pick up the tune, and the piano and strings trade it off as the melody is offset rhythmically in shifting meters; the accompaniment grows dense and dissonant.
"Sweet and Singing": Slower, with shifting meters; the melody begins in the piano and flute, then the strings take it over and new percussion instruments are heard (celeste, glockenspiel, and thunder sheet). The music slows and softens to a dreamy *pianissimo*.
Cadenza: A long trill introduces a mini-cadenza for piano, which leads to the coda.
Coda ("Fast and Furious"): The full orchestra builds to a rhythmic and loud (*fff*) frenzy, followed by a long *decrescendo*. The movement closes with a soft bass-drum roll and another mini-cadenza, this one aleatoric (the pianist repeats notes "in any order to control cluster chords" in the piano's low range). Repeated notes die away to a final soft chord.

Chapter 62

New Sound Palettes: Mid-Twentieth-Century American Experimentalists

"I thought I could never compose socially important music. Only if I could invent something new, then would I be useful to society."

—John Cage

KEY POINTS

- Contemporary music often calls for innovative and highly virtuosic instrumental or vocal effects that challenge performers to new technical levels.

- Composer John Cage used a specially modified **"prepared" piano** to simulate the sound of the **Javanese gamelan**, an ensemble of metallic per-

cussion instruments played in Indonesia (on the islands of Java and Bali, in particular).

- In his four books of madrigals, which treat the voice as a virtuosic instrument, composer George Crumb set texts by the Spanish poet Federico García Lorca.

Since the beginning of recorded history, musicians have been expanding their sound-production resources—by inventing new scales and harmonies, developing increasingly complex and versatile instruments, and training their bodies to sing and play in experimental ways. In order to do so, they have reached out to other cultures for inspiration, but also taken advantage of the inventiveness of their fellow musicians. The mid-twentieth century was an especially fertile time for musical expansion in North America, and we will consider examples by two composers who shaped such expansion: John Cage and George Crumb.

Early Experiments

Henry Cowell

Two earlier composers in particular helped shape the pioneering genius of John Cage. One, Henry Cowell (1897–1965), was drawn toward a variety of non-Western musics. His studies of the musics of Japan, India, and Iran led him to combine Asian instruments with traditional Western ensembles. Cowell also experimented with foreign scales, which he harmonized with Western chords. Several of his innovations involved the piano; these include **tone clusters** (groups of adjacent notes played with the fist, palm, or forearm) and the plucking of the piano strings directly with the fingers. This novel approach to the piano helped to inspire Cage's idea of the "prepared piano," which we will encounter below.

Tone clusters

The most serious proponent of microtonal technique was Harry Partch (1901–1974), who developed a scale of forty-three **microtones** to the octave in the 1920s and adapted Indian and African instruments to fit this tuning. Among his original instruments are cloud-chamber bowls (made of glass), cone gongs (made of metal), and gourd trees. Such instruments make melody and timbre, rather than harmony, the focus of his music.

Microtones

The Music of John Cage

Cage represents the type of eternally questing artist who no sooner solves one problem than presses forward to another. His works explored new sounds and concepts that challenged the very notion of what makes up music. Probably his most important contribution, and one that shaped many strands of music in the second half of the twentieth century, was the idea of **chance**, or **aleatoric**, music. His experimental compositions and writings defined him as a leader in the postwar avant-garde scene.

Sonatas and Interludes

Sonatas and Interludes represents Cage's crowning achievement for the prepared piano, approximating the subtle sounds of the Javanese gamelan and preserving the effect of music floating above time. There are sixteen sonatas in this set, ordered in four groups of four, and separated by interludes (LG 55). Cage provides detailed

In His Own Words

" Once in Amsterdam, a Dutch musician said to me, "It must be very difficult for you in America to write music, for you are so far away from the centers of tradition." I had to say, "It must be very difficult for you in Europe to write music, for you are so close to the centers of tradition."

—*John Cage*

John Cage (1912–1992)

Born in Los Angeles, Cage exhibited an early interest in non-Western scales, which he learned from his mentor, Henry Cowell. He soon realized that the traditional division between consonance and dissonance had given way to a new opposition between music and noise, as a result of which the boundaries of the one were extended to include more of the other.

In 1938, Cage invented what he called the "prepared piano," in which various foreign substances were inserted at crucial points in the strings of a grand piano. From this instrument came a myriad of sounds whose overall effect resembled that of a Javanese gamelan. Cage wrote a number of works for the prepared piano, notably the set of *Sonatas and Interludes*. His interest in indeterminacy, or chance, led him to compose works in which performers make choices by throwing dice.

Cage maintained an intense interest in exploring the role of silence, which led to a composition entitled *4'33"*, without any musical content at all, consisting of four minutes and thirty-three seconds of "silence." The piece was

first "performed" by the pianist David Tudor in 1952. He came onstage, placed a score on the piano rack, sat quietly for the duration of the piece, then closed the piano lid and walked off the stage. Cage viewed *4'33"* as one of the most radical statements he had made against the traditions of Western music, one that raised profound questions. What is music, and what is noise? And what does silence contribute to music? In any case, *4'33"*, which can be performed by anyone on any instrument, always makes us more aware of our surroundings.

MAJOR WORKS: Orchestral music • Piano music, including *Music of Changes* (1951) • Prepared piano works, including *Bacchanale* (1940) and *Sonatas and Interludes* (1946–48) • Percussion works, including *First, Second, Third Construction* (1938, 1940, 1941) • Vocal works, including *Aria* (1958) • Electronic music, including *Fontana Mix* (1958), *Cartridge Music* (1960), and *HPSCHD* (for harpsichord and tapes, 1969) • Indeterminate works, including *4'33"* (for any instrument, 1952) • Writings, including *Silence* (1961), *Notations* (1969), *Themes and Variations* (1982), and *I–VI* (1990).

LISTENING GUIDE 55

 1:23

Cage: Sonata V, from *Sonatas and Interludes*

DATE: 1946–48 (first performed 1949)

OVERALL STRUCTURE: 16 sonatas, in four groups of 4, each group separated by an interlude

What to Listen For

Melody	Irregular phrases, small-range, undulating chromatic line; second section is more disjunct.
Rhythm/ meter	Opening with regular movement, then changing rhythmic flow, seemingly without a clear meter.
Harmony	Minimal sense of harmony; dissonant ending.

Texture	The focus is on linear movement.
Form	Binary structure (**A-A-B-B**).
Expression	Evokes ethereal, otherworldly sounds.
Timbre	Piano produces percussive effects, both pitched and nonpitched; varied tone quality and pitches.

0:00   **A section**—18 measures, grouped in irregular phrases (4 + 5 + 4 + 5 = 18).
Opening of sonata, with regular rhythmic movement and two-voice texture:

(una corda pedal)

An irregular sense of meter develops.

0:12   Upper line is sustained over a moving lower line (in last 9 measures).

0:20   **A section** repeated.

0:38   **B section**—22½ measures, in irregular phrases (4 + 5 + 4 + 5 + 4½ = 22½).
Rests break the music into sections.

0:46   Quicker tempo, lines are more disjunct and accented.
Second half of **B section**, with more disjunct lines and accents:

0:55   Sustained dissonance at the closing.

1:00   **B section** repeated.

instructions at the beginning of the score, indicating that forty-five of the piano's eighty-eight keys should be prepared by inserting nails, bolts, nuts, screws, and bits of rubber, wood, or leather at carefully specified distances. The effect is var-

John Cage's prepared piano works call for screws, nails, and other materials to be inserted between the strings.

ied, depending on the material inserted, its position, and whether the soft pedal is depressed. Some strings produce a nonpitched, percussive thump, while others produce tones whose pitch and timbre are altered. This music is not concerned with the simultaneous sounding of pitches (harmony) but rather with timbral effects and the rhythmic grouping of sounds.

Sonata V is short but highly structured; its overall shape is binary (a prevalent form in the Baroque and Classical eras), with each section repeated (**A-A-B-B**). The sonority of the prepared piano is almost ethereal. Here and elsewhere, Cage's music for prepared piano is made of wholly original sounds that delight the ears and, as intended by the composer, "set the soul in operation."

George Crumb and Avant-Garde Virtuosity

Avant-garde musical styles call for a new breed of instrumentalists and vocalists, and a new arsenal of unusual techniques, to cope with the music's performance demands. The music of George Crumb, for example, draws from art music traditions, folk themes, and non-Western sounds. Crumb displays a real talent for turning ordinary instruments, including the voice, into the extraordinary. His imaginative music resounds with extramusical and symbolic content that infuses it with a deep meaning waiting to be unlocked.

Caballito negro (Little Black Horse)

Caballito negro (LG 56) is the last of three songs in Crumb's second book of madrigals. All three are set to poetry by Federico García Lorca, and are scored for soprano with metallic percussion instruments and a flute or piccolo. The piccolo player uses a technique called **flutter-tonguing**: quickly moving the tongue as though "rolling an R" while blowing into the instrument. In Caballito negro, a hair-raising image of death, Crumb extracts only the two refrains from the poem, alternating between them: "Little black horse, where are you taking your dead rider? Little

In His Own Words

" I think composers are everything they've ever experienced, everything they've ever read, all the music they've heard.... I think there's a lot of music that has a darker side and maybe some of this music influenced me."

—George Crumb

George Crumb (b. 1929)

Crumb studied at Mason College of Fine Arts in Charleston, West Virginia, and earned graduate degrees at the University of Illinois and University of Michigan. He taught composition in Colorado and New York before he was appointed to the University of Pennsylvania, where he remained until he retired in 1999. Crumb has shown a special affinity for the poetry of Federico García Lorca, the great poet killed by the Fascists during the Spanish Civil War. Among his works based on García Lorca's poetry is the song cycle *Ancient Voices of Children*, which abounds in a number of unusual effects. He also set García Lorca's poetry in his four books of madrigals, in which he explores *Sprechstimme* (spoken melody), quarter tones, and a "white" tone (without vibrato) for the voice.

Crumb's music is focused on creating new sonorities as well as exploring theatrical concepts. In *Echoes of Time and the River*, for which he won a Pulitzer Prize in 1968, performers whisper and shout as they move around the stage. His music is charged with emotion, which derives from a highly developed sense of the dramatic. His use of contemporary techniques for expressive ends is extremely effective with audiences.

MAJOR WORKS: Orchestral music, including *Echoes of Time and the River* (1967) • Vocal music set to García Lorca poetry, including four books of madrigals (1965–69) and *Ancient Voices of Children* (1970) • Chamber music, including *Black Angels* (for electrified string quartet, 1970), *Lux aeterna* (*Eternal Light*, for voice and chamber ensemble with sitar, 1971), *Vox balaenae* (*The Voice of the Whale*, for amplified instruments, 1971) • Music for amplified piano, including two volumes of *Makrokosmos* (1972–73), *Music for a Summer Evening* (1974), *Zeitgeist* (1988), and *Otherworldly Resonances* (two pianos, 2003) • Other piano music.

This Italian stamp celebrates the centenary of the Spanish poet Federico García Lorca. The background depicts the Andalusian countryside with horsemen and Gypsy women.

cold horse. What a scent of knife-blossom!" Most phrases end with a downward melodic line, on ominous words. The rhythmic treatment might remind you of the galloping horse in Schubert's equally chilling *Elfking* (Chapter 36), and the vocalist is even asked to whinny like a horse.

Both Cage and Crumb rely on the extraordinary creativity of others for their works to be successful, whether through modeling or through virtuosic performance. And this necessity of collaboration between composer and performer is one of the characteristic (and most wonderful) aspects of music, especially in an age of specialization and experimentation.

CRITICAL THINKING

1. What kinds of new techniques have modern musicians needed to learn in order to perform avant-garde music?

2. Compare Crumb's idea of madrigal with the Farmer song in Chapter 16. What is similar, and what is different?

YOUR TURN TO EXPLORE

Choose an instrument that you find interesting (the human voice can count!), and try to find examples of musicians pushing the technical possibilities of that instrument. What kinds of extended techniques can you discover? Do they have a significant expressive potential, and if so, how? Do you think those techniques could find a place in your favorite repertories? Can you envision other techniques that might be musically expressive?

LISTENING GUIDE 56

1:32

Crumb: *Caballito negro* (*Little Black Horse*)

DATE: 1965

GENRE: Song, from *Madrigals*, Book II

What to Listen For

Melody	Highly disjunct; extended techniques (flutter-tonguing, glissandos, whispering).	**Expression**	Grimly playful; very animated.
		Timbre	Bright, hard, metallic quality.
Rhythm/ meter	Regular pulsations, no firm sense of meter.	**Performing forces**	Soprano voice, piccolo, percussion (marimba, glockenspiel, antique cymbals).
Harmony	Atonal.		
Form	Three-part (**A-B-A′**).	**Text**	Text by Federico García Lorca.

	TEXT	TRANSLATION
0:00	Caballito negro.	Little black horse.
	¿Dónde llevas tu jenete muerto?	Where are you taking your dead rider?
0:30	Caballito frío.	Little cold horse.
	¡Qué perfume de flor de cuchillo!	What a scent of knife-blossom!
0:55	Caballito negro . . .	Little black horse . . .
	Caballito frío . . .	Little cold horse . . .
	Caballito negro . . .	Little black horse . . .

Opening of song, with pounding rhythm in piccolo and percussion, disjunct vocal line, and flutter-tonguing in piccolo:

Return of opening line, with the vocalist neighing like a horse:

Javanese Gamelan

isteners at the 1889 Paris World Exhibition were captivated with the spectacle of Javanese dance and the accompanying orchestra called gamelan. French composer Camille Saint-Saëns observed that it was "a dream music which had truly hypnotized some people." From that time on, many composers have looked to the music of Southeast Asia and Oceania for inspiration in their own works. American West Coast musicians in particular had the opportunity to experience the gamelan on their own turf: in California, Santa Barbara–based composer/ethnomusicologist Henry Eichheim (1870–1942) brought Indonesian instruments back from his travels in the 1920s and also adopted elements of Balinese music in his work. Beginning in 1940, touring Javanese ensembles traveled up the coast from Los Angeles. These events caught the attention of experimental composers Henry Cowell, who taught a class on "Music of the World's Peoples" at the New School for Social Research in New York, and Lou Harrison (1917–2003), who wrote a number of works for Javanese-style instruments. John Cage, a devotee of Cowell and Harrison, was certainly not blind to these influences, and he too undertook a study of Asian cultures. The prepared piano technique Cage devised owes a significant debt to gamelan music, in both texture and timbre, although the sounds are achieved in quite a different way.

The gamelan, an orchestra of metallic percussion found on the Indonesian islands of Java, Bali, and Sunda, is comprised of melodic-percussive instruments, each with its own function. The music is generally performed from memory, passed on through oral tradition from master musician to apprentice. It is only in recent years that a notational method has been devised. Gamelan music is often heard in ritual ceremonies, including court performances (there are four princely courts in central Java alone), and in *wayang*, or shadow-puppet theater.

The performance of a shadow-puppet play would normally begin in the early evening with an overture and continue until dawn. A master puppeteer operates the puppets from behind a screen, narrates and sings the songs, and signals the gamelan—here, soft and loud metallophones (tuned metal bars struck with a mallet), gongs of various sizes, wooden xylophones, and drums—when to play. Our selection is an overture (called *Patalon*) to a

A gamelan, with metallophones, playing for a meeting of OPEC (Organization of Petroleum Exporting Countries) in Jakarta.

shadow-puppet play. Like many Javanese dramas, the story comes from the great Hindu epic *Ramayana*, the story of King Rama, whose wife Sinta is kidnapped by an evil king named Rahwana. (Java today is predominately Islamic, although Hindu and Buddhist beliefs are also important to the culture.) In this play, the evil king's brother is cast out of the kingdom for suggesting that Rahwana return Sinta to her husband.

In Javanese music, the interaction of the melodic movement with a cyclical rhythmic structure determines the form of the work. Here, the melody is based on the pentatonic scale (notes 1, 2, 3, 5, 6, or C, D, E, G, A). The work unfolds in sections, with the drum marking the transition between sections. The first, including an introduction, is slow and stately—the melody can be heard in the highest-pitched metallophone, which sounds each note of the pentatonic pattern twice. When the singer enters, he elaborates on the melody in quite a different way from the instruments, but both singer and instruments converge on accented notes. At dramatic moments in the text, the accents can jolt the listener. A fast-paced and excited closing section signals the entrance of the dancers and puppet characters.

Wayang 🎧

What to listen for:

- Pentatonic (five-note) melodic patterns.
- Rhythmic cycles that develop in complex polyrhythms.
- Sectional alternations between loud and soft instruments.

Javanese shadow-drama puppets of King Rama, hero of the Hindu epic *Ramayana*, and his wife Sinta (left), who is kidnapped and later recovered.

A slow introduction features the high-sounding metallophone outlining the melodic pattern; the voice soon enters, elaborating on the main melody, which is punctuated by gongs.

A drum cues the transition to the next (faster) section; a loud-style section follows, featuring the first four notes of the melody and the gong playing on most main notes.

A transition leads to a soft-style section, featuring quieter instruments and the voice (with dramatic accents and leaps; the dynamic level grows, with loud instruments; recording fades out.

Chapter 63

Staged Sentiment: Bernstein and American Musical Theater

"Any composer's writing is the sum of himself, of all his roots and influences."

—Leonard Bernstein

KEY POINTS

- The roots of American musical theater lie both in vaudeville shows and in European operetta.
- **Musicals** feature romantic plots (some taken from novels), comic moments, appealing melodies, and large ensembles and dance numbers; the dialogue is mostly spoken.

- The "golden age" of the American musical, the mid-1900s, was characterized by composer-lyricist teams (George and Ira Gershwin, Lerner and Loewe, Rodgers and Hammerstein).
- Leonard Bernstein, a versatile conductor and composer, wrote the music for *West Side Story*, which transports the Romeo and Juliet story into New York City and its gang warfare.

American musical theater is, like jazz, a tradition that is both rooted in the United States and tremendously influential and popular throughout the world. From the beginning, composers and lyricists of the **musical** (as it's most commonly known) have sought to make their themes current and vital, relevant to the concerns of their society. One such theme is urban life and especially urban violence, as we saw in Gershwin's *Porgy and Bess*. Another powerful treatment of that theme was understood as pathbreaking from the start and continues to influence theatrical multimedia today: *West Side Story*, a collaboration between composer Leonard Bernstein, lyricist Stephen Sondheim, and choreographer Jerome Robbins—three of the most talented artists of the mid-twentieth century.

Musical Theater in North America

Although theatrical productions were banned in most of the earliest North American colonies on religious and moral grounds, by the early nineteenth century immigrant musicians were helping to build a tradition of musical theater in North America. In the mid-1800s, New York became the cultural center of the country. In midtown Manhattan, the heart of the theater district, theaters lined the wide street called Broadway. Here and throughout the country, minstrel shows were giving way to vaudeville; these productions still featured some blackface, but more and more the characters were taken from new immigrant populations from Italy, Eastern Europe, and Asia. While some musical routines were parodies of the "funny way" the immigrants talked and behaved, often the actors themselves were immigrants, and the music could be sentimental and nostalgic as well as humorous—continuing a tradition established by Stephen Foster in an earlier generation (see Chapter 37). The vaudeville tradition expanded in New York into the variety show, which continued to offer musical and theatrical sketches, now often strung together by a loose topical theme.

The American musical theater of today developed both from the variety show and from the operetta tradition of late nineteenth-century European composers such as Johann Strauss Jr. and the team of W. S. Gilbert and Arthur Sullivan (*The Pirates of Penzance*, 1879; *The Mikado*, 1885). The genre was revamped to suit American tastes, both by immigrant composers like Victor Herbert (*Babes in Toyland*, 1903) and by "locals" like Will Marion Cook, an African American composer whose *Clorindy, or The Origin of the Cakewalk* (1898) was both the first black production to play a major Broadway theater and the first musical to incorporate ragtime melodies and rhythms. By the 1920s, talented creative teams such as George and Ira Gershwin (*Lady, Be Good*, 1924) and Oscar Hammerstein and Jerome Kern (*Show Boat*, 1927) had ushered in what many consider the golden age of the American musical. In the ensuing decades, the musical established itself as America's unique contribution to world theater.

While plots for early musicals were often sentimental and contrived, this changed when composers looked to sophisticated literary sources (*Show Boat*, for example, is based on the Edna Ferber novel). After the 1940s, interest grew in adding more serious dramatic elements (for example, in the Richard Rodgers and Oscar Hammerstein productions *Oklahoma!* 1943; *South Pacific*, 1949; *The King and I*, 1951; *The Sound of Music*, 1959). Noted composers of musicals in more recent decades include Stephen Sondheim (*Sweeney Todd*, 1979; *Into the Woods*, 1988), who lifted the genre to new levels of sophistication; Andrew Lloyd Webber (*Cats*, 1981; *Phantom of the Opera*, 1986), who combined song and dance with dazzling scenic effects; and Claude-Michel Schonberg (*Les Misérables*, 1987, based on the Victor Hugo novel), who brought history alive with memorable songs. Jonathan Larson's hit show *Rent* (1996) is a modern rock opera based on Puccini's opera *La bohème*, and the Broadway hit *Wicked* (2003) derives from the classic book *The Wonderful Wizard of Oz* (1900, made into a movie with Judy Garland in 1939). Dance has taken precedence over story line in musicals like *Billy Elliot* (2005, with music by Elton John), and plays a striking role in *West Side Story*.

Maria (Elena Sancho Pereg) and Tony (Liam Tobin) in a 2012 Berlin performance of *West Side Story*.

In His Own Words

" This will be our reply to violence: to make music more intensely, more beautifully, more devotedly than ever before."

—*Leonard Bernstein*

Leonard Bernstein and *West Side Story*

Composer/conductor Leonard Bernstein dedicated his life to promoting concert music to the general public, through his accessible compositions and his far-reaching educational efforts. Bernstein was deeply influenced both by Gershwin's successes in expanding the jazz idiom and by Copland's ability to create soundscapes that could quickly be recognized as reflecting American ideals. His most enduring project was a collaboration with several outstanding creative minds of the mid-1900s, which brought the culturally profound story of Shakespeare's *Romeo and Juliet* into the violent gang world of New York.

Bernstein, along with lyricist Stephen Sondheim and playwright Arthur Laurents, had first intended to replace Shakespeare's warring families with Jewish and Catholic families living in the tenements of Manhattan's Lower East Side. As the project developed, choreographer Jerome Robbins joined the team and suggested shifting the location to the West Side, turning the families into juvenile gangs, a topic that was saturating the news in the mid 1950s: the result was two gangs called the Jets and the

Interface

Music as Literature

Have you considered where composers find inspiration for their story-based compositions? Some make up their own stories—a case in point is Russian composer Sergei Prokofiev, who in *Peter and the Wolf* created a modern children's folk tale. It should be no surprise that great literature has spawned countless operas, ballets, and programmatic orchestral works, as well as Broadway musicals. Some composers rely on the classics, as Purcell did for *Dido and Aeneas* (taken from Virgil's *Aeneid*), while others are inspired by new literary trends: Debussy's *Prelude to "The Afternoon of a Faun"* evokes a contemporaneous Symbolist poem of the same name. Verdi wrote operas on Shakespeare's tragedies *Macbeth* and *Othello*, as well as on the comedy *Falstaff*. Broadway musicals generally offered lighter fare, but composers and lyricists still occasionally looked to great writers (notably Shakespeare) for good stories—beginning with *The Boys from Syracuse* (1938), based on *A Comedy of Errors*, and Cole Porter's *Kiss Me, Kate* (1948), an updating of *The Taming of the Shrew*. These musicals enhanced familiar comedic plots with all the showy trappings of the golden era of Broadway: memorable tunes, spectacular chorus and dance sequences, and colorful costumes and sets, all with a feel-good story that ends happily.

The idea of a musical as tragedy was unheard of until Leonard Bernstein and Stephen Sondheim tested the waters with *West Side Story*, an updated version of Shakespeare's *Romeo and Juliet*. They wanted to tell a modern story not far removed from the opposing Capulets and Montagues. But was the public ready for a show that replaced the glamour and romantic clichés of the genre with the gritty reality of New York's street life? Critics and audiences alike were stunned by the electrifying dance sequences, choreographed by Jerome Robbins, and the violent onstage deaths of three of the show's lead characters, and *West Side Story* was immediately recognized as a bold step forward in musical theater. Then, as today, the familiarity of this tragic story of young love makes the show all the more compelling.

Modern composers of dramatic music continue to look to familiar literature—both comic and tragic—as a means to engage their audiences while pressing their eyes and ears to ever new sights and sounds. You might enjoy one of the recent operas based on famous books: for example, *Frankenstein* (1990), by Libby Larsen, on Mary Shelley's landmark horror novel; *Little Women* (1998), by Mark Adamo, on Louisa May Alcott's family tale; or *Moby Dick* (2010), by Jake Heggie, on the masterful novel by Herman Melville. Some contemporary musicals also look back to the classics. Surely

Artists, like composers, found inspiration in Shakespeare's tale of star-crossed lovers. *The Last Farewell of Romeo and Juliet* (1832), by **Francesco Hayez** (1791–1881).

West Side Story forged a path for one of the most intense and violent dramas that will ever grace the musical theater stage: the smash-hit show *Les misérables*, by Claude-Michel Schönberg and Alain Boublil and based on Victor Hugo's great novel, a show that resounds even louder and to a broader public through its spectacular 2012 film adaptation.

Sharks (a Puerto Rican group). Robbins was especially eager to depict the setting's "gritty realism," and encouraged Bernstein to incorporate not only elements of jazz and early rock-and-roll, but also Latino music like the mambo, an Afro-Cuban dance with a fast, syncopated beat that was extremely popular at the time.

This story of star-crossed lovers unfolds in scenes of great tenderness, with memorable songs such as *Maria*, *Tonight*, and *Somewhere* alternating with electri-

Leonard Bernstein (1918–1990)

As a composer, conductor, educator, pianist, and television personality, Bernstein enjoyed a spectacular career. He was born in Lawrence, Massachusetts, entered Harvard at seventeen, attended the prestigious Curtis Institute of Music in Philadelphia, and then became a disciple of conductor Serge Koussevitzky. At twenty-five, he was appointed assistant conductor of the New York Philharmonic. When a guest conductor was suddenly taken ill, Bernstein took over a Sunday afternoon concert that was broadcast coast to coast, and led a stunning performance. Overnight he became famous. Fifteen years later, he was himself named director of the New York Philharmonic, the first American-born conductor to occupy the post.

As a composer, Bernstein straddled the worlds of serious and popular music. He explored his Jewish background in his Third Symphony (*Kaddish*) and also tried his hand at serial composition. But he was rooted in tonality, as he demonstrated in his choral masterwork *Chichester Psalms*. Bernstein's feeling for the urban scene, specifically that of New York City, is vividly projected in his theater music. In *On the Town, Wonderful Town*, and *West Side Story*, he created a sophisticated kind of musical theater that explodes with movement, energy, and sentiment. His harmonies are spicily dissonant, his jazzy rhythms have great vitality, and his melodies soar.

MAJOR WORKS: Orchestral music, including three symphonies (*Kaddish*, 1963) • Choral works, including *Chichester Psalms* (1965) • Operas, including *A Quiet Place* (1983) • Musicals, including *On the Town* (1944), *Wonderful Town* (1953), *Candide* (1956), and *West Side Story* (1957) • Other dramatic stage works, including the ballet *Fancy Free* (1944), the film score *On the Waterfront* (1954), and a staged Mass (1971) • Chamber and instrumental music • Solo vocal music.

 Tonight, from *West Side Story*

---

fying dance sequences choreographed by Robbins. We will first hear *Mambo* (LG 57), part of the dance scene where Tony (former member of the Jets) meets Maria (related to the Sharks). To a lively Latin beat, the bongos and cowbells keep up a frenetic pulse under the shouts of the gang members and the jazzy riffs of the woodwinds and brass.

The *Tonight Ensemble* is set later the same day, after a fire-escape version of Shakespeare's famous balcony scene, where Tony and Maria first sing their love duet. As darkness falls, the two gangs anxiously await the expected fight, each vowing to cut the other down to size. Underneath the gang music, an ominous three-note ostinato is heard throughout. Tony sings the lyrical ballad *Tonight* over an animated Latin rhythmic accompaniment. The gang music returns briefly, after

Rival gangs (the Sharks and the Jets) dance in a 2007 production of *West Side Story*, performed in Paris.

which Maria and later Tony repeat their love song, their voices soaring above the complex dialogue in an exciting climax to the first act.

West Side Story was an instant audience success, and more than fifty years later remains a powerful work of musical theater, which has claimed its place in North American culture not only through the remarkable 1961 film adaptation, but also as a favorite of school and college theatrical groups. Yet it also caused controversy, both because of the focus on violence and gangs (and essentially sympathetic treatment of the gang members) and for what some considered a stereotypical portrayal of Latino characters. Certainly, however, it was a groundbreaking multi-media work, as well as a landmark in our society's continuing struggle with artistic depictions of violence.

CRITICAL THINKING

1. How did the tradition of North American musical theater change through the 1900s?

2. In what ways was *West Side Story* significant? What issues of race and ethnicity does it raise in ways that are similar to, and different from, *Porgy and Bess*?

YOUR TURN TO EXPLORE

Choose a musical or multimedia work that addresses violence explicitly. What attitude do the performers project toward that violence, and what do you think they want listeners to understand about it? How does sound—rather than just the meaning of words—contribute to the performers' message about violence? Do you think that message is legitimate? What problems do you see with either its style or its substance?

LISTENING GUIDE 57

 5:26

Bernstein: *West Side Story*, excerpts

DATE: 1957

GENRE: Musical theater

CHARACTERS: Maria, Puerto Rican sister of Bernardo
Tony, former member of the Jets
Anita, Puerto Rican girlfriend of Bernardo

Riff, leader of the Jets
Bernardo, leader of the Sharks

Act I: The Dance at the Gym, *Mambo*

1:48

What to Listen For

Melody	Disjunct, syncopated riffs (short ideas).	**Expression**	Frenetic Latin dance with excited voices and hand clapping.
Rhythm/ meter	Fast-paced Afro-Cuban dance; highly rhythmic with much syncopation.	**Timbre**	Brass and Latin rhythm instruments (bongo drums, cowbells) featured.
Harmony	Sweetly dissonant.	**Text**	Lyrics by Stephen Sondheim.
Texture	Dense and polyphonic.		

0:00   Percussion introduction, eight bars, with bongos and cowbells; very fast and syncopated.

0:07   Brass, with accented chords; Sharks shout "Mambo!," followed by a quieter string line, accompanied by snare drum rolls; accented brass chords return; Sharks shout "Mambo!" again.

0:28   High dissonant woodwinds in dialogue with rhythmic brass.

0:33   Trumpets play a riff over *fff* chords:

Woodwinds and brass alternate in a highly polyphonic texture.

1:00   Rocking two-note woodwind line above syncopated low brass:

1:13   Solo trumpet enters in a high range above a complex rhythmic accompaniment:

Complex *fortissimo* polyphony until the climax; rhythm slows as music dies away at the close.

Act I: *Tonight* Quintet

3:38

What to Listen For

Melody	Speechlike exchanges; soaring lines in love duet.	**Texture**	Complex and polyphonic; simultaneous lines.
Rhythm/ meter	Fast, accented, and rhythmic dialogue; ominous three-note ostinato; duple-meter love song in regular phrases, with gentle, offbeat accompaniment.	**Form**	32-bar popular song form (8-bar sections, **A-A'-B-A''**, starting at 1:26).
		Expression	Breathless gang dialogue.
Harmony	Some unison singing; tonal but modulating.	**Performing forces**	Men's chorus as gangs; Maria (soprano) and Tony (tenor), with orchestra.

Setting: The neighborhood, 6:00–9:00 p.m. Riff and the Jets, Bernardo and the Sharks, Anita, Maria, and Tony all wait expectantly for the coming of night.

0:00   Short, rhythmic orchestral introduction featuring brass and percussion, based on a three-note ostinato:

Gangs sing in alternation.

0:07   **Riff and the Jets**
The Jets are gonna have their day tonight.

Riff and the Jets
The Puerto Ricans grumble: "Fair fight."
But if they start a rumble,
We'll rumble 'em right.

Bernardo and the Sharks
The Sharks are gonna have their way tonight.

Bernardo and the Sharks
We're gonna hand 'em a surprise tonight.

Continued on next page

0:29	**Riff and the Jets** We're gonna cut them down to size tonight	**Bernardo and the Sharks.** We said, "O.K., no rumpus, No tricks." But just in case they jump us, We're ready to mix. Tonight
0:43	**All** We're gonna rock it tonight, We're gonna jazz it up and have us a ball! They're gonna get it tonight; The more they turn it on, the harder they'll fall!	Unison chorus, more emphatic and accented; with accented brass interjections.
	Riff and the Jets Well, they began it!	**Bernardo and the Sharks** Well, they began it!
	All And we're the ones to stop 'em once and for all, Tonight!	
1:09	**Anita** Anita's gonna get her kicks tonight. We'll have our private little mix tonight. He'll walk in hot and tired, so what? Don't matter if he's tired, As long as he's hot. Tonight!	Opening melody now in uneven triplet rhythm, sung sexily:

1:26	**Tony** Tonight, tonight, Won't be just any night, Tonight there will be no morning star.	**A section** (8 bars):

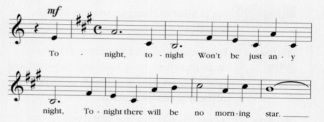

	Tonight, tonight, I'll see my love tonight, And for us, stars will stop where they are.	**A′ section** (8 bars); higher range, more emotional.
1:52	Today the minutes seem like hours, The hours go so slowly, And still the sky is light . . . Oh moon, grow bright, And make this endless day endless night!	**B section** (8 bars); strings in canon with voice. **A″ section** (8 bars); reaches climax, then cuts off.
2:15		Instrumental interlude.
	Riff (to Tony) I'm counting on you to be there tonight. When Diesel wins it fair and square tonight. That Puerto Rican punk'll go down, And when he's hollered "Uncle," We'll tear up the town!	Return to opening idea, sung more vehemently.

Ensemble finale

Maria sings *Tonight* in a high range, against simultaneous dialogue and interjections over the same syncopated dance rhythm that accompanied Tony's solo; dramatic climax on last ensemble statement of *"Tonight!"*

Maria (warmly)

2:41   [**A**] Tonight, tonight

Won't be just any night,

Tonight there will be no morning star,

[**A′**] Tonight, tonight,
I'll see my love tonight,

And for us, stars will stop
Where they are.

Riff: So I can count on you, boy?
Tony (abstractedly): All right.
Riff: We're gonna have us a ball.
Tony: All right.
Riff: Womb to tomb!
Tony: Sperm to worm!
Riff: I'll see you there about eight.
Tony: Tonight . . .
Jets: We're gonna jazz it tonight!
Sharks: We're gonna rock it tonight!

Anita

Tonight, tonight, late tonight,
We're gonna mix it tonight.

Sharks

They're gonna get it tonight!
They began it, they began it,

Tony and Maria

3:07   [**B**] Today the minutes seem like hours,

Anita ⎡ Anita's gonna have her day,
Anita's gonna have her day,
Bernardo's gonna have his way tonight, tonight,
Tonight, this very night,
We're gonna rock it tonight.

The hours go so slowly,

Sharks ⎣ They began it . . .

And still the sky is light.

Jets ⎡ Tonight! They began it,
And we're the ones to stop 'em once and for all!
The Jets are gonna have their way,
The Jets are gonna have their day,
We're gonna rock it tonight. Tonight!

[**A″**] Oh moon, grow bright,

Sharks ⎡ They began it,
We'll stop 'em once and for all.
The Sharks are gonna have their way,
The Sharks are gonna have their day,
⎣ We're gonna rock it tonight, tonight!

And make this endless day endless night,
Tonight!

Chapter 64

Less Is More:
Reich and Minimalist Music

"The sounds that surrounded Americans from 1950 through 1980—jazz and rock-and-roll—cannot be ignored. They can be refined, filtered, rejected, or accepted in part, but they can't be ignored, or you're an ostrich: you're ill-informed."

—Steve Reich

KEY POINTS

- Throughout the 1950s, the twelve-tone method gained prestige because of its perceived "scientific" nature.

- Some composers who rejected twelve-tone methods but did not find older tonal approaches satisfying developed **process music** and a style eventually called **minimalism**.

- Minimalist works rely on consonant musical elements repeated and gradually changed over extended time frames: an example is American composer Steve Reich's *Electric Counterpoint*, for multiple guitars.

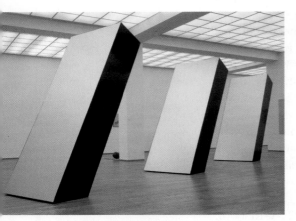

Ronald Bladen (1918–1988) illustrates the clean lines and simplicity of minimalist art, in *Three Elements* (1965).

We may value a piece of music because it has a "good tune." Composers often try to come up with one, or some melodic element that will hook the listener and make their work memorable, and all of us have experienced what Germans call an "ear-worm"—a melody that burrows into our brain and won't go away. Our idea of what makes a good tune, however, is shaped by both our cultural and our historical circumstances: Josquin, Mozart, and Billie Holiday built their hooks in drastically different ways. And musicians have sometimes attempted to redefine the possibilities of how music can hook us, as Schoenberg and Stravinsky did. This search for new hooks continues into the present, with one noteworthy approach coming from the tradition of process music and minimalism.

From Twelve-Tone to Process and Phase

The twelve-tone compositional approach of Schoenberg and his students became widespread in the 1940s and 50s: musicians valued not only the new expressive avenues it provided but also the nature of its method. At a time when Western society equated science with progress, the scientific rigor of serial music lent it a prestige

Steve Reich (b. 1936)

Reich, born in New York City, was most influenced in his early musical thinking by hearing Stravinsky's *Rite of Spring* and the music of Bach as a fourteen-year-old. After playing the drums in several bands during his college years (he has also cited jazz as an essential influence), he studied modernist composition at the Juilliard School (in New York) and Mills College (in California) in the 1950s. But when one of his teachers advised him, "If you want to write tonal music, why don't you write tonal music?" he took it as a challenge to go in a new direction. Reich worked with several pioneers of process music (especially Terry Riley and Philip Glass) in San Francisco and later New York in the 1960s, holding day jobs as a taxi driver and furniture mover before his reputation eventually began to allow him to live on commissions and recording/concert income.

Illness prevented him from spending more time in West Africa to study Ewe drumming in 1971. Back in the States, he also soaked up influences from Balinese gamelan ensembles based in California, and formed Steve Reich and Musicians, the primary group that has interpreted his works. Another important cultural influence for Reich has been his Judaism: one of his prominent choral works is a setting of Hebrew psalms (*Tehillim*, 1981) that takes Jewish cantillation (chant) formulas as the inspiration for repeating and layering vocal lines. *Different Trains* (for string quartet and recorded voice, 1988) reflects on both his personal experience and that of European Jews at the time of Nazi Germany; it was awarded the Classical Music Grammy in 1990 and has been called by one critic "the only adequate musical response to the Holocaust." Reich is acknowledged by many innovative composers, including members of the rock band King Crimson, as one of the most influential musicians of the twentieth and early twenty-first centuries.

MAJOR WORKS: Tape music: *It's Gonna Rain* (1965) and *Come Out* (1966) • *Piano Phase* and *Violin Phase* (1967) • *Drumming*, for pitched and unpitched percussion (1970–71) • *Music for 18 Musicians* (1976) • *Tehillim*, for voices and ensemble (1981) • *Different Trains*, for string quartet and tape (1988) • *WTC 9/11*, for string quartet and tape (2010).

in both European and American institutions. Some composers continued writing in tonal styles that were tuneful in pre-modernist terms, but their music was often characterized as backward-looking by those who argued for novelty.

Within modernist musical institutions, however, some became dissatisfied with serial music's implicit lack of a harmonic center, and decided to develop an approach that would treat stable harmonies in an entirely new way. The result was **process music**: a composer chooses a very simple and harmonically clear musical idea—one or two chords, or a few notes forming a consonant snippet—and repeats it over and over again, gradually changing or elaborating it. The goal was to make the musical unfolding transparent to a listener: as one of the pioneers of this method, Steve Reich, described it, "To facilitate closely detailed listening, a musical process should happen extremely gradually . . . so slowly and gradually that listening to it resembles watching the minute hand on a watch—you can perceive it moving after you stay with it a little while."

Process music

One way Reich and other experimental composers—such as Terry Riley (b. 1935) and LaMonte Young (b. 1935)—developed process music in the early 1960s was by using technology. They would record a musical idea on a loop of magnetic tape (a technology developed during the Second World War and made increasingly cost-effective through the 1950s) and play several copies of that loop simultaneously, slowly changing the tape speeds in order to combine the loops in various ways; this process was known as **phase music**. Some of Reich's early phase works were created entirely on tape, but he later experimented with having live musicians replicate the process, playing the same music and gradually speeding up or slowing down so that they would go "in and out of phase."

Phase music

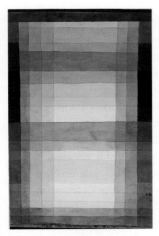

As in Reich's phase music, the overlapping geometric shapes in this watercolor by **Paul Klee** (1879–1940) blur the colors of the rainbow.

African Influence

Reich's approach shifted in 1970 when he encountered a musical tradition of West Africa: the percussion ensembles of the Ewe people of Togo, Benin, and Ghana. Ewe drummers had developed a performance method called **polyrhythm**, in which each musician plays a unique rhythm pattern continuously. While each pattern starts at a different point, they all interlock under the leadership of a master player in the group. (For a parallel African tradition, see the Encounter on p. 388.)

After just a month of listening and playing with drummers in Ghana, Reich was struck by the similarities between the Ewe style and his ideas about phase and process music. On his return to the United States, he was eager to incorporate what he had learned in West Africa, but in his own way:

> The least interesting form of influence, to my mind, is that of imitating the sound of some non-Western music. . . . Alternately, one can create a music with one's own sound that is constructed in light of one's knowledge of non-Western structures. . . . One can study the rhythmic structure of non-Western music and let that study lead one where it will while continuing to use the instruments, scales and any other sound one has grown up with. This brings about the interesting situation of the non-Western influence being there in thinking, but not in sound.
>
> This is a more genuine and interesting form of influence . . . the influence of non-Western musical structures on the thinking of a Western composer is likely to produce something genuinely new.

The structural complexities in Ewe music also led Reich to think about process music differently, eventually concluding that "as the texture gets more filled up, as it gets richer, it becomes less possible and less necessary to follow the process." This more developed process-influenced style has come to be called **minimalism**.

Minimalism

Electric Counterpoint

One of Reich's new directions took him to a series of works he called "counterpoint." The last of these, *Electric Counterpoint* (1987) for twelve guitars, is the most nuanced and complex (LG 58). The work is traditionally performed by one live guitarist playing along with up to fourteen tracks he or she has prerecorded—this is how Pat Metheny, the renowned jazz guitarist for whom Reich wrote *Electric Counterpoint*, premiered the work—but it can also be played by an ensemble of live guitarists. The work is in three movements, labeled "fast"– "slow"– "fast" and thus harking back to the overall structure of the Baroque concerto, of which we will consider the third. In the repetitive nature of the initial musical idea we can hear "process" elements of Reich's earlier style, and the device of canon is another Baroque feature. Ambiguity and complexity are introduced by the layering of instruments in different ranges, and by small shifts in the musical patterns; eventually the ambiguity is resolved as the instrumental layers "peel off."

Electric Counterpoint reveals a very different approach to harmony from the goal-oriented tonality of the pre-modernist period. On the other hand, the consonant nature of the work distinguishes it from the modernist goal of emancipating dissonance. This is why process/phase works have sometimes been seen as the beginning of a postmodern trend, though again, the definition of postmodernism in music is elusive. The hook of music like *Electric Counterpoint* depends less on the initial musical idea, which is not especially memorable, and more on the way that idea is gradually combined with itself to reveal its layered possibilities—the essence of counterpoint since the beginning of the Western polyphonic tradition.

In His Own Words

" It became clear to me after Ghana that I was going to use my own instruments, not theirs. . . . What one learns from African (or Balinese) music is how it's put together, how to organize sound."

—*Steve Reich*

4:25

LISTENING GUIDE 58

Reich: *Electric Counterpoint*, III

DATE: 1987
GENRE: Chamber work for guitar and tape

What to Listen For

Melody	Short melodic ideas repeated as an ostinato.
Rhythm/meter	3/2 meter, 12 "pulse-units"also presented as 6/4 and 12/8; regular rhythms with varying patterns and accents in syncopation.
Harmony	Diatonic, mostly static with some subtle shifts; predominant chords are C major, B minor, E minor.

Texture	Highly polyphonic, with canons.
Form	Through-composed.
Expression	An almost trance-like effect from the gradual addition and combination of regular patterns; striking moments created by subtle changes.
Performing forces	Live guitarist playing with 12 prerecorded tracks (2 bass guitars and 10 guitars).

0:00   Five guitars enter in turn with repetitions of the same short musical idea in canon.

0:43   Bass guitars play a shortened musical pattern that gradually builds to a complete melody at 0:58; it then repeats this melody.

1:06   Three-chord strumming pattern begins in one guitar track, slowly building to a three-track canon.

2:17   Harmony in the strumming tracks changes, then changes back and forth regularly between original and new strumming harmony.

3:20   Bass guitar patterns and strumming tracks gradually fade out; the original pattern moves higher and higher in pitch until it suddenly stops at 4:21.

Beginning of piece:

CRITICAL THINKING

1. What are some of the main characteristics of process and phase music, and how did it differ from the twelve-tone tradition it rejected?

2. How did non-Western music influence Reich's minimalist style?

YOUR TURN TO EXPLORE

Find examples of polyrhythm in different musical traditions, such as those in sub-Saharan Africa (Ewe drumming, the "thumb piano" called mbira), those connected to the diaspora of African people throughout the world (Afro-Cuban music, jazz), Carnatic music of southern India, gamelan music of Indonesia. How are the rhythmic patterns similar to and different from the rhythms we have studied so far? What do you find distinctive about the melody, and how does it connect to the layered rhythms? What parallels can you find between the polyrhythmic tradition you are exploring and *Electric Counterpoint*?

East African Drumming

Since the era of late nineteenth-century European coloni-zation known as the New Imperialism—and the 1889 Paris World Exhibition, where musicians and nonmusicians alike first experienced music and dance from cultures across the globe—an aura of mystery has surrounded the little-known regions of sub-Saharan Africa. Although French composers like Camille Saint-Saëns and Maurice Ravel were charmed by the music of Arab northern Africa, music of the sub-Saharan colonies was viewed as "primitive" for its lack of melodic and harmonic content. This "primitivism" soon took hold in the arts world, however, influencing early twentieth-century art-ists and musicians toward non-Western ideals of abstraction—among them painter Paul Gauguin, who was attracted to the simplic-ity of Tahitian life, and Igor Stravinsky, whose *Rite of Spring* drew on pagan themes to reach new heights of rhyth-mic complexity (Chapter 53).

From the early twentieth century, composers have continued to look beyond Western musical ideas and constructs; some, like John Cage and Steve Reich, intro-duced Asian and African ele-ments in their own works. Reich claims that when he first saw notated music from Ghana, in West Africa, he realized it was composed of repeat-ing patterns that were superimposed on each other. "That was a real eye opener," he said. "I thought it would be best if I went there and played it myself." These patterns became part of Reich's phase technique. Upon his return from Ghana, he wrote *Drumming,* a large-scale percussion ensem-ble work for tuned bongos, marimba, and glockenspiel as well as voice; the use of all-tuned instruments lends interest not only to the dense polyrhythms but also to the short, repeated melodic patterns.

We will investigate here the music of another African nation: Uganda, a land-locked country in East Africa, bordering Kenya and Lake Victoria. The Ugandan people—representing many different cultures—have felt influences from the Arab world, from Indonesia, and also from their British colonizers. The modern Republic of Uganda was formerly subdivided into a number of powerful kingdoms, each with its own court and ruler. We will hear music from one of these courts, performed by a royal drum (entenga) ensemble of six musicians playing fif-teen drums. Four musicians play on twelve melody drums that are grad-uated in size and tuned to the pitches of a pentatonic scale, while the other

Members of the entenga drum chime ensemble of Uganda.

Large and small laced drums with sticks from Uganda.

4 tuned drum players:

II — IV — I — III

1 2 3 4 5 1 2 3 4 5 1 2

lowest middle highest

2 bass drum players:

VI V

two accompany on three unpitched drums (see chart below; note that they are sharing drums). The melody drums, called drum chimes, are conical in shape with cowhide skins laced tightly over both ends; their folk-song melodies are played with long, curved beaters.

Our example, *Ensiriba ya munange Katego*, tells the story of a subchief named Kangawo who wears a leopard-skin headband for good luck. One night, his precious headband disappears, and he feels so unprotected without his charm that he falls ill and dies. In the performance, the players of the melody drums enter one after another, first striking the sides of their drums. One plays a melody pattern, which is then doubled an octave lower by another player. Then the other melody players enter in turn, playing new patterns. Once the melodic ideas are established, the large bass drums enter, punctuating the complex, polyrhythmic fabric with strong strokes. When the players move their sticks

to the middle of the drum head, the volume increases and the individual melodies can be heard more clearly. This music is transmitted by oral tradition: an apprentice musician learns the repertory and technique by sitting beside an accomplished drummer, and so maintaining a vestige of Uganda's rich cultural past.

Ensiriba ya munange Katego 🎧

What to listen for:

- Pentatonic, gapped melodies in interlocking patterns.
- Developing complex polyrhythmic structures, with interlocking rhythmic patterns.

Players begin to establish rhythmic patterns by striking the sides of their drums, making a clicking sound.
The drum chime players move one at a time to the drum heads, introducing several melodic ideas; the lower-pitched drum player moves to the drum head, adding depth of sound.
The texture thins as lower-pitched drums drop out; one melodic pattern is heard above the others.
One drummer moves his sticks to the side of the drum (clicking), as the tempo slows to the end.

Chapter 65

Returning with Interest: Dylan, Corigliano, and Postmodern Reworkings

"I always conceive a piece as a different set of challenges."

—John Corigliano

KEY POINTS

- Musicians often pay homage to or elaborate on earlier composers' ideas.

- Bob Dylan is one of the most inventive singer-songwriters of the last century, and his distinctive vocal and poetic styles have influenced many other musicians. One of his most treasured songs

is *Mr. Tambourine Man*, made most popular by the folk-rock group the Byrds.

- John Corigliano, a prominent contemporary American composer, composed a song cycle using the evocative lyrics of selected Dylan songs, including *Mr. Tambourine Man*.

In His Own Words

66 They're just songs—songs that are transparent so you can see every bit through them."

—Bob Dylan

The ability to control creative content is both artistically and financially crucial to an artist's success. Laws concerning copyright and the unauthorized use of other artists' materials have become increasingly strict in the last century. It was not always so: in earlier times, using material by another musician in your own work was considered a tribute to a skilled predecessor. This was true especially if, in the words of a contemporary of J. S. Bach, you "returned with interest": that is to say, if the material was integrated and expanded so that it reflected a new creative perspective. Indeed, contemporary musicians often cull from each other's ideas, and the possible resources have grown in recent decades as boundaries between art and commercial music have been crossed. We will consider one remarkable example that links songwriter Bob Dylan with composer John Corigliano.

Bob Dylan as Singer-Songwriter

Beyond his important role in social protest in the 1960s, Dylan has rightly gained a reputation as an outstanding singer-songwriter. His musical style is distinctive: his voice exploits a unique nasal timbre, and a song's texture is sometimes very simple (homophonic, just a singer and a guitar) and other times fairly complex (polyphonic, with electric instruments, percussion, even saxophones and other winds). The form and melody of his songs are always irregular and surprising, coming close to predictable models but always being "tweaked" for expressive

Bob Dylan (b. 1941)

Dylan has been on the music scene since the early 1960s. Born in Minnesota, he dropped out of college after his freshman year and moved to New York, where he played in Greenwich Village and met his idol, folk singer Woody Guthrie. Dylan soon began making a name for himself as a songwriter and singer of protest songs. His first notable song was *Blowin' in the Wind*, which hit the charts in a cover by Peter, Paul, and Mary. His personal style—a raspy voice accompanied by acoustic guitar—changed in 1965 when he went electric. The next decade marked an era of experimentation and alienation from the mainstream, in which this second-generation Russian-Jew became a born-again Christian.

Since then, Dylan has edged his way back into the main current with a hectic international touring schedule and new protest songs: he won a Grammy Lifetime Achievement Award in 1991, concurrent with his release of *Masters of War*, about the beginnings of war with the Middle East. In recent years, Dylan has enjoyed a renewed popularity: his 2006 album *Modern Times* was nominated for three Grammys, and in 2009 he received a National Medal of Arts and in 2012 the National Medal of Freedom. His recent song *Things Have Changed* (from *Wonder Boys*) won both an Academy Award and a Golden Globe. Dylan is a force to be reckoned with, viewed by many as one of the most important cultural and musical figures of the twentieth century.

SELECTED RECORDINGS: *Mr. Tambourine Man*, from *Bringing It All Back Home*; *Blowin' in the Wind* and *Masters of War*, from *The Freewheelin' Bob Dylan* (1963/2004); *Beyond Here Lies Nothin'*, from *Together Through Life* (2009).

effect. Dylan's texts are also extraordinary, full of imagery that borrows from several poetic traditions, and using forms and metric patterns that are also just a little short of regular. Some consider him one of the greatest American poets of the twentieth century.

Dylan's *Mr. Tambourine Man*

Written between 1964 and 1965 and recorded for his album *Bringing It All Back Home*, this is one of Dylan's most evocative songs (LG 59). The beginning is immediately unusual because it presents what turns out to be a refrain, although we don't know this for sure until the text and music return. The refrain consists of two musical phrases, which begin the same way but end differently—the first one inconclusively (with an "open cadence"), the second more firmly (with a "closed cadence"). (The text of each phrase also begins with the same words, "Hey! Mr. Tambourine Man," and ends differently.) This type of phrase pair is also common in the eighteenth-century Classical style of Mozart and Haydn.

Each of the verses that alternate with the refrain is a different length. Again we hear two distinct musical phrases, but unlike the refrain, both phrases end inconclusively (with an open cadence)—requiring the refrain to follow and "close" the musical as well as the textual verse. Though the musical elements of this song are simple, the way Dylan deploys them is very nuanced, emphasizing the poetic text through irregular rhythms and melodic ideas.

The song reached its greatest success in a 1965 cover version by the Byrds, who added electric guitar and drums to Dylan's simple voice-and-acoustic-guitar instrumentation and thus pioneered the influential genre of "folk rock." Many other musicians have covered Dylan's song since, but perhaps the most imaginative take was by a composer outside the folk *or* rock tradition—John Corigliano, one of the most lauded composers of our day.

Milton Glaser (b. 1929) paid homage to songwriter Bob Dylan in this famous 1967 silhouette featuring psychedelic hair.

LISTENING GUIDE 59 5:26

Dylan: *Mr. Tambourine Man*

DATE: 1965

GENRE: Folk song

What to Listen For

Melody	Regular four-measure phrases in the chorus; verses have more variety in phrasing, with repeated musical ideas.
Rhythm/meter	Straightforward duple meter; no accented backbeat.
Harmony	Accompanied by simple chords (I, IV, V).

Form	Verse/chorus, with four vocal verses, each longer than the last, and one instrumental verse.
Expression	Text may refer to loneliness or an escape from life.
Timbre	Raspy vocal quality; acoustic guitar, harmonica.
Text	By Bob Dylan.

0:00   Guitar introduction (4 measures).

Chorus (16 measures)

0:05   Hey! Mr. Tambourine Man, play a song for me,
I'm not sleepy and there is no place I'm going to.
Hey! Mr. Tambourine Man, play a song for me,
In the jingle jangle morning I'll come followin' you.

Verse 1 (20 measures)

0:30   Though I know that evenin's empire has returned into sand,
Vanished from my hand,
Left me blindly here to stand but still not sleeping,
My weariness amazes me, I'm branded on my feet,
I have no one to meet,
And the ancient empty street's too dead for dreaming.

Chorus

1:00   Hey! Mr. Tambourine Man . . .

Verse 2 (24 measures)

1:26   Take me on a trip upon your magic swirlin' ship,
My senses have been stripped, my hands can't feel to grip,
My toes too numb to step, wait only for my boot heels
To be wanderin.'
I'm ready to go anywhere, I'm ready for to fade
Into my own parade, cast your dancing spell my way,
I promise to go under it.

Chorus

2:00   Hey! Mr. Tambourine Man . . .

Verse 3 (26 measures)

2:25   Though you might hear laughin', spinnin', swingin' madly across the sun,
It's not aimed at anyone, it's just escapin' on the run.

And but for the sky there are no fences facin',
And if you hear vague traces of skippin' reels of rhyme
To your tambourine in time, it's just a ragged clown behind.
I wouldn't pay it any mind, it's just a shadow you're
Seein' that he's chasing.

Chorus

3:02   Hey! Mr. Tambourine Man . . .

3:25   Instrumental verse/chorus (Dylan on harmonica).

Verse 4 (32 measures)

4:08   Then take me disappearin' through the smoke rings of my mind,
Down the foggy ruins of time, far past the frozen leaves,
The haunted, frightened trees, out to the windy beach
Far from the twisted reach of crazy sorrow.
Yes, to dance beneath the diamond sky with one hand waving free,
Silhouetted by the sea, circled by the circus sands,
With all memory and fate driven deep beneath the waves,
Let me forget about today until tomorrow.

Chorus

4:51   Hey! Mr. Tambourine Man . . .

John Corigliano and the Contemporary Song Cycle

Corigliano writes highly imaginative scores that are rooted in the language of the past but at the same time redefine traditional genres like the symphony and the concerto. His music is widely performed by the premier artists of our time, and he often writes works for specific ensembles or individuals based on his subtle understanding of their musical capabilities.

Corigliano's *Mr. Tambourine Man*

When Corigliano was commissioned by singer Sylvia McNair in 2000 to write a song cycle for her recital at New York's Carnegie Hall, he wanted a poet who spoke universally across generations. He decided to investigate the works of Bob Dylan. He found Dylan's poems beautiful, immediate, and eminently suitable to his musical style. But he had no intention of using any of Dylan's familiar melodies, nor did he wish to suggest a popular or rock style: "I wanted to take poetry I knew to be strongly associated with popular art and readdress it in terms of concert art."

Corigliano first wrote the song cycle for voice and piano, but then orchestrated it to add color and dimension. He selected seven poems for the cycle, which begins with *Prelude: Mr. Tambourine Man*, described by the composer as "fantastic and exuberant." This is followed by five more reflective songs that take the listener on an emotional journey, starting with innocence (*Clothes Line*), then developing an

John Corigliano (b. 1938)

Corigliano was born into a musical family: his father was the concertmaster of the New York Philharmonic and his mother was an accomplished pianist. After his studies at Columbia University and the Manhattan School of Music, he worked as a producer for Leonard Bernstein's Young People's Concert Series. A New Yorker all his life, he has held teaching positions at the Manhattan and Juilliard Schools of Music, and at Lehman College of the City University of New York. Corigliano has won every distinguished award possible for his music, including an Academy Award for the film score to *The Red Violin* (1999) and a Grammy Award for his song cycle *Mr. Tambourine Man*.

Throughout his career, Corigliano has explored diverse styles, including atonality, serialism, microtonality, and even chance music. He has written concertos for luminary performers such as violinist Joshua Bell (*The Red Violin*), flutist James Galway (*Pied Piper Fantasy*), and percussionist Evelyn Glennie (*Conjurer*). His stage works include *The Naked Carmen* (1970), an eclectic rock opera fashioned after Georges Bizet, and *The Ghosts of Versailles*, which, using contemporary serial language, looks back to Mozart's operas and presents ghosts of both historical and operatic characters in the French royal palace at Versailles.

MAJOR WORKS: Orchestral music, including *Pied Piper Fantasy* (for flute and orchestra, 1981) • Concertos, including Concerto for Violin and Orchestra: *The Red Violin* (2003) • Choral music, including *A Dylan Thomas Trilogy* (a choral symphony, 1960–76) • Vocal music, including *Mr. Tambourine Man: Seven Poems of Bob Dylan* (2000) • Wind ensemble music • Stage works, including *The Naked Carmen* (1970) and *The Ghosts of Versailles* (1991) • Film music, including *The Red Violin* (1999) • Chamber music.

---

awareness of the world (*Blowin' in the Wind*), followed by political fury (*Masters of War*) and a premonition of an apocalypse (*All Along the Watchtower*), culminating in a victory of ideas (*Chimes of Freedom*). The cycle closes with a *Postlude* set to *Forever Young*, which Corigliano calls a "folk-song benediction." The songs are unified by recurring motives; each introduces a short idea in the accompaniment that is picked up as important melodic material in the next song.

We will hear the *Prelude* (LG 60), a quirky and wonderfully effervescent setting of *Mr. Tambourine Man*. After the dreamy opening that presents the first verse, the music moves along athletically, with disjunct, angular lines, asymmetrical phrasing, and a Broadway-style delivery of the text. There is no obvious melodic "borrowing": only the words and the prominent tambourine connect this dramatic setting to the Dylan original. The same mysterious mood returns to close off the song, and swirling instrumental lines produce effective word-painting.

Although Corigliano said that he "decided to not hear [the original Dylan songs] before the cycle was complete," *Mr. Tambourine Man* in particular was such a popular song (especially in the Byrds' version) in the 1960s that he likely heard it at some point, and he may have carried some memories of the text-setting rhythms into his composition. What do you think? Do you hear any connections? Is Corigliano (who had Dylan's permission to "re-set" his text) "returning with interest"?

CRITICAL THINKING

1. What are some distinctive aspects of Dylan's vocal, musical, and poetic styles?
2. How does Corigliano's approach resemble the various art-song traditions we have seen so far? How is it similar to and different from Dylan's musical and text-setting approach?

LISTENING GUIDE 60

Corigliano: *Prelude, from Mr. Tambourine Man: Seven Poems of Bob Dylan*

DATE: 2000 (voice and piano); orchestrated in 2003

GENRE: Song cycle

MOVEMENTS: **Prelude: Mr. Tambourine Man**   *All Along the Watchtower*
                Clothes Line   *Chimes of Freedom*
                Blowin' in the Wind   *Postlude: Forever Young*
                Masters of War

What to Listen For

Melody	Speechlike delivery; very disjunct with asymmetrical phrases; jazzy, "natural" vocal style with slides between pitches.
Rhythm/ meter	Alternates slow, free, and quick rhythmic sections with syncopation, shifting meters, and accents; jazzy feel.
Harmony	Chromatic and spicily dissonant.
Texture	Largely homophonic.
Form	Modified verse-chorus structure.
Expression	Dreamy, mysterious mood at opening and closing; quirky and frenetic; increasing dynamic level; various special effects; word-painting (using a real tambourine).
Performing forces	Orchestra, including harp, piano, alto and baritone saxophones, and tambourine.
Text	Poems by Bob Dylan (1964) in verse-chorus form.

0:00   Instrumental introduction.   Undulating winds, with sustained strings punctuated by harp.

       Verse 1

0:15   Though I know that evenin's empire has returned into sand,   Sung freely, like recitation; rushing upward.
       Vanished from my hand,   Slower, leading to a long note.
       Left me blindly here to stand but still not sleeping.   Recitation-like.

0:42   My weariness amazes me, I'm branded on my feet,   Long vocal slide upward; sustained chords.
       I have no one to meet
       And the ancient empty street's too dead for dreaming.   Slows, with repeated text ("dreaming"); low chords, then undulating accompaniment.

Opening speechlike vocal line:

      Though I know that eve-nin's em-pire   has re-turned_ in-to sand, _

1:27   Instrumental introduction.   Quick and rhythmic; high woodwinds with tambourine; dissonant.

       Chorus

1:43   Hey! Mr. Tambourine Man, play a song for me,   Fast and highly syncopated; disjunct, wide-ranging line; tambourine is prominent.
       I'm not sleepy and there is no place I'm going to.
       Hey! Mr. Tambourine Man, play a song for me,   Momentum grows.
       In the jingle jangle morning I'll come followin' you.

Opening of chorus; disjunct, syncopated, with shifting meters:

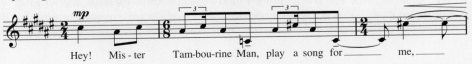

     Hey!   Mis-ter   Tam-bou-rine Man, play a song for ____   me, ____

Continued on next page

Verse 2

1:58   Take me on a trip upon your magic swirlin' ship,
         My senses have been stripped, my hands can't feel to grip,
         My toes too numb to step, wait only for my boot heels
         To be wanderin'.
         I'm ready to go anywhere, I'm ready . . . to fade
         Into my own parade, cast your dancing spell my way,
         I promise to go under it.

Louder, with rising instrument lines; wide leaps in vocal line; prominent brass and percussion.

Energetic and *fortissimo*.

Syncopated figure moves into chorus.

Excited melodic line for verse 2, with swirling accompaniment:

Chorus

2:20   Hey! Mr. Tambourine Man . . .

Chorus is repeated; much syncopation.

Verse 3

2:37   Though you might hear laughin', spinnin', swingin'
            madly across the sun,
         It's not aimed at anyone, it's just escapin' on the run . . .
         And if you hear vague traces of skippin' reels of rhyme
         To your tambourine in time, it's just a ragged clown behind.
         I wouldn't pay it any mind, it's just a shadow you're
         Seein' that he's chasing.

More dramatic; shrieking vocal quality; percussive (vibraphone and piano) sound; instruments with running passages. Softer, high woodwinds and tambourine. Tambourine rolls.

Verse 4 (partial)

2:58   Yes, to dance beneath the diamond sky with one hand waving free,
         Silhouetted by the sea, circled by the circus sands,
         With all memory and fate driven deep beneath the waves,
         Let me forget about today until tomorrow.

Loud and dramatic again, with running instrumental lines; voice has wide leaps.

Suddenly quieter and slower. Undulating woodwinds, like opening; repeated text ("until tomorrow").

3:52   Instrumental interlude.

Brief instrumental passage, quick and syncopated.

4:03   . . . I'm not sleepy and there is no place I'm going to . . .

Vocal line is slow and free over rhythmic accompaniment; dies out with woodblock beats.

YOUR TURN TO EXPLORE

Find a musical work that draws significantly on earlier models, whether through digital sampling or any other "re-use" of melody, harmony, lyrics (even covers of songs can count, especially if there is a clear modification of the original; see, for example, the Byrds' cover of *Mr. Tambourine Man*). Are there repertories/styles that rely more on borrowing than others? Why do you think the musicians have chosen to borrow specific ideas? What new elements are added to the borrowed material, and for what expressive goals? Do you think the borrowing successfully "returns with interest"?

Chapter 66

Neo-Romantic Evocations: Higdon and Program Music into the Twenty-First Century

"Music written now reflects now.... People are into variety ... even in their concert experiences.... Many folks want a mix of musics. And many young composers are picking up on this."

—Jennifer Higdon

KEY POINTS

- Some recent compositional trends speak to audiences alienated by highly intellectual modernist music.
- **Neo-Romanticism** favors the lush harmonic language of the late Romantic era: the music is mostly tonal, chromatic, and highly virtuosic, with innovative timbral combinations.
- Neo-Romantic works often feature program elements connected with a personal story, as in Jennifer Higdon's tone poem *blue cathedral*.

One trend in recent concert music, labeled neo-Romanticism, is represented by composers who embrace aspects of nineteenth-century orchestral sound. Among those aspects is program music, which as we saw in earlier chapters was very important to Romantic composers, from both a personal and a nationalist perspective. This importance has endured to the present, as musicians continue to draw on their biographical and cultural experiences as sources for expression. The example we will consider, by Jennifer Higdon, aims to "modernize" the nineteenth-century orchestral tradition. It also shows an influence of non-Western cultures that has lasted beyond John Cage, and that reflects the never-ending search for new ways to expand and renew the tradition of concert music for the twenty-first century.

A New Romanticism?

We have traced several different approaches to making music new in the early twentieth century—and indeed, the multiple facets of modernism were very important to artists and their audiences. But the style that had developed in the 1800s never really went away; great works by renowned composers such as Beethoven, Brahms, Verdi, and Wagner were performed in concert halls and opera houses even as the modernists were proposing new alternatives. Some early twentieth-century composers continued to update the Romantic style, building on the luxuriant orchestral tradition as well as the chamber genres that had been constantly evolving since the generation of

Haydn and Mozart. One of the most prominent exponents of this continued commitment to Romantic ideals was American composer Samuel Barber (1910–1981), whose elegiac and well-loved *Adagio for Strings* (1936) is suffused with the feeling and grand gestures of the nineteenth century, and whose songs continue the multinational tradition of setting intense poetry to sweeping and beautiful melodies.

The music of Barber and others who upheld key elements of Romanticism was dismissed as regressive and antiquated by those who considered modernism the only legitimate artistic pathway into the twentieth century. The advent of postmodern styles, however, induced composers to look again to the past for inspiration—sometimes with an ironic or detached perspective (often the case with quotation music; recall Bartok's use of Shostakovich's tune in the *Concerto for Orchestra*), but sometimes with respect and perhaps even a touch of nostalgia for the expressive power of the Romantic style. In the last quarter of the twentieth century and into the twenty-first, orchestral repertories have been revitalized by this reclaiming of nineteenth-century harmonic and melodic language in a new context, one that takes into account the complexities of a postmodern world—an approach commonly known as **neo-Romanticism**.

In Her Own Words

“ Can music reflect colors and can colors be reflected in music? . . . I often picture colors as if I were spreading them on a canvas, except I do so with melodies and harmonies, and through the peculiar sounds of the instruments themselves."

—*Jennifer Higdon*

Jennifer Higdon and *blue cathedral*

Hailed by one critic as a "savvy, sensitive composer . . . with a generous dash of spirit," Jennifer Higdon is one of the most widely performed of living American composers. Her music is richly neo-Romantic, displaying an innovative sound palette that has been described as "very American." We will consider her orchestral work *blue cathedral* (LG 61), which is already garnering status as a classic.

Written in 2000 to commemorate the anniversary of the Curtis Institute of Music in Philadelphia, *blue cathedral* is an orchestral tone poem with a subtext of personal grief over the untimely death from skin cancer of the composer's younger brother, Andrew Blue Higdon. Higdon explains that she was contemplating the remarkable journey of life. The title incorporates her brother's name, and she also provides evocative imagery to help us understand the broader goals of her composition:

Jennifer Higdon (b. 1962)

Born in Brooklyn, New York, Higdon pursued music studies at Bowling Green State University and then completed graduate degrees in composition at the University of Pennsylvania, where she studied with George Crumb (see Chapter 62). She claims that "the sheer number of Beatles tunes I listened to helped me to realize the ability of music to communicate." Higdon has been recognized with prestigious awards: she received the Pulitzer Prize in 2010 for her Violin Concerto, written to show off Hilary Hahn's talents (p. 40). Since 1994, she has taught composition at the Curtis Institute of Music in Philadelphia.

Higdon's extensive output spans most genres, including orchestral music and compositions for her own instrument, the flute. Her "American" sound harks back to that of Aaron Copland, on which she imposes her own highly colorful timbral palette as well as dense textures and wide-ranging dynamics. Some works, like *blue cathedral*, exude a rich lyricism and shimmering beauty, while others, like *Fanfare Ritmico* and the Percussion Concerto, are more propulsive. Her rooting in tonality as well as the familiar quality in her music help mark her as a neo-Romantic.

MAJOR WORKS: Orchestral music, including *Fanfare Ritmico* (2000), *blue cathedral* (2000), *Concerto for Orchestra* (2002) • Concertos for oboe (2005), percussion (2007), and violin (2008) • Works for wind groups, including soprano saxophone concerto (with wind ensemble, 2009) • Chamber music, including *Amazing Grace* (for string quartet, 2002) • Choral works, including *Southern Grace* (1998) • Vocal works, including *Dooryard Bloom* (for baritone and orchestra, 2004).

Blue . . . like the sky. Where all possibilities soar. Cathedrals . . . a place of thought, growth, spiritual expression . . . serving as a symbolic doorway into and out of this world. I found myself imagining a journey through a glass cathedral in the sky. . . . The listener would float down the aisle, moving slowly at first and then progressing at a quicker pace, rising towards an immense ceiling which would open to the sky. . . . I wanted to create the sensation of contemplation and quiet peace at the beginning, moving toward the feeling of celebration and ecstatic expansion of the soul, all the while singing along with that heavenly music.

The tone poem opens to shimmering, bell-like timbres (known as tintinnabulation) sounded over softly muted strings. An intimate dialogue ensues between an ethereal solo flute (the composer's instrument) and solo clarinet (her brother's instrument).

Throughout, there is a sense of continual expansion and ascent as the work builds toward several stirring climaxes. The open string sonority is "very American" in its evocation of Aaron Copland's characteristic orchestral sound, while plaintive solos are heard from darker instruments, like the English horn, viola, and cello (Higdon notes that she is "hyper-aware of color"). Near the end, more soothing colors appear, in the guise of pitched crystal glasses (a finger is run around the rims) and the chiming of some fifty Chinese reflex balls, played by most of the orchestra's musicians, a borrowing from Asian soundscapes.

In her use of characteristic tone colors and biographical elements, Higdon maintains the tradition of program music that spurred nineteenth-century composers to such imaginative heights. Her approach, popular with modern audiences, has helped to keep the tradition of concert music vital and relevant to our day.

Jennifer Higdon's *blue cathedral* evokes colorful Impressionist images like *Cathedral of Rouen: Full Sunlight, Blue Harmony and Gold* (1894), by **Claude Monet.**

CRITICAL THINKING

1. What are the qualities that make a musical work neo-Romantic?
2. How does Higdon evoke non-Western timbres in *blue cathedral*?

LISTENING GUIDE 61   🎧 6:18

Higdon: *blue cathedral,* excerpt

DATE: 2000

GENRE: Orchestral tone poem

What to Listen For

Melody	Languorous, lyrical lines; ascending ideas.
Rhythm/ meter	Mostly in 5/4 with a veiled sense of bar lines; some shifting meters.
Harmony	Prominent use of major triads but with no strong sense of key center.
Texture	Homophonic, focuses on individual lines and duets.
Form	Sectional, with a rondo-like structure.

Expression	Transcendent mood; includes several climaxes.
Timbre	Juxtaposes instrument families: metallic percussion, solo woodwinds, dark instruments, brass chorales.
Performing forces	Large orchestra with many percussion instruments (crotales, celesta, marimba, vibraphone, bell tree, chimes, triangle, tuned glasses, Chinese reflex balls).

Continued on next page

A section

0:00   Gentle, bell-like tintinnabulation, then muted lower strings, with two-note descending motive.

0:47   Solo flute with rising line, accompanied by muted string chords; no sense of pulse.

1:14   Solo clarinet answers, with harp and string accompaniment.

1:30   Duet between flute and clarinet in overlapping high-range lines:

2:18   Violin solo joins with ascending lines; builds to a large *crescendo* into the next section.

B section

3:07   Wavering horn chords alternate with open high strings; more rhythmic and syncopated:

Builds to a loud climax as strings ascend, punctuated by brass.

4:12   *Fortissimo* climax, then fades quickly.

4:23   **A section** returns briefly; a falling motive in strings.

C section

4:50   A sustained pitch and rhythmic percussion chords introduce solo instruments;
        plaintive English horn is accompanied by harmonics on harp and percussion in open fifths:

Other solo instruments enter one at a time (viola, piccolo, cello, oboe, bassoon) over now-syncopated
accompaniment; crotales (antique cymbals) add a bell-like timbre.

6:13   Builds to a gentle climax, with syncopated chords continuing; our recording fades out.

YOUR TURN TO EXPLORE

Find a recent instrumental work that has an evocative title and/or a specific program. What musical elements does the composer use to convey that title or program? How does the availability of increasingly diverse musical styles in the twenty-first century give contemporary musicians more expressive options? What kinds of musical colors and devices might you choose to describe your emotional response to something that deeply concerns you today?

Chapter 67

Underscoring Meaning: Music for Film

"So much of what we do is ephemeral and quickly forgotten . . . so it's gratifying to have something you have done linger in people's memories."

—John Williams

KEY POINTS

- A film's music sets the mood and helps establish the characters and a sense of place and time.

- There are two principal types of music in a film: **underscoring** and **source music.**

- The film music of John Williams uses full orchestral resources and **leitmotifs** (recurring themes) associated with characters or situations.

- Chinese composer Tan Dun has blended Asian and Western musical resources in his works, especially the soundtrack to *Crouching Tiger, Hidden Dragon.*

Multimedia has often been a powerful way to express emotion, as we have seen with opera and ballet: several creative individuals collaborating on a total effect can produce extraordinary results. We can see this perhaps most clearly in contemporary multimedia: dramatic musical resources pioneered onstage have been transformed for the screen—film, television, and video games—so successfully that their emotional effects can stay with us for years. We will consider the work of two of the most prominent film composers of our day: John Williams, who has shaped decades of blockbuster movies with his imaginative soundtracks; and Tan Dun, whose creative blending of Chinese and Western elements helped make several martial arts films a worldwide success.

Sound and Film

Music has played an indispensable role in creating some of the most memorable moments in film history. The opening of *2001: A Space Odyssey* (1968), the Paris montage from *Casablanca* (1942), and the shower scene in *Psycho* (1960) are all accompanied by music that has become an integral part of American culture. A composer's choices of style, instrumentation, and emotional quality are critical in fulfilling the director's vision. Even the absence of music in a scene or an entire movie (as in Alfred Hitchcock's *Lifeboat,* 1944) can contribute to the overall tone of the film.

Most Hollywood films use music to reflect the emotions of a given scene. John Williams, for example, guides us at the end of *E.T.: The Extra-Terrestrial* (1982)

Elijah Wood as the heroic hobbit Frodo Baggins, in *The Lord of the Rings* trilogy (2001–03).

Underscoring and source music

from sorrow at the apparent death of E.T. through joy at his recovery, excitement at the chase scene, and sadness at his final farewell. Howard Shore's scores to *The Lord of the Rings* trilogy help establish the dark, brooding mood surrounding Frodo's quest, but also bring out the contrasting moments of humor and tenderness.

Composers can create irony by supplying music that contradicts what is being shown, a technique called "running counter to the action." Perhaps the best-known musical/visual contradiction is the chilling climactic scene of *The Godfather* (1972). While filmgoers hear Bach organ music played during a baptism, they watch the systematic murders of Michael Corleone's enemies being brutally carried out. A number of action films since the 1990s, including Quentin Tarantino's *Pulp Fiction* (1994) and *Kill Bill, Vol. 1* and *Vol. 2* (2003–04), contain scenes of graphic violence accompanied by lighthearted rock music. This jarring contrast produces a sense of black comedy and raises questions about the superficial treatment of violence in today's media.

Music can help create a sense of place and time, as do the bagpipes in *Braveheart* (1995) and the guitar in *Brokeback Mountain* (2005). The instruments do not have to be authentic but can merely suggest a time period. In *Avatar* (2009), a small choir sings in "Na'vi"—a language developed exclusively for the movie—in keeping with the film's setting in a future utopia.

There are two main types of music in a film. **Underscoring**, which is what most people think of as film music, occurs when music comes from an unseen source, often an invisible orchestra. Music that functions as part of the drama itself is referred to as **source music**. For example, someone may turn on a radio, or a character may be inspired to sing. In *Rear Window* (1954), director Alfred Hitchcock employs only source music, which emanates from the various apartments on the main character's block. In *Boyz 'n the Hood* (1991), source music of classical, jazz, Motown, and rap helps define the figures of the story.

John Williams: *Star Wars* and Beyond

Leitmotif

It is difficult to overestimate the importance of composer John Williams to film music. His mastery of the techniques of **leitmotif** (a theme associated with a particular character) has defined the concept for our century; in *Jaws* (1975), for example, a scary two-note oscillating motive warns the audience of the shark's presence when the characters onscreen are oblivious to the danger, greatly intensifying the dramatic effect. Williams is often credited with the revival of the grand symphonic film score, writing unforgettable themes set in an accessible, neo-Romantic idiom. In keeping with postmodernist trends, he looked back to the familiar clichés and emotional appeal of older films. He also contributed to the 1980s hunger for sequels in movies like *Star Wars, Superman, Raiders of the Lost Ark,* and *Jurassic Park.*

The soundtrack to George Lucas's *Star Wars* has been called the greatest multi-film score ever written. Several factors support this claim, including the unity Williams (perhaps inspired by Wagner's *Ring* cycle) achieves through multiple leitmotifs that return in the sequels and prequels. Each motive in the *Star Wars* series—the opening fanfare (which becomes Luke Skywalker's theme), the "force" theme associated with the Jedi and Obi-Wan Kenobi, Yoda's gentle melody, Princess Leia's Romantic tune—supports the general nature of that character. Yet these motives can also be transformed to reflect totally different events. The theme for Luke Skywalker can sound sad or distorted when he is in trouble, triumphant when he is victorious. One of the finest musical moments occurs in *The Return*

John Williams (b. 1932)

A native of Long Island, Williams moved to Los Angeles as a youth, where he studied at UCLA. He then attended New York's Juilliard School, after which he worked as a jazz pianist. He began composing for television in the 1950s, and shifted to the big screen in the 1960s, when he wrote a series of scores for disaster films like *Jaws*. By the end of the 1970s, Williams had established himself as Hollywood's foremost composer, with three blockbusters to his name: *Star Wars*, *Close Encounters of the Third Kind*, and *Superman*. During the 1980s, he scored such box-office hits as the two *Star Wars* sequels, the *Indiana Jones* trilogy, and *E.T.*, and in the 1990s *Home Alone*, *Jurassic Park*, and *Schindler's List*, among many others. More recent scores include those to the first three *Harry Potter* films. In addition to this amazing lineup, Williams has also written classical works, including fanfares for the Olympics and inauguration music for President Barack Obama (*Air and Simple Gifts*). He served as the director of the Boston Pops Orchestra from 1980 to 1993.

Williams's film music explores the Wagnerian ideas of extended chromatic harmony and the use of leitmotifs—themes that represent a person, object, or idea—throughout a work. His writing is highly lyrical, providing us with eminently memorable themes that capture our imagination.

MAJOR WORKS: Orchestral works, including *Winter Games Fanfare* (1989), *Summon the Heroes* (1996), and concertos for various solo instruments • Chamber music, including *Air and Simple Gifts* (2009) • More than 90 film scores, including *Jaws* (1975), *Close Encounters of the Third Kind* (1977), *Star Wars* (1977, trilogy), *Superman* (1978), *Raiders of the Lost Ark* (1981), *E.T.: The Extra-Terrestrial* (1982), *Jurassic Park* (1993), *Schindler's List* (1993), *Harry Potter and the Sorcerer's Stone* (2001), *War Horse* (2011), *Lincoln* (2012) • Television series and themes, including *Gilligan's Island* (1957–60).

---

of the Jedi (1983). At the death of Darth Vader, his once terrifying theme is transformed into a gentle tune played by the woodwinds and harp.

Vader, the character whose rise and fall spans all six *Star Wars* movies to date, does not have a distinguishable theme until *The Empire Strikes Back* (1980, now designated episode V owing to the prequels); his ominous-sounding theme, the

Luke Skywalker and Darth Vader duel with light sabers in *The Empire Strikes Back.*

LISTENING GUIDE 62

 3:02

Williams: *Imperial March*, from *The Empire Strikes Back*

DATE: 1980

GENRE: Film score

What to Listen For

Melody	Accented, disjunct melody; two-measure phrases.
Rhythm/ meter	Quadruple meter, with repeated rhythmic ostinati.
Harmony	G minor theme, with some chromaticism.

Form	Theme and variations.
Expression	Menacing and marchlike.
Performing forces	Full orchestra; brass is featured.

0:00   Introduction—rhythmic ostinato accompaniment sets the ominous mood; stuttering pattern, with repeated notes in horns, strings, and timpani.

0:09   Main theme is introduced by trumpets and other brass, in G minor, with stuttering accompaniment underneath:

12-measure statement (4 + 4, then last 4 repeated).

0:37   Accompaniment pattern; then other brass instruments join; fanfare builds in a *crescendo*.

0:46   New ostinato pattern: each downbeat is answered by a busy three-note motive in flutes, then strings.

1:04   Theme is varied in horns, played softly with an elongated note at the end of each two-measure phrase; new busy accompaniment is heard underneath.

1:37   Returns to opening stuttering accompaniment, then rises a whole step.

1:47   Theme in trumpets, returns to G minor, with full orchestra playing ostinato accompaniment.

2:14   Theme in horns, with full orchestra playing *fortissimo*.

2:33   Stuttering accompaniment passage, leads to coda.

2:42   Coda—varied brass statement of the theme grows dissonant; whirling strings lead to a final full orchestral statement of the ostinato.

Imperial March   *Imperial March* (LG 62), is first heard when he makes his appearance here, and its various motives are associated with this character throughout the rest of the films (in the prequels, they foreshadow who will become Darth Vader). The march begins with an incessant stuttering rhythmic accompaniment that sets the mood for the powerful brass melody, which recurs in various guises. The minor tonality contributes to the dark character of the march, as do the occasional chromaticism and low-instrument timbres. A middle section introduces a lighter, more disjunct ostinato that accompanies an unpredictable French horn statement of the theme in which some phrase endings are elongated. This uncertainty gives way to the commanding opening music and theme statement, and the march finishes with a *fortissimo* pounding of the ostinato. The *Imperial March* has made its determined way into the public consciousness, heard often at sporting events between rival teams, in covers by rock bands, and as a favorite ringtone.

Tan Dun: Blending East and West

Like John Williams, Tan Dun is both a critically recognized composer of art music and an award-winning writer of film scores. In 2000, he won an Academy Award for the score to *Crouching Tiger, Hidden Dragon,* a martial arts fantasy directed by Ang Lee and featuring stunning visual and action sequences. Tan Dun creates a fascinating, postmodern blend of Asian and Western musical traditions, including both avant-garde and popular elements, and employing Chinese and Western musical instruments. The well-known Chinese American cellist Yo-Yo Ma is featured throughout, the cello heard in combination with an **erhu**, a Chinese   **Erhu** two-stringed violin. The cello's melodic material includes slides and ornaments typical of the vocal style heard in Beijing Opera (see Encounter, p. 254).

Based on a series of novels by Wang Du Lu, *Crouching Tiger, Hidden Dragon* involves two sets of star-crossed lovers caught up in a complex story of obligation and revenge, mysteries and miracles, moral codes and gender expectations. Our selection, entitled *Farewell* (LG 63), combines two melodies that represent the lovers Jen Lu and the bandit king Lo, played by the cello and erhu and accompanied by a Western string orchestra with Chinese percussion instruments. The principal (cello) melody's two phrases are heard repeatedly against the ostinato lament of the erhu. Entering at the cadence of the cello's first phrase, the erhu counter-melody also has two phrases that overlap and encircle the cello's line. You will hear that each entrance of the erhu begins with the same three pitches (A–C–D),

Tan Dun (b. 1957)

Born in Hunan Province in China, Tan Dun grew up during the Cultural Revolution (1966–76). When he was sent to work in the rice fields of a commune, his early love of music spurred him to organize a musical group there with whatever resources and people he could find. Eventually he was able to study music formally at the Central Conservatory of Beijing; after hearing Beethoven's Fifth Symphony for the first time, he was inspired to join the "new wave" of Chinese musicians who wished to explore Western music. In 1983, the Chinese government banned public performances of his own music (calling it "spiritual pollution"), prompting him to leave for New York to pursue a PhD in composition at Columbia University. There, he discovered avant-garde composers like John Cage and Steve Reich and continued his efforts to merge disparate musical styles and cultures.

In recent years, Tan Dun has created a number of celebrated works. His opera *Marco Polo,* which mixes Western avant-garde techniques with the vocal style of Beijing Opera, won the prestigious Grawemeyer Award; another opera, *The First Emperor,* about the first ruler of unifed China (246–221 BCE), was commissioned by the Metropolitan Opera in New York, with tenor Plácido Domingo singing the title role. *Symphony 1997 (Heaven, Earth, Mankind)* was written for a momentous modern occasion: the ceremony marking the return of Hong Kong to China. Tan Dun's interest in multimedia is evinced not only in his film music but in his *Internet Symphony No. 1 (Eroica),* commissioned by Google/YouTube for the first collaborative online orchestra. For this work, musicians from around the world sent videos of their playing, and the best were selected by YouTube voters to take part in a performance at Carnegie Hall, with the composer conducting. His highly successful martial arts film scores have been excerpted in a new work, *Martial Arts Trilogy.*

MAJOR WORKS: Four operas, including *Marco Polo* (1995) and *The First Emperor* (2006) • Orchestral music, including *Symphony 1997 (Heaven, Earth, Mankind), Internet Symphony No. 1 (Eroica)* (2009), *Martial Arts Trilogy* (2013) • Concerto for String Orchestra and Pipa (1999) and Piano Concerto: *The Fire* (2008, written for Lang Lang) • Film soundtracks, including *Crouching Tiger, Hidden Dragon* (2000), *Hero* (2002), *The Banquet* (2006).

LISTENING GUIDE 63 2:25

Tan Dun: *Farewell,* from *Crouching Tiger, Hidden Dragon*

DATE: 2000

GENRE: Film score

BASIS: Book by Wang Du Lu

What to Listen For

Melody	Singing cello line and lyrical erhu counter-melody; expressive rising-fifth interval begins the main theme and is heard frequently throughout.
Rhythm/ meter	Duple-meter melody accompanied by irregular pulses in Chinese hand drum.
Harmony	Consonant accompaniment.
Texture	Mostly linear, with two main lines.
Form	Theme and variations; a two-phrase melody is varied in pitch, range, and dynamics.
Expression	Lush string timbres and varied dynamics; accelerating movement in accompaniment.
Performing forces	Cello (played by Yo-Yo Ma) and erhu (Chinese fiddle), accompanied by hand drum and Western orchestra.

0:00   Love theme played by cello, with interval of a rising fifth (pitches D–A): theme heard in two phrases, accompanied by sustained strings and hand drum. Higher-pitched erhu improvises an expressive countermelody against cello line; it also begins with a rising line (pitches A–C–D).

0:34   Variation 1—duet continues between cello and erhu, with differing pitches; drum accompaniment moves slightly faster.

1:05   Variation 2—duet is closer to original statement; more expressive and louder, with quicker drum accompaniment.

1:38   Two varied statements of the second phrase, with quickening drum part.

2:07   A wavering between two pitches at the closing.

Chow Yun-Fat and Zhang Ziyi battle on the branches of bamboo trees in Ang Lee's *Crouching Tiger, Hidden Dragon* (2000).

which are central to much of the film's thematic material. The cello closes with a two-note motive associated with the powerful sword known as the Green Destiny (scheduled to reappear in an upcoming sequel). In this free mixture of Western harmony and popular music, avant-garde timbres, and ethnic Chinese sounds, Tan Dun creates an appealing new sound world.

The history of film music is now over a century old. During this time, the medium has attracted many of the world's best-known composers, including several we have met: Aaron Copland, George Gershwin, Leonard Bernstein, Silvestre Revueltas, and Philip Glass. The Hollywood industry also supported a number of soundtrack specialists, who in addition to John Williams include Max Steiner (*Gone with the Wind*, 1939), Miklós Rózsa (*Ben-Hur*, 1959), Bernard Herrmann (*Vertigo*, 1958; *Psycho*, 1960), and Elmer Bernstein (*To Kill a Mockingbird*, 1962; *Ghostbusters*, 1984). While each composer brought an individual sound to his art, three general tendencies can be observed: the incorporation of the principles established by Wagner's music dramas; the assimilation of ever-changing trends in popular music; and the constant search for fresh, new sounds, including resources from across the globe. After one hundred years, film music remains a strong, vibrant medium and an integral part of the art of filmmaking.

CRITICAL THINKING

1. How does the music for films contribute to their stories?

2. How does Tan Dun bring two distinct musical styles and sound worlds together?

YOUR TURN TO EXPLORE

Choose a favorite film and watch it a couple of times, paying attention to the use of sound. Which types of music discussed in this chapter are employed? Are there particular moments when you think sound and music are used most effectively? Conversely, can you identify moments where you feel the music is not effective for the dramatic purpose? How might a different choice at that point improve the effect?

Video Games

We have seen that throughout the Western tradition, musicians have helped to shape entertainment technology; and, as we learned in Chapter 15, mathematical/logical skills often go hand in hand with musical ability (training in one tends to reinforce strengths in the other). It's therefore not surprising that music plays an important role in gaming—not just in soundtracks to enhance the gaming experience (as they do films) but also in games and apps for portable devices that are tied to music-making.

In 2005, the game *Guitar Hero* (and related multiplayer spin-offs like *Rock Band*)—designed by students of Tod Machover at MIT Media Lab (p. 366)—became a worldwide sensation: one or more specially designed controllers synchronized the player's actions as closely as possible with a soundtrack featuring musical hits of the time. Though that game faded away after a few years, other sound-related games have since been developed, and some of the most interesting come from a company called Smule. The company's co-founder and creative director, Ge Wang, is a composer and computer scientist (and professor at Stanford University) who has also directed "laptop orchestras" that mix technology with creative sound generation.

Smule specializes in creating apps for portable devices (primarily iOS) that are designed for sharing music across the Internet: players can upload their music to the "cloud" and not only listen to other contributions but combine them with their own, allowing for long-distance polyphonic interchanges. The first app developed by Smule, Ocarina, is on the iTunes store's "Top 20 Downloads of All Time" list. This is yet another, technologically enhanced spin on the opportunity for friendship through sound, and this one can forge worldwide connections, since language differences won't get in the way. Other music-related apps (SoundCloud, for example, which allows you to comment on as well as share musical compositions) also take advantage of the astounding reach of social networking.

Video games have long employed source music to help give more satisfying feedback to a player's actions (think of the sounds that characters make when a button is pressed to make them "jump," or the fanfare you hear at the end of a level, or sounds that accompany significant moves in puzzle games) and underscoring to add inten-

Members of Stanford University's Laptop Orchestra press the boundaries of how people make electronic music.

sity and meaning to the flow of action in a role-playing game. But underscoring in games is slightly different from that in films: the player's choices open up a much more dynamic set of musical options, so the composer needs to be able to create shorter musical tracks that can be combined in flexible ways. This means that no two players will hear exactly the same combination of underscoring and source music within a well-crafted game; and in a way, each player contributes uniquely, through his or her choices, to the sonic aspect of the gaming experience. Might we consider this a sort of performance, or even composition?

Among the most respected composers of video game music is Japanese native Nobuo Uematsu (b. 1959), best known for his highly successful *Final Fantasy* series in the 1990s. A self-taught pianist, he has also written for anime and other types of film and played in a rock band. For the last decade, Uematsu has presented live orchestrations of his music in sold-out concerts throughout the world. His musical influences range from British and American rock of the 1970s to traditional music (Japanese but also Celtic), jazz, and late Tchaikovsky.

We will hear the well-known "Aerith's Theme," from *Final Fantasy VII* (1997). Aerith was one of the three original playable characters in the game; unusually, she dies, and this may have contributed to players' extraordinary emotional investment in her character and theme (or leitmotif). This theme not only prepares you for the story of the game when it's heard during the starting sequence, but also reinforces your emotional

engagement when elements of the theme return during the flow of play.

Uematsu's success with his orchestral concerts have demonstrated the crossover appeal between video game music and live choruses and orchestras. Another prominent game-music composer, Jeremy Soule (*Elder Scrolls V—Skyrim*, 2011), recently performed and recorded his first symphony, with the help of social media and the crowd-sourcing site Kickstarter. Rather than wait for a commission, he called on fans who knew his game-scoring work to help him hire an orchestra of his own. Perhaps this kind of crowd-sourcing of patronage might become one of the ways computers and the Internet will continue to transform the making and consuming of music in the twenty-first century.

"Aerith's Theme" 🎧

What to listen for:

- Large orchestra with distinct use of timbres and dynamics.
- Mostly arpeggiated primary theme contrasted with mostly stepwise secondary theme.
- **A-B-A′-B′** form.

After a stepwise introduction in which winds and strings alternate, the arpeggiated primary theme is pre-

sented first in the piano and then with doubling in various orchestral voices. Musical lines are passed among the orchestral families, creating a clear homophonic texture in which the theme is always easy to follow. After the primary theme, a contrasting theme expands on the stepwise intro. Uematsu then returns to the primary theme in elaboration, and finally builds up to a grand version of the stepwise theme, adding a short coda that echoes the intro.

Ge Wang, co-founder of the software startup Smule, turned an iPhone into an instrument called an ocarina, which he plays here at the Macworld Expo 2009 in San Francisco.

Chapter 68

Icons in Sound: Tavener and Postmodern Orthodoxy

"I hope that my music resembles 'icons in sound,' insofar as I see music as a 'window of sound' onto the divine world."

—*John Tavener*

KEY POINTS

- Alongside the concert tradition, composers have continued to write expressive music for their religious communities.

- Like the Western Christian tradition, the Greek Orthodox tradition has roots in Jewish practice, but it developed in significantly different ways over the centuries.

- English composer John Tavener's music employs concepts and specific traits of Orthodox ritual to convey a spiritual intensity that is designed to transcend individual religions.

W e have seen that while religion was probably the most important concern of Western society before about 1800, in the century that followed, Europeans embraced secular music and also concert performances of sacred works (as with Fauré's *Requiem* and Boulanger's *Psalm 24*). The arts (especially music) themselves could even be felt to satisfy the human desire for experience that is "beyond this world." Musicians were thus given more and more opportunities to work in secular contexts, and as a consequence much of the repertory we encounter today has a nonsacred purpose. Still, composers have never stopped focusing on spiritual goals. We will examine one distinguished example, John Tavener, whose deeply meaningful works are a spiritual response to an increasingly secular world.

Frank Stella's (b. 1939) minimalist sculpture *The Chapel of the Holy Ghost* radiates a mystical spiritualism.

Spiritual Minimalism

Tavener was a prominent exponent of a branch of minimalism often referred to as **spiritual**, or **holy**, **minimalism**. Developed mostly at the hands of European composers, this is a nonpulsed music inspired by religious beliefs and expressed in deceptively simple—and seemingly endless—chains of modal or tonal progressions. Representatives of this deeply meditative music include the Polish composer Henryk Górecki (b. 1933), whose Symphony No. 3 (for soprano and orchestra, 1976) features modern sound masses couched in a slow-moving, tonal language; and Estonian Arvo Pärt (b. 1934), whose works (*Kanon Poka-*

janen, 1997; *Berlin Mass*, 1992) intersect the fervent mysticism of Russian Orthodox rituals with elements of Eastern European folk music and Gregorian chant. Tavener's style infuses elements of neo-Romanticism with a devout spiritualism.

Tavener and Greek Orthodoxy

Born and raised in the Presbyterian tradition, Tavener evinced an interest from an early age in Christian mysticism. When he encountered the Greek Orthodox branch of Christianity, he was so moved by its spiritual message that he converted to that faith, undertook a systematic study of Greek Orthodox plainchant, and set about creating music for its services.

Although the Greek Orthodox and Western Christian chant traditions stem from the same Jewish roots over two thousand years ago, they developed in significantly different ways. This was in large part because the Eastern Christian Church separated from the Western in 1054 and then spread into Asia and eastern Europe. The two churches differed in ritual practices: for example, Latin was the language of worship throughout the Western church, while the Eastern church developed rituals in the local languages (most prominently Greek and Russian). The melodic formulas of Greek Orthodox chant were also closely tied to the scales and modes of local Greek and Byzantine tradition, which include intervals smaller than half steps (**microtones**) and rhythms that differ sharply from Western notions of duple and triple regularity.

Tavener's sacred music draws not just on Greek Orthodox chant but on the patterns of repetition that Orthodox ritual implies, aiming toward a mystical effect of timelessness. Beyond his settings of Orthodox texts, his instrumental compositions tend to refer directly to imagery or beliefs central to Orthodox Christianity—

John Tavener (1944–2013)

Born in London, Tavener was quickly identified as a piano prodigy. From the age of sixteen he was active as a church organist, and he continued his education in keyboard and composition at London's Royal Academy of Music. His early successes (the cantata *The Whale*, 1968; *A Celtic Requiem*, 1969) showed the modernist influences of Stravinsky and Olivier Messiaen and received wider attention by being recorded on the Beatles' Apple Records label. His growing fame led to commissions for theatrical music, but after converting to Greek Orthodoxy in the mid-1970s, Tavener refocused his attention on mystical texts and topics.

After a decade dedicated almost entirely to choral music, his *Protecting Veil* for cello and orchestra (1987) expanded his style into instrumental genres, resulting in a series of instrumental works likewise concerned with Orthodox imagery. One of his shorter sacred works, *Song for Athene* (1994), was heard by millions at the close of the funeral service for Princess Diana on September 6, 1997; its text, "Alleluia. May flights of angels sing thee to thy rest," is taken from Shakespeare's *Hamlet* and from the Orthodox Vigil Service. In more recent years, Tavener sought to combine the spiritual messages of many faiths into large-scale religious works: the most monumental is *The Veil of the Temple* (2004), for four choirs, several orchestras and soloist, and an overall duration of at least seven hours. Tavener was elevated to the British knighthood in 2000.

MAJOR WORKS: Settings of Greek Orthodox rite (*The Liturgy of Saint John Chrysostom*, 1977; *The Vigil Service*, 1984) • Choral works on broader sacred themes (*Resurrection*, 1989; *The Apocalypse*, 1993; *The Beautiful Names*, 2007) and shorter anthems (*The Lamb*, 1982, to a poem by William Blake) • Instrumental compositions based on images from Orthodox Christianity (*The Protecting Veil*, 1987; *The Last Sleep of the Virgin*, 1991; *Theophany*, 1993) • Dramatic works on sacred themes (*Mary of Egypt*, 1991; *The Play of Krishna*, 2012).

This Greek Orthodox icon portrays Mary as the well of life; from the Basilica of St. George in Madaba, Jordan.

especially the idea of the icon, or key image that represents an aspect of the divine (the Protecting Veil of the Mother of God, for example, which inspired Tavener to write a work for cello and orchestra with that name).

A Hymn to the Mother of God

We will examine Tavener's *Hymn to the Mother of God*, scored for two six-voice choirs (LG 64). This hymn is from a service that is celebrated several times during the Greek Orthodox liturgical year, most notably on Sunday in Great Lent (a period of fasting before Easter); the text is attributed to Saint John Damascene, who lived in the eighth century. It's one of the most beloved of the hymns celebrating Mary as Mother of God, a central tenet of the Greek Orthodox as well as Catholic faith.

Characteristic of Tavener's choral works is the presence of **drones** (continuous pitches held while other musical lines interweave, occasionally providing moments of intense dissonance within the slow-moving counterpoint) and harmonies based on Greek Orthodox modes that avoid the progressions of major/minor harmony and create an almost static effect. The use of short repeating musical ideas recalls organum and also the procedures of minimalism. You may hear some similarities with two other sacred compositions dedicated to Mary we have encountered—the organum *Gaude Maria virgo* from the 1200s and Josquin's *Ave Maria . . . virgo serena* from the late 1400s. This stylistic link is purposeful, since Tavener specifically looked to medieval and Renaissance polyphony for his choral writing. Like the Josquin motet, this *Hymn* alternates more homophonic with more polyphonic passages; but the harmonies and dissonances are distinctly modern.

As he continued in his quest for spiritual creativity, Tavener began to understand that "no single religion could be exclusive. . . . All religions are in the transcendent way inwardly united beneath their outward form." With this perspective, he began to incorporate sacred texts from several traditions into his vocal works (for example, he included a part for a pow-wow drum in *Hymn of Dawn*, a "mystical love song inspired by texts from the American Indians, Saint John's Gospel, the Sufis and the Hindus"). Still, the composer remained resolute in letting his own Orthodox sensibility govern his musical choices: spiritual identity served as a touchstone of his creative success.

CRITICAL THINKING

1. How did Tavener achieve his musical connection with Greek Orthodox Christianity?
2. What are some similarities and differences between *A Hymn to the Mother of God* and the examples of medieval and Renaissance polyphony we have encountered?

YOUR TURN TO EXPLORE

Seek out recordings of works in the spiritual minimalism tradition that borrow from Greek Orthodox and/or Russian Orthodox sacred music. Note musical details such as instrumentation, melody, harmony, texture. How do these works resemble and differ from the examples from Western Christian traditions we have examined, or sacred music from your own experience (Christian or otherwise)?

LISTENING GUIDE 64   2:36

Tavener: *A Hymn to the Mother of God*

DATE: 1985

GENRE: Hymn

What to Listen For

Melody	Stepwise and very narrow range; clear syllabic text setting.
Rhythm/ meter	Free rhythm, varying groups of rhythmic patterns; unmetered.
Harmony	Diatonic and modal, parallel triads and other third-related "stacked" intervals; contrasting and slightly more chromatic harmonies in second section.

Texture	Homorhythmic and parallel motion in each choir; polyphony is achieved through rhythmically displaced canon between the two choirs.
Form	**A-B-A′**.
Expression	Mystical and almost chantlike.
Performing forces	Twelve voices in two choirs, each SAATBB.
Text	Greek Orthodox hymn, attributed to St. John Damascene.

Section A

0:00 In You, O Woman full of Grace,
The angelic choirs and the human race,
All creation rejoices!

First choir enters with parallel triadic intervals and drones; second choir follows slightly after with the same notes (rhythmic canon at the dotted-half note), creating almost an "echo effect"; starts softly and builds to very loud.

0:45 Combined choirs end on an F major triad, a striking consonance after the dense weaving and overlapping dissonances; pause.

Section B

0:55 O sanctified Temple,
Mystical Paradise, and glory of Virgins.

Harmony shifts to an A-flat major triad; first choir is again followed by second choir singing same notes at the same time difference; slightly more chromatic; dynamics soft throughout.

1:25 Again choirs "meet" on a consonant triad, this time E-flat major; again a pause.

Section A′

1:36 In You, O Woman full of Grace,
All creation rejoices.

Begins the same way as the opening; builds more quickly to loud, original phrase is shortened; choirs join on a B-flat major triad.

2:09 All praise be to You!

Melodic high point is reached on "All," and dynamics increase until the choirs join again on an F major triad. Tavener adds a long pause into the score at the end.

Beginning of soprano line in each choir:

Chapter 69

Reality Shows: Adams and Contemporary Opera

"Whenever serious art loses track of its roots in the vernacular, then it begins to atrophy."

—John Adams

KEY POINTS

- Operatic composers sometimes choose historical topics, seeking to convey emotional truths through semi-fictional accounts of past events.

- American composer John Adams's eclectic approach combines elements of minimalism with traits of neo-Romanticism, forging a post-minimalist style in his recent opera *Doctor Atomic*.

Verdi once said that in musical theater, "it may be a good thing to copy reality; but to invent reality is much, much better." And operatic composers and librettists—like directors and their teams in film—have often sought deeper truths in stories based in fiction rather than fact. History, however, has also regularly been present in opera, since the actions of significant individuals have long fascinated us. In recent years, several composers have taken recent historical events as the basis for operatic treatment. Operas are not documentaries, however: much of the content of a "historical opera" is based on the creativity of librettist and composer, rather than on documented dialogue between real-life individuals. The goal of these works is to evoke the intensity and complexity of the time and the emotions felt by the historical actors, rather than to provide a factually accurate account. One noteworthy example is *Doctor Atomic*, a collaboration between composer John Adams and provocative playwright/director Peter Sellars.

In His Own Words

66 [I am] a very emotional composer, one who experiences music on a very physical level. My music is erotic and Dionysian, and I never try to obscure those feelings when I compose."

—John Adams

John Adams and Post-Minimalism

Minimalism has exerted a great influence on a variety of composers. Perhaps the most versatile of these "post-minimalists" is John Adams, whose works have gained wide appeal in large part because of their combination of accessible melodies and harmonies with intense, deeply expressive contemporary devices. Adams infuses the minimalist style with traits of neo-Romanticism, illustrated in his recent opera *Doctor Atomic*.

John Adams (b. 1947)

Adams was educated at Harvard University, where he was steeped in serialism. In his dorm room, though, he preferred to listen to rock: "I was much inspired by certain albums that appeared to me to have a fabulous unity to them, like . . . *Abbey Road* and *Dark Side of the Moon*." In 1972, he drove his VW Beetle cross-country to San Francisco, where he began teaching at the San Francisco Conservatory of Music, and quickly became an advocate for contemporary music in the Bay Area.

Adams first gained notice with two hypnotic minimalist works—*Phrygian Gates* (for piano, 1977) and *Shaker Loops* (for string septet, 1978)—then earned a national reputation with *Harmonium* (1980–81) and *Harmonielehre* (1984–85, which pays homage to Arnold Schoenberg), both written for the San Francisco Symphony. He attracted much attention with his opera *Nixon in China* (1987), on the historic visit of President Nixon in November 1972. The works that followed show an increasing awareness of the sumptuous orchestration and expressive harmonies of neo-Romanti-

cism, including his next opera, *The Death of Klinghoffer* (1991), based on the 1985 hijacking of a cruise liner by Palestinian terrorists. The 2000 *El Niño*, a Nativity oratorio modeled on Handel's *Messiah*, has texts culled from English, Spanish, and Latin sources. Both these recent stage works were collaborations with stage director Peter Sellars.

Adams won a Pulitzer Prize for *On the Transmigration of Souls* (2002), commissioned to mark the first anniversary of September 11, 2001, setting texts based on victims' names. His latest opera, *Doctor Atomic*, may be his most dramatic work yet.

MAJOR WORKS: Stage works, including *Nixon in China* (1987), *The Death of Klinghoffer* (1991), *El Niño* (2000), and *Doctor Atomic* (2005) • Orchestral works, including *Short Ride in a Fast Machine* (1986), *Tromba lontana* (1986), and *City Noir* (2009) • Chamber music, including *Phrygian Gates* (1977), *Shaker Loops* (1978), and Chamber Symphony (1992) • Vocal works, including *On the Transmigration of Souls* (In Memory of September 11, 2001—for chorus, children's chorus, and orchestra, 2002) • Tape and electronic works.

Doctor Atomic

For his third opera, Adams chose as his subject the awe-inspiring creation of the atomic bomb by a team of scientists, headed by physicist J. Robert Oppenheimer, working at the Los Alamos Laboratory in New Mexico. Peter Sellars's fascinating libretto is based on the memoirs of the project's scientists and some declassified government documents, as well as the poetry of John Donne, Charles Baudelaire, and the sacred Hindu scripture *Bhagavad Gita* (*Song of God*), the last three all literary texts well known to Oppenheimer. Adams's rich and dark score is complex texturally, as are his very human and well-developed characters.

Bhagavad Gita

The opera focuses on the last days and hours before the first atomic test on July 16, 1945. In Act I, chorus members sing of their hopes and fears about the invention—a twenty-one-kiloton atomic weapon. Oppenheimer, struggling with his conscience, sings a stunning aria that carries us to the depths of his soul as he looks with awe and trepidation at his creation.

In Act II, we learn that the test will go on while scientists worry about fallout: no one really knows what to expect, but one team member speculates that the atmosphere itself might catch on fire. Tension mounts as the chorus sings, "At the sight of this," a dramatic text from the *Bhagavad Gita* describing the moment when Krishna, an avatar (or incarnation) of Vishnu, reveals himself as the Supreme God, the all-powerful creator and destroyer of the world (LG 65). Adams's spine-chilling chorus conveys the apprehension and terror of those about to witness the historic blast. The fearsome text is declaimed on repeated notes in short phrases, punctuated with offbeat brass and percussion accents. An unsettling refrain ("O master") recurs with even shorter, more dissonant tones. At the close, the crowd responds

Gerald Finley as physicist J. Robert Oppenheimer in the San Francisco Opera production of *Doctor Atomic*.

to the immense buildup of tension with mere utterances over distorted electronic sounds. The effect is thoroughly compelling.

The opera's last scene depicts the moments before the detonation, when a rocket sends out a two-minute warning and Oppenheimer sings, "Lord, these affairs are hard on the heart." The scientist recalls the Hindu text again to describe the explosion: "If the radiance of a thousand suns were to burst at once into the sky, that would be like the splendor of the mighty one."

In *Doctor Atomic*, Adams has taken a hugely complex subject that draws together science and art, and presented it in a multilayered, eclectic score that offers much to the imagination as well as to the ears. The topic of the opera also raises complex moral (and perhaps political) questions: What does it mean to make art about such a destructive and lethal technology? Do we run the risk of losing track of the horrors that followed these experiments (the bombing of Hiroshima and Nagasaki) by focusing on an individual's struggles through beautiful music?

Several of Adams's works have caused controversy, including his opera *The Death of Klinghoffer*, based on an episode in which Palestinian militants kidnapped a cruise ship and killed one of its Jewish passengers. Some saw it as a nuanced treatment of a complex global political problem, others were disturbed at what they felt was too sympathetic a portrayal of the terrorists and their cause. Still, Adams is hailed as one of the most masterful contemporary composers in part because he constantly seeks to make his music relevant to the concerns of the twenty-first century.

CRITICAL THINKING

Comparing styles 7: Contemporary choral music

1. What kinds of stories have contemporary composers chosen for their operas?

2. How does *Doctor Atomic* create an artistic reading of the story of Oppenheimer and the Los Alamos atomic-bomb project?

YOUR TURN TO EXPLORE

Find an opera or other dramatic/multimedia work that takes a historical event as a starting point and provides an artistic interpretation of that event. How are different individuals characterized through music (high or low voice types, instrumental timbre for accompaniment, tuneful or dissonant melodies)? How do you think the composer wants us to interpret the event—is his or her artistic reading an appropriate interpretation given the historical facts? What recent event do you think might lend itself to operatic/dramatic treatment, and what kinds of musical choices would you make to convey the story?

4:05

Adams: *Doctor Atomic*, "At the sight of this"

DATE: 2005

GENRE: Opera

SETTING: Los Alamos, New Mexico, 1945

LIBRETTIST: Peter Sellars

CHARACTERS: J. Robert Oppenheimer, a physicist (baritone)
Kitty Oppenheimer, his wife (mezzo-soprano)
General Leslie Groves, U.S. army engineer (bass)
Edward Teller, a physicist (baritone)
Robert R. Wilson, a physicist (tenor)
Jack Hubbard, chief meteorologist (baritone)
Captain James Nolan, an army officer (tenor)
Pasqualita, the Oppenheimers' maid (mezzo-soprano)

Krishna displayed in his universal form as Vishnu, from the Sri Srinivasa Perumal Temple in Singapore.

Act II, scene 3, chorus: "At the sight of this"

What to Listen For

Melody	Short, choppy phrases with declaimed text, much repetition of ideas.
Rhythm/meter	Syncopated, with many offbeat accents.
Harmony	Sharply dissonant.
Form	Verse/refrain structure with repeated sections and text.
Expression	Fiery mood; mysterious electronic sounds.
Timbre	Prominent timpani and brass.
Performing forces	Chorus and orchestra.
Text	*Bhagavad Gita*, Chapter 11.

A section

0:00 At the sight of this, your Shape stupendous,
Full of mouths and eyes, terrible with fangs.

Loud, fiery mood; offbeat horn accents.
Chorus with short phrases, recitative style.

Opening of chorus, with text declaimed together:

Refrain

0:27 O O O O O.

Regular harsh chords on the main beats against a syncopated accompaniment.

A section, elongated

0:41 At the sight of this, your Shape stupendous,
Full of mouths and eyes, feet, thighs and bellies,
All the worlds are fear-struck, even just as I am.

A section repeated with harsh, offbeat, accented dissonances.

Refrain

1:06 O O O O Master.

Single chords again on the main beats.

Continued on next page

Choral refrain, invoking Vishnu:

B section

1:19   When I see you, Vishnu, when I see you omnipresent,   Connected chords, descending and chromatic,
        Shouldering the sky, in hues of rainbow.   against syncopated accompaniment.

Refrain

1:35   O O O O Master.   Single chord interjections again; active accompa-
                                            niment leads back to the **A section.**

A section

1:48   At the sight of this, your Shape stupendous,   Repeated choral section; dissonant string chords.
        With your mouth agape and flame-eyes staring—
        All my peace is gone; O, my heart is troubled.

Refrain

2:13   O O O O Master.

B section

2:26   When I see you, Vishnu, omnipresent, flame-eyes staring,   Connected chords as in the last **B section.**
        All my peace is gone, is troubled.

B section, with sustained chords:

2:43   **Coda**   Disjunct high woodwinds, with agitated,
                                                  accented accompaniment.

3:00   Vocables: "Ee ee" (women)/"Do" (men).   Electronically generated sounds accompany
                                                  the vocables.

The Notation of Pitch

Musical notation presents a kind of graph of each sound's duration and pitch. These are indicated by symbols called **notes**, which are written on the **staff**, a series of five parallel lines separated by four spaces:

Staff

A symbol known as a **clef** is placed at the left end of the staff to determine the pitch names. The **treble clef** (𝄞) is used for pitches within the range of the female singing voice, and the **bass clef** (𝄢) for a lower group of pitches, within the range of the male singing voice.

Clefs

Pitches are named after the first seven letters of the alphabet, from A to G. (From one note named A to the next is the interval of an **octave**.) The pitches on the treble staff are named as follows:

Pitch names

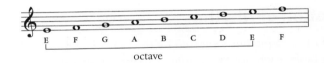

And those on the bass staff:

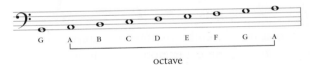

If you need to notate pitches above and below these staffs, short extra lines called **ledger lines** can be added:

Ledger lines

Middle C—the C that, on the piano, is situated approximately in the center of the keyboard—comes between the treble and bass staffs. It is represented by either the first ledger line above the bass staff or the first ledger line below the treble staff. This combination of the two staffs is called the **great staff** or **grand staff**:

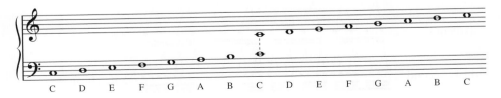

Accidentals   Signs known as **accidentals** are used to alter the pitch of a written note. A **sharp** (♯) before the note indicates the pitch a half step above; a **flat** (♭) indicates the pitch a half step below. A **natural** (♮) cancels a sharp or flat. Also used are the **double sharp** (×) and **double flat** (♭♭), which respectively raise and lower the pitch by two half steps—that is, a whole step.

Key signature   In many pieces of music, where certain sharped or flatted notes are used consistently throughout, these sharps or flats are written at the beginning of each line of music, in the **key signature**, as seen in the following example of piano music. Here, the sharp symbol on the F line means that every F in the piece is played a half step higher, the black key F♯. Notice that piano music is written on the great staff, with the right hand usually playing the notes written on the upper staff and the left hand usually playing the notes written on the lower:

Chopin: Prelude in E Minor

The Notation of Rhythm

Note values   The duration of each pitch is indicated by the type of note placed on the staff. In the following table, each note represents a duration, or **value**, half as long as the preceding one:

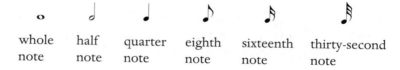

| whole note | half note | quarter note | eighth note | sixteenth note | thirty-second note |

In any particular piece of music, these note values are related to the beat of the music. If the quarter note represents one beat, then a half note lasts for two beats, a whole note for four; two eighth notes last one beat, as do four sixteenths.

Notes   *Beats*
                                                       (in quadruple, or 4/4, time)

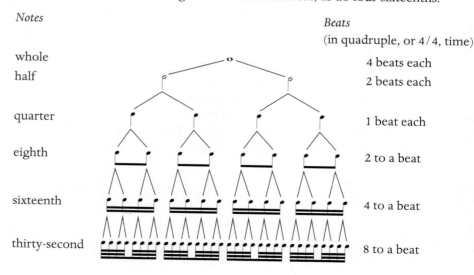

whole   4 beats each
half   2 beats each

quarter   1 beat each

eighth   2 to a beat

sixteenth   4 to a beat

thirty-second   8 to a beat

When a group of three notes is to be played in the time normally taken up by only two of the same kind, we have a **triplet**, indicated by a 3.

Triplet

If we combine successive notes of the same pitch, using a curved line known as a **tie**, the second note is not played, and the note values are combined:

beats: $4 + 4 = 8$ $2 + 4 = 6$ $1 + ½ = 1½$

A **dot** after a note enlarges its value by half:

Dot

beats: $2 + 1 = 3$ $1 + ½ = 1½$ $½ + ¼ = ¾$

Time never stops in music, even when there is no sound. Silence is indicated by symbols known as **rests**, which correspond in time value to the notes:

Rests

| whole rest | half rest | quarter rest | eighth rest | sixteenth rest | thirty-second rest |

The metrical organization of a piece of music is indicated by the **time signature**, or **meter signature**, which specifies the meter: this appears as two numbers written as in a fraction, to the right of the key signature. The upper numeral indicates the number of beats within the measure; the lower one shows which note value equals one beat. Thus, the time signature 3/4 means that there are three beats to a measure, with the quarter note equal to one beat. In 6/8 time, there are six beats in the measure, each eighth note receiving one beat. Following are the most frequently encountered time signatures:

Time signature

duple meter	2/2	2/4	
triple meter	3/2	3/4	3/8
quadruple meter		4/4	
sextuple meter		6/4	6/8

The examples below demonstrate how the music notation system works. The notes are separated into measures, shown by a vertical line (called a **bar line**).

Mozart: *Ah! vous dirai-je Maman* (tune of *Twinkle, Twinkle, Little Star* and the *Alphabet Song*)

Clef: Treble
First pitch: C
Key signature: none = key of C major
Meter: Duple (2/4)

This is the original piano version of the tune, composed by Mozart. Notice how turns decorate the familiar melody on the recording.

Brahms: *Lullaby (Wiegenlied)*

Clef: Treble

First pitch: A

Key signature: 1 flat (B♭) = key of F major

Meter: Triple (3/4)

Other features: Begins on an upbeat, after two rests.

This is the original vocal version by Brahms, sung in German. You may know the English lyrics.

Battle Hymn of the Republic (Civil War song)

Clef: Treble

First pitch: G

Key signature: none = key of C major

Meter: Quadruple (4/4)

Other features: Many dotted rhythms.

This is a nineteenth-century brass band version of the tune from the Civil War era. The band plays only the familiar chorus on the recording.

Greensleeves (English traditional song)

Clef: Bass

First note: E

Key signature: 1 sharp (F♯) = key of E minor

Meter: Sextuple (6/8)

Other features: Begins on an upbeat, has dotted rhythms and added accidentals.

This Elizabethan-era song is played here on classical guitar.

absolute music Music that has no literary, dramatic, or pictorial program. Also called *pure music.*

a cappella Choral music performed without instrumental accompaniment.

accelerando Getting faster.

accent The emphasis on a *beat* resulting in its being louder or longer than another in a *measure.*

accompagnato Accompanied; also a *recitative* that is accompanied by orchestra.

accordion A musical instrument with a small keyboard and free-vibrating metal *reeds* that sound when air is generated by pleated *bellows.*

acoustic guitar A *guitar* designed for performance without electronic amplification.

acoustic music Music produced without electronics, especially amplifiers.

active chords In the *diatonic* system, chords that need to resolve to the *tonic chord.* These include the *dominant* and *subdominant* chords.

adagio Quite slow.

aerophone Instruments such as a *flute,* whistle, or *horn* that produce sound by using air as the primary vibrating means.

agitato Agitated or restless.

Agnus Dei The last musical section of the *Ordinary* of the *Mass.*

alap A free, unmetered, and often improvisational introductory section to an Indian classical composition.

alla breve See *cut time.*

allegro Fast, cheerful.

Alleluia An item from the *Proper* of the *Mass* sung just before the reading of the Gospel; *neumatic* in style, with a long *melisma* on the last syllable of the word "Alleluia."

allemande German dance in moderate *duple meter,* popular during the Renaissance and Baroque periods; often the first *movement* of a Baroque *suite.*

alto Lowest of the female voices. Also *contralto.*

amplitude See *volume.*

andante Moderately slow or walking pace.

answer Second entry of the *subject* in a *fugue,* usually pitched a fourth below or a fifth above the subject.

anthem A religious choral composition in English; performed liturgically, the Protestant equivalent of the *motet.*

antiphonal Performance style in which an ensemble is divided into two or more groups, performing in alternation and then together.

antique cymbals Small disks of brass, held by the player (one instrument in each hand), that are struck together gently and allowed to vibrate.

aria Lyric song for solo voice with orchestral accompaniment, generally expressing intense emotion; found in *opera, cantata,* and *oratorio.*

arioso Short, *aria*-like passage.

arpeggio Broken chord in which the individual pitches are sounded one after another instead of simultaneously.

art song A song set to a high-quality literary text, usually accompanied, and intended for concert performance. See also *Lied* and *mélodie.*

a tempo Return to the previous tempo.

atonality Total abandonment of *tonality* (which is centered in a *key*). Atonal music moves from one level of *dissonance* to another, without areas of relaxation.

augmentation Statement of a *melody* in longer note values, often twice as slow as the original.

aulos *Double-reed* pipe; played for public and religious functions in ancient Greece.

automaton (plural is **automata**) Mechanical device, sometimes musical.

avant-garde French term that refers to new styles and techniques in the arts, especially in the early twentieth century.

backbeat In rock and roll and related *genres,* the second and fourth *beats* of the *measure.*

bagpipe Wind instrument popular in Eastern and Western Europe that has several tubes, one of which plays the melody while the others sound the *drones,* or sustained notes; a windbag is filled by either a mouth pipe or a set of *bellows.*

balalaika *Guitar*-like instrument of Russia with a triangular body, fretted neck, and three strings; often used in traditional music and dance.

ballad A form of English street song, popular from the sixteenth through the eighteenth centuries. Ballads are characterized by narrative content and *strophic form.*

ballad opera English comic opera, usually featuring spoken dialogue alternating with songs set to popular tunes; also *dialogue opera.*

ballet A dance form featuring a staged presentation of group or solo dancing with music, costumes, and scenery.

banjo Plucked-string instrument with round body in the form of a single-headed drum and a long, fretted neck; brought to the Americas by African slaves.

bar form Three-part **A-A-B** form, frequently used in music and poetry, particularly in Germany.

baritone Male voice of moderately low range.

bar line See *measure line.*

bass Lowest of the male voices.

bass clarinet *Woodwind* instrument, with the lowest range, of the *clarinet* family.

bass drum *Percussion instrument* played with a large, soft-headed stick; the largest orchestral drum.

basso continuo Italian for "continuous bass." See *figured bass*. Also refers to a performance group with a chordal instrument (*harpsichord, organ*) and one bass melody instrument (*cello, bassoon*); also *continuo*.

bassoon *Double-reed* woodwind instrument with a low range.

bass viol See *double bass*.

baton A thin stick, usually painted white, used by a *conductor*.

beat Regular pulsation; a basic unit of length in musical time.

bebop Complex *jazz* style developed in the 1940s.

Beijing opera A form of entertainment from Beijing (Peking), China, with music, mime, stylized gestures and dance as well as colorful masks and costumes.

bel canto "Beautiful singing"; elegant Italian vocal style characterized by florid melodic lines delivered by voices of great agility, smoothness, and purity of tone.

bell The wide or bulbed opening at the end of a wind instrument.

bell tree Long stick with bells suspended from it, adopted from *Janissary music*.

bellows An apparatus for producing air currents in certain wind instruments (*accordion, bagpipe*).

bent pitch See *blue note*.

big band Large *jazz* ensemble popular in the 1930s and 40s, featuring sections of *trumpets, trombones, saxophones* (and other *woodwinds*), and rhythm instruments (*piano, double bass, guitar*, drums).

big-band era See *Swing Era*.

binary form Two-part (**A-B**) form with each section normally repeated. Also *two-part form*.

bluegrass *Country-western* music style characterized by quick *tempos*, improvised instrumental solos, and high-range vocal harmonies.

blue note A slight drop of pitch on the third, fifth, or seventh note of the scale, common in *blues* and *jazz*. Also *bent pitch*.

blues African American form of secular *folk music*, related to *jazz*, that is based on a simple, repetitive poetic-musical structure.

bodhran Hand-held frame drum with a single goatskin head; used in Irish traditional music.

bongo A pair of small drums of differing pitches, held between the legs and struck with both hands; of Afro-Cuban origins.

bourée Lively French Baroque dance type in *duple meter*.

bow A slightly curved stick with hair or fibers attached at both ends, drawn over the strings of an instrument to set them in motion.

brass instrument Wind instrument with a cup-shaped mouthpiece, a tube that flares into a bell, and slides or valves to vary the pitch. Most often made of brass or silver.

brass quintet Standard chamber ensemble made up of two *trumpets, horn, trombone*, and *tuba*.

bridge Transitional passage connecting two sections of a composition; also *transition*. Also the part of a string instrument that holds the strings in place.

Broadway musical A work of *musical* theater that is performed in New York City's major theater district (Broadway).

buffo In *opera*, a male singer of comic roles, usually a *bass*.

bugle *Brass instrument* that evolved from the earlier military, or field, *trumpet*.

cadence Resting place in a musical *phrase*; musical punctuation.

cadenza Virtuosic solo passage in the manner of an improvisation, performed near the end of an *aria* or a *movement* of a *concerto*.

call and response Performance style with a singing leader who is imitated by a *chorus* of followers. Also *responsorial singing*.

camerata Italian for "salon"; a gathering for literary, artistic, musical, or philosophical discussions, notably the Florentine Camerata at the end of the sixteenth century.

camp meeting A musical gathering where hymns, spirituals, and folk songs were sung; popular in nineteenth-century America.

canon Type of *polyphonic* composition in which one musical line strictly imitates another at a fixed distance throughout.

cantabile Songful, in a singing style.

cantata Vocal genre for solo singers, *chorus*, and instrumentalists based on a lyric or dramatic poetic narrative. It generally consists of several *movements*, including *recitatives, arias*, and ensemble numbers.

cantor Solo singer or singing leader in Jewish and Christian liturgical music.

cantus firmus "Fixed melody," usually of very long notes, often based on a fragment of *Gregorian chant*, that served as the structural basis for a *polyphonic* composition, particularly in the Renaissance.

carol English medieval *strophic* song with a *refrain* repeated after each stanza; now associated with Christmas.

castanets *Percussion instruments* consisting of small wooden clappers that are struck together; widely used to accompany Spanish dancing.

castrato Male singer who was castrated during boyhood to preserve his soprano or alto vocal register; prominent in seventeenth- and early eighteenth-century *opera*.

celesta *Percussion instrument* resembling a miniature upright *piano*, with tuned metal plates struck by hammers that are operated by a keyboard.

cello See *violoncello*.

chaconne Baroque form similar to the *passacaglia*, in moderately slow *triple meter*, featuring *variations* that are based on a repeated chord progression.

chamber choir Small group of up to about twenty-four singers, who usually perform *a cappella* or with piano accompaniment.

chamber music Ensemble music for up to about ten players, with one player to a part.

changing meter Shifting between *meters*, sometimes frequently, within a single composition or *movement*; also *shifting meter*.

chanson French *monophonic* or *polyphonic* song, especially of the Middle Ages and Renaissance, set to either courtly or popular poetry.

character piece A short, lyric piano work often with a descriptive title; popular in the nineteenth century.

chart Colloquial or *jazz* term for a score or arrangement.

chimes *Percussion instrument* of definite pitch consisting of a set of tuned metal tubes of various lengths suspended from a frame and struck with a hammer.

choir A group of singers who perform together, usually in parts, with several on each part; often associated with a church.

chorale Congregational hymn of the German Lutheran church.

chorale prelude Short Baroque *organ* piece in which a traditional *chorale* melody is embellished.

chord Simultaneous combination of three or more *pitches* that constitute a single block of *harmony*.

chordal *Texture* comprised of *chords* in which the *pitches* sound simultaneously; also *homorhythmic*.

chordophone Instrument that produces sound from a vibrating string stretched between two points; the string may be set in motion by bowing, striking, or plucking.

chorus Fairly large group of singers who perform together, usually with several on each part. Also a choral *movement* of a large-scale work. In *jazz*, a single statement of the melodic-harmonic pattern.

chromatic *Melody* or *harmony* built from many if not all twelve pitches of the *octave*. A chromatic scale consists of an ascending or descending sequence of half steps.

clarinet *Single-reed* woodwind instrument with a wide range of sizes.

clavichord Stringed *keyboard instrument* popular in the Renaissance and Baroque that is capable of unique expressive devices not possible on the *harpsichord*.

clavier Generic word for *keyboard instruments*, including *harpsichord*, *clavichord*, *piano*, and *organ*.

climax The high point in a melodic line or piece of music, usually representing the peak of intensity, *range*, and *dynamics*.

coda The last part of a piece, usually added to a standard form to bring it to a close.

codetta In *sonata-allegro form*, the concluding section of the *exposition*; more broadly, a brief *coda* concluding an inner section of a work.

collage A technique drawn from the visual arts whereby musical fragments from other compositions are juxtaposed or overlapped within a new work.

collegium musicum An association of amateur musicians, popular in the Baroque era. Also a modern university ensemble dedicated to the performance of early music.

col legno *String instrument* technique in which the strings are hit with the wood of the bow.

comic opera Comprising English *ballad opera*, Italian *opera buffa*, French *opéra comique*, and German *Singspiel*.

commedia dell'arte Type of improvised drama popular in sixteenth- and seventeenth-century Italy; makes use of stereotyped characters.

common time See *quadruple meter*.

computer music A type of electro-acoustic music in which computers assist in creating works through sound synthesis and manipulation.

concert band See *wind band*.

concertina Small, free-reed, *bellows*-operated instrument similar to an *accordion*; hexagonal in shape, with button keys.

concertmaster The first-chair violinist of a symphony *orchestra*.

concerto Instrumental genre in several *movements* for solo instrument (or instrumental group) and *orchestra*.

concerto form Structure commonly used in first movements of concertos that combines elements of Baroque *ritornello* procedure with *sonata-allegro form*.

concerto grosso (also *ensemble concerto*) Baroque concerto type based on the opposition between a small group of solo instruments (the concertino) and *orchestra* (the ripieno).

concert overture Single-movement concert piece for *orchestra*, typically from the Romantic period and often based on a literary program.

conductor Person who, by means of gestures, leads performances of music ensembles, especially *orchestras*, *bands*, or *choruses*.

conga Afro-Cuban dance performed at Latin American Carnival celebrations. Also a single-headed drum of Afro-Cuban origin, played with bare hands.

congregational singing Simple worship music, often monophonic, in which the church congregation participates; often associated with Lutheranism and Calvinism. See also *chorale*.

conjunct Smooth, connected *melody* that moves principally by small *intervals*.

consonance Concordant or harmonious combination of *pitches* that provides a sense of relaxations and stability in music.

continuo See *basso continuo*.

contour The overall shape of a melodic line. It can move upward or downward or remain static.

contrabass See *double bass*.

contrabassoon *Double-reed* woodwind instrument with the lowest *range* in the woodwind family. Also *double bassoon*.

contralto See *alto*.

contrapuntal *Texture* employing *counterpoint*, or two or more melodic lines.

contrary motion Motion in opposite directions between individual parts in a *polyphonic* work.

contrast The use of opposing musical elements to emphasize difference and variety.

cornet Valved *brass instrument* similar to the *trumpet* but more mellow in sound.

cornet à pistons French term for a soprano-range brass instrument similar to a *trumpet*; it first appeared c. 1830 in Europe when valves (pistons) were developed.

cornetto Early instrument of the brass family with woodwind-like finger holes; developed from the cow horn but was made of wood.

countermelody An accompanying *melody* sounded against the principal melody.

counterpoint The art of combining in a single *texture* two or more melodic lines.

countersubject In a fugue, a secondary theme heard against the *subject;* a countertheme.

country-western Genre of American popular music derived from traditional music of Appalachia and the rural South, usually vocal with an accompaniment of *banjos, fiddles,* and *guitar.*

courante French Baroque dance, a standard *movement* of the *suite,* in *triple meter* at a moderate tempo.

cover Recording that remakes an earlier, often successful recording with the goal of reaching a wider audience.

cowbell Rectangular metal bell struck with a drumstick; used widely in Latin American music.

Credo The third musical section of the *Ordinary* of the *Mass.*

crescendo Growing louder.

crossover Recording or artist that appeals primarily to one audience but becomes popular with another as well (e.g., a *rock* performer who makes *jazz* recordings).

Cublism Early twentieth-century art movement begun in Paris, characterized by the fragmentation of forms into abstract or geometric patterns.

cut time A type of *duple meter* interpreted as 2/2 and indicated as ¢; also *alla breve.*

cyclical form Structure in which musical material, such as a *theme,* presented in one *movement* returns in a later movement.

cymbals *Percussion instruments* consisting of two large circular brass plates of equal size that are struck sideways against each other.

da capo An indication to return to the beginning of a piece.

da capo aria Lyric song in *ternary,* or **A-B-A,** form, commonly found in *operas, cantatas,* and *oratorios.*

decrescendo Growing softer.

development Structural reshaping of thematic material. The second section of *sonata-allegro form;* it moves through a series of foreign keys while *themes* from the *exposition* are developed.

dialogue opera See *ballad opera.*

diatonic *Melody* or *harmony* built from the seven pitches of a *major* or *minor scale.* A diatonic scale encompasses patterns of seven *whole steps* and *half steps.*

Dies irae Chant from the *Requiem Mass* whose text concerns Judgment Day.

diminuendo Growing softer.

diminution Statement of a *melody* in shorter note values, often twice as fast as the original.

disjunct Disjointed or disconnected *melody* with many leaps.

dissonance Combination of tones that sounds discordant and unstable, in need of resolution.

divertimento Classical instrumental genre for chamber ensemble or soloist, often performed as light entertainment. Related to *serenade.*

divertissement Grand genre of the French Baroque, characterized by spectacle and grandeur, intended for light entertainment or diversion.

Divine Offices Cycle of daily services of the Roman Catholic Church, distinct from the *Mass.*

dolce Sweetly.

dominant The fifth scale step, *sol.*

dominant chord *Chord* built on the fifth scale step, the V chord.

double To perform the same *notes* with more than one voice or instrument, either at the same pitch level or an *octave* higher or lower.

double bass Largest and lowest-pitched member of the bowed string family. Also *contrabass* or *bass viol.*

double bassoon See *contrabassoon.*

double exposition In the *concerto,* twofold statement of the *themes,* once by the *orchestra* and once by the soloist.

double reed A *reed* consisting of two pieces of cane that vibrate against each other.

double-stop Playing two notes simultaneously on a string instrument.

downbeat First *beat* of the *measure,* the strongest in any *meter.*

doxology A prayer of thanks to God, sung after a *psalm* or at the close of the *Magnificat.*

drone Sustained sounding of one or several pitches for harmonic support, a common feature of some folk musics.

dulcimer Early folk instrument that resembles the *psaltery;* its strings are struck with hammers instead of plucked.

duo An ensemble of two players.

duo sonata A chamber group comprised of a soloist with piano. Also, in the Baroque period, a *sonata* for a melody instrument and *basso continuo.*

duple meter Basic metrical pattern of two *beats* to a *measure.*

duration Length of time something lasts; e.g., the vibration of a musical sound.

dynamics Element of musical expression relating to the degree of loudness or softness, or volume, of a sound.

electric guitar A *guitar* designed for electronic amplification.

electronic music Generic term for any composition created by electronic means.

electronische Musik Electronic music developed in Germany in the 1930s that uses an oscillator to generate and alter waveforms.

embellishment Melodic decoration, either improvised or indicated through *ornamentation* signs in the music.

embouchure The placement of the lips, lower facial muscles, and jaws in playing a wind instrument.

encore "Again"; an audience request that the performer(s) repeat a piece or perform another.

English horn *Double-reed* woodwind instrument, larger and lower in *range* than the *oboe*.

English madrigal English secular *polyphonic* song (for two to six voices) developed from the Italian *madrigal*; often lighter and less serious, featuring *refrain* syllables (fa-la-la); largely cultivated by amateurs.

ensemble concerto See *concerto grosso*.

episode Interlude or intermediate section in the Baroque *fugue* that serves as an area of relaxation between statements of the *subject*. In a Baroque *concerto*, the free and inventive material that alternates with returns of the *ritornello*, or instrumental refrain.

equal temperament Tuning system (used today) based on the division of the *octave* into twelve equal *half steps*.

espressivo Expressively.

ethnomusicology Comparative study of musics of the world, with a focus on the cultural context of music.

étude Study piece that focuses on a particular technical problem.

euphonium Tenor-range brass instrument resembling the *tuba*.

exoticism Musical style in which *rhythms, melodies,* or instruments evoke the color and atmosphere of far-off lands.

exposition Opening section. In the *fugue*, the first section in which the voices enter in turn with the *subject*. In *sonata-allegro form*, the first section in which the major thematic material is stated. Also *statement*.

Expressionism A style of visual art and literature in Germany and Austria in the early twentieth century. The term is sometimes also applied to music, especially composers of the Second Viennese School (Schoenberg, Berg, Webern).

falsetto Vocal technique whereby men can sing above their normal *range*, producing a lighter sound.

fantasia Free instrumental piece of fairly large dimensions, in an improvisational style; in the Baroque era, it often served as an introductory piece to a *fugue*.

fiddle Colloquial term for *violin*; often used in traditional music. Also a medieval bowed string instrument.

fife A small wooden transverse *flute*, with fewer holes than a *piccolo*, traditionally associated with the military.

figured bass Baroque practice consisting of an independent bass line that often includes numerals indicating the harmony to be supplied by the performer. Also *thorough-bass*.

film music Music that serves as either background or foreground for a film.

flamenco A musical dance style from Andalusia (in southern Spain), often associated with Gypsy performers, featuring improvisational singing, finger snapping, foot stomping, and guitar strumming.

flat sign Musical symbol (♭) that indicates lowering a pitch by a *half step*.

fluegelhorn Valved brass instrument resembling a bugle with a wide bell, used in *jazz* and commercial music.

flute Soprano-range *woodwind* instrument, usually made of metal and held horizontally.

flutter-tonguing Wind instrument technique in which the player's tongue is fluttered as though "rolling an R" while he or she blows into the instrument.

folk music See *traditional music*.

folk rock Popular music style that combines folk music with amplified instruments of *rock*.

form Structure and design in music, based on repetition, contrast, and variation; the organizing principle of music.

formalism Tendency to elevate formal above expressive value in music, as in twentieth-century *neo-Classical* music.

forte (*f*) Loud.

fortepiano Forerunner of the modern *piano* (also *pianoforte*).

fortissimo (*ff*) Very loud.

four-hand piano music Chamber music genre for two performers playing at one or occasionally two pianos, allowing for home or *salon* performances of orchestral arrangements.

French horn See *horn*.

French overture Baroque instrumental introduction to an *opera, ballet,* or *suite,* in two sections: a slow opening followed by an *Allegro,* often with a brief reprise of the opening.

frequency Rate of vibration of a string or column of air, which determines *pitch*.

fugato A fugal passage in a nonfugal piece, such as in the *development* section of a *sonata-allegro form*.

fugue *Polyphonic* form popular in the Baroque era, in which one or more themes are developed by imitative *counterpoint*.

fusion Style that combines *jazz* improvisation with amplified instruments of *rock*.

galliard Lively, *triple-meter* French court dance.

galop A fast-paced, duple-meter dance popular in the mid-niineteenth century, with a galloping kind of step.

gamelan Musical ensemble of Java or Bali, made up of *gongs, chimes, metallophones,* and drums, among other instruments.

gapped scale A scale that lacks some pitches of the seven-note *diatonic* scale; for example, a five-note (*pentatonic*) scale has gaps.

gat An Indian classical work or section of a work with rhythmic patterns established by a drum; see also *tabla*.

gavotte *Duple-meter* French Baroque dance type with a moderate to quick *tempo*.

genre General term describing the standard category and overall character of a work.

gigue Popular English Baroque dance type, a standard *movement* of the Baroque *suite*, in a lively *compound meter*.

glass (h)armonica A musical instrument invented by Benjamin Franklin, made from tuned glass bowls of graded sizes that are rubbed on the rim with wet fingers.

glee club Specialized vocal ensemble that performs popular music, college songs, and more serious works.

glissando A rapid slide through pitches of a *scale*.

global pop Collective term for popular third-world musics, ethnic and traditional musics, and eclectic combinations of Western and non-Western musics. Also called world beat.

glockenspiel *Percussion instrument* with horizontal, tuned steel bars of various sizes that are struck with mallets and produce a bright metallic sound.

Gloria The second musical section of the *Ordinary* of the *Mass.*

gong Percussion instrument consisting of a broad, circular metal disk suspended on a frame and struck with a heavy mallet; produces a definite pitch. See also *tam-tam.*

gospel music Twentieth-century sacred music style associated with Protestant African Americans.

grace note Ornamental note, often printed in small type and not performed rhythmically.

Gradual Fourth item of the *Proper* of the *Mass*, sung in a *melismatic* style, and performed in a *responsorial* manner in which soloists alternate with a choir.

grand opera Style of Romantic *opera* developed in Paris, focusing on serious, historical plots with huge choruses, crowd scenes, elaborate dance episodes, ornate costumes, and spectacular scenery.

grave Solemn; very, very slow.

Gregorian chant *Monophonic* melody with a freely flowing, unmeasured vocal line; liturgical chant of the Roman Catholic Church. Also *plainchant* or *plainsong.*

ground bass A repeating *melody*, usually in the bass, throughout a vocal or instrumental composition.

güiro An idiophone of Latin American origin, comprised of a hollow gourd with notches, across which a stick is scraped.

guitar Plucked-string instrument originally made of wood with a hollow, resonating body and a fretted fingerboard; types include *acoustic* and *electric.*

guitarrón A large, six-stringed bass *guitar*, common in *mariachi* ensembles.

habanera Moderate *duple-meter* dance of Cuban origin, popular in the nineteenth century; based on a characteristic rhythmic figure.

half step Smallest *interval* used in the Western system; the *octave* divides into twelve such intervals; on the piano, the distance between any two adjacent keys, whether black or white. Also *semitone.*

hammered dulcimer Metal-stringed instrument with a trapezoidal sound box, struck with small hammers; an *idiophone.*

harmonica Mouth organ; a small metal box on which free reeds are mounted, played by moving it back and forth across the mouth while breathing into it.

harmonics Individual, pure sounds that are part of any musical tone; in string instruments, crystalline pitches in the very high *register*, produced by lightly touching a vibrating string at a certain point.

harmonic variation The procedure in which the *chords* accompanying a *melody* are replaced by others. Often used in *theme and variations* form.

harmonium *Organ*-like instrument with free metal reeds set in vibration by a *bellows*; popular in late nineteenth-century America.

harmony The simultaneous combination of notes and the ensuing relationships of *intervals* and *chords.*

harp Plucked-string instrument, triangular in shape with strings perpendicular to the soundboard.

harpsichord Early Baroque *keyboard instrument* in which the strings are plucked by quills instead of being struck with hammers like the *piano.*

heterophonic *Texture* in which two or more voices (or parts) elaborate the same melody simultaneously, often the result of *improvisation.*

hip hop Black urban art forms that emerged in New York City in the 1970s, encompassing *rap* music, break dancing, and graffiti art as well as the fashions adopted by the artists. The term comes from the strings of *vocables*, or nonsense syllables, used by rap artists.

homophonic *Texture* with a principal *melody* and accompanying *harmony*, as distinct from *polyphony.*

homorhythmic *Texture* in which all voices, or lines, move together in the same *rhythm.*

horn Medium-range valved *brass instrument* that can be played "stopped" with the hand as well as open. Also *French horn.*

hornpipe Country dance of the British Isles, often in a lively *triple meter*; optional dance movement of solo and orchestral Baroque *suites.* A type of *duple-meter* hornpipe is still popular in Irish traditional dance music.

hymn Song in praise of God; often sung by a whole congregation.

idée fixe "Fixed idea"; term coined by Berlioz for a recurring musical idea that links different *movements* of a work.

idiophone Instrument that produces sound from the substance of the instrument itself by being struck, blown, shaken, scraped, or rubbed. Examples include bells, rattles, *xylophones*, and *cymbals.*

imitation Melodic idea presented in one *voice* or part and then restated in another, each part continuing as others enter.

Impressionism A French movement developed by visual artists who favored vague, blurring images intended to capture an "impression" of the subject. Impressionism in music is characterized by exotic *scales*, unresolved *dissonances*, parallel *chords*, rich orchestral tone color, and free *rhythm.*

improvisation The creation of a musical composition while it is being performed, as in Baroque *ornamentation*, *cadenzas* of *concertos*, *jazz*, and some non-Western musics.

incidental music Music written to accompany dramatic works.

inflection Small alteration of the pitch by a microtonal *interval.* See also *blue note.*

instrument Mechanism that generates musical vibrations and transmits them into the air.

interactive performance Computer-supported, collaborative music-making that includes live performers interacting with computers, interconnected performance networks, and online improvisation.

interlude Music played between sections of a musical or dramatic work.

intermezzo Short, lyric piece or *movement*, often for piano. Also a comic *interlude* performed between acts of an eighteen-century *opera seria*.

interval The distance and relationship between two *pitches*.

inversion Mirror or upside-down image of a *melody* or pattern, found in *fugues* and *twelve-tone* compositions.

Irish harp Plucked-string instrument with about thirty strings; used to accompany Irish songs and dance music.

irregular meter An atypical metric scheme, often based on an odd number of *beats* per *measure* (e.g., 5/4, 7/8, 11/4).

Italian overture Baroque *overture* consisting of three sections: fast-slow-fast.

jam band A group that focuses on live performance rather than commercial recordings. Jam bands, such as the Grateful Dead and Phish, combine different musical traditions, most notably *folk*, *jazz*, *rock*, and *country-western*, in a highly improvisational and expressive style.

Janissary music Music of the military corps of the Turkish sultan, characterized by *percussion instruments* like the *triangle*, *cymbals*, *bell tree*, and *bass drum* as well as *trumpets* and *double-reed* instruments.

jarabe Traditional Mexican dance form with multiple sections in contrasting *meters* and *tempos*, often performed by *mariachi* ensembles.

jazz A musical style created mainly by African Americans in the early twentieth century that blended elements drawn from African musics with the popular and art traditions of the West.

jazz band Instrumental ensemble made up of reed (*saxophones* and *clarinets*), brass (*trumpets* and *trombones*), and rhythm sections (*percussion*, *piano*, *double bass*, and sometimes *guitar*).

jig A vigorous dance developed in the British Isles, usually in *compound meter*; became fashionable on the Continent as the *gigue*; still popular as an Irish traditional dance genre.

kabuki A genre of Japanese musical theater with elaborate costumes and makeup.

Kapellmeister A German term referring to the leader of a musical chapter, either at court or at a church.

kettledrums See *timpani*.

key Defines the relationship of *pitches* with a common center, or *tonic*. Also a lever on a *keyboard* or *woodwind* instrument.

keyboard instrument Instrument sounded by means of a keyboard (a series of keys played with the fingers). See also individual types.

key signature Sharps or flats placed at the beginning of a piece to show the *key* of a work (there are no sharps or flats if the key is C major or A minor).

koto Japanese plucked-string instrument with a long rectangular body, thirteen strings, and movable bridges or frets.

Kyrie The first musical section of the *Ordinary* of the *Mass*. Its construction is threefold, involving three repetitions of "Kyrie eleison" (Lord, have mercy), three of "Christe eleison" (Christ, have mercy), and again three of "Kyrie eleison."

largo Broad; very slow.

Latin jazz A *jazz* style influenced by Latin American music, which includes various dance rhythms and traditional *percussion instruments*.

Latin rock Subgenre of *rock* featuring Latin and African *percussion instruments* (*maracas*, *conga drums*, *timbales*).

legato Smooth and connected; opposite of *staccato*.

leitmotif "Leading motive," or basic recurring *theme*, representing a person, object, or idea; widely used in Wagner's *music dramas*.

librettist The author of a *libretto*.

libretto Text or script of an *opera*, *oratorio*, *cantata*, or *musical* (also called the "book" in a musical).

Lied German for "song"; most commonly associated with the solo *art song* of the nineteenth century, usually accompanied by *piano*. See also *art song*.

Lieder Plural of *Lied*.

liturgy The set order of religious services and the structure of each service, within a particular denomination (e.g., Roman Catholic).

lute Plucked-string instrument of Middle Eastern origin, popular in western Europe from the late Middle Ages to the eighteenth century.

lyre Ancient plucked-string instrument of the *harp* family, used to accompany singing and poetry.

lyric opera Hybrid form combining elements of *grand opera* and *comic opera* and featuring appealing melodies and romantic drama.

madrigal Renaissance secular work originating in Italy for voices, with or without instruments, set to a short, lyric love poem; also popular in England.

madrigal choir Small vocal ensemble that specializes in *a cappella* secular works.

madrigalism A striking effect designed to depict the meaning of the text in vocal music; found in many *madrigals* and other genres of the sixteenth through eighteenth centuries. See also *word painting*.

maestoso Majestic.

Magnificat Biblical text on the words of the Virgin Mary, sung polyphonically in church from the Renaissance era on.

Magnus liber organi The Great Book of Organum, compiled by resident composers at Notre Dame in Paris during the eleventh and twelfth centuries.

major-minor tonality A harmonic system based on the use of *major* and *minor scales*, widely practiced from the seventeenth to the late nineteenth century. See also *tonality*.

major scale Scale consisting of seven different pitches that comprise a specific pattern of *whole* and *half steps* (W-W-H-W-W-W-H). Differs from the *minor scale* primarily in that its third degree is raised half a step.

mandolin Plucked-string instrument with a rounded body and fingerboard; used in some *traditional musics* and in *country-western* music.

maqam An Arabic mode or scale.

maracas Latin American rattles (*idiophones*) made from gourds or other materials.

march A style incorporating characteristics of military music, including strongly accented *duple meter* in simple, repetitive rhythmic patterns.

marching band Instrumental ensemble for entertainment at sports events and parades, consisting of wind and *percussion instruments,* drum majors/majorettes, and baton twirlers.

mariachi Traditional Mexican ensemble popular throughout the country, consisting of *trumpets, violins, guitar,* and bass guitar.

marimba *Percussion instrument,* a mellower version of the *xylophone*; of African origin.

masque English genre of aristocratic entertainment that combined vocal and instrumental music with poetry and dance, developed during the sixteenth and seventeenth centuries.

Mass Central service of the Roman Catholic Church.

mazurka Type of Polish folk dance in *triple meter.*

measure, or bar Metric grouping of *beats,* notated on the musical staff with *bar lines.*

medium Performing forces employed in a certain musical work.

medley A composition built on a series of well-known tunes that may be loosely connected or from different sources.

Meistersinger A German "master singer," belonging to a professional guild. Meistersingers flourished from the fourteenth through the sixteenth centuries.

melismatic Melodic style characterized by many notes sung to a single text syllable.

melodic variation The procedure in which a melody is altered while certain features are maintained; often used in *theme and variations* form.

mélodie An accompanied French art song of the nineteenth and twentieth centuries; the French parallel to the German *Lied.*

melody Succession of single *pitches* perceived by the ear as a unity.

membranophone Any instrument that produces sound from tightly stretched membranes that can be struck.

metallophone *Percussion instrument* consisting of tuned metal bars, usually struck with a mallet.

meter Organization of *rhythm* in time; the grouping of *beats* into larger, regular patterns, notated as *measures.*

metronome Device used to indicate the *tempo* by sounding regular *beats* at adjustable speeds.

mezzo forte (**mf**) Moderately loud.

mezzo piano (**mp**) Moderately soft.

mezzo-soprano Female voice of middle range.

microtone Musical interval smaller than a *semitone* (*half step*), prevalent in some non-Western musics and some twentieth-century music.

MIDI Acronym for Musical Instrument Digital Interface; technology standard that allows networking of computers with electronic musical instruments.

minimalism Contemporary musical style featuring the repetition of short melodic, rhythmic, and harmonic patterns with little variation. See also *post-minimalism, spiritual minimalism,* and *process music.*

Minnesingers Late medieval German poet-musicians.

minor scale Scale consisting of seven different pitches that comprise a specific pattern of *whole* and *half steps* (W-H-W-W-H-W-W). Differs from the *major scale* primarily in that its third degree is lowered half a step.

minstrel show A late nineteenth-century American entertainment featuring white performers in blackface acting out stereotypes of African American slaves.

minuet An elegant *triple-meter* dance type popular in the seventeenth and eighteenth centuries; usually in *binary form.* See also *minuet and trio.*

minuet and trio An **A-B-A** form (**A** = minuet; **B** = trio) in a moderate *triple meter;* often the third movement of the Classical *multimovement cycle.*

modal Characterizes music based on *modes* other than major and minor, especially the early church modes.

mode *Scale* or sequence of notes used as the basis for a composition; major and minor are modes.

modernism Early twentieth-century movement in the arts and literature that explored innovative, nontraditional forms of expression. See also *postmodernism.*

moderato Moderate.

modified strophic form Song structure that combines elements of *strophic* and *through-composed* forms; a variation of strophic form in which a section might have a new *key, rhythm,* or varied melodic pattern.

modulation The process of changing from one *key* to another.

molto Very.

monody Vocal style established in the Baroque era, with solo singer(s) and instrumental accompaniment.

monophonic Single-line *texture,* or melody without accompaniment.

motet *Polyphonic* vocal genre, often secular in the Middle Ages but sacred or devotional thereafter.

motive Short melodic or rhythmic idea; the smallest fragment of a *theme* that forms a melodic-harmonic-rhythmic unit.

movement Complete, self-contained part within a larger musical work.

mp3 A file-compression format applied to audio files; short for Moving Pictures Expert Group 1 Layer 3.

muezzin A male crier who sounds the Muslim call to prayer from the top of a mosque.

multimovement cycle A three- or four-movement structure used in Classical-era instrumental music—especially the *symphony, sonata, concerto*—and in *chamber music*; each movement is in a prescribed *tempo* and *form*; sometimes called sonata cycle.

multiphonic Two or more pitches sung or played simultaneously by the same voice or instrument.

musical Genre of twentieth-century musical theater, especially popular in the United States and Great Britain; features spoken dialogue and a dramatic plot interspersed with songs, ensemble numbers, and dancing.

music drama Wagner's term for his operas.

music video Video tape or film that accompanies a recording, usually of a popular or *rock* song.

musique concrète Music made up of natural sounds and sound effects that are recorded and then manipulated electronically.

mute Mechanical device used to muffle the sound of an instrument.

neo-Classicism A twentieth-century style that combined elements of Classical and Baroque music with modernist trends.

neo-Romanticim A contemporary style of music that employs the rich harmonic language and other elements of Romantic and post-Romantic composers.

neumatic Melodic style with two to four notes set to each syllable.

new age Style of popular music of the 1980s and 90s, characterized by soothing *timbres* and repetitive forms that are subjected to shifting variation techniques.

New Orleans jazz Early *jazz* style characterized by multiple improvisations in an ensemble of *cornet* (or *trumpet*), *clarinet* (or *saxophone*), *trombone, piano, double bass* (or *tuba*), *banjo* (or *guitar*), and drums; repertory included *blues, ragtime,* and popular songs.

ninth chord Five-note *chord* spanning a ninth between its lowest and highest *pitches.*

nocturne "Night piece"; introspective work common in the nineteenth century, often for piano.

Noh **drama** A major form of Japanese theater since the late fourteenth century; based on philosophical concepts from Zen Buddhism.

nonlexical syllable Syllable that does not carry specific meaning; a nonsense syllable.

nonmetric Music lacking a strong sense of beat or meter, common in certain non-Western cultures.

non troppo Not too much.

note A musical symbol denoting *pitch* and *duration.*

oblique motion Polyphonic voice movement in which one voice remains stationary while the others move.

oboe Soprano-range, *double-reed* woodwind instrument.

octave *Interval* between two notes eight diatonic pitches apart; the lower note vibrates half as fast as the upper and sounds an octave lower.

octet *Chamber music* for eight instruments or voices.

ode Secular composition written for a royal occasion, especially popular in England.

offbeat A weak *beat* or weak portion of a beat.

opera Music drama that is generally sung throughout, combining the resources of vocal and instrumental music with poetry and drama, acting and dancing, scenery and costumes.

opera buffa Italian comic opera, sung throughout.

opéra comique French comic opera, with some spoken dialogue.

opera seria Tragic Italian opera.

operetta Small-scale operatic work, generally light in tone, with spoken dialogue, song and dance.

ophicleide Nineteenth-century *brass instrument* (now obsolete) with *woodwind* fingering holes; used by Berlioz, among others; the parts are usually played today on *tuba.*

Opus number (Op.) A number, often part of the title of a piece, designating the work in chronological relationship to other works by the same composer.

oral tradition Music that is transmitted by example or imitation and performed from memory.

oratorio Large-scale dramatic genre originating in the Baroque, based on a text of religious or serious character, performed by solo voices, *chorus,* and *orchestra*; similar to *opera* but without scenery, costumes, or action.

oratory A prayer chapel within a church; the origin of the genre term *oratorio.*

orchestra Performing group of diverse instruments in various cultures; in Western art music, an ensemble of multiple strings with various *woodwind, brass,* and *percussion instruments.*

orchestration The technique of setting music for instruments in various combinations.

Ordinary Sections of the Roman Catholic *Mass* that remain the same from day to day throughout the church year, as distinct from the *Proper,* which changes daily according to the liturgical occasion.

organ Wind instrument in which air is fed to the pipes by mechanical means; the pipes are controlled by two or more keyboards and a set of pedals.

organum Earliest kind of *polyphonic* music, which developed from the custom of adding voices above a *plainchant*; they first ran parallel to the chant at the interval of a fifth or fourth and later moved more freely.

ornamentation See *embellishment.*

ostinato A short melodic, rhythmic, or harmonic pattern that is repeated throughout a work or a section.

overture An introductory *movement,* as in an *opera* or *oratorio,* often presenting melodies from *arias* to come. Also an orchestral work for concert performance.

panharmonicon An automatic instrument designed to simulate a whole *orchestra* using *organ* pipes and mechanical percussion devices. Beethoven's *Wellington's Victory* was originally written for the panharmonicon.

panpipes Wind instrument consisting of a series of small vertical tubes or pipes of differing length; sound is produced by blowing across the top.

pantomime Theatrical genre in which an actor silently plays all the parts in a show while accompanied by singing; originated in ancient Rome.

parlor song A song, generally accompanied by piano, intended for home entertainment; the term is particular to nineteenth-century America.

part book A bound music book—either print or manuscript—with music for a single vocalist or instrumentalist.

part song Secular vocal composition, unaccompanied, in three, four, or more parts.

partita See *suite*.

pas de deux A dance for two that is an established feature of classical ballet.

passacaglia Baroque form (similar to the *chaconne*) in moderately slow *triple meter*, based on a short, repeated bass-line melody that serves as the basis for continuous variations in the other voices.

passepied French Baroque court dance type; a faster version of the *minuet*.

Passion Musical setting of the Crucifixion story as told by one of the four Evangelists in the Gospels.

pastorale Pastoral, country-like.

patron (patroness) A person who supports music or musicians; a benefactor of the arts. See also *patronage*.

patronage Sponsorship of an artist or a musician, historically by a member of the wealthy or ruling classes.

pavane Stately Renaissance court dance in *duple meter*.

pedal point Sustained *pitch* over which the *harmonies* change.

penny whistle See *tin whistle*.

pentatonic scale Five-note pattern used in some African, Far Eastern, and Native American musics; can also be found in Western music as an example of exoticism. See also *gapped scale*.

percussion instrument Instrument made of metal, wood, stretched skin, or other material that is made to sound by striking, shaking, scraping, or plucking.

perfect pitch The innate ability to sing any pitch without hearing it first.

performance art Multimedia art form involving visual as well as dramatic and musical elements.

period-instrument ensemble Group that performs on historical instruments or modern replicas built after historical models.

phrase A musical unit; often a component of a *melody*.

pianissimo (pp) Very soft.

piano (p) Soft.

piano Keyboard instrument whose strings are struck with hammers controlled by a keyboard mechanism; pedals control dampers in the strings that stop the sound when the finger releases the key.

pianoforte Original name for the *piano*.

piano quartet Standard chamber ensemble of *piano* with *violin*, *viola*, and *cello*.

piano quintet Standard chamber ensemble of *piano* with *string quartet* (two *violins*, *viola*, and *cello*).

piano roll A perforated paper roll that was recorded and then capable of playing back mechanically on a player piano.

piano trio Standard chamber ensemble of *piano* with *violin* and *cello*.

piccolo Smallest *woodwind* instrument, similar to the *flute* but sounding an *octave* higher.

pipa A Chinese *lute* with four silk strings; played as a solo and ensemble instrument.

pipe A medieval *flute* with three holes, blown at one end through a mouthpiece.

pitch Highness or lowness of a note, depending on the *frequency*.

pizzicato Performance direction to pluck a string of a bowed instrument with the finger.

plainchant See *Gregorian chant*.

plainsong See *Gregorian chant*.

plectrum An implement made of wood, ivory, or another material used to pluck a *chordophone*.

pluck To sound the strings of an instrument using fingers or a *plectrum* or pick.

poco A little.

polka Lively Bohemian dance; also a short, lyric piano piece.

polonaise Stately Polish processional dance in *triple meter*.

polychoral Performance style developed in the late sixteenth century involving the use of two or more *choirs* that alternate with each other or sing together.

polychord A single *chord* comprised of several chords, common in twentieth-century music.

polyharmony Two or more streams of *harmony* played against each other, common in twentieth-century music.

polymeter The simultaneous use of several *meters*, common in twentieth-century music and certain African musics.

polyphonic Two or more melodic lines combined into a multivoiced *texture*, as distinct from *monophonic*.

polyrhythm The simultaneous use of several rhythmic patters or *meters*, common in twentieth-century music and certain African musics.

polytonality The simultaneous use of two or more *keys*, common in twentieth-century music.

portative organ Medieval organ small enough to be carried or set on a table, usually with only one set of pipes.

positive organ Small, single-manual organ, popular in the Renaissance and Baroque eras.

post-minimalism Contemporary style combining lush harmonies of neo-Romanticism with high-energy rhythms of minimalism; John Adams is a major exponent.

postmodernism A movement in the arts and literature that reacts against early modernist principles through the use of classical and traditional elements. See *modernism*.

post-Romanticism A trend at the turn of the twentieth century in which nineteenth-century musical characteristics like *chromatic* harmony and expansive melodies are carried to the extreme.

prelude Instrumental work preceding a larger work.

prelude and fugue Paired *movements*, the prelude in a free form, the fugue in a strict, imitative form.

prepared piano Piano whose sound is altered by the insertion of various materials (metal, rubber, leather, and paper) between the strings; invented by John Cage.

presto Very fast.

process music A compositional style in which a composer selects a simple musical idea and repeats it over and over, as it's gradually changed or elaborated upon. See also *minimalism*.

program music Instrumental music endowed with literary or pictorial associations, especially popular in the nineteenth century.

Proper Sections of the Roman Catholic *Mass* that vary from day to day throughout the church year according to the liturgical occasion, as distinct from the *Ordinary*, in which they remain the same.

Psalms Book from the Old Testament of the Bible; the 150 Psalm texts, used in Jewish and Christian worship, are often set to music.

psaltery Medieval plucked-string instrument similar to the modern *zither*, consisting of a sound box over which strings were stretched.

pure music See *absolute music*.

quadruple meter Basic metrical pattern of four beats to a measure. Also *common time*.

quartal harmony *Harmony* based on the *interval* of the fourth as opposed to a third; used in twentieth-century music.

quarter tone An *interval* halfway between two notes a *half step* apart.

quintet *Chamber music* for five instruments or voices. See also *brass quintet, piano quintet, string quintet,* and *woodwind quintet*.

quotation music Music that parodies another work or works, presenting them in a new style or guise.

raga Melodic pattern used in music of India; prescribes *pitches*, patterns, *ornamentation,* and extramusical associations such as time of performance and emotional character.

ragtime Late nineteenth-century piano style created by African Americans, characterized by highly syncopated melodies; also played in ensemble arrangements. Contributed to early *jazz* styles.

range Distance between the lowest and highest *pitches* of a melody, an instrument, or a voice.

rap Style of popular music in which rhymed lyrics are spoken over rhythm tracks; developed by African Americans in the 1970s and widely disseminated in the 1980s and 90s; the style is part of the larger culture of *hip hop*.

rebec Medieval bowed-string instrument, often with a pear-shaped body.

recapitulation Third section of *sonata-allegro form,* in which the thematic material of the *exposition* is restated, generally in the *tonic*. Also *restatement*.

recitative Solo vocal declamation that follows the inflections of the text, often resulting in a disjunct vocal style; found in *opera, cantata,* and *oratorio*. Can be *secco* or *accompagnato*.

recorder End-blown *woodwind* instrument with a whistle mouthpiece, generally associated with early music.

reed Flexible strip of cane or metal set into a mouthpiece or the body of an instrument; set in vibration by a stream of air. See also *single reed* and *double reed*.

reel Moderately quick dance in *duple meter* danced throughout the British Isles; the most popular Irish traditional dance type.

refrain Text or music that is repeated within a larger form.

register Specific area in the range of an instrument or voice.

registration Selection or combination of stops in a work for *organ* or *harpsichord*.

relative key The major and minor key that share the same *key signature*; for example, D minor is the relative minor of F major, both having one flat.

repeat sign Musical symbol ($\|$: :$\|$) that indicates the repetition of a passage.

Requiem Mass Roman Catholic *Mass* for the Dead.

resolution Conclusion of a musical idea, as in the progression from an *active chord* to a *rest chord*.

response Short choral answer to a solo *verse*; an element of liturgical dialogue.

responsorial singing Singing, especially in *Gregorian chant,* in which a soloist or a group of soloists alternates with the choir. See also *call and response*.

rest chord A chord that achieves a sense of *resolution* or completion, normally the *tonic*.

restatement See *recapitulation*.

retrograde Backward statement of a *melody*.

retrograde inversion Mirror image of the backward statement of a *melody*.

rhyme scheme The arrangement of rhyming words or corresponding sounds at the end of poetic lines.

rhythm The controlled movement of music in time.

rhythm and blues Popular African American music style of the 1940s through the 60s, featuring a solo singer accompanied by a small instrumental ensemble (*piano, guitar, double bass,* drums, tenor *saxophone*), driving rhythms, and *blues* and pop song forms.

rhythmic variation The procedure in which note lengths, *meter,* or *tempo* is altered. Often used in *theme and variations* form.

riff In *jazz*, a short melodic *ostinato* over changing harmonies.

ring shout Religious dance of African American slaves, performed with hand clapping and a shuffle step to *spirituals*.

ritardando Holding back, getting slower.

ritornello Short, recurring instrumental passage found in both the *aria* and the Baroque *concerto*.

rock A style of popular music with roots in rock and roll but differing in lyric content, recording technique, song length and form, and range of sounds. The term was first used in the 1960s to distinguish groups like the Beatles and the Rolling Stones from earlier artists.

rocket theme Quickly ascending rhythmic melody used in Classical-era instrumental music; the technique is credited to composers in Mannheim, Germany.

Rococo A term from the visual arts that is frequently applied to mid-eighteenth-century French music, characterized by simplicity, grace, and delicate *ornamentation*.

romance Originally a *ballad*; in the Romantic era, a lyric instrumental work.

rondo Musical form in which the first section recurs several times, usually in the *tonic*. In the Classical *multimovement cycle*, it appears as the last *movement* in various forms, such as **A-B-A-B-A**, **A-B-A-C-A**, and **A-B-A-C-A-B-A**.

round Perpetual *canon* at the *unison* in which each voice enters in succession with the same melody (for example, *Row, Row, Row Your Boat*).

rounded binary Composition form with two sections, in which the second ends with a return to material from the first; each section is usually repeated.

rubato "Borrowed time," common in Romantic music, in which the performer hesitates here or hurries forward there, imparting flexibility to the written note values.

rural blues American popular singing style with raspy-voiced male singer accompanied by acoustic steel-string *guitar*; features melodic *blue notes* over repeated bass patterns.

sackbut Early *brass instrument,* ancestor of the *trombone.*

sacred music Religious or spiritual music, for church or devotional use.

salon A gathering of musicians, artists, and intellectuals who shared similar interests and tastes, hosted by a wealthy aristocrat.

sampler Electronic device that digitizes, stores, and plays back sounds.

Sanctus The fourth musical section of the *Ordinary* of the *Mass.*

sarabande Stately Spanish Baroque dance type in *triple meter*, a standard *movement* of the Baroque *suite.*

SATB Abbreviation for the standard voices in a *chorus* or *choir*: soprano, alto, tenor, bass; may also refer to instrumental ranges.

saxophone Family of *single-reed* woodwind instruments commonly used in *wind* and *jazz bands.*

scale Series of pitches in ascending or descending order, comprising the notes of a *key.*

scat-singing A *jazz* style that sets syllables without meaning (*vocables*) to an improvised vocal line.

scherzo Composition in **A-B-A** form, usually in *triple meter*; replaced the *minuet and trio* in the nineteenth century.

secco *Recitative* singing style that features a sparse accompaniment and moves with great freedom.

secular music Nonreligious music; when there is text, it is usually in the vernacular.

semitone Also known as a *half step,* the smallest *interval* commonly used in the Western musical system.

septet *Chamber music* for seven instruments or voices.

sequence Restatement of an idea or *motive* at a different pitch level.

serenade Classical instrumental genre that combines elements of *chamber music* and *symphony,* often performed in the evening or at social functions. Related to *divertimento.*

serialism Method of composition in which various musical elements (*pitch, rhythm, dynamics, timbre*) may be ordered in a fixed series.

seventh chord Four-note combination of notes consisting of a *triad* with another third added on top; spans a seventh between its lowest and highest notes.

sextet *Chamber music* for six instruments or voices.

sextuple meter Compound metrical pattern of six *beats* to a *measure.*

sforzando (*sf*) Sudden stress or accent on a single note or chord.

sharp sign Musical symbol (♯) that indicates raising a pitch by a *half step.*

shifting meter See *changing meter.*

side drum See *snare drum.*

simple meter *Meter* in which the *beat* is divided into two, as in duple, triple, and quadruple meters.

sinfonia Short instrumental work, found in Baroque *opera,* to facilitate scene changes.

single reed A *reed* consisting of one piece of cane vibrating against another part of the instrument, often a mouthpiece.

Singspiel Comic German drama with spoken dialogue; the immediate predecessor of Romantic German *opera.*

sitar Long-necked *chordophone* of northern India, with movable frets and a rounded gourd body; used as a solo instrument and with *tabla.*

ska Jamaican urban dance form popular in the 1960s, influential in *reggae.*

slide In bowed string instruments, moving from one pitch to another by sliding the finger on the string while bowing.

slide trumpet Medieval *brass instrument* of the *trumpet* family.

snare drum Small cylindrical drum with two heads.

solfège French term referring to a pedagogical system for learning music by assigning syllables to scale tones (*do, re, mi, fa, sol, la, ti*).

son A genre of traditional Mexican dances that combine compound duple with triple meters.

sonata Instrumental genre in several *movements* for soloist or small ensemble.

sonata-allegro form The opening *movement* of the *multimovement cycle,* consisting of themes that are stated in the first section (*exposition*), developed in the second section (*development*), and restated in the third section (*recapitulation*). Also called sonata form.

song cycle Group of songs that are unified musically or through their texts.

soprano Highest-ranged voice, normally possessed by women and boys.

soul A black American style of popular music, incorporating elements of rock and roll and *gospel*.

source music A film technique in which music comes from a logical source within the film and functions as part of the story.

sousaphone *Brass instrument* adapted from the *tuba* with a forward bell that is coiled to rest over the player‚Äôs shoulder for ease of carrying while marching.

spiritual Folklike devotional genre of the United States, sung by African Americans and whites.

spiritual minimalism Contemporary musical style related to *minimalism*, characterized by a weak pulse and long chains of lush progressions—either *tonal* or *modal*.

Sprechstimme A vocal style in which the melody is spoken at approximate pitches rather than sung on exact pitches; developed by Arnold Schoenberg.

staccato Short, detached notes, marked with a dot above them.

staff The five parallel lines on which notes are written.

stanza A unit or verse of poetry; also a *strophe*.

statement See *exposition*.

steel drum A *percussion instrument* made from an oil drum, developed in Trinidad during the 1930s and 40s.

stopping On a *string instrument*, altering the string length by pressing it on the fingerboard. On a *horn*, playing with the bell closed by the hand or a *mute*.

strain One of a series of contrasting sections found in rags and marches; in *duple meter* with sixteen-measure themes.

stretto In a *fugue*, when entries of the *subject* occur at faster intervals of time so that they overlap, forming dense, imitative *counterpoint*. Stretto usually occurs at the climactic moment near the end.

string instruments Bowed and plucked instruments whose sound is produced by the vibration of one or more strings. Also *chordophone*.

string quartet *Chamber music* ensemble consisting of two *violins*, *viola*, and *cello*. Also a multimovement composition for this ensemble.

string quintet Standard chamber ensemble made up of either two *violins*, two *violas*, and *cello* or two violins, viola, and two cellos.

string trio Standard chamber ensemble of two *violins* and *cello* or violin, *viola*, and cello.

strophe A unit or verse of poetry; also a *stanza*.

strophic form Song structure in which the same music is repeated with every stanza (strophe) of the poem.

Sturm und Drang "Storm and stress"; late eighteenth-century movement in Germany toward more emotional expression in the arts.

style Characteristic manner of the presentation of musical elements (*melody, rhythm, harmony, dynamics, form*, etc.).

subdominant Fourth scale step, *fa*.

subdominant chord Chord built on the fourth scale step, the IV chord.

subject The main idea or *theme* of a work, as in a *fugue*.

suite Multimovement work made up of a series of contrasting dance movements, generally all in the same *key*. Also *partita*.

swing *Jazz* term coined to describe Louis Armstrong‚Äôs style; more commonly refers to *big band* jazz.

Swing Era The mid-1930s to the mid-1940s, when *swing* was the most popular music in the United States. Important musicians of the era were Louis Armstrong, Duke Ellington, and Benny Goodman.

syllabic Melodic style of one note set to each text syllable.

Symbolism Literary movement that paralleled *Impressionism*, in which poetic images were invoked through suggestion or symbol rather than literal description.

symphonic poem One-movement orchestral form that develops a poetic idea, suggests a scene, or creates a mood, usually associated with the Romantic era. Also *tone poem*.

symphony Large work for *orchestra*, generally in three or four *movements*.

symphony orchestra See *orchestra*.

syncopation Deliberate upsetting of the *meter* or pulse through a temporary shifting of the accent to a weak *beat* or an *offbeat*.

synthesizer Electronic instrument that produces a wide variety of sounds by combining sound generators and sound modifiers in one package with a unified control system.

tabla Pair of single-headed, tuned drums used in north Indian classical music.

tabor Cylindrical medieval drum.

tala Fixed time cycle or *meter* in Indian music, built from uneven groupings of *beats*.

tambourine *Percussion instrument* consisting of a small round drum with metal plates inserted in its rim; played by striking or shaking.

tam-tam A flat gong of indefinite pitch. See also *gong*.

tape music Type of *electronic music* in which sounds are recorded on tape and then manipulated and mixed in various ways. See also *musique concrète*.

tempo The rate of speed or pace of music.

tenor Male voice of high range. Also a part, often structural, in *polyphony*.

tenor drum *Percussion instrument*, larger than the *snare drum*, with a wooden shell.

ternary form Three-part (**A-B-A**) form based on a statement (**A**), contrast (**B**), and repetition (**A**). Also *three-part form*.

tertian harmony *Harmony* based on the *interval* of the third, particularly predominant from the Baroque through the nineteenth century.

texture The interweaving of melodic (horizontal) and harmonic (vertical) elements in the musical fabric.

thematic development Musical expansion of a *theme* by varying its melodic outline, *harmony*, or *rhythm*. Also *thematic transformation*.

thematic transformation See *thematic development*.

theme Melodic idea used as a basic building block in the construction of a piece. Also *subject*.

theme and variations Compositional procedure in which a

theme is stated and then altered in successive statements; occurs as an independent piece or as a *movement* of a *multimovement cycle*.

theme group Several themes in the same *key* that function as a unit within a section of a form, particularly in *sonata-allegro form*.

third *Interval* between two notes that are three *diatonic* scale steps apart.

thirty-two-bar song form Popular song structure that subdivides into four sections (**A-A-B-A**) of eight measures each.

thorough bass See *figured bass*.

three-part form See *ternary form*.

through-composed Song structure that is composed from beginning to end, without repetitions of large sections.

timbales Shallow, single-headed drums of Cuban origin, played in pairs; used in much Latin American popular music.

timbre The quality of a sound that distinguishes one voice or instrument from another. Also *tone color*.

timbrel Ancient *percussion instrument* related to the *tambourine*.

timpani *Percussion instrument* consisting of a hemispheric copper shell with a head of plastic or calfskin, held in place by a metal ring and played with soft or hard padded sticks. A pedal mechanism changes the tension of the head, and with it the *pitch*. Also *kettledrums*.

Tin Pan Alley Nickname for the popular music industry centered in New York from the nineteenth century through the 1950s. Also the style of popular song in the United States during that period.

tintinnabulation A bell-like style developed by Estonian composer Arvo Pärt, achieved by weaving conjunct lines that hover around a central pitch; from the Latin word for bell.

tin whistle Small, metal end-blown *flute* commonly used in Irish traditional music.

toccata Virtuoso composition, generally for *organ* or *harpsichord*, in a free and rhapsodic style; in the Baroque era, it often served as the introduction to a *fugue*.

tom-tom Cylindrical drum without snares.

tonal Based on principles of major-minor *tonality*, as distinct from *modal*.

tonality Principle of organization around a *tonic*, or home, pitch, based on a *major* or *minor scale*.

tone cluster Highly dissonant combination of *pitches* sounded simultaneously.

tone color See *timbre*.

tone poem See *symphonic poem*.

tone row An arrangement of the twelve *chromatic* pitches that serves as the basis of a *twelve-tone* piece.

tonic The first note of the *scale*, or *key*; *do*.

tonic chord *Triad* built on the first scale note, the I chord.

traditional music Music learned by *oral transmission* and easily sung or played by most people; may exist in variant forms. Also *folk music*.

transition See *bridge*.

transposition The shifting of a piece of music to a different pitch level.

tremolo Rapid repetition of a note; can be achieved instrumentally or vocally.

triad Common *chord* type, consisting of three *pitches* built on alternate notes of the *scale* (e.g., steps 1-3-5, or *do-mi-sol*).

triangle *Percussion instrument* consisting of a slender rod of steel bent in the shape of a triangle, struck with a steel beater.

trill Ornament consisting of the rapid alternation between one note and the next.

trio An ensemble of three players.

triple meter Basic metrical pattern of three *beats* to a *measure*.

triplet Group of three equal-valued notes played in the time of two; indicated by a bracket and the number 3.

trombone Tenor-range *brass instrument* that changes pitch by means of valves.

troubadours Medieval poet-musicians in southern France.

trouser role In Classical *opera*, the part of a young man, written for a soprano or mezzo-soprano singer.

trouvères Medieval poet-musicians in northern France.

trumpet Highest-pitched *brass instrument* that changes pitch by means of valves.

tuba Bass-range *brass instrument* that changes pitch by means of valves.

tutti "All"; the opposite of solo.

twelve-bar blues Musical structure based on a repeated harmonic-rhythmic pattern, twelve measures long: I–I–I–I–IV–IV–I–I–V–V–I–I.

twelve-tone music Compositional procedure of the twentieth century based on an ordering of all twelve chromatic pitches (in a *tone row*), without a central pitch, or *tonic*, according to prescribed rules.

two-part form See *binary form*.

underscoring A technique used in films in which the music comes from an unseen source.

unison "Interval" between two notes of the same pitch (for example, two voices on the same E); the simultaneous playing of the same note.

upbeat Last *beat* of a *measure*, a weak beat that anticipates the *downbeat*.

variation The compositional procedure of altering a preexisting musical idea. See also *theme and variations*.

vaudeville A light comedic variety show with music featuring popular song, dance, comedy, and acrobatics; flourished in the late nineteenth and early twentieth centuries.

verismo Operatic "realism," a style popular in Italy in the 1890s, which tried to bring naturalism into the lyric theater.

vernacular The common language spoken by the people as distinguished from the literary language, or language of the educated elite.

verse In poetry, a group of lines constituting a unit. In liturgical music for the Catholic Church, a phrase from the Scriptures that alternates with the *response*.

vibraphone A *percussion instrument* with metal bars and electrically driven rotating propellers under each bar that produces a *vibrato* sound, much used in *jazz*.

vibrato Small fluctuation of pitch used as an expressive device to intensify a sound.

vielle Medieval bowed-string instrument; ancestor of the *violin*.

vilhuela A type of Mexican *guitar* with a rounded back, common in *mariachi* ensembles.

villancico Devotional song, often for Christmas, from Latin America.

viola Bowed-string instrument of middle range; the second-highest member of the *violin* family.

viola da gamba Family of Renaissance bowed-string instruments that had six or more strings, was fretted like a *guitar*, and was held between the legs like a modern *cello*.

violin Soprano, or highest-ranged, member of the bowed-string instrument family.

violoncello Bowed-string instrument with a middle-to-low range and dark, rich sonority; lower than a *viola*. Also *cello*.

virginal A small keyboard instrument on which the strings run at right angles to the keys; popular in the sixteenth and seventeenth centuries.

virtuosic Demanding remarkable technical ability.

virtuoso Performer of extraordinary technical ability.

vivace Lively.

vocables Nonsense, or *nonlexical*, syllables, lacking literal meaning.

vocalise A textless vocal melody, as in an exercise or concert piece.

voice In a *fugue*, a melodic line. Keyboard fugues of the late Baroque period, such as those by J. S. Bach, commonly have four distinct voices even though they are played by a single musician.

volume Degree of loudness or softness of a sound. See also *dynamics*.

Wagner tuba A *tuba* developed specifically for Wagner's opera cycle *The Ring of the Nibelung*; the instrument was adopted by other late nineteenth-century composers.

waltz Ballroom dance type in *triple meter*; in the Romantic era, a short, stylized piano piece.

whole step Interval consisting of two *half steps*.

whole-tone scale Scale pattern built entirely of *whole-step* intervals, common in music of the French Impressionists.

wind band Instrumental ensemble ranging from forty to eighty members or more, consisting of wind and *percussion instruments*. Also *concert band*.

woodwind Instrumental family made of wood or metal whose tone is produced by a column of air vibrating within a pipe that has holes along its length.

woodwind quintet Standard chamber ensemble consisting of *flute, oboe, clarinet, bassoon*, and *horn* (not a woodwind instrument).

word painting Musical pictorialization of words as an expressive device; a prominent feature of the Renaissance madrigal.

work song Communal song that synchronized group tasks.

xylophone *Percussion instrument* with tuned blocks of wood suspended on a frame, laid out in the shape of a keyboard and struck with hard mallets.

yangqin A Chinese hammered *dulcimer* with a trapezoidal sound box and metal strings that are struck with bamboo sticks.

zapateado A lively Spanish and Latin-American dance style that features foot-stomping patterns.

zither Family of string instruments with a sound box over which strings are stretched; they may be plucked or bowed. Zithers appear in many shapes and are common in traditional music throughout Europe, Asia, and Africa.

Credits

Photos

Chapter banner: Amy White & Al Petteway/Getty Images; page 3: Digital Vision; 4: UIG via Getty Images; 5: UIG via Getty Images; 6: AP Photo/Gina Gayle; 7: MCT via Getty Images; 8: Henning Larsen Architects; 12: (top) Scala/Art Resource, NY; 12: (bottom) Pete Saloutos/Corbis; 15: Fernand Ivaldi/Getty Images; 16: FRANCOIS LENOIR/Reuters/Landov; 20: © The Museum of Modern Art/Licensed by Scala/Art Resource, NY(c) 2010 Artists Rights Society [ARS], NY/VG Bild-Kunst, Bonn; 24: Newark Museum/Art Resource, NY; 27: The Museum of Modern Art/Licensed by SCALA/Art Resource, NY. (c) 2010 The Andy Warhol Foundation/ARS, New York/Trademark, Campbell Soup Company. All rights reserved; 29: Wilfried Krecichwost/Corbis; 31: Owen Franken/Corbis; 32: Pete Leonard/Corbis; 34: Lebrecht Music & Arts; 37: (top left) Ethan Miller/Corbis; 37: (top right) Photo of EJ Jones courtesy of Kim Hill; 37: (bottom left) Sean Drakes/LatinContent/Getty Images; 37: (bottom right) Bruno De Hogues/Getty Images; 38: Insightfoto.com; 40: (top left) Sigi Tischler/epa/Corbis; 40: (bottom left) Courtesy of Julie Spring/ Photo by Lindsay Lozon; 40: (top right) Reuters/Corbis; 41: (top left) Courtesy of Mr. D. Owsley; 41: (top right) Getty Images; 42: (bottom) Chris Stock/Lebrecht Musc & Arts Library; 42: (top) Dave Benett/Getty images; 43: (top left) Lebrecht Music and Arts Photo Library; 43: (top right) Courtesy of Frank Salomon Associates; 43: (bottom) Chris Stock/Lebrecht Music & Arts; 44: (top left) Soren McCarty/WireImage/Getty Images; 44: (top right) Royalty-Free/Corbis;. 44: (bottom left) Photo courtesy of Sue Burrough; 44: (bottom right) Photo by Ron Lipson; 45: Time Life Pictures/Getty Images; 46: NBC via Getty Images; 47: Washington Post/Getty Images; 48: Jay Blakesberg; 49: Getty Images; 50: Photo by Mark Lyons. Courtesy of Cincinnati Symphony; 52: Chris Christodoulou; 54: Getty Images AsiaPac; 55: (bottom left) The Iveagh Bequest, Kenwood House, London, UK/The Bridgeman Art Library; 55: (bottom right) Pablo Picasso, The Old Guitarist, late 1903-early 1904. Oil on panel. 122.9 × 82.6 cm. Helen Birch Bartlett Memorial Collection, 1926.253, The Art Institute of Chicago. Photography © The Art Institute of Chicago. (c) 2010 Pablo Picasso/Artists Rights Society (ARS), New York; 56: (top left) AFP/Getty Images; 56: (center left) Getty Images.

58: bpk, Berlin/National Portrait Gallery/Jochen Remmer/ Art Resource, NY; 58: Art Resource, NY; 58: Lebrecht Music & Arts; 58: Album/Art Resource, NY; 59: Terrestrial globe, detail: angel playing trumpet, 1683, Coronelli, Vincenzo Maria (1650–1718)/Bibliotheque Nationale, Paris, France/© Christian Larrieu/The Bridgeman Art Library; 60: Scala/Art Resource, NY; 61: Art Resource, NY; 62: (bottom) By permission of The British Library; 62: (top left) Eileen Tweedy/The Art Archive at Art Resource, NY; 62: (center left) Eileen Tweedy/The Art Archive at Art Resource, NY; 63: Hermitage, St. Petersburg, Russia. Scala/Art Resource, NY; 65: Public Domain; 66: Bibliothèque Municipale, Laon, France. Photo: Eric Lessing/Art Resource, NY; 68–69: (top banner) Manuel Cohen/The Art Archive at Art Resource, NY; 68: Universal Images Group/Art Resource, NY; 69: © Christine Osborne/CORBIS; 70: Erich Lessing/ Art Resource,

NY; 71: The flight into Egypt, possibly from the Abbey Church of St. Germain des Pres in Paris, c. 1247 (stained glass), French School, (13th century)/Germanisches Nationalmuseum, Nuremberg (Nuernberg), Germany/The Bridgeman Art Library; 73: View of the cathedral exterior from the Left Bank, completed c.1330 (photo) (see also 54953)/Notre Dame, Paris, France/Peter Willi/The Bridgeman Art Library; 73: © DeA Picture Library/Art Resource, NY; 75: (bottom) Kharbine-Tapabor/The Art Archive at Art Resource, NY; 75: (top) Alfredo Dagli Orti/The Art Archive at Art Resource, NY; 76: (top) By permission of The British Library; 76: (bottom) Bibliothèque Nationale, Paris, France [Ms Fr. 22546, fol. 74]. Snark/Art Resource, NY; 78: Anthony Scibilia/Art Resource, NY; 80: (top) MThe Rustic Concert, the Song (oil on panel) (pair of 19949), Italian School, (16th century)/Musee de l'Hotel Lallemant, Bourges, France/Giraudon/The Bridgeman Art Library; 80: Hermitage, St. Petersburg, Russia. Scala/Art Resource, NY; 82: (bottom left) Kharbine-Tapabor/The Art Archive at Art Resource, NY; 82: (bottom right) © Lebrecht Music & Arts; 83: Hamburger Kunsthalle, Hamburg, Germany/The Bridgeman Art Library; 85: Leemage/Universal Images Group/Getty Images; 86: (top left) Cimabue, Giovanni (1240–1302)/Galleria degli Uffizi, Florence, Italy/Giraudon/The Bridgeman Art Library; 86: (top right) Raphael (Raffaello Sanzio of Urbino) (1483–1520)/Alte Pinakothek, Munich, Germany/Giraudon/The Bridgeman Art Library; 87: The Granger Collection, New York; 92: (top) Scala/Art Resource, NY; 92: (bottom) Istituto dei Padri dell'Oratorio, Rome. Photo: Scala/Art Resource, NY; 94: Erich Lessing/Art Resource, NY; 96: akg-images; 98: Ullstein bild.

100: Gianni Dagli Orti/The Art Archive at Art Resource, NY; 100: St. Teresa of Avila (1515–82) (oil on canvas) (b/w photo), Goya y Lucientes, Francisco Jose de (1746–1828) (attr. to)/Chateau de Villandry, Indre-Et-Loire, France/Giraudon/The Bridgeman Art Library; 100: Erich Lessing/Art Resource, NY; 101: Album/Art Resource, NY; 102: Erich Lessing/Art Resource, NY; 103: (top left) Ric Ergenbright/Corbis; 103: (top right) © Araldo de Luca/CORBIS; 104: A Young Lady Seated at a Virginal, c.1670 (oil on canvas), Vermeer, Jan (Johannes) (1632–75)/National Gallery, London, UK/The Bridgeman Art Library; 105: The Galerie des Glaces (Hall of Mirrors) 1678 (photo), Mansart, Jules Hardouin (1646–1708)/Château de Versailles, France/Peter Willi/The Bridgeman Art Library; 106: The Metropolitan Museum of Art, H. O H. Havemeyer Collection. Image copyright © The Metropolitan Museum of Art/Art Resource, NY; 109: (top) DEA/G. DAGLI ORTI/Getty Images; 109: (bottom) Album/Art Resource, NY; 110: bpk, Berlin/Hamburger Kunsthalle/Hanne Moschkowitz/Art Resource, NY; 114: Louvre, Paris, France/Giraudon/The Bridgeman Art Library; 115: © Royal Academy of Music Coll/Lebrecht/ The Image Works; 116: The Death of Dido (oil on canvas), Sacchi, Andrea (1599–1661)/Musee des Beaux-Arts, Caen, France/Giraudon/The Bridgeman Art Library; 118: Saint Thomas's Church and Saint Thomas's School, where Bach was a singer, colored engraving, 1749/De Agostini Picture Library/The Bridgeman Art Library; 119: © Lebrecht/The Image Works; 123: Cameraphoto Arte, Venice/Art Resource, NY; 124: Portrait of

Index

Page numbers in **boldface** indicate a definition; page numbers in *italic* indicate an illustration.

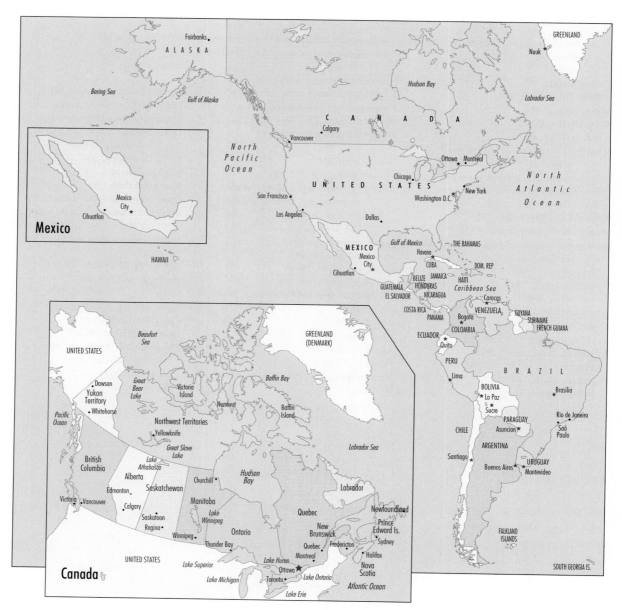

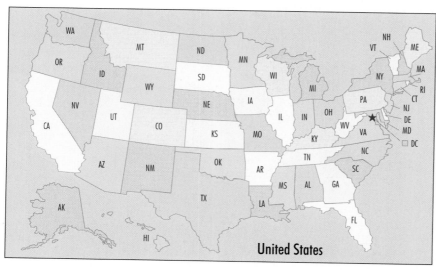